NATURALISTS' GUIDE to Fresh-Water AQUARIUM FISH

By J. J. HOEDEMAN

Photos by A. van den Nieuwenhuizen

STERLING PUBLISHING CO., Inc., New York

Oak Tree Press Co., Ltd London & Sydney

OTHER BOOKS OF INTEREST

The Guppy: Its Life Cycle
The Siamese Fighting Fish: Its Life Cycle
Color Guide to Tropical Fish
Tropical Fish Identifier
Tropical Fish in Your Home

Translated by Manly Banister

Edited and adapted for American readers by Louisa Bumagin Hellegers

The author and publishers would like to thank the following people for their kind assistance in the preparation of this volume over the past few years: the group of translators who worked with Mr. Hoedeman on the original translation; Manly Banister, for his special efforts in straightening out translation problems; Braz Walker of Waco, Texas, for his work as American Consultant and for answering our many queries; Anthony Evans of "Petfish Monthly," London, England, for his work as British Consultant and for bringing important controversies to our attention; Dr. James Atz of the American Museum of Natural History for his help in pointing out ichthyological difficulties; Dr. Herbert Axelrod of New Jersey for his comments on the Cardinal Tetra; Earl Schneider of New York for his continual faith and encouragement; and A. van den Nieuwenhuizen for providing 117 color photographs additional to those that appeared in the Dutch edition.

All technical and scientific drawings and photographs, as well as all photographs of habitats (all artwork besides actual photographs of fish), by the author.

Originally published under the title, "Elseviers Aquariumvissen Encyclopedie" by Elsevier Nederland N.V., Amsterdam.

Additional material for Chapter 7 taken from the book, "Elseviers Pocketboek voor de Aquariumliefhebber," written by J. J. Hoedeman, and published by Elsevier Nederland N.V.

Contents

... The Spleen ... Lymph Glands ... Heart and Blood Vessels
... The Heart ... Nervous System and Sense Organs ... Brain
and Spinal Cord ... Organization ... Simple Sense Organs ...
Sight and Eyes ... The Lateral Line Organ ... Organ of Hearing
and Balance ... The Weberian Apparatus

Fishes . . . The Transportation of Tropical Aquarium Fishes
. . . Fishing Expeditions and Exploring the Land

Publisher's Note

As its title implies, this book is a guidebook—a book to be read, consulted, and referred to over and over again by aquarists, naturalists and fish hobbyists. But, it is also a guidebook in a very different sense. Ichthyology and the aquarium hobby are wide-ranging fields of continual research and constant new discovery. New fish imports, although welcomed as the backbone of the hobby, often bring with them more questions than answers—who are their relatives? what habits do they have which might relate them to known fishes? should they be classified among existing species? or are they truly new species? if new, where and how do they fit into the over-all picture?

Are these questions that concern a hobbyist? Shouldn't they be left for "scientists" to answer? Our contention is that these are, indeed, queries that are not only important, but also necessary for every aquarist to face. The problems that arise in classification and nomenclature should certainly be of interest to every reader, and it is our hope that the historical and scientific backgrounds put forth in this book will serve to educate serious hobbyists and, perhaps, guide them to answers. Ichthyological study will stand still unless new discoveries are pursued and new data filed.

As is inevitable in any lengthy scientific work, there are controversial questions raised in this volume that are typical of the field. Scientists are in conflict about certain points—and where this occurs, we have not presumed to answer the questions outright, but rather to present points of view (sometimes ones with which the author himself does not agree) that within the context of the entire book might be a guide to why there are problems and where one might begin to look for answers. The naming of *Barbus* and *Puntius* species is one instance, and the Guppy, named by some *Lebistes reticulatus* but by others, *Poecilia reticulata,* is another. When and if such discussions can be concluded once and for all depends on well researched fact and constant and painstaking work.

This book is conveniently divided into two very different, but interconnected sections designed to provide readers with as all-encompassing a view of fish as possible. Part I deals with the evolution, distribution, anatomy, and life processes of fish, as well as with the relationship of fish to science and of fish to man. A chapter on general aquarium care is of special importance.

Part II, on the other hand, is an alphabetical, fully illustrated catalogue of hundreds of the best known and most often kept aquarium fishes. Here, a thorough discussion of the habits, coloration, temperature and breeding requirements, and any special points of interest regarding those aquarium fishes you probably have or will have in your tank is presented.

Following Part II is a Bibliography of reference works that the author has used, which may be of interest for further study. Completing the book is a detailed Glossary-Index with definitions of those scientific terms that entered into the discussions and descriptions of fish throughout the book.

This book, now published for the first time in English, offers more expanded, up-to-date and comprehensive information for aquarists than ever before presented in a single volume. It *is* a guidebook—use it as such, and the world of fishes will be more than simply a leisure-time hobby.

Author's Preface

This volume is a new, totally revised and updated edition of the fifth printing of the Dutch *Encyclopedia of Fresh-Water Fish*, of 1948 to 1956, and its sequels, under the titles: *Encyclopedie voor de Aquariumhouder* and *Elsevier's Aquariumvissen Encyclopedie*. The material, gathered for over 40 years, is largely based on my own experiences with the various individual species in home aquariums, including background information gathered during my 13 years as curator of fishes at the University of Amsterdam.

A great deal of additional material has, furthermore, been compiled from audience questions during the many lectures that I have given for aquarist societies, both in the Netherlands and abroad. From the questions asked, it became clear that most aquarists do need more information about their pet fish than a brief description and a nice photograph, even if the photograph is in color.

Although the additional background information I supplied here is based on scientific material and pertinent literature, I have attempted to express everything in non-scientific, generally understandable terms.

The introductory chapters, which, in a way, open the gates to better understanding of the "way of fishes," are of great help in aquarium keeping, even though this might not be obvious at first glance. Especially concerning newly imported fishes, about which hardly anything is known, any background knowledge a hobbyist gains will help find the proper ways of handling the fish. This is not merely my theory, but has proved to be true from thousands of letters and personal communications I have received from my readers.

A further advantage this book certainly has for the reader is the introduction of field notes and observations, giving some idea of how aquarium fishes live in nature and the sometimes extreme ranges of circumstances they overcome at different times of the year. How much more satisfying it is to know not only with *what* one is dealing, but also why and how.

To help in using the book, the species are arranged systematically, and, in addition, an extensive, alphabetical Glossary-Index is provided. The information supplied about each species has been brought up to date to the time of printing in 1973. Unfortunately, the rapid growth of the hobby and, particularly, the great number of newly imported species—several each week—cannot be coped with in any book. The speed with which new information about classification and nomenclature is being discovered and researched is phenomenal, and even a book just off the press is likely to have missed some new occurrence. The general information here, however, will help the user of this book to find the nearest relatives of any newly imported species, so that he will know how to handle his acquisitions.

I am greatly indebted to Dr. Nijssen and Dr. Isbrücker of the Fish Department of the Taxonomic Institute of the University of Amsterdam, and to many others, for their kind co-operation in bringing this volume up to date.

I also greatly appreciate and anticipate receiving any constructive information on the subject of aquarium fish, and am always willing and anxious to communicate with aquarists who want to co-operate in improving this text for an eventual second American edition.

J. J. Hoedeman
Abcoude, Holland
May, 1973

PART I.

1. HOW IT

ALL BEGAN

Considering the vast number of living fish species today, we could begin by saying that we are living not in the Age of Aquarius, but in the age of aquariums! Among the invertebrates, the insects (arthropods) as a group are richest in species. Among vertebrates, however, the award goes to the fishes. For several million years, they have been several times more numerous in species than all the rest of the vertebrates put together.

During that long-ago geological era known as the Age of Reptiles, both land and sea were mastered by mighty creatures of tremendous size, great reptiles that played, fought, fed, starved, lived and died in the primordial slime of the world's endless swamps and seas. The reptilian group, though still with us, is diminishing in both size and numbers, so that the earth is now dominated for the most part by mammals. The dominant order of these mammals, of course, is man, who outnumbers all the other mammals inhabiting the planet. That is to say, man is more numerous in individuals, even though not in number of species. Urged on by an illogical impulse to spread out, man has slowly taken possession of the entire globe, exterminating those animals that might have competed with him and, thus, disturbing the delicate balance of nature.

However, there are fishes in all the waters of the earth. With so much ocean—and so many rivers, lakes, streams and ponds—fishes have always had more room to expand in than land animals have had. This includes man, who is now, in fact, seriously considering the sea as *Lebensraum* for the excess population sure to come in the future.

Yet, despite vast diversity of shape and coloration among fishes, the variety is limited. Whatever a fish may look like, it never loses the look of a fish. We must ask ourselves, then, how fish first chanced to become fish. The next few chapters will try to clarify this.

The Branches of the Animal Kingdom

The primary division of nature is into two realms—that of plants and that of animals. The origin of life will be discussed later, and briefly, for there is not room here to go deeply into this complex problem. Table 1–1 shows the distinct animal groups with which we are familiar. The first forms of life were single-celled organisms, capable of performing the essential functions—that is, feeding, elimination, growth, and biological reproduction. The members of this enormous realm of single-celled beings are sometimes difficult to classify as plant or animal. Their common name is PROTISTA; when they are obviously plants, they are called PROTOPHYTA, when animals, PROTOZOA.

A second main stage in the animal kingdom is formed by the METAZOA. These are composed of several to many cells and include all animals other than PROTOZOA. The sponges, PORIFERA, are the simplest representatives of this branch of life, after which come the coelenterates (COELENTERATA), animals having a body cavity. These differ markedly in their physical make-up—their anatomy and embryology—from the higher forms. They possess only two germinal layers (DIBLASTERIA). (Detailed explanation of terms is given in the Glossary on page 1118.)

For the remainder, the table is self-explanatory. Animals with three germinal layers (TRIBLASTERIA) may either have a body cavity or may not have one. A transition is found among worms (VERMES). Flatworms and roundworms have no body cavity, while millepedes ("thousand leggers") and all the higher species do. All these lower forms of life have more significance for the aquarist than would appear on the surface. They serve as food for aquarium fishes, but often, too, they are parasites or in some other way dangerous enemies of the brood. This holds true also for other lower animals, the arthropods in particular, as well as for molluscs (MOLLUSCA).

A number of criteria are common to the remaining groups of animals. One of these is the presence in the body tissues of the chemical substance creatine. To such animals the name CREATINARIA has been given. They include the echinoderms (ECHINODERMATA) and the chordates (CHORDATA). The latter include a group of worm-like animals (HEMICHORDATA), the tunicates (UROCHORDATA or TUNICATA), the lancelets (CEPHALOCHORDATA), and the vertebrate animals proper (VERTEBRATA), to which fish belong.

15

1 *Protophyta* - Unicellular plants

1 *Protozoa* - Unicellular animals

Metazoa - Multi- and polycellular animals

Diblasteria (with two germ layers)

2 *Coelenterata* - Sea anemones, jellyfish and hydroids

3 *Porifera* - Sponges

Triblasteria or triploblasts (with three germ layers)

4 *Coelenteria* (without a body cavity)

5 *Plathelminthes* - Flat worms

6 *Nemathelminthes* - Round worms

Coelomaria (with body cavity)

7 *Annelida* - Ringed or segmented worms

8 *Arthropoda* - Jointed-limbed animals

9 *Mollusca* - Molluscs, shell fish

11 *Echinodermata* Starfish, sea urchins, etc.

10 *Creatinaria* (with creatine in the tissues)

Hemichordata Acorn worms

Urochordata Tunicates

Cephalochordata Lancelets

12 *Chordata* Chordates

Vertebrata Vertebrates: fish, amphibians, reptiles, birds, mammals

Table 1-1. Synopsis of the relationships between the groups of the animal kingdom. The figures correspond to the figures in Table 1-4, The Evolution of Fish.

The Story Told by the Crust of the Earth

The Appearance of Life

The question of when, how, why and from where the life surrounding us has come into being is not for most of us a subject of very deep thought. Life is—and we accept it. Nevertheless, scientists have long been challenging themselves to find a rational explanation to add to what has been supplied us by religious faith. It is beyond the scope of this book to go deeply into the matter, but a few thoughts on the subject will not be amiss.

The first life form to appear on earth was "living protein" (amino acid), the basic building block of every living thing. From these proteins arose the single-celled creatures. Later, these formed aggregates or colonies of themselves, and then they took on the form of multicellular plants and animals.

For the present, we can only assume that this process took place more than 3,000 million years ago, and that it took this long for the world of primitive organisms to develop. Events are more clearly seen, however, in the geological era called the PROTEROZOIC—the age of primitive animals and single-celled organisms.

Before this—a considerably long time before—in a period during which the earth itself was undergoing the process of formation, many circumstances combined to make life on earth impossible. This most ancient period in the earth's history, a step in the marching pageant of time before the appearance of life on the globe, is called the AZOIC or ARCHAIC, the age of no life. In Table 1–2 the names of the different periods are listed one under the other at the left. It may be asked how the divisions happened to be made in this way, not so much in regard to the names themselves, but to the periods of time they indicate. The terms Azoic and Proterozoic, for example, refer to periods involving certain changes or formations of the earth's crust. The same is true of the other periods—each one involves some major change in the earth's crust or climate.

This simplified discussion hardly indicates the difficulties in setting up a system like this. Yet, plain logic underlies it. Man has always tried to arrange things into groups and classes—to bring wide-ranging things into smaller compass—so that he can see them as a whole and understand them.

Era	Period	Epoch	Time (in million years) (Duration)	(Total)	Climate and Events	Development of Plants and Animals
Neozoic	Quaternary	Holocene	7.5	7.5	Postglacial Ice Ages.	Recent man, Cro-Magnon, Neanderthaler (Iron, Bronze, Stone Ages), Primitive men, highest primates.
		Pleistocene	13.5	21		
	Tertiary	Pliocene	7.5	28.5	Shaping of the earth into its present form; the last violent period of mountain raising; wide climate changes; shifting of the poles.	Complete collapse of the Age of Reptiles; further development of modern mammals; disappearance of the giant ratites or flightless birds; development of toothless birds.
		Miocene	10	38.5		
		Oligocene	5.5	44		
		Eocene	16	60		
Mesozoic	Secondary	Cretaceous	60	120	Great floods; formation of chalk; alpine mountain forming; the Carboniferous Tethys Sea largely disappears; rather cool climate.	First angiosperm plants, first heartwood trees; decline of numerous groups of invertebrate sea dwellers, sea reptiles, bi-pedal saurians, flying reptiles; marsupials, insectivores.
		Jurassic	40	160	Calm period; great deserts vanish; coal formation; warm climate.	Horsetails (*Equisetum*), tree ferns, conifers, resin formation with inclusions (insects, etc., fossilization); hey-day of the Age of Reptiles; more birds and mammals.
		Triassic	40	200	No ice ages.	Gymnosperms appear; the first quill-worts; giant horsetails; seed ferns; cactus-like plants; formation of coral reefs; strong development of ammonites.
Palaeozoic	Primary	Permian	30	230	Still-active earthquakes, mountain forming; dry, deserts and salt lakes (salt deposition); Permocarboniferous ice age.	Extinction of Carboniferous flora; first conifers; cephalopods dominate the sea; huge insects; land lizards, water reptiles; mammal-like reptiles; first true birds and mammals.
		Carboniferous	70	300	Violent earthquakes; huge coal formations; volcanic eruptions; warm.	Explosive development of land plants, tree ferns, horsetails; seed ferns; wide development of sea urchins, etc.; decline of the trilobites; many land insects; first reptiles.
		Devonian	50	350	Continuous floods, followed by mountain raising; greatest geological revolution; volcanic activities.	Warm climate, partly dry; regionally luxuriant plant growth on a broad scale on land; water plants and herbs; first insects and amphibians.
		Silurian	40	390	Formation of Caledonian mountains; at first still warm; in second half, dry, desert climate.	First land plants, algae and mosses; in water all invertebrates and many new varieties of fish; eurypterids (giant water scorpions).
		Ordovician	90	480	Shallow seas and flat continents, one northerly and one southerly, divided by a narrow equatorial ocean.	After ice age, a uniformly warm climate; no land flora, only extensive water life; first fishes.
		Cambrian	70	550	After an early ice age, a mild climate, no ice age; many deserts; warm seas to both poles.	Exclusively algae in seas and marshy coastal areas; all phyla of lower marine animals already present; trilobites already strongly developed.
Archaeozoic		Proterozoic	1450	2000	Pre-history of the earth very eventful since formation of the crust; subject to long periods of warmth and cold.	Traces of first unicellular animals; worm tracks; reef corals.
		Azoic	1000	3000		

Table 1-2

The crust of the earth is built up in layers, one on top of the other, like a multi-decked sandwich. The formation of crustal layers was by no means a peaceful process. It was accompanied by cataclysm, by the bursting-out of the crust, resulting in the thrusting-upward of some parts, and the caving-in of others. This process, repeated again and again, forced the breaking-up of the primordial continent and the drifting-apart of its separate elements. At that time, about one third of the earth was land, the remaining two thirds, water.

The Geological Time-Scale

An investigation of the results of cataclysmic upheaval of the earth's crust brings to light evidence of drastic changes at various times. Besides those changes due to climate (ice ages and deluges), many volcanic eruptions and upheavals on a grand scale folded the upper crustal layers into mountain ranges. Moreover, there were cosmic changes. It is clear that in Archaic times a great, continental land mass existed, surrounded by a vast body of water. The separate continents, as we know them today, had not yet come into being. Without discussing this aspect further, suffice it to say that investigation has indicated that the moon in those primitive ages may have been created from the earth itself, ripped from the parent bosom by unleashed cosmic forces, and hurled into the sky to persist there for ages as a satellite to the earth. However the moon was formed, the consequences have been and still are of far-reaching significance.

Naturally, life as it existed in the various geological eras was strongly affected by these events. Based on the greatest geological events since the cooling-off of the earth's crust, five geological eras can be differentiated. Each era has been divided into periods of time; each period, in turn, has been sub-divided into epochs, and these sometimes are still further divided into ages (see Table 1–2 for a geological history). A thorough study of this material is far beyond the scope of this book, but it is useful to have a general idea of the tremendous lengths of time required for certain changes to take place. How much variation there was in the lengths of the individual eras can be judged from the given figures. The variation is also visualized schematically in Table 1–4 connecting the development of the earth with the history of its fish population.

However, a comparison of the different diagrams and tables reveals a certain connection, and a discussion of this will be undertaken wherever it has bearing on the story of the fish. The connection between geological development and the distribution of the different groups of animals is certainly a strong one and more will be said about this.

Although the Glossary explains the geological terms, there is more to be said about them here. The names were derived from the names of the places where the given crustal layer was first observed being squeezed upward to the surface by tectonic movements in the crust itself. The specific layer, formed at a given time in the earth's history, corresponds to the geological era naming it. (See Table 1–2 for a brief characterization of the various periods and epochs.)

The earliest, oldest rock is more than 3,000 million years old and was formed in the Azoic or Archaic era in which not a vestige of life existed on earth. The eras following this begin to show traces of life. The first of these, called the Proterozoic, is the period during which life of the most primitive sort began. It follows from this observation that the creation of life on this planet occurred about 3,000 million years ago. Animals with skeletons of silicate, the RADIOLARIA, that dwelt on earth then have descendants surviving into our present day.

The following era concerns us more deeply. This is the PALAEOZOIC, which lasted 300 million years. In this period, higher forms of life entered the living scene. The six periods of the Palaeozoic were each terminated by cataclysm, a world-wide catastrophe accompanied in most cases by a vigorous shaking-up of the earth's crust, which could not fail to have a profound effect on the living creatures involved. These events are recorded in the layers of the crust. Some layers contain the remains of living things, petrified bones—and sometimes flesh—called fossils.

Fossils

For a very long time, men have been confronted by the fossilized remains of life from long-forgotten times. Ancient Greek writers, such as Xenophanes and Herodotus (about 500 B.C.), mention, in their histories, fossils, which they thought were the buried remains of giants. It is now known that these fossils were parts of the skeletons of huge animals. Fossils are the remains of plant or animal organisms that used to live in prehistoric times, which have somehow been preserved in the rock. The glacial plains of Siberia provided a mass grave for gigantic animals called mammoths. For some unknown reason, these animals died by the thousands and all at once. In the deep-freeze conditions prevailing, their bodies were preserved in a frozen state in their entirety to this day. Not only can the contents of their stomachs still be in-

Illus. 1-1. How a fossil looks when removed from the rock formation. The organic materials of the live tissues are changed into silica and lime by the process of fossilization. The fossil is usually of a different coloration and composition than the enclosing rock. This is *Cephalaspis salweyi* from the Silurian period in England.

vestigated, but even the flesh has remained edible after many millions of years in the ice. For many years, the tusks of these Siberian fore-runners of the elephant were traded as ivory, and the ivory was used in the famous Chinese ivory carvings. Many fossils, however, are no more than petrified remnants, more or less complete. Sometimes they are merely carbon impressions imbedded in layers of rock, as is the case with plants and lower invertebrate animals. Even traces of single-celled creatures have been preserved. And who has not heard of the ants, bees and other insects, perfectly preserved and visible inside lumps of amber?

The connection between geological events, the extinction of certain groups of plants and animals, and the rise of new groups is quite clear (see Table 1–4). It must be kept in mind, however, that only a slight chance exists for any given animal to become fossilized. Second, as a result of earthquakes and volcanic activity, a large part of those that do succeed in becoming fossils are destroyed. Third, only a tiny fraction of the existing fossils is ever discovered in the crustal layers that have been accessible to research. Even so, the amount of such material so far recovered is vast, but only a small part of it has been investigated so far.

It is expected, of course, that, in time, the science of palaeontology —that is, the study of fossils—will reveal a great deal more information about the life that existed on earth in the past. However far scientists progress, their knowledge is bound to remain incomplete.

You can get a graphic idea of this by comparing the history of life on earth to a bush with its roots in the ground, a short stem, and then many branches and twigs. Of this bush, only the tips of the youngest shoots are seen, with bits of old branches and a few glimpses of the roots here and there, while the remainder is completely invisible. The problem, then, is to reconstruct the shoots in their proper sequence on a stem that has to be entirely re-created. It is an almost impossible task. In the same way, researchers find themselves in disagreement on many points when they attempt to trace the origin of plants and animals through certain characteristics.

Many centuries passed before Alessandro Alessandri (about A.D. 1500) recognized one real origin of fossil material. He theorized that some fossils were the remains of victims of the Biblical flood! At present, it is known that more than one terrible deluge has ravaged the earth. When many plants and animals fell victim to them, undoubtedly other events led to their preservation as fossils. It happens even now that animals are drowned in mud, in asphalt pools, and in liquid resin. Perhaps, in due time, they will be dug up as fossils.

Once the geological time-scale had been set up and the crustal layers subsequently named and dated, the task of applying a date of origin to the fossils that had been found became not too difficult. Still, it was not as simple as all that, either. Imagine the crust of the earth being torn open in an earthquake, exposing a wide gap that through erosion becomes a deep, wide rift, cutting through layers of rock piled one on the other throughout many tens of millions of years. A plant may be blown by the wind, or an animal fall to the bottom of such a chasm and, in the course of events, fossilize there. Suppose another earthquake then closes the rift and, after a few million more years, the site is again brought to light and worked on by scientists. When the fossil is found, the researcher is faced with a problem—can the fossil actually be dated in respect to the age of the layer in which it is found, or is it not a product of some far later age? Such problems do occur in the field of palaeontology.

It was not until the second half of the 18th century that palaeontology developed into a major science. And then, it was due to the contributions of the great research scientists such as Buffon, Cuvier and Lamarck (see Chapter 5). Palaeontology provides vast insight into the development of life on earth, into evolution, and it reveals that all higher forms of life have developed from lower forms—that is, from more primitive forms. At that time, this was revolutionary thinking, for the Bible and the story of creation that it presented were accepted literally by most people, and it was held true that all present-day animals have been on earth since the very beginning. Modern interpretations of Genesis, however, no longer allow conflict between the Bible story and the teaching of evolution.

It is not surprising that people at first did not know what to do about the fossils they found, though they appreciated their obvious importance. It took time and study for them to rationalize their way out of the thicket of ignorance and misunderstanding into a world of scientific observation. The palaeontological interpretation of fossils has now definitely proved the theory of succession of groups of animals, as well as the development of higher, more complex groups from simpler forms. More of this will be considered in connection with the descriptions of groups of fishes.

How Fishes Developed

The first fishes date back perhaps 500 million years. At that time, life had been in existence for as much as four times that long, yet the waters still contained only the lower forms of life. However, a new form of organization appeared among fishes. Their physical construction underwent a remarkable change into a more advanced form in a comparatively short time.

The most striking difference that can be observed is the absence, and then later the presence, of a spinal column. This difference forms the basis of the division of the animal kingdom into vertebrates and invertebrates—those having and those not having a backbone. The development of the spinal column was a great step forward in the evolutionary history of animals.

The Origin of the Spinal Column

Fossils have always been an essential aid in tracing and reconstructing the steps of evolutionary development. Slight chance exists of ever finding fossils of the immediate ancestors of the vertebrates. The reason is simple: their boneless bodies had nothing much to fossilize. Among present-day fauna, however, there are still some remarkable groups of animals which are probably very closely related to those primordial forms and which quite possibly can lift the veil now hiding the origin of the spinal column.

Illus. 1-2. This schematic cross-section through a young vertebrate shows the main positions of the various organs and the external openings. The figures stand for: 1. nostril. 2. mouth opening, connecting with 3. the pharyngeal cavity with gill slits. 4. the heart. 5. the lung (in fish, developed, in different ways, into the swim bladder). 6. liver. 7. gall bladder. 8. stomach. 9. pancreas. 10. spleen. 11. intestine. 12. anal opening or cloaca. 13. urine duct. 14. kidney. 15. sex organ. 16. chorda dorsalis (notochord). 17. esophagus (gullet or forestomach). 18. spinal cord, contained in the spinal column. 19. auditory organ. 20. brain. 21. eye.

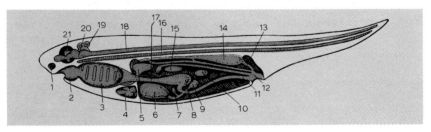

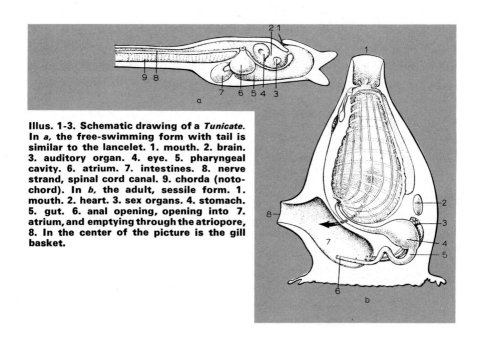

Illus. 1-3. Schematic drawing of a *Tunicate*. In *a*, the free-swimming form with tail is similar to the lancelet. 1. mouth. 2. brain. 3. auditory organ. 4. eye. 5. pharyngeal cavity. 6. atrium. 7. intestines. 8. nerve strand, spinal cord canal. 9. chorda (notochord). In *b*, the adult, sessile form. 1. mouth. 2. heart. 3. sex organs. 4. stomach. 5. gut. 6. anal opening, opening into 7. atrium, and emptying through the atriopore, 8. In the center of the picture is the gill basket.

Vertebrates still in the embryonic stage develop inside their bodies a fluid-filled tube that is closed at both ends. As the fluid is under pressure, this primitive kind of spinal column is reasonably stiff. In fact, the name for this tube is the notochord, the CHORDA DORSALIS, called chorda for short. Animals having a chorda are called chordates (Chordata). All vertebrates have chordae and are, thus, chordates. However, there are two known groups of animals, the Hemichordata and the Urochordata, which, though ranked among the invertebrates, at one stage of their development possess a structure corresponding to the chorda of the higher animals.

Hemichordata are peculiar, worm-like animals which, at first glance, are similar to lobworms and have the same living habits. Although these creatures can be considered a class apart, next to the chordates, they do possess a pronounced chordal structure. It is, however, very small and extends only about half the length of the body. The remaining organization of the creatures is a great deal like that of chordates. They seem to belong to a special, degenerate group having the same ancestral line as the higher vertebrates, though science is still unsure of the precise relationship.

Urochordata—also called Tunicata because of the tunic-like sheath enveloping the body—are also fascinating animals which, in many respects, may be compared with the lancelet (see below). The larvae, as well as the adult stages of freely-living species, have a chorda in the tail region of their bodies (in the adult sessile forms, the entire tail is lost). These creatures are also considered degenerate offshoots from the primary developmental line of vertebrates.

For a long time, a third group was considered as belonging to these primitive chordate species, namely, the lancelets or Cephalochordata. Actually, these are not true fishes, but by agreement, they are considered as such, since they are regarded as degenerate descendants of the earliest chordates that were classed among the fishes.

Obviously, in one way or another, the forerunners of vertebrate animals showed a certain correspondence with these strange chordates from primitive times at some stage of their development. The science of embryology can be a guide in this respect.

The question of how the internal skeleton came into being must now be considered. The chorda, the first part of the structure to be laid out, forms the focus around which the vertebrae develop. Points are created along the length of the chorda, into which are deposited lime salts secreted by the body. First formed are small bits of cartilage, four for each vertebra. Two are on the dorsal (back) and two on the ventral (belly) side. These grow into rings around the chorda, forming different types of vertebrae in accordance with the line of evolution involved. To some, ribs are attached (fishes also have ribs). The finer points of the physical structure of fishes will be treated later in Chapter 3.

Forerunners of the True Fishes

Up to now, scientists have had but a slight foothold on the evolutionary situation. Clearer and more palpable evidence, however, is provided by the vertebrate group, in which the fishes take first place, not only because they are the first and oldest forms, but also because they indisputably possess the largest total number of species among vertebrates.

The first fish life was characterized by the lack of true jaws, and for this reason they were called jawless (AGNATHA), as opposed to those that had jaws (GNATHOSTOMATA). The study of fossils has revealed that the transition from jawless to jawed fish was not nearly as spectacular as had been believed.

The earliest fishes, primitive chordates, lived on plankton. For this, they needed a rather large head with a mouth opening surrounded by a kind of sieve. The primitive fishes had a cartilaginous gill basket with the double function of taking oxygen from the water and sieving from the water the micro-organisms they fed upon. This gill basket is still preserved in surviving jawless fishes, presumably unchanged in form. In jawed fishes, this structure is also still quite apparent, though it is only in the embryo that it is found complete.

The gill basket became the starting point for the development of jaws, as can be determined from fish embryos. Several of the frontal elements of the gill basket developed loose positions, perhaps to enable them to chop up the larger food-creatures that got into the basket. In the course of evolution, this type of jaw has further developed in numerous directions (see Chapter 3—*The Anatomy of Fish*).

The most primitive chordates, then, were divided into two groups, jawed and jawless. In the same stage of development, a new characteristic developed—a skull. This characteristic permits a distinction between animals having a skull and those having none, the CRANIATA and the ACRANIA, respectively.

Among the chordates, the lancelets (Cephalochordata) have already been mentioned. Though they have no actual skull, they form a remarkable group of creatures that has been researched by many scientists. They have actually been so thoroughly investigated that, on the basis of strange characteristics, they have been given all kinds of names, each based on one or another of the anatomical characteristics. Here are some of them: LEPTOCARDII (tube hearts), for the slightly differentiated, elongated heart; MARSIPOBRANCHII (pouch-gilled), for the sack-shaped gills; CIRROSTOMI (eyelash-mouthed) for the crown of thread-like protrusions around the mouth opening. In recent classifications, lancelets are mostly grouped under Amphioxi, in the order Amphioxiformes, derived from the species name *Amphioxus lanceolatus* (synonyms are *Branchiostoma lanceolata* and *Asymmetron lanceolatum*). Hence, it seems that the lancelets do not form a separate group, but should rather be regarded as fish-like animals (but having an original line of their own) that have lost the ability to form a solid skull, rather than as a group that *does not yet* have a skull. There is a striking similarity between lancelets and lampreys in the larval stage.

Evolution of the spinal column from the chorda has already been discussed. However, before that development took place, there was a still greater step taken from the invertebrate stage to the chordate, and this needs further explanation. In Table 1–1 illustrating the relationships between the races composing the animal kingdom, the group Creatinaria is found under item 10. Investigation of the sequence from invertebrates to vertebrates among various groups of lower animals (worms, crab-like creatures and primitive chordates) revealed, rather unexpectedly, that it was the Echinodermata (item 11 in the chart) from which the fishes and other vertebrate animals are directly descended. This is an interesting subject, but it cannot be gone into more deeply here. However, the connection is obvious from the presence of creatine in the tissues of the echinoderms. Creatine is not found in any other invertebrate group. Other points of similarity will be dealt with in Chapter 5.

The First Fishes

To obtain a good grasp on the story of fish, it is necessary to go back into the CAMBRIAN period (see Tables 1–3 and 1–4), which was about 550 million years ago. Not much material has been preserved from the early Cambrian period, but fossils from the late Cambrian and ORDOVICIAN periods provide a fair degree of insight. It is simple to conclude from this that the origin of fish-like creatures dates back at least to the Cambrian.

The Hemichordates and Urochordates are probably also offshoots from this ancestral line, a supposition supported by abundant fossil material from the Ordovician. At the beginning of this period, a fairly well differentiated fauna of fishes existed along with the invertebrate groups. These fishes were characteristically provided with sturdy armour and are called Ostracodermi (item 13 in Table 1–3). These are the first animals that can be clearly defined as fishes. They were probably still without jaws, resembling the present-day lamprey and the hagfishes. The development of these fishes is considered to have occupied that space of time from the late Cambrian or early Ordovician to the end of the latter period. Only three lines of this oldest branch of fish survived into the SILURIAN period. Interestingly enough, the whole process took place in fresh water, which is contradictory to what has been said about the sea previously. Fish life had its start in

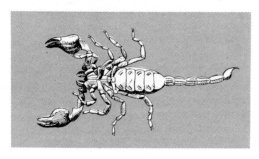

Illus. 1-4. Likeness of the scorpion. The enormous water scorpions of the Silurian made life so difficult for the earliest fishes that they had to be provided with skin armour in order to survive the unequal battle.

28

CLASS	SUB-CLASS	SUPER-ORDER	ORDER
Bony Fish			
13 Ostracodermi*	Cephalaspida*		Amphioxiformes / Petromyzontiformes
	Pteraspida* / Anaspida*		Myxiniformes
14 Osteichthyes	15 Crossopterygii*	16 Dipnoi*	Dipteriformes* / Ceratodiformes
		17 Rhipidistia*	Porolepiformes* / Osteolepiformes* / Amphibia, etc. (18)
		19 Actinistia*	Coelacanthiformes
	20 Actinopterygii	21a Actinopteri — Ostariophysi	22 *Siluriformes* / 23 *Cypriniformes* / 24 *Characiformes*
		Cladistia	25 *Polypteriformes*
		Osteoglossi	26 *Osteoglossiformes* / 27 *Notopteriformes* / 28 *Mormyriformes*
		Elopoidei	29 Elopiformes / 30 Anguilliformes / 31 Clupeiformes
		Salmonoidei	32 Salmoniformes / 33 Esociformes

retractores arcuum branchialium ---- ↑ absent / ↓ present

CLASS	SUB-CLASS	SUPER-ORDER	ORDER
14 Osteichthyes	21b Acanthopterygii	Holostei s.s.	34 Amiiformes / 35 Lepisosteiformes
		Paracanthopteri	36 *Mugiliformes* / 37 Batrachoidiformes / 38 Gobiesociformes / 39 Gadiformes
		Pseudacanthopteri	40 *Beloniformes* / 41 *Cyprinodontiformes*
		Acanthopteri	42 *Gasterosteiformes* / 43 *Syngnathiformes* / 44 *Ophicephaliformes* / 45 *Mastacembeliformes* / 46 *Perciformes* / 47 *Tetraodontiformes*
Cartilaginous Fish			
48 Placodermi*	Antiarchi*		Asterolepiformes*
	Arthrodira*	Coccostei*	Coccosteiformes*
		Holocephali	Chimaeriformes
49 Acanthodii*			Acanthodiformes* / Climatiiformes*
50 Chondrichthyes → Selachii		Protoselachii*	Xenacanthiformes* / Cladoselachiformes*
		Euselachii	Heterodontiformes / Lamniformes / Squaliformes
		Hypotremata	Torpediniformes / Rajiformes

* means extinct   *italics* mean true aquarium fish

Table 1-3

29

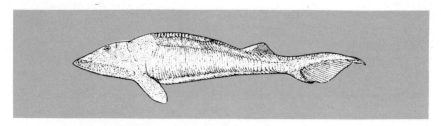

Illus. 1-5. *Hemicyclaspis* was an armoured, cephalaspid fish of the Ordovician period. Its single nostril lay between its two small eyes.

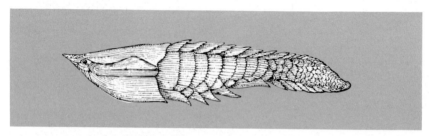

Illus. 1-6. *Anglaspis* also lived in the period of the earliest development of fish. It was a pteraspid with twin nostrils, as are found in present-day armoured catfish.

fresh water, and though it adapted to and differentiated in sea water, the earliest fossils of importance undoubtedly originated in fresh water. More about this later.

Although the great variety of forms in the Ordovician period should have made a much greater number of groupings, the fossilized material has been divided into only three classes: Cephalaspida, Pteraspida, and Anaspida (see Table 1–3). Because of its organization, a sub-division of the Cephalaspida, the Coelolepida, is regarded as containing the original forms of the Ostracodermi. The Coelolepida, however, became extinct towards the end of the Silurian—at least, no fossils of the group have been found in later periods. Some specimens must have survived, nevertheless, for it is supposed that the lancelets and the lampreys (Amphioxiformes and Petromyzontiformes) are offshoots from these early Coelolepida.

The derivation of lancelets—skull-less animals—from early fishes that did have a skull, gives these creatures a special place. It must be assumed that lancelets—true fishes by definition—acquired their present shape through specialization and degeneration. This kind of development—having the period of immaturity indefinitely prolonged—is a typical one in evolution and is called NEOTONY, or sometimes PAEDOMORPHOSIS and PAEDOGENESIS.

Three classes of Ostracodermi (item 13 in Tables 1–3 and 1–4) were differentiated during the Silurian. The first was the Cephalaspida, tiny, armoured fishes with a broad, thick, bony shield over the skull. As stated before, these can be considered ancestors of the lamprey (Petromyzontiformes), among others.

The second class, the Pteraspida, developed a trunk-shaped mouth opening underneath the head. The edges of the mouth were provided with bony plates set with very fine, rasping teeth. In this respect, they show an unmistakable similarity to the present-day, armour-clad catfish, the Loricariidae (see page 358). The Pteraspida are the ancestors of today's hagfish (Myxiniformes).

The third class, the Anaspida, resemble our present-day fishes far more than the other two classes. They lived from the end of the Silurian to the end of the DEVONIAN. Up to now, no trace of them has been found in rocks laid down after that period.

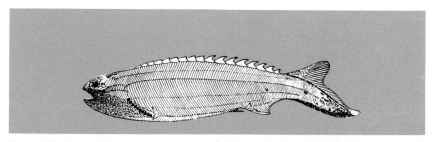

Illus. 1-7. *Pterolepis,* an anaspid ostracoderm of the same early Ordovician period. Its shape shows that it was a good swimmer. Note the series of holes for gill openings, which gives them a certain resemblance to the lampreys.

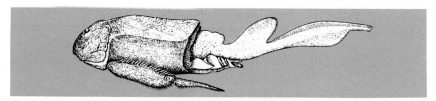

Illus. 1-8. *Bothriolepis* was undoubtedly a remarkable dweller of the Devonian fresh waters. The head-thorax region is enclosed in heavy, bone armour, while the rear part of the body and the tail are not.

The First Fishes with Jaws

As mentioned earlier, the difference between fishes without jaws and those possessing jaws is merely one of degree. The limits were so vague that at first certain groups were classed among the jawless fish, until it was ascertained later that they did have jaws. Fish with jaws are called Gnathostomata to differentiate them from Ostracodermi (called Agnatha). This differentiation, however, appears not to hold good when the pertinent fossil material is studied. (See items 14 through 50 in Table 1-3 for the fish groups having jaws.) Without going more deeply into the evolution of the jaw, suffice it to say that an abundance of oversized food animals in the environment of these first fishes made it necessary for part of the gill basket to become freely moveable so as to accommodate the larger sizes.

In phylogenetic arrangements (or phylogenies), the Placodermi (item 48 in Table 1-3) are usually discussed immediately after the Ostracodermi. This example will be followed, though this group and its offshoots, the sharks and other cartilaginous fishes (which, though interesting, are of no direct importance to aquarists), are found to have originated in the order shown in the table—that is, after the bony fishes.

During the Ordovician, the fishes with jaws became masters of the water. Their variety of form increased rapidly, as if nature were experimenting with new ways of development. Entire groups soon died out, either because of poor adaptability, because they were killed off by other animals, or, because they starved for lack of nourishment in an environment that was otherwise suitable. Finally, a certain balance was established, and the various forms became suited for survival in their surroundings. The Placodermi (item 48) had already appeared on earth in the Silurian. Early in the Devonian, two groups split off from the main stem. These were the Antiarchi and the Arthrodira, which, in turn, can be differentiated into a number of clearly distinguishable orders. Two of these are the Asterolepiformes and the Coccosteiformes. The drawing of *Pterichthyodes* in Illus. 1-11 gives an impression of these Devonian fish. *Pterichthyodes* was a bottom-dwelling fish, while *Coccosteus* was a good swimmer. The powerfully developed armour with which both were clad kept them secure in their environment. A remarkable change that first appeared in the Antiarchi was the breaking-up of large bony plates into many smaller ones, thus greatly improving the ability of the fishes to manoeuvre in the water. The cranial bone still remained as a single, large plate which covered more

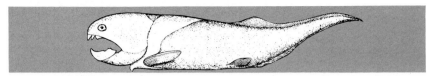

Illus. 1-9. *Dinichthys* **was one of the first fish to dare the open sea. It was a large fish and most likely a fearful predator. At first, fish probably did not constitute its prey, but other sea dwellers, such as octopi and crab-like creatures, did.** *Dinichthys* **is classed among the arthrodirous placoderms.**

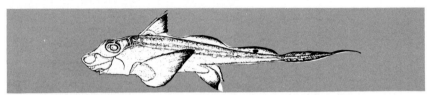

Illus. 1-10. *Chimaera* **is representative of an old family probably dating from before the migration of the sharks to sea, where they mainly developed into a group of fish living on the continental shelf and feeding on bottom-dwellers.**

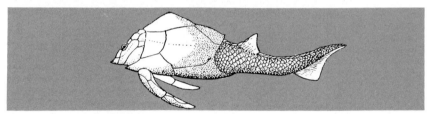

Illus. 1-11. *Pterichthyodes* **was a rather small, bottom-dwelling, Devonian representative of the placoderms.**

than two thirds of the entire length of the body. Incidentally, although the Chimaerae, or Holocephali, are usually placed at the end of the system of cartilaginous fishes, in this work we place them before the real shark-like fishes, since they are, presumably, the direct descendants of the Arthrodira.

The especially strong development of the jaws, which, among other things, made *Coccosteus* one of the greatest pirate fish of its time, obviously leads to the Acanthodii (item 49). The Acanthodii, in fact, split off at the same time as the specialized placoderms developed—towards the end of the Silurian. Acanthodii must be considered the direct ancestors of today's cartilaginous fish. The two most important orders are named in Table 1–3—the Acanthodiformes and the Climatiiformes. These were clearly already shark-like fishes that had adapted themselves to the salt-water environment, since fresh-water habitats could not provide them with enough room or food. The remaining groups are, to this day, predominantly dwellers of the shallow stretches of fresh water which, in that time, were much more far-reaching.

33

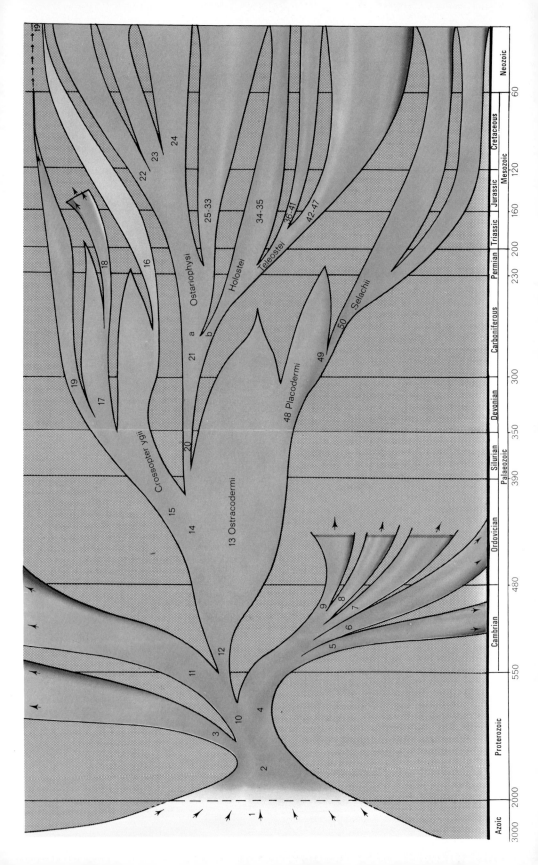

Table 1-4. Schematic survey of the developmental history of fish. Although the chart looks as if everything is known about this development, this is a personal interpretation of the data. However, these data are far from complete. The intention here is to give a hypothetical picture that deviates in a number of points (which will be discussed and accounted for more thoroughly in the text) from the current "family tree of fishes." The figures apply to a connection with the various parts of the text; items 13 to 47 inclusive are the groups towards which attention will be directed in this book. The column footings are meant only as a simple guide with regard to the groups concerned.

Cartilaginous Fishes

At the end of the Silurian, shark-like fishes—a direct branch of the Silurian placoderms (item 48)—appeared on the scene. They were still fashioned upon a bony skeleton and covered with solid, dermal armour. Some twenty million years later, in the Devonian period, typical sharks were present (under item 50, the Chondrichthyes). They were Xenacanthiformes, which died out as an order, but whose pre-served fossils clearly show the process of diminishing ossification of the internal (axial) skeleton. In contrast to earlier views that the skeleton of bony fishes derives from the cartilaginous fish, it is now certain that all primitive fishes, long before the shark-like fishes appeared, were pro-vided with a well ossified, internal skeleton. The degeneration of the axial skeleton of bony fishes is probably due to the environment, sea water.

The CARBONIFEROUS fauna already counted among its members one of the first representatives of modern cartilaginous fishes, the sea-dwelling shark *Pleuracanthus*. This fish is notable for its completely straight tail fin, while the internal skeleton had not yet degenerated into cartilage.

The small group most closely resembling present-day sharks is made up of such forms as *Cladoselache*, which dates back to the Carboniferous and the PERMIAN. Collectively, these two groups are known as Proto-selachii, or primitive sharks, as compared with the modern sharks, or Euselachii. In contrast to the Xenacanthiformes sharks, *Cladoselache* and

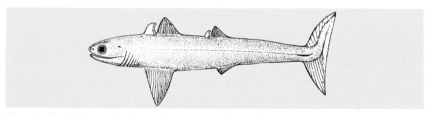

Illus. 1-12. *Cladoselache* is a famous fossil shark from the Carboniferous and Permian periods.

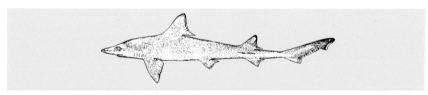

Illus. 1-13. *Mustelus* is a modern shark in which, compared to *Cladoselache,* the lengthening of the snout is striking. This gives the mouth an under-positioned character, typical of present-day sharks.

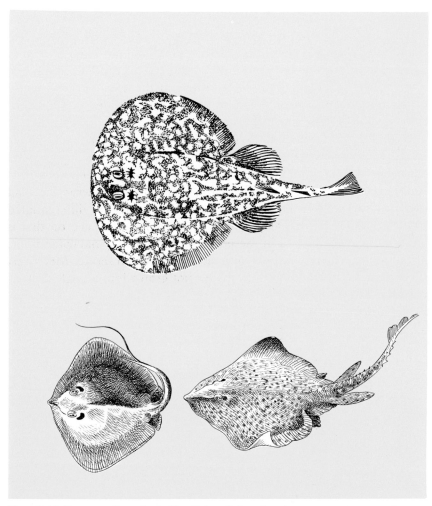

Illus. 1-14. Rays are flat, shark-like fishes living, for the most part, on or close to the bottom. The Devilfish (*Manta* ray), though absolutely harmless and living on plankton, is one of the few species dreaded by fishermen. These creatures can measure nearly 8 metres (26 feet) across the fins and weigh as much as 2 tons. Most species, however, are smaller but some, especially those living in river mouths and smaller fresh waters, are rightly dreaded because of their poison caudal spine. This spine is not confined to the Stingray alone. Illustrated here, to give an idea of their shape, is a species of *Torpedo* (top), then the Stingray (bottom left) and the Skate (bottom right).

its relatives had a tail end that was bent sharply upward and which ran through to the uppermost lobe of the caudal fin. The lobes of the caudal fin were, however, pretty well symmetrical.

Today's sharks and rays are direct descendants of the oldest Euselachii that used to populate the seas from the Carboniferous period onward.

It was not until the Permian period that these fishes and the marine reptiles began to compete with each other. As the latter preferred to inhabit the coastal regions, the sharks were driven out into the oceans. From the end of the Carboniferous to the end of the Palaeozoic era, many new species appeared, in addition to the then already clearly differentiated offshoot of the Arthrodira, the Chimaerae (Chimaeriformes). The sharks and the rays are descended from these two large groups. The sharks chose to live in the open sea, while the rays, for the most part, lived on the continental shelves. Many of them lived around the mouths of rivers and some have remained faithful to their aboriginal fresh-water habitat—or have returned to it. The Chimaerae that had diverged earlier from the placoderms (Arthrodira), are differentiated from the remainder of cartilaginous fishes by having a chorda that is either not enclosed at all in the bony structure of a spinal column, or, at the most, is merely a slight suspicion of such a structure. Moreover, the two halves of the pelvic girdle have not grown into a single unit, as with the Selachii.

The True Bony Fishes

The fishes under discussion up to now have been called cartilaginous fishes, as opposed to the bony fishes, or fishes with hard skeletons. For a long time, it was thought that the presence of the bony skeleton was a step upward in the scale of evolution from the cartilaginous fishes. This does not, however, appear to be true as bony fishes *have* been found among the earliest fishes, the oldest known group, the Ostracodermi, and even among most of the Placodermi.

Glance at Table 1–4 which bears the coded numbers given in Table 1–3. Groups 14 through 47 are collectively called the Osteichthyes, whose origin in time was somewhere in the Ordovician period. These represent the first and most important branch of the Ostracodermi (item 13), which roamed the waters of earth long before the cartilaginous fishes appeared. As some specimens with a calcified skeleton are found among cartilaginous fishes, so among bony fishes are also found numerous groups and kinds having a poorly developed or degenerate skeleton. This phenomenon, especially observable in the sturgeon, will be discussed more fully later on. At any rate, the assumption that the line of evolutionary development went from cartilaginous to bony fishes—for a long time considered a valid thesis—must certainly be revised.

One of the principal differences between the two main kinds of fishes today is the possession by bony fishes of an air or swim bladder. Shark-like fishes have neither air nor swim bladder.

Illus. 1-15. *Cephalaspis* **lived towards the end of the Ordovician period, but, in respect to build and armour, could be classified without much difficulty among present day armoured catfish.**

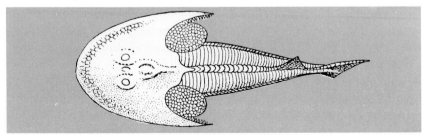

The land environment of the first fishes, and of the first bony fishes as well, can be compared with today's broader stretches of marshland, and this surely contributed to the development of an auxiliary respiratory organ. It would seem to be absurd to connect this development with feeding, but not so much if we consider that the most primitive creatures had to do everything with their intestines, from digesting their food to simple breathing. It may be assumed that algae, the principal food of the early fishes, was not only used by the fishes for nourishment, but also as the source of most of the oxygen their bodies required. At that time, the gills were still primitive and served mainly to excrete carbon dioxide resulting from oxidation of the food in the metabolic process. This kind of intestinal respiration is considered the oldest method of providing for the body's oxygen requirement. To a certain extent, this made these fishes independent of the oxygen content of the water they lived in. There are fishes still living today in oxygen-poor environments, which depend on a similar method of intestinal respiration. Among these are the armoured catfishes, loaches, and other fishes of this type.

This explains why an auxiliary respiratory organ was developed to enable the fishes to remain in even the worst kind of water for an indeterminate length of time. Protrusions from the intestine were established as reservoirs for air and oxygen, and these gradually developed into air bladders and lungs.

Chapter 3 will deal more fully with the intestinal tract, air bladder and respiratory systems, but it seems useful to mention here that the term swim bladder or air bladder is not entirely appropriate. Actually, there are two kinds of air bladders, one of which serves as an auxiliary respiratory organ or air reservoir. The other, however, is connected with the hearing organ and serves as a kind of sonic receiver. Its function is not only that of a receiver, but also that of an instrument of emission, for it can send out a series of vibrations by means of the bladder, which is often embedded in a bony capsule. In murky waters where visibility is poor, this sonic system is a most useful instrument.

If it is stated that the road from water to land passed through the lungs, it is about the same as saying, "The way to a man's heart is through his stomach." Of course, it is odd to say that it was necessary for fishes to develop air-breathing apparatus that would give service outside the water, so that they could develop into amphibians. Air breathing was apparently not developed to conquer new realms, but rather to escape from a drying-out pool to another with more water.

This long stride from water to land took place towards the end of the Palaeozoic era, during the Carboniferous and Permian periods. The terrestrial climate was still warm and, particularly, damp. Towards the end of the Permian, the climate turned dry, so that the first amphibians must have had a difficult time. The passing from aquatic to terrestrial life took place so rapidly, however, that the first reptiles also developed as early as the Carboniferous. Owing to their physical structure, they were adapted to life on land and could survive even the great drought at the end of the Palaeozoic era. The amphibians, as an evolutionary line, did not accomplish much.

Although it seems obvious that intestinal pouches of the swim-bladder type must have preceded the lung-type respiratory organ, no convincing evidence of this has yet been found in fossil relicts. Fossils from the Ordovician period already show an obvious lung development.

Lobe-Finned Fishes and Lungfish

Following the Ordovician and Silurian periods, two markedly different types of fish fauna developed, fresh-water bony fishes, and cartilaginous marine fishes. The division is a generalized one, but it is based on solid principle, nevertheless. In the beginning, the fresh-water fishes living in marshes and rivers had to use the intestinal tract for breathing. The skin and, later on, other auxiliary breathing mechanisms made it possible for them to live in waters that were sometimes heavily polluted and poor in oxygen. Lung-like organs developed from the intestinal pouches, with which the first group of true bony fishes deriving from the ostracoderms were provided. This was better than the rather simple—even though effective—intestinal method of respiration. It allowed them to take in air from above the surface and to live on it while remaining submerged for long periods of time. This old group of fishes was named, for a characteristic common to a great number of forms, the lobe-finned fish, or Crossopterygii (item 15 in Table 1–3). Towards the end of the Silurian and during the Devonian period, three distinct groups of these diverged from the main stem. One of these, the lungfishes (Dipnoi), flourished briefly during the Carboniferous. One of its branches, the formerly large group of Dipteri, became extinct. The other branch, the Ceratodi, managed to survive and is still represented among the fish fauna of Africa, South America and Australia (see page 307).

The second important offshoot from the lobe-finned fishes took place in the Devonian (items 17 and 19 in Table 1–3), when the lungfish

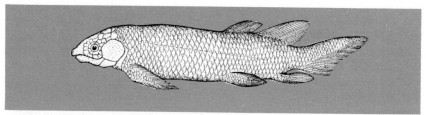

Illus. 1-16. The oldest known fossil lungfish, *Dipterus,* has two dorsal fins and an up-thrust tail with the caudal fin located on the under side. It clearly possessed lobed anal, pelvic and pectoral fins. It lived during the Devonian and Carboniferous periods.

Illus. 1-17. There is remarkably little difference between this recent Australian lungfish, *Neoceratodus,* and *Dipterus* of the Carboniferous period. The tail has become straight and the median fins are arranged around the end of it in a continuous fringe. The paired fins are still lobed.

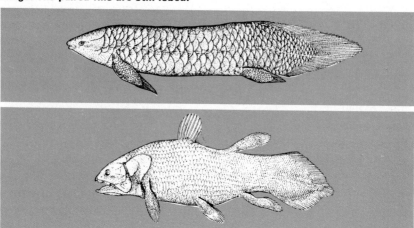

Illus. 1-18. This was drawn by White from the first dead specimen of the recent *Latimeria* to arrive in England. The photo in Illus. II-5 was made from a better preserved, later specimen. Nevertheless, the resemblance between *Latimeria* and Carboniferous *Dipterus* is remarkable.

Illus. 1-19. Another lobe-finned fish from the Devonian was *Osteolepis,* which is even more primitive than *Dipterus.* The osteolepid line may have given rise to the amphibians, especially frogs and toads.

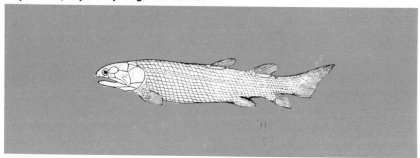

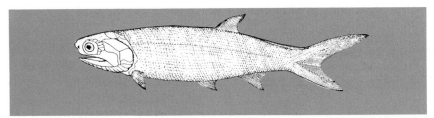

Illus. 1-20. *Palaeoniscus,* an important fossil fish for many palaeontologists and ichthyologists, has been found in great numbers, well preserved, in rocks of the Carboniferous to the end of the Cretaceous. Many of its characteristics have been thoroughly studied, not always the case where most fossils are concerned.

Illus. 1-21. The Spoonbill or Paddlefish, *Polyodon spathula,* is a remarkable fish living today in the Mississippi River Basin. It is classed among the relatives of the sturgeon and other chondrostean fish. *Palaeoniscus* is a distant ancestor.

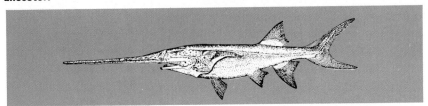

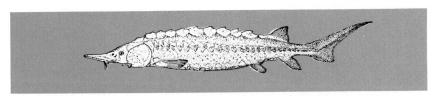

Illus. 1-22. The sturgeons, Acipenseridae, represent an undoubtedly very old group, directly descended from the early bony fishes, but typified by a degenerative ossification of the axial skeleton. The species illustrated is a *Scaphyrhynchus* from North America. Of the external bony armour, this fish still retains a number of rows of so-called ganoid scales.

Illus. 1-23. *Polypterus* is an extant genus from a previously renowned group of fishes, related, on one hand, to the sturgeons and, on the other, to the higher bony fishes, especially item 20 in Table 1-3.

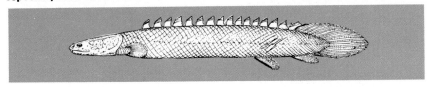

types developed typical fins from which the name of the entire group was derived. The first group (item 17) is of overwhelming importance to the history of the animal kingdom, because from this group developed all later groups of land animals, by way of the sequence of amphibians (item 18), reptiles (with birds as an offshoot), and mammals, among which, on biological grounds, man is also counted.

Some time before the first group, the Rhipidistia, diverged from the main evolutionary line, there appeared some rather large, remarkable fishes, the Actinistia (item 19), with a somewhat better developed type of lobate fin. These were the first bony fish, flourishing towards the end of the Palaeozoic era, that chose the depths of the sea for their habitat. For a long time it was thought that they had become extinct during the CRETACEOUS period, until a catch of the first live specimen of *Latimeria*, made in 1938 near the South African coast in fairly deep water, proved the supposition to be in error.

The Origin of Terrestrial Animals

Perhaps of even greater significance than the capture of the first living Latimeria known to man is the group of Rhipidistia, mentioned above. They, too, were fishes with lobate fins, but ample proof exists to lead to the assumption that the land environment was conquered by two groups deriving from them, the orders Osteolepiformes and Porolepiformes. These gave rise to two different groups of amphibians still surviving—respectively, the Anura and the Urodela. The Anura are possibly the direct ancestors of the reptiles. Present-day frogs and toads are known by this name, while salamanders are included with the Urodeles.

It is notable that frogs and toads in the larval stage have tails like salamanders, which they lose upon joining the ranks of the land animals. The most ancient reptiles had very long tails, of course, as do many modern reptilian types. Salamander-like animals keep the tail throughout their lives and thus form an offshoot from the evolutionary line which, so far, has produced no higher genetic forms. The possibility still exists, however, that these creatures may have given rise to some typical land reptiles that have not yet been recognized as being divergent from them.

44

2. DISTRIBUTION OF FISH POPULATIONS

Continuing with the development of fish life, some unusually interesting sidelights illumine the situation in various parts of the world.

Of course, fishes that have been imported from Asia bear little resemblance to those from tropical Africa or South America. For example, take a spot in Asia and another in Africa where the environment is practically the same. It would seem that a certain *Barbus*, living in Asia, would find its counterpart in an environment of Africa. Since it does not occur there, it becomes obvious that the same type of fish is not reproduced everywhere in the world. To each its own. Each part of the world has its own development of fish life, reflected, more or less, in the way the fish population is distributed throughout the all-encompassing oceans.

Ichthyogeography

Literally, ichthyogeography refers to the geographical distribution of the different families of fishes throughout the course of time. Every geologic age had its own distribution of the fish population, discovered by palaeontologists in their never-ending search through the rocks of prehistoric ages. It is no less difficult today to determine accurately which fishes are native to which regions than it is to make an educated guess from fossil remains. However, much can be learned from the different geological formations that help us to create a picture of the existing situation. Pictures reproduced in the form of even incomplete diagrams help to explain the tremendous, upward-surging development of fish life.

Compare today's geological layer—that is, the existing lakes, rivers and seas that are reasonably accessible to research—with the layers of long-vanished eras. If scientists know so little about today's geological layer, how is it possible that they can know much of anything about those of the far-distant past? The ravages of time have removed part of the evidence, while another great part, in the older layers, is buried under layers of more recent deposits.

History

The prominent name in the field of distribution is that of Alexander von Humboldt (1769–1859), whose book *Kosmos* was the first attempt to create a field of study concerning the distribution of plants and animals. A world traveller, von Humboldt picked up information wherever he went, slowly building random bits of information into a cohesive whole, until he had laid the foundations for a new branch of science, biogeography. Charles Darwin (1809–82) built the structure of his own ideas on the sturdy foundation laid by von Humboldt. Von Humboldt keenly discerned the relationship between conditions required for existence, climate, type of ground, and so on. Later, it was these activities of von Humboldt that assured the success of Darwin's journey on the "Beagle" to all the then-odd parts of the world. There were other researchers, such as Adalbert von Chamisso, who travelled from 1815 to 1818, and Dumont d'Urville, who made three trips around the world between 1822 and 1840. This research added further rungs to the ladder of development, and, therefore, to modern marine research and knowledge of the distribution of plants and animals.

The laying of the trans-Atlantic cable brought further facts to light. Life was discovered at deeper depths in the ocean than had ever been thought possible. The mere fact that life could exist in the impenetrable dark and under the crushing pressure of the ocean depths was enough to set the scientific world agog. Expeditions, one after another, set out to gather material and study this astounding discovery. Wyville Thomson led the "Challenger" expedition from 1872 to 1876 and the Norwegians undertook their Arctic expedition from 1876 to 1878. In the next year, from 1878 to 1879, the Swedish Vega expedition followed upon the finds of its predecessors.

Other expeditions came along thick and fast. Max Weber led the Siboga expedition at the turn of the century, and the Snellius and Dana expeditions practically overlapped at the end of the 1920's. The Dana expedition is of particular interest to ichthyologists, for it was on this trip that the Danish scientist, Johannes Schmidt (1877–1933), solved the riddle of the reproduction of the eel.

These were by no means all of the expeditions that researched this field. Many more were undertaken into almost inaccessible parts of the world and many brave scholars lost their lives in the pursuit of knowledge. (More on the contributions of these expeditions will be covered later.)

The Habitat

It soon became clear to researchers that, if they wanted to find a certain fish, they had to go to the place where that fish was known to live. In other words, each kind of fish is closely confined to a certain geographical area. The specific living area of a given fish is referred to as its "habitat"—the area it inhabits. (Maps throughout this book illustrate the habitats of the various fishes.) The question naturally arises—why is *this* particular fish confined to *that* particular area? How is such an area determined? Take the Tuaregs, for example. These hardy desert dwellers consider the whole Sahara Desert as their home. Wherever you travel in the Sahara, sooner or later you will come upon some representative of the Tuareg people. The Sahara is their habitat.

In the same way, a given kind of fish, through generations of exposure to climatic and regional conditions, becomes accustomed to, and actually a part of, the large number of BIOTOPES (bios=life, topos= place), regions of uniform environmental conditions, that constitute its habitat. A given biotope supports such plants and animals as are physically adapted to the conditions the biotope has to offer. Many factors, of course, can alter the constitution of a particular biotope from year to year.

We learn from fossils in rocks that different species of fishes than we now know used to inhabit the earth and that many living species are relatively new in the grand scale of evolution. Moreover, scientists have discovered that existing fishes which inhabited a certain region in those times now occupy totally different areas. At some point between then and now, the whole population picked up and migrated to a new biotope. It is not possible to say with 100 per cent accuracy how or why this took place in the past, but with the guidance of the principles of evolution, scientists can get a glimmering of understanding. At the same time, the distribution of fish populations also serves to direct our research into the evolution of the given fishes.

Discounting overseas migration, why are species of animals in North America close in kin to animals dwelling in Siberia? Why is it that a species becomes extinct in the region where it originated, yet continues to flourish elsewhere? To solve such problems, scientists penetrate deeply into the evolutionary aspect of the matter and somehow derive an acceptable theory.

Isolation

In the ages of greyness surrounding the development of life on our planet, when the first plants and animals were coming into being, the world was theirs alone. These first creatures were confined to the water —the land was an inhospitable place for their development. The remote descendants of these same creatures are still found everywhere in the oceans of the world.

Why isn't every living species found anywhere and everywhere, then? In trying to find an answer, consider the fresh-water fishes. Sea water is an insuperable barrier to the migration of fresh-water fishes, because such fishes cannot live in the strong brine of the ocean. Therefore, they remain land-locked—isolated by the surrounding areas of land. In the history of evolution, this isolation of habitats occurs frequently. For example, when the Sunda Shelf sank, the connection was broken between the Asiatic mainland and the islands of Sumatra, Java, and so on, which now remain to mark the spot. This had to affect the fish population.

If a certain group of animals is totally destroyed in a given area by a cataclysm, natural or otherwise, then that particular group will never spontaneously develop there again. The primary fresh-water fishes will be replaced by other fish groups, called secondary fresh-water fishes. Australia, incidentally, furnishes a splendid example of this secondary population situation.

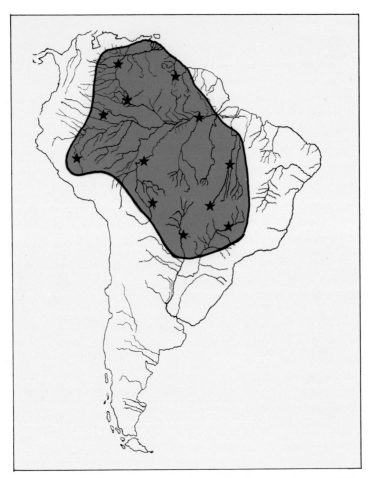

Illus. 2-1. Example of a distribution pattern. The distribution of random fish species is outlined and from this, it is obvious that the region of dispersal actually consists of a series of sampling places (localities). Presumably, the same species also inhabits the regions between these localities. A distribution area thus constitutes a number of sampling places, mutually interconnected by unexplored regions. In certain cases, the species may no longer be present in the inbetween regions, in which case a splitting-up of species into local varieties may have occurred.

Biogeographical Regions

The activities of men like von Humboldt and Darwin have led to the division of the earth's surface into "biogeographical regions," each one inhabited by its own characteristic types of plants and animals. The most striking example of this is the region of Australia, which has native to it such marsupials as the kangaroo and the wombat, as well as the egg-laying mammal known as the duck-billed platypus. These strange creatures exist nowhere else in the world, though other strains of marsupials are known elsewhere—for example, the various opossums of North, Central and South America.

There was much disagreement among scientists, however, on a positive classification of the various regions. Bird specialists tended, for instance, to differ in their ideas of classification from specialists involved with other animals, on the one hand, and from those scientists concerned with botanical considerations, on the other. The most difficult problems of this type lay in archipelagos—the Indonesian-Australian Archipelago being the research territory of Max Weber (1852–1937) and of his pupil, L. F. de Beaufort (1879–1968).

Illus. 2-2. Survey of the biogeographical regions. The heavy line is the so-called Line of Holmes, based on over-all distribution patterns of animals. The line separates the northern continents (Arctogaea) from those in the southern hemisphere (Neogaea and Notogaea). The broken lines denote boundaries of continental shelves based on general faunistic and floristic bioassociations. The figures correspond to those in the table on page 52.

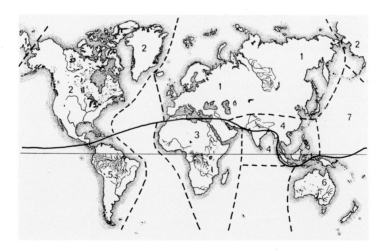

From the positions of the continents today, it has been inferred that in Palaeozoic times, all were connected into a single, huge continent, which Sir Edward Suess named Gondwanaland, after a district in India. On the map on page 51, the position of the primordial, equatorial ocean, named Tethys, is indicated by the Holmes line, the irregular, heavy line drawn across the middle of the map, dividing the north and south regions of the earth. The same line indicates the approximate division of the southern part of Gondwana and the northern part, called Eria or Angara.

Consideration of the creation of the present-day world divisions and of the composition of the plant and animal worlds leads to the determination of seven general biogeographical regions:

PRIMARY LAND DIVISIONS	GENERAL BIOGEOGRAPHICAL REGIONS	LOCATIONS
Arctogaea	1. Palearctic area	Europe, North Africa and Asia north of the Himalayas
	2. Nearctic area	North America and Greenland
	3. Ethiopian area	Africa, south of the Sahara, Arabia and Madagascar
	4. Oriental area	Asia south of the Himalayas
Neogaea	5. Neotropical area	South America
Notogaea	6. Australian area	Australia and New Zealand
	7. Pacific area	Polynesia and Oceania and the Pacific Islands up to Hawaii

The two island regions tangent to the shores of the prehistoric continents—that is, Indonesia-Australia and the Caribbean—must be considered areas of transition or mixing, where a change-over is being made from the flora and fauna of one to that of the other, with elements of both being present.

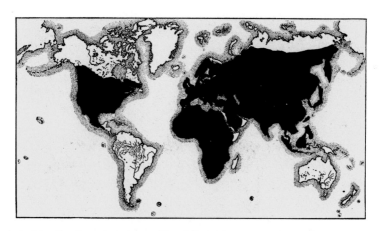

Illus. 2-3. Distribution of the carp-like fishes (Cypriniformes) extends over all of Arctogaea with the exception of those regions covered for extended periods of time with ice and snow, and the desert regions.

Illus. 2-4. The distribution of characins (Characiformes) points towards an origin in Gondwana, especially in the Ethiopian region. Penetration into North America is obviously a recent occurrence.

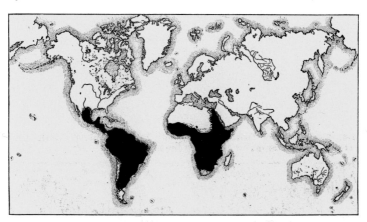

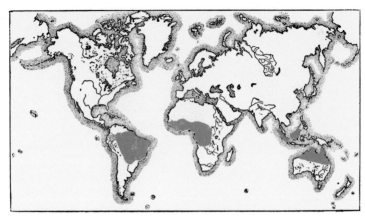

Illus. 2-5. The ancient group Osteoglossiformes obviously originated in Gondwana. The recent varieties must be considered relicts of a former hey-day.

Illus. 2-6. The pike-like fish (Esociformes) have a typical distribution in the temperate and colder areas of the northern hemisphere.

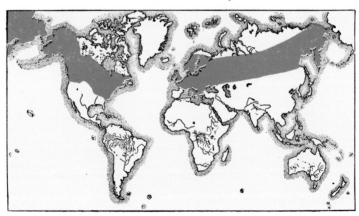

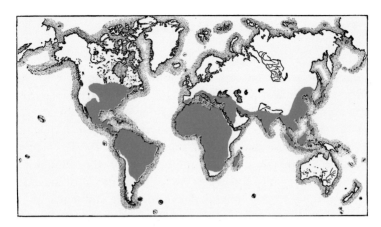

Illus. 2-7. The toothcarps (Cyprinodontiformes) also originated in southern Gondwana. They did not penetrate into the north until more recent times. The relative salt tolerance of a number of species of this order can certainly not explain a migration by sea to the various islands, as has been suggested by some scientists. The recent distribution, however, is certainly not so difficult to explain (see also page 739).

Illus. 2-8. The rather young group of perch-like fishes(formerly called Labyrinthici), which have a remarkable breathing-labyrinth, must be regarded, without any doubt, as primary fresh-water fish, which originated in Africa.

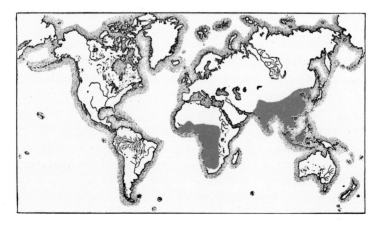

Influences on Distribution

It should be clear by now that numerous factors influence the distribution of the world's fish population. The largest factor is the place of origin, for it influenced the very coming into being and subsequent development of fish. A not insignificant rôle is played, too, by the survival factor and the adaptability of a species to changing conditions. Changes in climate, influenced by the changes in the general divisions of land and water areas, from the most archaic times to the present, have also exercised considerable influence in making the present distribution of the fish population what it is.

Historical Influences

In prehistoric times, the land and water masses were distributed differently than they are today. The first three maps of the world on pages 58 and 59 sketch the successive changes in land distribution in the Devonian, Permian, and Cretaceous periods. Compare these land arrangements with fish development discussed in Chapter 1. In Devonian times, the main land mass was a large, northern continent, accompanied by several large islands, and a much larger, southern continent corresponding in position to the modern continents of South America, Africa, Antarctica, Australia; and India. Compare Illus. 2–9 with this land situation, and you will quickly see why present-day lungfishes, for example, have such a remarkable distribution.

During the Permian period, the most outstanding change occurred in the existing land mass. The continent of Antarctica came into existence and extended from the polar region to the great area presently occupied by Australia. During the Cretaceous period, the old southern continent broke into three large masses, roughly corresponding to the present land distribution. Note that the land-bridge then extended between Asia and the Australian continent. There have been further changes since, of course, and the continents, writhing and twisting like living things, have in certain places alternated between submergence in the sea and emergence into a state of dry land.

Generally speaking, however, the present arrangement corresponds pretty well with the situation existing during all of the NEOZOIC period. The first part of this period coincided with the breaking-up of the land masses during the Cretaceous period when, coincidentally, a radical change took place in the development of fresh-water fishes. At the time that present-day Africa broke away from the continent we now call South America, the catfishes, inhabiting a wide area of the southern continent, were split into two groups.

These historical influences, though mostly traceable to geologic changes, are to a large extent also due to climatic changes. The circumstances of earlier epochs have already been briefly scanned. The warm climate of the Devonian period turned into the Silurian-Devonian ice age, which was characterized by continuous floods and violent volcanic activity. It was during this time that the Caledonian Alps in Europe, North Africa, and Siberia were formed. In the second half of the period, the already worn-down Appalachian Mountains of North America were given a new existence through further folding and upheaval of the land. In Australia, too, enormous, new mountain ranges were created by the seismic convulsions of the planet.

The Devonian period lasted 40 million years, but the distribution of land and water during that time as shown on the map on page 58 is, nevertheless, only a presumption of what the real situation must have been.

Various scientific findings lead to the belief that fish life began on the southern, primordial continent, somewhere around or during the Devonian period. To say, however, that fish life originated in Africa (for which there is considerable evidence) is not entirely correct. If the hypothesis is maintained that a primordial continent called Gondwanaland existed, and may have continued to exist in the same form throughout the time from the Cambrian or early Ordovician to the Permian period, it must also be asserted that fish life had its beginnings in Gondwanaland.

By this time, however, southern Gondwana and Angara to the north were already divided into small land masses, separated from each other by the teeming waters of the Tethys, the equatorial sea, which wound around the earth at its equator.

During the Carboniferous period, this sea withdrew more and more from northern lands which, in fact, were undergoing a period of rising. Already parts of the land which later became Europe were dry. Up to the Cretaceous period, no trace has been found of a land-bridge between Gondwana and Angara. A land-bridge is necessary to further the distribution of fresh-water fishes which are barred, you will remember, from entering the dangerous, salty ocean waters. Findings now tend to show that fish life was transmitted from Gondwana to

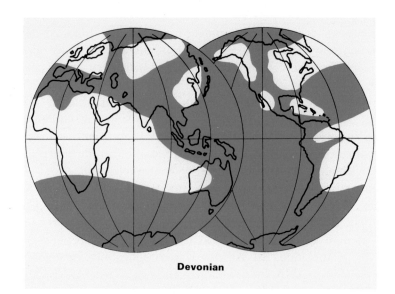

Devonian

Illus. 2-9. The earlier division of water and land deviated in important respects from that of today. On the basis of geological investigations, it has been determined which parts of the recent continents and oceans, respectively, were flooded by

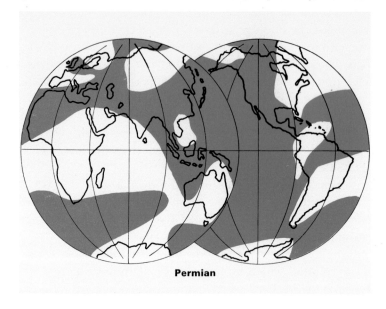

Permian

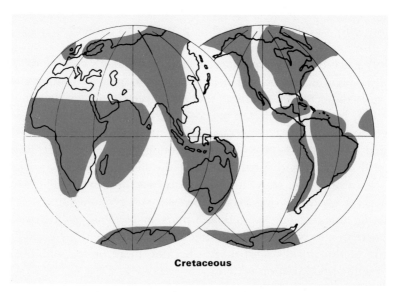

Cretaceous

the sea or were above it. The maps graphically present an idea of the water/land division during the Devonian, Permian, Cretaceous, and Tertiary periods.

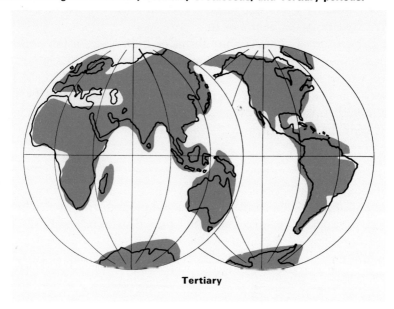

Tertiary

Angara only during the Cretaceous period, a hypothesis that fits well with other available facts.

Only since the Cretaceous period have the world's continents taken on their present shapes and locations. India, part of southern Asia, was still connected to Africa at that time (see the Cretaceous map on page 59), but the final break had occurred between Africa and South America. During the Cretaceous period, also, South America was still divided by a broad course of water running north and south. Eurasia was still connected to Australia along the belt of Indonesian islands, but the western link with North America was broken off. The eastern connection via the Bering Strait, however, still remained.

During the TERTIARY period (see map on page 59), which was the first part of the Neozoic continuing from the Cretaceous period, the picture of the world's land masses became more or less stabilized to that range of distribution which exists today.

The present-day Mediterranean Sea and the Russian-Asiatic lakes to the east are the final remnants of primordial Tethys. The peninsula now occupied by India had been a part of Africa, whose connection was destroyed by continental drift.

At this period of change many forms of fresh-water fishes and land animals found their way from Gondwana to the virgin land to the north. Coincidentally, too, Asia and Australia severed their land connection. The only land communication that still existed between Eurasia and America was by means of the islands spaced like stepping stones near the Bering Strait.

Salt Tolerance

Although it is not possible in this volume to delve too deeply into the many other factors influencing population distribution, the important part played by water salinity in the distribution of fresh-water fishes around the world cannot be overlooked. Up to a point, fresh-water fishes and non-swimming land animals can be compared. A salt-water sea or ocean is an insuperable obstacle. This means that primary fresh-water fish distribution can only occur overland, from river to river, from pond to lake, by flood and, sometimes, by waterspout. A land-bridge is normally a partially submerged mountain range. River systems can and do occur in such a range but, unless there is a flow-through of fresh water along the length of the land-bridge, there is little chance that they will indeed provide a negotiable passage for fresh-water fishes.

It has been shown that fishes originated in fresh water, so that, except for a few, all members of the primary groups are true fresh-water denizens. These fishes are called "primary fresh-water fishes" after Myers (1938), as opposed to "secondary fresh-water fishes," which can also survive in salt or brackish water. Salt water is fatal to many kinds of fishes, especially to the Ostariophysi. Since about 90 per cent of all existing fishes belong to this group, the remaining 10 per cent, which can live in salt water, are especially important in the proliferation of the fish population throughout the world.

A third group, the peripheral fresh-water fishes (so-called by Nichols, 1928), includes those groups of species which spend a large part of their life cycle in salt water, but which are still distinguishable from the marine species or groups to which salt water is not fatal. The division into categories of fresh-water and salt-water fishes is reinforced by differing constructions of the fishes' kidneys. The structure of the kidneys of fresh-water fishes is more primitive than that of marine fishes, another argument for the fresh-water origin of such fishes. (Anatomy is covered in Chapter 3.)

The majority of aquarium fishes (except for the sea-water aquarium fishes) that are now available on the general market are primary fresh-water fishes. This includes, for example, the lobe-finned fishes, the lungfishes, the catfishes, with the exception of some orders which are peripheral fresh-water fishes—that is, the loaches, carp-like fishes and the characins. The toothcarps and the cichlids are secondary fresh-water fishes and the sticklebacks, the atherinids and the gobies belong to the peripheral category.

Climate

Climate has a tremendous influence on many fish populations. The water temperature, in particular, is of great importance. Aquarists know only too well that aquarium water must be heated for most aquarium fishes from distant, tropical waters. The majority of imported fishes require a temperature ranging from 18–28 °C (64–82 °F).

The temperature may be allowed to fluctuate a few degrees either way, so far as individual species are concerned, but if a number of fishes originating in widely separated areas are kept in the same aquarium, the temperature differential, either upwards or downwards, must indeed be very small if the optimum temperature for all is to be maintained.

Looking at the various distribution maps, most of which are based

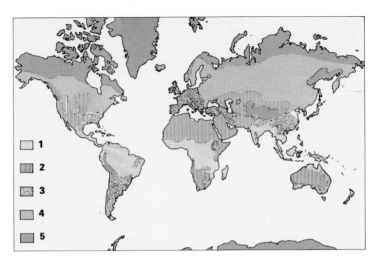

Illus. 2-10. A simple climate map. The world climate is differentiated into five types: 1. the tropical rain climate. 2. dry climate, hence deserts and steppes. 3. temperate rain climate. 4. snow-forest climate and 5. snow or arctic climate. Of these, in connection with the places of origin of most aquarium fish, the most important are the tropical rain climate and the temperate rain climate.

on facts concerning the different families, it appears that, within a given continent, population distribution is often limited by what seem to be invisible factors. For a clear example of this, consider the distribution of the *Botia* group (see map in Illus. II–73). Some species, at least, seem to object less to a lowering of the temperature than to diffusion into western desert and steppes regions. In comparison, the boundary in Asia of the habitat of the Danionini (see Illus. II–97) seems to lie north of the 20th parallel of latitude, a point at which the temperature drops too low to support the life cycle of the fish.

The best illustration of climatic influence is found in the distribution of the pike group. Pike (Esociformes, see map, Illus. 2–6) are typical inhabitants of the northern temperate zone, in the regions of coniferous and deciduous trees. Their distribution area is limited on the north by the encroachment of cold and on the south by temperatures that are sub-tropical. Except for the temperature, there seems to be nothing to stop their spreading even farther southward. A comparison of the climate map with the distribution of this particular population, in fact, shows that these fishes dwell in a climate that has no dry season, but is an Arctic-forest climate that extends across Canada and as far south as the temperate, rainy area in the United States south of the Great Lakes.

From a climatological standpoint, scientists observe that the distribution of certain fish populations parallels the spread of typical climatic regions, though this is less the case with families and larger groups than it is where genera and species are concerned. A family, of course, can be made up of more than one genus which, by specialization and conditioning, are able to populate different climatic regions. Every biotope, however, is typified by some kind of a micro-climate—a climate within a climate—that also makes adjustment to the habitat possible.

Tied closely to climate in any distribution area is the existing vegetation, which is a product of the climate. Many aquarium fishes come from regions of tropical rain forests, which provide ideal living conditions for them. But, there are other more or less important considerations. For instance, if a species in a given area finds competition too strenuous, it must either flee that area or become extinct. From a study of the distribution and life pattern of today's lungfishes, we know that they are fiercely competitive, for they can inhabit the most improbable biotopes even under the most competitive conditions. Such life patterns were developed gradually. The ancestors of the present-day lungfishes lived in free, open water. With the onset of the dry season, they moved to other, better watered areas. That they no longer make such dry-season migrations indicates that they have adapted to the impossibility of such migrations in the dry season. Instead, they accustomed themselves to retreating beneath the mud bottom, where sufficient moisture manages to collect to permit their survival. There is not enough to live fully—only enough to exist with all bodily functions practically at a standstill and the creature itself in a state of suspended animation for the duration of the dry spell.

Possibilities for Adaptation and Distribution

Fishes have certain possibilities available to them for adapting to changing circumstances. Such changes have appeared regularly in the history of the earth and have often resulted in the extinction of a large group. Any of the factors dealt with so far could be responsible for such an extinction. The animal must either have a built-in adaptability that will allow him to survive the change, or it must, if the change comes about slowly enough to allow time, escape the suddenly inimical environment. In case of escape, the group, for the most part, will survive. The more gradual the change, the more ways become

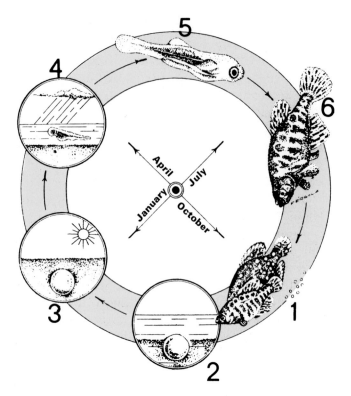

Illus. 2-11. Among aquarium fish are a number of the so-called annual fish, which have a life cycle of about one year. Immediately before the dry season in October, mating (1) takes place. The eggs are burrowed into the mud bottom of the biotopes (2), where they remain (3) four to six months. As soon as the water evaporates during the dry season, the parent fish die. The young do not hatch out (4) until the first rains fall in April. The larvae (5) develop quickly into adult fish (6) within a period of, again, about a half a year, thus closing the life cycle. Hence, these fish never know their parents. (See also page 798, *Cynolebias bellottii*.)

available for the fishes to respond to the situation, either by flight, by assuming control through physical adaptation to the new environment, or by giving up altogether and taking the road to extinction.

If the sea should suddenly flood the biotope of a primary fresh-water fish, the result will always be fatal, as will a sudden drought. If salt water seeps gradually into a fresh-water area, slowly turning the water brackish, the population has a choice of flight (migration), or adaptation to the saline content of the water. We shall see later on that such adaptation is impossible for primary fresh-water fishes. That the ancestors of present-day marine fishes adapted themselves to the increasing salinity of the world's oceans is a somewhat different thing. Secondary fresh-water fishes and fishes of the peripheral group have shown that they are unaffected by changes in salinity.

(Note on page 269 that this same theory of gradual replacement is also used to acclimate tank fish from salty or brackish water to fresh water.)

Individual eccentricities in the life patterns of popular aquarium fishes are generally traceable to an earlier adaptation to environment. For instance, the annual dry season marks the end of the life cycle for several egg-laying toothcarps. They mate just before the onslaught of dry weather and bury their eggs in the mud. (More about this under *Cynolebias*, *Aphyosemion* and *Nothobranchius*.) When the first patter of tropical rain puts an end to the dry spell, the eggs come to life and the young fish hatch out. These fish never know or have any contact whatever with their parents—who are dead and gone long before they come to life—but the fact that the eggs manage to hatch at all can only be the result of parental care. Many types of fishes from the savannah regions have learned to adapt in this way to the periodic dry spells.

The result of environmental adaptation appears in many guises, generally in the shape of the body, which will be discussed in Chapter 3. It was important to fish life that environmental adaptation developed at an exceptionally early stage in the earth's history, when the environment consisted of the primordial, tropical swamp. Adaptation to these surroundings was effected by means of a simple, but operable, intestinal respiratory system. Present-day descendants of those primitive fishes still possess that same, perfectly working, intestinal respiratory system, supported in many cases by dermal respiration (breathing through the skin). One very singular result of environmental adaptation is the development of the Weberian apparatus, the structure which connects the air bladder with the ear in the Ostariophysi (see page 133).

Early Distribution

It is interesting to consider just how the earliest fish populations in prehistoric times were distributed. The full story eludes us, however, like the fading of a radio signal, when we are forced to depend on the evidence provided by fossils in the rocks. Conclusions drawn from such evidence are not necessarily false, but hardly any clue has been found that sheds light upon the shadowed way of life in the pre-Cretaceous period.

There are indications that fish life originated in the southern primordial continent, Gondwana, and from there were scattered over the earth. One view on the order of appearance of the classes and orders of fishes has already been advanced—that catfishes followed directly after the lobe-finned fishes and the lungfishes.

A series of fossils showing a continuation of development of form has been found for the lobe-finned fishes and the lungfishes. These fishes occurred sporadically over the whole of Gondwanaland. In the present-day continents which formerly comprised this southern, primordial land mass, relics of those ancient times are still found in an occasional isolated species tucked in among the current fauna.

Scientists do not know of any forms of catfishes bridging the gap between Ordovician and Cretaceous times. Still, the structure of the dermal ossification of some ostracoderms and placoderms, for example, *Alaspis* and *Ophiolepis*, is identical with that of the Porolepiformes and that of *Hypostomus, Ancistrus, Pseudacanthicus* and *Corydoras* (from Ørvig, 1957) among others. A fossil from the TRIASSIC period, described as *Phanerorhynchus*, could very well be a catfish. And so, there are a few clues—vague enough to be just scarcely visible, but still better than nothing.

The conclusion may be reached that catfish are the oldest ostariophysans and belong to a type in between the ostracoderms, on the one hand, and the higher bony fishes, on the other. They flourished, to begin with, throughout Gondwana, except for the region now occupied by Australia, unless they were driven from there by some overwhelming cataclysm, and so no trace remains.

This view is supported by the fact that the oldest known fossils, dating from the Cretaceous period and representing the Ostariophysi, must be considered as catfish. The Characidae, generally considered to be older, occur as fossils only since the late Tertiary period (the end

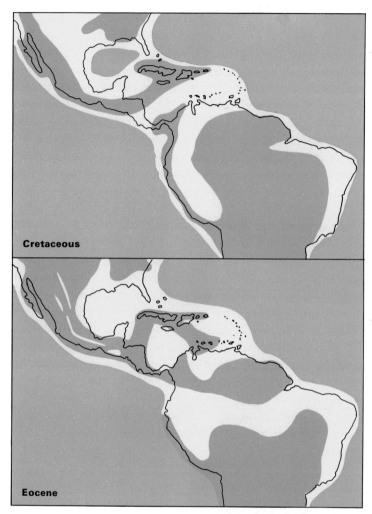

Illus. 2-12. The data upon which these two maps are based are particularly interesting. They show that in Central America, changing land connections have existed between North and South America. The continental shelf (yellow) and the land above water (green) were, as always, surrounded by a deeper sea (blue). In the Cretaceous period, both these parts of the world were continuously separated by a shallow sea. During the Eocene (beginning of the Tertiary), a part of the Isthmus of Panama and Guatamala apparently connected the Guiana Highlands with the island region of the Caribbean Sea. In the Cretaceous, there already existed a connection between these islands and the western land belt of North America. For the distribution of the toothcarps, among others, this connection has been essential. These islands were undoubtedly populated at that time by toothcarps and cichlids from South America.

of the Neozoic). Of course, this does not lead to a final conclusion, but the implication is certainly striking. It is also worth noting that these late-Tertiary fossils of Characidae come from Brazil and Egypt.

Another order of primary fresh-water fishes, the Osteoglossiformes, also inhabited the broad stretch of archaic Gondwanaland con-temporaneously with the lungfishes. In contrast to the rather small catfishes, these fishes grew to considerable size—typical of inhabitants of large, open rivers. A few species still exist in Africa, South America, and the Indonesian-Australian Archipelago. The striking thing about comparing these 50-million-year-old fossils with later forms is that there is hardly any difference between them, in spite of the great length of time that separates them.

During the break-up of Gondwanaland and the approach of North and South America towards each other, the region of the Caribbean experienced some turbulence. Throughout the Cretaceous period, an equatorial sea passage remained open between the Americas, south of Cuba and Jamaica, where present-day Central America is. Several times during the EOCENE period, the rising of the north-south mountain range closed off the sea passageway, shifting it towards the Amazon delta. In the late Tertiary period, after alternate breaching and re-folding of the mountain range, the final land connection between North and South America, as we now know it, came into being. The effect of the isthmus on the exchange between northern and southern animal groups was very great, and the Caribbean islands were, at that time, largely populated with animal groups incapable of migrating across the sea.

Illus. 2-13. Rapids and waterfalls cannot hold back the salmon as they move against the current in their mating migration towards the cold, mountain waters.

Distribution Patterns of Fresh-Water Fish

Most fresh-water fishes spend their entire lives in the same water, the same river basin, the same biotope. Some fishes, however, spend part of their life cycle in one environment and the remainder in a totally differing biotope. Two such creatures, the eel (Anguilliformes) and the salmon (Salmonidae) are striking examples of this. The eel hatches and develops from the larva in sea water, but eventually, as a young member of its species, seeks the fresh-water rivers and streams of the various continents. Eels continue to grow for a few years in the fresh-water environment, until they become sexually mature adults. At this point in their lives, they are instinctively impelled to return to the sea, where they will eventually spawn.

On the other hand, salmon hatch out in mountain streams and spend their youth in fresh water. When they have grown large enough to brave the perils of the sea, the salmon set forth, living for a period of years in the ocean. The full-grown fish ultimately returns to its home waters, to the very stream (or fish hatchery) in which it was hatched. Regardless of the difficulties that lie in the way, such as waterfalls, rapids, and dams, the salmon fight their way upstream, leaping water-

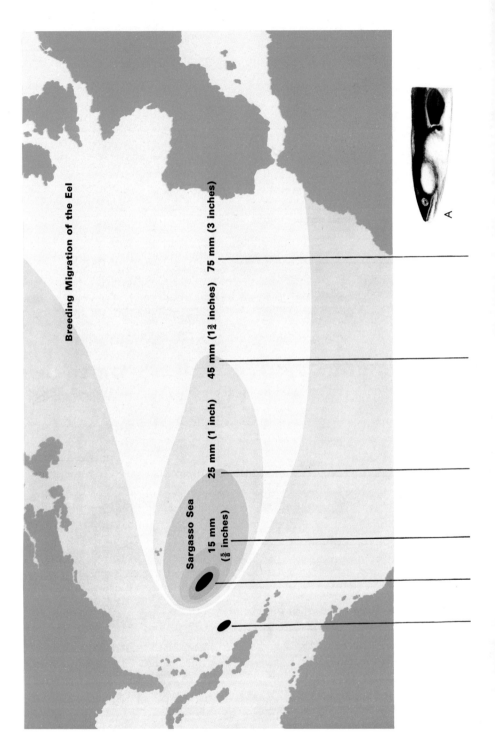

Breeding Migration of the Eel

75 mm (3 inches)

45 mm (1¾ inches)

25 mm (1 inch)

15 mm (⅝ inches)

Sargasso Sea

A

70

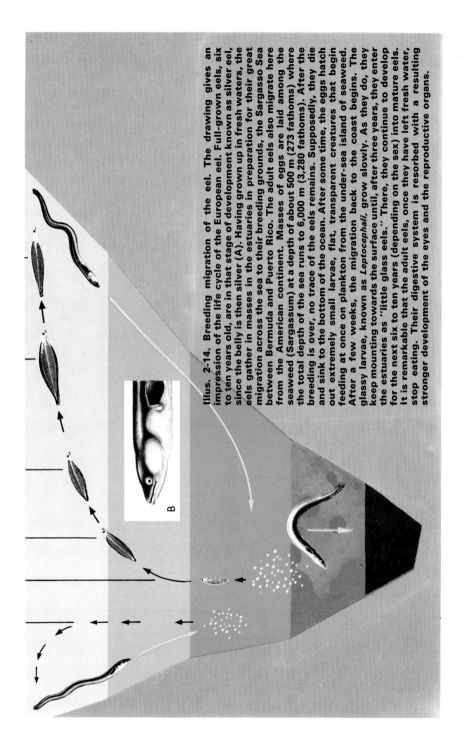

Illus. 2-14. Breeding migration of the eel. The drawing gives an impression of the life cycle of the European eel. Full-grown eels, six to ten years old, are in that stage of development known as silver eel, since the belly is then silver (A). Having grown up in fresh waters, the eels gather in masses in the estuaries in preparation for their great migration across the sea to their breeding grounds, the Sargasso Sea between Bermuda and Puerto Rico. The adult eels also migrate here from the American continent. Masses of eggs are laid among the seaweed (Sargassum) at a depth of about 500 m (273 fathoms) where the total depth of the sea runs to 6,000 m (3,280 fathoms). After the breeding is over, no trace of the eels remains. Supposedly, they die and sink to the bottom of the ocean. After some time, the eggs hatch out extremely small larvae, flat, transparent creatures that begin feeding at once on plankton from the under-sea island of seaweed. After a few weeks, the migration back to the coast begins. The glassy larvae, known as *Leptocephali*, grow slowly. As they do, they keep mounting towards the surface until, after three years, they enter the estuaries as "little glass eels." There, they continue to develop for the next six to ten years (depending on the sex) into mature eels. It is remarkable that the adult eels, once they have left fresh water, stop eating. Their digestive system is resorbed with a resulting stronger development of the eyes and the reproductive organs.

71

falls and struggling over fish ladders (a series of steps in a dam which help them climb upstream) until they again reach the place where they first saw life. There they mate and deposit their eggs in the cold, oxygen-rich, mountain water.

Both the salmon and the eel die almost immediately after mating, their ultimate purpose in life fulfilled. The background and development of such life cycles and the distribution patterns resulting from them are more comprehensible when we take into consideration historical distribution—especially the division of land and water areas due to continental drift. They are, however, phenomena that can stand considerable more study and research before they are fully understood.

Horizontal Distribution

To distinguish between horizontal and vertical distribution is rather strange, since the latter is a part of the former. For a long time, it was incomprehensible that many aquarium fishes—particularly the older ones—could die on the plane trip from the place where they were caught to their destination. A special examination, however, finally revealed that the swim bladder had burst. All happened to be species with a closed air bladder system. As the fishes were transported by air, the sudden drop in air pressure of the climbing plane caused the pressure to mount inside the bladder, until the bladder ruptured. Younger fishes hardly suffered at all from the change in air pressure, nor did species having a continuous, open connection between the swim bladder and the intestines.

It follows, then, that fishes are capable of dispersing horizontally over their entire distribution area, though they are actually impeded by the several ecological factors which we have already examined.

Just exactly what is the direct cause of distribution of any species? Take the first fishes, developing in the stagnant or slow-flowing waters of a flooded swamp—small, quiet fishes, browsing on the bottom where micro-organisms abound as food. If the supply of food to which they are accustomed becomes exhausted, the fishes might travel elsewhere in search of it. First, of course, they will try other food within their environment. If a fish does not like what it finds, it will search elsewhere for what it likes. The first migration, then, is undertaken for reasons of survival—to keep from starving to death.

While searching for a suitable habitat, the fish may be confronted with some circumstance that makes it necessary to adapt. Thus, through processes of natural selection, one part of the original population begins to follow a new and different way of life, while the few remaining behind still find sufficient food for their needs. Differentiation and specialization, caused by scarcity of food, were the first steps in fish evolution. Food has always been, and will always be, a worldwide problem for all species of animals. So long as a given area is capable of supporting a given number of living organisms, changes taking place in the combination of species will not affect the total number of organisms, if all other factors remain the same.

A second direct cause of migration is a threat to safety. If the existence of an animal is threatened in any way, it will seek safety in flight. A large group will spread out in alarm, darting in all directions to find a way out. Some will succeed. In those who do, secondary adaptations will often run parallel with the first. The development of surface armour by the first real fishes was probably an adaptation intended to protect the naked body against continuous attacks from the giant water scorpions of those times.

Vertical Distribution

Fish life exists from the highest mountain streams in the world down to the deepest abysses in the ocean. Fishes, therefore, also have a vertical distribution. The spread of fishes into areas other than those in which fish life first developed is largely the result of the two factors

Illus. 2-15. The transition between a highland and a lowland plain is usually characterized by a series of rivers with waterfalls and rapids, which, in the tropics, house abundant fish life. Particularly evident are those species that feed on the algae growing on the masses of rock.

mentioned above—a scarcity of food and a threat to safety. (In this book, we are not concerned with ocean fishes, which is a gigantic subject in itself.)

In tropical regions, a given species does not usually drift away from the same kind of biotope. The need for expansion, however, caused by overpopulation, malnutrition, and competition for survival, can cause a part of the population to break away in search of a fuller satisfaction of its needs upstream. With recently developed species, it is hardly possible to differentiate between populations at different levels in the river. Yet, with older fishes, it is often evident that a species has developed into a number of clearly recognizable sub-species. This is particularly true of catfishes and loaches. It is obvious, then, that the population of small mountain streams arrived originally from the lowlands by a process of gradual colonization of the main river bed and its tributaries.

A remarkable phenomenon concerning almost all fishes, but especially fresh-water fishes, is that they will continue to struggle against the current and give up only when exhausted to the point of being absolutely unable to continue the struggle. Many typical inhabitants of running water, on the other hand, are somehow able to attach themselves to the bottom by suction, so that they can rest and gather renewed strength for another bout with the force of the water. These fishes are often called bad swimmers, in contrast to good swimmers that inhabit quiet, open waters.

Loaches have a trick of hiding behind and under rocks on the bottom while they rest. The rocks divert the force of the current and create a quiet backwater in which the fish can recover strength without exerting effort.

Although good swimmers occur in open and smoothly flowing water, they nevertheless avoid rapids. A moderately fast flow of water will not stop many species from migrating, but generally fish prefer the quiet, open waters, flooded areas, pools and lakes. Many species experience an instinctive urge to migrate in the mating season.

It is difficult to determine, simply from the description of a biotope, whether it is a suitable place for reproduction. In many cases, it is not, a completely different environment being required in the mating season than at other times. This depends, of course, on the species concerned, but the matter is basically one of instinct—nobody knows better than the fish that their ordinary environment of free, open water will be unsuitable for their progeny in the first days of their existence.

Illus. 2-16. The Nile Basin between Lake Victoria and Lake Albert is surrounded by a savannah region. Here, numerous biotopes of best-known, African aquarium fish, from the labyrinth fish to the cichlid, are found.

Illus. 2-17. The widespread Finnish lakes form an ideal habitat for pike. There, they can hunt to their heart's content for the abundant minnows.

Illus. 2-18. Schematic view of a river course, which can be divided into three main sections. The upper reaches, origin, or young river, located in the high mountain range, is characterized by a considerable fall and, hence, a fast current, with waterfalls and much broken rock, and a surrounding landscape that is practically without flora.

The second section, the middle reaches or mature river, causes valley formation in the midst of the mountain range, sometimes waterfalls and especially rapids. The landscape usually has a well developed flora, in the tropics' dense forests, alternating with savannahs. In the terminal section, the lower reaches or old river, the current is medium to slow because of the slight fall of the river bed. The stream meanders a great deal and runs out into the sea over a delta. The power of the water causes a great shifting of rocks from the high mountains towards the sea, beginning with large boulders, which later become tumbling rocks, and finally, are ground down fine to gravel and sand. Along with the rock, of course, there is also a large quantity of organic matter and dissolved salts.

Natural Environment

The term "natural environment" means characteristic surroundings in open country where, with the influence of climate and soil composition, a basic unit of living space is created. The flora and fauna within the unit form a complex whole, so that altogether four factors compose the environment: composition of the soil, climate, plants, and animals. The earth as a whole forms a natural environment for everything that dwells upon it. The world scene is then divided into many smaller areas set apart by natural boundaries. The various land regions and the oceans of the world are different kinds of environment which whittle down into further sub-divisions of constantly diminishing area. The biogeographical regions thus constitute the first, rough divisions, each being made up of smaller environmental areas. You can work efficiently with the environmental unit, but the size of such a work unit depends entirely on the approach to it. A geographer, for instance, with bigger things in mind, will generally mark out a larger area than will the ecologist, whose interest is more concentrated. The ecologist's viewpoint may be more interesting, in fact, for its very smallness brings home all the more forcibly such comprehensible data as the vegetation and animal population peculiar to that area. Within such an environment, a certain interdependence binds the plants and animals, and existence is quiet and harmonious. Of course, the quiet and harmony are disturbed from time to time by outside influences, but if change in climate is at fault, the status quo will in time re-assert itself. Even the seasonal changes in climate are an intrinsic part of the local environment. The plants and animals within that environment have adapted themselves to the changing seasons. If there are animals present that do not get along so well in a dry spell, they will either try to find satisfactory surroundings elsewhere, or will establish a means of survival that will do until the proper climate comes around again. (Note the lungfishes.)

Another approach towards natural environment shows clearly that a very small environmental unit can be a highly suitable habitat for some species. On the other hand, such places are far too precarious for other species, which travel from such small areas to outlying units around them. For this reason, then, the ecological unit of the natural environment is divided into a number of the typical, small areas called biotopes. An aquarium is, in fact, a biotope and the plants and animals brought together in it form a BIOCOENOSE, or interdependent community of diverse organisms, if the individuals and the elements of their surroundings have been chosen wisely.

Illus. 2-19. The desert oases form a marvelous biotope for certain fish which have remained as relicts of the period when the region was still connected with the great rivers. The water supply origin is now mostly subterranean, for rain hardly ever falls there.

It ought to be clear by now that the natural life found in a given place developed as it did because of a specific succession of historical circumstances. It would not be sensible to say that African animals are not found in a certain biotope in South America because they could not get along in that environment. The aquarium is an experimental station proving just the opposite. The existing distribution of plants and animals throughout the world has come about as a result of all kinds of factors, each of which served its purpose in pushing development in the direction it has gone. Wherever the environment is the same, the same creatures can live together, so there is no real objection to keeping fishes from different parts of the world in the same aquarium so long as that miniature biotope fulfils the environmental requirements for each individual concerned.

While this explains how a given distribution pattern comes into being, it also explains how it is possible for a certain discontinuity to take place. Actually, every distribution area for every species consists of a larger or smaller number of interdependent biotopes. If a number of biotopes situated in the midst of others should disappear, the distribution area can lose its identity as a united whole composed of individual biotopes. The remaining biotopes now may become so far separated that the original exchange of organisms and species can no longer take place. When this sort of a situation seems to become permanent, there is only one result—differentiation. This is one set of circumstances which can lead to the development of new species.

Biological harmony prevails within any given biotope or natural environment. This means that the plants and animals of the biotope are mutually supportive in their relationships and can expect a beneficial return from the biotope. Also, the possibility of maximum food provision is evident. Since two kinds of plants or animals hardly ever require the same food, a variation in the make-up of the population is possible. Should any part of the living order vanish for any reason, its place is immediately filled by other forms.

In any given biotope, some types of fishes live on algae and others on vegetation. Still others—and not only very young fish—feed exclusively on micro-organisms. Other species live on worms, slugs, insect larvae and various crustaceans. Then, there are a number of rather powerful fish of prey, and these eat anything they can sink their teeth into.

A natural order made up in this way brings harmony with it, and all kinds of circumstances assure the proper maintenance of natural selection. The fish of prey play an important rôle in this regard, since they devour the weak and sickly members of other species.

Examples of Biotopes

To give an idea of the great variety of biotopes found in the open country, a few are illustrated here in color. Keep these in mind when setting up a home aquarium, but do not expect to reproduce anything like a natural biotope. The situation is often better, however, for public aquariums because of the space involved. If sufficient room is available, provide a large, above-water environment imitating river-

Illus. 2-20. The so-called winter dry climate is characterized by this type of landscape, which is seldom cultivated—heath with birches and bushes, peat bogs—with frost in the winter and rather warm, damp summers. In the open landscape only a few fish are found, for example, pike and mud minnows.

Illus. 2-21. The fast-flowing streams in the alpine landscape form the habitat for, among others, the oxygen-requiring trout. The water there is always clear and cold and contains little food. The insect world above the water usually forms the most important food source for these fish.

bank vegetation and flowering plants. Put these under a high, glass roof to provide natural lighting. Under such a roof, fruit flies for the insect-eating species can also be bred. (See also pages 292 to 294.)

Illus. 2-22. On the mud banks of many tropical rivers, especially in the estuarial regions, are flood forests of mangroves, which have rhizophores (aerial roots) to supply them with the oxygen they need. Here are the breeding grounds of many marine fishes which know that their offspring are safe in the nourishing fresh and brackish waters.

Fish Populations

In the natural state, most aquarium fishes live together in large groups. Only a few live alone or as small families. A fish population develops through the reproduction of fish that have grown up in the given place which is their natural environment. It depends on the species, but generally young fishes seek out a different biotope from that of maturing fishes. The life story of the eel is an excellent example of this. Before mating, the adult eel travels under its own power to the Sargasso Sea where the event takes place. Here, the eel larvae come out of the eggshell and begin the long trek that takes them to the fresh waters of the continental rivers and streams.

Another example is the birth biotope of migratory aquarium fishes, such as the *Pyrrhulina* and *Copella*. This is often a muddy, savannah pool where most of the enemies of the young fish are unable to live, but where there is sufficient food for the youngsters to grow on. When the fish get bigger, they penetrate farther into the biotope and populate somewhat deeper water. In some species, fish of only one size can be caught in a given place.

From the viewpoint of heredity, the population of a species forms a unit embodying certain characteristics of the population as a whole, though not all such characteristics may be present in any single individual.

In tropical savannah regions situated high above sea level many river systems are interconnected and thus distribution (migration) of the species over the entire system of waterways becomes possible. Such interconnection, however, usually occurs only during an exceptionally heavy rainy season which has resulted in floods. Sometimes, over a long period of relative dryness, no adequate connection exists between the waterways, and a kind of population estrangement may then occur. This, of course, results in the formation of new species. If, after a long period of time, these areas are again connected by waterways, the separated populations mix again, sometimes bringing about interesting results.

Fish Communities

In their natural environment, many aquarium fishes share their habitat with fishes of other species. For example, *Barbus sophore* is described as being caught in its natural state along with *Barbus gelius, Barbus guganio, Barbus ticto, Brachydanio rerio, Esomus danricus, Rasbora daniconia, Chela laubuca*, its relatives. The loaches, *Noemacheilus botia* and *Noemacheilus denisoni*, the catfish *Mystus tengara* and the Snakehead Fish *Ophicephalus punctatus* also belong to this community. The Snakehead Fish is the predatory pike in this community which takes care of the natural selection of its members. This fish, of course, would be a drastic upset to the order of an aquarium, but all the other species mentioned are perfectly suitable for a community aquarium. Unfortunately, not all of them are yet commercially available.

The description of *Rasbora heteromorpha* on page 520 provides a second interesting fish community, and elaborate data on the environment. This information is invaluable in setting up an aquarium representative of one particular locality. Unfortunately, the captors do not always include a documented report with their catch, and, as a result, the aquarist may become the victim of withheld information.

3. THE ANATOMY

OF FISH

Taking everything that has been written over the years concerning the anatomy of fish, an entire volume devoted to the subject would not be sufficient to exhaust the resources. It is, therefore, a rather precarious undertaking in a work such as this to attempt to condense, from the vast body of available knowledge, only such information as may be of interest to the aquarist, and so ignore many facets of the study that might be of equal or greater importance. Nevertheless, some knowledge of the external as well as the internal structure of the fish is indispensable to the serious aquarist. Hopefully, however, the information in the following pages will be considered only as an extremely brief introduction to this many-sided subject.

Body Shapes

It is not enough simply to say that fish are vertebrates, but the word vertebrate must be defined. All vertebrates have in common the external characteristic of a symmetrically constructed body plus the internal characteristic of a spinal column. The differences between invertebrate and vertebrate creatures and the transition from the former to the latter have already been discussed. Now, we shall consider more closely the details pertaining to the spinal column—that is, the skeleton or bony framework. In fish, this is popularly known as "the fishbone."

Fish occupy a unique position among vertebrates. In the first place, they form, as a group, the ancestral forerunners of all the remaining vertebrates. In addition, they are distinguished from other vertebrates by the fact that their entire life cycle (with, of course, certain exceptions) is spent in water. This wet environment is necessary to fish because— and again a general statement—their skin lacks a horny layer which might protect them against drying out. Two other features making water a necessary environment for fish are their gill breathing and their lack of a constant body temperature. Although some of these characteristics are shared by the amphibians, fish are undeniably recognizable for what they are. In spite of the enormous differences in body shape exhibited by all kinds of fish, there is never any difficulty recognizing a fish as a fish.

Illus. 3-1. The skeleton of a perch as an example of a bony fish shows all the important parts: a. intermaxillary bone. b. upper jaw. c. eye socket. d. fin-ray bearers. e. spiny rays of the first dorsal fin. f. fin membrane. g. branched fin rays of the second dorsal fin. h. neural spine of vertebra. i. lower jaw. j. bones of the gill cover. k. shoulder girdle. l. pelvic girdle. m. pectoral fin. n. the thoracic pelvic fin. o. hemal spine with fishbone. p. rib. q. vertebral body. r. anal fin. s. spinous process of hemal arch. t. hypural complex. u. caudal fin.

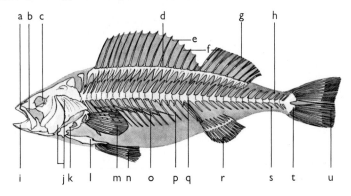

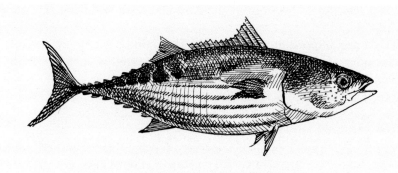

Illus. 3-2. The typical, streamlined body structure of a mackerel.

Streamlined Shape of the Body

Although there are exceptions, fish can generally brave any current in their environment. As far as modern fish are concerned, the ideal body form has finally achieved its ultimate in the well known spindle shape, a fine example of streamlining. In spite of the many variations of streamlining that have developed, fish still have not attained the wealth of form exhibited by the mammals. Perhaps water resistance played the prevailing rôle in this, for water provides many times more resistance to movement than does air. Even in more highly developed animals that have chosen to return to the water for their habitat, the spindle shape is evident (penguins and seals, for example). Of course, the streamlined fish possesses a head, a trunk, and a tail, although it is difficult to tell where one part leaves off and the next begins. The fins serve as propelling and stabilizing members.

The design occurring most frequently among the earliest fishes involved the many variations on the basic theme of the spindle shape. In principle, a fish is highest and thickest just behind the head. Fishes of this type are especially good and tireless swimmers, and usually, all fishes living in the open sea have such a spindle-shaped body. This is also typical of fishes that live in schools—such as the mackerel, herring and tuna. These fishes have an advantage over the shark, because they possess an internal air bladder that allows them to hover or float at some given depth in the water. The shark has no air bladder and the moment it stops swimming and loses forward momentum, it sinks to the bottom. However, the degree of importance of the swim bladder to marine fishes is still not well understood. It does not, in any case, seem particularly essential to mackerel which rest in great numbers on the sea bottom of the continental shelf during the winter months.

The most important variation on the spindle shape is flattening of the sides. This causes the body to become higher in proportion to its width or thickness. Fishes of this shape usually live in calm waters, where it is easy for them to maintain themselves in proper balance.

Arrow-Shaped Body Construction

The living habits of many species of fishes have resulted in the development of a shape like that of an arrow. These are predatory fishes which, literally, flash upon their prey like an arrow shot from a bow. They are actually not such good swimmers in the sense of being distance swimmers, but they are swifter and more active in short spurts. The best known representative of this group is the pike, which shoots out of its hiding place to fall upon prey swimming by, and thus goes about its job very differently from the bass, which is also a predator. The arrow-like body structure includes a powerfully developed tail and a substantial caudal fin. At the same time, the dorsal and anal fins are situated farther to the rear. The pike-type fish is found in practically all known families of fresh-water fishes and in some marine varieties. In general, they are dwellers of the upper water layers, and many of them are even surface fishes.

Eel-Shaped Body Construction

Several environments have provided the opportunity for the development of an eel- or worm-shaped body. The most outstanding example of this is, of course, the eel. There are many species among aquarium fishes that have this body build, or one similar to it, with more or less emphasis on the many possible variations. The body can be flattened on the sides, resulting in a ribbon shape which, combined with perfect streamlining, is found in the knife fishes. The deep sea also contains many species with this body build.

Flattened Body Shapes

Among the earliest fishes, which were all bottom-dwellers, were many having a depressed—that is, a dorso-ventrally compressed—body (flattened back to belly and spread out from side to side). This is an easily understandable structure which has remained unchanged by evolution to present times. It ranges from a simple flattening of the very large head—as in the more primitive forms—to a flattening of

86

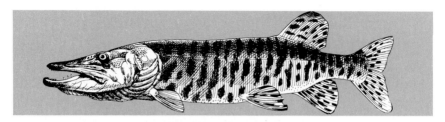

Illus. 3-3. Typical, arrowy body structure of a pike.

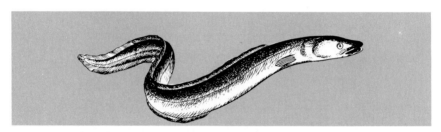

Illus. 3-4. Eel-shaped body structure of the European species *Anguilla anguilla*.

Illus. 3-5. The extremely flattened (depressed) body of the ray makes it possible for this creature to lie on the sandy bottom and, almost invisible in its surroundings, to wait for passing prey.

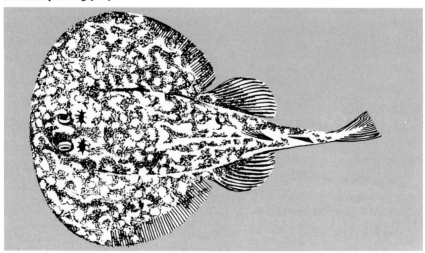

Illus. 3-6. The laterally compressed structure of the Angelfish.

the entire body, as exemplified by the skates and rays. Many varieties of this type are found in numerous families, especially featuring the more or less severely flattened breast and abdominal areas which characterizes fishes living at or close to the bottom. Among aquarium bottom-dwellers, the flattening is limited to no more than a broad, flat belly surface. Catfishes are an example.

Compressed Body Structure

A common variation of the typical streamlined body is the high body build, always coupled with a severe flattening of the sides. Many species of this type are known among aquarium fishes, including the numerous characins—for example, the Disc Characin and hatchet fishes—and many perch-like fishes—such as the Angelfish and the

Discus Fish. In their natural stagnant-water environment, these fishes are able to maintain their balance while motionless, so that they can hide among the stems and ribbon-like leaves of water plants. Their natural camouflage for this is usually heightened by the appearance of a number of dark, vertical stripes on the lighter-toned body.

Special Body Shapes

Although a thorough investigation of different body shapes is not intended here, something should be said about the strange paths nature has trod in the development of body form when it has been a matter of adaptation to a sometimes hostile environment.

The idea of body armour for protection of the soft parts is a very old one, and there are numerous variations to this among fishes. Among fresh-water fishes, the catfishes include a great variety of forms. Indeed, a number of varieties living in brackish water are also of a bizarre nature, such as the trunkfishes, the blowfishes, the Bullhead or Miller's Thumb, as well as sea horses and pipefishes. Observe, however, that all these strange shapes are related to the creature's adjustment to the struggle for existence. The deep sea contains the queerest possible forms of all, of which only the Sea Devil, or Angler Fish, will be mentioned. The best known European species is an Angler Fish *(Lophius piscatorius;* the American counterpart is *Lophius americanus)* and consists of a head with an enormous maw. On the head is a single dorsal fin ray that has been deformed into the shape of a fishing rod.

Illus. 3-7. The Sea Devil is more head than fish.

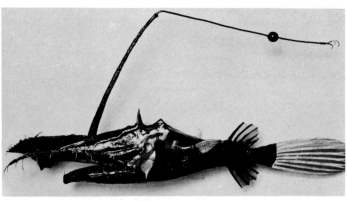

Skeleton and Fins

The household term for the skeleton and fins of a fish is an inclusive one—"fish bones"—but far from definitive or scientific. Actually, the expression is misapplied when the skeleton is being referred to as such. The frame or internal skeleton is the entirety of tissue which is more or less substantially stiffened with lime salts and which lends support to the body of a fish (or of a higher animal). The spinal column is built up around the chorda dorsalis (see page 25). The development of the parts of the skeleton will not be too fully treated at this point, not, at least, beyond what will prove useful in the discussion and treatment of the various families of aquarium fishes. This applies especially to the upcoming sections of this chapter.

The most important sub-divisions of the skeleton or frame are the spinal column, the cranium, and the skeletons of the paired and unpaired fins. All sub-divisions of the skeleton serve as points of support for and places of attachment for the connective tissue and muscles.

Development of the Spinal Column

The spinal column—also known as the axial skeleton—is the most important part of the internal skeleton. Around the chorda dorsalis of young animals, two pairs of concentrations of connective tissue develop at regularly spaced intervals from the centralmost mesoblastic tissue (the MESENCHYME), which, by deposition of lime, can turn into cartilage and bone. The first blocks of cartilage to take shape in a cartilaginous fish remain cartilage throughout its life, while in most bony fishes they more or less quickly calcify and stiffen into bone. Sometimes, the cartilage stage is entirely by-passed, as it was with the primeval bony fish.

The number of vertebrae equals the total number of body segments, the muscle bundles, each vertebra lying between two such segments. Half the vertebral placement of one segment overlaps half the following segment, etc. The segments are separated from each other by membranous connective tissue, the so-called SEPTA (singular: SEPTUM).

On the vertebra itself, a number of protrusions, called PROCESSES, can be distinguished. In most cases, these are well developed and give support to the fins, among other things. These protrusions are evident on each side of each vertebra, both above and below. The upper pair of processes on each vertebra form an arch on the dorsal side of the spine, called the NEURAL ARCH. The lower or ventral pair of processes form an arch on the ventral side of the spine, called the HEMAL ARCH. Both arches usually bear spiny pieces of bone, the neural and the hemal spines. The neural arch of the vertebra encloses the spinal cord, while the hemal arch encloses the arteries. The spinal cord was first constricted and, in many cases, almost completely replaced by the series of vertebral bodies. In most cases, the constriction turned entirely to bone leaving no canal through the middle of the vertebrae.

Because, in the case of fishes, the tail muscles are so active, the alternating construction of the muscle segments and vertebrae is especially functional. Two consecutive vertebrae must be moved with respect to each other, which is possible only if both are controlled by the same bundle of muscle fibres. As far as the septa are concerned, these can be distinguished as vertical and horizontal. The vertical septa lie partly crosswise to the lengthwise axis of the body, both dorsally and ventrally, above and below the spinal column. The horizontal septa lie between the spinal column and the sides of the body. They serve for the attachment of muscles and are often strengthened by

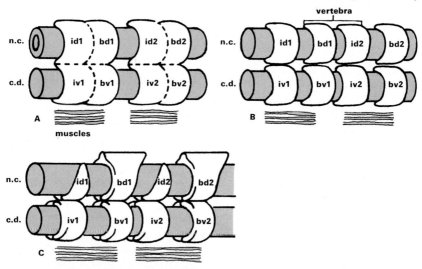

Illus. 3-8. Three sketches of the development of the vertebral bodies around the nerve cord (n.c.) and the notochord (c.d.). In stage A, pieces of cartilage are formed per each muscle segment, four pieces on both sides—an interventral (iv) and a basiventral (bv) piece around the chorda, and an interdorsal (id) and a basidorsal (bd) piece around the nerve cord.

In stage B, the basal parts of the first muscle segment have shifted towards the inter parts of the second segment. In stage C, a vertebra is formed from parts of two succeeding segments; in the basidorsal parts the primordium of the neural spine already shows.

small ossifications, the ribs. Fish can possess ribs that are directed dorsally (towards the back) as well as ventrally (towards the belly and enclosing the abdominal cavity). The first are usually short, while the latter are long.

The number of vertebrae is constant for a given species; within groups, however, it is sometimes variable—up to about 400 for sharks, to 120 for eels, and between 35 and 100 for most fishes. In a few groups, there are only a small number of vertebrae—only 14 or 15 in the backbone of the sea horse, for instance.

Extremities of the Spinal Column

In the forepart, the spinal column continues on in the form of the skull, while at the rear, it develops into the caudal fin. The median fins are inserted above and below the tail section, while in the trunk, the extension of the spine occurs in the limbs, the motile accessories of the fins.

Since the connection of the skull to the spine is fixed in the skeleton of the fish, the head remains immovable, whereas among the higher animals, especially the quadrupeds, this is not so. Although in principle the atlas-axis complex is present in fish, the bones are fused together into a single unit.

The end of the spinal column usually features a terminal vertebra, to which the caudal fin is attached. We shall return to this subject shortly. The unpaired and paired fins start out as folded skin which, during their development, are supported by the vertebral processes.

The Cranium

The head of a fish is constructed around a cartilaginous case (CHONDROCRANIUM) that is stiffened by dermal ossification (forming the OSTEOCRANIUM). The chondrocranium is formed very early and develops into a rigid brain case, more or less heavily ossified, depending on the group to which the fish belongs.

The dermal ossification of the skull does not pass through a cartilaginous stage, but originates directly from ossification of certain connective tissues. These ossified connective tissue patches are laid down in various places inside and outside the cartilaginous cranium.

Among the earliest fishes, the Ostracodermi and the Placodermi, the osteocranium (formed by dermal ossification) must have been of considerably greater importance than it is to most latter-day fish. As noted before, the armoured catfish with its durable skin armour

92

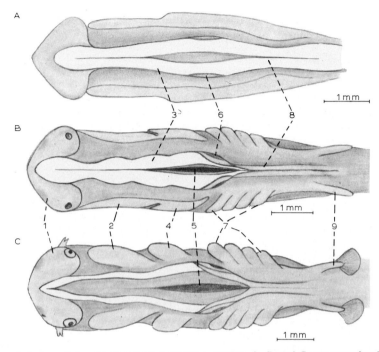

Illus. 3-9. Larval development of *Callichthys,* stages A, B and C representing larvae of respectively 2.7 mm (1/10 inch), 3.1 mm (about $\frac{1}{8}$ inch), and 3.5 mm (about $\frac{1}{7}$ inch). From this, it may appear that development progresses very rapidly. 1. snout plate (ethmoidal plate). 2. the primordium of the jaw. 3. trabecula, cartilaginous strand between the anterior and posterior part of the cartilaginous skull. 4. tongue bone arch, hyoid arch. 5. pituitary opening. 6. position of the auditory capsule. 7. gill arches. 8. end of the chorda, parachorda. 9. developing pectoral fins.

is a splendid example of an extended, over-all osteocranium, while the internal skeleton of these fishes is also well ossified. Any lesser ossification of the axial or dermal skeleton must be considered a reduction from the norm, or, if you will, a degeneration, or in most instances, the maintenance of an embryonic stage, or an arrested juvenile stage (see neoteny and paedomorphosis, page 31). A diminishing of the amount of bone in the body occurred very early in the evolution of fish. The head has remained longest, well protected by its sturdy armour of bone.

The primitive, cartilaginous skull is never completely closed; there are always one or more openings, in the roof of the skull, which are called FONTANELS. The osteocranium, however, can completely overgrow these openings. At the back of the skull—the occipital region—there is an opening to permit passage of the spinal cord. This is the FORAMEN MAGNUM. Below this is located a basal conical unit that forms

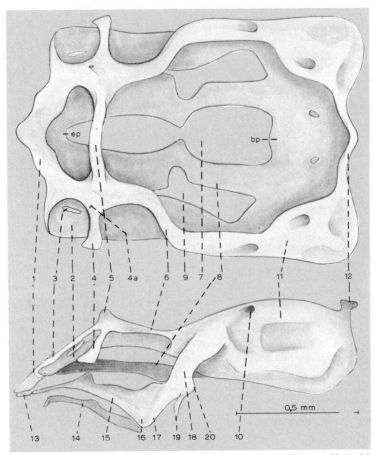

Illus. 3-10. The cartilaginous skull of *Callichthys*, larva of 10 mm ($\frac{3}{8}$ inch) total length. Skull viewed from above and from the left. In this stage, about the maximum cartilage formation has been reached. The dermal ossification begins to show as small platelets (see Illus. 3-11). 1. lamina precerebralis. 2. nostril. 3. nasal cartilage. 4. septum (partition) between eye and nose (lamina orbitonasale) with 4a. orbitonasal opening for optic nerve. 5. epiphyseal arch, across the skull, connecting the orbital cartilage rods (6). 7. hypophyseal foramen. 8. trabecula. 9. sphenoid fissure. 10. foramen for orbitonasal nerve. 11. auditory capsule. 12. Arabecula. 13-20. cartilaginous elements of jaws and attachment of the jaw to the skull (after Hoedeman, 1960).

94

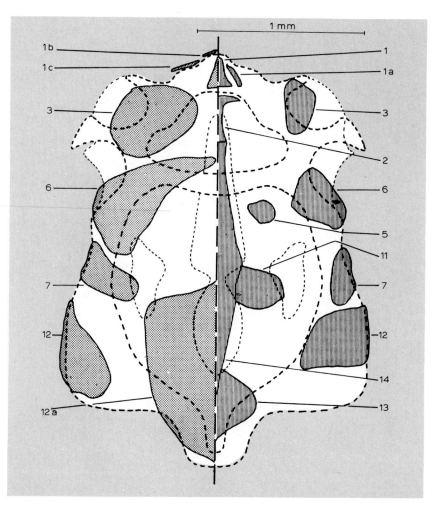

Illus. 3-11. Outline of the cartilaginous skull (chondrocranium) of a young (15 mm or ⅝ inch long) specimen of *Callichthys,* in which are indicated the places where ossification has already begun. The left side in dorsal view, right side in ventral view (after Hoedeman, 1960).

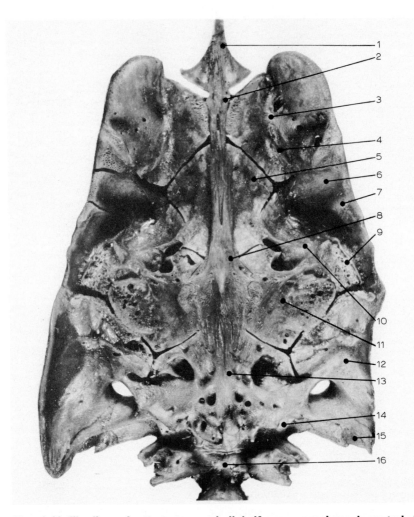

Illus. 3-12. The floor of a *Hoplosternum* skull, half-grown specimen, in ventral view for orientation of the positions of the various bone elements. 1. snout plate (ethmoideum). 2. ploughshare bone (vomer). 3. lateral ethmoid. 4. anterior (pterygoid) articulation of jaw suspensorium with the lateral ethmoid. 5. orbitosphenoid bone. 6. frontal bone. 7. sphenoid bone. 8. palate bone (parasphenoid). 9. sphenotic articulation of the hyomandibular arch. 10. lachrymal bone (pleurosphenoid). 11. prootic. 12. pterotic. 13. basal occipital bone (basioccipital). 14. lateral process of the first vertebra. 15. bony cap of the auditory passage (opistotic). 16. second vertebra.

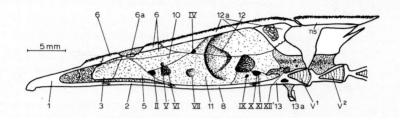

Illus. 3-13. Medial sagittal section through the skull of *Hoplosternum* showing principle elements of craniovertebral connection. Only the first vertebra has fully ankylosed with the skull. Figures as in Illus. 3-12. 6a. frontal aperture. 12a. skull cap bone (supraoccipital). 13a. hemal arch of the first vertebra, ns is nuchal shield, V^1. first vertebra, V^2. second vertebra. The Roman numerals indicate the nerve passages. II. optic nerve. V. triplet nerve (trigeminus). VI. eye muscle nerve (abduscens). IV. pulley nerve (the trochlear nerve). VII. facial nerve (facialis). IX. taste nerve (glossopharyngeus). X and XI. mixed nerves (vagus and accessorius). XII'. branch of the nerve strand to the Weberian apparatus.

the connection with the first vertebra. In many fishes—especially fresh-water bony fishes—this basal cranial unit is ankylosed (fused solidly) with a number of the anterior vertebrae to form a rigid complex. Among the Ostariophysi, the Weberian apparatus (the connecting structure between the air bladder and the ear) is housed in this complex.

The skull is, of course, also where the sense organs are lodged—hearing (the otic region), sight (the orbital region), smell (the olfactory region), and taste/touch (the ethmoidal region). It is also the place for the entire hub of the nervous system, the brain itself.

The Median or Unpaired Fins

Fins are characteristic of fish. The median (middle-line) fins include one or more dorsal fins, anal fins, and, at the conclusion of the spinal column, a caudal fin. The structure of the ultimate vertebra is very interesting. It may actually be a complex of vertebrae terminating the spine and onto which the caudal fin is adjusted. This is called the HYPURAL BONE, or, the HYPURAL COMPLEX, which is formed of the expanded and more or less fused hemal spines of the last few vertebrae, and therefore becomes a firm support for the caudal fin.

97

The Hypural Bone

Among fish developing quickly and having heavy ossification of the spinal column, the terminal vertebra is broadened out vertically into a flat, triangular bone. Among other groups, a hypural complex is formed, consisting of two or more modified vertebrae. The kind of hypural bone or complex present depends on the living habits, environment, and rate of bone development of the type of fish concerned (cf. Hoedeman, 1960, 1961). In a number of groups, the formation of vertebrae seems to go on endlessly, while in others the spinal column tends to taper down to very thin, long, terminal vertebrae, often ending in a hair-thin, whip-like tail. Although the axial skeleton often determines the outward appearance of the caudal fin, it is far from always evident externally whether an asymmetrical fin is attached to an also asymmetrical vertebral extremity.

Spines and Fin Rays

Fish fins are built up of elements that are grown together in pairs (LEPIDOTRICHIA), the origin of which can be traced back, for example, in most armoured catfishes. These lepidotrichs are transformed bony dermal SCUTES (in Latin, *scutum* means shield) which, in the armoured catfishes, fill in as FULCRA (modified scales or scutes) in the azygous area of the back, where the lateral scutes meet. The same applies to the spines. The segmentation of spines and fin rays begins at the extremities, which explains why the spines of the callichthyids, for example, do not show any segmentation. Rapid ossification forestalls segmentation, and in this case, ossification begins before segmentation starts.

Support for the Fin Rays

The fins are made up of dermal elements and bone formations. Their connection with the spinal column is provided by fin ray supports, or RADIALS. In the embryonic stage, these are cartilaginous rods set along the vertebral axis, one between each pair of neural spines, and, for the anal fin, between each pair of hemal spines, for the length of the fin.

The Limbs or Paired Fins

Most fish possess pectoral fins and ventral fins. These can diverge greatly in development. In the process of reduction, the ventral fins are most likely the first to disappear; the pectorals seldom are lost

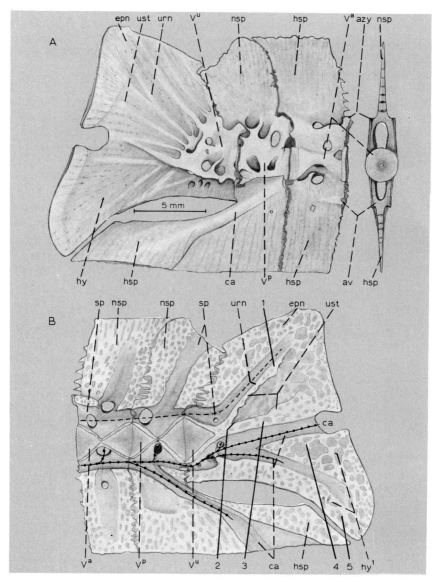

Illus. 3-14. Hypural complex (end of the tail) of *Hypostomus plecostomus*. A. lateral view of the last three vertebrae, with front view of the penultimate vertebra. B. the same vertebrae in median sagittal, showing the canals for the caudal artery (ca) with its branches (↦⟶⟶), and of the spinal cord and urostyle.

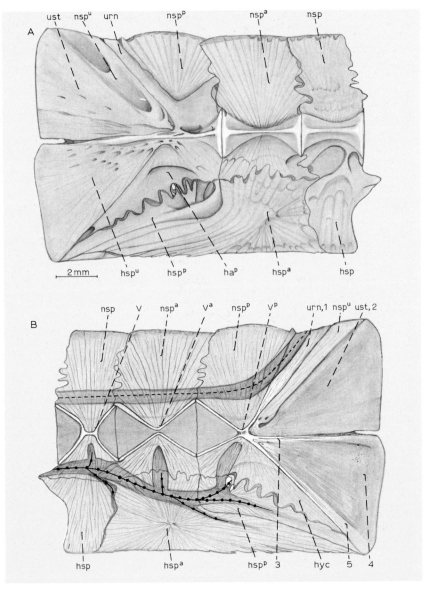

Illus. 3-15. Ultimate vertebrae of *Tetraodon oblongus,* for comparison with the hypural complex of *Hypostomus plecostomus*. A. right lateral view. B. sagittal section.

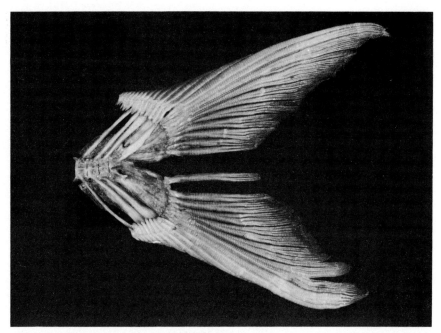

Illus. 3-16. Skeleton of a fish caudal root showing the gradual transition of the fulcra through unbranched into branched fin rays.

entirely. The placement of the paired fins is also subject to variation. Some systematic classifications are even based largely on the placement of the ventral fins which, remarkably enough, can be pushed far forward between the pectoral fins, and in some groups even as far forward as beneath the throat. This is the case, for example, in some labyrinth fishes.

The spines and fin rays of the paired fins are formed and developed in the same way as the median fins. However, their symmetry is often disturbed. The fin ray elements form a supporting complex usually from elements of the internal skeleton combined with external (dermal) ossification. These supporting complexes are called the SHOULDER GIRDLE and the PELVIC GIRDLE, corresponding to the same structures in higher vertebrates.

The Shoulder Girdle or Pectoral Girdle

In the beginning, the pectoral fins probably developed in the same way as the supporting elements of the median fins, simply having a point of contact with the spinal column. In most fishes, a part of the

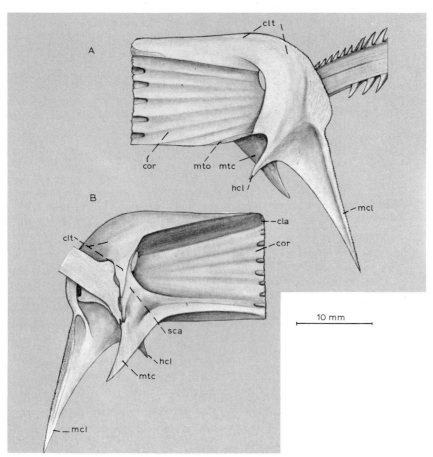

Illus. 3-17. Left half of the shoulder girdle of *Pterodoras granulosus* (342 mm or 13½ inches total length). A. ventral view. B. dorsal view. cla is claviculum (collarbone); clt is cleithrum; cor is coracoideum; hcl is hypocleithrum; mcl is metacleithrum; mtc is metacoracoideum; mto is mesocoracoideum; sca is scapula.

shoulder girdle belonging to the internal skeleton can also be distinguished, as opposed to those elements which must be considered dermal (skin) ossifications. In the cartilage stage, two shoulder blades (SCAPULAE) and two bones resembling a crow's beak—the CORA-COIDEA—appear. The dermal skeleton consists of a pair of bony plates (CLEITHRA), running vertically directly behind the heart, and a pair of narrow collarbones (CLAVICULAE), running downwards under the gills, but the whole complex is complicated and highly variable in shape. In some groups, dermal ossification plays a greater part in the complex than the internal bones of the axial skeleton. The result, however, is always a good support for the active pectoral fins.

102

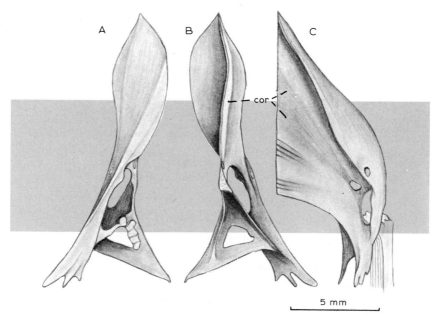

Illus. 3-18. Right half of the shoulder girdle of *Eutropiellus debauwi* (163 mm or 6⅔ inches total length). A. dorsolateral view. B. ventrolateral view. C. dorsal view. cor is coracoideum.

The development of the forelimbs is an important one, as the larval fins make a half turn—that is, the upper edge of the embryonic fin flap turns towards the outside, while the lower edge turns inward so as to lie against the body. The ventral or pelvic fins, which develop later, continue to maintain the embryonic position—that is, the outer edge of the fin flap remains on the outside or turns slightly forward. The development of arm and leg movements was preceded for a long time by this opposite rotation of the foremost and hindmost limbs. Have you ever wondered why your forearm bends forward and your lower leg bends backwards—the two movements being precisely opposed to each other? We would certainly look a lot different than we do if our arms and legs were attached to our bodies so that both pairs of limbs bent in the same direction. Of course, there was an entirely different purpose motivating this early, embryonic rotation. For the fish, the rotation had a certain practicality. Although it is not entirely clear, it appears that, first, the rapid development and the placement of the pectoral fins and, second and probably most important, the position assumed in the water by the larval form, have had something to do with this rotation.

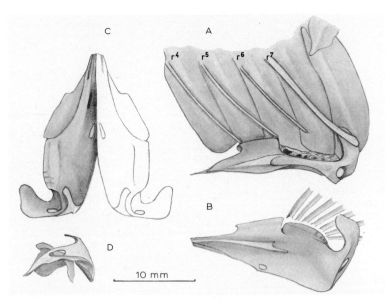

Illus. 3-19. Pelvic girdle of *Callichthys* (187 mm or 7⅜ inches total length). A. inner side of ventral body scutes with the right half of the girdle in position, showing the attachment to the ribs (r⁴ to r⁷). B. dorsal view of the right half of the girdle. C. entire girdle in ventral view. D. posterior view of the right half with the ventral side turned upward.

The Pelvic Girdle

The support elements for the ventral fins are, in principle, brought about in the same manner as those of the pectoral fins. Two rods of cartilage initially grow out into almost triangular plates, enclosed in muscle tissue. Usually, these plates grow together in front and, in the case of catfishes, among others, they form a rigid, pelvic girdle. In most fishes, however, the pelvic girdle stays far behind the shoulder girdle, and ossification is limited in many cases. Among sharks, lungfishes, and a few bony fishes, the pelvic girdle remains cartilaginous.

In the rest of the fishes, the pelvic girdle becomes ossified, but remains simple and free-moving in the muscle tissue. As a rule, there is no connection between it and the spinal column. Exceptions to the rule include many catfishes, especially the armoured catfishes, as has been demonstrated (Hoedeman, 1960, 1961). Among these fishes, a situation develops—similar in some amphibians—in which a number of ribs are connected directly to processes on the girdle.

The pelvic fins develop the same way as the median and pectoral fins. The first fin ray is often a spine.

104

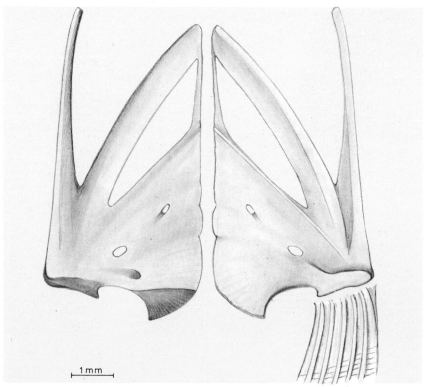

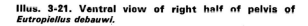

Illus. 3-20. Pelvic girdle of *Diplomyste papilosus*.
left, dorsal view; right, ventral view from below.

Illus. 3-21. Ventral view of right half of pelvis of
Eutropiellus debauwi.

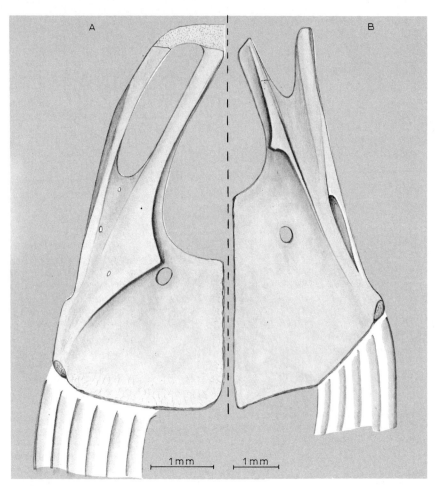

Illus. 3-22. Pelvic halves of: A. *Glyptosternum* in ventral view and B. *Gagata* in dorsal view (family Sisoridae).

106

Skin and Scales

The best protection animals have against outside influences of all kinds is the organic system of tissue layers and their associated structures. In fish, perhaps one of the most important functions of the skin is to protect the fish against drying out and against the incursion of all kinds of parasites. Pigmentation occurs in the skin as protection against high intensity of light, and an important support of this protection is found in the origin and development of dermal ossification—that is to say, in the bony plates and scales. It has already been shown that cooperation between the internal skeleton and the bony elements formed by the skin plays a large part in the formation of the skull, the limbs, the girdles, and the median fins. The skin can play a prominent rôle in respiration (skin-breathing) by absorbing oxygen and giving off carbon dioxide. From the beginning, the skin has naturally been the location where the sense organs are most substantially developed. As an auxiliary organ to the kidneys, the skin can serve to expel or drain off excess salts and waste products from the body.

The skin is not composed of homogeneous tissue, but consists of three layers—the superficial mucous membrane, the outer skin or EPIDERMIS, and the innermost layer, the DERMIS or CORIUM. Actually, the epidermis is the most important layer, not only because it contains the mucous cells that secrete the outer covering of slime, but also because it contains poisonous glands and many sensory end buds.

The epidermis is a continuous layer of epithelial cells covering the whole body, including the body openings. In fish, the epidermis is nothing more than a simple layer of living cells containing normal protoplasm. Since cells become lost at the surface because of wounds or other damage, the epithelial cells are replaced from underneath. Serious injuries sometimes make restoration of the epidermis difficult, if not impossible, and this can prove fatal to the fish.

Skin Glands

Perhaps the most important glands in the epidermis are, from the fish's view, the mucous cells which secrete and maintain the outermost mucous layer. They occur in great numbers on every part of the body. Next in importance is a large number of glands—actually, poison glands—that excrete alkaloids. The secretion may range from a light irritant to a strong poison. Also found here are several types of nerve cells, directly or indirectly involved with the lateral line organ.

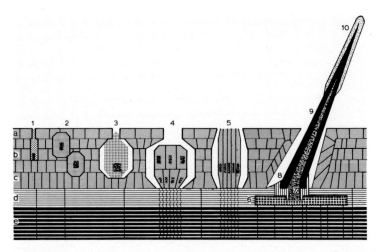

Illus. 3-23. Schematic cross-section through the skin of an armoured catfish showing the various tissue layers and cells. a to c are outer skin (epidermis) which forms the not-shown slime layer. a. surface layer of slightly squeezed cells. b. central sheath of three cell layers which enclose: 1. slime cells. 2. pigment cells. 3. gland cells (poison cells). 4 and 5. two types of sensory cells. c. basal epithelial layer, connecting with d. surface layer of the actual skin (dermis), containing mainly blood vessels, connective tissue, and pigment cells. e. lower corium layer, with strong connective tissue fibres, bound by cross fibres; carries and develops the bony scutes (6), which develop from a number of bony rings (pediments), each of which can bear a dermal tooth. These teeth consist of (7) a pulp cavity inside the dental body (9), which is closed off at the tip by an enamel cap (10). The whole dental structure is anchored to the scute (6) with connective tissue fibres.

Corium

The dermis or corium varies greatly in thickness, but, unlike the epidermis, it is usually homogeneous in structure. It is built up of layers of connective tissue formed from the middlemost germ layer. Among higher vertebrates, the dermis is leathery in composition. It has a different structure in fish, however, and dermal ossifications are formed from it—the bony plates, the skin denticles, and the scales. The development of these dermal ossifications is especially easy to follow in the armoured catfishes. In the rest of the fishes, where this type of ossification is limited to the head and a few other parts, the development of dermal ossification is harder to follow.

Dermal Armour

In discussing the development of fishes (see page 28), it was shown that dermal armour was found among the earliest fishes. Similar external skeletal structures, therefore, must be considered as very primitive in origin. The formation of "ordinary" scales, although they are created in a similar manner, came later. The bony plates in the fish's skin (Callichthyidae, Loricariidae, Amphiliidae, etc.) originate from small, bony rings (pediments) in the corium layer. Two or more of these rings, fused into a unit by the depositing of lime, form a bony scute or plate. Dermal denticles are usually formed on the surface of the plates by the uppermost layer of the corium. Since these dermal denticles are identical in structure and development to the regular jaw teeth, they are considered equivalent to them. A tooth such as this is made up of a basal unit, of the tooth itself, consisting of DENTINE with a pulp-filled central cavity, and of a layer of tooth enamel on the outside. The base of the tooth is fastened to the basal plate with stiff strands of connective tissue in such a way that it remains moveable. The greater part of the embryonic denticles on the bony plate is usually lost, but a number of them do develop into stiff teeth and spines.

Scales

In the range of development between heavy bone armour and bare skin, scales present a middle path between functional protection and maximum flexibility of the body. Had dermal ossification in the earliest fishes developed into a stiff armour-plating with little ability to flex, the undermost layers of bone would soon have lessened in rigidity. In

Illus. 3-24. Two examples of so-called cycloid scales and a ctenoid scale. a. *Erythrinus*. b. *Copeina*. c. *Nannaethiops*.

a   b   c

one group of fish, close-fitting, dermal armour was finally formed of small bony plates with a complete surface layer of dentine and enamel (ganoid scales). By further reduction of the dentine and enamel layer, the current, commonly occurring scales, composed of a flexible, bony material, came into being. In all cases of a close-fitting skin covering, the plates or scales are arranged in rows that overlap like rows of roof tiles.

Note that ordinary scales are never found on catfishes. Catfishes are either bare-skinned or armoured with bony scales or bony plates armed with spiny denticles. From this, only one conclusion can be drawn—that there surely have been no recent catfishes that have given rise to other fish groups. Any such possible relationships must be sought for in times long past.

Musculature

We are all acquainted with the flesh of fish, the part we customarily eat. It is composed of bundles of muscles that lie in a compact mass under the skin. If, for example, we fillet a cooked fish or clean a smoked salmon, we can clearly see that the flesh on both sides is arranged in an upper-and-lower division, separated by the previously mentioned membranes or septa. At the same time, it can be clearly seen that the flesh on the abdomen, where the body cavity is located, is thinner

Illus. 3-25. Sketches of the way in which the muscle bundles run in *Hoplosternum*. A, B. median sagittal and lateral sections at a and b in section D. C. enlarged view of the caudal region, D. E. horizontal sections at d and e in section A.

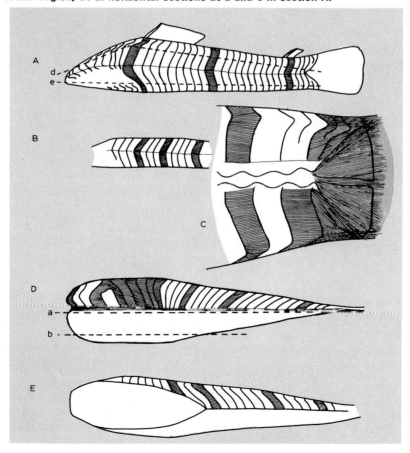

than on the back. The center of gravity of most fish, then, lies above the bodily axis (middle-line), so that, if a fish gets sick, it is no longer in condition to maintain its balance and turns upon its side, or even completely over, with the belly upward.

Balance is normally maintained by the stabilizing surfaces and steering equipment—the median and paired fins.

If we strip the skin from a fish, we can then clearly see that the muscle bundles also have a vertical division in which the different segments are divided into zig-zag shapes by the septa. The muscle segments or plates (MYOMERES) are thus the scale-like pieces of flesh which, when cooked, easily separate from each other along the separating membranes (both vertical and horizontal septa). The zig-zag forms are directly related to the form and placement of the vertebrae with which they correspond. In the early stages, the skin is also folded in accordance with the same pattern and this gives rise to the pattern in which dermal armouring develops.

This type of muscle—the so-called striated muscle—is controlled directly by the motor nerves. In addition to these axial body muscles, this type also includes the muscles of the eyes, gills and fins.

Smooth muscles (unstriated), on the other hand, operate with regard to the digestive system, the reproductive organs, the swim bladder and the lungs.

Electrical Organs

Muscle fibres in general are elements adapted to rapid chemical reactions. Chemical energy is translated into muscle contractions, or, in the case of electrical organs, by means of a modification of the muscle tissues into a kind of electrical element—a condenser which can be charged and discharged at will. The electrical organs are thus muscle bundles that have a specialized function, developed from striated body muscle. The muscle plates are arranged in accordance with the principle of the voltaic pile or galvanic battery and do, in fact, operate in the same way to accumulate and discharge a sometimes very powerful electric current. The well known Electric Ray fish (*Torpedo torpedo*) can discharge a current of 200 volts with a force of 2000 VA (volt-amperes or watts) into its immediate surroundings. This is enough to stun or even kill an approaching enemy.

Electrical organs of the same kind that occur in rays and various Ostariophysi in primitive times evidently protected many an ostracoderm from its enemies.

Respiratory and Digestive Organs

These two systems are mentioned in the same breath, not only because they are closely interwoven with each other, but also because both developed out of the same original organ. In the development of fishes, we saw that even the most primitive fishes possessed an apparatus that was suited both for obtaining nourishment from food and oxygen from the water. This PRIMITIVE INTESTINE or GILL BASKET further developed along several lines. In many cases, however, the dual function of the intestinal canal has been retained (consider INTESTINAL RESPIRATION). The original, embryonic intestine has two ends—an inlet and outlet (in the more primitive organism, there was only one opening for both functions). The inlet developed into a mouth, and the outlet into the anal opening. All functions for breathing and digestion, excluding those of some of the auxiliary respiratory organs, take place between these two openings.

Mouth and Teeth

The evolution of the mouth in vertebrates is a most interesting phenomenon, and it is a pity that it cannot be discussed more fully here. At first, the mouth was simply an inlet for the water that contained both oxygen and food, but soon, the fish had to develop some kind of action in the mouth that would permit it to take in special foods that were not suspended in water. So, the first fish mouths were under-positioned RASP MOUTHS, and the edges were provided with dermal denticles, or rasp-like teeth. Stiffening of the mouth with cartilaginous elements followed as a necessary evolutionary step, thus producing real jaws. In fact, ossification of these cartilaginous elements led to the formation of such jaws as are found in the bony fishes. The lining of the oral cavity with skin tissue gave rise to the development of teeth, which appeared in several different ways in several different places in the oral cavity, not simply confined to the jaws.

MOUTH GLANDS, or buccal glands, are of little interest where fishes are concerned. The watery environment kept the oral cavity moist, thus making salivary glands superfluous. One of the few glands that did develop—for instance, among the adult, parasitic hagfish and the lampreys—gives off an anticoagulant fluid that prevents coagulation of the blood of its prey.

A TONGUE comparable to that of the more highly developed verte-brates is also lacking in fishes. In some families, a structure similar to a tongue has developed in the bottom of the oral cavity, as in the archer fishes (see Toxotidae on page 947).

The TEETH, as already mentioned, developed from the skin. Because the mouth opening was clad inside with epidermis, teeth could develop anywhere at all in the mouth. They most frequently occur on the jaws, however, but can also appear on the bony palate and the pharyngeal bones, as well as on other areas covered with oral mucous membrane. The throat, or pharyngeal, teeth of the carp-like fishes are also true teeth, constructed of dental bone (dentine). These teeth develop on the edges of the pharyngeal and, especially, the hypopharyngeal bones, or, as among the cichlids, all over the surface of the pharynx. Carp-like fishes have no teeth on their jaws, their absence being made up for by the pharyngeal teeth in the gullet.

Pharyngeal Cavity (The Throat and Gills)

In fish, the oral cavity connects through the pharyngeal cavity to the esophagus, which, in turn, is connected, by way of a pair of dorsally lying ducts (the Eustachian tubes), with the auditory organs and a ventrally lying canal (DUCTUS PNEUMATICUS or air duct), connecting with the lungs or air (swim) bladder. In fish, the entire space between the mouth and the pharynx is known as the PHARYNGEAL CAVITY. In the second or rear half of this cavity lie the GILL ARCHES, which are cartilaginous elements. The GILL LAMELLAE were formed from the primordial intestine and are richly supplied with blood, serving for the exchange of gases. In very young fish, as well as in degenerated groups, each gill arch has its own outlet opening. Among the bony fishes, a gill cover or OPERCULUM is formed on the outside, providing only one opening for the rearward emission of the breathing water.

On the oral-cavity side of the gill arches are small processes, known as GILL RAKERS, which serve as food strainers. Their purpose is partly to protect the delicate gill lamellae and partly to trap microscopic food particles and pass them on to the pharynx.

Swim Bladder and Lungs

It will probably never be discovered whether the auditory organ developed before the air bladder (the swim bladder) or lungs. Let us start with the supposition that breathing by means of the skin and the intestinal canal was effective enough to fulfil the oxygen need of the first bottom-dwelling fishes. For these fishes, whose eyesight was possibly limited, a superior development of the organ of hearing was more important than an air reservoir. It is, moreover, now clear that two types of air bladders, or air chambers, must be distinguished. The first and undoubtedly oldest type is a bilateral protrusion of the esophagus or fore-gut, derived from the rearmost embryonic gill pouches. The second type constitutes the actual swim bladder and is a protrusion at the end of a more or less long ductus pneumaticus. In some cases, the situation is not very clear, because not only is there a change of form, but also because the various chambers and air bladders lie close together and are sometimes fused into each other.

The original, bilateral air chambers which, among the ostariophysans, are connected to the hearing organ by means of the Weberian ossicles, are also found in a number of families which do not belong to this group, such as the Mormyridae. It can be asked whether these

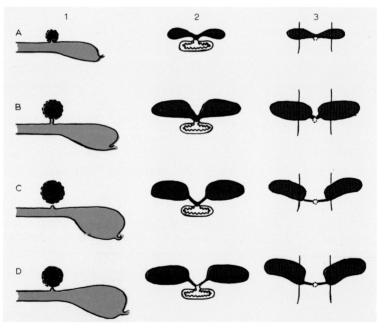

Illus. 3-26. Development of the two lateral air sacs in *Callichthys*. The different stages are: A. total length of fish 4.3 mm (about $\frac{1}{5}$ inch). B. 18 mm ($\frac{23}{32}$ inch). C. 40 mm ($1\frac{19}{32}$ inches) and D. 78 mm ($3\frac{1}{16}$ inches). The cross-sections are made: 1. vertically through the gullet. 2. vertically crosswise through the connecting duct to the intestine. 3. horizontally through the middle of the bladders.

lateral "ballast tanks" play a possible rôle in maintaining balance by communicating faulty body angles to the ear labyrinth, or whether there is a possible connection between these structures and the maintenance of balance in running water. It has been determined that in many varieties of fishes these twin air chambers (whether or not encapsulated in a bony structure) are connected with the outer world by means of a membrane, and, in many cases, there is also a connection with the lateral line organ. On the other hand, there is a direct or indirect connection with the ear. With the aid of this apparatus, the fish can receive vibrations from their surroundings (*see also*, under *Nervous System and Sense Organs*, Hearing, on page 126).

It is certain that these air chambers have no hydrostatic function. Such a function, however, can be ascribed to the true swim bladder, because, although general agreement as to the function of the swim bladder has not yet been reached, it is certain that, in addition to a respiratory function, the swim bladder may eventually serve a hydrostatic function. In various groups, the swim bladder serves exclusively as a means of communication. With the bladder, the fishes make vibrations which are easily propagated through the watery medium to reach like-voiced species-companions. These receive the vibrations in their own swim bladders, which now become hearing bladders. The vibrations, inaudible to the human ear, are of considerable special use for the fishes. In the first place, they let the fishes continue to maintain a contact with each other that would otherwise be poor in the often murky waters, especially since the eyesight of these primitive varieties is usually poorly developed. Also, the vibrations permit the parents to remain, in a simple way, in contact with their young, which, as can be observed in the aquarium, react promptly to the vibratory signals. In this connection, see also the discussion of the Weberian apparatus (page 133).

There are two types of swim bladders. Many species of fishes have a swim bladder that is connected to the intestinal canal. Another group has a swim bladder which lost its connection with the intestinal canal very early on. The fish of the first group (which are called physostomi) quickly adapt themselves to changes in pressure by taking on or being relieved of gas through the connecting duct to the intestine. Fishes of the second group (which are called physoclysti) are not able quickly to diminish or increase the amount of gas in the swim bladder, but can, by means of a special structure called the OVAL ORGAN add to or reduce the gases in the swim bladder. That this type of swim bladder serves as an auxiliary respiratory organ, especially for deep-water dwellers, perhaps appears in the high percentage of oxygen (up to 90 per cent) that is found in such cases. For shallow-water species, the swim bladder gas usually consists mostly of nitrogen (up to 96 per cent), and in this agrees pretty well with the usual composition of air.

At the present time, LUNGS occur only in a few living fish species. In primitive times, possession of lung-like organs was, however, a common occurrence. At present, it is not completely clear whether the lungs of fishes, at least of present-day species, are strictly the same as the lungs of higher vertebrates. In either case, the discharge of the esophagus is into a ventrally located pneumatic duct, which leads to the lung sacs, which in turn lifts upward to a position (dorsal) above the intestine. Why these lung sacs open abdominally into the esophagus is not clear, but perhaps this has some connection with the position maintained by young fishes. In the larval stage of most of these groups of fishes, the young are suspended by threads on the head, the body consequently being vertical. We can thus assume that the intestinal protrusion developing in the larval stage occurs ventrally and in later stages, as the fish swims freely about, it turns laterally upward. If this is so, and if the lungs of fishes are the homologues of those of the higher vertebrates, this explains, at the same time, the peculiar structure in men and mammals in which the air duct lies in front of the gullet, with all the consequences deriving therefrom.

Gullet and Gastrointestinal Canal

In fishes, just as in other vertebrates, the esophagus, with its important appendages and protrusions, connects with the mid- and hind-gut. The transition from fore- to mid-gut is formed by the gullet and, if present, a stomach. It is usually a wide, elastic, strong, muscular duct which turns into the stomach without any line of demarcation. The walls of the stomach, which is sometimes a U-shaped sac, are richly provided with a layer of digestive glands which secrete the gastric juices. At the transition from stomach to mid-gut is a ring-muscle, the PYLORUS, and right at the start of the mid-gut, ducts from the gall bladder and the pancreas discharge. In many fishes, the pylorus has a varying number of blind sacs.

Depending on the diet of the fish, the digestive tract is constructed in different ways. Many species (lampreys, lungfishes, sea horses, wrasses, and numerous carp-like fishes and catfishes) are lacking a stomach—for others, the place where kneading, mixing, and pre-

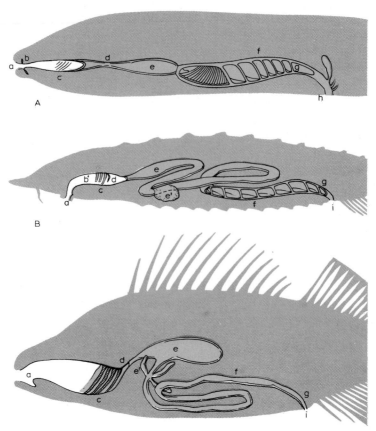

Illus. 3-27. Diagrams of digestive tracts of A. lungfish *(Protopterus)*. B. sturgeon. C. bony fish in general (perch). The various parts are: a. mouth. b. nostrils. b'. spiraculum (breathing duct). c. gill slits. d. esophagus. e. stomach. e'. pyloric ceca. f. intestine with spiral in A and B. g. rectum. h. cloaca. i. anal opening (anus).

digestion of food takes place—so that the fore- and mid-gut are connected without any clear line of demarcation. Except for the pyloric blind sacs, which actually have the same internal structure as the stomach, an enlarging and lengthening of the digestive tract is found in all kinds of folds of the intestine, or, as in the case of sharks, by a spiral valve inside the gut. Furthermore—just as among mammals—the intestinal canal of flesh-eaters is short, that of plant-eaters very long, while that of the species that live off bits of food material that have sunk to the bottom is longest.

The mid-gut ends, finally, in the very short, straight hind-gut, opening to the outside through the anal opening (anus) just in front of the anal fin.

118

In addition to the already-mentioned glands for digestion in the stomach, the gall bladder, the pancreas, the liver and the spleen also play important rôles.

DIGESTION in fishes is carried on as follows (in principle, it is the same as the process among higher vertebrates). The food, depending on the species, enters the stomach as fine particles (as, for example, in eaters of plankton, or carp-like fishes which grind food fine in the mouth) or large chunks (as, for example, piranha or perch and pike), and is broken down to a near-liquid mass by the stomach juice. The stomach juice of fishes is not always an acid, but can also be alkaline. The process of digestion takes a long or short time depending on such factors as the temperature and the kind of food. After going through the stomach (or if no stomach is present), the food passes into the alkaline vicinity of the mid-gut where the secretions of the pancreas further break down the proteins, fats and carbohydrates. The gall bladder also excretes bile especially for the conversion of fat. Certain enzymes finally convert the predigested food particles into materials that can be absorbed through the intestinal wall into the bloodstream and then be transported throughout the body. The liver, which lies in the abdominal cavity and is usually reddish brown, serves as a storage place for food reserves. It contains oil rich in vitamin D, carbohydrates and proteins which, in time of food scarcity, are released into the blood. In this respect, aquarists can vacation without worry if no means are provided to feed the fish while they are gone. Fish can, if well fed and healthy, subsist for weeks on their reserve, which in many cases is particularly necessary.

Bile is made by the liver and is stored in the gall bladder. The pancreas is an especially important gland for digestion, and another of its functions is the secretion of insulin. The spleen, a dark red organ, plays a rôle in the formation of new blood corpuscles.

The Excretory Organs

By embryological predisposition, excretory and sex organs are closely connected with each other. Nonetheless, they will be discussed separately here, as far as is possible.

The excretion of waste, where this concerns the intestinal system and digestion, can be treated briefly. Indigestible materials are cast out through the anal opening in a very simple manner.

The KIDNEYS are quite significant to fishes, especially fresh-water fishes, for one of their most important tasks is to keep the body salts the body fluid in balance with the water in which the fishes live. Sea fishes, which live in water having a higher salt concentration than is possessed by their own bodies, have a tendency to give off water from their body to the surrounding water. Among fresh-water fishes, which have a higher salt concentration in the body, the tendency is to continually take up more water into the body. The function of the kidneys is, among other things, to maintain the required balance.

Thus, the structure of the kidneys, especially of the renal tubules, is again an indication of the fresh-water origin of fish life.

The way the kidneys function is very complicated. In principle, the blood flowing through the kidneys rids itself of a surplus of water and of poisonous break-down products (a combination of nitrogenous materials, such as uric acid), which are conducted as urine to the exterior by means of ducts.

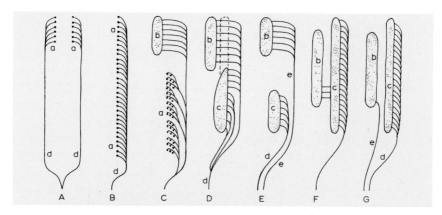

Illus. 3-28. Layout and development of the urogenital system of fish. A. embryonic, primitive kidney (idealized pronephros), which forms kidney ducts along left and right sides of the vertebral column, emptying into the urinary bladder through the paired ureters. B. ideal theoretical situation with a single tubule (renal corpuscle) for each vertebra (only the right half is drawn). C. the anterior renal corpuscles develop into gonads; multiplication of posterior tubuli tending to share duct with the gonads. D. further development of gonads and the kidneys. E. development of separate single ureter and duct for genital products marks the general situation in amniotes. F. situation in lungfish, where the genital products drain through the nephric ducts. G. situation with most bony fishes, in which a separate genital duct evolves, releasing the archnephric duct for original urinary function. a. renal corpuscles; b. testis (gonad); c. kidney; d. ureter; e. sperm duct (oviduct).

Reproductive Organs

As already said, the reproductive organs are most closely connected with the ureter and the kidneys. Actually, both are constructed embryonically on the same plan and, therefore, have been quite sensibly named the UROGENITAL SYSTEM (sometimes called GENITOURINARY SYSTEM). From an originally large number of tiny renal tubules, some of the foremost are transformed, respectively, into TESTES or OVARIES, which maintain, wholly or partially, their own drainage tubes, but which always, however, discharge into the ureter. In many varieties is found a CLOACA, an end-opening into which, in addition to the hind-gut, the ureter and the sperm duct or oviduct also discharge. This development in bony fish is unique.

First of all, it must be made clear that among mammals the sexes—males and females—are always separate (barring some extreme exceptions, such as sex reversal and hermaphroditism). The heredity chromosomes dictate the sex although a variety of hormones also control the process of physical and sexual development.

The reproductive organs, male (testes) as well as female (ovaries), produce sex cells or GAMETES, exactly as it is done by the higher types of plants. The male gametes are sperm cells, the female, the egg cells. Fish eggs are called SPAWN, while the male sperm is called MILT.

Scientific terminology refers to the two as OVUM (p. OVA) and SPERMA, respectively. Since the sperm cells are capable of active and independent movement and are similar to microscopic, single-celled organisms, they are often called sperm animals or SPERMATOZOA. A fusion of the two produces a fertilized egg cell from which a young animal can develop. Of considerable importance are some structures and deviations of construction among fishes, especially in connection with egg-laying and live-bearing species.

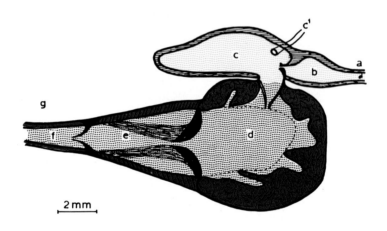

2 mm

Illus. 3-29. Sketch of a median cross-section through the heart of *Callichthys* (187 mm or 7⅜ inches long), seen from the left side. The blood enters the heart at a, through the body veins (ducti Cuvieri) into the anterior chamber (sinus venosus) b, and passes several valves to the second chamber (atrium) c. Among these catfish (and many others) the vein from the lower jaw c¹ directly enters the atrium. The blood leaves the atrium through valves into d, the third chamber (ventriculum), the strongly muscled, sponge-like, actual heart pump which pumps the blood between two large, sac-shaped valves towards the so-called conus arteriosus e (the ventricle valves are attached to the wall of the conus with sturdy bundles of muscles), which forces the blood, with its ring-shaped muscular wall pulsing, through a last pair of valves in the unmuscled bulbus arteriosus f, which connects by way of an opening in the shoulder girdle g with the gill arteries.

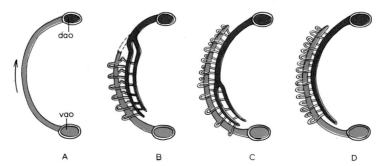

Illus. 3-30. Blood flow along the gill arches. A. the embryonic condition with continuous aortic arch from ventral (vao) to dorsal aorta (dao). B. in sharks, the
afferent vessel (blue) is formed from the aortic arch, whereas the paired efferent
vessels (red) are newly formed; these connect with the ventral vein by means of
fine ducts. C. a transitional condition found in several early bony fishes, many
catfishes, and the sturgeon; the separated ventral and dorsal parts of the aortic
arch grow out and connect through a series of fine ducts. D. condition in most bony
fish; the embryonic arch gives rise to the efferent vessel (red); the afferent vessel
(blue) is a new formation.

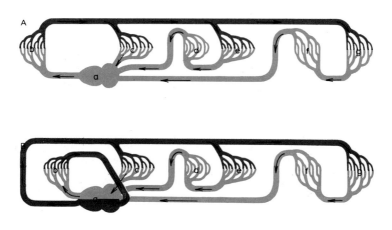

Illus. 3-31. Sketches of blood circulation, *A* among fish, *B* among adult amphibians.
The circulation of blood in fish is separated into an oyxgen-poor circulation to the
heart and from the heart to the gills, and a circulation rich in oxygen from the gills
to the head, body and organs. In amphibians, the oxygen-rich blood in the heart
(which has separate chambers) is mixed with oxygen-poor blood. In higher
vertebrates, the chambers of the heart are completely separated and no mixing of
veinous and arterial blood takes place. Since among fish the blood has to flow
through three capillary systems, the pressure is low and the speed of flow is small.
The various parts of the system are: a. the heart. b. gills or lungs. c. body. d. hepatic
system. e. digestive system. f. renal system. g. caudal section with posterior limbs.
Blue is oxygen-poor blood that is rich in carbon dioxide (CO_2); light red is blood rich
in oxygen and poor in CO_2; dark red is mixed blood.

123

Blood Circulation

The function of the circulation of the blood is principally to transport nourishment to the cells of the body. Among vertebrates, this nourishing circulation is particularly ingenious and effectively organized. The circulation is kept in motion by means of a circulation pump, the heart.

Blood

The blood circulating throughout the body consists of a basic fluid (PLASMA) in which are dissolved the blood proteins (ALBUMIN, GLOBULIN, and FIBRINOGEN). The proteins are formed in the liver. Fibrinogen, which is a coagulant protein, is of great importance in case of a wound, when the bloodstream must be shut off.

In addition to these materials, the blood plasma contains not only chemical compounds—salts, hormones, and enzymes—but also the red and white blood corpuscles (ERYTHROCYTES and LEUCOCYTES). The red corpuscles are oxygen-carriers, and perform perhaps the most important task of the circulatory system.

The Spleen

The most important control of blood cell production is the spleen, where both red and white blood cells are formed. Old red blood cells are broken down in the liver and their pigments appear in the bile.

Lymph Glands

Although fish do not have lymph glands comparable in structure to those of mammals, their place is taken by an extensive SYSTEM OF LYMPH VESSELS. The most important task of the lymph cells is to render invaders (bacteria) harmless.

Heart and Blood Vessels

Blood circulation takes place by means of a system of large and small blood vessels. There is a to-system and a fro-system—an arterial system and a venous system—and in addition to these, a system of capillaries which penetrates into all parts of the body. These ensure that the nourishing stream reaches every part of the system of cells.

The Heart

In order to keep the circulation in motion, a heart (pump) is provided, a powerful, hollow muscle in fishes, rather varied in structure, but in accordance with the same principle as in higher vertebrates. In invertebrates as well as in lancelets, a series of valve-like structures in the main artery serves the pumping purpose, but in other kinds of fishes, the heart is an individual unit, which lies beneath the pharynx in the rear end of the head, just in front of the shoulder girdle. The heart originally consisted of four chambers placed one after the other, a situation still found in the embryonic stage. It is actually a large tube divided into compartments separated by valves. By means of alternating contractions, it pumps the blood in a forward direction. The heart is actually a double-action pump (both sucking and forcing), for by contraction of the rear portion (two chambers), blood is forced into the frontal chambers, while by relaxing the rear chambers, blood is sucked into them.

The chambers of the heart from back to front (in the direction of the blood flow) are called: SINUS VENOSUS, a thin-walled sac having few muscles, connected to the veins of the body and the liver; ATRIUM, also thin-walled but somewhat more muscled, which lies in front of the sinus venosus and is separated from it by a pair of so-called sino-atrial valves; VENTRICLE, thick-walled, strongly muscled, the main pumping station, and, again, separated from the second chamber by a pair of atrioventricular valves; CONUS ARTERIOSUS, a narrow, thick-walled tube with a varying number of valves. Farther forward, the pump system connects to the main artery.

The ARTERIAL SYSTEM is not very complicated among fishes. The oxygen-poor blood completely surges from the heart through the VENTRAL AORTA (an abdominally located artery) and along the gills, where an exchange of gases takes place, through the DORSAL AORTA (the artery located down the back) and next, through a number of smaller arteries and into the capillaries in order to provide every part of the body with nourishing, oxygen-rich blood. The arterial blood for the head, body, tail and internal organs branches off from the dorsal aorta, after, of course, it has passed through the gill vessels (and among lungfishes, after passing through the lungs, because the lungs are actually substitutes for a set of gill arches).

The VENOUS SYSTEM serves to return the blood, now poor in oxygen and nourishment, back to the liver and heart, in order to complete the circulation. There are several venous circulatory systems to be distinguished: the HEPATIC-PORTAL SYSTEM, in which the nourishment-supplying liver is included; the ABDOMINAL SYSTEM for most of the head and body; and the RENAL-PORTAL SYSTEM for the tail region and kidneys.

Nervous System and Sense Organs

Single-celled organisms are, even though only one cell is concerned, able to react to stimuli. Of course, this is also true of higher animals, such as fish, but the plan of organization is so much more complicated that certain groups of cells have been devoted to certain specific tasks. The numerous activities of these various cell complexes are controlled by a specialized group of cells. The directing complex of cells, called the nervous system, is built up of nerve cells. The nervous system is divided into the CENTRAL NERVOUS SYSTEM, including the brain and spinal cord, and the PERIPHERAL NERVOUS SYSTEM, to which all remaining nerve elements belong. As a complete system, it consists of many specialized nerve cells, NEURONS, which can be called the basic elements of the entire apparatus. A neuron consists of a cell having long and short, thread-like protrusions which meet in a kind of relay station, called a SYNAPSE. The network of neurons and synapses extends over the entire body.

Some nerves end in sense organs, terminal knobs or RECEPTORS, for receiving impulses from outside or inside the body. Other nerves end in muscles, glands, capillaries, pigment cells, and so forth, and are called MOTOR-NEURONS; the organs receiving the impulses (muscles, glands, etc.) are called the EFFECTORS.

Impulses start at the sense organs and can reach an effector by way of the central messenger service, the nerve fibres and cells. However, a stimulus from a sense organ is not automatically conveyed through the nervous system to an effector—that would limit the possible activities to the number of receptor-effector connections, which do indeed exist in the form of "reflex" connections—but the nervous system also co-ordinates and regulates the activating of the effectors. A very complicated but refined course is taken by way of the synapses. These synapses or relay stations work most selectively in the sense that impulses are passed on after "consulting" other synapses that may also have received "messages" for the same nerve cell. The final impulse incorporates the combined message.

As a consequence of this co-ordination, the action of an impulse upon a sense organ is not limited to two possibilities (the activating or non-activating of an effector); the impulse can either receive support from other synapses or be radically blocked, and thus result in no reaction.

126

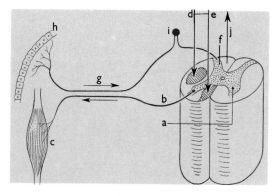

Illus. 3-32. Diagrammatic representation of a horizontal (coronal) section through the spinal cord. The nerve cells in the spinal cord form the grey matter that takes on a butterfly shape in cross-section. From the anterior (motor) horn (a) come the motor-nerve fibres (b) which innervate the muscles (c). In the white matter run the so-called pyramidal tracts (d), bundles of ascending and descending nerve fibres (e), connecting with the cerebral cortex, transmitting sensory information from sensory receptor cells (h), such as the skin. These sensory impulses are relayed by fibres (g) over nerve ganglions (i) to the posterior (sensory) horn (f). These impulses are then relayed to the brain (cortex) through sensory tracts (j) in the posterior grey column; from there, a motor impulse can again be issued.

In addition to a regulation of the organs and elements of the body by means of the nervous system, there also exists a second, more slowly working system. This functions on the basis of material secreted by the endocrine glands, the HORMONES, which, through the circulatory system, can act upon other organs by either applying a braking effect or by activating them.

Contrary to old ideas that impulses are passed on in an electrical way, it appears that, for the most part, transmission functions on a chemical basis. The substance released at the synapse which causes the transfer from one neuron to another is called the NEUROHUMOR.

Brain and Spinal Cord

It has already been said that the central nervous system consists of a stiff tube or nerve strand with the brain in front as the control point and the spinal cord leading off to the rear through the neural arches of the spinal column. Within the spinal cord run two main strands, the dorsal and the ventral horns. The dorsal horn is the seat of all the sensory-organ fibres, the cells of which meet in GANGLIA. The ventral horn is the seat of all motor-nerve fibres with cell bodies in the spinal cord. The cephalic nerves can also be split into dorsal and ventral strands. In the tail, the spinal column (NOTOCHORD) runs out into a thin, so-called UROSTYLE, which is usually bent upward by the extension of the underlying vertebral outgrowths.

Primordially, among the ancestors of the fishes, the nervous system had developed along lines of more or less random reflex reactions. The chordates must have been the first to require controlled reactions for the hunting and consumption of food; this resulted in a concentration of specific nerve cells in the head, the frontal end of the central nervous system, which gradually transformed into the main control point, the brain.

It is interesting to follow the embryological development of the brain, which develops much more quickly than any other organ. Beginning as a simple thickening of the neural tube, an increase in size causes the anterior end to fold downward. This end is the primitive forebrain (PROSENCEPHALON), separated at the fold or first flexure from the midbrain (MESENCEPHALON). The first differentiation in the forebrain are two lateral, forward-directed protrusions, the smell-, taste-, and touch-organs of the head, and an anteroventral pair containing the optic nerves. This point is later called TELENCEPHALON, which, together with the interbrain or THALAMUS bordering directly on it, forms the forebrain.

Farther back are the midbrain and the cerebellum (METENCEPHALON) together with the lengthened medulla (MYELENCEPHALON), forming the so-called RHOMBENCEPHALON.

Organization

The nervous system is thus a complex of nerve cells (neurons and ganglia) whose primary task is to create a connection between the sense organs, stimulus receivers (receptors) and the organs, tissues, muscles and glands, etc. (effectors) to be activated. In the second place, the nervous system co-ordinates and regulates the various stimuli and reactions; in the third place, it maintains, as an autonomous system, reactions which can neither be interrupted nor voluntarily regulated, such as respiration and digestion, and transmits, as the occasion requires, impulses to certain glands.

The nervous system of vertebrates can be divided into a central nervous system which consists of an accumulation of inter-connected neurons and ganglia which connect with bundles of long, thin nerve fibres from the peripheral nervous system. These nerve fibres connect to the sense organs, vital organs and muscles, etc. The peripheral nervous system thus functions as an impulse conductor. An impulse in a nerve fibre either is or is not aroused by a stimulus, without gradation; the stimulus is either completed or not completed. Furthermore, the power that conducts the impulse along a fibre is not variable in strength, although impulses vary in frequency. Impulses pass through the synapses in one direction only, so that the synapses can be considered more or less as rectifier cells. The synapses can also work selectively, and, for example, pass on impulses separately when several follow upon each other. On the other hand, a series of weak impulses can be strengthened by the synapse. It is all rather complicated, but what has been given here is sufficient background to permit continuation of the story.

Simple Sense Organs

The reception of stimuli takes place in vertebrates by means of SENSORY CELLS, generally grouped in sense organs. According to their type, sensory cells are sensitive to physical or chemical stimuli and are connected to nerves which pass impulses on to the brain by way of the spinal cord. There, a reaction is determined and transmitted as necessary to any part of the body that is able to offer defence.

Taste is located in taste buds, which are principally situated in the mouth, but among fish can be distributed over the entire skin. According to their type, the taste buds are sensitive to various chemical stimuli. In catfishes, for example, these little organs are numerous and extremely sensitive on the underside of the snout, around the mouth, often on the fleshy lips, and even along the flanks of the body.

Smell is generally poorly developed among fishes, and to a large degree, this function is performed by the taste buds. Lungfishes and their relatives, however, have a more or less well developed sense of smell. Fish have a series of cells in the external nostrils which are very well developed and direct in their operation and which work entirely on their own (a very original situation), because they are connected by long nerve fibres directly to the olfactory control point (LOBUS OLFACTORIUS) of the brain.

Sight and Eyes

Fish possess a pair of eyes (some remarkable exceptions—blind, cave-dwelling fish—are left out of this discussion), which lie on either side of the head in orbital cavities. The function of the eyes will not be discussed further here, but a few particulars concerning fish eyes are indeed interesting.

The placement of the paired eyes on either side of the head, as it occurs in most fishes, is the cause of their only limited forward vision. The almost cone-shaped eye lens of the fish in normal resting position lies forward, which focusses the eye on the nearby field of vision. In order to see farther, the lens is moved to the rear. Bottom-dwellers are generally equipped with very small eyes and their ability to see is quite limited. Most fishes, however, have eyes that are proportionally large to very large, with a somewhat better sight capability. Some species, such as the archer fishes (see page 948, *Toxotes*), can see especially well, even above water.

Certain tests have shown that many fishes are able to distinguish form and coloration, which is extremely useful not only in the search for food, but also during mating, as coloration and pattern can play an important rôle in the mating season. It has even been shown that the observable spectrum for fishes extends farther than for the human eye, extending into the ultraviolet.

The Lateral Line Organ

A sense organ that is unique among fish and water-dwelling larvae of amphibians is formed by receptor cells (NEUROMASTS) which are located in certain places in the skin. In fishes, they are usually concentrated in a lengthwise direction in the middle of the sides (the lateral line), as a kind of canal which extends on the head into a canal system of particularly great significance (there is no equivalent among higher animals). The single nerve cells are quite similar to those of the taste organs, and in fact, they are both sometimes combined. The most important task of the lateral line organ, however, seems to be to receive vibrations from and provide awareness of currents in the surrounding water.

This sensory system registers surrounding obstacles so precisely

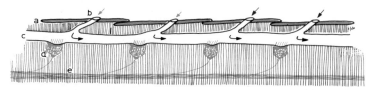

Illus. 3-33. Sketch of the lateral line organ of a fish (cross-section): a. scale. b. pore in scale. c. main canal of the lateral line organ. d. receptor cell (neuromast). e. bundle of nerve fibres. The arrows indicate the direction of water flow. In most fishes, the lateral line organ has various types of receptor cells among which are the taste buds.

that blind fish (sightless by nature or having been blinded) can swim about in a thickly-planted tank without ever bumping into an obstacle (see page 633, *Anoptichthys jordani*). The lateral line organ also plays a significant rôle as an organ of balance; the connection is made through the continuous canal system in the head along nerve fibres to the paired auditory organ. For example, this helps a fish to quickly regain its balance after being put out of balance by having a small piece of metal attached to it. The auditory organ, the paired ear labyrinths, is actually nothing more than a further developed and specialized extremity of the lateral line organ, situated in the skull.

Organ of Hearing and Balance

In fish, we look in vain for an external ear, such as is found in most higher vertebrates. Upon closer examination, however, we do indeed find a well developed internal ear, a sensory organ located in so-called AUDITORY CAPSULES on either side of the skull, directly under the brain.

From its build and structure, it can be clearly deduced that this internal ear developed as the frontal end of the lateral line. Here, too, are neuromasts that react to vibrations and movements in a labyrinth filled with lymphatic fluid. These neuromasts are directly connected to the auditory nerves. The entire bilateral organ consists of fine, bent tubes—two vertical and one horizontal, each at right angles to the other two. Simply stated, all three tubes, called semicircular canals, may be compared to a carpenter's level; they are mutually connected. This ear labyrinth has a number of thickenings or sacs, a UTRICULUS, a SACCULUS, and a further protrusion from the latter, a LAGENA. The sensory cells are crowded together, tiny ovals (MACULAE) on the bottoms of these sacs. During the embryonic development, a calcareous jelly is formed in this space, which solidifies to ear-stones or OTO-LITHS. The shape of the otoliths can be considered a useful distinguishing

131

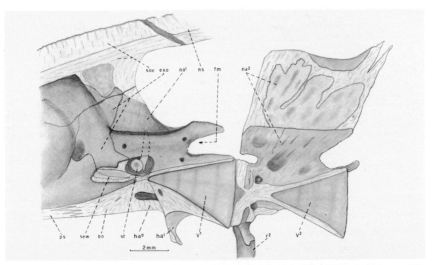

Illus. 3-34. This detail of skull cross-section (see Illus. 3-13) of *Hoplosternum* with the anterior vertebrae (V^1 and V^2) clearly shows the location of the auditory apparatus and the Weberian ossicles (further details in Illus. 3-35). Abbreviations: bo. basioccipital, basic bone of the skull, fused with the anterior half of the embryonic first vertebra. exo. exoccipital (auditory capsule). fm. foramen magnum (opening in the skull for admitting the spinal cord). ha. hemal arches of basioccipital and first vertebra. na. neural arches of the first and second vertebrae. ns. nuchal bone, a dermal ossification behind the skull. ps. parasphenoid (second basal bone of the skull). r. rib (second vertebral expansion is very strongly developed). sew. sinus endolymphaticus weberi (see text). soc. supraoccipital (uppermost posterior bone of the skull). st. stapes (of the auditory organ, fused with the second bone that is opposite the air bladder). V. vertebral body, respectively of the first and second complete vertebrae. It is possible that the second vertebra (V^2) originated from embryonic elements of the second and third vertebrae.

characteristic of species. Also, in many cases, it is possible to tell the age of the fish from the number of growth rings in the otolith.

The ear labyrinths serve as balance sensors, and it has long been a question whether the sense of hearing in fishes may be compared in any way with that of the higher vertebrates. It is presently known that fish are not only able to receive sound vibrations, but also that in many cases these are of a frequency range beyond that detectable by the human ear.

An external auditory canal, whether or not homologous with the Eustachian tube of higher vertebrates, has developed in many fishes; however, it sometimes has a very distinct structure and function. Embryologically, this canal develops from the sixth pair of gill pouches, which in most fishes do not develop in a respiratory function, but have been transformed into air sacs which, in some Ostariophysi, bear a relationship to the Weberian apparatus.

The Weberian Apparatus

A peculiar auditory function can be ascribed to what is called the Weberian apparatus, as found in numerous variations in the Ostariophysi and actually in modified form in various other families of fishes. The Weberian is a peculiar and unique apparatus in Ostariophysi—a chain of tiny bones (ossicles) which form a moveable connection between the air or swim bladder and either the endolymphatic or the perilymphatic cavity of the auditory organ. This allows the swim bladder undoubtedly to function as an amplifier of vibrations which, along with other vibrations, are picked up by the body. A solely hydrostatic function, therefore, is not the purpose of the gas bladder in fishes possessing the Weberian apparatus, although it seems very likely to be

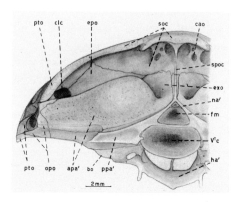

Illus. 3-35. Posterior view of the skull (detail from Illus. 3-34), after the second vertebra has been removed. The bony capsule (apa) of the left air bladder is clearly seen, anteriorly surrounded by some extensions of the skull bones (epo, opo, pto) enclosing the auditory apparatus; cao. opening for cephalic artery; ppa'. posterior process of the vertebra. Further abbreviations as in Illus. 3-34.

Illus. 3-36. Detail in the same direction as Illus. 3-35, cut down to the Weberian ossicles. From this it can be seen that in the armoured catfish (Callichthyidae), the chain of Weberian ossicles consists of a single, boomerang-shaped element on each side. These are not directed posteriorly but dorsally, whereas they are opposite the wall of the bladder (indicated by a dotted line). Since the bony capsules slant somewhat to the rear (see Illus. 3-37 and 3-38), they are only partly shown in this section. Abbreviations as in Illus. 3-35.

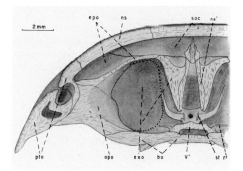

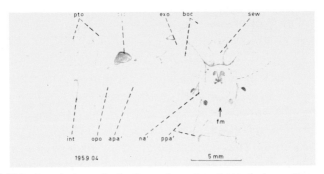

Illus. 3-37. This dorsal view of a horizontal section through the auditory region of *Hoplosternum* shows a detail of the same area as Illus. 3-36. The air bladder capsule (left half) extends laterally to the wall of the skull where its oval opening (int is introitus) is closed by a membrane. In front of the capsule lies a vertical canal for articulation of the cleithral process of the shoulder girdle (clc). Other abbreviations as in Illus. 3-36.

utilized by those which regularly frequent a certain water level. That the combined gas bladder/Weberian apparatus, moreover, is typical of fresh-water fishes (the ostariophysans as a group comprise more than 90 per cent of all fresh-water fishes) points in a further direction.

Although many attempts have been made to relate the elements of the Weberian apparatus with those of the hearing apparatus of higher animals, no agreement has yet been reached on the subject. Obviously, the starting point of both systems has to be the same, but differentiation and adaptation to completely different circumstances has resulted in structures differing greatly in details. A structure closely approaching the original situation in fish is found in catfishes and among some loaches. The apparatus is best known and most thoroughly investigated in rather specialized and relatively advanced carp-like fishes and catfishes and the illustration of this organ repeatedly presented in textbooks gives a very one-sided impression.

Earlier, we mentioned two types of air or swim bladders—the bilateral, anteriorly situated one and a usual medial, unilateral bladder, posteriorly located. In most catfishes, most loaches and a number of carp-like fishes, a pair of air bladders develops from the primordial last pair of gill pouches, just in front of or in the middle of and above the first vertebra. Gradually, these air bladders became enclosed in a bony capsule (formed by the lateral vertebral processes) which open laterally, just behind the hind margin of the posterior cranial bones, and which are closed off by a membrane. The space in the cylinder, around the air bladder, is filled with lymphatic fluid (and is now comparable to the perilymphatic space).

134

Interestingly, the bilateral air bladders, which have lost their embryonic connection with the esophagus, are located immediately behind the auditory apparatus. The blind sac (SINUS ENDOLYMPHATICUS WEBERI) originating in the two auditory capsules, extends as far as the perilymphatic space of the bladder capsules. In an early embryonic or larval stage a strand of connective tissue develops between the left and right walls. The fibre attachments located on the wall of the endolymphatic blind sac are the first to ossify into oval bony plates (possibly homologous to the CONCHAE STAPEDES of higher vertebrates). The remaining part of the connective tissue strand ossifies a little later into a small, triangular piece of bone varying in size and shape. Both left and right triangles are attached with one corner to a median point of the vertebral body. The long arms of the triangular bones lie against the air bladder of either the left- or right-hand capsule. The capsule thus has a membrane on the outside and, at the same time, a connection to the lateral line organ. In the developmental series of Ostariophysi, we immediately see that the distance between the auditory capsules on the one hand and the air bladder (either bone enclosed or not), on the other, becomes steadily greater. The number of vertebrae that fuse (ankylose) to the base of the skull in order to stiffen the whole also increases, and it is obvious that to bridge over this distance between auditory organ and either air or swim bladder, more elements are continually required. The elements taking part in this bridging operation are vertebral processes, the chain called Weberian ossicles, which are only partially homologous to similar bones among the remaining vertebrates.

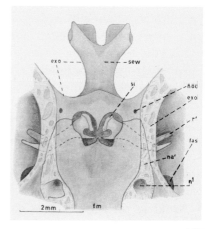

Illus. 3-38. Enlarged detail of Illus. 3-37 showing the Weberian apparatus in dorsal view. The Y-shaped ossification of the sinus endolymphaticus weberi (sew) is attached to the exoccipital bone (exo). The auditory nerve runs through the opening (noc) in the front of this auditory bone. Posteriorly, in the bottom of the ossified capsule, lies the foramen for the larval connection of the two lateral air sacs (fas) with the esophagus, which quickly disappears as the fish grows up.

4. THE LIFE

OF THE FISH

Fishes occupy a special place in the broad realm of vertebrate animals, because they are bound to an existence in the primordial element —water. There are exceptions, of course, and there are some other vertebrates—mammals, reptiles and birds—that spend their entire life cycle in water. Even though some may look like fish—the dolphin and the whale, for instance—they differ from fish in that they are warm-blooded air breathers instead of cold-blooded water breathers. Among true fish, however, there are exceptions—lungfishes that travel over land or bury themselves for an entire season in mud.

Furthermore, fish form perhaps the most economically significant group of animals for man. Rich in protein, their bodies serve as food for human beings, fertilizer for fields, and lately, a kind of fish-flour has been produced that may some day go far towards feeding the world's hungry population.

As far as their life cycle is concerned, fish differ especially from all higher vertebrates in that they are absolutely bound to the water. During mating, eggs are deposited and are usually fertilized outside the mother's body. Fish eggs hatch rapidly and the larvae are self-supporting within a very short time. The struggle for life, however, is the same for fish as for any other group of animals, as they must learn to adapt to the changes and vagaries of a totally hostile environment.

Certain phases of the life cycle of the fish are of special interest to aquarists. Let us now go over these.

Life Processes

The struggle for existence is highlighted by a number of processes that completely control the life of the fish. The most important of these are: adaptation to the environment; the environmental factors of climate, water composition, natural enemies, etc., with the resulting continual search for food; and the ultimate goal of the life cycle— reproduction.

Adaptation to the Environment

One aspect of vital significance in the struggle for existence is the necessity for species and populations to adjust their way of living to certain and sometimes strongly variable environmental conditions. Various adaptations are discussed in this book, such as the final development of the spinal column, of the jaws, the distribution patterns, the diversity of body forms, the dermal armour of bony plates or scales, the development of various types of respiratory organs, digestive systems adapted to varied diets, and for particular higher developments and functions, special air chambers such as the swim bladder and lungs and, of course, the special structures in the reproductive system. The development of particular sensory organs has also made many adaptations possible.

The Search for Food

Aquarists know that fish do not require regular feeding. They can live for a reasonably long time on an unbalanced diet and, when healthy, they can go without food for a rather long time. In a correctly balanced aquarium, there is always something edible for the fish to find, so that it scarcely ever becomes a matter of live or starve for them.

There is no "feast" in nature. Daily life consists of the eternal hunt for food. The predator is constantly lying in wait or searching the environment for prey. The digestive process is connected with the kind of food consumed. A predatory fish, like the pike, quickly swallows the catch, then rests for a long period of time in the reeds while it digests its dinner. For the carp, on the other hand, the search for edible morsels continues all day long, without stop, its stomach going through a process of continuous digestion of the small particles delivered to it.

It can only be mentioned at this point that the creatures in open nature do not have it as easy as those in an aquarium. From this, we

Plate 4-1. *Nothobranchius rachovi,* **spawning in the bottom humus layer.**

can learn that a strictly measured diet works better for aquarium fishes than allowing them to swim about among an excess of food. (See page 292 for a complete description of appropriate aquarium food.)

Reproduction

If mating is considered to be the principle objective of the life cycle, then it is plain that this life process is of the greatest interest, both for the aquarist and for science. Without reproduction, there can, of course, be no struggle for survival to preserve the species, as Charles Darwin pointed out. We shall soon see that, from a biological point of view, reproduction for maintaining the species is not a process that stops with the act of mating.

Sexual Activity

The term "sexual activity" is used here to indicate the complex of processes and activities which must be completed by both sexes of a species in order to assure both the production of progeny and the safety of their progress for some time along the dangerous path of life. This complex of actions falls into a number of phases which are briefly outlined here. Each phase could provide enough material for a 200-page book, so only the most important points are touched upon, but in such a way as to give a satisfactory, clear picture of the most interesting aspects of aquarium-keeping. (See also the accounts devoted to the various species in Part II.)

Development to Maturity

It is important for an aquarist to know when a given fish is mature or "ready for breeding." Breeding is not a simple task, even for the skilled breeder. The largest factor is the degree of maturity of the fish, and this is not always obvious from the size or length. Generally, too, there is too little information on imported fish for us ever to estimate the possible age or the size to which a given specimen might grow. The age of the fish is usually quite important. If this is unknown, we must resort to the experience obtained from other, related forms. We are bound, then, by those characteristics that may be visible and sometimes by habits which provide us with the indications we are looking for. Experience acquired by close observation is more valuable in this respect than the experience we may have gained simply by years of fish-keeping.

In the case of some species, males and females, upon reaching a certain age or size, can be clearly differentiated. The distinction is different for many other species, however, in which the sexes are difficult or impossible to tell apart. Experience may sometimes give us a clue to the sex, or perhaps a visible roundness of the belly will give it away and let us know that we have a female. Sometimes, however, the difficulty is insurmountable. As a guide, material which points up the distinguishing characteristics of the sexes of various species of fish is included whenever known in Part II of this book.

Courtship Activity

An interesting, though sometimes misleading, aspect of mating biology is the so-called courting, a subject that has been written and philosophized about a great deal. With most aquarium fishes, the real mating comes after a varying number of preparatory activities loosely labelled as "courtship." In general, it appears that the number of eggs laid is in inverse ratio to the intensity of the courtship. That is to say, fishes having a simple prelude to the act of mating lay the largest number of eggs (see page 147, *Parental Care among Fish*).

The mating preparations represented by courtship can assume many forms, but, in every case, there is one or another stimulus that leads directly to mating. Fishes may be divided, according to these activities, into species that build nests, species that seek out special spawning grounds, and still other species that scatter their eggs and milt at random, without bothering further with the process.

Although the first category, compared with the so-called free-layers, is in the minority, detailed study shows that many more species, including most of the free-layers living in large groups and schools (herring, mackerel, cod, etc.), provide more of a certain form of parental care than has been suspected. Parental care, as exercised by the various forms, is dealt with in detail on page 147.

Mating

When a given species has completed the courtship activity peculiar to it, mating follows as the high point of the cycle. Differing from species to species, the procedure of mating follows a fixed pattern, and we can even attach a certain systematic qualification to the pattern of mating. Within a group of closely related forms, the mating pattern is similar. In Part II, necessary attention is devoted to certain aspects of the mating of various fishes.

Generally speaking, the female is stimulated at a certain stage to expel or lay her eggs, which are immediately fertilized by the male. For some species, mating is carried on in groups; in others, the female is accommodated by several males; and in still others, one male serves to fertilize the eggs of several females. Interesting divergences are found in forms where internal fertilization takes place, or where the female takes up in the oviduct the sperm capsules (SPERMATOPHORES) from the male, in order to deposit them, along with the ripe eggs, in a suitable place. It is precisely such variations as these that make a study of the process of mating so interesting. Wherever possible, these divergent aspects are treated with the depth and detail they deserve.

141

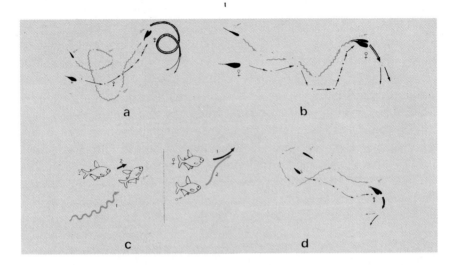

Illus. 4-1. Courting patterns in the characins. Various patterns of approach and courting movements can be recognized, each of which is typical for a species or genus or complex of related forms. Pattern a applies to the complex in which *Hyphessobrycon bifasciatus, H. flammeus* and *H. griemi* belong; b applies to many *Hyphessobrycon* species, especially of the *H. callistus* group and related *Megalamphodus* species; c shows the fluttering dance of the male in *Hyphessobrycon* and *Megalamphodus* species, which directly precedes mating itself; d is the mating procedure.

Illus. 4-2. With many nest builders, the just-hatched larvae hang from tiny threads, as if to dry, for several days before swimming freely about.

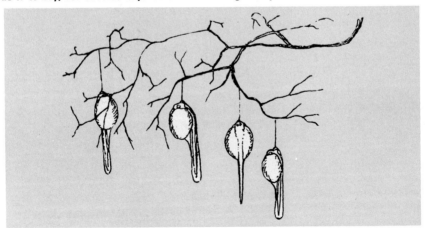

Protection and Care of the Eggs and Larvae

When an organism is in an environment which is, for the most part, hostile, a primitive reaction is to develop some method of parental care and protection. Co-operation of both parents beyond the actual period of mating is necessary for the protection of the offspring.

When the first fish struggled to survive in the primordial swamps, it was obviously advantageous for them to bring the eggs up to the oxygen-rich surface waters. The development of a bubble-nest at the surface made this possible (in the case of *Callichthys, Hoplosternum,* and the Anabantidae, among others). Some even adopted the practice of attaching their eggs to leaves overhanging the water in open air (*Copella, Pyrrhulina,* etc.). This meant that the eggs, not being immersed in the water, had to be kept wet. In all these cases, one or the other parent is obliged to stand guard and perform the necessary function to care for the nest and spawn. In order to keep the eggs from being carried away by fast-running water, the eggs have a sticky coating or sometimes fine threads, so that they automatically attach themselves to stones or plants. Cichlids discovered many kinds of protective measures to care for their spawn, forced entirely by the circumstances of the environment. (For greater detail on this subject, consult the section on parental care on page 147 and also refer to the individual species described in Part II.)

Development from Egg to Fish

An egg expelled by a female is a single cell that must fuse with a male sperm cell to be able to develop further. The process by which the male cell nucleus fuses with that of the egg is called "fertilization" and it normally takes place at the time of mating. Eggs that somehow escape fertilization first turn milky white, then become mouldy. Such obviously unfit eggs are removed from the viable spawn by the parents.

A newly-expelled egg cell is provided with a thin cell membrane that encloses the protoplasm. This cell protoplasm or cytoplasm is the basic material of the cell, and contains a so-called nucleus. The sperm consists of a "head" and a "tail"; the head penetrates the membrane of the egg cell and the tail remains outside. The membrane "closes" after a single sperm cell has penetrated.

In principle, egg cells are formed in the same way as sperm cells, from the same primordial germ cells, developing in the gonads (see section on the kidney, page 120). Sexual products are excreted through special tubes, after which fertilization and fusion of the two cells takes place.

Eggs, Embryos, and Larvae

When a sperm cell has fused with an egg cell, the fertilized egg then contains the hereditary factors donated by both parents. The number of "heredity carriers," or GENES in the egg cell is thus double, so that the cell is then called a DIPLOID CELL. Then follows the process of initial cleavage, too complicated for detailed consideration here, resulting in the formation of a clump of cells enclosing a cavity called the MORULA STAGE (BLASTULA). After cleavage and blastula formation, the major event (gastrulation) follows, where a part of the outermost layer of cells is turned inside so as to lie against another part of the same layer. In this way, a double-walled ball or two-layered embryo is formed around a cavity that has one opening to the outside. This GASTRULA is, in principle, the physical make-up of the lowest of metazoan animals, the Coelenterata—a phylum of invertebrates that includes corals, sea anemones, jellyfish, etc. During this development, the original cavity is entirely pushed out and the new space is, in fact, the primitive gut.

After the gastrula or beaker stage, a fast development of the embryo follows. The young fish is provided with a food supply in the form of a yolk sac.

144

It is usually at this stage that the larvae emerge from the protective eggshell and attach themselves to the glass of the aquarium or to plants with some kind of a sticky organ. Hanging in this way, the larvae continue to subsist on the nutriment provided by the yolk sac, until they are ready to make their first, timid attempt at swimming. By the time the yolk sac is used up, they must start searching their surroundings for food, which consists of microscopic particles and the one-celled plant-like and animal-like organisms.

In the aquarium, as well as in the breeding tank, the aquarist must take it upon himself to provide food over and above what the tank population of micro-organisms can offer. The best food is infusoria (protozoan creatures which depend on decaying organic matter for survival) from pond or ditch water. Collect samples of the water, dredging up a little muck from the bottom and, with a knife blade, scrape the stems and underside of leaves of water plants into the collecting vessel. In a gallon glass jar covered with a plate of glass, the aquarist can "farm" his own infusoria in the original ditch water. In a day or two, the vessel will be swarming with a swollen population of minute creatures, and these can be transferred from time to time to the aquarium water to provide the living food that the young fish (the FRY) need. In nature, only a small number of the larvae grow to maturity, but under artificial conditions providing utmost protection and a maximum food supply, a much larger number of the young fish will thrive into maturity.

Young and Adult Fish

In nature, young fish normally gather in schools, hunting together for food. There is a basic and primitive urge for safety that causes weak and vulnerable creatures to collect in crowds, each member strengthened, as it were, by the presence of his comrades. This pattern is still retained in certain highly developed species—the school fishes. Also, the schools of fry inhabit those areas of the biotope that provide them with their preferred kind of food. These are the shallow, peaceful places, abounding with organic refuse. As soon as the fry grow a little larger, a need for greater food-bulk arises, and this can be satisfied only by larger food animals living in some other part of the biotope. Half-grown fish need still a different kind of food and they forage about until they find that part of the biotope which can supply them with it. There they stay, at least for the time being. When the fish is full-grown, it acquires still other needs and in order to be satisfied must normally inhabit the more dangerous areas of the biotope.

Owing to the above factors, as well as to the preference of certain types of fish for one or another part of the biotope, naturalists divide native waters into both vertical and horizontal zones of habitation. It should be pointed out for aquarists that it is desirable to collect a combination of fishes into one tank so that each depth of the aquarium has its own population. In other words, there should be a separate population of fish to inhabit the surface waters, another for the middle depths, and still another of bottom-dwellers to roam the floor of the tank.

By the time the creatures have reached a certain stage of maturity, noticeable differences begin to appear. Sometimes a difference distinguishing the sexes shows up, a difference in fin shapes, in size, coloration, and so forth. Sometimes there is no visible, external difference, but the actual difference is internal. Sexual maturity of females is normally manifested in a rounded belly.

Natural Selection and Cross-Breeding

When fish reach sexual maturity, they pair off and a period of biological mating begins. It is a remarkable thing that fish of the same species always find each other in the pairing-off process, even in the midst of a numerous and varied population. Although cross-breeding of different forms can take place in nature, such an occurrence is the result of several irregular factors in the normal course of events.

Darwin, the father of evolutionary thought, was one of the first scientists to study and explain this phenomenon.

In a population of any given species, only a small number of individuals attain adulthood and the consequent ability to reproduce. Considering the fact that individual variation is always present, it is possible for a number of original characteristics, present in the population as a whole, to be lost, or even to be intensified, among part of the offspring. Successful variants will, in time, influence the character of the general population.

It can also happen that the individuals of an original population become separated from the others for some time. This prevents an exchange of characteristics, making it possible for the separated populations to develop in different directions. Population fractions of this kind are called sub-species.

As soon as such sub-specific individuals are again brought into contact with each other, the chance is very great that cross-breeding will take place.

Parental Care among Fish

Over a century ago, in 1859, the appearance of a certain book became a "world-shaking event." The title of the book was: *On the Origin of Species by Means of Natural Selection, or the Preservation of Favoured Races in the Struggle for Life.* The author of this book with such a wide-ranging title was hardly known at that time—Charles Robert Darwin. That this book quickly aroused a great deal of controversy in some circles is quite understandable, considering the sociological views and the criteria for belief that held sway at that time. Fragments of the title have become catch-words for the ignorant—"natural selection" and "the struggle for life"—while "survival of the fittest" from the text became another mere cliché uttered without the least understanding of what the whole thing is all about. The more excitable of Darwin's detractors even put words into his mouth, accusing him of saying that "man comes from apes"—something that Darwin, careful scientist that he was, never once said.

For purposes of this present study, we need to make a deeper excursion into an important part of the field—namely, the struggle for life in the animal kingdom.

Early youth is the most dangerous period of development, when every living thing runs the risk of falling prey to a hostile environment. Let us take the well known supposition, promulgated by Julian Huxley, at its face value—that all living organisms multiply in geometrical progression. Notwithstanding this, the population of a given species remains about constant in its biotope. It is obvious, of course, that many more young are produced than will ever live to maturity. Normally, if a couple reproduces *itself* with a single pair of offspring, the requirements of species survival are thereby satisfied. This is a "normal" situation. So, if a population of 1,000 specimens reproduces in the totality of its life cycle only 1,000 offspring, it will survive.

Nature has arranged things in such a manner that the Darwinian principle remains in force. If a single limiting factor is changed, then it becomes not only possible for the population to die out, but also, on the other hand, for it to increase in number. Significant examples of such a change in limiting factors are the Australian plague of rabbits, the introduction of muskrats and minks into England, the bringing of starlings and English sparrows to North America, and so on. Nonetheless, though momentarily staggered, nature recovers its balance rather quickly. A superfluity of numbers carries with it its own reprisal—starvation, disease, and other limiting factors assume control of the situation.

Besides the numerous limiting factors concerned—such as insufficient food, personal weakness, ill health of the individual, and so on—a large number of young fall prey to other animals, becoming food for them. Aside from the loss of individuals, nothing ecological is lost in the process, as the consumed parts serve a useful purpose and re-appear in some indistinguishable form on or within the person of the predator. Should all young of all species of animals invariably live to maturity, then long before this the biosphere of the earth would have become so overcrowded that it would be incapable of supporting life today.

For mere maintenance of the species, a pair of parents is obliged to produce no more than two young. This seems a small requirement, but it is not always easy to achieve even this much. There is a great chance that not a single offspring will live to maturity. On the one hand, nature takes young lives ruthlessly; on the other, it provides prodigally for success in carrying out the struggle for life, insofar as the species as a whole is concerned. Parental care is one of these provisions. There is a remarkable connection, already pointed out, between the quality of parental care and the number of fish eggs produced. Many species that provide nothing in the way of parental care try to second-guess nature by pouring out an overwhelming number of eggs to compensate for the intended lack of "post-natal" care.

Another question that concerns many aquarists is this: "Is it a natural phenomenon for many species to eat eggs, including their own?" Since a great many cyprinoids and other fishes (see, for example, *Barbus everetti* on page 459), including well fed specimens, do devour their own eggs while breeding, it is assumed that nature has evolved some other method for survival of the species. In any case, the urge for reproduction and preservation of the species, present in every other living creature, is apparently not present in the cyprinoids. Does this happen in the natural state as well? The answer to this question comes by providing the home aquarium with what these fishes need—a fairly dry beach with a sloping bottom.

In the natural state, the spawning grounds of many cyprinoids are banks, pools, flooded lands—areas where there is only an inch or so of water. Such places are never visited by adult fishes except during the mating season, and thus the progeny are well protected from the cannibalistic appetites of the parents. Call it what you will, the urge to eat their own eggs is simply an instinct for tidiness on the part of the parents, who consume anything at all that seems the least bit edible.

Though we cannot speak for exotic species (ornamental fish), we can accept that the so-called free-layer fishes of Dutch waters (and these are almost all cyprinoids) reproduce in a more or less identical manner—that is, by the depositing of eggs—as their relatives do in other places. The water in which the eggs are deposited is often so shallow that when the parent fish are mating, they splash right out of the water, and sometimes find themselves quite high and dry! Other than the natural protection against the rapacity of their parents which the shallow water offers the eggs, the continually rippling and pleasantly warm water of the shallows is ideal for the development of the eggs. It provides oxygen and warmth throughout the incubation period and supplies sufficient food for the young later, when they hatch out. In this way, most of the eggs survive—unless they happen to collide with any other natural enemies. It appears, for example, from the shoals of young fish appearing in the spring in Dutch waters, that the eggs and just-hatched young are less exposed to dangers than are the developing young and the half-grown fish. All in all, the continuation of the species is assured by all kinds of circumstances and, at the same time, over-population of the area is prevented.

Of course, it is hardly possible to reproduce accurately such circumstances in the aquarium except to a partial degree. Efforts undertaken in this direction—for example, replacing the recommended practice of "removing parent fish after mating" by allowing reproduction to happen in the aquarium in a more natural way— give the aquarist more pleasure and more affection for the objects of his study than is usually the case in breeding.

Lungfishes

The primitive environment and the first fishes have already been discussed (see page 28), but it will probably never be established that those first fishes enjoyed an elaborate amount of parental care. All indications, however, point in that direction.

About the same time that Darwin's famous book was published, a time that we now consider to have been one of great expansion in the field of natural research, three genera of fishes were discovered, one after another, totally divergent from ordinary types. They were so divergent, in fact, that scientists at first considered them to be amphibians, a misidentification that is still present in their generic names.

149

Illus. 4-3. The nest of a lungfish while guarding the larvae.

In 1836, the naturalist Johann Natterer discovered, in the Amazon River basin, a number of animals that he sent to the Zoological Museum in Vienna for scientific examination. In the same year, Dr. Fitzinger, specialist at the same institute, classified the creatures as *Lepidosiren paradoxa*. He was positively convinced that they were related to the North American amphibian genus *Siren*.

A year before, some animals had been taken from the Gambia River in West Africa. These were classified in 1839 by Dr. Richard Owen of the British Museum of Natural History in London as a second species, *Lepidosiren annectens*. However, Dr. Owen correctly assumed that the creature was a fish. Whether it was fish or amphibian, however, remained an open question for many years. In 1870, a third species was caught in Queensland, Australia, clearly related to the genus *Ceratodus*.

Ceratodus had long been known as a fossil fish, and, after an at-first sceptical reception of Dr. Kreft's (who also worked in Vienna) publication, in which he related the present-day lungfish to their ancestors of the Triassic, scientists slowly became reconciled to the conviction that these lung-breathing creatures belonged, in truth, to the class of fishes. Kreft called his fish *Ceratodus forsteri*, and in 1878, Castelnau demonstrated that there were enough differences between the living and the fossil lungfish to establish for the living species the generic name *Neoceratodus*.

What has all this to do with parental care? In one sense, nothing at all; but in another, a great deal. If we consider lungfishes as living fossils, then we can understand something of the archaic environment in which such creatures must have lived. We can then see that their adaptation to this strange environment must have required the development of a very special kind of parental care.

Once scientific interest in the lungfishes had been aroused, other expeditions were undertaken for the express purpose of finding out more about these remarkable creatures. In 1900, an expedition was taken into the area of the Gambia River by J. S. Budgett, who was particularly concerned about life in those wide stretches of marshland. Science has his accurate observations to thank for most of the existing knowledge about lungfishes. On a hot, August afternoon in 1900, with a temperature of 37.2 °C (99 °F) in the shade, an excited native fisherman came to tell Budgett that he had found the young of "*cambona*" (*Protopterus annectens*). In the marsh, about 3 m (10 feet) from the edge, the water in a small, oval pool in the dry ground, was in violent commotion. The watery upstir was caused by the thrashing tail of a fish standing on its head in the pool. The fisherman removed a handful of larvae from the water and Budgett observed them with astonishment. The clusters of external gills characteristic of the larvae of these fish were strongly reminiscent of similar organs of amphibians. The adult fish in the nest turned out to be a male. Though the pool was hardly a foot deep, the fish was about 60 cm (2 feet) long, and the total number of young it guarded was about 200.

(For a further description of marshy areas as primitive environments, refer to page 165, *Collecting Trips and Expeditions*. For adaptation to different conditions, see page 63, *Possibilities for Adaptation and Distribution*, page 77, *Natural Environment* and page 79, *Examples of Biotopes*.)

In 1931, Svenson (of Sweden) collected the final data in the same region where Budgett had operated. Knowing what to look for, he located without difficulty about 40 nests containing eggs and larvae. The mating period is stretched out over a month, beginning about two weeks after the sleep of dry-period estivation is broken by the first shower of rain. The sexual organs of the fish are fully developed during estivation, but the animal requires a little time after its long sleep to regain its strength. The young, originally provided with external gills for breathing during the rainy season, grow to 4 inches long within two months, whereupon they lose the external gills and develop lungs for breathing. In the autumn dry season, they act like adults and bury themselves in the mud, where they make themselves strong cocoons

151

from the slime on their skins. They live as fish of prey, on insects, frogs and other fish.

The Reproduction Migration

It has been shown that larvae in their most vulnerable stage live in a particular part of the biotope that provides them with both food and protection.

How does it happen that the young find themselves there? Many species tend to breed in places other than those in which they live. So, when the urge to mate comes upon them, part of the urge is to seek some other part of the biotope—or to go completely outside the biotope for the purpose of reproduction, as do the salmon and the eel, as extreme examples. This has special significance. Such migration is more common than might be thought. Based as it is, on instinct, it must be considered a kind of parental care. The spawning grounds reached at the end of the trek are particularly attractive in one way or another to the fish concerned and are suitable for the laying of eggs. This may be because the water is shallow (appealing to some fish), or particularly warm and affording plenty of hiding places for the young, and at the same time it is rich in oxygen and abundant with the necessary kind of food.

After fish spawn in shallow water, they may be seen floundering about, seeking an escape back into deep water. Under ordinary circumstances, the water where the eggs are laid is too shallow for large fish, hence the young are safe from predatory raids by their parents and others. Of course, the shore teems with raiders of its own, so the young fish are not entirely safe in their biotope, as the parents normally offer nothing further in the way of parental care.

Migration to the Marshes

The savannah regions and the overflowing banks of large rivers play important rôles in the life of the fish population. Two main types of aquatic environments are distinguished in the savannahs—still water and running water. Rivers, creeks and brooks are featured by running water, and their oxygen content is normal. The stagnant water of ponds, ditches, marshes and swamps is normally less richly oxygenated. Historically, the swamps represent a replica of the primordial environment. This leaves no doubt that an important part of the evolution of the higher vertebrate animals took place in an environment that was similar.

There are three distinguishable types of swamps, and this applies everywhere in the world, particularly in the tropical regions. The first type is the rain marsh or rain swamp. Caused by rain, this swamp is located so high above river level that it is never penetrated by river water, though excess water from the swamp can flow downhill to the nearest river.

The second type is the flood swamp. This occurs when rainfall raises the level of rivers, causing them to overflow their banks and inundate the surrounding countryside. When the river retreats within its banks, much of the flood water is left standing to stagnate and retain its own peculiar kind of life forms.

The third type of swamp is the pond swamp. This is a semi-permanent kind of swamp that may originate similarly to the flood swamp.

Naturally, the fish population in these three types of swamp is not exactly the same. The rain swamp has only a periodic connection with a river, when unusually heavy rains cause it to overflow and course towards the river, often across a broad strip of savannah, which does not have a firm river bed. While the overflow takes place, certain fish are able to cross over the wet savannah in order to spawn in the rain swamps.

The flood swamps also appear during the rainy season and are, actually, temporary enlargements of the rivers and their tributary creeks. The fish fauna sheltered there are potentially the same as in the main river, and large fish that go off into such areas do so only for the purpose of spawning.

The ponds or permanent river marshes may, in theory, also contain the same kind of fish as the river, but there are other restricting factors involved. Once the connection with the river is broken, the serene condition of the standing water rapidly declines, owing to the decrease in the oxygen content.

Oxygen Content as a Limiting Factor

Of the numerous species found in a savannah region, only a certain number are adapted to life there. First, many possible inhabitants may be provided with their oxygen requirement by other than normal means. These are called "primary swamp fish." Any species not so adapted may live in the swamp only so long as propitious conditions exist during the rainy season. Many species, not only during the mating season, but also in the rainy period, do look for richer subsistence among the flood waters than what the open water may have to offer

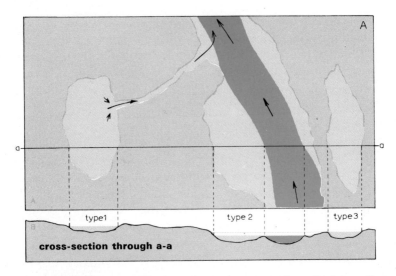

Table 4-1. Sketch of three types of marshes and swamps: A. vertical view. B. cross-section of the terrain along the line a-a indicated in A. Type 1 is the rain marsh, lying higher than the highest level of the river; hence, water can only flow down the river. Type 2 is the flood marsh, maintaining connection with the river, and type 3 is the pool marsh, that usually does not dry up completely.

Illus. 4-4. In the rainy season, despite its beauty, the jungle becomes less accessible owing to the treacherous water level. For the fish, however, it opens up a period of abundant food. This area is a typical biotope of the gymnotids.

154

Illus. 4-5. The interest of the fish in the flooded jungle during the rainy season also attracts men. Every angler is assured a good catch, regardless of how primitive his equipment.

them. As soon as the dry season begins, the water level retreats under the rays of the hot, tropical sun, and puddles and pools are cut off from the running water by strips of dry land. Before the last escape is cut off, most species go back to the river and its tributaries. The large number of fish left lazing in the pools and puddles must then be written off as dead, unless they are equipped with efficient, auxiliary respiratory equipment.

Adaptation to Oxygen-Poor Water

Typical swamp dwellers have adapted their breathing apparatus in relation to their special environment and are able to exist under conditions that would prove fatal to other species. It has already been mentioned that such adaptations must be considered very original (see pages 65 and 114). Many adaptations of the breathing potential, so characteristic of the primordial state, are lost in more advanced fishes who inhabit a "normal" environment that is rich in oxygen. Of course, no one will contend that terrestrial vertebrates developed from fishes as a result of adaptation to low-grade water. It is possible to say, though, that higher attributes have been acquired by reason of this

Illus. 4-6. At the approach of the dry season, the water pulls back. Everywhere are places where the fish flounder in an effort to escape back to the river, often in vain.

"happy accident" of environment. It is understandable that regularly occurring periods of drought within the environment have been a further stimulus for the transmigration of later stages of evolutionary development into land animals. It is also understandable from the standpoint of reproduction and protection for the helpless larvae which are dependent on moisture and oxygen.

Adaptation to a Drying-Out Biotope

Another restriction placed by nature on the swamp fish with regard to its biotope is evaporation of the swamp waters and the eventual drying up of the biotope. When there is no replenishment of water from stream or sky, there is no alternative for the swamp inhabitants except to dry up along with the swamp. Complete desiccation always results in death for the fish. Unadapted fishes soon die in the cramped pools and puddles, poisoning the water for the stronger fishes. The dying fish are a rich source of food for the species adapted to drying out. In the ultimate event of complete drought, however, they, too, must decamp for better pastures (one such fish is the armour-clad catfish which travels long distances overland in early morning hours, looking for hollows still containing a little water). Otherwise, the only recourse is to burrow in the mud, as the lungfishes do. There is still another kind of adaptation, namely that of the annual or seasonal fishes.

156

Annual Fishes

In the regions of periodic drought—in the pampas, the savannahs, and the overflow marshes—special adaptation to the peculiarities of environment is encountered.

Various members of the family Cyprinodontidae, the egg-laying toothcarps, have the unusual life cycle characteristic of annual fishes. Considering that every habitable spot on earth is inhabited, we keep running into fishes in the most out-of-the-way places. In the open, savannah-like regions of America and Africa live toothcarps that have adapted their whole life cycle to periodic drought. As far as is known, these creatures do not even venture out into free and open water, but stay in rain pools. After a drought, the whole land is dried out and nothing lives there, particularly fish. When the rainy season returns, however, and the first showers fall, the puddles swarm with fish within 24 hours. They are fish larvae, of course, but still fish.

Research has revealed that the eggs have lain in the mud of the bottom throughout the dry period. After an incubation period that sometimes lasts many months, they start to develop embryos and to hatch. The most well known species are those belonging to the genera

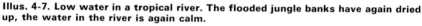

Illus. 4-7. Low water in a tropical river. The flooded jungle banks have again dried up, the water in the river is again calm.

Cynolebias and *Cynopoecilus* in South America and members of the genera *Aphyosemion* and *Nothobranchius* in Africa. In recent years, several different genera have been discovered, having the same life cycle and inhabiting similar biotopes.

These are extremely attractive fishes for the aquarist for several reasons. In the first place, the eggs can be transported "dry" over the entire world, and, as described above, within 24 hours of being placed in water, they will produce larvae. In a very short time, these grow up into the most handsome fish anyone could desire.

The Life Cycle of Annual Fishes

All species of annual toothcarps deposit their eggs on or in the bottom (bottom egg-layers) though the method of spawning may differ from species to species. In the end, all eggs laid must rest on the bottom, buried under the topmost layer of mud (in nature, this is peat mud). In the case of some species, the eggs are expelled and fertilized just above the bottom. Then male or female or both parents cover the eggs with soil by fanning their fins and stirring up the bottom. In other species, at the time of mating, the parents dive down into the soft, muddy bottom, making the egg-laying take place underground. Spawning may continue for several weeks, during which the biotope is drying up. By the time spawning is ended, so are the parents, gasping out their lives on the shimmering, waterless mud flats. These adult annual fishes themselves are not at all adapted to living in poor water and cannot endure drought. For them, the struggle for life is ended, but continuation of the species is guaranteed by the safety of the spawn buried in the mud of the bottom.

5. FISH

AND SCIENCE

Without going too deeply into the scientific aspect of fish study and culture, it is still possible to meet the demand of aquarists for more specific information about the background of their hobby. One question that keeps coming up concerns the names given to fishes— what purpose do such names serve? Another important question concerns the way of life of the different fishes; still another deals with the problem of "difficult" species in the matter of breeding. Moreover, the knowledgeable aquarist should be able to recognize species at sight, thus developing confidence in his own ability to tell one fish from another.

The science behind all this is called ichthyology *(ichthys* means fish in Greek). In accordance with a plan to treat the subject somewhat more fully than is usually done in popular handbooks, the following is a brief history of ichthyology and then a consideration of how newly discovered species are treated before being labelled with particular names.

Concise History of Ichthyology

The Egyptians of the time of the Pharaohs are famous not only for building pyramids that have withstood the ravages of 5,000 years of time, but also for their artistic accomplishments. They pictured the world of nature around them with a stylized but forceful imagery. Of particular interest to modern science is the complete picture of Nile fauna which they have bequeathed to us, and which is still an accurate catalogue of existing fish life. Several mummified fish specimens have also been preserved throughout the ages. Both the drawings of the fish and the mummies can be identified with species now inhabiting the Nile waters.

Of course, the Egyptians made no systematic study of their fish nor did they discriminate among them in any way, except to sort out the kinds that were good to eat.

The study of ichthyology actually began with Aristotle (384–322 B.C.), the most influential of all the Greek philosophers and the mentor of Alexander the Great. He should be considered one of the founders of biology, since he set up a system of methodical orderliness for differentiating the living organisms of his time. It is said that Alexander collected plants and animals on his campaigns and had them sent back for the edification of his old tutor.

In the middle of the 16th century, 2,000 years after Aristotle, a spontaneous interest in nature again rose up simultaneously in various places. In 1553, the Frenchman, Belon (1517–64), published an octavo volume of 448 pages entitled *De Aquatilibus*, in which he described 110 species of fishes from the Mediterranean Sea. In 1554–55, another Frenchman, Rondelet (1507–66), in his *De Piscibus Marinus* listed 244 species from the Mediterranean. None of these, of course, were species in the sense that we understand them today, but were different kinds of fishes—fishes different in appearance from one another.

The Italian, Salviani (1514–72), discussed sea life a little more extensively in his *Aquatilium Animalium Historia* (1554–58). Nearly a hundred years of silence then intervened, broken in 1643, when, under the protection of Prince Maurits of Nassau (1605–79), a kind of expedition was sent to Brazil. Among those who went along were George Marcgrave (1610–44) and William Piso (1611–78). Marcgrave's book, *Brasilianische Naturgegenstände* (1643), is illustrated with fine color plates of 86 of the 150 kinds of fishes described. This book constituted the first cumulative report on fishes outside the Mediterranean area.

In 1648, Piso re-edited Marcgrave's work under the title *Historiae Rerum Naturalium Brasiliae, libri VIII*. Apparently, the publisher, De Laet, of Leyden and Amsterdam, did not do the job to suit Piso, for, 10 years later, in 1658, Piso published a completely revised and enlarged edition, in which he included Marcgrave's work, under the title, *G. Marcgravii Historiae Rerum Naturalium Brasiliae*, commemorating, in this way, his deceased friend.

In 1686, *Historia Piscium* was published by two English researchers, John Ray (1628–1705) and Francis Willoughby (1635–72). Actually, the work was originally written by Willoughby under the title *Historia Piscium Libri Quatuor*, and was edited and published by Ray after the death of his disciple. In this book, for the first time, a distinction was made between cartilaginous and bony fishes.

More familiar names of this same period are those of Borelli (1608–79), Malpighi (1628–94), and Swammerdam (1637–80), all of whom were engaged in anatomical research.

Compilations

Present-day science regards Peter Artedi (1705–35) as the "father of ichthyology." A fellow-Swede and friend of Linnaeus, he was commissioned to catalogue the famous fish collection of Seba, a rich merchant of Amsterdam. Artedi drowned in an Amsterdam canal at the age of 29. The original memorial statue to Artedi is still located near the aquarium building of Amsterdam's zoological gardens, Artis. Artedi's treatment of the subject was so well done and approved that Linnaeus found it unnecessary to make any changes in it. Linnaeus prepared the manuscript for the printer and the book appeared in 1738 in Leyden under the title *Ichthyologia Sive Opera Omnia de Piscibus Scilicet*.

The work of Carl von Linné marks the beginning of a period of compiling activity in the field of ichthyology. To the scientific world, Linné is known as Linnaeus (1707–78) in accordance with the then popular custom of Latinizing names. As already mentioned, Linné edited Artedi's manuscript, at first without alteration.

Artedi had divided the world of fishes into five orders: the Malacopterygii, Acanthopterygii, Branchiostegi, Chondropterygii, and the Plagiuri. The last included whale-like animals—though these are actually mammals—because in Artedi's time, whales were considered to be fish. He further listed 47 genera and 230 species of fishes. The main feature of Artedi's system was the Latin nomenclature carrying the specification. This was a step ahead of the practice common at that time of applying the vulgar or popular name. Linnaeus and later workers based their descriptions on those of Artedi. (See the chapter *Nomenclature and Systematics* on page 171.)

Linnaeus' own famous work, *Systema Naturae*, went through 12 editions, a "best seller" for his time. In 1758, in the 10th edition, Linnaeus definitely introduced binomial nomenclature (double names) for all animals. The section on fishes in *Systema Naturae* is based entirely on Artedi's work. Linnaeus considered it necessary to change only a single name—*Lepturus* into *Trichiuris*. Moreover, he added 17 new names: *Chimaera, Tetraodon, Diodon, Centriscus, Pegasus, Callionymus, Uranoscopus, Cepola, Mullus, Teuthis, Loricaria, Fistularia, Atherina, Mormyrus, Polynemus, Amia*, and *Elops*. These modifications executed by Linnaeus in Artedi's work were ineffective and, in the end, no improvement. In the 12th edition, without rhyme or reason, he changed a number of names, violating the well chosen binomial (dual) nomenclature of his 10th edition. This, however, hardly affects the great merit of his work and the valuable service he rendered to science— foremost of which was his binomial nomenclature, and second of which was the introduction of the generic concept into biology.

Another contemporary of Linnaeus worth mentioning is the German scientist, Gronow, who worked in the Netherlands. This reference is not to Lorentz Theodor Gronow, but to his father, Johannes Fridericus, known as Gronovius, the Latinized version of his name. Father and son are often mistaken for each other, where their publications in the field of ichthyology are concerned. Laurentius Theodorus (1730–78) dried fish skins as herbarium specimens, but the publication, *A Method of Preparing Specimens of Fish by Drying Their Skins* (Philosophical Transactions of the Royal Society of London, 1742), was written by his father, Johannes Fridericus Gronovius (1690–1760). Laurentius was only 12 years old at that time. The collection of herbarium fishes started by Johannes Gronovius has been preserved in good condition. It served as a source for Günther's *Catalogue of the Fishes of the British Museum*.

Other contemporary scientists working with fishes were Johann Frederick Gmelin (1748–1804), who tried to bring Linnaeus' *Systema Naturae* up to date in a 13th edition. However, his lack of expertise caused this work to be soon forgotten. A more deserving compilation written by Marc Elezier Bloch (1723–99) was published by a publisher, author and professor in Leipzig, Johann Gottfried Schneider (1750–1822): *M. E. Blochii Systema Ichthyologiae Iconibus cx. Illustratum*

(1801). Bloch, a physicist, was 56 years of age when his first work on ichthyology appeared. The compilation, usually referred to as "Bloch, ed. Schneider, 1801," describes 1,519 species with excellent illustrations. Considering that the author was well along in years when he became interested in fishes, his compilation is unique, although his system is rather artificial.

A more original work was produced by the French scientist Lacépède. During the French Revolution, he was deprived of his full name and title—Bernard Germaine Etienne de la Ville-sur-Illon, Comte de La Cépède—and was thereafter called, simply, Citizen Lacépède. Even though he worked under unsatisfactory circumstances, his *Histoire naturelle des poissons* (5 parts, 1798–1802), became the forerunner of Cuvier & Valenciennes' monumental work under the same title. He described 1,463 species. Because of numerous mistakes and faulty illustration, and, no doubt, because the work of Cuvier & Valenciennes, in 22 parts, eclipsed it, this by no means undeserving book failed to gain attention.

In his *Règne animale* (1817), Cuvier introduced comparative anatomy and palaeontology to support his system. In 1828, the first part of the *Histoire naturelle des poissons* appeared, mentioning Valenciennes (1794–1865) as co-author. The first part, however, was composed entirely by Cuvier. Both men worked on Parts 2 through 9, but individual chapters are attributed to one or the other of the authors. Parts 10 through 22 were written by Valenciennes alone. Valenciennes was Cuvier's pupil and, after Cuvier's death in 1832, the younger man carried on the work and completed it—that is, he added a cumulative index as a finishing touch, even though the work itself was not entirely finished. The incompleteness of the work is ascribed to a dispute with the publisher. In all, 4,514 species are described, but sharks, ganoids, flatfishes and eels are not included.

According to a ruling of the International Commission for Zoological Nomenclature, the various species newly described should be attributed to either one of the authors. It is thus erroneous to refer to the authorship of Cuvier & Valenciennes when referring to a particular species. Correctly, the species in question should be ascribed either to Cuvier or to Valenciennes, depending on the location of the description within the work—the part and the page containing it. Cuvier & Valenciennes' *Histoire naturelle des poissons* is still the standard work for ichthyological studies and shall probably continue to be so, irrespective of the many fine books that have been published since. Do not forget that Cuvier was first to relate fish fossils to living fishes. Yet, it was (John) Louis

(Rodolphe) Agassiz (1807–73) who finally drove home the idea that fossil fishes were of significant use in the development of a natural system. In laying out the principles of LEPIDOLOGY—the study of (fish) scales—Agassiz defined the system of the four basic types of fishes, distinguished according to the scalation and the structure of the scales. His extensive knowledge of fossils, however, was not coupled with enough familiarity with recent forms, so that his system is not infallible. Still, as shall be seen, his command over the material was, perhaps unwittingly, greater than his successors begrudgingly admitted.

Johannes Müller (1801–58) brought light to a different aspect in his study specializing in Agassiz's groups of Ganoidei. Müller's work, *Über den Bau und die Grenzen der Ganoiden, und über das Natürliche System der Fische* (1844), is regarded as one of the most important for systematic arrangement. In it, the author introduces the structure of the heart and the relation of the cranial blood vessels as new criteria for a system of classification.

Science is also indebted to Müller for a closer study of the swim bladder and the small duct connecting it to the intestine, the ductus pneumaticus. He divided the Teleostei into two categories: those fishes with a permanent duct connection between the swim bladder and the intestine, which he called physostomi, and those without this duct (where such an embryonic duct is lost at any early stage of development), which he called physoclysti. As will be discussed later, such a division is, up to a point, a completely unnatural one.

The last, serious effort made to catalogue all the known fishes on earth was made by Albert (Carl Ludwig Gotthilf) Günther (1830–1914). His *Catalogue of the Fishes of the British Museum*, 8 parts in quarto (1859–70), lists 6,843 species and 1,682 doubtful species. It is still one of the basic works for ichthyological studies.

This actually brings us up to date. More recent works should be considered more as summarizing efforts than as compilations. The number of known species was estimated in 1910 at 12,000, and this figure has surely doubled since then, in spite of the thorough revision of the specific taxonomy (species concept), due to research in the areas of genetics, distribution, natural environment, and so on. Many of the older, so-called morphological species, were found to belong to one variable, biological species. Although numerous old species were gathered into one common species in this manner, the present number of known biological species of fishes can well be set at about 25,000.

Collecting Trips and Expeditions

Collection of specimens on which investigations were based was formerly a haphazard process. Crew members of merchant ships and warships picked up random specimens here and there and took them home as curiosities from far lands. It was not until later that collecting gradually became more organized. The knickknack cabinets of rich merchants with a bent towards scientific curiosity provided specimens for deliberate investigation.

Collecting got itself upon a firm footing when it was finally taken over by professional biologists and people of scientific interest and training. As far as ichthyology was concerned, Europe became the

Year	Research Terrain	Expedition, etc.	Processors and Publications
1798–1801	Egypt	The French Army Expedition to Egypt under Napoleon Bonaparte.	Geoffroy-St. Hilaire, 1809, 1827.
1817–20	Brazil	Spix and von Martius' Journey in Brazil.	Spix & Agassiz, 1829.
1835–39	Guianas	Schomburgk's Journeys in Guiana and to the Orinoco.	Schomburgk, 1841.
1840–44	Guyana (British Guiana)	ibid., in Guyana.	Müller & Troschel, 1848, and others — +
1865–66	Brazil	The Thayer Expedition to Brazil under Louis Agassiz.	Eigenmann, 1908, 1914 — +, and others — +
1873— +	India	The Yarkand Expeditions (Mission).	Day, 1876, 1878.
1888–89	Indonesia	A Journey to the Dutch East Indies.	Weber, 1890; Weber & De Beaufort, — +
1888–90	East Africa	A Journey undertaken by F. Stuhlmann to the coastal region of East Africa.	Pfeffer, 1893.
1895–96 (1899–1900) (1904–05)	Tanzania	Expeditions to Lake Tanganyika by J. E. S. Moore. by W. A. Cunnington.	Boulenger, 1898, 1900, 1901. 1906, — +
1896–99	Patagonia	Princeton University Expedition to Patagonia.	Eigenmann, 1909, 1910, — +
1903, 1907, 1909	New Guinea	Dutch Expeditions to New Guinea under Arth. Wichmann.	Weber, 1908, 1913, Weber & De Beaufort, 1911, — +
1905–12	West Africa	Gruvel Missions, Expeditions along the West Coast of Africa.	Pellegrin, 1914 — +
1907–08	Central Africa	German Central Africa Expedition.	Pappenheim & Boulenger, 1914.
1908	Guyana (British Guiana)	Indiana University and Carnegie Museum Expedition to Guyana.	Eigenmann, 1909, 1912, — +, Myers, —
1911	Brazil	The Stanford Expedition to Brazil.	Starks, 1913.
1918–19	Andes Mountains	The Irwin Expedition of Indiana University.	Eigenmann, 1919 — +
1920–21	Andes–Amazon	"Centennial" Expedition of Indiana University.	Allen, 1942.

Table 5-1

dominant scientific hub, inspired by the work of Artedi, Linnaeus, and, later, by Bloch, Cuvier, Valenciennes, and many others. Exploring expeditions were organized by men who later became famous. The table on page 165 summarizes some of these expeditions.

At the end of the 19th and the beginning of the 20th century, when overseas shipping improved, the number of expeditions suddenly increased spectacularly. Not all expeditions were actually concerned with the collection of scientific data, as the purpose of such expeditions was generally economic or political. It was not until later that these expeditions took on a purely scientific character; whatever economic purpose was involved took a back seat to the scientific purpose. People wanted to know all about every creature that lived on earth. The table on page 165 only goes to 1921, which does not mark the end of expeditions and collecting trips, but was a point of change, after which the character of expeditions changed. Concerning fresh-water fishes, no large-scale expeditions have been undertaken since that time. On the other hand, the number of small-scale, specialized collecting trips has grown to such enormous proportions that it would be impossible to list them all.

The importing of aquarium fishes is strictly a business enterprise and, as such, will be discussed in Chapter 6.

Literature Regarding Fish

When knowledge reaches the point that it overflows the 22 parts of Cuvier & Valenciennes' *Histoire naturelle des poissons*, the time for specialization has come. First, one can systematically collect and study the fishes native to a certain area or areas. Next, one can further specialize in the various aspects of ichthyology, built upon the basic findings of early scientists.

As will be seen in the next chapter, insight into scientific development became much deeper towards the end of the 19th century than it had been even three decades earlier.

In the Indonesian-Australian Archipelago, the matter was taken firmly in hand by the Dutch physician Pieter Bleeker (1819–78), during his stay there from 1842 to 1860. His famous atlas, illustrated with hundreds of excellent color plates, was, unfortunately, never completed. Titled *Atlas ichthyologique des Indes Orientales Néerlandaises* (36 parts in folio, 1862–78), it is a compilation of several hundred of Bleeker's earlier, published works. The area he chose to explore had been a virgin one up to this time, so that he was free to go about it as he thought best. As a result, many East Indian species are labelled with his authorship.

Moreover, the *Atlas* is still a basic work for the Indonesian Archipelago. A follow-up on Bleeker's work was *Fishes of the Indo-Australian Archipelago* (1911–57), by Weber & De Beaufort, comprised of 13 parts. The first part deals exclusively with Bleeker and his published works. The 13th part was published in 1957.

Africa is the hunting ground of many researchers. The Belgian ichthyologist, George Albert Boulenger (1858–1937), studied, among other things, the fauna of the Democratic Republic of the Congo (formerly the Belgian Congo). He published a *Catalogue of the Fresh-Water Fishes of Africa* (4 parts in octavo, 1911–16). Still a standard work for Africa, it has been enlarged by numerous authors, including Jacques Pellegrin (1892–1917).

South American fishes—including fresh-water species—were studied by Carl Hubbs Eigenmann (1863–1927) and his many students. His *Fresh-Water Fishes of British Guiana* (1912) is a priceless acquisition for aquarists. His monograph on toothcarps, which will be discussed later, is also a valuable work. A more broadly based, fundamental work on South American fishes was written by Alexander von Humboldt (1769–1859). After him, David Starr Jordan (1851–1931) and many of his pupils published a series of papers based on material collected by Agassiz.

Illus. 5-1. It is important for the naturalist to be able to distinguish various kinds of landscapes. A quiet bog pond, surrounded by bushes and birches, indicates acidulous water in which insect life is especially abundant. In the temperate lowland districts, such bog ponds generally have no connection with open water and are not populated by fish. Occasionally, such fish as, for example, mud minnows (Umbridae), can be found in them.

For information on the fishes of Brazil, we must go as far back as 1855 for works by Comte François L. de Laporte de Castelnau (1812–80). After his first treatises on South America, however, he turned his attention to Australia. The name of Franz Steindachner (1834–1919) is also well known; in fact, a list of his papers alone would take up more than 20 pages. His papers concerning South America were particularly based on fishes collected by Johann Natterer. More recent works have been published by Henry Weed Fowler (1878–1968) and Alipio de Miranda Ribeiro, with particular emphasis on the area south of the Amazon, and by George Sprague Myers and his pupils, covering other districts, particularly the Guianas.

North America also provided an ample study area for numerous explorers. The studies here were strictly localized at first, such as the exquisitely illustrated articles of Charles Alexander Lesueur (1778–1846) on the fishes in the Great Lakes and in the state of Ohio. Samuel Rafinesque-Schmalz (1783–1842) also studied Ohio fishes, as did Jared Potter Kirtland (1793–1877). Sir John Richardson (1787–1865) chose to study the Great Lakes and Canada, John Edwards Holbrook (1797–1871), the state of South Carolina, and Louis Agassiz, Lake Superior. Spencer Fullerton Baird (1823–87) and Charles Frédéric Girard (1822–95) joined forces to describe a great portion of the fish fauna of the United States. Edward Drinker Cope (1840–97), an all-round naturalist, dealt with the carp- and the perch-like fishes of the United States.

Charles Henry Gilbert (1859–1928) published *A Synopsis of the Fishes of North America*, which was conceived by Herbert Edson Copeland (1849–76) and completed with the collaboration of David Starr Jordan. Later, Gilbert studied the fishes of Alaska and Central America. The second, enlarged edition of the *Synopsis*, edited by Jordan & Evermann (Barton Warren Evermann, 1853–1932) was the 4-part, standard handbook, *Fishes of North and Middle America*.

Europe, which has been the subject of intensive study ever since Artedi, still lacks a practical compilation of its fish fauna. The book by Harry Govier Seeley (1839–1909), titled *The Freshwater Fishes of Europe*, although still used for fresh-water fishes, is most incomplete and, now, obsolete. There is a Dutch booklet by Heinrich Carl Redeke (1873–1943), which appeared in 1941, that gives a brief, historical review of ichthyology in the Netherlands. A revised edition of this part of the *Fauna van Nederland* would, in no way, be a luxury. For other European countries, only a few names are mentioned here, as thousands of publications have been issued by countless authors: Steindachner

(Germany, Austria, Hungary, the Balkans); Heckel and Kner (Germany, Austria); von Siebold (Central Europe); Bocage and De Brito Cappello (Spain and Portugal); Kröyer and Bilsson (Scandinavia); Yarrell, Turton, Couch, Day (England), and many others.

Asiatic fishes were studied extensively by Francis Hamilton (1762–1829)—better known as Hamilton-Buchanan—and the result of his studies were published in the form of a book titled *An Account of the Fishes Found in the River Ganges and Its Branches* (1822). Francis Day (1829–89) compiled his numerous papers into a book entitled *Fishes of India, Being a Natural History of the Fishes Known to Inhabit the Seas and Fresh Waters of India, Burma, and Ceylon* (1875–78).

The school of Sunder Lal Hora (18?–195?) contributed a great deal to the knowledge on Southeast Asia. The vast territory had been but randomly explored, until one of the most important books covering the fishes of that area was produced by John Treadwell Nichols (1883–   ), *The Fresh–water Fishes of China* (1943).

For a long time, Japan has been a subject of ichthyological interest. Studies on the fish fauna were published, among others, by Carl Pehr Thunberg (1743–1828), Herman Schlegel (1804–84), Günther, Gill, Hilgendorf, Döderlein, and many others. Lately, the work has been taken over by Japanese ichthyologists. The classic foundation work, however, remains that of David Starr Jordan and John Otterbein Snyder, and consists of many treatises and "lists" of Japanese fishes, issued in 1901.

Australia must not be overlooked, even though it has always been something of a stepchild to ichthyologists. In addition to Bleeker, Weber, De Beaufort and others who studied the Indonesian-Australian Archipelago, Frederick Wollaston Hutton (1836–1905), Theodore Nicholas Gill (1837–1914), William Macleay (18?–18?), John Douglas Ogilby (18?–1916?), Allan R. McCulloch (18?–19?) and others investigated the fish fauna of the Australian continent and of New Zealand.

Taxonomic Studies

There has been a tendency lately to review and survey certain groups of fishes to arrive at a better knowledge of their life, their propagation and their geographical distribution.

In view of the enormous volume of available material, it is urgent to adapt the various descriptions of fish fauna to one another. Since the monumental work of Cuvier & Valenciennes was published,

169

Illus. 5-2. If there is such a bog pond nearby, the fortunate aquarist is assured of a year-round sufficient food supply for his aquarium fish. The larvae of many insects, such as beetles and dragon-flies, are dangerous predators, however, so that care must be exercised in using these as food animals. The larger fish, such as cichlids, nevertheless, can thrive on them.

ichthyologists have been engaged in studying smaller groups on a world-wide scale. In order to map out the distribution of a certain family of fishes around the world, all the literature ever published on members of that family must be read. Being unaware of or neglecting any publication concerning the fishes of certain areas, and lack of insight into the laws governing geographical distribution have often led to the same fish being given two names. Early authors were usually satisfied to indicate the place of origin of a fish as "India," "Africa," "North America," etc. This was often due to the absence of more exact data as to where the fish was in fact found.

Among the many hundreds of world-wide reviews of fish groups, there are a few that concern aquarists: Samuel Garman (1846–19?) wrote a review of toothcarps, *The Cyprinodonts* (1895); Ellis reviewed *The Gymnotid Eels of Tropical America* (1913); Eigenmann published *The Cheirodontinae, A Subfamily of Minute Characid Fishes of South America* (1915), and *The American Characidae* in 5 parts (1917, 1918, 1921 and 1927, the fifth part produced in collaboration with Myers, 1929). Charles Tate Regan (1878–1943) was the author of many reviews on almost all groups of bony fishes.

Nomenclature and Systematics

The fancy words at the heading of this section simply mean "naming" and "classification." The two are inseparable, of course, as there could be no classifying without names, and the names would have no meaning at all if they were not fitted into some kind of a system that related them to each other.

Up to now, we have discussed the development of the science of fishes, but have dealt only with the names of those scientists or researchers whose names were used in labelling the fishes. Now, the time has come to examine very closely the names of the fishes themselves. All the fishes we are about to discuss have names, sometimes even two or three names. This does not include, of course, the popular names given to fishes in various countries, but the international, scientific names that identify the same fish in every country in the world.

Aquarists often speak of *Barbus conchonius* or *Aphyosemion australe* without realizing that the double names indicate the exact place the fish occupies in the system of classification. By "exact place" is meant its position in the widely ramified family tree of the fish population of the world, which reveals its relationship to the nearest form-types and families.

Of course, the place a fish holds in the system is of minor importance to the aquarist. At times, however, that very knowledge can spell the difference between success and failure when the aquarist finds himself face to face with certain problems. It is, for instance, a good thing to know something about the fish in question, whether it is a cichlid or a characin, a toothcarp or a carp, a labyrinth fish or a bass, and so on. Classification is also useful when you happen to run across a newly imported fish about which nothing is known. If its place in the system can be determined, then information on related species can be applied by inference, so that you are not completely in the dark in regard to the way in which the new fish should be treated.

Setting up a system can be dry and tedious work, but it can also be a lively occupation, depending entirely on how you go about it. It need not be just a matter of fumbling through ancient, yellowed, musty folios or among flasks and jars of preserved materials. Modern research involves study of the living creatures and their ways of life, so that it is not only desirable, but also necessary, for systematists who would "do their fish" in a proper manner to keep them under control in an aquarium, so as to be in a position to solve whatever problems may come up.

More than once, aquarists, as well as other naturalists, have discovered matters of great scientific importance simply by constant and sympathetic observation of their respective broods.

Naming the Fishes

A teacher standing in front of his class runs the chance of finding more than one John, Peter, Tom, Paul, Harry, Dick, Jane or Mary among them. Fortunately, each has his or her own family name, and that goes far towards making it possible to tell the children apart. In the same way, even though the aquarist may give pet names to some of his fishes, he generally distinguishes among them by using the official Latin names.

Although the nomenclature devised by Linnaeus was not the first practical attempt at classification, it is the one that has been adopted. His concept of binomial nomenclature was introduced in the 10th edition of his *Systema naturae*, which appeared in 1758 and still serves as a basis for zoological nomenclature. It has been adopted by international agreement, which provided for permanent control by a committee handling all pertinent problems as they arise. It is also the duty of the committee always to keep the system of nomenclature up to date.

In principle, the names of fishes, as well as the names of all plants and animals, are made up in much the same way as those of the schoolchildren. The only difference is that the more important name (which relates to the surname) takes the first position. It is as if Harry Jones, for instance, were to be called Jones Harry, which is, to be sure, the way he is listed in the telephone directory. The more important name, called the "generic" name—that is, the name of the GENUS—always begins with a capital letter, thus: *Brachydanio*. The "specific" name—that is, the name of the SPECIES to which the fish belongs—follows, as *albolineatus*. The specific name begins with a lower-case letter, never with a capital. Genus and species names, also, are invariably printed in *italic* type. When written by hand, they are underlined, to set them apart from other written words on the page.

The full, scientific name of a fish consists of four parts: the name of the genus, the name of the species, the name of the "author," and the year. The year marks the time of the *first* scientific description of the fish. The author is the scientist (often the discoverer) who wrote up

172

and published the first description. The specific name is given by the author in accordance with factors characterizing and distinguishing this particular specimen from other species of the same genus which have already been described and published. Naturally, the author always seeks a relationship between his find and some known genus of fishes. For example, *B. albolineatus* (never begin a sentence with a single specific name; the specific name must be accompanied by the generic name or the first initial of the generic name, because a specific name is often used for more than one genus) was described in 1860 by Blyth as *Nuria albolineata*. The genus *Nuria* was already known to science. It comprises various small rasboras and danios, and Blyth assigned his fish to this group. To point out its difference from the other fishes of this genus, he gave it the name *albolineata*. Nevertheless, the present complete official name of this fish is *Brachydanio albolineatus* (Blyth, 1860). The change came about because it was later found that the fish did not belong to the genus *Nuria*, but was related to *Danio*. The generic name *Brachydanio* was found to determine its geneological place even more accurately, and this is the name that was ultimately adopted.

Since departure was made from Blyth's naming of *Nuria albolineata* and it is now called *Brachydanio albolineatus* (in Latinized names, the ending of the specific name must agree in gender with the generic name), the author's name and the year must stand in parentheses. This shows that the combination of the name does not derive from Blyth, but from another author, while Blyth is still given credit for the first announcement.

Another example of this is *Rivulus urophthalmus* Günther, 1866. In this case, the combination of generic and specific names was given by Günther, and, therefore, his name and the year are not enclosed in parentheses.

Wherever the discoverer is the author as well and his name is mentioned in connection with a genus or higher unit of the system, it should not be enclosed by parentheses. Why should the author and year be mentioned, anyway? This can be explained by an example. In a treatise on some *Rivulus* of the Antilles (Hoedeman, 1958, *Rivulid Fishes of the Antilles*—Stud. Fauna Curaçao), the distribution area of *Rivulus holmiae* had to be determined. In 1949, Dr. Leonard P. Schultz (Washington D.C.) reported on a collection of fish from Margarita Island (Venezuela) and classified a number of specimens as *Rivulus holmiae*. This species was first described in 1909 by Eigenmann, from Guyana (British Guiana). Therefore, the complete name is *Rivulus holmiae* Eigenmann, 1909. On closer examination,

173

Schultz' specimens were not identical with *holmiae*, but they represented a local variety of *Rivulus harti* (Boulenger, 1890). Obviously, the correct reference to the specimens in question should be: *Rivulus holmiae* Schultz, 1949 (non Eigenmann, 1909).

A scientific compilation of the data regarding *R. harti* would thus look as follows:

Rivulus harti (Boulenger, 1890)

Haplochilus hartii Boulenger, 1890, Trinidad

Rivulus harti De Beaufort, 1940, Margarita Island

Rivulus holmiae Schultz, 1949, Margarita Island

Rivulus harti Hoedeman, 1958, Margarita, Trinidad, Tobago, etc.

For another nomenclatural problem, see the discussion of *Barbus* vs. *Puntius* on page 451.

So, to avoid misunderstanding, it is customary in scientific works, to give the specimen's name complete with author and year. In aquarium literature, confusion of names occurs inevitably unless all the names are used and are thoroughly verified. Moreover, it is confusing if photographs are published and the name of the fish is given in the caption without the name of the author or person responsible for the naming, particularly when the person's name is cited later. It should be a matter of editorial responsibility to see that the names are properly added.

How did such a method of naming ever come to pass? As already mentioned, Artedi gave his species Latin designations, as the Latin language was at that time generally and internationally understood by the educated classes. This was a great step forward, as the descriptions that existed before Artedi were so different and varied that no two publications could be compared with each other.

Linnaeus chose Artedi's designations for the binomial nomenclature of fishes. With the generic name representing several characteristics, followed by the specific name which, essentially, has a more limiting function, this system permits an endless number of combinations to exist. That is why it is still in force.

The sudden bursting forth of activity in natural science research in the 18th and 19th centuries and the lack of international co-ordination of these activities, led to unwitting duplication of work, several researchers dealing simultaneously with the same plants and animals and giving them different names. It became necessary, therefore, to create commissions for botanical and zoological nomenclature to develop order out of the chaos. The task is still not accomplished by a long shot and the arbitration committee still has its hands full of daily work. This shows the important position that nomenclature holds internationally, a condition that also pertains, but perhaps to a lesser degree, to systematic classification.

Systematic Classification

Ever since thinking men began to ask questions of the world around them, there has been a need for some kind of system of classification that would reduce much into little. In no other way could man fit the sprawling events of nature into the limited capacity of his mind. The first thing he did, probably, was to divide things into what was edible and what was not. This was the most primitive of classifications and, to primitive man, the most useful. Man's next step towards differentiation may have been to decide between what was living and what was not, and to further sub-divide the living into what was animal and what was plant.

The origin of the present system of natural sciences is not known to derive from any given individual, though a few names have come down to us in ancient writings. It appears that even in the most remotely past times, men were concerned with this question of classification. It may well be asked if classifying things is really so important as all that. And the answer is that it is indeed—even for the aquarist.

The importance of systematic classification for the natural sciences— and for all sciences—can be understood to some extent if we consider how many hundreds of species of aquarium fishes have been described in the course of time. Obviously, each fish must have a name—were this not so, we could neither talk nor write about them. Good illustrations can play an important part, but without the use of names, we would soon get bogged down in descriptive verbiage, trying to get across the idea we are talking about. Classification and nomenclature go hand-in-hand and are inseparable. Do not think that a name, once adopted, is revised by some whim of the classifier, though this may occasionally seem to be so. Rather, at some point, a line had to be drawn to put an end to some untenable situation that kept clouding the issue more and more. Some aquarium fishes are known by a variety of names, simply because a hard-and-fast line of nomenclature has not yet been laid down for them.

Systematic classification and nomenclature are not an end in themselves, but only a means to an end—that end being to expand our knowledge of the living world. Consider them the same as ruled lines on a sheet of paper, which are but a means to guide your pen in clear, legible writing.

One of the many striking examples of the need for—as well as the very real economic importance of—a system of classification and correct nomenclature follows. A certain insect was causing a great deal of damage, in agriculture and, in particular, in horticulture. A campaign of extermination was undertaken, but soon proved a failure. Further study by experts in classification showed that the suspected insects were not at fault at all—they were harmless, and even useful, creatures. The real culprit was a migrant sub-species that could hardly be distinguished from the useful insects. Large sums of money had been expended on the extermination of harmless creatures only to find that the brigand doing all the damage had escaped unscathed.

Ichthyological Research

The simplest way for the reader to gain insight into the scientific work going on behind the scenes is to follow the course of a typical research situation, from collecting the material to processing and storing it for future use by other scientists. Within the parameters thus established, the experience of some scientists shows the following steps to be in order: collecting the material—preserving it—transporting it to the laboratory—working up the collected data—releasing and publishing the results—long-term storing of the material—and finally, arranging the stored material so that particular items can readily be found again.

Each phase is subject to certain norms. If any one of the steps is omitted or becomes lost, the final result is bound to be the worse for it. Obviously, old-time collecting and processing did not come up to the high standards demanded today. The aquarist will often have to bear the brunt of such a situation.

For greater clarity, consult the schematic representation of the process in Table 5–2. Phase 1 indicates the route travelled by the collected material. Phase 2 shows the processing of the material, and Phase 3, the steps taken by the processed data towards final publication. The whole process is further divided into steps, marked *a* through *w*.

Phase 1 begins in the realm of nature, *(a)*, where the fish is caught by a collector or expedition, *(b)*. The fish may either be transported alive for the trade, or preserved for scientific research, *(c)*. The latter should be supported by detailed documentation, such as photos of the habitat, specifications of the native water, etc., *(d)*. The fishes are then sorted out and sent on to the ichthyological department of an institute, but not without each specimen being clearly marked, *(e)*. After arrival at its destination, the collection is roughly sorted out according to the data gathered in the field by the collector, *(f)*. These are recorded, and then the material is definitely and carefully sorted, *(g)*, and processed, *(h)*.

Processing leads us into Phase 2 of the research, done by the ichthyologist. Each and every part of the collection is preserved in a separate jar (a stoppered bottle), as it will eventually have to go into storage, *(s)*. For the preserving phase, *(r)*, the specimens must be tagged, the label showing the scientific name, the collection number, and the place

177

Table 5-2

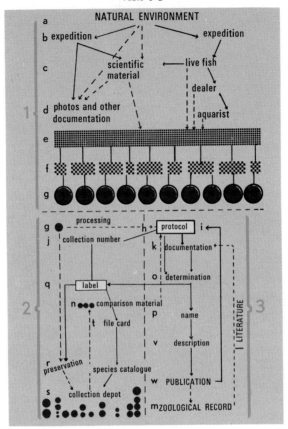

where the specimen was found. The last items are easy to derive, as collection numbers are only serial numbers from a register of numbers, and the place of discovery is also known. The scientific name, however, must be checked out first, *before* it is written on the label.

This is a moment of crucial interest, for how is the name to be found and why must it be given? Dealing first with the latter, no two kinds of animals bear the same name. A certain name, therefore, refers only to a certain kind of animal. Actually, the name itself is not the essential thing—it is the differentiation of one fish from another that is important. Thus, *Rivulus agilae* refers to a fish different from *Rivulus holmiae*. Determination, therefore, involves designation of the kind of fish that this particular one is, in relation to all other kinds. However, it will become obvious that there is more than that to a name. Finding the proper name is also a subject of some interest. For more about this, see page 205.

Determining the name—which must be done in Phase 3 of the research—requires a lot of pertinent data, which are listed on a record form (protocol), *(i)*. These data comprise information obtained from comparative material from previous collections, *(n)*, and from the literature, *(l)*. The two underlie the documentation that leads ultimately to the designation of the name, the determination, *(o)*. The label, *(q)*, can now be written, the fish preserved, *(r)*, and placed in the storeroom, *(s)*, to be taken out again later for reference as comparative material, *(n)*. For guidance in the storeroom, each jar must be registered or "booked in" on a card, *(t)*, with its full label. The card is then inserted into the card record file. This is, in fact, all that needs to be known to make the method of determination clear.

The data collected can, however, contain useful information on the fishes of a certain area. It may be thought necessary to release this information in a report, *(w)*. This must be done if any new material has come out about a fish, or if the fish is a new species or a form not yet described and named. In such a case, the scientist involved must name the new species and provide a description of it, *(v)*, which gives a clear idea of what it looks like. The publication is then sent on to other ichthyologists, and a reference to the article is included in the section Fishes (Pisces) of the *Zoological Record*, *(m)*. This is a yearbook listing all publications on fishes that have been released in the course of the year. The *Zoological Record* is an indispensable aid to any worker in search of literature that will tell him whether or not a given fish has been reported on before.

Equipment for Fish Research

Some equipment is needed for the examination and study of a fish collection: trays for sorting, preservatives, tweezers, dissecting needles, fine scissors, small sharp knives, and sometimes dyes, as well as a great number of smaller items. The most essential device for examining fishes smaller than 6 inches (most aquarium fishes) is a binocular stereomicroscope, also called a stereoscopic microscope or analytical microscope. For larger specimens, a precision vernier caliper is used for making fine measurements, and a slide rule for calculating the ratios. A miniature camera kept in permanent readiness for picture-taking is also useful.

The Microscope

First, the size of all specimens included in the collection must be accurately measured. Specimens that have withstood preservation

179

Illus. 5-3. Pre-sorting a collection of fishes, work that requires a ready knowledge of the various families. Recognition of the members of the armoured catfish family is difficult only where very young specimens are concerned.

poorly, or which have dried out or are otherwise damaged should be discarded. Measurements must be made somewhat as a dressmaker measures—that is, not just in the length, but in every important proportion. Measuring the parts of tiny specimens with the caliper would not be too accurate; however, a machinist's rule used in conjunction with the stereoscopic microscope will let you measure lengths right down to a tenth of a millimetre, or less, depending on the magnification employed.

The stereoscopic microscope is, in fact, a means towards extending and sharpening the eyesight. It is provided with twin eyepieces, one for each eye, coupled, through a set of prisms, with the twin objective lenses. The twin sets of lenses provide for the stereoscopic (three-dimensional) effect in viewing the object, and the complex arrangement of lenses and prisms allows wide field of view and brilliance of the image. At high magnifications (over $200\times$), the effect of stereoscopic vision is lost, but it is no longer necessary when working this small.

Small fishes are always examined under the stereo-microscope. At low powers of magnification, such as are generally used in measurement and dissection (from $6\times$ to $24\times$), there is ample working space between the objective lenses and the object being viewed for you to use dissecting needle and scissors when necessary.

Microscopes of this kind can be bought in many designs at many prices. The finer the instrument, the more costly it is, and the more precision-working are the accessories that come with it. For working with small fishes, the microscope stage should be equipped with a sliding attachment on the stand so that it can be moved up and down or secured firmly in place, as desired. In some models, the optical device itself is designed to move up and down over a fixed stage. The stage itself should contain a kind of sub-stage—that is, a revolving turntable having a spherically convex underside fitting into a concavity in the sub-stage. This specially-designed ball fitting allows the sub-stage to be turned or inclined at any required angle. The fish is attached to a needle which, in turn, is attached to the revolving, swinging stage so that, in fact, the specimen hangs practically free in space.

For taking measurements, the fish is placed horizontally—that is, the vertical and lengthwise axes of the fish lie in a horizontal plane that is perpendicular to the central axis of the twin microscopes. After sticking the fish on the needle, the ball-joint stage is revolved in the horizontal plane to bring all parts of the specimen under examination without having to re-set the fish on the needle, thus avoiding making unnecessary holes which would only damage the specimen.

The top part of the microscope containing the optics is attached to a slide similar to that on the stage and can be fixed at different heights to suit the convenience and stature of the seated user. A rack-and-pinion device permits the optics to be raised or lowered by simply

Illus. 5-4. The stereo-binocular microscope with lamp providing top light on the stage.

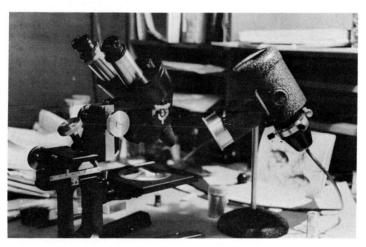

turning a hand wheel. The microscope is roughly focussed by means of the first slide; then, final, fine focussing is accomplished by means of the rack-and-pinion mechanism.

In addition, the entire optical arrangement of the instrument can be moved forward and back and from side to side, by manipulating various controls, thus bringing every part of the stage into its field of view, one part at a time. The rack-and-pinion devices responsible for forward and lateral movement of the optics are fitted with precision scales, permitting highly accurate measurements in the horizontal plane. A cross-hair reticle is located in one eyepiece of the lens-system. By centering the cross-hairs sharply on one end of the specimen to be measured, and by then moving the optics by means of the required rack-and-pinion device, the measurement is made when the cross-hairs are viewed with the other end of the specimen. The correct length is read directly from the precision scale attached to the movement control. Since the forward-and-back movement is also equipped with a scale the same as the scale for lateral movement, vertical measurements of the specimen can also be made, without having to change the set-up.

The procedure described above is suitable for moderate magnifications. Five-power oculars (5× magnification) are generally used in combination with an objective lens system having a magnifying power of 1 (same size), for a total magnification of 5×. (The magnifying power of a microscope is obtained by multiplying the magnifying power of the objective by the magnifying power of the eyepiece. In this case, $1 \times 5 = 5 \times$.) In addition, a 4-power objective will give a total magnification of 20 times ($5 \times 4 = 20 \times$), and a 10-power objective will provide 50 diameters (50×) of magnification. This is quite enough for most work. By using eyepieces of 10 and 20 magnifications with the same objective, total magnifications up to 200× are possible.

Fish are practically always examined under the stereoscopic microscope by direct lighting of the object. The ordinary microscope generally employs sub-stage illumination which passes the light through the object, which is generally cut into thin slices with a MICROTOME (an instrument for cutting sections for microscopic examination) for the purpose. Sub-stage illumination can also be used with the stereoscopic microscope, as it is needed for examination of scales.

The Slide Rule

In order to compare the data from specimens of different lengths, we have to express all the measurements taken from the fish in a so-called standard length, the proportionate length of the head compared to the standard length of the fish, expressed in percentages. The standard length is measured from tip of snout to base of caudal fin (since the caudal fin is liable to be damaged in many preserved specimens).

The actual length measurements cannot be compared, but the derived proportion rates, expressed as percentages of the standard length, do indeed have a comparable relationship.

Simple as they are, these calculations normally take up considerable time. Therefore, it is suggested that you use a slide rule. With this instrument, you can do 8 or 10 such calculations in a minute, simply reading off the correct proportions, once the slide rule has been adjusted to the standard length.

35-mm Camera with Fine-Grain Film for Preserved Specimens

The last essential piece of equipment is a camera, permanently fixed above the microscope stage, ready for instant use. If you see something under the lens that needs further study, you can take a few shots in a few seconds and keep on working with the specimen. On the record you are keeping of your work, next to the fish data, enter the information concerning the photos taken. The films should be serially numbered, regardless of the factory numbering on the film itself. If the field of view is not too small, often a number can be lettered on a small piece of card and laid beside the specimen to be included on the negative. Fine-grain film is suggested, even though it is rather slow in speed. For still subjects such as this, the exposure-length is of no concern anyway, and such film gives the sharpest picture for producing the largest blow-up when prints are made. Lens-extension tubes are available for use with some cameras for making extreme close-ups; for others, there is a bellows attachment. If the lens of your camera is non-removable, you will have to use a special close-up lens fitted over the front of the taking lens. These are available in diopter-powers allowing a full range of magnifying powers. The best camera to use is a single-lens reflex, or S.L.R., one that focusses and views the subject through the taking lens; otherwise, careful measurement of the camera-to-subject distance must be made, which, in extreme close-ups, is a major source of mistakes and spoiled negatives. In any case, use one of the smaller stops or diaphragm openings your lens affords in order to achieve the greatest possible depth of field.

For other photographic purposes, make good use of a copying stand. This stand can be a wide, plywood base fitted with a vertical column, containing sliding and rack-and-pinion devices to which the camera can be fixed in a vertical position. These devices aid in adjusting the camera in rough focussing. The camera should be fitted with the bellows mentioned above, between the camera-box and the taking lens, or with the lens-extension tubes, which are also effective, but rather limited and more difficult to use.

Place the preserved subject to be photographed on the base and light from both sides with photo flood lamps angled at 45°. Focus the camera carefully by racking the bellows in or out until the subject is clearly in focus when you look into the through-the-lens view finder. If the bellows is long enough, up to about 20 cm or 8 inches, you can produce a direct magnification of about 2.5 × with nothing more than the standard, 50-mm taking lens of your camera. This is the size of the image on the negative, of course. At 10 magnifications in the enlarger, this can be increased to about 25 ×, and so on. Somewhat larger magnifications can be achieved by equipping the lens with one of the wide range of close-up lenses available in addition to the bellows. A photo dealer can answer all questions about cameras, lenses, exposures, and so on.

Photographing Live Fishes

You may, at some point, wish to photograph a live specimen. Although other cameras can be used, a single-lens reflex (S.L.R.) 35-mm camera is also best for live fish photography. Modern S.L.R.'s have automatic lenses which normally keep the diaphragm open to admit maximum light for focussing. This closes down to the selected aperture or f-stop when the shutter is released. Without attachments, normal lenses usually focus to about 45 cm (18 inches), which is about right for a fairly large cichlid. Close-ups of smaller fishes need the addition of either close-up lenses, bellows or extension tubes in order to allow closer focussing. Close-up lenses, which attach to the front of the lens, are easiest to use while maintaining fully automatic operation of the lens. Automatic extension tubes also allow auto-operation, but non-auto extension tubes are less expensive. Bellows are usually non-automatic. The better viewing brightness of automatically operated lenses is a distinct advantage in photographing small moving subjects, such as fishes.

Fish can be photographed in their home aquarium, although many photographers prefer a separate photographic aquarium in which the fish can be confined near the front glass by a moveable glass partition.

This keeps the fish from moving in and out of focus. Another method is to pre-focus your camera on an area which the particular fish you are photographing frequently passes.

The best lighting is provided by electronic flash. Flash after flash can be taken without bulb replacement, and the flash duration is usually less than 1,000th of a second, freezing even the fastest action. The shade of the light matches daylight film. Lighting should be from above the tank, or above and just in front, to avoid reflections from the glass. An aperture of $f8$ or smaller (a higher number) should be used to increase depth of focus. It is wise to shoot an experimental roll of film to determine the proper light-to-subject distance and proper f-stop.

First Phase of Research—Collecting the Material

Table 5–2 shows the first research phase, consisting of seven steps, a through g. At the same time, g is the first step of Phase 2.

The Natural Environment for Fish

Actually, scientific research begins the moment you set foot on the bank of the water course where you want to start collecting. Collecting is bound to make you aware of the nature of the environment the fish live in. To understand fish customs fully, you must learn as much as you can about their habitat, because only when you are thoroughly familiar with the habitat can you hope to start collecting with any possibility of success.

Suppose you are in Surinam, a tropical country, formerly called Dutch Guiana, located on the north coast of South America, between Guyana (formerly British Guiana) on the west and Cayenne (French Guiana) on the east. Surinam is bordered on the north by the Atlantic Ocean and on the south by Brazil. The entire highland, the Guiana Plateau, which extends far into Venezuela, is one of the oldest land masses on earth.

Behind a flat coastal area not more than a few miles wide, there lies a broad stretch of lowland that rises gradually to form a chain of hills. At about 200 m (650 feet) altitude is a region of waterfalls. The plateau averages about 500 m (1,650 feet) altitude. Surinam is rocky, with sandstone plateaus at higher altitudes. There is hardly any limestone. The climate is tropical, featuring 200 days of rain per year, and a daily average rainfall of just under 7 cm (3 inches). The temperature ranges between 22 and 30 °C (72–86 °F). Broad rivers drop almost perpendicularly from the highlands to the coast. The fish fauna

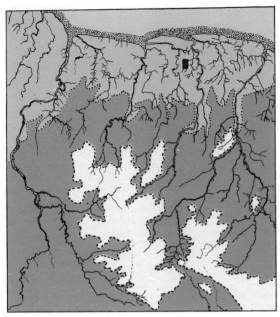

Illus. 5-5. Map of Surinam indicating the most important rivers and their tributaries, the 200-metre (717-foot) altitude line (....) and the 500-metre (1,800-foot) altitude line (------). The red rectangle indicates the location of the detail map on page 187.

in the rivers are clearly differentiated between highland and lowland fauna, the borderline being at the altitude of the waterfalls, the 200-m (650-foot) level.

Three types of forests are distinguishable: first, there are the river forests with boggy soil, usually very dark, with thin underbrush, where the *Mora excelsa* tree is dominant (hence, the name *Mora* forest); second are mixed forests in higher regions, with drier soil, less dark than the *Mora* forest, with thicker underbrush. *Mora* is found here, too, along with other plants; and third are *Eperua* (or wallaba) forests, on very high ground with dry soils.

There are also big, boggy forests, where the manicole palm *(Euterpe oleracea)* flourishes. Temperature in the Guianas is fairly constant, varying by not more than 2 °C (3.6 °F) over the year from the 22–30 °C (72–86 °F) range.

The forest swamps never run deeper than 2 feet of water over a very deep bottom of mud and decaying plants. The waters lie still under a canopy of high trees which shut out the winds, so that the water quality is bad, the oxygen content is low, and the water is

186

yellow. Except during the rainy season, the water contains 20 ml (1.2 cubic inches) of oxygen per 100 litres (26.42 U.S. gallons) and as much as 1,000 ml (61 cubic inches) of carbon dioxide to the same amount. During the rains, there is a slight improvement, but only in the surface water. As a rule, the water in the swamps is stagnant and only during the rainy season is it flushed out by creeks and rivers.

Remarkably, in spite of these conditions, a rich variety of fishes populates these waters, most of the species being equipped with an auxiliary respiratory organ. Fishes from these swamps, as well as from the grass swamps, include *Pyrrhulina, Copella, Hoplias, Erythrinus, Callichthys,* and *Hoplosternum.* Others not equipped with auxiliary respiratory organs are *Poecilia, Micropoecilia, Hemigrammus, Aequidens,*

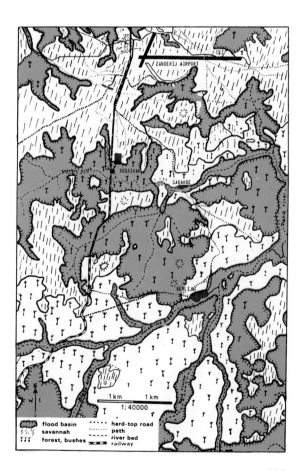

Illus. 5-6. Detail from the map on page 186, with the close vicinity of the Zanderij Airport and camp Bosbivak, in addition to the sites of Sabakoe and Berlijn.

and *Crenicichla*. Many other species find their way into the swamps from the rivers during the rainy season, but they cannot survive there for long. It is necessary, therefore, to use caution in drawing conclusions, for, obviously, shortly after the rainy season, many species of river fishes are likely to be found in the swamps. Including them in a roster of native fishes would provide a false picture. Thus, not all fishes caught in the swamps at any one season are typical of the local fauna, for they could not exist in that environment throughout the entire year. Some species use this period for breeding, but a large proportion of their offspring die later when drought comes and the water in the swamp returns to its "natural "condition, which is to say, poor in oxygen. The conclusion, then, is that it is essential to collect the fishes at various times of the year. Each collection must be kept separate from the others and tagged to indicate where and when, to the exact hour of the day, the fishes were caught.

In describing the habitat of a certain species or variety, it is most helpful to characterize the area concerned. Surinam, the main site of this example research expedition, can be roughly divided into low country and high plateau region.

The following data are important to record in describing the localities where your fishing takes place:

1. Soil composition
2. Climate
3. Vegetation } the bioassociation, or biocoenotic
4. Fauna
5. Food: Plants and animals, quality and quantity available (from stomach contents)
6. Enemies and competing varieties
7. Numbers of a given kind (solitary fish, schools, small groups, couples, masses)
8. Size (age) most frequently found of a species
9. Density of population desired by the species, or of the part of the population to which they belong

In connection with the last point, a certain feeling for sociological factors plays a not-unimportant part. In laboratory experiments, as well as in aquariums, it can be observed that some fish, solitary members of their kind, do not feel at ease alone, and seek the company of other fish of their own or a related species. If they find none relevant to themselves, they pine away. At the other extreme, however, it can be observed that a fish will fiercely protect its own territory. If another fish intrudes, the first will fight for his domain, which will, in the course of such events, fall to the stronger.

Now, let us take a little closer survey of the typical landscape of Surinam, before we concern ourselves with a more limited locale. On the whole, the coastal area is flat. Ten kilometres (6.2 miles) from the coast, the sea is only 3 fathoms deep (about 5.5 m or 18 feet). Mud-flat deposits are formed mostly by water streaming westward from the mouth of the Amazon, and their broad banks are overgrown with a luxuriant tangle of mangrove forests. So heavy is the deposit of slimy mud that even the river mouths are forced westward, as the map in Illus. 5–5 clearly shows. The coastal stretch is about 50 km (about 31 miles) wide and slowly climbs uphill into the higher savannah region. At the 200 m level (about 650 feet), there are waterfalls. The rim of the plateau is at an altitude of 500 m (about 1,650 feet).

The savannah is a billowing stretch of land located higher than the swamps but below the jungle of the highlands. Vegetation consists mostly of hard grass and low shrubs with big patches of bare sand meagerly spotted with pioneer growth. In the lower areas and along the rivers are fairly thick forests.

The plateau is covered with a thick, tropical, virgin forest. The highest peak of the Wilhelmina range is 1,280 m high (4,200 feet), while the average height is 650 m (2,132 feet). The great rivers, which originate on the southern slope of the chain of mountains stretching east and west, fall in practically a straight line down to the coast. As the grade is steep, the current is strong. After reaching the 200-m level (650 feet), the fast currents diminish. Most of the big rivers continue their flow in sharp bends, frequently changing course through the savannah. This savannah area will be the subject of our study.

The map in Illus. 5–6 is a greatly enlarged representation of the region indicated in the map in Illus. 5–5 as a small, red rectangle. The mapped terrain lies between Zanderij I and Zanderij II, with the hamlets Sabakoe and Berlijn in the middle. It is a small area of savannah, in the basin of the Para River, one of the last tributaries of the Surinam River. On the right a bit of the Para River is shown.

A particularly interesting catch was made in this region. The fishing trips started out from Bosbivak, located 1.5 kilometres (a little under a mile) west of Sabakoe. Sabakoe Creek runs by here and to the south lies Saramacca Creek, into which the smaller Blaka Creek empties. The two creeks are strikingly different in coloration, because of the difference in vegetation at their sources. Sabakoe Creek is brownish— and is, therefore, known locally as Coca-Cola Creek—whereas the

Illus. 5-7. At this point, the 15-cm (6-inch) deep creek with a sandy bed crosses a footpath in the sandy soil. The water is nearly glass clear.

water of Saramacca Creek is yellowish. In spite of coloration, however, the water of both creeks is clear as glass. The source of these rivers, located in an area measuring about 150×300 m ($500 \times 1,000$ feet), is the source of some of the many creeks that feed Sabakoe River. The terrain is shown in Illus. 5–7, 5–8, 5–9, and 5–10. In early morning, looking towards the savannah, one can make out the edge of a forest of *Mauritia* palms in the distance. The rising sun, while still low on the horizon, lights the trees from below, so that the dry, underfoliage is clearly visible. Bushes are scattered sparsely over the grassy savannah. Some 60 m (200 feet) beyond, the view changes. The savannah lies bare and flat, criss-crossed by sandy paths. During the rainy season, these paths become sparkling streamlets, draining away the excess rain water. About 60 m (200 feet) southward lies a broad, sandy path, a rill of hastening wavelets, no more than 2.5 cm (one inch) or so deep. In the wet season, this patch may be as wide as 8 m (25 feet). Just beyond the point where the stream is its broadest, it is crossed by a dirt road; just beyond the road is a marshland that stays wet throughout most of the year and, in the rainy season, is flooded. The river bed suddenly narrows now, passes through a thick forest of palm, and emerges on the other side of the woods as a typical woodland creek with fairly deep water having transparent, brownish yellow coloration. The creek then spreads out into a marshy area with no clearly defined bed. Part of the water flows off westward and disappears among the brushwood. Another part continues southward and then makes a bend eastward. Here, the brush grows out from the banks, meeting over the stream, covering it almost entirely. The swampy area has a mud layer of decayed vegetation 50 cm (20 inches) deep. The water above the muddy bottom is clear, however, and canes stick out above the surface, so that the water is thick with a floating carpet of algae and bladderwort (*Utricularia*), forming an excellent shelter for the teeming population of many kinds of fishes. Such places are excellent for fishing.

The creek continues to course through the bog until at last it loses its identity and sinks into the soggy, forest soil. In the forest, the natives have laid down a walkway of tree trunks, over which they can scurry. The ground under the trunks is wet throughout most of the year and supports a mass of small fishes. During the mating season, when the water is somewhat higher, this forest is an ideal breeding ground for many species. Such an environment is a typical one for aquarium

Illus. 5-8. Continuation of the savannah creek among the undergrowth as Coca-Cola Creek. The water is clear, the ground under it is colored brown by humus.

Illus. 5-9. Right next to camp, Sabakoe Creek is nothing more than a damp spot on the sand; farther on, it becomes somewhat narrower and a little deeper and disappears among the bushes. A short distance beyond, it re-appears again as the so-called Coca-Cola Creek.

fishes and from it the aquarist can glean a few ideas of the kind of habitat his pets are accustomed to. The environment is usually quite different from what the average aquarist thinks it is, and certainly different from what may be found in home aquariums. Very few species live in open water; most of the popular aquarium fishes feel more at home in rubbishy spots where they can look for food among the algae and decaying vegetation. The periodic changes in the water level, the drying-out of bits of land and their later reflooding, causes a proliferation of bacteria and other micro-organisms. There are hardly any real water plants here, except for *Utricularia* and a water lily here and there—circumstances ideal for small fishes. Somewhat farther on, in the larger creeks, the growth of water vegetation is more profuse, but that is where the larger fishes live, and these are of no concern to the aquarist.

After the fishing spot has been adequately examined, the catch can start, whether for scientific or trade purposes. There are, of course, many ways to catch fish, but if they are to be caught alive and unhurt, they must be outmanoeuvred. Their coloration must be examined and noted *before* sending them off to base headquarters, either alive or preserved.

Expeditions and collecting trips are undertaken for the purpose of collecting data and specimens which, after processing, give an idea of the variables which the fishes are up against in nature. A tropical fish dealer must know where to set up for a catch that will include the fishes in greatest demand. The collected data take on many forms. Soil, water and air samples have to be examined in addition to specimens of the local plants and fauna. Study of the landscape—a science in itself—has to be supported by photographs of the terrain. Aerial photographs are a great help in making maps of the area. Needless to say, such charts are invaluable in making further excursions.

Much important material from Surinam was provided by Mr. J. Van der Kamp of Amsterdam, from 1954 to 1957, and by Mr. H. P. Pijpers of Paramaribo, between 1957 and 1962. Before leaving for Surinam, Mr. Van der Kamp was asked to explore certain typical sites where it was particularly expected that information could be collected about the youth-development stages of some species of armoured catfishes that had been a source of interest for many years. It was expected that they would be inhabiting the humus layer on the bottom of shallow water with either a weak current or none at all, and in marshy stretches. Screening the mud through a large sieve produced some small catfish, along with other fishes that were often hard, if not impossible, to come by. By noting the date and the time of day, conclusions could be drawn concerning the breeding time. Besides, the almost complete developmental series that was obtained allowed aquarists to gain a good insight into the formation of the armour. Also, the line of growth could be followed. Because of the strictly

Illus. 5-10. In the savannah country is the almost-dry bed of Sabakoe Creek, which is used as a road in the dry season. In the rainy season, it is a good-sized stream.

limited area of operations of this expedition, it was possible to research the findings in extraordinary detail. On the other hand, there was a disadvantage in being unable to make a clear comparison between this area and the nearby Para River basin. Moreover, the catch was not complete enough to give a full picture of the fish population. Nevertheless, for a number of species, knowledge of the milieu and of the conduct and relationship of the fishes with other species, as well as many other biological aspects of the situation, was considerably expanded. Mr. Pijpers remedied the shortcomings in later expeditions.

Scientific material is anything that serves to enrich the content of human knowledge. Thus, it includes not only the fishes preserved on the spot with all the necessary information jotted down, but also the live fishes processed for transporting to civilization, for further observation and study of their habits.

The value of such specimens is greatly enhanced wherever the background documentation is complete and accurate. Specimens unsupported by documentation can hardly claim to be scientific material, any more than a fish itself could, swimming about in its natural habitat. Unless the place and time of catching a specimen are clearly indicated and a reference is made to the field diary, the importance of the specimen is largely lost.

If all this has been done, the mass of collected scientific material is in a condition fit to be called a collection. This brings us close to the end of the first phase of research, the collection of the material. At this stage, the collector forwards the specimens and data to an elaborator, who sorts out the data and issues the results obtained from them.

The scientific material, then, consists of specimens preserved immediately on the spot and at the base camp, where fresh preservative fluid is added. Liquid-proof paper and lead pencil should be used for labels. The label attached must either show the important data concerning the sample and the place where it was caught or it may simply contain a number referring to the field manual, where these data have been set down. The same purpose can be achieved by including in the package containing the fish a number, made of metal or plastic, which refers, of course, to data recorded elsewhere. If the collecting expedition is in the field a considerable length of time, it is prudent and safe to check the state of the preserved specimens at intervals and to add fresh preservative whenever it seems necessary. An incision is usually made in the belly of larger specimens and an injection with preservative is given to prevent intestinal decomposition and to inactivate the gastric juices.

An example of the process involved in recording scientific data can be seen in the first collection of Mr. Van der Kamp, which contained, among other things, the following samples from Surinam:

SAMPLE 1: Bosbivak Zanderij, stations 1–7, 28 April 1956.

SAMPLE 2: Bosbivak Zanderij, stations 8–11, 29 April 1956.

SAMPLE 3: Coropina Creek, stations 12–15, 20 May 1956.

SAMPLE 4: Road Paramaribo to Zanderij, near Onverwacht, station 16, 20 May 1956.

SAMPLE 5: Coropina Creek, near Republiek, station 17, 11 October 1956.

SAMPLE 6: Coropina Creek, near Republiek, stations 18–21, 12 October 1956, evening.

SAMPLE 7: Road to Domburg, km 8, station 22, 27 January 1957.

SAMPLE 8: Bosbivak Zanderij, stations 23–27, 12–13 February 1957.

Each sample is provided with a reference to one or more of the stations 1 through 27. These are the sampling places (stations) accurately described in the field record. The usefulness of these brief notations is readily apparent.

A list of these places, called the station list, can be incorporated into a publication, saving the need for repetition. Following are three examples of such data concerning the stations:

Station 2: Bosbivak Zanderij, Surinam, 28/4/56, 13.00 h, brook A, bog behind the fence along the boardwalk west, water level 24 cm, Coca-Cola coloration, sandy bottom, current 0.8m/sec, photos Z-1.04-1.11, color slides K-1.03-1.05.

Station 6: Bosbivak Zanderij, Surinam, 28/4/56, 22.00 h, brook A, near bridge to Coca-Cola Creek, water level 65 cm (strongly swollen, rainy season set in), coloration clear as glass, sandy bottom, current 2.15 m/sec, photos Z-1.17, K-1.08-1.09.

Station 7: Bosbivak Zanderij, as station 6, 10.00 h, 29/4/56, water level normal again, about 25 cm, clear, sandy bottom with remnants of plants, current 0.2 m/sec, slide K-1.10.

It can be readily seen from the above that many changes take place within 24 hours of the onset of the rainy season. In less than 10 hours, the water level in the creek can rise 40 cm (16 inches), while the current speed rises to twice its original velocity. After a lapse of another 10 hours, everything is practically back to what it was originally, the current being even slower than it was to start with. Obviously, this has an effect on the life of the fishes in that area, many of whom, in fact, die by being stranded when the water subsides—thus falling prey to birds and other animals, or becoming desiccated in the sun. During the rainy season, irregular flooding and subsidence of the flood waters over certain patches of land occur repeatedly. This is accompanied by varying or changing water levels in the flood area which must be adapted to, in order to survive. It is only natural, then, that many species have adapted to these environmental alterations.

The first job is a preliminary sorting out of the collection as delivered (see *e* in Table 5–2) and dividing of the material into smaller series *(f)*, for each sample includes many different species. These must then be sorted out and put into separate jars, each of which must be provided with all the available data pertaining to it. Here is an example of the make-up of a sample:

SAMPLE 1: Bosbivak Zanderij, 28 April 1956.

Station 1: 2 *Hoplosternum*, 7 *Aequidens*, 30 *Pyrrhulina*

Station 2: 8 *Rivulus*, 9 *Pyrrhulina*, 2 young *Aequidens*

Station 3: 11 *Pyrrhulina*, 24 young *Aequidens*

Station 4: 7 *Pyrrhulina*, 2 young *Aequidens*

Station 5: 12 *Rivulus agilae*, 4 *Pyrrhulina*

Station 6: 1 *Aequidens*, 1 *Erythrinus*, 1 big *Pyrrhulina*

Station 7: 1 *Hoplosternum*, 16 *Aequidens*, 10 *Pyrrhulina*

This sample as a unit gives a picture of the fish community living in a circumscribed area, and of the dominant species there. In decreasing order, there were 72 *Pyrrhulina*; 52 *Aequidens*, mostly young ones; 20 *Rivulus* of two different species; 3 *Hoplosternum*, and 1 *Erythrinus*—a total of 148 specimens. *Pyrrhulina* is clearly in the majority, comprising almost 50 per cent of the specimens, so this area could be said to be a *Pyrrhulina* community. *Aequidens*, with 35 per cent of the population, is second; and *Rivulus*, with 13.5 per cent, is third.

The following is an analysis of a sample from more open water:

SAMPLE 3: Coropina Creek, 20 May 1956.

Station 12: 82 *Aequidens*, 1 *Erythrinus*

Station 13: 14 *Gymnotidae*, 1 *Aequidens*

Station 14: 1 *Hoplosternum*, 2 *Hoplias*

Station 15: 2 *Rivulus*, 19 *Hemigrammus*, 8 *Pyrrhulina*

All this adds up to 83 *Aequidens*, 19 *Hemigrammus*, 14 *Gymnotidae*, 8 *Pyrrhulina*, 2 *Rivulus*, 2 *Hoplias*, 1 *Erythrinus*, and 1 *Hoplosternum*, totalling 130 specimens. Because this community is dominated by *Aequidens*, which comprises nearly 64 per cent of the population, this species can give its name to the community. Obviously, the figures, though they show the number of fishes caught, are not exactly representative of the population, but they do suggest a pattern deserving of closer scrutiny.

196

Second Phase of Research—Elaboration of the Material

The material must now be worked over, preserved, and roughly sorted. After arrival at the ichthyological laboratory, it is given its final sorting (steps *a* through *g*). As it is not possible to work up all the samples at once, the undetermined collection must be safely stored, together with the field reports. The state of preservation must be checked again before the provisional storing of the samples.

Let us now follow the processing of a species chosen for immediate handling. The material derived from the second phase of the research will pertain to the third phase. These two phases are so closely connected with the material, however, that it is necessary to jump back and forth between the second and third phases. Before going into detail, let us scan the last phase, *g* through *w*.

The figures obtained from the material (sizes and ratios) are entered on a list (official record), *(h)*. The samples are given a collection number, *(j)*, also entered on the list, *(h)*. The data appearing on the list can later be included in the report, *(i)*. Data concerning sampling place and other documentation (photos of the environment, etc.) can also be used in the official record, which is also referred to as the protocol, *(k)*. Before the report is made up, previous publications, *(i)*, must be consulted, a list of which can be found in the *Zoological Record*, *(m)*. For comparison, it is desirable to examine material from one's own storage facilities, *(n)*. If this is not available, specimens may be borrowed for study from zoological institutes. After these preliminaries, the species under scrutiny is ready to be determined, *(o)*, and given a name, *(p)*. This name is entered on the label, *(q)*, that is put into the jar with the specimens, which are preserved, *(r)*, and placed in the storage room. A card, *(t)*, containing the data on the label is then inserted into a species catalogue, *(u)*, for easy reference. We can now proceed with the description of the material, *(v)*, for an article to be published in a relevant scientific journal, *(w)*, reference to which is later published in the *Zoological Record*, *(m)*.

A few remarks will clarify the processes in Phase 2. The material under study, *(g)*, includes perhaps 10 samples from 16 different places, including specimens of *Rivulus*. The measurement of each specimen is taken with the binocular stereoscopic microscope; the jar in which the fishes are kept is provided with a label, *(q)*, filled with fresh preservative fluid, sealed with paraffin wax, *(r)*, and deposited in the storeroom, *(s)*, for later reference. The owned material used for comparison, *(n)*, is also placed in the storeroom. Specimens received as loans are

Illus. 5-11. The place where scientific material is kept. In a collection depot such as this, the fish are kept in stoppered bottles filled with alcohol for more detailed research and as comparative material.

returned to their original institutions. The place in the storeroom where a specimen can be found (shelf, etc.) is noted on the file card, *(t)*, which is inserted in the alphabetical species catalogue, *(u)*.

Collection Numbers

The jars are numbered serially—the serial number is the so-called collection number, *(j)*—and these numbers are entered into a register. The register shows the chronological order of receipt of the material. Moreover, it provides a rapid survey of the composition of the various collections. The numbers on the labels, furthermore, prevent confusion—you will not mix up one sample with another collected from the same place. The collection number is also noted on the file card, as well as on the label. A collection number is, moreover, a safe guide for concise reference in the article to be published.

Labelling

Each jar must be provided with a label pasted to the *inside* (for example, with egg-white, which is alcohol-proof) together with a second, identical label which is loosely put in the jar along with the material. This second label is merely a safety measure in case one of the labels becomes blurred (this is not likely to happen with present-day writing materials, but only time can tell for sure what they will look like in 100 years). The collection number provides additional reference, in case both labels become illegible.

Preservation

Bottling, *(r)*, has the same purpose as, for instance, the pickling or salting of herring—to prevent decay. Since aquarium fishes are not preserved for human consumption, they are usually stored in a solution

198

of 70 per cent alcohol. Some workers prefer a solution of formalin, or one made up of a mixture of formalin and alcohol. The glass jars must be closed tightly with ground-glass stoppers and further sealed with paraffin wax or another kind of greasy wax. Great care should be applied to the sealing as any slight opening to the interior of the bottle would allow the alcohol to evaporate, and the preserved specimen would wither and become useless.

Storage Facility

Proper storage, *(s)*, is essential. The material is to be used again at some future time, perhaps as scientific evidence for publication, or for closer comparison and study. For this purpose, the storeroom must be provided with shelving equipment of wood or steel. The jars are arranged on the shelves in groups according to families, and alphabetically within the families according to genus and species. If, for instance, a collector wishes to check on what kind of *Rivulus* is in storage for comparison with new varieties of this genus, he checks the shelf or rack involved and finds all the *Rivulus* species neatly arranged in their jars. Where several jars contain the same species, these are neatly grouped and separated from the others by a narrow space.

To find your way about in such a storeroom, you must be familiar with the system used; or, you must use an index of the generic names in alphabetical order with rack and shelf numbers. To make sure you have overlooked nothing, you can consult the card file, where rack and shelf numbers are also shown.

The Card File

At the same time that the labels are typed, a file card is filled in with the identical text. This card is placed in a file arranged alphabetically according to genus and species. Thus, each jar or bottle has a separate card in the file. The card file represents the collection. To give some idea of how far along such a file can be carried, just consider that the ichthyological card file of the Zoological Museum of Amsterdam contains over 25,000 cards. Other important collections are located at the British Museum (Natural History) in London, at the Smithsonian Institution, Natural History Department, Washington, and the Musée d'Histoire Naturelle in Paris. The filing system will be referred to again in the section Species Catalogue below.

In addition to the card file—that is, the alphabetical species catalogue—a second file is kept of type species. This file could have pink cards to distinguish them from the white cards of the other file. These cards refer to the samples (jars) containing the specimens upon which the description of a new species is based. The type catalogue is prepared in duplicate, one set arranged alphabetically (like the catalogue of species), the other arranged by orders and families, so that the material available in the collection of any group can be readily checked.

Species Catalogue

This is the main catalogue, *(u)*, in which the cards are filed alphabetically. It provides a complete picture of the available material. The disadvantage of such a system is, however, that it is likely to become outdated, strange though this may seem. In 1883, when the first cards for the collection of the Museum of Amsterdam were written, the species were labelled with the names then current. Many names have since been changed and the process is still going on. It would be quite cumbersome to keep changing the names of the entries as fast as new names are coined. The names on the cards would then no longer correspond to those on the jars. An expedient was found—inserting reference cards into the file, referring to the older names. If any jars are withdrawn from storage for additional study or comparison, the name on it can be updated. Material of historical significance—such as that used for describing the type—should, however, keep the original name.

Third Phase of Research—Development of the Publication

The lower-right section of Table 5–2 shows the steps to be taken for eventual publication of the data.

The Protocol

This is a most important part of the official record—a list of all the data, which should be so clearly stated that it permits comparison of various specimens. The protocol is a pre-printed form, *(i)*, designed especially for fishes. It contains the following items: collection number; total length; standard length (that is, length without the caudal fin, which is sometimes damaged); sex (if it can be ascertained); number of rays and spines in the dorsal fin and the anal fin; lengths in tenths of a millimetre—for comparison to be converted into per cent or per mille (1/1,000) of the standard length—measured from snout to root of the dorsal fin, anal fin, ventral fin; the length of the head; the greatest body height; the caudal length; height of the tail; length of snout; diameter of the eye; head width between the rims of the eye sockets; the number of scales lengthwise and vertically; the number of scales around the tail; the number of teeth in the jaws, etc.; and, at last, a column listing the photos of the details, if any were made.

After noting all the data concerning a sample of a population, proceed to the determination of the species. As a rule, additional documents, *(k)*, and literature, *(l)*, have to be consulted. Where possible, specimens from stores at hand or elsewhere must be used for comparison.

Documentation

While requested comparative material is still on the way from the institutes, the building up of documentation can be started, *(k)*, beginning with the figures included in the protocol. Unusual features discovered at the first examination should now be closely scrutinized (for example, an intersexual individual intermediate in sexual characteristics between a typical male and a typical female). Diagrams of characteristic traits can be roughly plotted to check which are typical and constant and whether they show any difference between the sexes. External sexual characteristics can be defined. Photos (last column of the protocol) are most valuable. When familiarity with the material has been gained, the next investigation should concern the recent distribution of the species and any natural barriers opposing it. For example, it may be stated that the fish do not live at altitudes above the lowlands and that they prefer moderate currents or stagnant water. The literature concerning such sites should be looked up and checked.

Literature

Naturally, all that has been written on the subject in hand cannot be found in a manual, but is contained in an enormous number of journals. It is customary to exchange reprints with specialists working in the same field, and this helps materially in providing the foundation for literature data, *(l)*. Files of such reprints, if systematically kept, would make it possible to look up all reprints on any subject—say, the pyrrhulinids—in chronological order. With luck, there will be a large number of reprints on the subject, but sometimes only very little information can be located. To continue, it is necessary to check whether any reprints are available not dealing with a restricted group, but rather with fishes from a certain area. Such reprints would be filed under the name of the country (or zone). To find out whether anything had been written about pyrrhulinids, for example, check ichthyological/faunistic reports from Surinam and the surrounding countries. Since it is known approximately where these fish are to be found, you certainly would not look for them in Africa or Australia. It takes years of experience to acquire knowledge, but by then you will have a stock of ready information practically at your fingertips.

Assume that you have succeeded in finding a publication on the fish fauna of Surinam, which mentions three species of pyrrhulinins. This serves as a guide to where the fish in question may belong. The word "may" is used, because it is possible that it does not belong to any of the three species, or it may fit in between two of the earlier-described species in such a way that it begins to seem as if the three forms are due for a more thorough examination. This would be to ascertain whether they really are three distinct species, or merely three varieties of a single species. For this, the variation range for all three species must be defined on the basis of the measures on the protocol.

Often, closer scrutiny of a certain area from which, previously, two different "species" have been described reveals a third form in a position between the previous two, as if it were some kind of transitory form. While the characteristics of the first two species described were so sharply differentiated that discrimination between them seemed justified, the discovery of the third variety leads to the conclusion that the characteristics gradually pass over into each other so that no sharply delineated limit can actually be drawn. The number of fin rays in the different fins is often a reliable feature for determining different species. (See page 938 for the method used for counting fin rays).

Nevertheless, it has been shown that the genus *Rivulus* shows a tendency to develop larger fins (with more rays) when the fish inhabits waters at higher altitudes. Lowland varieties, living where currents are slow, possess smaller fins—that is, fins having a shorter base and fewer rays—unlike other fishes that grow long fins from a short base and few, but long, rays. A good example of this is *Betta splendens*.

Similar alteration of most specific traits can often be found in different environments. Any one trait is seldom constant enough to prove useful in the discrimination of species. *Pyrrhulina*, for example, has a constant number of scales around the body and the caudal root, common to all its species. This safely differentiates it from, for instance, *Copeina*.

We cannot yet relax from the search for literature. We have to know whether any of our differential varieties has already been described elsewhere. For this purpose, we can rely on the excellent help of the *Zoological Record*.

Hoar, W. S. (3). Photoperiodism and thermal resistance of goldfish. Nature, Lond. 178 : 364–365.

Hoar, W. S. see Keenleyside, M. H. A.

Hoar, W. S. see Mahon, E. F.

Hobbs, D. F. Do newly introduced species present a separate problem? Proc. N.Z. Ecol. Soc. No. 2 1955 : 12–14.

Hochman, L. ' Der Beitrag zum Erkennen des Wachsens und der Nahrung der Barbe. [Barbus barbus (Linné)] in Soretkafluss. Acta Univ. Agric. Silv., Brunn No. 2 1955 : 147–159. 3 figs. [German summary.]

Hoedeman, J. J. (1). Barbus kahajani n.n. for Barbus tetrazona. Aquarium Den Haag 26 : 288–289 1 fig.

Hoedeman, J. J. (2). Nannaethiops geisleri, eine neue Art aus dem Kongo, nebst einer Übersicht über die Arten der Sippe Nannaethiopidi. Aquar. Terrar. Z. 9 : 259–261 1 fig.

● Hoedeman, J. J. (3). Hyphessobrycon rubrostigma, neue Species. Eine höchst interessante und farbenfreudige Form der Callistus-Gruppe aus Kolumbien. Aquar. Terrar. Z. 9 : 312–313.

Holmes, W. & Moorhouse, D. E. The peri-renal tissue of Protopterus. A contribution to the history of the adrenal. Quart. J. micr. Sci. 97 : 123–154 11 figs.

Homma, Y. Further additions to " A list of fishes collected in the Province of Echigo including Sado Island. Jap. J. Ichthyol. 5 : 59–60.

Hora, S. L. (1). Some observations on the trout farm and hatchery at Achhabal, Kashmir. J. Bombay nat. Hist. Soc. 53 : 390–396.

Hora, S. L. (2). Food of the whale shark, Rhinecodon typus (Smith): evidence of a Jataka sculpture, 2nd century B.C. J. Bombay nat. Hist. Soc. 53 : 478–479 1 pl.

Hotta, H. see Iwai, T.

Howard, G. V. A study of populations of the Anchoveta, Cetengraulis mysticetus based on meristic characters. Bull. Inter-Amer. Tuna Comm. 1 1954 : 1–24, 3 figs.

Hubbs, Clark (1). Records from east Texas of three species of fish, Hadropterus maculatus, Etheostoma histrio and Etheostoma barratti. Texas J. Sci. 4 1952 : 486.

Hubbs, C. (2). Relative variability of hybrids between the minnow, Notropis lepidus and N. proserpinus. Texas J. Sci. 8 : 463–469.

Hubbs, C., Kemp, R. J. & Gray, C. E. Three Shiners, Notropis ortenburgeri, N. maculatus, and N. blennius, added to known East Texas fauna. Tex. J. Sci. 8 : 110–112.

Hubbs, C. & Strawn, K. Interfertility between two sympatric fishes, Notropis lutrensis and Notropis venustus. Evolution 10 : 341–344.

Hubbs, Clark see Jurgens, K. C.

Hubbs, Clark see Strawn, K.

Hubbs, C. L. (1). The distribution of macrourids. Publ. Un. int. Sci. biol. (B) No. 16 1954 : 62–64.

Hubbs, C. L. (2). Hybridization between fish species in nature. Syst. Zool. 4 1955 : 1–20 8 figs.

Hubbs, C. L. & Crowe, W. R. Preliminary analysis of the American Cyprinid fishes, seven new, referred to the genus Hybopsis, subgenus Erimystax. Occ. Pap. Mus. Zool. Univ. Mich. No. 578 : 1–8.

Hubbs, C. L. see Miller, R. R.

Hublon, W. F. and others. Fifth progress report on salmon diet experiments. Fish Comm. Res. Briefs 6 No. 2 : 10–14 1 fig.

Huish, M. T. see Berry, F. H.

Humm, D. G. & Young, R. S. The embryological origin of pigment cells in platyfish-swordtail hybrids. Zoologica, N.Y. 41 : 1–10 2 pls. 1 fig.

Huro, J. see Gamulin, T.

Hussain, S. S. see Raj, B. S.

Iga, T. see Yanai, T.

(Ignatyeva, G. M.) (1). [Fermentsecretion during the hatching in embryos of Acipenseridae.] C.R. Acad. Sci. URSS. 100 1955 : 1199–1202. [In Russian.]

(Ignatyeva, G. M.) (2). [The role of membranes in discharging the hatching ferment in embryos of sturgeons.] C.R. Acad. Sci. URSS. 107 : 493–496. [In Russian.]

Illus. 5–12. Three pages from the Zoological Record (fish section) for 1956. The heavy dots indicate the places where the article referred to in the text appears in the three main sections of the Record.

Africa, Cadenat (5); Senegal coast, Cadenat (1); Sierra Leone, Cadenat (2); South Africa, Smith, J. L. B. (2) & (3); East London, S. Africa, Smith, J. L. B. (5); Mocambique, Smith, J. L. B. (1); Madagascar, Smith, J. L. B. (6); Bahamas, Böhlke (5); Surinam, Boeseman (3); Brazil, Lopez, A.; Puerto Rico, Böhlke (1); Costa Rica, Briggs; Gulf of Mexico, Bigelow & others; Bullis & Arnold; Mead & Nicholson; Rousseteil; Schultz & Springer; Peru, Koepcke; Hawaii, Jordan & Evermann; Strasburg; Tahiti, Chabonis; Pacific, Randall (2); Rivas (3); Central Pacific, King & Ikehara; Java Sea, Klausewitz (2); New Guinea, Beaufort; Philippines, Randall (5); Bombay, Klausewitz (3); Ceylon, Deraniyagala (4); Silva, P. H. (1), (2); Smith, J. L. B. (4); Indian Ocean, Bertelsen & Marshall; Chabanaud (1); Grottanelli; Smith, J. L. B. (8), (9); Maldives, Deraniyagala (1); Mauritius, Baissac (1).

South Temperate. — Uruguay, Buen (1); Chile, Yanez; Tristan da Cunha, Rowan, M. K. & A. N.; Australia, Whitley (6); E. Australia, Whitley (4); New Zealand, Cunningham; Garrick; Moreland; Whitley (6); Tasmania, Cowper.

c. FRESHWATER

General. — Occurrence of marine forms in freshwater, Boeseman (2); Herre & Boeseman; northern limits for Cyprinid fishes in Manitoba, Keleher; determining factors in distribution of fishes in Uttar Pradesh rivers, Raj & Husain; origin of New Zealand fishes, Allen, K. R.

Palaearctic. — Scotland, Friend; Jersey, Sagi; Belgium, Leloup, E. & Konietko; Germany, Gottschalk; Spain, Klausewitz (1); North west Spain, Margalef; Dolomites, Marcuzzi; Roumania, Bacescu & Mayer; Banarescu (1); Leonte & Ruga; Popescu & Ruga; Vasiliu; Czechoslovakia, Dobsik & Libosvárský; Oliva (2) & (3); Slovakia, Balon & Mink; Moravia, Kux; Lusely; Transylvania, Müller, G.; Iran, Iraq, Israel, Fowler & Steinitz; Latvia, Ivanauskas & others; Central Asia, Turdakov & Piskarev (6); Russia, Zhukov; Amur river, Nikol'skii (1) & (5); Georgia, Russia, Elahidge; Azerbaidzhan, Abdurakhmanov, Y. A. (1);

Kirghiz Republic, Turdakov (1) & (3); Turdakov & Piskarev (2) & (3); Tyurin (1).

Nearctic. — Saskatchewan, Atton & Johnson; British Columbia, Lindsey (2); N. America, Hubbs & Crowe; Iowa, Bailey; Virginia, Robins & Raney; Carolina, Crawford; Texas, Jurgens & Hubbs; Hubbs, Clark (1); Hubbs, Kemp & Gray; Ohio and Mississippi valleys, Trautman; Alabama, Florida and Georgia, Bailey & Gibbs; Florida, Böhlke (4).

Ethiopian. — Nile, Greenwood (3); Uganda, Greenwood (4); Lake Victoria, Greenwood (1); Lake Tanganyika, Poll; Lake Nyasa, Fryer (1) & (3); Jackson; Zambesi river, Fairweather; Nigeria, Clausen (2); Congo, Hoedeman (2).

Central America. — Mexico, Buen (2); Miller, R. R. (2); British Honduras, Fowler (3).

South America. — Meinken (1); Venezuela, Böhlke & Myers; Inger; Surinam, Boeseman (3); Colombia, Hoedeman ● (3); Brazil, G:mes (1) & (2); Myers & Weitzman; Schultz; Travassos (3); Rio Paraiba, Travassos (1); Argentina, Nichols (1).

Oriental — Patna, India, Sarkar; Ceylon, Deraniyagala (3); Fernando (3); Malaya, Brittan; Tweedie (2); Sumatra, Klausewitz (3); Meinken (3).

Australian region and Polynesia. — New Guinea, Boeseman (1); Nichols (2); Whitley (8); Australia, Whitley (7); New Zealand Cunningham.

d. FOSSIL

General. — Evolution of vertebrates, Romer; morphology and phylogeny of Agnatha, Balabai (1) & (2); evolution in Subholostei, Schaeffer; origin of cyclostomes, Bystrow (1); habitat of earliest vertebrates, Denison; histology of bone, Enlow & Brown; dermal bone patterns, Parrington; destruction of bone by fungoids, Bystrow (2); radioactive specimens, Bowie & Atkin; brachythoracid parasphenoid, Kulczycki; nature of " electric " or sensory organs, Bohlin; nature of " electric " or sensory organs in Ostracoderms, Cory.

Palaeozoic. — Devonian, Attridge; Bowie & Atkin; Bystrow (3); Fletcher; Gross (1); Kondratyeva & Obruchev;

INIOMI

SUDIDAE

Chlorophthalmus japonicus sp. nov. off Okitsu, Japan, Kamohara (3) p. 1 figd.

MYCTOPHIDAE

Diaphus gigas from Prov. Tosa, Japan, Kamohara (3).

Electrona rissoi salubris recorded from New Zealand, Moreland.

Lampanyctus bensoni recorded from Suruga Bay, Japan, Kuroda (2).

Myctophum punctatum presence of golden coloured pigment in retina, Denton & Warren.

†Rhinellus (?) africanus sp. nov. U. Cretaceous Morocco, Arambourg p. 121 text-fig. 57 pp. x, xi.

Rhinoscopelus oceanicus sp. nov. Hawaiian Isl., Jordan & Evermann p. 168 [omitted from Vol. 41, 1904].

NOTOSUDIDAE fam. nov.

Notosudis status of known specimens discussed, Krefft & Maul; N. lepida sp. nov. eastern North Atlantic, Krefft & Maul p. 306 figd.

APLOTOPTERIDAE

Anolopterus farao recorded from Kamchatka, Anon (5).

MIRIPINNATI ord nov.

MIRAPINNIDAE fam. nov.

Mirapinna esau gen. et sp. nov. North Atlantic, Bertelsen & Marshall p. 4 figd.

TAENIOPHORIDAE fam. nov.

Taeniophorus gulosus gen. et sp. nov. north west of Seychelles, Bertelsen & Marshall p. 8 figd.; P. brevis sp. nov. Indian Ocean, Bertelsen & Marshall p. 10 figd.

Taeniophorus festivus gen. et sp. nov, Indian Ocean, Bertelsen & Marshall p. 6 figd.

ALEPISAURIDAE

Alepisaurus ferox reported from Tristan da Cunha, Rowan, M. K. & A. N.

PARALEPIDIDAE

Paralepis rissoi kröyeri recorded from Kamchatka, Anon (5).

Uncisudis gen. nov. p. 90 type U. longirostra sp. nov. p. 91 figd. Madeira, Maul (2).

OSTARIOPHYSI

CYPRINOIDEA

CHARACIDAE

Key to genera of the Acestrorhynchinae, Fernandes Yepez (2).

Xenurobryconini a new tribe with key to species, Myers & Böhlke.

Alestes dentex biometric study, Gras.

Anopticthtys = Astyanax, Sadoglu; A. jordani histology of eyes, Lüling (2); photosensitivity compared with that of Cheocobarbus geertsii, Thines (1).

Argonectes anapioensis et sp. nov. Rio Orinoco, Venezuela, Böhlke & Myers p. 2 figd.

Astyanax mexicanus, breeding experiments with river and cave ("Anopticthtys") forms, Sadoglu; A. (Poeciliurichthys) potaroensis recorded from Surinam, Boeseman (3).

Bryconamericus deuterodonoides caudovittatus subsp. nov. Venezuela, Inger p. 435.

Cheirodon axelrodi sp. nov. Brazil, Schultz p. 42; C. axelrodi see Hyphessobrycon cardinalis.

Copella gen. nov. type Copeina compta Myers, Myers (5) p. 3.

Creatochanes affinis new Venezuelan record, Inger; habitat, food, Geisler & Bolle.

Hyphessobrycon cardinalis sp. nov. Brazil, Myers & Weitzman p. 1; description, Meinken (2); supposed provenance Upper Rio Negro system, Ladiges; breeding in aquarium, Zühler; H. heterorhabdus, figd. in colour, Timmerman; H. rennei observations on breeding, Anon (4); H. rubrostigma, sp. nov. ● Colombia, Hoedeman (3) p. 312 figd.

Microcatelurus English translation of original description, Myers and Bohlke.

Moenkhausia miangi new Venezuelan record, Inger.

Pogonocharax see Esomus, Cyprinidae.

†Procharax sp. nov. type P. minor sp. nov. L. Tertiary Brazil, Santos & Travassos p. 190 1 pl.

The "Zoological Record"

Annually, the Natural History Department of the British Museum in London, in conjunction with the Zoological Society of London, publishes a yearbook, the *Zoological Record, (m)*. For each division of the animal kingdom, it contains an alphabetically arranged list of all publications issued during the preceding year. The entries under one author's name bear serial numbers for the articles published by him during that period. See Illus. 5–12 for a sample page from the fish section of the alphabetical, author index. Notice that a paper by Hoedeman is marked with a dot in the margin. The entry refers to the new description of *Hyphessobrycon rubrostigma*. It was the third article published by this author in 1956. Illus. 5–12 shows a second sample, a page from the systematic section, where the same article is found under *Characidae* (characins). Finally, in order to deal with the matter from the geographic angle, a list is made up by distribution (see Illus. 5–12). The article in question is listed again under *South America*. Authors who have dealt with a subject can be traced through the *Zoological Record*, which shows where and when an article on a given subject appeared.

The next step is to borrow literature on the subject in question from a library or libraries. If it is not available in one's own or in the museum's library, then it must be borrowed elsewhere. It may take weeks to secure the needed material, but when it is all finally on hand and has been read, determination can be started.

Comparative Material

When dealing with fishes from Surinam, it is desirable to take earlier determined material and add it to the protocol list for comparison purposes, *(n)*. Perhaps more interesting is to list material from Guyana (formerly British Guiana). From such a comparison, it can be determined in how many aspects the species are the same or different. If the differences are clear-cut enough, the new material might be considered a deviant variety or sub-species, or, it may be shown to what extent the forms are related. In research, one purpose, among others, is to obtain an accurate picture of the natural relationship between the fishes, and for this reason we must find the connection between distribution and populations, which can sometimes become unclear if, without thorough study, deviant varieties are described as new species.

If there is no comparative material available in your own collection, it should be borrowed from institutions.

Determination

Having researched, studied, read and digested the material, we are now ready to proceed with determination, *(o)*. This step should carry with it assurance that our material is similar to some fish that has been described before, or, on the contrary, that it represents a new variety not yet reported on. In the latter case, we have to specify its relationship to earlier described varieties and species and to point out the one to which it is most closely related. Then a description and definition of the fish must be drawn up, a name given to it, and all this released in a publication.

Name and Nomenclature

Giving a fish a new name sounds simpler than it really is. If we are certain that our material is to be given a new name, *(p)*, then a meaningful one must be chosen. There are, after all, rules laid down by an international committee which must be adhered to. The Rules of the International Commission on Zoological Nomenclature go into great detail and discussion of them would lead too far afield. It may be mentioned only that the name must either be in Latin or it must be Latinized. It must not have been used before, and it should be applied to one specific specimen called the TYPE SPECIMEN, or HOLOTYPE. This specimen must be representative of the new variety in every respect, whether it be male, female or bisexual. The specific description is based on this unique specimen, although it can apply to other suitable specimens, called the PARATYPES. Such type material is the most important part of any collection and not only should the reference material regarding them be typed on red cards, but also the lids of the jars containing the specimens should be painted with red lacquer. Another requirement is that all type specimens must be deposited in approved institutions where they can be made available to research workers at any time.

Note that the TYPE SPECIES is not the same as the type specimen. The type species is that species of a genus upon which the generic name depends. It usually contains the most exemplifying characteristics of the genus.

When the new name has been determined, the labels and cards may be typed up (see *q* in Phase 2).

Description

The description and definition of a new variety, *(v)*, must be like a diagnosis—that is, it must contain the criteria that differentiate the species from all its nearest, related species. Often it is accompanied by an illustration, which can be either a drawing or a good photograph. Further, particulars of the population represented by the holotype are noted down so as to create as exhaustive a report as possible. Following the technical details, as much as possible in the way of specific biological data is added. Moreover, a description of the environment can sometimes more clearly distinguish a certain species from a near relative than the most detailed description of the fish itself.

Publication

The climax of research is the report of the scientific results obtained. This includes publication, *(w)*, in a journal that is sent to all important institutions. As a rule, such scientific journals are published by the institutions themselves, not for commercial purposes but for trading information with each other. They receive in return many scientific journals from the institutions on their exchange list. Hardly any institution could afford subscriptions to the thousands of journals published all over the world. On the other hand, a moderate budget permits the institution to publish a periodical of its own, the circulation of which is amply compensated for by the flood of reports and journals they receive in return.

Finally, the journal (or a special reprint from it) is submitted to the editors of the *Zoological Record*, who will include the title and subject of the published material.

The Natural System

Now that science is about to reach a point at which the inventory of all living organisms is nearing completion, the task of systematicists (taxonomists) is getting to be less a job of describing a species and more a case of identifying specimens. In other words, it is time for closer co-operation between biologists in the field and those in the institutions. During the lifetimes of Alexander von Humboldt and Charles Darwin, natural history was equivalent to ecology—that is, the study of relationships between organisms and their natural environment. It was, primarily, the observation of nature. Later, field work was gradually relegated to the background and the workshop of biologists was set up in laboratories and museums. Interest was focussed on the individual specimen, which was studied over and over again, down to the smallest detail, but its relationship to nature, its habitat and its natural activities were neglected. At times, certain aspects of the study of natural science dominated others, so that eventually all co-operation ceased among specializing biologists.

Is there anyone who observes living beings in their true shape, in association with plants, animals and environment? Certainly not the morphologist or the physiologist, but only an experienced naturalist, nature lover, forester, or any other person who feels an affinity with nature.

Aquarists will find it difficult to grasp the nature of their tropical pets, about which they know too little. Still, if they do not mind the trouble of observing them and of reading all that has been written about them, they can acquire a better understanding of them than many scientists possess. It is the organism, not the individual specimen, that is worth knowing—the variety, the species, the group to which it belongs and the place it occupies in nature.

The large amount of data compiled by specialists of all kinds makes it difficult to obtain even a rough idea of the stage of development of modern science. Hence, there is a revival going on of the old struggle to get a clear view of nature and of the facts underlying its phenomena, and the attempt is being made by simply condensing the scientific findings. The material collected by the field biologist (the scientific collector) has value only when it is supported by full ecological data, for the development of a species must have an ecologic background.

These data are indispensable for the definition of a true biological species. Collected material has scientific value only if it consists of a large series gathered in various periods or at different times of the year, and is accompanied by the documentation mentioned above. Exception can be made to the rule in certain cases, such as if a specimen is so markedly different that it is obvious that it is something special (*Latimeria*, see page 44).

Also, the lack of a few of the required data should not always be reason enough to prevent your describing the material if it is otherwise good and appears to warrant a new description. Circumstances are not always ideal. Therefore, it would be a mistake to cast aside significant communication as falling short of the scientific desideratum as long as the main condition controlling the circumstances is that the material should contribute to the knowledge available to science.

Fishes are only a part of the animal kingdom, but they do have a place of their own in it. Man has spent ages trying to define this position. Pliny (A.D. 23–79) set up a simplistic system of classification that divided the animal kingdom into "land animals," "water animals," and "creatures of the air." Naturally, fishes were included under "water animals." As this system was too general to be considered satisfactory for very long, better methods of classification were sought. By and large, agreement has at last been reached on a classification that is in keeping with the following arrangement.

Fishes are vertebrates, differentiated from the other vertebrates, mammals and birds, by a number of characteristics. In general, it is not difficult to draw a boundary line separating the groups of higher animals from others. As will be shown, however, the assignment of a certain animal to a given place in the system is never a certainty. It would seem as if nature went all out to prevent us from compartmentalizing the world of creation. Some animals and some plants cannot easily be classified and are difficult to assign to their proper place. This is not only an intriguing situation; it provides an opportunity to test the value of the system.

The very elements or building blocks of a system are the different species composing it. For the sake of order, distinction must be made between the units, in the same way the grocer must keep order among the several hundred items he sells. He separates sugar and salt, beans and rice, cheese and sausage, large and small boxes, according to their contents.

What, in fact, is a species? The word simply means "kind," the latter having a more general meaning. It is therefore simpler for the grocer than it is for the nature lover, but even he must use caution. If he has a thousand boxes in stock, all the same size but differing in contents, it is simple to separate them into categories or areas of content, so long as the boxes are suitably labelled.

If we are given the job of sorting out 100 different objects according to any arbitrary system of our own, we have a choice of ways for doing it. Books can be separated by size, or alphabetically by name of author, title or subject matter. In large libraries, card files are kept on books in all of the last three categories.

A natural system such as this is developed in the course of time and must take into account every aspect in which relationship plays a principal rôle. It would be silly to classify fishes by size, and even more so by coloration. Well, then—how should a sensible system take hold of the situation?

In the first place, we must understand what is meant by a species. Nature lovers may well have a vague idea of what it is, but they may find it hard to define. Even men of science are still debating the exact meaning, and the species concept for some groups is not altogether acceptable for other groups. But, scientists will, eventually, come to whole-hearted agreement on what should be. Linnaeus considered the species to be the organisms created by God. He said, "We distinguish as many species as the Lord created in the beginning." Originally, there was one pair of each species, or kind. With the progress of science—particularly with the acceptance of the theory of evolution— the notions held by scientists have been thoroughly changed as compared to the originally accepted, stringent principles. For scientists today, the biological species has become the most important building block of systematics in a natural arrangement. The hundreds of books and articles on the subject are witness to the fact that it is not a simple thing to state, but it can be said that any group of individuals in free nature having no association with the individuals of any other group, is a true species—a kind unto itself. Such a definition offers possibilities and is open to various interpretations.

Working with the building block, the SPECIES, the first step is to group related species into a system based on relationships. The species are combined to form GENERA (the plural form of GENUS), and several genera make a TRIBE. Several tribes form a SUB-FAMILY; a number of sub-families are a FAMILY; families collectively form SUB-ORDERS, which combine to make ORDERS. Orders are ultimately classed under a few main groups. A SUPER-SPECIES is a monophyletic group of closely related and largely or entirely allopatric species, which have no nomenclatural recognition, but are useful in zoögeographical studies.

If you take a close look at the arrangement, you will note that uniformity has been introduced linguistically into the different designations by adding certain endings to specific ranks of the classification. The stem is usually derived from a generic name belonging to the group. Attaching the suffix *-ini* indicates the tribes, *-inae* the sub-family, *-idae* the family, *-oidea* the super-family, and *-iformes* the order. This enables us to see, from the ending, which taxonomic group name is referred to. (Some authorities consider sub-order to be the next higher taxon after family, but there is no recommended ending for it. Greenwood, Rosen, Weitzman and Myers, 1966, used the ending *-oidei* for sub-order. Since a classification will seldom, if ever, contain both suborders and super-families, many authorities consider the two terms to be interchangeable.)

Almost all the ichthyologists mentioned up to now set up systems of their own. For the most part, these were based on existing systems which they modified in the areas of their own specialization. No general agreement has yet been reached, particularly where details are concerned. Still, on the whole, the various systems do not show any essential difference since the work of Johannes Müller (1808–88). His work, published in 1841, *Über den Bau und die Grenzen der Ganoiden und über das Natürliche System der Fische,* is the first system to be built on a scientific foundation. Müller divided fishes into six sub-classes: 1. Dipnoi (lungfishes); 2. Teleostei (recent bony fish); 3. Ganoidei (sturgeons, etc.); 4. Elasmobranchii or Selachii (cartilaginous fishes, or sharks and rays); 5. Marsipobranchii or Cyclostomi (pouch-gilled or cyclostomes); 6. Leptocardii (lancelets). All six groups are still valid as taxonomic entities.

Other systems were introduced later by the following authors: Regan (1929–30), Goodrich (1909, and later), Jordan (1923, and later), Stensiö (1921, 1927, and later).

Regan's system was presented in a large number of articles. In shortened form, it looks as follows:

Class Marsipobranchii   Class Pisces
     ”   Selachii   Sub-class Palaeopterygii
   Sub-class Trematopnea   ”   Neopterygii
      ”   Chasmatopnea   ”   Crossopterygii

Regan's strong point was his new nomenclature, derived generally from anatomical or morphological characteristics. This is why it does not appeal very much to the uninitiated.

One of the most recent and, at the same time, the most usable systems was worked out by Berg in 1940. One of its advantages is that it can be readily understood by non-professionals, because the names of the units of classification are derived from the name of a known member of that group.

This system gained ground because Berg derived the group names from known generic names, and further, because of his elaborate diagnosis for each taxonomic unit. The value of his nomenclature was particularly proved in zoögeography, because even non-proficient persons could easily become familiar with the terms. Much abbreviated, his system looks like this:

Sub-race Acrania (class Amphioxi)	(Series Pisces)
" Craniata	Class Pterichthyes
Super-class Agnatha	" Coccostei
Class Cephalaspides	" Acanthodii
" Petromyzontes	" Elasmobranchii
" Pteraspides	" Holocephali
" Palaeospondyli	" Dipnoi
" Myxini	" Teleostomi
Super-class Gnathostomata	Sub-class Crossopterygii
	" Actinopterygii

To gain insight into things, we must always compare two "things" with each other. For this, specific characteristics are used. Two objects may have numerous identical traits, but there will be one trait different. In such a case, they are not similar, but they differ from each other. On page 160, the early classifiers were mentioned. It was remarked that, in 1686, Ray & Willoughby differentiated between cartilaginous fishes and bony fishes. This division still holds, though the essential part of it has come to be viewed in a different light.

It had been assumed at first that cartilage preceded bone in the scale of evolution. At present, the two structures are considered to have undergone parallel development, so that bone and cartilage are equally old, historically speaking. True bone develops from embryonic cartilage. It eventually becomes ossified in the fishes that possess a bony skeleton at some stage of development. There is ample evidence that both cartilaginous and bony fishes developed from progenitors having bony skeletons, at least in the adult stage. The staying-behind of the calcification process in cartilaginous fishes is a retention of the juvenile stage of development (neotenic development).

211

Nevertheless, we must face the fact that cartilaginous fishes and bony fishes represent two distinctly separate groups in our recent animal kingdom.

Thanks to the introduction of palaeontology into ichthyology by Cuvier and Agassiz, the classification systems have changed considerably for the better, as the developmental steps leading back in time to primordial progenitors could at last be traced and these then connected to form a natural sequence.

6. FISH, MAN AND ECOLOGY

There is more to the relationship between man and fish than is contained in an aquarium. Fish have always played a supreme rôle in the life of man, starting as an important source of food. However, as the first and oldest vertebrates, they hold still another place in the over-all picture of man's evolution and pose more of a threat to the existence of man than might at first sight seem probable.

Counting fresh and salt waters, fish inhabit about 75 per cent of the earth's surface. In ancient times, it was the fish who left the water to develop legs and walk upon dry land and so paved the way for the higher forms of life to come. And, those fish who stayed behind populated the abysses of the world's greatest oceans.

This is, indeed, something for the aquarist to ponder—that fish are anything but objects to be scorned, for they have, by their very existence, earned our respect.

Dwellers of the Deep Sea

Peace hovers over the earth's surface, compared to the ear-shattering racket made by the denizens of the deep in the mighty abysses which they inhabit.

The Abysses of the Oceans

The deep sea is not considered to begin until a depth of 200–500 metres (650–1,600 feet) has been reached. Usually, the continental shelf, which varies in depth from place to place, is not taken into consideration. The deepest abyss of the oceans is in the Marianas Trench in the Pacific, just north of Ulithi atoll. It measures a depth of 36,198 feet—over 10 kilometres (almost seven miles)! It is known that pressure increases by 1 atmosphere (14.7 lbs. per square inch) for each 10 metres (about 33 feet) of underwater descent, so that, at a depth of 10 kilometres, a pressure of about 1,000 atmospheres prevails. How is life possible in such an environment? Light cannot penetrate below the 200-metre (650-foot) level. At 10 metres (33 feet), the red wavelengths have been filtered from the light; at 50 metres (about 164 feet), the yellow has been absorbed, and only a vague, blueish purple remains.

In spite of these extreme conditions—enormous pressure and lack of light—the largest of all the environments on earth is far more uniform in its potential for life than most other terrestrial biotopes. Over the total expanse of oceans, as well as in the deeps, the temperature range is practically constant at 0–4 °C (32–39.2 °F), and the salt content is almost constant at 34.5 *pro mille* or per thousand. As a result of these two factors, the speed of ocean currents is so small that it can be measured in centimetres per second (cm/sec). Of course, there are exceptions to all these circumstances. None the less, it is possible that the deep-sea population is more or less cosmopolitan. There are exceptions to this, too. Creatures living beyond the normal depth (in the abysses), as deep down as 200–6,000 metres (650–19,700 feet), do not differ much from each other, whether they live in the frozen sea at the pole or at the equator. Yet living creatures in the deep-sea troughs 6,000–11,000 metres deep (19,700–36,000 feet) (the so-called trenches), can have so adapted themselves to the heavier pressure and somewhat higher temperature that a divergent group has developed. This group is no longer able to leave the abyss and, for that reason, becomes different from similar life forms in the regular sea depths or in other trenches. Such isolation occurs even more frequently in environments on the terrestrial surface, where more and greater barriers may be erected. The sea, for instance, is an insurmountable obstacle for fresh-water fish.

What Creatures Dwell in the Deeps of the Ocean?

For a long time, it was thought that the fauna of the deep sea were as old as the earth itself. There are, however, grounds to believe that, on the contrary, the deep-sea population developed from creatures of the upper strata in relatively recent geological periods. The deep sea was even considered a refuge for groups of fishes which could not stand up to the competition of younger groups. The last word has certainly not yet been said about this. It has been firmly established that a few supposedly extinct animals (the lobe-finned fish *Latimeria*, the snail *Pilina*, and the crinoid sea lily *Pentacheles*) still exist at great depths, whether or not their retreat was to clear the field for other groups in their original environment. Remarkably enough, the original environment of the lobe-finned fish, *Latimeria*, was a continental, fresh-water surrounding. What the direct cause may have been, that not only drove these fresh-water denizens into the sea but also changed them into creatures that could be classified with the deep-sea fauna, is not yet entirely clear. Perhaps the current increase in deep-sea research will reveal the answer.

Fish are the principal dwellers in the sea, yet fish life does not occur below the 6,000-metre (19,700-foot) level, so far as is known today. As an exception to this, the fish *Bassogigas* was hauled up in 1952 from a depth of about 7,000 metres (22,950 feet). Naturally, trustworthy conclusions cannot be drawn from a few dips of the deep-sea trawl in the enormous expanse of the ocean, and many surprises still await us. Nevertheless, data of this kind permit saying that fish are rare below 6,000 metres and that life (exclusively animal life, of course, because plants cannot exist owing to the lack of light and bacteria are still the only forms of plant-like life to be found here) is represented by sea anemones, sea cucumbers, bivalve shellfish, crustaceans and chaetognathous bristle worms. If we expect these creatures to be completely different in appearance from those in the upper reaches of water, we are fooling ourselves. Similarly formed beings are also found near the surface. One might wonder how it is possible for a creature living under hundreds of atmospheres of pressure to be brought to the surface where there is but one atmosphere weighing upon it. In such cases, caisson disease (the bends) is sure to be brought on, the same way that it

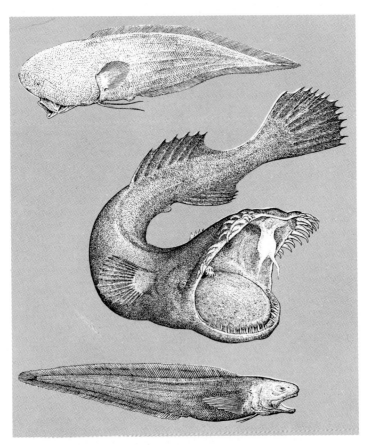

Illus. 6-1. From top to bottom: A blind fish, *Typhlonus,* with an inferior, protruding mouth, was caught at a depth of 5,090 m (3,040 fathoms) in the Celebes Sea. The Galathea expedition caught a strange fish at a depth of 3,590 m (2,833 fathoms) in the Pacific Ocean, off the coast of Central America. This *Galathaeathauma axeli* has, unlike the related Angler Fish (see text), the luminous "bait flap" hanging from the roof of its mouth. This way, it is naturally less vulnerable. The whole apparatus works like a mouse trap.
Bassogigas is the name of a fish which was caught at a depth of about 7,100 m (4,250 fathoms). The similarity of this species to some cod-like fishes from coastal waters is remarkable.

happens in man with a sudden pressure variation of a few atmospheres. Only a very slow reduction in pressure makes a live ascent at all possible for any creature.

Deep-Sea Exploration

The first expeditions confronted by these circumstances found that hauling the net up too fast caused the fish literally to explode. If the fish had a swim bladder, it popped out of its mouth and burst, and often the entire body was torn apart by the always-present gases expanding suddenly instead of slowly dissipating through the walls of the body.

It is first necessary to ascertain the depth of water beneath the keel of the ship. Today, this is accomplished by means of sonar signals. The old sounding method of heaving a weight on the end of a line is wholly impractical here, because of the drift of the lead and the miles of line that would have to be paid out and retrieved. Sonar operates on an echo principle. Although water quickly loses its ability to transmit light to greater depths, it is an eminently suitable medium for the propagation of sound waves. A vibration or tone sent out from the ship speeds through the water, in horizontal as well as vertical directions. Upon striking rocks or the bottom, the vibration is reflected back to its source—the ship. The time required for the sound wave to go and return, after a little figuring, determines the distance between the ship and the reflecting object or bottom, hence the depth of the water.

Once the distance to the bottom has been determined, a drag or trawl net is lowered on a special steel cable. The problems that came up in connection with this and confronted the deep-sea pioneers have been overcome today, and expensive equipment is seldom lost to the sea any more.

Now, what about the enormous pressure affecting the creatures living in these depths? We can hardly understand how the organs can adapt to it. Although it is known that a fish's body consists of about 99 per cent water, and water is practically incompressible, there still remains the puzzle of the exchange of gases as well as that of the deposition of lime in the body, in which the exchange of carbon dioxide plays so great a rôle. Carbon dioxide under such high pressure becomes fluid or even turns solid.

It used to be thought that food was provided for these ultra-deep-sea fishes by a rain of dead organisms from the higher water levels to the lower ones. However, this appears to be false. In normal circumstances, the dead organisms would be devoured by the population of their own high-water levels before any could sink to feed the hungry below. Hardly anything sinks to the bottom except the calcareous skeletons of micro-organisms, the cast-off shucks of crustaceans in metamorphosis, the plates of horn and the lime-based scales of squid, along with plant wastes and the droppings of the upper-level inhabitants. The main source of deep-sea food seems to be bacteria feeding on the waste mentioned above.

As said before, the creatures in the bottommost layers of water do not differ much from their relatives in continental waters. The most remarkable difference, however, is that the fishes are blind. Starfish and similar surface creatures also lack visual equipment. Furthermore, coloration is usually lacking entirely and the animals are almost completely transparent.

In the depths of the sea, there is an in-between zone of 200–3,000 metres (650–9,750 feet) where, opposed to both the surface and the deeps, coloration is present, visual ability develops, and many creatures possess light-emitting organs. It is obvious that sight is of value only where there is light, but where does the light come from? It seems that the phosphorescent organs are only partially responsible for the total quantity of light; some of it comes from luminescent bacteria sustained there, but this is really a subject in itself. Certain animals, fishes as well as crustaceans, are able to emit luminous clouds as a means of defence and to frighten off or delude would-be attackers.

Luminous Fishes

There are mainly two types of luminous fishes known to science. The first type possesses light-emitting spots, which look like a ship's port holes, in the skin. The second type develops projections upon which the light-emitting organs are hung like lanterns. The second type uses its lantern not so much for the purpose of lighting its way, but to attract prey. These fishes are related to the sea devils or Angler Fish of European coastal waters. Also, this Angler has an organ on its head that looks like a fishing rod with a piece of bait. It lets the glowing thing dangle in front of its large, open mouth with the obvious result that other fish, seeing it, are fooled into thinking it something to eat— then down the hatch! Attracted by the bait, the prey have paid the price of curiosity.

What is particularly striking in a comparison between surface and deep-sea creatures is the great development of all kinds of thin protuberances and appendages and the appallingly fragile structure in general. The possibility of creatures so equipped existing at all in the deep-sea environment is due to the perpetual calm that reigns. There is never, or hardly ever, a movement of the water, no waves to strike, no ebb and flow of the tides, only cold and the eternal dark. Does life in that total black-out bring no problems with it? How do the males find the females? How do the parents protect their young? Indeed, though many are equipped with light-emitting organs, these are by no means all the fishes, and even these organs provide no guarantee of contact between the sexes in the case of sluggish or unmoving creatures. Here, too, nature has hit upon something—something that has been most strikingly taken care of in the case of the deep-sea devils (among others, the genus *Linophryne*). Each large, plump female is always found with a male stuck fast to her body, completely grown together with her, flesh into flesh. These are the so-called dwarf males, which remain considerably smaller than the females. They are wholly parasitic on the female and their only purpose in life is to make reproduction possible.

A more common and, according to recent research, very widely spread means of making contact between creatures of the same kind is by sound. This means of communication is used so widely that scientists are wont to say that the surface of the earth is a haven of rest compared to the confounded racket perpetrated by the dwellers of the deep. Indeed, most of the noises they make are of a frequency inaudible to human ears. With this kind of capability, the creatures possess a means of communication par excellence. Nature, of course, hit upon this idea a long time before it ever occurred to modern man.

Modern, Deep-Sea Research

How do we come to know all this and what is the use of it? The deep-thinking reader asks the first part of this double-barrelled question, while the more practical person concerns himself with the latter part. It cannot be said beforehand with certainty whether such research will ever have a practical, economic use for all branches of science. Usually, however, each branch of science has its own economic significance, and this is just as true for deep-sea research.

When the first deep-sea expedition, the so-called "Challenger" expedition, set sail in 1872 under the leadership of Sir C. Wyville Thomson, hardly anything was known about life in the oceans, let alone about life in the deep sea. Opinions were divided on the subject, and none was based on factual observation. With still comparatively

primitive means, the ocean was dredged and fished and good use was made of some experiences of earlier pioneers in the field. It quickly became obvious that hempen rope was unsuitable and the hawsers were replaced with piano wire. Research of the ocean floor and the taking of samples were turned to practical use in the laying of the trans-Atlantic telephone cables. Sonar was used for the first time in World War I. Today, an even better method is generally used to track down schools of fish (economic significance). Based on the propagation of sound waves in water with a speed of about 1,500 metres (4,900 feet) per second, a depth of 1,500 metres is sounded in two seconds—one for the sound wave to go down and one for the echo to return—a task that formerly took several hours with the sounding line. Now it can be understood how a ship today, travelling at normal speed, can, by means of continuous emission of sonar signals, accurately map the profile of the ocean floor without the use of manpower. One of the most important results of depth measurement is that we now know precisely that the continents each lie upon a plateau bordered by up to 200 metres (650 feet) of ocean depth; then, suddenly the real ocean basin begins at a slope of 10° or more, the bottom inclining downwards to a

Illus. 6-2. The struggle for existence in the deep sea is a harsh one. Plant life is impossible there, so that the fish must devour each other. It is not always the small that feed the larger, as shown in this photograph. Seen here, among other things, is the substantially larger Narwhal Fish *(Bregmaceros macclelandi,* 3) falling prey to the much smaller, Black Swallower *(Chiasmodon niger,* 9). The stomach- and body-walls of this fish are so elastic, that the much larger prey can entirely vanish (9). The pale Roundmouth *(Cyclothone signata,* 1 and 5) is one of the numerous representative species which grows only 5 cm (2 inches) long. It lives mainly on small crustaceans. In the dark of the abyss also lives the hatchet fish *(Argyropelecus hemigymnus,* 2 and 11), a gleaming silver fish with many toned "lights" among the silvery scales. The Deep-Sea Gourmand or Hammerjaw *(Omosudis lowi,* 4) prefers squid. The Long-Armed Cuttle Fish (6) has luminous organs on two of its tentacles. The Viperfish *(Chauliodus,* 7) has luminous teeth which attract its prey. *Photostomias guernei,* the Loose-Jawed Fish (8), has rows of porthole-like lights along its belly. The upper jaw of the mouth of the Swallower Eel *(Gastrostomus,* 10) has a luminous edge that is capable of being opened enormously wide. All special equipment is designed to attract and overpower prey in these gluttonous depths.

depth of about 5,000 metres (about three miles), which is the average depth of the ocean.

The in-person descents into the depths by William Beebe and others must be considered a second series of underwater research. In contrast to the operations of the "Challenger" expedition and the others following, in which nothing more than instruments was lowered into the depths, the Beebe expedition went down equipped with human eyes to actually see what was going on under water. Beebe was one of the first to descend to a depth of 800 metres (2,600 feet) in a steel sphere provided with small peepholes set with quartz glass. What he and his associates observed there was a revelation to the entire, scientific world. It is no wonder that his example was followed, in January, 1960, in a very spectacular way by Jacques Piccard, who established an unbeatable record by descending to the ocean's greatest depths in the Marianas Trench. Accompanied by a colleague in a special diving vessel, the bathyscaphe, he descended to a depth of nearly 10,500 metres (over $6\frac{1}{2}$ miles) in the so-called Challenger Deep in the Marianas Trench. They saw many hitherto unknown creatures; the results of this expedition alone would fill a book.

Finally, it should be noted that deep-sea research has contributed a great deal to our knowledge of earth magnetism and volcanic activity, both of which are subjects of practical consideration and deserve more thorough investigation, as does the ocean as a source of food for all mankind.

Fish as Food

In prehistoric times, fish were a welcome and important source of food for the tribes of men. Naturally, since their first appearance, fish have fed many, though not all, other groups of animals. It is true, too, that fish also eat fish.

The value of fish as food is due to the natural make-up of the muscle tissue of fish, composed mostly of easily digestible protein that has no rival elsewhere in the plant or animal kingdom. Special materials of nutritional value in the flesh of fish, in addition to protein, cannot be obtained from the meat of other types of animals, dairy products, or vegetables.

For the growth of healthy people, fish is still an irreplaceable food which must be managed sensibly. A great many animals have become extinct in the relatively short period of man's existence on earth, either directly or indirectly because of man. It is certainly unthinkable that fish life should be eradicated merely through lack of sufficient controls on the fishing industry. For such scientific control, it is necessary first to study the habits of fish, and not only those of food fish, but also those of the fish that serve as food for fish.

World Fisheries

In 1883, one of the greatest scientists of that time, Thomas Henry Huxley (1825–95), stated his opinion, at the time of the fisheries exhibit in London, that all the great fishing grounds were probably inexhaustible. We know now, of course, that this was a mistaken opinion. Undoubtedly, the statement would have been true if the same fishing methods were still in use everywhere in the world. However, the increase in world population and the intensification of fishing methods that has gone hand in hand with it has already (and long since) brought numerous fishing grounds to the brink of danger.

Each year, approximately 40 million tons of fish are caught and used as food, either fresh or preserved, by various peoples. However, all this fish can only supply about 10 per cent of the world's need for protein. The most important fishing countries are Japan, Peru, China, Russia, the United States and Canada.

The activities of the fisheries are spread out over the continental plateaus and the coastal waters to a depth of about 350 metres (about 1,150 feet). So far as is known, these are the most satisfactory and

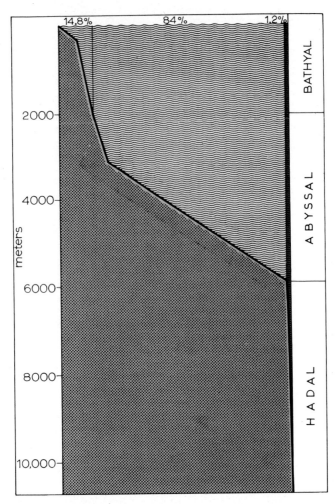

Illus. 6-3. Schematic survey, in cross-section, of the average depth of the different zones of the oceans. Of the total surface, 14.8 per cent covers depths of less than 2,000 m (1,200 fathoms) (bathyal); 84 per cent of all ocean surface covers deeps between 2,000 and 6,000 m (3,600 fathoms) (abyssal). The greatest deeps claim only 1.2 per cent, and are called trenches. The oceans take up more than two thirds of the total surface of the earth, and the 84 per cent abyssal, or actual deep sea, thus represents the greatest, single, ecological domain.

224

Illus. 6-4. A method of catching fish often used in rivers and shallow coastal waters by primitive peoples. A fence-like obstacle, made of branches and the like, is installed in the water. The fish are driven against it by the current. Protected from the sun by slanted, woven roofs, the fishermen catch the fish with hooks, nets and spears. This construction is in Thailand.

rich-in-food regions of the sea, with a still-abundant fish life. Heavier catches and sometimes inconsiderate competition, however, actually threaten these fishing grounds. Whole fleets move into them, mother ships with a flotilla of fishing craft and scouts, often accompanied by floating canneries where the catch is immediately processed. Even aircraft and helicopters are used to spot schools of fish from the air, and enormous trawling nets immediately go to work. Automation helps. Underwater television cameras hooked up to computers direct the trawlers as soon as suitable and desirable schools of fish have been located.

Fisheries Research

Naturally, science has also made itself master in this field. First, scientific methods were used to increase the size of the catches, and that is still keeping the fisheries' biologists busy. These biologists are equally busy with the question of how to nullify the threat to the existence of the fish. Many fishing fleets must continually travel farther and farther from home to harvest a good catch. The Japanese and Russians fish in every ocean in the world.

Increasing catches of tuna, for example, seem not to diminish their population. It has been asserted that these fish stand up well to the demand, and the more efficient methods are not hurting. However, the waters are, in fact, being over-fished—and by methods sometimes unworthy of men.

The modification of fishing grounds is one of the biologists' most important problems. On specially set-up vessels, actually floating laboratories, the biologists work to determine where to send their fishing fleet for the best chance of a catch. International co-operation has also become necessary in this field. In spite of the violent competition of the fleets of different nationalities, each of them realizes that this is a world-wide concern and of the greatest importance to the future population of the world.

How Man's Interference Threatens Fish Life

One of the most striking examples of this kind of disturbance of the hydro-ecological balance is Lake Kariba in Rhodesia. The dam was completed in 1959, forming a lake with a surface area of about 5,000 square kilometres (1,930 square miles), which made it the largest in the world. An insignificant, floating water plant, the Brazilian floating fern, imported long before from South America and barely holding its own in the river, found its opportunity in the nutritionally overloaded waters of the lake. In May, 1960, the fern covered an area of almost 220 square kilometres (85 square miles), and by 1962 it had spread out over 20 per cent of the lake's surface, in a layer at least 15 cm (6 inches) thick. It is so compact that a man can walk on it. The water under the layer is deprived of all light, and all the fish die from lack of oxygen.

Certain developments in Surinam over the years show that the scientific investigation of a given region is not only an enormous task that may last for generations, but that it also results in man's inter-ference with nature, which can have unhappy consequences. It also shows how a small fish species can often be important to the livability of a region and the health of its population. Moreover, it has also become evident that the building of a dam can be the signature on the death warrant for many species of fishes accustomed to spawning in the upper reaches of a river.

In addition, the progress of scientific research in Surinam gives an idea of what is involved generally in an exploration of any new area.

The first explorative journey into Surinam was made by a woman of Swiss extraction, Maria Sybilla Merian (1647–1717), who studied and illustrated the insects and their host plants, butterflies, and food plants of Surinam.

Maria Sybilla's work led to further journeys and research by men such as Pieter Cramer, Caspar Stoll, Scheller and Fermin.

Further studies of Surinamese fauna continued into the 19th century. In 1887, Kappler published the best review of the fauna of Surinam to date. Later studies included work on mosquitoes (Wepster, 1925, and Van der Kuyp, 1950) and birds (Penard brothers, 1908, and Haverschmidt, 1955).

Fish did not receive much attention until Pieter Bleeker wrote several papers on a limited number of groups in 1862-73. In his thesis treating the South American catfishes, Van der Stigchel (1946) described a number of species occurring in Surinam, whose presence had already been reported by Eigenmann (1912) in *The Freshwater Fishes of British Guiana*. Boeseman has been working since 1948 on old and recent collections of Surinamese fishes, while the author himself has, since 1952, been especially occupied with the fresh-water fishes of that region.

Many groups of animals, however, have not yet or have barely been studied, while a few fragmentary reports and communications have appeared on spiders, shellfishes, crustaceans, thousand-leggers and mites.

All in all, the knowledge of the animals of Surinam is not nearly as comprehensive as it should, and could, be. Such knowledge would be beneficial to the Surinamese economy and, more important, to the people themselves.

Dam-Building and its Consequences

What is going to happen now in this primary stage of the development of scientific investigation of Surinam? Driven by economic necessity, a surface area of not less than 1,500 square kilometres (about 580 square miles) has been flooded. In truth, this is a rather small part of the total area of Surinam which is about 160,000 square kilometres (about 27,000 square miles). It does fulfil, however, the greatest expectations of flora and fauna. The drowned forests alone certainly already represent a fortune, but this is not included among the consequences sure to result from such disturbance of the ecological balance—a disturbance that will reach out far beyond the flooded area. All this, however, was desirable in the interest of providing energy for the needs of a combined American-Surinamese company for the exploitation of the aluminum-bearing ore in the rock layers. The plan in question, known as the Brokopondo Plan, included provisions for the construction of a dam on the Surinam River.

It is interesting to examine more closely and to weigh the economic advantages and the ecological consequences that can result from the building of such a dam, especially in light of the slight factual knowledge of the local flora and fauna and the experiences met with in other districts following the building of dams and the flooding of entire regions of land. The following quotation, a statement by Professor Dr. George S. Myers of Stanford University, California, may be cited in this connection:

"In building any dam which will destroy or endanger migratory food fishes, it is necessary to weigh the potential value of the dam against the potential value of the self-renewing, food-fish resource—not only for the present but for the next thousand generations. Our children's children, in a world so full of people that every food resource is precious, may curse us for some of the dams to which we now point so proudly."

The first consequence following closure of the dam and the shutting off of the river shows up in the downstream part of the river itself. Since filling the lake behind the dam removes a great deal of water from the river, a lot less remains for the downstream region. The low- and high-tide lines at the mouth of the river are, as a result of this and other things, displaced inwards towards the land, while a not inconsiderable silting-up of a great part of the coastline takes place. Furthermore, the normal flood region of this part of the river, in the wet season, is practically non-existent. It is precisely that flood region

228

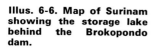

Illus. 6-6. Map of Surinam showing the storage lake behind the Brokopondo dam.

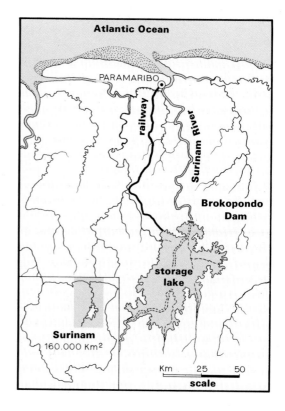

Illus. 6-7. Diagram of a large part of the storage lake of Brokopondo, in which the palm trees are more than half drowned, causing them to die off soon.

which is essential to the proper maintenance of fish life, as most species find their natural spawning and feeding grounds there. And, not to be overlooked are the changes in the river bottom and in the vegetation along the banks that follow.

As predicted, the flow below the dam decreased in quantity, a consequence of the water being taken up by water plants and of the evaporation of further enormous quantities. Naturally, men cannot live on the land covered by the water behind the dam, so that at one blow, the land was lost to cultivation, forestry and mining. Moreover, it is yet to be seen whether lake fishing will yield a greater return or whether it will just equal that of the river and its tributaries.

Experience has shown that in dammed lakes, trees of the original vegetation die very quickly, but the treetops continue to stick up out of the water for many years, and finally break off at the waterline. The trunks, shut off from air, continue to stand indefinitely. The complete bulldozing of the land to be flooded therefore becomes necessary before dam-building. Instances are known in which the forests were only partially cleared away, and these later damaged the dams when high winds ripped the trunks from the bottom and literally rammed them against the construction.

As soon as the original vegetation in the lake has died off, a process of "land formation" sets in due to a deteriorative sinking-away of the land, a reaction that develops harder and faster where the bank is a long, straight line. Thousands of small islands thus appear along the bank, and many native plants simply take advantage of the opportunity to find a new footing where they can multiply at will. By way of swamp and marsh, a dry-land vegetation soon begins to develop.

Producers and Carriers of Disease

No more suitable environment for mosquitoes and other disease carriers can be imagined than those swamp- and marsh-plants that sprout up in dammed-up localities. Naturally, diseases such as malaria, yellow fever, filariasis (thread-worm), dengue (pronounced dengh-y) fever, and schistosomiasis can be handled by modern medical science, but if the simplest way to fight such diseases is to clear out the breeding places of the carriers, or to keep them from forming, we begin to wonder. . . .

The destruction of breeding places of harmful producers and carriers of disease can be done mechanically by draining the swamps or by excavating and fencing them off. Dryness makes it impossible for the organisms and carriers to reproduce, while deep water is not a suitable environment for them, either.

An exhaustive inventory of the animal life of the area to be flooded would indicate that the use of a biological control can hardly be the answer. If the situation is completely investigated, it may be possible to use a locally occurring species—fish in particular—to exterminate carriers. Such fish studies have shown, among others things, that it is the little fish that have no economic value that can play an important rôle in this regard.

Summarizing, the advantages of a dam and its lake in the tropics should be weighed against a number of biological-ecological factors which work out as disadvantages, such as: loss of tillable land, forest trees, and mining possibilities; providing breeding places for disease-carrying insects; damage to the conditions for fish life; the falling-off of downstream flood terrain (in itself a disadvantage for soil, vegetation, spawning and feeding grounds for fish); damage to the dam itself (land formation, hindrance to drainage, increased evaporation because of floating plants, etc.; decreased lake capacity due to silting-up).

connection between water-level, plant-ecology and malaria control

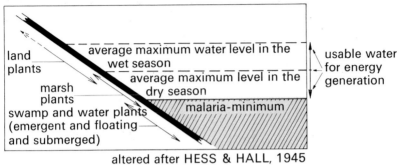

altered after HESS & HALL, 1945

Table 6-1. Indicates which are the critical water-lines of the storage lake of Brokopondo. Beneath the line "malaria-minimum," a considerable portion of the shore zone dries out—at least, is transformed into marsh—and malarial mosquitoes appear in great numbers. The minimum level for proper functioning of the power station must consequently lie above this. The other two lines speak for themselves.

Fish as Disease Fighters

Many diseases, especially in the tropical regions, are caused by micro-organisms and worm-like animalculae that are carried by insects. One of the first things to be done upon opening up a wild region is to undertake warfare against the insects. It is still a point of strife among scientists as to just how good insecticides are as offensive weapons in the fight to control insects. At first full of promise, insecticides brought with them some entirely unexpected and decidedly dangerous after-effects. A biological control was considered by many to be safe and wholly effective. That fish could play a rôle in this has, among other things, been clearly proven in Surinam.

Although many fish live on insects—or, at least, insects form an important part of their diet—we shall limit ourselves here to the genus *Rivulus*, because the author's own extensive material on this genus has been fully researched.

The Significance of "Rivulus" in Insect Control

Rivulus is just about the only genus of toothcarp that is represented by various species everywhere in the waters of Surinam. In nearly every sample from the savannah country, several specimens are present, which is the reason for choosing this genus to work over more thoroughly and to attempt to trace its distribution and migration throughout the Guianas.

232

In accordance with the exact data regarding catch locations, it can be further confirmed at what distance from the coast and at what altitude the fishes were caught. From this it can be construed that within a species, as well as within the genus as a whole, a tendency exists for the number of rays in the dorsal and anal fins to increase with an increase in the altitude of the catch location. In other words, in the higher-lying regions where the drop in the river is greater and the resulting stronger current makes more powerfully-built fins a necessity, the specimens do have larger fins, containing more rays than specimens from the lowlands.

Table 6–2. CORRELATION BETWEEN THE NUMBER OF FIN RAYS AND THE DISTANCE FROM THE COAST AND THE ALTITUDE OF THE CATCH LOCATION IN THE GENUS *Rivulus* FROM THE WATERS OF SURINAM.

Number of specimens in samples	Dorsal fin rays			Anal fin rays			Distance in km (miles) from coast		Altitude in metres (feet) above the sea	
	Variation	Mean	Standard deviation	Variation	Mean	Standard deviation	km	miles	m	feet
(a) 16	9–10	9.95	0.002	15–17	16.00	0.040	100	(62½)	100	(325)
(b) 11	9–11	10.10	0.135	15–17	16.09	0.060	130	(81¼)	150	(490)
(c) 12	9–11	10.50	0.151	16–18	16.78	0.049	130	(81¼)	550	(1,807)
(d) 19	10–12	10.80	0.120	15–18	16.41	0.116	250	(156¼)	1,000	(3,250)

Without paying attention to the species, this table shows that the mean number of rays in the dorsal and anal fins increases with the altitude above sea level of the place of origin.

Finally, to follow up on what species are represented in the material, it is first necessary to see how many different varieties or species are contained in it, and whether they are merely a few varying specimens of the same species or several species living together. One of the most important criteria for distinguishing a true species is the ecological factor of whether the specimens live together in the same biotope. Even two quite closely related varieties, sub-species or species, are normally not found in the same environment.

In *Rivulus*, the head scalation seems to form a pattern that gives an insight into the evolution of this species. There are three basic types of head scalation, the first of which was found in two Cuban species—in well known *Rivulus cylindraceus*, or Cuban Rivulus, described originally by Poey in 1861, and *Rivulus marmoratus*, described in 1880, also by Poey. Later, both species were considered synonymous, but the notable difference in pattern of the frontal scalation now leaves no doubt about the two being distinct species.

Closer examination of the frontal scalation shows a basic pattern, centering around a cross line formed by the longitudinal axis and a line connecting the rear margin of the orbits. In this area lies a scale that is overlapped all around by other scales. This central scale is designated by the letter *a*, and the encircling scales proceeding outward from it are, respectively, designated: *b, c, d, e, f, g* and *h*; *a, b, g* and *h* lie on the median line, while the remaining scales are placed to the left and right of it. (See section on *Rivulus* on page 804.)

Two types of frontal scalation are represented in the Cuban *Rivulus* spp., which belong, respectively, to the *d*-type and the *e*-type. The third type was found in material from Surinam, the *f*-type.

On the basis of scale pattern, three groups could be distinguished in the material from Surinam, plus a fourth group of specimens which do not belong to any specific type, or which showed head scaling so irregular that they could just as well be assigned to one group as to another. These were hybrids or cross-breeds, and this cross-bred material of necessity provided the key to further research.

An investigation of the stomach contents of various *Rivulus* species has clearly shown that over 75 per cent of the diet of these fish, regardless of species, consists of mosquito larvae and eggs. It is not an overstatement to say that *Rivulus* is one of the genera of fishes worth their weight in gold where public health is concerned. They do live, of course, in a region where the population is assailed by these sometimes harmless but often very dangerous insects. Mosquitoes are carriers of malaria, yellow fever, filariasis, dengue fever, and are probably also carriers of animal diseases. In order to keep these sources and carriers of disease within bounds, it is necessary that their natural enemies—fishes, especially—be allowed to reproduce in full measure. More effective than constant control of mosquitoes and their larvae by insecticides is undoubtedly the maintenance of an effective level of fish life, with emphasis on the species—such as *Rivulus*—which live almost exclusively on mosquito larvae.

The fish situation, especially in the case of rivulins, is seriously threatened in the dry season by birds which thoroughly clean these fishes out of regions that are drying up, such as the savannah marshes. Large-scale excavations of drainage ditches and canals would give the fish a means of escape from these birds, which are practically their only real enemies. Then again, draining the water from large areas of marshy terrain which are ideal breeding grounds for mosquitoes should work to hold these insects in check.

In addition to *Rivulus* species, which can certainly stand up to all kinds of environmental changes better than is generally supposed, Surinam provides a rather large number of fishes which feed, to a considerable extent, on insect larvae. These fishes are: *Trichomycterus*, *Pimelodella*, *Charax*, *Hemigrammus*, *Hyphessobrycon*, *Pristella*, *Lebiasina*, *Piabucina*, *Poecilia* (formerly *Lebistes*), *Anableps*, *Geophagus*, *Cichlasoma*, and *Dormitator*, plus the previously-named callichthyids and gymnotids.

The introduction of insectivores, especially larvae-eating fishes from other parts of the world, although often recommended is certainly not necessary and could even have fatal consequences for the native fish life. The introduction, a few years ago, of an African cichlid, a *Tilapia* species, into the Nickerie region, will long be remembered by the Surinamese. These fish, not part of the native fauna, made themselves so at home in the new environment that they were not only fiercely competitive with many native species, but drove them out and just about eradicated them.

Fish as Enemies and Parasites

There is an exception to every rule, and while it is true that fishes in general are useful, harmless and otherwise important to men, a few groups do, however, bear a certain hostility to men and animals. In addition to these, there is a small parasitic group that may be called something more than merely unpleasant.

When we think of hostile fishes, we think first of the dangerous, man-eating sharks and the aggressive barracudas. These live in the open sea and are actually a menace only to swimmers and bathers along certain coasts, and, naturally, to the victims of shipwreck. Thus, they are not a danger that imperils mankind in general. The same is true of the other hostile fishes, for the danger they present is really a defence for protection against other animals, or even against men who threaten their security. Viewed in this light are many of the poisonous fishes. On the other hand, the piranhas are both aggressive and dangerous. These are flesh-eating characins infesting South American waters. Attacking in great numbers, they will devour any man or animal venturing into their habitat.

Unpleasant and to a certain extent dangerous are the so-called URINOPHILES, members of the catfish family Trichomycteridae, which, when the opportunity presents itself, will penetrate the urinary tract of men and animals. Further examples could be brought forth, but let us concern ourselves more with the importance fishes have for us— and not only for the aquarist, of course.

Aquarium Fishes as a Hobby

From the ancient Egyptians, from the Aztecs and the Chinese, to modern western Europe and its aquarists, keeping fishes has been an enjoyable pastime. A rough estimate of the number of families in western Europe where one or more aquariums are found comes quite close to a half million.

History

Archaeological research has clearly shown that aquariums existed in ancient Egypt. It is asserted that the basins and vessels in which the fish were kept had an exclusively practical use in the kitchen—the Egyptians kept food fishes in a simple way by putting them into an aquarium to await the cook. This doubtless happened, but there are enough indications to show that the custom of keeping fish was adopted by many solely for the pleasure of looking at them, more in the same sense that we keep them today in an aquarium. Well known, too, are the fish pools in the gardens of ancient Rome and its surroundings, as have been brought to light in the excavation of Pompeii. Such fish pools were called PISCINAE (derived from *pisces* meaning fish). Although the Romans had considerable experience with the upkeep of fish in their so-called VIVARIA (*vivarium* means literally a place for keeping or maintaining live creatures), they cannot be considered the forerunners of today's true aquarists.

At the time of the Spanish conquest of Mexico, on the other hand, the fish reservoirs found there were being used for observing fish. The famous Aztec ruler, Montezuma, had artificial reservoirs and basins in his gardens, filled with fresh and salt water, in which fish and waterfowl could be kept for breeding and study. During the Middle Ages, the Chinese were already exceptionally interested in goldfish. The numerous breeds which, since about 1600, have been and are still being imported into Europe, are famous. The first exact information on the keeping and breeding of fishes in glass tanks (aquariums) by the Chinese dates from 1369. The earthenware industry was already making at that time—during the reign of the Emperor Hung-Wu—special "fish glasses" in which decorative fish and water plants were kept. The breeds obtained a firm foothold in Europe when Madame de Pompadour received a gift from the French-India Company in

1750—a number of brilliant Goldfish in the then-already world-famous "dragon globes" (a fine, porcelain vase, globular in shape and decorated with a dragon motif).

During the 15th century, the Chinese art of fish breeding was introduced into Japan. Whereas in China the fish were bred for coloration, the Japanese devoted themselves to producing all kinds of unusual shapes. The Veiltail, Stargazer, Telescope Fish, Lionhead- and Egg-Goldfish are all results of centuries of trial breeding of the ordinary Chinese Goldfish.

As far as can be traced, the first glass aquarium in Europe was in the shape of a glass globe (the still more or less current type of fish bowl) by a glass blower at Grimnitz (1572), on the order of Dr. Thurneysser, physician in ordinary to the Elector of Brandenburg. This monstrosity, which might have been more appropriate as an "instrument of torture" to our modern view, provided a place for a bird in the middle, with space round it for water and fish.

Such a glass is, as an aquarium, worthless. Not until 1666 was it written into a book by Leonhard Baldner that it is possible to keep fish in glass vessels and, thus, to observe their conduct. The then rather popular fish (a large loach, *Misgurnus fossilis*), known as the Weather Fish or Loach, is perhaps one of the first fish known to help pave the way towards more modern ideas of fish culture. About 1778, in France, information was released by the Abbé Dicquemarre, who described how he kept sea creatures and plants alive in artificial tanks for purposes of scientific research.

For the scientific research of water life, however, all kinds of glassware have long been used to keep the creatures brought in from the wild alive, if they have to remain for a few hours or days in the laboratory. Antonie van Leeuwenhoek kept his "microbes" in earthenware vessels. Not until after the discovery of the solution of gaseous oxygen and carbon dioxide in water by Priestly and Scheele (18th century), and other great men such as Lavoisier, Spallanzani, and Von Humboldt, was the necessity understood for changing the water—and how to change it—in the then more and more common fish bowls. The Dutchman Ingenhouss (beginning of the 19th century) has clearly shown by his investigations that the respirational interchange between plants and animals (absorption of carbon dioxide by plants, the exhalation of carbon dioxide by animals, the giving-off of oxygen by plants, and the inhalation of oxygen by animals) also holds true for the tiny, underwater world of the aquarium. At that time, a so-called "biological balance between plants and animals" was being industriously sought, and it was the Englishman Ward who, in 1841, mentioned a fresh-water aquarium, stocked with fish and provided with water plants, in which the water stayed fresh for a "long time." Ward's experiments can be considered as pioneering for the aquarist. In 1842, Johnston did the same thing for sea water as he demonstrated that algae under the influence of light make water keep fresh for an unlimited time. P. H. Gosse also has a name in this field, and in 1850 he presented a discussion of Rotifera. He had been able to observe these quite well in the aquarium for several years, since various water plants, of which he named *Vallisneria*, *Myriophyllum*, *Nitella* and *Chara*, had kept the water "pure" all that time. The term "aquarium" appears to have been first used by Gosse in 1853. We have read in earlier writings about the "vivarium" and even about the "aqua-vivarium," but not about the "aquarium." By definition, an aquarium is a space enclosed entirely with glass, or partially with opaque material, and filled with water, in which water life can be observed.

The Beginning of the Hobby

The patriarch of European aquarists was undoubtedly the German Rossmässler, who published his famous book, *Der See im Glase (The Lake in Glass)*, in 1856.

This beginning of aquarium literature was not followed in the Netherlands until about 25 years later, when the first original Dutch book, *Het zoetwater aquarium (The Fresh-Water Aquarium)* by C. J. den Hollander (1900) was published. It has had a continuously good mention in the press, and even today is still regularly reprinted, though in a somewhat revised form. The *Aquariumboekje (The Little Aquarium Book)* by Heimans appeared in 1912, and in 1925, the well known work *Mijn aquarium (My Aquarium)* by Portielje appeared in the series of Verkade albums. For the Netherlands, the heyday of the aquarist burgeoned between World War I and World War II, while in England and Germany aquariums were found in many households even before that.

In a very short time, the different types of aquariums have gone through a period of tremendous development. At first, there was a special place on the (gold)fish bowls—the round, ball-shaped vases—for very bad drawings of the plants and animals to be seen inside. The first aquarium with a flat, glass pane was a wooden tank with a piece of window glass at the front, a type, perhaps, that deserved a

Plate 6-1. *Geophagus brasiliensis* is one of the magnificent cichlids that hail from a large part of South America.

Plate 6-2. *Geophagus jurupari* is also native to a large part of South America, Brazil and the Guiana Highlands.

better future than it had. Leakage occurred from insufficient sealing and protection of the wood against water. With modern paints and lacquers, better results can be achieved in this respect, especially because wood is easily worked with (by do-it-yourselfers) and because it is a good insulator against heat loss. Nevertheless, all-glass aquariums quickly appeared on the market—moulded glass tanks that had many unpleasant properties—but they became rather popular because they gave, in any case, a better view of what was going on inside them, and they did not leak. At the least, moulded glass can suddenly crack to pieces, usually as a result of internal stresses arising from poor construction or from not being evenly supported.

The so-called angle-iron aquarium, consisting of a rectangular steel frame with a metal bottom and "walls" of window glass, made its appearance in the 1920's and had a great deal to do with the upsurge in the hobby. It was no longer necessary to confine aquariums to a certain size, for it was now possible, without much expense, to have an aquarium custom-made to any desired length, width or height. With a special filler (a kind of putty), the panes were set firmly into the frame and all made watertight. Also, heating the water for the tropical fish that had, meanwhile, become more and more popular, was a less troublesome problem than in the all-glass aquarium.

The First Aquarium Fish

In the meantime, what about populating the aquarium? In the beginning, it was usually with numerous varieties of goldfish. Later, ordinary native fishes and other creatures from local ditches and ponds were also kept in aquariums. Interest in salamanders (newts) has never been very great, although Heimans' book, *In sloot en plas (In Ditch and Pond)*, did a great deal in broadening the ordinary aquarist's interest towards other water dwellers.

Since 1869, when a fish entirely different from the goldfish—namely, the handsomely-hued Paradise Fish *(Macropodus opercularis)*—was imported into France from China, this fish has made a veritable triumphal march over the entire world. This was the result not only of a relative unconcern of this species for the temperature of the water, but also of the interesting, never-before-heard-of method of reproduction. As so-called labyrinth fishes are equipped to take oxygen from the air above water, they made few or no demands on the condition of the water they lived in, and were thus sturdy fish. Regularly, they surprised their owner with a nest of foam bubbles, in which

241

Illus. 6-8. Whether considered beautiful or ugly, this Veil-Finned Angelfish is obtained through selective breeding.

hundreds of little eggs were laid, cared for and watched over by the parents. The Paradise Fish is still considered one of the most beautiful, easiest to keep, and most interesting of the exotic, ornamental fishes. The species which belong to the same group are: the Siamese Fighting Fish *(Betta splendens)*; the Dwarf Gourami *(Colisa lalia)*; the Blue Gourami *(Trichogaster trichopterus)*; and the Pearl Gourami *(Trichogaster leeri)*. These were imported in later years and have found a regular place in the aquarists' tanks ever since, as has also been the case with many other species. These species, however, as well as other labyrinth fishes with an auxiliary respiratory organ (the so-called labyrinth, under the gill covers), required a higher temperature than the Paradise Fish, which thrived summer and winter at room temperature.

The true tropical aquarium entered the scene in this period and all kinds of heating systems were devised to keep the water at a constant temperature of about 22–24 °C (72–75 °F). The most obvious method was to place a heat source under the aquarium, and thus oil or kerosene lamps and burners came into use. To let a flame play directly against the bottom of an all-glass aquarium was naturally undesirable, so sand baths, among other things, were used. The aquarium was set in a metal box containing sand, beneath which the burner was placed. The metal-bottomed aquariums allowed the application of heat

242

directly against the bottom without the interposition of anything else. With the development of electricity, these bottom-heaters became obsolete and the use of a submerged electrical heating element was universally adopted. While the burners had required constant attention to keep the temperature from a sudden rise or fall due to fluctuations in the flame, the electrical elements could be accurately regulated with a thermostat, and a heater kept inside each tank. Today, heating is no longer a problem. The lucky owners of hothouses even use space heating, so that aquariums kept in them no longer require individual heating equipment.

While Europe was laboriously pioneering against all the problems of the cold-water aquarium—such as changing the water, keeping the temperature sufficiently low in the summer months, and finding suitable food for the native fishes—the enterprising Chinese had already instituted in the great cities of Asia—Singapore, for example—a large-scale trade in tropical fishes. After World War I, when shipping to and from Indonesia (the former Dutch East Indies) was resumed, the Dutch aquarium trade took its first tottering steps along the road that would lead to great success. Numerous tropical fishes were offered for sale to aquarists, at first at exorbitant prices. People were not yet fully aware that the beauty of form and coloration, which could be seen

Illus. 6-9. The Angelfish *(Pterophyllum scalare)* has been kept so long as an aquarium fish that all kinds of breeding products have been obtained, such as these jet-black pigmented "black Angelfish."

in the aquariums of well known zoological gardens, was also available to anyone who took the trouble to set up an aquarium at home.

Large aquariums have undoubtedly had a certain influence on the public and have stimulated the hobby. Public aquariums were opened in London (1850), Vienna (1860), Paris (1861), a first exhibition of aquariums at the World's Fair in Paris (1867), Berlin (1869), Naples (1874), Heligoland (1874), and Amsterdam (1882). Although most of these public aquariums concentrated on salt-water and sea-dwellers, there was always a section devoted to fresh-water fishes. Among the exotic species encountered in these aquariums were the labyrinth fishes, such as the Paradise Fish, *Macropodus opercularis* (since about 1870), the Siamese Fighting Fish, *Betta splendens* (1874), the Blue Gourami, *Trichogaster trichopterus* (1896), the Pearl Gourami, *Trichogaster leeri* (ca. 1900), the Dwarf Gourami, *Colisa lalia* (1903), all from Southeast Asia. A spectacular fish from South America is the Angelfish or Scalare, *Pterophyllum scalare* (kept without interruption since 1911 at the Artis Aquarium in Amsterdam and by hobbyists), and that attractive, live-bearing fish from Trinidad, the Guppy or Millions Fish, *Poecilia* (formerly *Lebistes*) *reticulata* (1908).

From Central America in 1909 came the Swordtail, *Xiphophorus helleri*, which bears living young like the Guppy and is beginning a veritable march of triumph. This species is not very susceptible to temperature change and can be kept by the hobbyist in an unheated aquarium in a heated room. It appears to be able to withstand a nightly drop in temperature to about 15 °C (59 °F), and it has been found that for this and other tropical species of fishes, a constant day and night temperature is not suitable. In the tropics, too, some waters can cool off sharply during the night, and for this type of fish a nightly lowering of the temperature by a few degrees seems desirable. Earlier, people did not know much about the origin and the natural circumstances under which the fish lived, neither dealers nor hobbyists. They had to puzzle things out and experiment, with temperature as well as with food. The collected works on aquarium fish in those days were based almost exclusively on experience, not on exact data regarding origin and environment. Naturally, the collectors often made mistakes and, of course, were far from always successful at breeding certain species, a failure that was not displeasing to the trade. For example, in the 1930's, a story made the rounds to the effect that the Chinese in Singapore were selling exclusively males or females from any given species so that they could limit their breeding territory. This may indeed have happened once, but in general it was nonsense. Also, the supposed sterilization of fish to prevent propagation appeared to exist in the imagination of those hobbyists who, for one reason or another, had not been successful in breeding their fish.

A similar thing happened, for example, with *Rasbora heteromorpha*, a lovely fish from tropical Asia, that was first introduced into Europe in 1906, but could not be bred. Each month, hundreds of pairs passed through the trade, still being imported, without any having brought forth progeny in the few years they lived before dying a natural death. In fact, nothing was known about this fish, except that it was practically always offered by the trade at high prices. It took until 1932 for people in the Netherlands to discover that, kept in a small school of 8 to 10 specimens, these fish bred spontaneously and en masse but only in the mating season.

In the case of the too-well-known Zebra Fish, *Brachydanio rerio*, which was imported in 1905 and began spontaneously to reproduce, the fall-off in quality is so great in tank-bred specimens that, not only does the attractive, golden yellow of the light stripes fade to an undistinguished, dirty white, but also even the relative measurements of the fish are changed. Fishes imported from the wild, accustomed to being swift swimmers in schools in clear, open water, after a few generations in the aquarium generally change into distinctively plumper creatures exhibiting a stumpier body build. Fishes like the Zebra, for sale everywhere at low cost, are not attractive to the aquarium trade any longer and further importation of these species is not being considered. As for the Guppy, the Millions Fish, which has shown itself to be indestructible, the same is also true. Not a single importer or dealer any longer considers it financially worth-while. A pity, really, for the true hobbyist would gladly pay a reasonable price for such re-imports.

In the last few years before World War I, it was the German importers who had spread their nets out over the world. Singapore, Rio de Janeiro, Georgetown, Lagos, and other sources of the aquarium-fish trade provided many attractive species. Besides the well known Red Tetra from Rio (Flame Tetra, U.K.), *Hyphessobrycon flammeus* (1920), southern South America yields *Aphyocharax rubripinnis* (1906), a fish that, considering its place of origin, appears to be kept as a subtropical species. From the tropical waters of that part of the world came many fishes at that time well known to hobbyists, such as the Head-and-Tail-Light Tetra, *Hemigrammus ocellifer* (1910), the Pristella Tetra,

Pristella riddlei (1924), the Armoured Catfish, *Corydoras paleatus* (1908), from the environs of Rio de Janeiro and numerous members of the family of cichlids, to which the already-named Angelfish belongs. From West Africa came the Cape Lopez Lyretail, *Aphyosemion australe* (1920).

More than ever, this hobby is increasing throughout the world and is clearly on the way to a still-to-be-determined crest of popularity. Naturally, the great number of organized hobbyists has had an influence on the importation of many species of fish, and new varieties are continually being imported in greater numbers. All in all, it looks as if the hobby is progressing towards a flourishing future all over the world.

Aquariophiles

Most aquarium owners—they cannot be called real hobbyists—will put together a heterogeneous collection of fishes which came originally from totally different biotopes, and which then must adapt themselves to what is often an unsuitable environment. The real aquarists—only a small percentage of the total number—practice their hobby in a scientifically more responsible way. They try to imitate, as closely as possible in their tanks, the natural environment of a certain fish species by the composition of the water and by the planting, lighting and temperature, so that the fish can live there under optimum conditions and ultimately propagate.

The swiftly rising interest in salt-water aquariums must be mentioned, even though it is a relatively new branch of the hobby. The keeping of tropical marine fish poses problems, indeed, which the quasi-aquarist generally cannot master. The almost unbelievably striking beauty of these fishes, however, promises that the salt-water aquarium will appear more and more in the home until it quietly supersedes the tropical fresh-water aquarium altogether.

The Importance of Environmental Conditions in Exporting Aquarium Fishes

Can you imagine the enthusiasm of aquarists, upon reading expedition reports from the far tropics about fish found in small, water-filled hollows in tree trunks, while there is no water at all in the local surroundings? Or of fish which, in the damp, early morning travel great distances overland from one creek to another? Or of fish on an annual trek from rivers and streams to lands that become flooded in the rainy season, a trek regularly followed at the end of the rainy season by a return journey of the same masses of fish to the open, free water of the creeks, a trek which can keep the fish from drying out during the dry season? But why do some species remain behind in the steadily shrinking ponds and pools, many until they die? And what of the riddle of the burgeoning fish life within 24 hours after the first rains sweep across the dry stretches of the savannahs, that for months had been deprived of all water? How is it possible for young life suddenly to develop from fish eggs buried in the mud months before?

These are only a few of the countless questions that crop up in reading the field notes of those who catch fish. Human striving to solve puzzles of this kind has contributed to elevating the hobby to its present level. People want more than an aquarium with beautiful plants and flashing fishes—they want to *know*! An important science has undoubtedly developed as a result of this. It would hardly be possible, without a great deal of trouble, at any rate, for scientists to keep in aquariums all the different fishes that are available, in order to study their activities. The science of the behavioral study of animals is already quite old, and it can now be revived with fresh interest in the field of water dwellers.

Surinam, to name a region which is attracting more and more interest from both scientists and hobbyists, consists largely of marshy lowlands of a type that may properly be called extremely primitive. What goes on there in the broad, marshy coastal strip is extremely intriguing to nature lovers. On the basis of numerous investigations into the rock layers, fossils and such, the conclusion may be reached that conditions in these marshes cannot differ remarkably from the marshy regions that existed during the age of coal formation, the Carboniferous period. In general, the water there is poor in oxygen, the gas which is essential to the respiration of all living organisms. Moreover, that same water is poisoned by an excess of carbonic acid gas and sulphides. Yet, there is life there—and how!

One of the first investigations to take place, of course, was to find out how a fish that normally took in oxygen from the water through its gills could live here. It appeared that, in the case of the fishes living here, gill breathing played a subsidiary rôle and that these fishes were endowed with a kind of lung breathing, which made them capable of taking oxygen directly from the air above the water. Among these fishes, the gills serve principally to expel the waste product of respiration, carbon dioxide, back into the water, thus ridding the body and the blood of it. An old enemy of aquarists, the so-called autumn plague, was a problem in former times that has more recently been solved. Overpopulation, insufficient circulation of the water, not enough light, and other such factors caused carbonic acid poisoning in autumn in the aquariums of many fishes that either did not live under such conditions in the wild so that they could have adapted to it, or were, indeed, immune to it, owing to some adaptation or other. It all boiled down to the fact that the survivors were not entirely dependent on the oxygen dissolved in the water.

How did these adaptations come about? From the standpoint of a marshy environment, which must be considered the oldest type of biotope for fish life, and taking into consideration that the intestine has always played a large part in the development of the respiratory organs, it is highly probable that the first fishes, in their need for oxygen, provided for this in a simple way by gulping air and swallowing it, thus absorbing the oxygen present in the intestinal canal.

Later, projections developed on the intestine, reservoirs for storing a quantity of air to be used as needed. These reservoirs were the forerunners of the swim bladder as well as of the lung. Numerous freshwater fishes still living today use intestinal respiration. These are, in general, the species that have remained faithful to the primitive environment of their ancestors. Many of their offshoots preferred, however, the clear, flowing water of streams and rivers, which has no oxygen problems, at least, not in unspoiled nature. In civilized countries, oxygen has again become a problem for fishes, now that more and more pollution and poisonous wastes are occurring in rivers because of discharges from factories and especially chemical industries.

No organ declines so quickly as one for which there is no longer any use. So, these descendants of the swamp dwellers quickly lost their
248

ability for intestinal respiration. The embryonically developing swim bladder, however, is normally preserved, and even today, practically all bony fishes are equipped with a swim bladder (see page 114).

Perhaps still more practical and possibly even older is the method adopted by several catfishes, which combines feeding and breathing (oxygen need) by scraping living algae from plants and stones with a specially-equipped mouth. The algae contain a reasonable amount of pure oxygen, which finds its way directly into the fish's intestine where it is used immediately. If circumstances in an aquarium become unacceptable for most fishes, and even if some die, there is no reason to be alarmed in respect to the intestinal breathers. They come up to the surface at regular intervals to gulp air, unless they are prevented, in which case, unfortunately, they drown. These fishes are so thoroughly adapted to the direct use of atmospheric air that they are incapable of otherwise supplying their need, even in oxygen-rich water. It does sound strange that this type of fish can actually drown.

Practically the same thing applies to the lungfishes, representatives of a very old group, which possess true lungs. They are fishes, but at the same time they belong to a group from which the very first amphibians developed, and thus were a preliminary step in the development of land animals, the higher vertebrates. It is, of course, not true that fishes developed lungs specifically to forward an ambition to migrate to the land, but it is likely that fishes equipped with lungs did pioneer the way from water to land without consciously being aware of it. Today, too, groups of fishes are known that are so independent of the water that they go out on land to hunt for insects and worms. How about the larvae of these fishes with lungs and intestinal-organs of respiration— how do they get along? All fish larvae are primarily equipped with gills, which are developed more and more as the fish concerned belongs to a group of a higher order. Among the most primitive varieties, shortly after birth, the complete exchange of gases by means of the gills disappears entirely. The gills change, as the type of specimen requires, into lung- or intestinal-breathing equipment (which in some cases is supplementary). From this it can be concluded, among other things, that "ordinary," gill-breathing fishes—the less primitive species, that is—are to be considered, in the light of evolution, as creatures that have retained the breathing habits of youth (a so-called neotenic development of the respiratory apparatus).

Very closely connected with respiration are the general procedures of breeding—that is, the care bestowed on the progeny. Fishes capable of living in an unsatisfactory environment (in water that is oxygen-poor, dirty, and often polluted with the products of decomposition) always wait for a conducive period before devoting themselves to reproduction.

Therefore, we come across various species of catfishes in Surinam that continue to live under the most unsatisfactory circumstances by means of intestinal respiration. In the dry season, these fishes walk on dry land, migrating from practically dried-up puddles to damper territory, which is usually only another dried-out puddle having slightly more water in it.

Note, however, that as soon as the rainy season sets in, these fishes prepare to breed. For this, they build a nest on the surface, made up of all kinds of little bits of water plants and bank grasses. The male then blows a great number of air bubbles under the nest, each of which has a thin skin of sticky saliva so that the bubbles will not spatter off from each other. These nests made of plant pieces and air bubbles sometimes measure more than 30 cm (12 inches) across and 10 cm (4 inches) high. Mating takes place under the nest, during which a large number of eggs issue from the female and are fertilized by the male. Both parents gather up the eggs in their mouths and spit them out into the nest. The larvae that emerge from the eggs after a few days find, in the "fresh" rain water of the rainy season, plenty of oxygen to support their larval gill-breathing. Very soon, however, the intestinal-breathing equipment develops and they are no longer dependent on a satisfactory environment, insofar as providing themselves with oxygen is concerned.

The Transportation of Tropical Aquarium Fishes

Sometimes, somewhat large sums of money were paid for a pair of small, tropical fishes. Not only was the rarity of such fishes responsible for these exorbitant prices, but the real culprit was the high cost of transportation from the place of origin to the shop of the small dealer. How often it happened that out of a shipment of hundreds of fish, a mere dozen were delivered alive! Often, not a single fish survived the long boat journey. Disease and improper care were the causes in the beginning, and the Red Sea, where extremely high temperatures were encountered, became the burial place of hundreds of beautiful, exotic fish. Not a single firm was willing to insure against the risks of transportation, so that the selling price of the few specimens surviving the voyage had to cover the damages incurred.

Then, shipping was gradually placed in experienced hands and, with the help of air pumps and chemicals, such success was achieved on the voyages that, finally, as much as 30 per cent of the shipment arrived safely.

The principal cause of the great loss heretofore suffered began in the improper or inexperienced handling of the fish as they were caught in their natural surroundings. The fishermen knew nothing about the fish they caught and often dumped them all together into large cans without giving a thought to the possibility that one species might devour another. Transporting large and small fishes together resulted in serious impairment of the resistance the fishes had possessed in their country of origin. Also, as a result of loading the cargo on board as quickly as possible and getting it on its way in a hurry, many fishes died. Finally, taught by experience and loss, the shippers developed a method of transportation which still operates today without great losses.

The shipping of aquarium fishes from the catch location to the dealers begins with the fishermen. The fishermen are so instructed that they possess a fairly accurate knowledge of the different kinds of fish they are catching. The species are roughly sorted out on the spot and packed in double-walled fish tanks, which prevent too-rapid temperature changes during the trip from the catch location to the reception stages. From these reception stages in the wilderness, the fish are taken to special fish ponds or large, concrete tanks belonging to the exporter, where they have an opportunity to adapt themselves and to recondition themselves from possible damage incurred in transport so far. After remaining a few weeks in these quarantine tanks, the fish are ready for shipment and orders can be processed. Going by size, a few dozen specimens of a given species are put together in a plastic bag with only a small quantity of water. Before the bags are closed, the air in them is replaced with pure oxygen. The bag is then closed air- and water-tight with an elastic band. A number of these bags are packed in boxes made from or lined with polystyrene, and, in a few days, the shipment goes by air to the importer.

The great advantage of this method is that, despite the rather high cost of air freight, the business becomes considerably more lucrative. In the first place, only a very little water is necessary, which naturally keeps down the weight and allows relatively lower transportation costs. In the second place, only a short period of time is required for the entire shipping procedure, so that the fish no longer have to undergo months or weeks of unsatisfactory conditions. The small amount of water with pure oxygen above it prevents the fish from dying from lack of oxygen, while the polluting gases from the exhaled breath (carbon dioxide) are absorbed by the chemicals dissolved in the water.

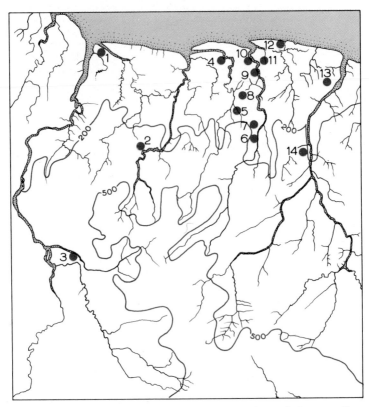

Illus. 6-10. Survey map of Surinam, on which are indicated the sampling places of popular aquarium fish of the last few years: 1. Nickerie region. 2. Langasula on the Coppename. 3. Airstrip, catch region between the Coeroeni and the Lucie rivers. 4. Groningen. 5. Guiana Gold Placer. 6. Cable Station. 7. Browns Road. 8. Zanderij Airport. 9. Paranam. 10. Paramaribo, in the vicinity of where many well known species have been caught. 11. Laarwijk. 12. Wiawia marshes. 13. Albina. 14. Gran Creek, in the Marowijne (Maroni River) region. Surinam is bounded on the west by the Courantyne River, the border with Guyana. In the east, the border with French Guiana is formed by the Marowijne (Maroni River). In the south, the border with Brazil runs over the Tumucumaque mountain range. On the map are also given the course of the 200-metre (720-foot) line, so important to fresh-water fish, which forms the boundary between the marshy savannah and the real Guiana Highlands, and is also the region of large waterfalls and rapids. The 500-metre (1,800-foot) line of a few mountain ranges on the plateau is also shown.

Fishing Expeditions and Exploring the Land

The aquarium trade is continually trying to open up new territories where perhaps unknown and attractive new fishes may be found. How such exploration is usually carried out can be learned by reading the following about an expedition by Mr. H. P. Pijpers of Paramaribo to the southern part of Surinam. The trip was undertaken from the Coeroeni region, where an airstrip had been established in 1959.

This expedition's plan was to find suitable terrain in the drainage basin of the Sipaliwini River and the Paru savannah for establishing a new airstrip for future fish explorations. The group set out on January 27, 1961, in five Guianese dugout canoes. Two days later, after traversing first a large waterfall and rapids and then another quieter waterfall, the men stopped for the night. The first catch was made and a pot was filled with "anjoemara" *(Hoplias malabaricus* and *H. macrophthalmus,* of the family Erythrinidae).

The journey continued with other difficulties to overcome: hazardous rocks, dangerous rapids, tangled plant growth, heavy rains. Along the way, however, the men did catch and preserve fish species for later

Illus. 6-11. The ghost pond from Pijpers' report (see page 255), the place where *Hyphessobrycon georgettae* was found.

253

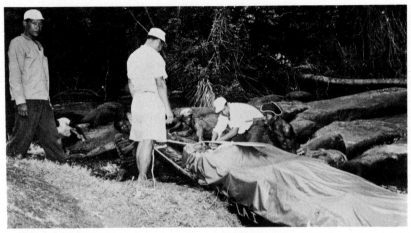

Illus. 6-12. Most of the time is naturally spent conquering all kinds of obstacles in the river. Small rapids make it necessary to partially unpack and to carry the dugouts over the rocks.

scientific research. In fact, by the time they were nearing their destination about a week later, some truly splendid specimens had been caught.

Finally, the expedition reached the first savannah, which turned out to be totally unsuitable for an airstrip—enormous boulders were scattered throughout. They continued on to the second savannah which seemed, at first, more suitable for the airstrip.

Meanwhile, Mr. Pijpers began extensive exploration for unknown species of fish. Taking a dip net and several companions, he set off to discover a new fish, which indeed he did—later named *Hyphessobrycon georgettae*.

The first day, Pijpers collected at least 500 specimens of a basically orange-red fish, although some were lighter than others. It seemed to have the pool all to itself, for although he found it everywhere, even in open stretches, he found no other species with it.

As the second savannah also turned out not suitable for the airstrip, the group moved on. Pijpers carefully put his fish into empty petroleum containers to transport them back to Paramaribo. Before leaving, however, he caught several hundred more fish and photographed the accompanying plant life. This time, however, Pijpers also caught several other species along with his red one, especially in the middle of the pool, in deeper water, where the temperature range was 23–24 °C (73–75 °F).

At the location where the airstrip was finally constructed, an isolated fish pool was found, where Mr. Pijpers also caught some fishes. While the airstrip was being constructed, he was still busy catching fishes— this time from the Sipaliwini itself. Following is the review of the fish Pijpers caught, which gives a good idea of the procedure involved with an interesting collection. This list was drawn up by Pijpers on the basis of questions posed by the author.

REVIEW OF FISH CAUGHT

1. Correct or supposed name: No. 1 unknown, No. 2 *Hemigrammus?* No. 3 *Copeina arnoldi?* (*Copella arnoldi*)
2. Date and time of catch: Feb. 12, 1961, at 4:00 p.m.
3. Catch location: Airstrip, Sipaliwini (see photo biotope)
4. Geographical location: Known, see map
5. Upper or lower river: Ghost pond in midst of jungle without connection with creek or river
6. Strong or weak current: Stagnant

Illus. 6-13. Rapids are the typical habitat of many fishes, especially catfishes. However remarkable it may seem, they are very good swimmers, although only for a short distance at a time. Many species can suck themselves fast to a rock with the help of their suction-cup mouth. The rocks in these rapids, where the water is always rich in oxygen, are generally heavily covered with algae, and it is these algae that form the principal food of numerous fishes. This is Four-Brothers Creek in the Sipali River region, Surinam.

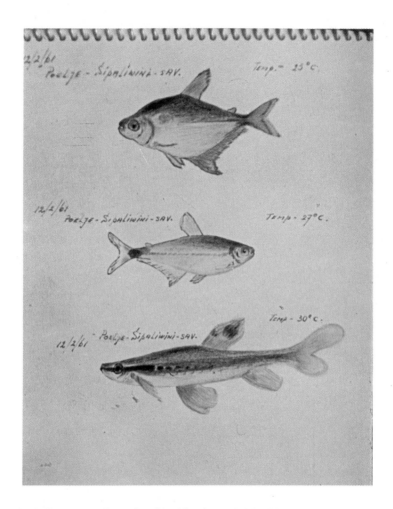

Illus. 6-14. Two pages from the sketchbook carried by Pijpers, which was of great value in working out the collected scientific material. Sketches with natural coloration of just-caught fish can be of inestimable value in later research.

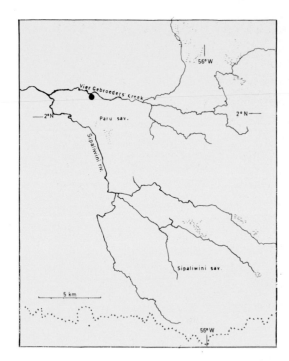

Illus. 6-15. Map of the southwestern part of Surinam, the region explored by the expedition, showing the Paru savannah, Sipaliwini savannah and indicating (•) the type locality of *Hyphessobrycon georgettae.*

7. Open water: For all three species, yes
8. In middle or near shore: 1. Middle deeper, 2. middle under surface, 3. all at the edges
9. Jungle creek, marsh, savannah: Spring pond? Not sure, see report
10. Clear or turbid: Clear
11. Ebb or flow: —
12. Rainy or dry season: Dry season
13. Temperature, bottom conditions: 1. 25 °C, 2. 27 °C, 3. 30 °C (1. 77 °F, 2. 81 °F, 3. 86 °F)
14. Altitude above sea level: About 250 m (900 feet)
15. School or surface fish: All three in schools
16. Is one more sporadic: All three numerous
17. Together with what: *Hoplias malabaricus?* (see preserved material)
18. Young specimens, breeding place: Not observed
19. Which plants, aquarium plants: Wild rice, many species of *Myriophyllum*, many grasses

20. What food for fish: Flies, dragon-flies, probably many other insects
21. What is pH, water coloration, taste, smell: Deep black, bad rain water? Light, marshy smell
22. Depth: In middle, 1 metre ($39\frac{1}{4}$ inches)
23. How fish was caught: Drag net, dip net, cast net
24. How transported: In munition drums, in plastic bags by air to Paramaribo
25. Bank vegetation: Saw grass, wild rice, and high forest
26. Environs dangerous?: 1 small alligator seen, no boa constrictors, many wasps and frogs
27. For further data, see photographs and report.

NOTE: This form is for three kinds of fish.

HPP Made up at Brownsweg, 4/6/1961

Collected by: Pijpers, H. P.

(Signed) H. P. Pijpers

Such well documented material, which is really not ordinary, gets immediate attention as soon as it arrives at an aquarium or ichthyological laboratory. Pijpers' material was sorted out by the author of this book the very first day, preservation taken care of (in fresh alcohol), and all characins (except for a few duplicates) were sent to Dr. Géry (France), who has been specializing for years in this group of fish. The remaining material was taken in hand by the author. The following correspondence concerning the *Hyphessobrycon* species which were found on the journey is also quite interesting.

Letter to Dr. Géry

Amsterdam, 17 April, 1961

Dear Jacques:

I have just received from Pijpers a fine shipment of fishes from the Sipaliwini region. The shipment is accompanied by beautiful black-and-white and color photographs and numerous interesting ecological data. I have sorted out the characins for you, which I am sending in the same mail with this letter. I call your attention principally to the little, red *Hyphessobrycon*, which bears promise of being something new. According to Pijpers, they do not grow any bigger. I have not spent much time looking over the other characins, but I guess there are quite a few new things among them.

I hope you can find time to look into this shipment with some priority and let me know if a second visit to this region should prove rewarding. Pijpers (and myself too, naturally), are very anxious to hear what name should apply to the little, red *Hyphessobrycon*.

I am sending five samples from different localities; the data are on the packing list under the respective, specified numbers. Presently, I am quite occupied in working out the ecological data accumulated some time ago by Van der Kamp, and more recently by Pijpers.

There is still a lot to be done on this Surinam material.

Cordially, JJH

Letter from Dr. Géry

Strasbourg, 20 April, 1961

Dear J.J.:

Many thanks for your interesting letter of the 17th, last. The package with the samples has not yet arrived. Thus, I cannot say anything definite about the reddish tetra, but suppose that it may be *Megalamphodus roseus*, which I described in my article, "New *Cheirodontinae* from French Guiana." Unfortunately, I could not bring them to Europe alive.

. . . etc.

Best wishes, Jacques

Letter from Dr. Géry

Strasbourg, 23 April, 1961

Dear J.J.:

Pijpers made an unusually interesting catch in the Paru savannah and I was quite excited to lay eyes on a number of varieties I had never seen before. First of all, my apologies for my supposition that the red *Hyphessobrycon* could be *Megalamphodus roseus*. It has the same red color, but I agree with you that it is indeed a *Hyphessobrycon*, and an entirely new species, as well.

Below is a tentative list of the species collected by Pijpers in the Sipaliwini region:

Sample 1. Paru, 4 *Curimatopsis* sp. In this genus, there is always the chance of finding something special. I will study them more closely, together with my own material.

Sample 2. Sipaliwini, 1 from the *Hemiodus microlepis* group. I think that this is a new form or species as well, with a squamation unlike that of *argenteus* and *microlepis*.

Plate 6-3. One of the magnificent characins, a real acquisition for the hobby, photographed later in a special aquarium. Géry described it later as *Poptella* sp.

Sample 3. Sipaliwini, 2 *Parodon guyanensis* Géry, new for Surinam, and 4 *Ephippicharax* (= *Poptella?*).

Samples 4 and 5. Sipaliwini, 4 and 1 *Brachychalcinus (guianensis?)*. Much finer material than that from the Lucie River that you sent some time ago. I think that it deserves to be illustrated (Boeseman surely gave none?).

Sample 6. 5 young *Mylinae* (spotted) + 7 larvae??. Sipaliwini. This sample is very interesting because they have the sex characteristic of *Utiarichthys* (fewer scales in front of the ventrals than in *Myleus*). In any case, it is something new for Surinam, if they are not young of the Pacu.

Sample 7. 3 *Moenkhausia lepidura* group, Sipaliwini, very interesting material for revision of the *lepidura* group. If the forms are sympatric[1], it is a new species.

Sample 8. 15 *Moenkhausia* new species, Sipaliwini. I believe this is the species on which I have an article lying about for the past year, under the new name *Moenkhausia georgetti*. It is closely related to *shideleri*.

[1] From the same distribution area.

261

Sample 9. 12 *Astyanax*, Sipaliwini, two species, to be determined.

Sample 10. 1 *Hemigrammus*, closely related to *ocellifer*, Paru savannah. It seems strange, since *ocellifer* is a coastal form.

Sample 11. 2 *Hemigrammus*, Paru savannah, maybe new, too.

Sample 12. Young *Hyphessobrycon bentosi* group. Sipaliwini. These lovely little tetras with pseudotympanum and red fins are probably the real *rosaceus*.

Sample 13. *Hyphessobrycon* sp. nov., *callistus* group. Paru savannah. This is undoubtedly Pijpers' greatest discovery. A small species, the males having many tiny hooks on the anal fin. The pink coloration is most prominent on the posterior of the body. Contrary to all other species of the *callistus* complex, which have 26 to 28 anal fin rays (also *Megalamphodus*, etc.), there are only 19 to 21 rays here.

I would like to ask you to reserve two or three pages in your Bulletin of Aquatic Biology for the official description, solely for the last species. I hope to send you the article within the next few weeks. Any further information concerning the biotope and the exact locality (I take it that the Paru savannah has some relationship to the upper reaches of the Tapanahony) will be welcome. What do you think of the name—I hesitate between *paruensis*, *pijpersi* and *georgetti*[2] (after my wife).

With our best regards,
Georgie and Jacques

Dr. Géry's article on *Hyphessobrycon georgettae*, as the red fish was finally called, appeared in "Notes on the Ichthyology of Surinam and other Guianas. 7. *Hyphessobrycon georgettae* sp. nov., a dwarf species from southern Surinam."

---

[2] This incorrect gender was later corrected by the author to *georgettae*.

7. GENERAL AQUARIUM CARE

Proper care and maintenance of an aquarium are dependent upon many factors, not the least of which is your awareness of what is required for your fishes. Spending a lot of money certainly is not necessary for the full enjoyment of beautiful and interesting fish; spending time and thought are much more valuable. Indeed, there is no better teacher than experience, although logical thinking can provide satisfactory answers to many questions. You should, in fact, immerse yourself in many facets of the hobby, because your knowledge of how to set up the aquarium is as important as your knowledge of the fishes themselves.

The purpose of this section is to outline generally some of the basic requirements for setting up a well functioning and decorative aquarium for the fishes that you choose as your pets. More specific information about how to care for the various species is outlined in Part II under the descriptions of the individual species.

The Tank

It is taken for granted that you will purchase a tank from a shop specializing in aquarium supplies, or obtain one from a friend or acquaintance. Be certain, of course, to choose a tank which, in dimensions and proportions, is suitable for the place in which you plan to keep it.

There are a great variety of ready-made tanks available, but, if necessary, you can have a tank made to order. The rule to go by, however, is to try to have a water-surface area that is in keeping with the water volume. A very high, narrow tank is undesirable; it should preferably be broader than high. The length of the tank is unimportant in this regard.

Double strength crystal glass, which is higher quality and stronger than ordinary window glass, is suitable for most aquariums up to 35 cm (14 inches) in height. Plate glass 6 mm ($\frac{1}{4}$ inch) thick is suitable for most aquariums 40–45 cm (16–18 inches) in height. From 45–55 cm (18–22 inches), 10-mm ($\frac{3}{8}$-inch) plate glass is recommended, and from 55–75 cm (22–30 inches) in height, 12-mm ($\frac{1}{2}$-inch) plate glass should be used. Exceptionally long tanks should be braced by a cross-bar in the middle at the top.

Many tanks now are either all glass or have stainless steel, rust-proof frames. If your tank has an angle-iron frame, be sure that the frame is

Illus. 7-1. Modern aquariums usually have an external metal frame. The panes are set into a framework of angle iron and are made water-tight by means of a special aquarium cement (a kind of putty that is water-resistant). The advantage of these aquariums is that the panes are absolutely flat and do not distort as the all-glass aquariums do. Moreover, the possible dimensions of the framework aquariums are limitless. The thickness of the glass is dependent on the size (height) of the aquarium.

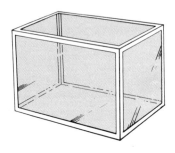

sturdy and not rusty; otherwise, scour it clean and paint it with red lead. Make sure, too, that the bottom has no holes or breaks in it and is not rusty. If the bottom is faulty, in some cases you can fix it by installing a new bottom plate—or a plate of glass—sealing it firmly with aquarium lute (cement) or silicone rubber sealant. The panes must be whole, of course, and still have some soft cement holding them in the frame (you should be able to stick a pin into the cement easily). In case of doubt, remove the panes and re-set them in the frame with fresh cement.

First cement in the largest panes in the front and back and then the smaller side panes. The thickness of the layer of cement you use depends on the size of the aquarium, but the minimum thickness should be 3–10 mm ($\frac{1}{8}$–$\frac{3}{8}$ inch), as considerable pressure is exerted by the water contents.

Fill the tank completely with water, so that the fresh cement squeezes down. If you have just set the glass in place, the tank may start to leak a little. However, this leakage will soon stop, provided that the cement is not too hard. In any case, always fill the tank in the garden or on a balcony or porch. If the tank stands a few days—without leaking—with this pressure from its water contents, then bring it indoors to begin the actual setting-up.

Location and Exposure to Light

The location of the tank is extremely important, especially if it is exposed to daylight, for if it is, care must be taken that light from the south or east does not enter the frontal pane. The usual placement is in a corner, with the aquarium generally set up against the wall, at an angle of 90° to the windows.

If so suitable a light angle is not possible, you can successfully make use of artificial light, wholly or partially, whether it is daytime or nighttime. This is often more convenient and certainly simpler, because you have complete control of the angle of the light, which is certainly not the case with daylight. Some experimenting in this regard is necessary to achieve the needed results.

Placement of the source of illumination over the aquarium calls for a great deal of attention. Today, fluorescent tubes in a metal reflector are most often used. This is certainly a good, usable source of illumination, but it can be substituted for by several incandescent light

265

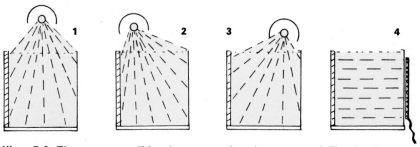

Illus. 7-2. These are possible placements for the source of illumination over the aquarium.

bulbs. If you place a light in the middle and above the aquarium (see 1 in Illus. 7–2), or over the rear area (2), the fish swimming at the back of the tank will be well lighted, but in all other parts of the tank, they will show up as silhouettes. Placement of fluorescent lighting above and in front of the tank is more suitable (3). In certain cases, such as an observational or photographic tank, lighting must come through the frontal pane (4), with tube lights paralleling the vertical edges of the frontal pane. The light then falls only upon that side of the fish which is observed through the frontal pane. However, such lighting is not so pleasant for the fish, who are used to the light coming from above. Also, the fish have a tendency to turn head-on towards the light, or the other way around, and thus avoid exposing their flanks to the light.

Setting Up the Aquarium

Sand

As soon as you are ready to begin putting the aquarium in order, first gather the materials before you empty the tank and bring it inside. For making a bottom soil, you need, first of all, some sand. Calculate the quantity by multiplying the length of the tank by the width (in cm) by 5, then divide by 1,000. This formula gives the number of litres of sand required. To convert litres to gallons, multiply by 0.2642.

If you want a light soil rich in food elements, mix a part of the sand with leaf mould or peat moss. (The peat moss must first stand a few days in water; the part that settles to the bottom is ready for use and will not float.) If you use nothing but sand, it must be well washed—in buckets, under running water until no more dirt or foam comes to the surface—and spread out on the bottom of the tank in a layer running from 3–6 cm ($1\frac{3}{16}$–$2\frac{3}{8}$ inches) thick, sloping upwards from front to back. If you decide to mix the sand with leaf mould or peat moss, divide the washed sand into two equal parts and lay the bottom soil down in two layers. The bottommost layer is composed of sand mixed with leaf mould or peat moss, and on top of it is a layer of just sand.

Note, however, that using soil other than sand is not recommended for the beginner or inexperienced aquarist because of potential water pollution.

While the bottom is still soaking wet, you can begin immediately to fill the tank with water.

Water for the Aquarium

The composition of the aquarium water is important. Rain water is best, but it is simplest to use ordinary tap water. The latter is all right so long as there are not too many minerals and other things dissolved in it that might be harmful to the fish. Also, the use of tap water that issues from the faucet under high pressure can result in danger from gas embolism; so, first let the water stand in the tank or in an accessory vessel before letting the fish come in contact with it. This is called "ageing the water."

To avoid any problems, however, the use of rain water is exemplary, so long as it is collected in a certain way. Rain water that has flowed off a tin roof can have zinc dissolved in it, while other rain water, falling in an industrial district, can pick up poisonous impurities. So, wait for a good rain shower; after 10 minutes, collect the rain in a tent cloth or other non-metallic receptacle. Then, filter the water to remove suspended particles.

pH and DH

The acidity (pH) and hardness (DH) of the aquarium water are still other factors to consider in setting up your tank. The pH expresses both acidity and alkalinity, usually on a scale of 0 to 14, on which 7 represents the value for pure water at 25 °C (77 °F), or neutrality. Values less than 7 represent increasing acidity (3.1 for vinegar, 2.3 for lemon juice). Values greater than 7 represent increasing alkalinity.

Most fishes require neutral or slightly acid water. Where the pH of the water for a certain species is of particular importance, it is mentioned as part of the description of that species in Part II.

The hardness is an indication of the presence of calcium and magnesium salts in the water. A standard measure of water hardness is the soap test. The harder the water, the more soap is required to form a lather when soap and the water are shaken up.

Most fishes require soft water—that is, water whose hardness measure is no more than 5 to 10 degrees. You can purchase substances to soften your water, if necessary. Test kits are available to determine both pH and DH.

Filling the Tank

The best way to fill the tank is to put a bucket of water on a board supported by the edges of the tank (see Illus. 7–3) and to let the water run into the tank through a rubber siphon tube about 1 cm ($\frac{3}{8}$ inch) in diameter. In order to avoid stirring up the bottom soil and sand, insert a piece of glass or metal tubing bent into a half circle into the bottom end of the rubber tube, and then clamp the rubber siphon tube with a compression clamp until only a thin stream of water is slowly emitted. If the water still runs out too fast, turn a dish upside-down under the stream to help the first depth of water to run in without turning the whole tank into a mud puddle. The more quietly this is done, the better.

When, after some time, there is a 5-cm (2-inch) depth of water in the tank, the bottom soil at the back of the tank should be entirely

268

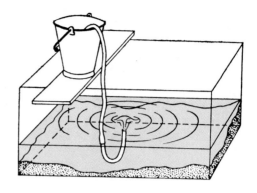

Illus. 7-3. Here is a simple method for filling the aquarium with water, without a drop spilling and without the bottom soil being stirred up by the water streaming in. At the same time, you can bring the water to the desired temperature by mixing cold water with hot. Do not hang an electric heating element in the water until at least half of it will be submerged.

under water. Stop for a while to give all the air trapped in the bottom soil a chance to rise out of it.

Acclimating Fish to Fresh Water

If you have primary or secondary fresh-water fish (see page 61) from salty or brackish water, you will have to make some adjustments. The correct procedure for acclimating fish from salty or brackish water to fresh water is through gradual replacement of the original water, removing perhaps 10 per cent at a time and replacing it with fresh. Make these changes on alternate days until the water is completely fresh. It is advisable to keep at least a couple of teaspoons of sea salt per gallon in water where brackish-water species are kept. Also, with some species, a replacement rate of 5 per cent would probably be advisable, although it is more time consuming.

Temperature and Heating

Today, the species which are being kept in amateur tanks are almost exclusively denizens of the tropics and sub-tropics. It goes without saying that a tank for such fish requires a rather constant water temperature of about 20–25 °C (68–77 °F). In houses with central heating, where the temperature is kept throughout the day at about 22 °C (about 70 °F), sometimes, such as when only sub-tropical fish are kept, no extra heating element is necessary. This temperature, however, is always slightly too low for tropical fish, and additional heating is desirable. In houses where the temperature is allowed to drop considerably at night, additional heating is necessary all year round.

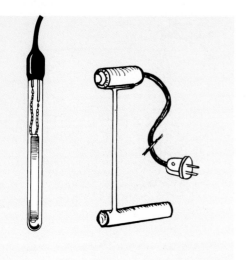

Illus. 7-4. The modern immersion-heating element for heating aquariums is not only nice to have but is also handy and safe. Moreover, it is far easier to regulate than other, non-electric heating devices. The simplest type is a plain, glowing heating element enclosed in a (glass) tube filled with fine sand (left). More satisfactory are the heating elements enclosed in metal tubing (right), which usually have a switch for a fixed capacity. A regulating screw that can be set and adjusted to any desired temperature makes this device equally useful for large or small tanks.

Heating Devices

The most common method in use today for heating aquariums is an electric heating element. Old-fashioned stove-oil or kerosene heaters, as well as gas burners, should not be so much as brought into the house if electricity is available. It is preferable—and less expensive—to pay the somewhat higher cost of electric heating than to suffer the misfortunes that may accompany the use of oil or gas. (See Illus. 7–4). The modern, electrical heating devices available today are perfectly safe.

The principle of aquarium heating is this: A special kind of conducting wire having great resistance to the flow of current is electrified and the electrical energy is given off as heat. The wire itself gets red hot (radiant heat). In the electrical immersion heater, either the heating coil is enclosed in a glass tube filled with insulating material, usually fine sand, or the immersion part possesses an element like that in an electric laundry iron. In other words, current is conducted through a medium having necessary resistance, so that heat is generated.

These modern heating elements give off heat to the water in which they are immersed and thus bring it up to the temperature required. To regulate the temperature, use an automatic regulator or thermostat which will cut the electricity off as soon as the desired temperature is reached.

270

Do not assume that a thermostat that works to an accuracy of 1/10 of a degree (or even more accurately) is any better than a coarser one adjusted to one degree. In the first place, it is undesirable for the thermostat to switch on and off every few minutes, and it is especially unnecessary to keep the temperature for the fish at so constant a level. This never happens in nature. A temporary (nightly) cooling-off of several degrees is not only completely normal, but often desirable as well.

The electrical apparatus—the heating element as well as the thermal switches—*must* be enclosed in a completely water-tight covering.

Install the heating device so that it is out of sight but still easily reached, preferably along one side of the tank, somewhat screened by water plants.

Auxiliary Equipment

In addition to the heating device, "auxiliary equipment" plays a constantly important rôle in the maintenance of your aquarium. By

Illus. 7-5. Circulation of the water is important in maintaining a certain balance between useful and non-useful materials in the tank and a correct build-up and removal of certain materials. This is done simply with a porous little brick (stone) attached to the air pump, pumping air into the water. The air rises in a series of bubbles, thus bringing about circulation of the water. With the help of a compression clamp on the air tube, the quantity of air bubbles can be regulated, thus the water circulation as well.

auxiliary equipment is meant the pump, which, by aerating the water, increases the tank's fish capacity; the filter, which helps keep the water clean by filtering out dirt; thermometers; glass pane scrapers; plant tongs; and various other small aids. A great variety of equipment is available on the market, some very handsome, many often very well thought out, but sometimes also completely worthless. Consider yourself warned.

Pump

In addition to the simple system of aerating an aquarium with the aid of an air stone (a cylinder of porous material with a stem to which the air line is attached) and a column of air bubbles (by means of which circulation of water does indeed take place and does bring oxygen down to the bottom of the tank), another system is coming more and

Illus. 7-6. The filter in its simplest form (a) consists of a round tank with a perforated bottom, hanging inside the aquarium, into which the dirty aquarium water is pumped. From the air pump is an air tube that is connected to a narrow tube (1) and goes through the vertical tube (2) by means of which the dirty water is lifted. The water then goes through (3) into the little tank (4). This tank is filled with a mass of filtering material that traps the suspended impurities, while the water returns to the aquarium through the holes (5) in the bottom of the little tank.
Better working and invisible outside (behind) the aquarium is the outside filter (b), consisting of a glass tank filled with layers of filter material (from top to bottom, usually glass wool wadding, active charcoal, and perhaps coarse sand or gravel). The dirty aquarium water enters through the small tube (2) via the opening (1) to the filter (3). The water sinks through the filtering layers and enters the wide tube where it is pushed up at (4) via (5) to the aquarium by the (at 6) introduction of air pressure from the pump.

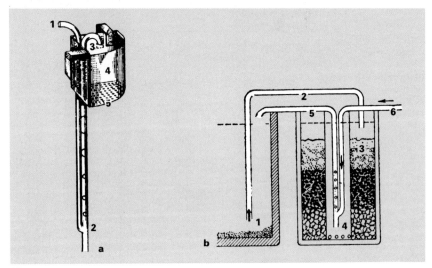

more into use. The aquarium water is pumped from the bottom and is allowed to flow back into the opposite corner of the aquarium. The result is the same, the effect less disturbing.

In the first place, the pump forces air through the water, supposedly to give off oxygen to the water. However, what happens is that an excess of carbon dioxide is prevented from accumulating while circulation in the aquarium brings the oxygen-poor/carbon dioxide-rich water from the bottom to the surface where it comes in contact with the outside air, so that an exchange of gases becomes possible. A more widespread use of the air stream supplied by the aquarium pump has turned it into a practically indispensable apparatus.

There are many kinds of pumps and it would lead too far afield to attempt to discuss them in detail here. There are three main types, the oldest of which worked by water pressure and is no longer in use. The second type is an ordinary piston pump, and the third, the diaphragm pump. This last works with an electro-magnet that moves quickly up and down behind a rubber plate (diaphragm) and, by means of check valves, produces a stream of air. It is, however, seldom very powerful and after some time most make an unpleasant humming noise. The old, trustworthy piston pump, however, is still in constant use and is operated by means of an electric motor.

Always take care that the pump itself is located at a higher level than the highest water depth in the aquarium. As soon as the pump stops, the temperature in the air tube drops, causing water to be sucked out of the aquarium. If the pump is located too low, a siphon is created which can tap off a considerable amount of water from the tank, through the air tube, and a small flood results.

Air-line filters containing activated carbon can be installed between the pump and the aquarium in order to avoid introducing polluted air into the aquarium (household air saturated with smoke and other smells). You can also provide the pump with an air-inlet from the outdoor air.

Filter

Building still further on this system, include a filter installation in the circulation tubes, so that the up-pumped water flows back into the tank as clean water—that is, water that has been rid of its suspended dirt and has, when necessary, been biologically cleaned.

The air-pressure principle for filters means that by introducing air underneath into a submerged tube, you can lift the water up with

273

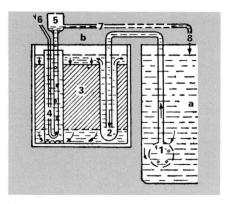

Illus. 7-7. A very efficient and all-purpose water filtering device is simple to make from a combination of the systems that have already been discussed. The aquarium (a) is provided with a filter tank (b) in which there are two tubes in addition to the mass of filtering material. The aquarium water comes into the first tube (2) by way of the perforated ball (1), leading to the filter. This tube (2) is closed at the bottom so that the only way out for the water is to overflow at the top. In addition to being a settling tank for suspended dirt, this tube also avoids the temporary lowering of the water level in the aquarium which causes the filter to run dry. This system is especially recommended for breeding tanks. The overflowing water in the first filter tube runs through the filter mass (3) into a space provided with a perforated bulkhead and can rise up in the second wide tube. Here it is pushed on up in the usual way by air pressure (via 6 and 4) to an overflow vessel (5). From here, the clean water flows back into the aquarium.

the rising air bubbles. However, it is important that the cross-section of the tube is not too large, because if it is, the air will go through without bringing any water up with it.

It is possible in this way to raise the water quite a distance above the water surface of the aquarium. During and just after this raising, the water comes into close contact with the air, and enables it to pick up oxygen. This has made this system the most used method of combined filtration and oxygenation.

There are two different types of filters—the inside filters and the outside filters. The outside filters were used first in the filtering of aquarium water. The level of water in both the aquarium and the filter are the same; by pumping water out of the filter, the water flows from the aquarium into the filter. Depending on the way the water passes through the filter, it is completely or partially purified. In the filter, a layer of glass wool wadding or synthetic fibre takes up the largest bits of dirt. Under that is a layer of active charcoal. This

274

charcoal provides an enormous surface by its porosity; here chemical and biological processes can transform harmful materials dissolved in the water into harmless and useful compounds. A condition for a good, biological cleansing is a uniform, not-too-fast flow of the water through the filter mass.

Although it is possible to pump the aquarium water to the filter, this is discouraged, because the stopping-up of the return flow or of the filter mass may cause the filter to overflow. In other words, pump water out of the filter but never out of the aquarium.

Inside filters are similar in principle to the outside filters just described and exist more for aesthetic reasons than for increased effectiveness. There are several forms of inside filters. See Illus. 7–6 for a detailed description of the two types of filters.

A very old filter system that focusses upon the biological cleansing of the water in the bottom soil (a system that most of the water-pipe purification installations come close to) is the bottom filter. At first, it was only a loose bottom piece, which was installed about 1 cm ($\frac{3}{8}$ inch) above the bottom of the aquarium. It was perforated with many tiny holes and upon it was placed the soil. Once the aquarium was set up, if water was pumped out of the double bottom, the aquarium water on top was forced to find a way through the soil layer, towards this open space. In practice, this system is quite satisfactory and it is sometimes used in a perfected form, with sections filled with active charcoal, or even the entire space filled with charcoal.

Other Useful Equipment

A bit of auxiliary equipment that is certainly necessary in the tropical aquarium is the thermometer. You do not need either a fever thermometer, nor an expensive mercury thermometer, but a quite simple alcohol thermometer which you can buy inexpensively in pet shops. In a larger tank, you may place two thermometers, one close to the bottom and the other at the surface, at least 20 cm (8 inches) from the tank heater. (In a tank with circulating water—that is, water moved by fish, filters or air stones—however, more than one thermometer is usually unnecessary as the moving water will become reasonably uniform in temperature.) A third thermometer can be helpful placed close to the heater, but it is not really necessary. Install these thermometers preferably so that they are not eminently visible through the front pane of the tank, but can be read through the side panels. The red column of these alcohol thermometers is very easy to see.

This kind of thermometer is naturally not officially tested, but you can do this yourself by checking the thermometer against a thermometer you know to be accurate. Deviations can often be corrected by carefully tapping the bottom of the thermometer on a table top so that the paper scale of degrees shifts slightly. If this is unsuccessful, note if the deviation is a full degree or more. Mark this on the thermometer itself to remind you to compensate for every reading. The thermometers are attached to the glass wall with special suction cups, so that they can be easily removed. In the course of time, the thermometer will become overgrown with algae and from time to time you will have to clean off the side to read it.

Pane scrapers, for removing algae from the glass panes, are available in many forms in fish supply shops. You can, however, remove algae quite satisfactorily with a single-edged razor blade. Be careful, though, not to scratch the inside of the panes. In many cases, rubbing with a cloth on the inside of the pane will be sufficient to remove the algae (under water, of course, and not too wildly, for then the water will splash over the edge). The fish know how to take care of the scraped-off algae, so that usually you do not have to siphon off the bottom afterwards. Other scraping devices are made of pieces of hard rubber or plastic, so that it is impossible to scratch the glass, not even if you scrape the pane vigorously. Never use scouring powders or chemicals.

Other aquarium accessories, such as plant tongs, for setting out water plants, and plant scissors for removing excess or rotting parts, are more or less luxuries. Sometimes, however, they are quite practical. More useful is the so-called bell trap, a glass bulb-tube for the removal of fish from the tank. In addition, a number of dip nets in various sizes and widths of mesh are standard equipment for any aquarist.

Welcome additions, also, are several small, glass tanks for keeping live food in and a small aquarium to provide accommodations for sick fish or for specimens that have been somewhat damaged by being transported.

Water Plants

Many of the water plants available for the aquarium are actually forms of land and marsh plants; a less significant number belong to the families of true water plants. This must be thoroughly understood if you want to attempt to create a biological balance in an aquarium, although an actual biological balance, even in an aquarium of formidable dimensions, is a practical impossibility. The enormous number of factors that must play a rôle in nature cannot be duplicated or even approximated in a small, under-water world, shut off from free nature.

Even so, an aquarium without plants is hardly thinkable, unless it is set up especially for fish that live in plantless water in the wild, but that is highly exceptional. In the aquarium, plants provide a place where the fish can find shelter from enemies or from daylight that is too bright. In the mating season especially, many lay their eggs among the plants so that their emerging offspring find an environment alive with a multitude of microscopically small organisms, their food.

Aquarium Architecture

Whether yours is a large or small tank, the first step in planting in an aquarium is to work out a plan or design of what you intend to do. The factors that you must consider are the plants at your disposal, the place in which the aquarium is to be located, the angle of the incoming light, and which fish you intend to put into the aquarium. Next, put in some stones and perhaps make a couple of terraces.

Terrace Shaping

The construction of terraces is not much of an art in itself for the individual, experienced hobbyist, because it is determined, for the most part, by a few basic principles of aesthetics.

In constructing terraces, always start from the viewpoint that symmetry does not give the right effect, and neither do perfectly straight lines. By dividing up the bottom, you may raise two thirds of it in the form of terraces. The principal thing in the construction of terraces is to prevent the raised ground from sliding down. Place pieces of stone so that, when leaning slightly backward, they are more than half buried in the ground. You should not stop up small tanks with large blocks of broken stone, nor, on the contrary, should you use stones that are too small for larger tanks.

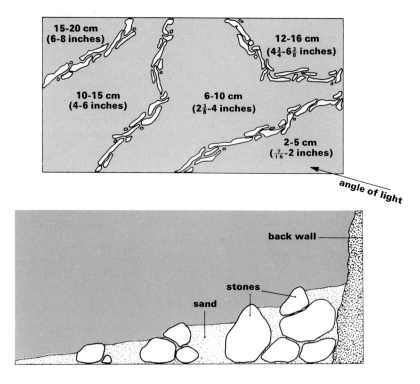

Illus. 7-8. Sketches for the construction of a terrace in the aquarium, connecting the back wall respectively with cemented down pieces of flagstone or an entire cement wall. In the first example, pieces of flagstone have also been used to hold down the ground, while the second example shows how a very solid terrace can be constructed with pieces of stone that are not too small. Even though the stones are dug out from under by the fish, no serious weakening takes place. In this case, the stones were first piled in place, and then the bottom soil (mainly sand) was poured in.

Setting the Plants

After your terraces are constructed, fill the aquarium with aged water (see page 267) to a depth of at least 15 cm (6 inches) above the bottom, and then carefully bring the plants into their appropriate positions according to the sketch you have made beforehand. In that way, the rooting plants will not uproot. You can bring in floating plants later on, when the water is filled to the proper level.

The rooting water plants must be planted or set in place. In doing this, do not damage the root system. Forcing the roots into the bottom layer or pulling up a rooted water plant in order to transfer it to another aquarium is often killing. Many species form a finely branched network of secondary roots and root hairs which are usually torn off;

278

they stay behind in the soil, stuck tightly to sand grains and between the particles of peat.

With many plants, it is better to dig them out, dirt and all. For fast growers, handling is naturally less important, but the existence of slow growers will depend on careful handling.

It is necessary to work carefully in planting. Before planting, roll the roots around a finger. Make a small hole, press the base of the plant deeply in with your finger, taking care not to break any stems or roots. Press soil around the plant, then carefully lift the plant up slightly, which will cause the rolled-up roots to spread out. Make sure that the roots do not appear above the sand.

Illus. 7-9. Planting lay-out for large aquariums, for example, 50 × 50 × 100 cm (20 × 20 × 40 inches). Constructing the terraces in such a way that they slope upwards from the direction of the incoming light results in the best illumination. The figures give the height of the terrace planes above the bottom. The advantage of these terraces in planting is readily observed, you can arrange the plants of various kinds in groups much more easily and more attractively, thereby taking account of their habits. Place low plants in front, or, if they are typical marsh plants inclined to bloom in shallow water, place them on the highest terraces. Put the other plants of normal height on the remaining terraces, taking account of satisfactory visibility and swimming space.

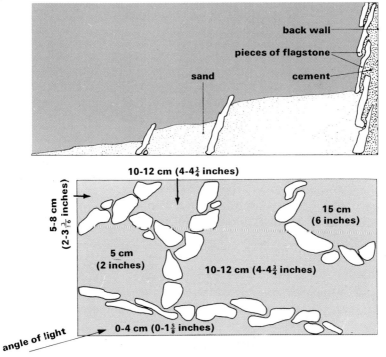

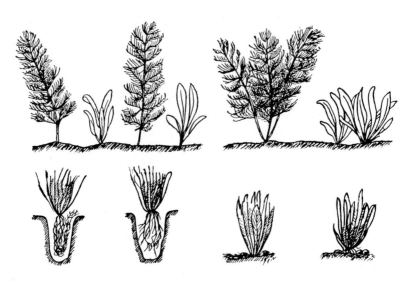

Illus. 7-10. How it must and must not be done! When planting an aquarium—large or small—never lay out the plant cuttings in alternate rows (top left), but arrange small groups of the same kind together (top right). In planting already-rooted plants, never thrust the roots into the soil so that the extreme ends turn upward (bottom left), but make a small hole with your hand and spread the roots out on the bottom of it. If the foot of the plant still remains a little under the sand, carefully lift the plant a little. The proper position (bottom right) is where the roots just fail to be visible.

Another factor in aquarium planting is mutual tolerance. Plants that require the same food in the same form compete with each other. The strongest ones win, though they may only be the species most numerous at that spot. As far as standing room is concerned, one plant can take so much light away from another that the latter suffers from it. When the plants are small, this will not happen.

When two *different* plant species look similar, they should not be planted close together. Also, never put two different plant species in alternating rows or mixed together in one bunch. Most plants are actually group plants—plants that grow close together or in bunches in nature; only a few plants are the solitary types.

Plants that customarily grow in groups must be planted in groups. These are principally water milfoil (*Myriophyllum*), a genus of submerged plant that is quite common in the northern hemisphere. Various types are known, all characterized by the small, hair-fine, divided leaves which are placed around the stem in whorls of four or five. European species are generally not especially suitable for the

280

tropical aquarium, but they may adapt. The American species do better: *M. hippuroides* (North America and Mexico), *M. pinnatum* (North America), and *M. brasiliense* (South America). *Myriophyllum* spp. can be formed into groups of five stems to make a lovely unit.

The same is true for the *Cabomba* species from America, of which two have been acclimated to the aquarium—*Cabomba aquatica* and *Cabomba caroliniana*. The first have more finely divided leaves than the latter. As soon as their submerged crowns reach the surface, the *Cabomba* species betray their relationship to the water lilies by producing round, floating leaves to support the above-water, handsome bloom stalk with white (*C. caroliniana*) or yellow-white (*C. aquatica*) blossoms.

The garland-forming *Elodea canadensis* (North America, imported to Europe a century ago; has since become a real pest in ditches and canals) is the best known of similar species. A more beautiful species for the tropical aquarium is *Elodea densa* (South America). Another is the African *Lagarosiphon muscoides*, or one of its varieties.

Illus. 7-11. *Lagarosiphon muscoides.*

Illus. 7-12. *Elodea canadensis.*

Illus. 7-13. *Elodea densa.*

Illus. 7-14. *Hydrilla verticillata.*

A very beautiful species of river weed is *Hydrilla verticillata* (Europe, Asia and Africa) which has whorls of five, or more often six to eight, dark green, finely toothed leaves at intervals along a slender stem.

For a long time *Cryptocoryne* spp. (water trumpet) have been among the most desired aquarium plants. The species *C. undulata* (top left in Illus. 7–15) has deep green leaves with wavy edges, a soft pink on the underside. *C. beckettii* (top right) has somewhat sturdier and broader leaves with a more lightly waved edge, while the large, broad leaves of *C. cordata* (bottom right) have long stems. These also have a reddish underside. The small species *C. nevillii* (bottom left) is especially suitable for foreground planting. The flowers of these plants open up under water when the water level is too high and then quickly rot away. When they are planted just below the surface, the blossoms open above water and remain for an extended time. The flowers are very attractive and possess the typical shape and manner of blooming of the arum types (arum is a kind of European herb with heart-shaped leaves).

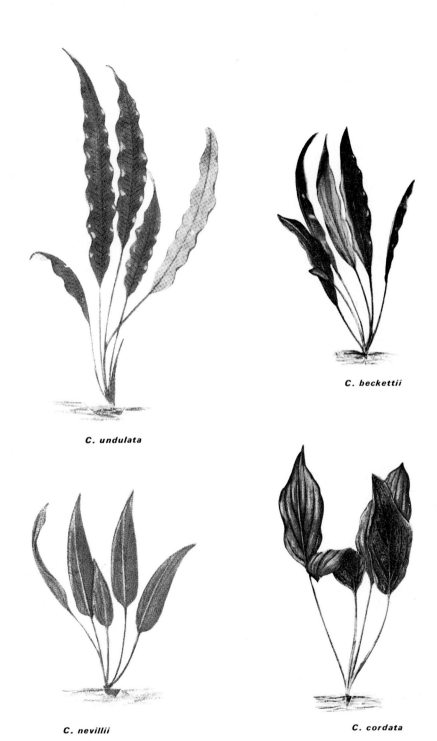

C. undulata

C. beckettii

C. nevillii

C. cordata

Illus. 7-15. *Cryptocoryne* species.

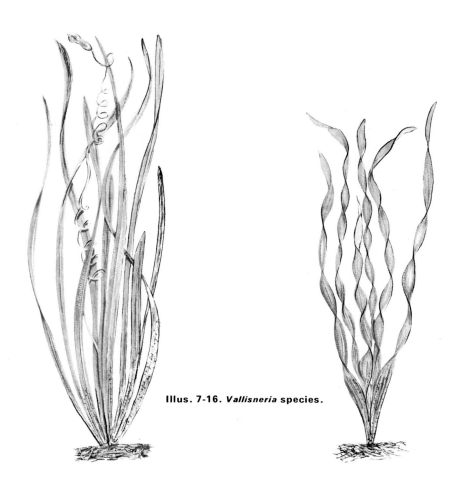

Illus. 7-16. *Vallisneria* species.

Vallisneria, called eel grass or Italian val, is one of the most popular aquatic plants. Native to the southern United States and southern Europe, *Vallisneria*, a grass-like plant, grows well in moderately lit or well lit spots.

The four-leaved water clover, *Marsilea quadrifolia*, can be a very ornamental aquarium plant on small terraces and also in the swampy areas of the marsh tank. Its relationship to the pill fern (see page 291) is clearly visible in its manner of growth and in the young leaves.

The members of the genus *Ceratopteris* are true ferns, hence not water ferns, although they have chosen the very wet environments of pools and marshes over living on land (above, left, in Illus. 7–18). *Ceratopteris thalictroides*, a floating plant, has an entirely different leaf

Illus. 7-17 (right). *Marsilea quadrifolia.*

Illus. 7-18. *Ceratopteris* species.

shape than its rooting, under-water varieties (top right) and goes under the name *C. thalictroides forma cornuta.* The more finely divided form from Sumatra (bottom), also *C. thalictroides*, is a typical under-water plant and is known as the oak-leaf fern.

285

Illus. 7-19. *Aponogeton elongatus.*

Illus. 7-20. *Aponogeton crispus.*

The *Aponogeton* species are handsome solitaries for the aquarium. *A. elongatus* (Illus. 7–19), with, at most, two or three plants forming a group, provide a wealth of fresh greenery among which the fish feel at home and show themselves off beautifully. *Aponogeton undulatus* and *A. crispus* (Illus. 7–20) are easily cross bred.

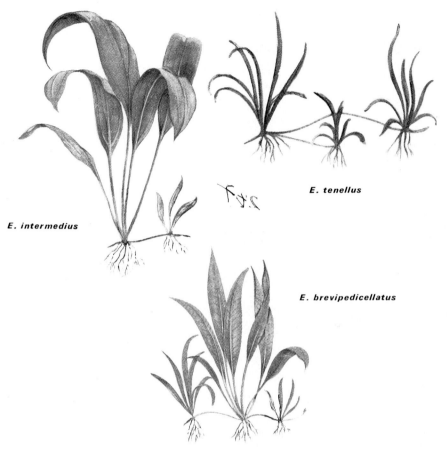

E. intermedius

E. tenellus

E. brevipedicellatus

Illus. 7-21. *Echinodorus* **species.**

The different *Echinodorus* species are especially suitable for terraces of medium height. *Echinodorus intermedius*, the so-called Amazon Sword Plant (left in Illus. 7–21) is the best known. *Echinodorus brevipedicellatus* (middle) becomes more robust and is quite suitable as a solitary plant, while the very small species *E. tenellus* (right) is best for planting in the foreground. The runners for vegetative reproduction can form an entire network, but can be kept well in control by timely cutting.

Small Aquariums

It is probably a great deal harder to plant a small aquarium than a large one. If you are not working exclusively with artificial light (which is often preferable to strongly varying natural light), you must take into

287

account the quantity and direction of the incoming light. If strong sunbeams are unavoidable, you should screen off the side where the sun enters with a group of sun-loving plants—for instance, *Vallisneria*— placed along the side pane. In this way, the light is so tempered that the other plants will not get too much sun. Remember that in the wild the sunlight falls upon the water from above, usually at a rather steep angle. The water above the plants, if they are not close to the surface, tempers the light sufficiently to counteract over-exposure. If the light comes in through the side walls of the aquarium, it is thus more direct.

In order to have the bottom surface as large as possible, make use of the "hill landscape," forming terraces (see page 277), which you may or may not firm up with rocks. A bottom soil sloping up to the rear not only gives more surface, but also enlarges the spatial action. Then, if you make the back corner lying farthest from the light somewhat higher than the back corner opposite, the result is certainly satisfactory.

Naturally, you cannot fill a small tank up too much with rocks. There is no set rule for this, but the sketches speak for themselves. An irregular bottom line gives you the opportunity to plant in groups. The frontal pane through which the interior can be seen should remain at least 90 per cent clear of growth. A symmetrical structure, furthermore, is to be discouraged, while too central a group planted in the middle of the tank is also not successful because it divides the field of view.

Illus. 7-22 (left). The under-water form of the moneywort (see Illus. 7-23) is an especially suitable and attractive addition to your aquarium. The fresh green of the leaves, lighter than in the land variety, is especially decorative with a background of yellow sandstone. Similar to the land variety, the plant branches out easily into an entire thicket, and is excellent for taking cuttings. From the nodes sprout fine, white rootlets.

Illus. 7-23. Moneywort *(Lysimachia nummularia)*, commonly occurring in ditches and ponds in polders and in marshy areas, is a creeping plant with round-oval leaves located in pairs along the stem. The flowers have four bright yellow calyces and attract many insects. At each node, the plant sends roots into the ground. It, therefore, does well in a rock garden. In marshy areas, it can grow entirely under water. See Illus. 7-22.

Illus. 7-24. *Chara* **(left) and** *Nitella* **(right).**

Planting Large Aquariums

In principle, setting up large aquariums requires the same work as setting up small aquariums, with the following exceptions: First, devise a more spacious composition—larger plant groups—and, second, put in several different species of plants. On the one hand, making terraces is simpler here, but on the other hand, the terraces should be well suited to their purpose, without hidden places into which the eye cannot penetrate.

Planting Study Aquariums and Breeding Tanks

The choice of plants for study aquariums and breeding tanks is broader than that for ordinary home aquariums, because a number of plants can be used which are not recommended for the home aquarium. Here, it is usually a matter of "breeding plants"—an assortment of extremely finely divided plants growing in a confused mass and offering necessary hiding places for the elder fish at the time of mating as well as for the eggs and the fry in the first weeks of their development. The plants known as thread algae are green algae (Chlorophyceae), which can form thick groves under certain conditions.

Among the weed families are also the whorl weeds, among which the genera *Chara* and *Nitella* are known as "breeding plants" (family Characeae). These filamentous algae, although extremely fine and tiny, are in some ways remindful of higher plants by the formation of fine offshoots and leaf-like protrusions.

The well-spring mosses are true mosses. The ordinary spring moss (*Fontinalis antipyretica*) is a cold-water plant from the northern hemisphere and in warmed breeding tanks lasts only a rather short time. Nonetheless, for a number of months it gives fish an ideal spawning place because you can plant handsome, dark green clumps of it.

289

Illus. 7-25. *Eichhornia crassipes.*

The water hyacinth (*Eichhornia crassipes*) belongs among those plants which are typical of watery environments, without, however, leading a submerged life. Originally a floating plant from the shallow and moderately flowing waters of tropical and sub-tropical America, it has been spread throughout other parts of the world by men. For the amateur naturalist, it is one of the most beautiful and attractive water plants, interesting for its hyacinth-like cluster of blossoms and the swollen stems which keep the plant afloat. For the aquarist, it is an especially ornamental plant which, on account of its enormous root system hanging down in the water, affords a welcome hiding and spawning place for the fish.

In addition to reproducing by seed, this plant also rapidly reproduces vegetatively by means of runners. As a consequence, in the wild, a watery area can quickly become covered with these plants. For the lakes themselves and for the movement of boats, in fact, in certain regions the water hyacinth has developed into an almost uncontrollable plague, its sole natural enemy being the manatee or water cow. It is, however, easy to keep under control in the aquarium.

The pill fern (*Pilularia globulifera*) is a fine plant which forms a dense network of roots and runners and which, as bottom cover, especially in the breeding tank, can provide shelter for eggs of the free-laying fishes.

Depending on the type of fish you intend to transfer to the breeding tank, your choice of plants is also limited, as certain fish prefer certain plants. In any case, most aquarium fish must have available a thick growth of fine-leaved plants, close to the bottom for bottom-layers or at the surface for surface-layers. Further plantings, too, must intercept light that is too bright, as most fish in the mating season seek shelter from the light. Remember, though, that a breeding tank must provide a satisfactory open space for swimming, as well as an unobstructed interior arrangement.

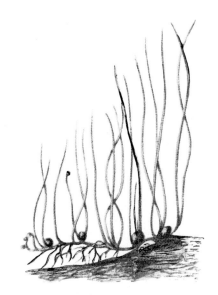

Illus. 7-26. *Pilularia globulifera.*

Feeding Your Fish

If all goes as planned for a few weeks after you have set up the aquarium, then it is most likely that the aquarium will continue to do well.

Your foremost task is, then, only to provide regular food. In this regard, you may think that you can get along well for a long time by providing dried food from a sack or box, but actually, you should only use dried food as an auxiliary in cases where it is needed. Primarily, you should provide your fish live food, which should be available practically throughout the entire year. Small crustaceans such as brine shrimp (*Artemia salina*) are very nourishing fish food. They are available either in egg form (which, in a dried state, is easily transportable and endures for long periods of time), which must be hatched before the shrimp can be fed to your fish, or in a frozen form. In addition, you can feed your fish waterfleas (*Daphnia, Cyclops, Bosmina*), mosquito larvae, gnats, flies, ants, worms, and so forth, or you can provide for the fish's need for protein by feeding them unsalted, fresh red meat or cooked white fish, which must not have any fat. The well known little white worms or *Enchytraeus* (fat fare) must certainly not be given every day. Cereals, such as bread crumbs or cookies, are among the worst and deadliest foods for the fish's digestive mechanism.

Tubifex worms, available in fish shops or, if you wish to catch your own, in shallow, muddy-bottomed bodies of water, are also excellent food for aquarium fishes. Be sure that the worms are clean, however, before you feed them to your fish.

Infusoria, protozoan animalcules found in any water capable of supporting life, is an important food, especially for very small fry who cannot yet consume larger foods.

You can catch other animal food yourself from ditches and ponds. When you do, expect there to be other water-dwellers of various kinds among the massive catch of waterfleas. For the most part, these will be tiny crustaceans, but also insect larvae. Some are dangerous, such as the larvae of the water beetles and the dragon-flies and the larvae and adult specimens of some crustaceans. However, there is no need to worry over this, for, when you deposit your catch in a white enamel bucket or

292

pan, you can easily recognize the dangerous guests from the drawings in Illus. 7–27.

The most important foods for your fish are crustaceans and insect larvae. Occurring quite commonly all over the entire world is the group of so-called waterfleas. These little creatures, in no sense fleas, are so-called "paddle-foot crabs," and they are found together in reddish clouds in the water (see Illus. 7–27, *Daphnia pulex*).

Mosquito larvae—actually, each developmental stage of the different gnats and mosquitoes—are perhaps an even better food. The life cycle of the common malaria mosquito (top right in Illus. 7–27), *Anopheles maculipinnis*, is shown in the numbered circle. The mosquito lays many

Illus. 7-27. For the aquarist who catches his own live fish food, here are some illustrations of useful and harmful creatures which can be dipped out of ditches and ponds with a dip net.

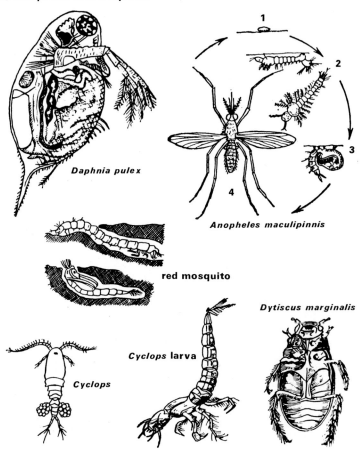

Daphnia pulex

Anopheles maculipinnis

red mosquito

Dytiscus marginalis

Cyclops larva

Cyclops

eggs on the water (1), from which develop the larvae (2), which after the necessary growth skin-shedding transform into the pupa stage (3), from which, finally, the mosquito again appears (4). The red mosquito larvae and pupae living in the soil (center left) are somewhat more difficult to catch.

Cyclops (bottom left) is an abundant genus with many species, also waterfleas, which can be caught periodically in great numbers. On the one hand, they form an excellent food, but on the other hand, at certain periods of development, the much smaller males can appear in great numbers and form, as gill-parasites, a troublesome and rather dangerous plague. However, you need not be too afraid of this. Indeed, beware of the larvae (bottom middle) and especially of the adult beetles (bottom right), *Dytiscus marginalis*. This so-called yellow-rimmed water beetle is one of the most universal fish enemies. For the smaller fish and especially for the young fry, the larvae are also a deadly danger.

Fish Diseases

When your fish are kept and handled properly, it is not very likely that diseases will develop. Most of the micro-organisms that occasionally attack fish are present in latent form in any tank, but only fish that are in poor condition will eventually be attacked by them. Healthy fish have a dermal protection in the form of a slime skin.

A parasite which, in comparison to other enemies of fish, can be destructive to the entire population of an aquarium is a micro-organism called velvet, *Oodinium pillularis*. These microscopically small beings have a latent stage in a capsule and do not transform into an active life form until the circumstances are satisfactory. The fish are attacked (a) generally by numerous spores of this remarkable creature —a being from the boundary region between plant and animal—which fastens itself all over the fish, even internally, to the layer of the mucous membrane. Wounds created by tissue damage are centers of infection which make the fish more sensitive to other unsatisfactory conditions. Young fish especially fall victim to this parasite, which further completes its life cycle outside the fish (c), where it reproduces by fission and may yield numerous progeny.

When you put food animals into the tank, there is a chance of your introducing other dangers for your fish. In general, it is recommended that you put all micro- and macro-plankton in a bucket with clean tap water before you put them into the tank. After the water has stood for 20 to 30 minutes, most of the dangerous organisms have probably moved to the walls of the bucket. The free-swimming animals are ready to be fed to your fish. In the author's opinion, the fear of disease is actually far worse than the possibility of the diseases' attacking the fish. But, when disease does occur, always try to remedy hopeless cases by taking the infected fish out of the community tank; try to avoid chemical treatment for the whole tank population. For many parasitic diseases, a raising-and-dropping-the-temperature cure works fine.

In summation, this section has introduced some of the general knowledge and conditions that are necessary for you to set up your aquarium. Specifics about individual species are covered under the descriptions of the species in Part II.

PART II—
CATALOGUE
OF FISHES

Illus. II-1. Tropical savannah.

The following descriptions are presented in an order based on the natural classification of fish, arranged in accordance with the latest scientific publications. The last word about such a system of classification has not yet been said. The guide line adopted in this presentation is based on the mutual relationship between fishes as expressed in certain common characteristics.

In addition to the well known and less well known aquarium fishes, some are included here that are not suitable for home breeding, but which either possess a peculiar interest for naturalists or are frequently shown in public aquariums. Of course, the naturalist wants to know more about these fishes than can be learned from the brief texts attached to the public tanks they swim in.

For convenience of reference, an alphabetical order of listing has been adhered to throughout, within the families and sub-families as well as the genera and the species. If this should cause a loss of the line of relationship, it will be made up for in the summary of each group. The alphabetical system is unexcelled as a means for ready reference.

PISCES

The fish kingdom is collectively called *Pisces*, Latin for "fish." Fishes are usually simply divided as they were by early scientific researchers—into two groups, the cartilaginous and the bony fishes. This appears to be a useful primary division. We have seen, however, that bony fishes were the first to appear on the world scene and that cartilaginous fishes were a subsequent stage of development. The cartilaginous skeleton could, in fact, be regarded as a degenerated adaptation to the environment, as the need for a solid, bony skeleton was not as imperative in the sea—at least, not in the deep waters where the shark-like fishes reside.

Furthermore, fishes are such a diversified assemblage, and differ in so many primary features, that a sub-division into five classes seems warranted. Also, in total number of species (about 20,000), fish far outnumber all other groups of vertebrates; the known number of species of amphibians is 3,000, of reptiles, 6,000, of birds, 9,000, and of mammals, 3,700.

Class Ostracodermi

These fishes, considered the first to appear on earth, have been discussed already (see page 28), so the discussion here will be limited to some points that clearly illustrate their relationship to higher groups of fishes.

Fossils preserved from the Ordovician period and later provide fairly exact information about the shape of these fishes. They varied from 5-15 cm (2-6 inches) long and had a relatively large head which, along with the body, was encased in thick, bony armour. The skeleton inside the body was also a bony one. Fins, if any, were invariably provided with a sharp, spike-like first ray. The mouth opening was usually round and, in most cases, was at the ventral side of the head. It was probably provided with a number of fleshy folds of skin so that the mouth could function as a sucker.

In fossils of ostracoderms, the only part of the fins preserved was the spine, probably due to fragmentary fossilization of the bony parts rather than to the absence, in these early fishes, of fine fin rays and intervening webs. It is not likely that such fragile parts would be preserved, but it is just as unlikely that these soft, fleshy parts were entirely absent in these first bottom-dwellers.

A comparison with modern fishes—and there seems to be no valid objection to making one—first brings to mind the armoured catfishes. Like the ostracoderms, most armoured catfishes have an inner skeleton and an outer encasement of armour. The big head is, for the most part, enclosed in a helmet of bony plates; the round mouth opening underneath the head is equipped with flabby suckers and poorly-developed jaws sparsely set with fine teeth. Because of the absence of jaws in the earliest ostracoderms, they used to be called *Agnatha*, meaning no jaws (*a* means no, *gnatha* means jaws). Obviously, the name does not fit all ostracoderms. The faintly-developed and poorly-ossified jaw of the earliest ostracoderms is found today in lancelets, rays and hagfishes, as well as in several catfishes of the family Trichomycteridae. Undoubtedly, the structure found in living groups is due to degeneration or reversion to the original, "primitive" trait. For a discussion of this phenomenon, see page 31.

The relationship existing between these primeval bottom-dwellers and the groups mentioned above exists also between the ostracoderms and later and present-day groups, such as loaches, the sturgeon-like fishes, and others. From the study of fossils, it appears that these fishes originated at the beginning of the Ordovician period. Toward the middle of that period, three distinct groups were differentiated—the classes Cephalaspida, Anaspida, and Pteraspida. In the chart showing the evolution of fishes and in the table on page 29, it can be seen that, according to the theory applied, these groups tend towards a connection with Amphioxiformes, Petromyzontiformes, and Myxiniformes. Many workers in this field feel that these surviving orders cannot be considered simply as living fossils and remains of the formerly flourishing ostracoderms.

The environment of the ostracoderms is fairly well known. Their armour was quite useful, just as functional, in fact, as that of the modern, armoured catfishes. Among their contemporary fauna were no higher forms that could have been the enemies of the ostracoderms, but certain of the lower groups did grow to enormous size and could have been dangerous to them. Though most lower animals showed a preference for the open sea, the first fishes developed in shallow, fresh water. This was also the habitat of the dangerous water scorpions or Eurypteridae, rapacious arthropods which usually grew up to a metre (39¼ inches) in length, although fossils 150 cm (about 5 feet) long have been found. Apparently, the armour of the tiny ostracoderms spared them from complete extermination by these water scorpions. Had this not been so, it is possible that the ostracoderms would have been wiped out and no higher vertebrates could then have developed. It seems, therefore, that man may owe his very existence to the bony armour of a tiny fish that swam in the waters of earth 500,000,000 years ago.

Towards the end of the Permian period, the water scorpions began to lose their dominant position. They diminished in size and, before the onset of the Devonian period, they disappeared completely as a specific group. The ostracoderms, however, continued to flourish.

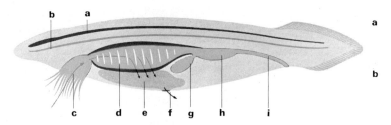

Illus. II-2. Schematic diagram of the lancelet, known by various names, perhaps as a reference to other species. *Branchiostoma lanceolata,* or *Amphioxus lanceolatus,* is actually only of superficial interest to us, as it is not suitable for the aquarium. See text. *a.* spinal column, nerve canal. *b.* chorda dorsalis. *c.* mouth opening with whip-like barbels around it. *d.* pharyngeal cavity or gill basket for sieving out live food (plankton). *e.* body cavity with open water exit *(f). g.* liver. *h.* stomach. *i.* intestinal canal and anal opening.

Order Amphioxiformes

This order includes the lancelets or Cephalochordata (see page 15), a peculiar and interesting group. The lancelets are quite suitable for the aquarium.

The lancelet is probably incorrectly considered to be a link between the invertebrates and the vertebrates. It lives in the sea, in shallow water along the coasts, has neither eyes nor limbs, has blood without coloration and a mouth that has no jaws, but is surrounded by tactile processes. It has no skeleton but has a chorda extending from head to tail. It is probably the classic example of one of the main principles of evolution, the phenomenon called *paedomorphosis* (see page 31). The development of the lancelet, which looks like the larva of a higher fish, stops at the point where the development of the true fish begins. Nonetheless, the lancelets grow into adulthood and are, of course, able to reproduce.

Order Petromyzontiformes

Another group that is perhaps just as remarkable as the lancelets is the lampreys. Although interesting from a biological viewpoint, they are hardly suitable for the usual home aquarium. They can, however, be seen in public aquariums.

The peculiarity in the life cycle of these fishes is that it is divided into five distinct periods which, in certain respects, correspond to those of the eel-like fishes. The first period, emergence from the eggs and the larval stage, lasts about half the entire life span. The metamorphosis from larvae living in the bottom to free-swimmers still living on plankton lasts a sixth of the life span. This is followed by a period of gluttony, during which the lampreys live as parasites on fishes and other living creatures. After a short mating season, they lay their eggs and die.

In the case of the well known, small lamprey (*Lampetra planeri*), these phases from egg to adulthood take three years—one year for full growth and almost two for the period of parasitism. After that, there is a short mating season. Matings usually last for a few consecutive days.

Order Myxiniformes

This is another group often found in public aquariums but never in the home aquarium. These hagfishes are marine, eel-shaped fishes, of which 25 species have survived as present-day fauna. They particularly dwell in colder seas at depths of 20–650 m (60–2,000 feet). Unlike the lampreys, they produce copious secretions of slime, and the well known Atlantic hagfish, *Myxine glutinosa*, if held in a container with 10 litres (about 10 gallons) of water, will turn the water into a gelatinous mass in a few seconds.

Class Osteichthyes

Glance at Table 1–3 on page 29 and the chart (Table 1–4) on pages 34 and 35. For the point where a connection is found with what are called the true bony fishes (Osteichthyes), we must go back into earth's history to about the middle of the Ordovician. Many links are missing from the chain, unknown or not yet discovered. Yet, there are indications that the most important divergence towards true bony fishes had, by this time, taken place. This offshoot from the ostracoderms, found under item 14, in Table 1–3, leads first to item 15, the Crossopterygii, or lobe-finned fishes. It is accepted that towards the end of the Ordovician—hence much earlier than is indicated by fossil material—the second important offshoot to spring from the ostracoderms was the Actinopterygii, item 20.

The Crossopterygii (item 15), including the lungfishes, broke away from the oldest line of fishes in the middle of the Ordovician period. They flourished exceptionally well during the Silurian, the Devonian, and the greater part of the Carboniferous.

The Crossopterygii (item 15) are included under the classification Osteichthyes (item 14), along with the remainder of the known bony fishes (but not the sharks, etc.). There are two more groups of Osteichthyes (Actinopterygii and Acanthopterygii), which differ from each other in many ways, yet one of them is actually of greater importance than has generally been recognized. The main stem, Actinopterygii (item 20), has been divided into two groups, items 21a and 21b. The first—Actinopteri (item 21a)—is principally the Ostariophysi, with a few groups stemming from it, and the second, stemming from the same, original stock, includes the Holostei and Acanthopterygii (item 21b). Conditions of environment and food supply caused a remarkable difference to develop between these two groups. The first group failed to develop certain muscles for retracting the gill arches, while these muscles, officially named *retractores arcuum*

304

branchialium, are definitely present in the second group. This is an important feature, which, in addition to a number of other characteristics, justifies this division.

The still much-used name, Teleostomi, which means literally "with an end-positioned (terminal) mouth," is a very misleading term for all these bony fishes. Many of the bottom-dwelling fishes certainly do not have an end-positioned mouth; indeed, the more primitive forms have just a mouth underneath the head (compare especially with the armoured catfishes and the loaches). Naturally, an end-positioned mouth has frequently developed from an under-positioned one, and sometimes, in unusual circumstances, development has been the reverse. However, as a general characteristic encompassing such a comprehensive group, this name is not tenable.

Sub-class Crossopterygii

The Crossopterygii, or lobe-finned fishes, actually form a main division of fishes of which practically the entire phylogenetic development is known. They have always been rather large fishes whose fossil traces have been clearly followed from the beginning of their existence into the Cretaceous. Thereafter, nothing more was ever found of them, until a miracle occurred, in 1938, off the coast of South Africa near East London. A live specimen of the famous *Latimera* (item 19) was caught in fairly deep water.

About the beginning of the Devonian, at the same time as the oldest lobe-finned fishes flourished, the environmental circumstances on the earth were such that serious attempts began to be made to adapt to the land (see page 32). Two groups are important in that connection, the lungfishes or Dipnoi (item 16) and the Rhipidistia (item 17), also known by other names, including bone-scaled fishes. This last group, as already mentioned, constituted the actual link with terrestrial vertebrates.

Naturally, this interesting group of fishes has received special attention from scientists and is still of great interest to them. As a result of different kinds of research and some remarkable characteristics, they were at first included under Choanichthyes, along with amphibians, because of the supposed presence of internal nostrils, called CHOANAE. It has, however, been unequivocally shown that of this group only the Rhipidistia have such internal channels connecting the nostrils to the oral cavity (see page 309). Moreover, these are the groups accepted as having formed the link with the terrestrial vertebrates (item 18) (Jarvik, 1942, and others).

Plate II-1. *Protopterus aethiopicus.*

Super-order Dipnoi

The old line of lobe-finned fishes developed an offshoot in the middle of the Carboniferous, of which some present-day fauna, the so-called lungfishes, still live in the southern hemisphere. They appeared as an evolutionary line some time in the Devonian (see the chart on page 34) and enjoyed a long period of growth during the Triassic and Jurassic, with a gradual reduction in numbers during the Cretaceous.

Plate II-2. *Protopterus annectens.*

Illus. II-3. *Neoceratodus forsteri*, the Australian lungfish. Note the large, round scales and especially the lobed pectoral fin. This is a half-grown specimen.

Order Dipteriformes

Most known fossil forms have been customarily grouped in this order. Living forms have been included in the order Ceratodiformes, below.

Order Ceratodiformes

The lungfishes living today can be regarded as relics from the vanished hey-day of this group. In spite of the apparent characteristics matching those of some modern fishes, Ceratodiformes possess peculiar anatomy and manner of activity, both of which are clearly very old and primitive. In any case, these fishes, limited to the southern hemisphere, live in South America, Africa, and a small region of Australia. The six species are included in two families: the Protopteridae (some authorities consider the correct family name to be Lepidosirenidae) with the species *Protopterus aethiopicus, P. amphibius, P. annectens,* and *P. dolloi* from Africa, and *Lepidosiren paradoxa* from South America; and the Ceratodidae, with only *Neoceratodus forsteri* in Australia. The last species, especially, is most like the lobe-finned ancestral line.

Ryder (1886) made the following observation concerning these fish: "*Ceratodus* (=*Neoceratodus*) actually looks like an embryo of a teleost (member of a sub-class or other division of fishes, called bony fishes, which comprises most living fishes) that has lost its yolk sac and

307

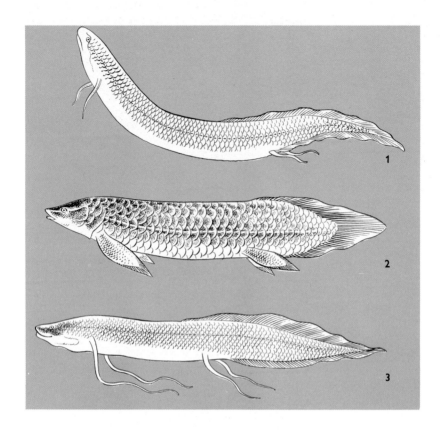

has grown into a big creature without losing a single one of the larval characteristics of the skeleton, but has acquired other traits, such as a more differentiated respiratory system. The tail has also remained in the stage of an embryonic salmon."

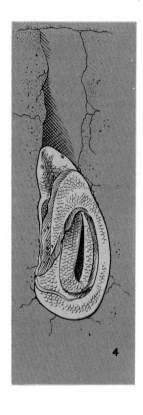

Illus. II-4. Lungfish.
1. *Lepidosiren paradoxa,* the Amazonian lungfish, grows to about 100 cm ($39\frac{1}{4}$ inches). Although it also occurs in the drainage basin, it prefers the regular, seasonally dry, flood pools.
2. *Neoceratodus forsteri,* the Australian lungfish, can grow to 175 cm (about 69 inches). It is a river dweller.
3. *Protopterus aethiopicus* is one of the four African lungfishes. It grows to about 100 cm ($39\frac{1}{4}$ inches).
4. A lungfish in its "cocoon" of hardened mud, in which it spends the dry season, without water. As soon as the first rains fall, the lungfish awaken from their dry sleep.

Super-order Rhipidistia

This very interesting group of fishes (item 17) developed from certain lobe-finned fish during the Devonian. The only fossil fish material discovered so far has been divided into two orders, the Porolepiformes and the Osteolepiformes, the first with two true representative families from the Devonian to the Permian (Porolepidae and Holoptychidae), the second with two other clearly distinguishable families (Osteolepidae and Rhizodontidae). As has been observed many times, these fishes are regarded as the direct ancestors of the first fishes that attempted to conquer the land. They all possessed lungs of the type found in the lungfishes and in many higher animals at a certain stage of their development. The Swedish biologist Erik Jarvik (1942 and later) has especially concerned himself with the finer structure of the head and snout of these fishes and the amphibious forms with which they are connected, as well as with current amphibians and reptiles. He has shown, in a thorough study and in a handsomely illustrated series of publications, that the rhipidistians possess a direct connection between the nostrils and the oral cavity, as is the case with the higher animals.

Class Amphibia

Perhaps the reader is surprised that anything is said here about amphibians. But, they hold a place in the story of fishes not only by reason of their direct branching off from the fish line, but also because there are always some aquarists who take an interest in frogs and toads and who have closely watched over their development in water. Also, we must not forget the salamanders, terrestrial amphibians which often pass through an aquatic stage during which they breathe by gills.

The absolute congruence of development of many fishes with the youth stage of amphibians is strikingly informative. Moreover, the breeding of tadpoles from frog spawn, to be used as food for larger fish, is a task for the advanced aquarist and is an unavoidable consequence of his avocation, particularly if he keeps larger species of fish.

Illus. II-5. *Latimeria chalumnae,* a fish believed long extinct, was caught at a depth of 70 metres (250 feet) off the coast of South Africa, near East London.

Super-order Actinistia

This last group of the lobe-finned fishes is quite similar to the old group of lungfishes. In fact, it is the first group to diverge clearly from the lobe-finned line early in the Devonian period. These peculiar fishes were thought to have died out long ago, for no fossils have been found dating later than the Cretaceous period. However, it set the scientific world agog when a live specimen was caught by a trawler near East London, close to the South African coast. The creature was 150 cm (about 5 feet) long, and, although it had been caught alive, it died on its way to port in East London. Because of its unusual nature, the curator of the East London Museum, Miss Courtenay Latimer, called upon the late Professor J. L. B. Smith of Rhodes University in Grahamstown, who identified it as a coelacanth, a group that had been considered extinct for more than 70 million years. It was given the name *Latimeria chalumnae* Smith, 1939, and was the sole representative of the so-called lobe-finned fish that man had ever set eyes on. Thanks to the efforts of Professor Smith, several other specimens of *Latimeria chalumnae* have since been caught, a valuable scientific achievement. These catches permitted study of the group with fresh material, so that far better insight into the structure was obtained than the best preserved fossil could afford, in which the soft parts were at best only fragmentarily preserved.

Professor Smith appealed throughout Africa and, as a result, an intense effort was made by fishermen to catch more of the elusive *Latimeria*. On December 20, 1952, a second specimen was caught, but it was different from the first one, as the frontal dorsal fin was absent. Professor Smith named it *Malania anjouanae* in grateful acknowledgement to Daniel François Malan, Prime Minister of South Africa (1948–54), who sent a seaplane to pick up the creature at the island of Anjouan (northeast of Madagascar), where it had been caught.

The fairly well known fossilized fish, together with the two specimens caught alive, are included in the order of Coelacanthiformes. Though it would be interesting, from a scientific viewpoint, to see a representative of this order in a public aquarium, not much chance of this exists. Coelacanthiformes seem to have made deep water their habitat, where they presumably took refuge in ages past from competing younger groups. Nevertheless, they are obviously of fresh-water origin.

Sub-class Actinopterygii

What are usually called the bony fishes are classified under Actinopterygii, or ray-finned fishes, in contrast to the Acanthopterygii (item 21b), or spiny-finned fishes. By today's standards, the division seems rather a strained one, but it will have to do until more is known about the correct relationship. The systematic classification of these groups given in Table 1–3, concerning the Actinopteri, has, for the most part, been based on the investigations of the author.

The principal division between items 20, 21a and 21b is based on the presence or absence of the retracting muscles of the gill arch (the *retractores arcuum branchialium*). This structure is closely connected with the development of the mouth and the oral cavity as well as with feeding habits. It is supported by other traits which confirm the validity of such a division. From Table 1–4, it can furthermore be seen that the division has to do with the fresh-water and salt-water environments. Apart from the orders listed in Table 1–3 which are concerned with our story—those in italic type being the ones to which true aquarium fishes belong—many other orders are also known, especially from extinct groups (followed by asterisks).

Without losing sight of the general aim, a word should still be said about those varieties that have become extinct fairly recently, because the information will prove useful later on. Although there is no factual evidence for the assumption, it is believed that the origin of the Actinopterygii should be sought in the Ordovician as a tiny branch of certain Ostracodermi (item 13). No fossils from the Silurian and Devonian periods have yet been found that could be regarded as related or intermediate forms. Only during the Carboniferous was there an abundant actinopterygian fauna, belonging particularly to the extinct order of Phanerorhynchiformes. The genera under this order were markedly similar to some of the present-day catfishes (armoured catfishes) and the sturgeon-like fishes. From the large parent race living in fresh water, two orders—Tarassiformes and Polypteriformes—broke away towards the end of the Jurassic period. In many respects, these are clearly related to the lobe-finned fishes. Two genera of Polypteriformes (item 25) still survive.

Another branch of Actinopterygii led, via the Saurichthyiformes, to the sturgeon-like fishes, the Acipenseriformes, and it is assumed, for reasons later clarified, that the main stem (item 21a) continued as Ostariophysi.

Another branch, which must have split off before the middle of the

313

Carboniferous period (21b in Table 1–4), is usually called Holostei, a name not altogether satisfactory. It is probable that the spike-finned fishes developed from this branch. Although ample fossil material has been found, dating from the Permian, Triassic, Jurassic, Cretaceous, and later periods, the connection is not very clear. The material, however, is promising.

Infra-class Actinopteri

This group, regarded as an infra-class, includes many orders preserved as fossils, all of which could be designated by the name Palaeopterygii, or primitive-finned fishes. They are forerunners or even contemporaries of the first real modern fishes. A well known order, recognized by numerous fossils from the Carboniferous · to the beginning of the Cretaceous period, is a herring-like fish called Palaeonisciformes. *Palaeoniscus* had a head still enclosed in sturdy, bony plates, and thickly-superposed ganoid scales covered the body. The scales were composed of an inner layer of bone and an outer layer of hard, shiny enamel. A contemporary cousin was *Stegotrachelus*, also herring-like, more coarsely built and slightly higher in body construction. Their shape shows that they were fast swimmers. The firm jaws set with sharp teeth indicate that they were ferocious killers. They must have been a frightful terror to the fry of their time. Another related family had a typically diamond-shaped, compressed, high body, such as *Cheirodus* of the family Platysomidae.

Presumably, the Palaeonisciformes played an important rôle and must have been the progenitors of several modern groups. Certain characteristics lead up to the Holostei (item 21b). It is doubtful, however, that they evolve from the sub-class Actinopteri (item 21a). The super-orders united in this sub-class in the table on page 29 share many characteristic traits. These do not agree, however, with the most typical traits of the Palaeonisciformes.

Super-order Ostariophysi

The enormous group of Ostariophysi, which includes almost all present-day fresh-water fishes, should, it is thought, be derived directly from certain ostracoderms of the Ordovician period. As can be seen in Table 1–3, the ancestral stem of the early ostariophysans produced an important offshoot (items 25 to 33), to which all other ray-finned fishes belong. The main group, however, split up in the course of the Triassic and Jurassic periods, until, in the Cretaceous, three different orders could be distinguished. These were the catfishes, the loaches and carp-like fishes, and the characins. It has already been shown that the fossil Phanerorhynchiformes from the Carboniferous period in England may be of considerable interest. These small fishes, though extremely specialized, show considerable similarity in build and armour to present-day catfishes and when collected with a recent fauna, they would no doubt be classed with the armoured catfishes. The idea of a genuine, though perhaps collateral, relationship should thus not be discarded (Hoedeman, 1959).

The three orders, Siluriformes, Cypriniformes, and Characiformes, derive from each other in this order, and together constitute the super-order Ostariophysi.

Recent research reveals that there is much evidence to separate the gymnotid fishes, hitherto regarded as degenerate characins, into a distinct order, Gymnotiformes, because they prove to be much closer to the ancestral stock of ostariophysan fishes. Furthermore, there are some other groups (orders) of fishes which turn out to possess a more or less developed Weberian apparatus (order Gonorhynchiformes, and probably others), justifying their inclusion under the Ostariophysi.

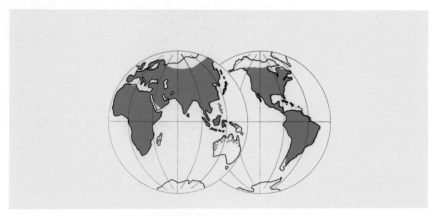

Illus. II-6. Distribution of catfish (Siluriformes).

Order Siluriformes

Catfishes, a fascinating group of remarkable fishes, are, for the most part, small dwellers of all kinds of fresh waters. This makes them most suitable for aquariums, where they are welcome not only for their queer, intriguing shapes, but sometimes also for their fine coloration, which especially accounts for their increasing popularity with aquarists. Moreover, scientists in the past few years have become more and more aware that a basic knowledge of the different families can cast an increasing amount of light on ichthyological problems of all kinds.

Catfishes are essentially at home in fresh water. The few species that live in the sea, not far off the coast, migrate up the rivers for mating.

The group includes the world's biggest contemporary fresh-water fishes, the Eurasian catfish *Silurus glanis* that may grow to a length of 3 metres (nearly 10 feet). (The giant Manguruyu, *Paulicea lutkeni*, a giant Amazonian catfish, may grow even larger. This is also true of *Pangasianodon gigas*, the huge "pla buk," a catfish found in the Mekong River in Southeast Asia. The osteoglossid *Arapaima gigas* also reaches similar proportions.) Others grow no longer than 25 mm (1 inch). Some are poisonous, others are parasitic, many are plant eaters, and others are voracious hunters.

Generally speaking, catfishes require very little oxygen and, with their special respiratory apparatus, they can live in very foul water. Some species not only can spend a long period of time on dry land, but can also walk, in a manner of speaking. Some species have developed a powerful, electricity-generating organ and all of them are equipped with the highly specialized Weberian apparatus (see page 133), which makes a kind of radar communication possible for them.

Catfishes live in practically any kind of water, from stagnant pools and slowly-evaporating ponds to big rivers, in which even swift-moving rapids provide no obstacle for them. Thus, they can be found living in waters that are uninhabitable for all other kinds of fish.

As far as distribution is concerned, catfishes are found everywhere in fresh water, as long as the temperature is not too low, as is clearly shown on the map in Illus. II–6. It is remarkable that only a few forms are found in the Australian region. (An acceptable explanation for this is given in Chapter 2, *Biogeographical Regions.*) The broad dispersal of catfishes is undoubtedly attributable to the age of the group.

Because catfishes encompass an enormous variety of forms, only a few traits are useful for typifying: head and body covered with bony plates, or body completely naked; no true scales; a varying number of barbels, or feelers, surrounding the mouth; a mouth which is not protrusile, though the lips often are; the premaxilla usually set with teeth, while the upper jaw is sometimes so. The vomer (ploughshare) bone of the skull forms the front part of the roof of the mouth and is usually toothed, as are also the pectoral spines. A so-called adipose fin is often present.

We shall discuss only a limited number of the great many known families, most of which include some interesting fishes for the aquarist to keep in his tanks.

Family Callichthyidae

The difference between armoured catfishes and the other catfishes is that the armoured catfish is clad in plates of bone instead of scales which protect the bodies of most fishes.

This family differs from the evenly armoured catfishes (family Loricariidae) in the structure and form of the bony dermal scutes. The armour (in Callichthyidae) is composed of small, banana-shaped plates that cover the flanks in only two lateral rows. In front, dermal scutes connect with the heavy skull bones. The upper rows of lateral scutes meet on the back, sometimes leaving a narrow, bare strip, occasionally filled in with small, round bony platelets. The armour on the flanks of the Loricariidae, on the other hand, is built up of more than two rows of bony plates.

The development, type and arrangement of the various bony plates and bits of bone serve as distinguishing characteristics for the species and genera within the family Callichthyidae.

The different bits of bone can be more or less "hairy"—that is, covered with rough (in many species), hair-like denticles. These projections are strongly developed in the males of some genera, particularly on the head and on the spines of the dorsal and pectoral fins.

The small, terminal mouth is directed downward and bears one or two pairs of barbels on the upper jaw and a single pair of slender barbels on the underlip. These barbels can be differently developed—in

Illus. II-7. Distribution area of the armoured catfish (Callichthyidae).

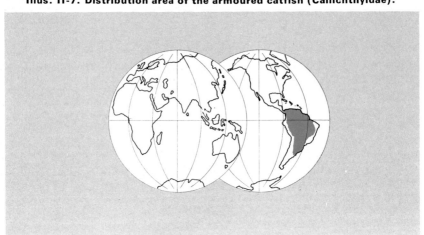

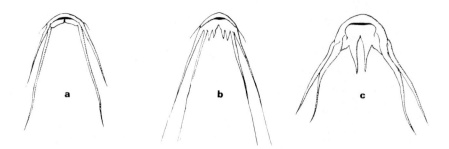

Illus. II-8. Underside of snout, showing placement and shape of the barbels of *a*. Callichthyinae. *b*. Dianemini. and *c*. Corydoradini.

the Callichthyini for example, the underlip has only flaps, whereas the Dianemini have short, barb-like growths and the Corydoradinae have really mobile little barbels.

As shown in Illus. II–8, these barbels provide an appropriate means of recognizing the different groups. The simplest (or least developed) are those of the genera *Hoplosternum* and *Callichthys*, which are made up of two pairs of well developed barbels and one pair of weakly developed barbels on the upper lip (jaw), with two (one pair) of fleshy flaps at the underlip. The arrangement is similar in the Dianemini, except that the barbels are somewhat longer and the fleshy flaps have grown out further into two pairs of short barb-flaps.

The sub-family Corydoradinae provides a different picture of the situation. Although the arrangement of barbels is similar in principle, the flaps on the underlip have become two short, solid barbels. At the same time, the small, slender threads on the upper lip are entirely lacking.

Sub-family Callichthyinae

The representatives of this sub-family are the most original and primitive forms of the family, larger and, therefore, less well known than the much smaller Corydoradinae. Two genera suitable for aquariums are known, *Hoplosternum* and *Callichthys*. The third genus, *Cascadura* Ellis, 1913, was found, on closer investigation, to be based on a specimen of *Hoplosternum* whose total length was 66 mm (2⅝ inches), and whose bony scales were not yet fully developed.

Within this sub-family, two tribes—the Callichthyini and the Dianemini—can be distinguished by means of the traits described above.

Tribe Callichthyini

These fish have a very unusual manner of adapting themselves to varying environmental conditions. Their ordinary habitat is the muddy bottom of slow-moving rivers, ditches, pools, and bogs, where they live mostly in large shoals. If disturbed in their element—where they can sometimes be caught by hand—they make grunting, squeaking sounds in outraged alarm. The sounds are made by gases forced from the respiratory system.

From time to time, Callichthyini approach the surface to take a gulp of air, whether the water is clear and oxygen-rich or foul and oxygen-poor. If the water is oxygen-poor, this performance is made more frequently, for the gulping of air is one of their breathing functions. The gut is lined with a web of small blood vessels which function like lungs in higher animals—that is, by removing the oxygen from the gulped air and absorbing it into the blood. This system is indeed useful in times of severe drought, when even the home waters dry up completely. Then, this intestinal breathing practically substitutes entirely for gill breathing. In Europe and Asia, the Cobitidae (see page 427) or loaches have a similar respiratory system, in which the air passes through the entire gastric channel and leaves through the anus, snorting and squeaking as it goes.

In periods of drought, Callichthyini sometimes migrate overland. Mawson (Science Magazine, December 25, 1880) published an eye-witness report of a migration of a specimen of *Hoplosternum* that had escaped from a jar in which it was being kept as a curiosity. On the ground, it jerked itself forward, supported by its pectoral spines, covering a distance of about 90 m (292½ feet) in two hours. *Hoplosternum* can also jump a few centimetres high in the same manner as skipjacks (any fish that jumps above or plays at the surface of the water; the name skipjacks is also used as a common name, in America, both for lake Silversides and for the so-called Ten-pounder, *Elops*). Forward movement was not a constant process, but after 5 or 10 seconds, in which a metre (39¼ inches) was covered, the creature paused for an equal interval of rest, and so on.

→

Illus. II-9. This photo gives a good idea of the type of marshy waters in which some species of *Callichthys* and *Hoplosternum* prefer to build their nests. The vegetation leaves scarcely an open spot of water visible. This is the Watrasneki Creek, Para River system, near Zanderij, Surinam.

Illus. II-10. Cross-sections through the body at various places to show the main differences in build: 1. through the head at the level of the eye, 2. just behind the gill openings, 3. just in front of the dorsal fin, 4. angle the snout makes in its length, respectively for the genera a. *Callichthys*, b. *Hoplosternum*, and c. *Corydoras*.

The way in which *Hoplosternum* builds its nest has been known for a long time. Hancock, who originally described the species *Hoplosternum littorale*, reported on its nest building in 1829, at a time when it was generally assumed by biologists that fish do not brood their spawn. Later, in 1886, Hancock's findings were confirmed and enlarged upon by Vipan (1886).

The tribe Callichthyini, including both genera, *Hoplosternum* and *Callichthys*, build a real nest from plant parts, mud, and an oral secretion. Thereafter, they blow air bubbles from their mouth secretion under the nest until it floats 5-10 cm (2-4 inches) above the surface. When the glued-together composite of the nest sets, it becomes rather solid and stays afloat. The nest measures 20 cm (8 inches) across.

Nest building is a job for the male. He cuts the plant parts with his pectoral fins and assembles the structure with his mobile barbels. Not until the nest is ready does he turn his attention to the females. Many times during construction of the nest, the females come nosing in, as if to see what is happening, only to be chased away by the builder until the job is finished.

When at last he is satisfied with what he has built, he accepts one of the females loitering near the nest. The female expels a number of eggs and catches them up in a kind of bag that she makes by folding her pelvic fins together. A varying number of eggs is carried into the nest by the female, who does this by turning over on her back, belly up. Before this, however, the male has deposited his milt among the bubbles of foam, while turned on his side or back. He keeps a sharp eye out to see that all the eggs are deposited in the nest. During this procedure, the female carries several hundred eggs into the nest, and the male covers them each time with bubbles. When all is done, the

322

pair usually stand by, keeping watch together. (Curiously enough, the mating season begins only after the onset of the rains.)

In contrast to some (perhaps all) *Corydoras* species, the Callichthyini are monogamous—that is, a single male takes a single female. Vipan (1886) maintained that the male was the sole protector of the nest, and this was frequently observed by aquarists later on. It is not known how long the brood takes to hatch, but the male guards the nest for about a month, and the progeny come swimming out when they are about 20 mm ($\frac{13}{16}$ inch) long. This conclusion was reached from a study of material collected in the Surinam River region, which contained a large number of young fish about that size. The armour is rather soft at this age, so that these youngsters are easy prey for hungry fishes.

What do Callichthyini eat? In aquariums, almost anything that is edible, and this is probably also true in the wild. Most catfishes are not very selective. Still, algae seem to make up a substantial portion of their diet. Care should be taken, therefore, to provide plenty of algae.

Illus. II-11. A place where, over a surface of at most 12 m² (125 square feet), no less than 17 bubble-nests of *Callichthys* were discovered. The depth of water above the mud layer of about 15 cm (6 inches) was not more than 30 cm (12 inches).

Genus *Callichthys*

Callichthys is represented by a single species divided into numerous sub-species—all so-called local varieties which used to have specific names of their own. This genus is even more widely distributed than *Hoplosternum*, and can be found in the regions shown on the map on page 318.

Callichthys callichthys (Linné, 1758)

This armoured catfish has received increasing attention only in recent years. It has taken a long time for aquarists to become interested in *Callichthys callichthys* especially because in time, it grows rather large. It does take many years, however, for a specimen to attain a maximum length of about 200 mm (8 inches). After a rapid growth period as a hatched larva, the species continues to grow at a calm, slow rate. It is certainly not difficult to breed, but the tank must be adapted to its needs.

The males have strongly-developed spines on their pectoral fins and they have a slight, orange-red tint. The males are usually more vivid than the females.

Illus. II-12. Detail of the tail region of *Callichthys*. Clearly the ossification of this specimen is complete, and the bony scutes overlap like roof tiles, and meet at the lateral line. Also note the overlap of the median bone plates of the back and belly regions into so-called fulcra, which turn into the outermost, spine-shaped rays of the caudal fin.

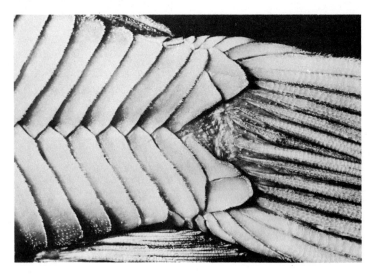

Illus. II-13. Development of the rows of bony plates in *Callichthys*. The youngest specimen is still entirely bare (*a* is 18 mm or $\frac{23}{32}$ inch) and no trace of skin folds is yet seen. Somewhat later (*b* is 35 mm or $1\frac{3}{8}$ inches), the skin is clearly set off in folds which correspond to internal muscle bundles, and not until a length of about 40 mm ($1\frac{19}{32}$ inches) (*c* is a young *Hoplosternum*, 40 mm or $1\frac{19}{32}$ inches long) does ossification start. The young of *Callichthys* and *Hoplosternum* can hardly be told apart before reaching a length of 40 mm.

Genus *Hoplosternum*

Of the many species that used to be described under this genus, only three remain today—*Hoplosternum littorale, H. magdalenae,* and *H. thoracatum.* Of course, a great many sub-species are still recognized, but only good was accomplished by clearing out the large number of inconveniently arranged synonyms.

Hoplosternum littorale (Hancock, 1828)
Brown Hoplo Catfish

This species has a wide distribution, from the island of Trinidad, through Venezuela and the Guianas, south to Buenos Aires and the region of the La Plata River.

The basic coloration is greyish brown, without spots. The back is a slightly darker brown. In the mating season, the pectoral fins of the male take on a blood red hue. Its length is up to about 200 mm (8 inches).

Plate II-3. *Hoplosternum magdalenae.*

Hoplosternum magdalenae Eigenmann, 1913
Striped Hoplo
Striped "Porthole"

Whether or not this is a true species, fish imported on several occasions from the region of the Magdalena River in South America, compare well with the original description by Eigenmann. As far as can be ascertained, they also fit the descriptions of the two better-known species, *H. littorale* and *H. thoracatum.*

Illus. II-14. *Hoplosternum thoracatum.*

Illus. II-15. Photo of the stage in which *Hoplosternum* has practically completely formed its skin-folds, having small skin denticles on the rear edges. Ossification into bony plates just set in. Total length of specimen is 40 mm (1$\frac{19}{32}$ inches).

Hoplosternum thoracatum (Valenciennes, 1840)

Hoplo Catfish

Spotted "Callichthys"

Spotted Panzerwels

The distribution of *Hoplosternum thoracatum* runs from Trinidad, Martinique, Venezuela, and the Guianas to Colombia and Brazil.

The general coloration is brownish with dark spots on the body and fins. The length is up to about 200 mm (8 inches). In the *Hoplosternum* species, the males have more heavily developed pectoral fins than the females. Young specimens, up to about 80 mm (3$\frac{3}{16}$ inches), are attractively patterned and quite lively.

Illus. II-16. Even while quite young, the sexes of *Hoplosternum thoracatum* are easily distinguished. Underside of the head of young specimens, *a*. male, 34 mm (1$\frac{3}{8}$ inches). *b*. female, 40 mm (1$\frac{19}{32}$ inches). and *c*. male, 58 mm (2$\frac{5}{16}$ inches).

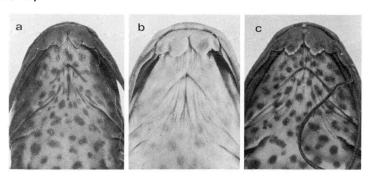

Plate II-4. *Dianema longibarbis.*

Tribe Dianemini

This group includes two genera—*Cataphractops* and *Dianema*—of which only a single species is accepted as an aquarium fish. (Another species, *Dianema urostriata*, has appeared in the United States and England from time to time. It is a striking fish, identical to *D. longibarbis*, except for a beautiful black and white striped caudal fin.)

Dianema longibarbis Cope, 1871
Porthole Catfish

Dianema longibarbis is similar to *Hoplosternum*, except that the body armour is somewhat less ossified, which gives the catfish a slightly different look. The bony plates are less conspicuous than in *Hoplosternum*, especially in half-grown specimens. Both *Dianema longibarbis* and *D. urostriata* are mid-water dwellers rather than bottom-dwellers.

Sub-family Corydoradinae

The armoured catfish of the *Corydoras* type, which up to now have been most popular and whose popularity is still growing at a remarkable rate, stem from *Hoplosternum*-like ancestors and are of about equal age. This may be assumed from their distribution throughout practically the entire region inhabited by the Callichthyini.

What has been said concerning the respiratory system, home territory, and biotope of the Callichthyinae is true, without much exception, for the *Corydoras* species. As far as breeding is concerned, especially in regard to nest building and care of the brood, much less is known, and that only of a few species. Vipan described in detail the breeding habits of *Corydoras paleatus*, while Carbonnier bred them in Europe as early as 1880.

Immediately after the dry season, apparently all callichthyids go about their mating. So far, no data have been collected as to whether or not those regions which have two wet seasons per year also have two mating periods.

Several males swim in company, getting all wound up by their mutual showing-off, while a single female swims among them, feeling about with her barbels. The males finally get themselves into such a state of commotion that they swim upon the female and attach themselves to her body in various places with their sucker-mouths. One of the males finally succeeds in getting to her head and then, with the aid of the spines on his pectoral fins, he clasps her barbels against her body and thus closely embraces her. Still holding her fast, he glides slowly down until he lies under her head, belly to belly with her. He then discharges his milt into the folded pelvic fins of the female, into which she lays five or so eggs a moment later. The female then goes to a stone or some other object which she had cleaned earlier, and attaches the eggs to it. Usually, an object close to the surface is chosen, but all the eggs of a mating session, which may number as many as 300, are not deposited in the same place. Fertilization takes place during the "embrace," otherwise there would be no reason for it. The act of holding on to the female by means of his sucker device excites the male into emitting the fertilizing milt, while the female gathers up the eggs in her folded, pelvic fins. The eggs are always fertilized by the time they are deposited, for, after they are put down, the male never comes close enough to the eggs for fertilization.

Therefore, no nest is made, unlike the *Hoplosternum* and *Callichthys*. Neither are *Corydoras* monogamous, at least not those species whose

329

mating habits are now known—mainly *Corydoras aeneus, C. melanistius* and *C. paleatus*. All three of these species are polyandrous—that is, one female to several males. This is well known to aquarists and appropriate provisions are made when breeding these species. This kind of mating is certainly not unusual in the animal kingdom, and it explains why no attention is paid to nest building or brood care by members of *Corydoras* species.

Once the eggs have been laid, neither parent bothers to give them a second thought, unless it occurs to one or the other to start eating them. A protection against this is that the parents prefer to roam along the bottom, far removed from the spawn that has been deposited higher up. Other fish, however, are just as likely to devour the spawn, unless some arrangement has been made to prevent this.

Although the full mating process is known for only a few *Corydoras* species, the same procedures, on the whole, apply to other species as well. Preferably, the breeding aquarium should be provided with a bottom layer of well-soaked peat dust, 5 cm (2 inches) thick. Clear water is a requirement, plus a thick plant growth along the tank sides. These usually lazy fish develop a surprising friskiness during the mating season. The actual mating is preceded by a rather long courtship period.

Mating is repeated regularly throughout several weeks, until a total of 100 to 200 eggs have been laid. The eggs are fairly large and sticky, and the young hatch out after 5 to 10 days. The fry are not difficult to raise, though they do grow rather slowly. There is no need to remove the parents. As long as the parents are given proper food, they will not eat their spawn or their offspring. It is an exceptionally attractive and pleasurable sight to see a crowd of these young little "vacuum cleaners" with their parents.

A number of catfishes, among them, for example, armoured catfishes, sometimes inhabit rather rapidly moving streams. Obviously, the male must take into account the fact that his milt can be easily whisked away by the current before he has a chance to fertilize the eggs. Certain fishes are known to take precautions against such an event by digging a pit in the sand. While the female deposits the eggs in the pit, the male takes a stand farther upstream and the current sweeps the released milt into the pit. Perhaps *Corydoras* has developed a similar practice.

Since about 1880, many aquarists have taken up with the species *Corydoras paleatus* especially. It is in every respect an attractive little fish that is well appreciated and all publications about it should be regarded as important. In particular, the tests made by Knaack (1955) have proved, once and for all, that the male sperm (if sucked up by the female) does not reach the eggs by way of the intestinal canal, and that only those which slide along outside her body are effective. All authors are unanimous in agreeing that the female sucks up the milt to release it through the gills, together with the breathing water. Using a fluorescent fluid, Knaack made the female's stream of respiration water visible. Normally it leaves through the gill openings in a slipstream that bends forward on either side of the body. While mating, the couple is surrounded by a diffuse cloud which envelops them and also penetrates into the sac formed by the female's pelvic fins. In an aquarium, no account is taken of currents in the water, which must occur in the wild. Moreover, it is assumed that the female consciously, or, at least, purposefully sucks up the milt in order to carry it further along. This may not be entirely true, but the inclination is to believe that the natural currents play a rôle and that this rôle is taken over in the aquarium by the current from the slipstream of breathing water. Tests made do not conclusively prove whether the female purposefully or instinctively sucks herself fast to the vent of the male.

Females have been repeatedly observed attaching themselves close to the male anal opening, or even sometimes to the side of the male, resulting in direct fertilization of the eggs. It is likely that absorption of the milt by the female is not a functional act, nor is its release with the breathing water. It seems more likely that the milt is sucked in during mating, along with the breathing water, so that some of it is bound to get into the oral cavity and be expelled through the gills.

If the female sucks herself onto the male, normal respiration of water streaming in through the mouth and out through the gills would not be possible. Still, most catfishes can modify their respiration by breathing in as well as out through the gills. This would also account for the increased respiration rate, which is invariably observed at such times. On the other hand, the agitation due to the mating process would also, presumably, accelerate the respiration rate to a certain extent.

In summation, then, the male approaches the female, clasps her head with his pectoral fins, and presses her barbels against her body. He then takes a position that can vary in a number of ways, and the two sink together to the bottom. In this position, which can last for as long as a minute, the female usually attaches herself with her sucker to the belly or the side of the male and the usual mouth-gill method of respiration is exchanged for a twice-as-fast method of breathing in and out through the gills. Consequently, turbulent currents, which envelop the whole couple but which are stronger around the female, are set up in the water. The direction of the current causes the male sperm to be carried into the bag formed by the female's pelvic fins, thus fertilizing the eggs contained there. The female then deposits the eggs by herself, usually at some distance from the bottom. The rather sticky spawn hatches out in 5 to 7 days or a little sooner or a little later.

Corydoras are not known to have any bad habits as aquarium dwellers. They are good scavengers, doing away with live food that creeps into the bottom. They also destroy planaria (small, soft-bodied, leaf-shaped, ciliated flatworms) and clean out the dangerous, blue algae. They keep the bottom loose and free of waste. This is not to say that they subsist only upon wastes of the communal aquarium. For them to thrive and breed, they must be fed as well as any other fish, but they are not picky eaters. Two tribes belong to this sub-family: the Corydoradini and the Aspidoradini. Not too many of the latter are seen in the aquarium trade, which is a pity, as they can be a nice little group showing much promise.

Tribe Corydoradini

Two genera of this group, *Brochis* and *Corydoras*, can be distinguished from the Aspidoradini (genus *Aspidoras*), as the nuchal (neck) scutes do not run through on the back but are interrupted by an extension of the occipital bone that joins the so-called pre-dorsal shield in front of the dorsal fin. The opening in the parietal bone is longitudinally oval-shaped (round in *Aspidoras*), a significant characteristic.

Plate II-5. *Brochis splendens.*

Genus *Brochis*

The only difference between these fish and *Corydoras* is that *Brochis* has a greater number of rays in the dorsal fin—10 to 12, as against 7 to 9 ramified rays in *Corydoras*—and a higher body. In general, what has been said about *Corydoras* species can also be applied to *Brochis*. Up to now, only one species of this genus, *B. splendens* has been imported. It may be hoped that a second species, *B. multiradiatus*, will also be made available, for it is quite pretty and a real asset to any aquarium.

Brochis splendens (Castelnau, 1855)
Emerald Catfish
Green Catfish

Brochis splendens is related to *Corydoras*, having a salmon belly and olive green flanks with a metallic sheen. Its length, including the tail fin, is about 70 mm (2¾ inches). The peculiarly elongated snout is found only rarely in *Corydoras* species.

Brochis splendens was formerly known among aquarists as *B. coeruleus*, but that name has been replaced by the older name of Castelnau.

333

Genus *Corydoras*

To the long, general review of this genus, it should be added that, in spite of their tropical origin, these fishes are very hardy, an observation based on experience with *Corydoras aeneus, C. melanistius,* and *C. paleatus.* Barlink (1963) reports eggs of an unnamed species hatching at a temperature as low as 7 °C (45 °F). Presumably, they belonged to the most southerly living species, *C. paleatus,* which must endure rather low temperatures in its native habitat. Nevertheless, it is not a good idea to experiment with this hardiness as it may result in the sacrifice of some fish.

The genus *Corydoras* has an extremely widespread distribution area, both horizontally and vertically, and is likely to live in all kinds of water, even more so than the Callichthyini. A reason for this may be that specimens of this species do not grow as large as the Callichthyini and can thus pass through narrow channels without trouble. On the other hand, *Corydoras* species do not seem to be able to travel over land as the Callichthyidae do.

More than 100 species and sub-species of *Corydoras* have been described, but not more than about 20 are known to aquarists and only a few of these have gained any great measure of popularity. Although a number of new varieties are described each year, a thorough review would probably reveal that the number of true biological species is actually very low. A newly-described "species" is usually a local variety. Such local varieties show considerable differences in a group as widespread as this. However, this is of little importance to the aquarist, for it is accepted that varieties or species existing under similar conditions in the wild will behave the same way in the aquarium, insofar as breeding is concerned.

When the first specimens of *Corydoras paleatus* were brought into Europe from the La Plata region in 1880, no one suspected that this little fish would stir up tremendous interest in the following century, even in scientific circles, or that it would lead to the importation of dozens of related species.

A number of *Corydoras* species are not named in the following pages—only the best known and most important ones are.

Many biologists are engaged in intensive study of this group: Knaack, 1955 and on; Rössel, 1961 and later; Nijssen & Isbrücker, 1967–72; Weitzman, 1954; and undoubtedly still others. A useful review will be published shortly for aquarists.

The *C. aeneus* Group[1]

Members of this group are distinguished from the other three *Corydoras* groups to be discussed by the absence of cross stripes on the caudal fin and a pronounced design of spots on body, head and fins. This group includes the species *C. aeneus*, *C. nattereri*, *C. melini*, *C. arcuatus*, *C. treitli*, and as offshoots of the group, especially *C. hastatus* and *C. elegans*. Most species within this group have no lengthwise stripe, but rather a conical blotch.

The *C. barbatus* Group

This group includes the species *Corydoras barbatus* and *C. macropterus*, from the region between São Paulo and Rio de Janeiro in southeastern Brazil. Günther proposed the sub-generic name *Scleromystax* for this group to distinguish it from the remaining *Corydoras* species, for *C. barbatus* and *C. macropterus* both show a strong deviation in several respects. Usually *Scleromystax* is fully recognized as *Corydoras*, and these two are no longer considered separate by scientists. However, this does not give a true picture of the real relationship, because the species *C. barbatus* and *C. macropterus* and possibly *C. elegans* appear to occupy a special place and, technically (by systematic classification), can be differentiated from the remaining *Corydoras* species. Moreover, their distribution suggests that they are an original (primitive) stock which was an offshoot from the evolutionary line very close to the callichthyids. The two representative species of the *C. barbatus* group are shown on the map in Illus. II–17 of the *C. paleatus* group under 1 and 2, because they are probably closer to this group than to the other two.

The *C. paleatus* Group

Of the four species belonging to this group, only *Corydoras microps* and *C. paleatus* are available.

The *C. punctatus* Group

This group is also called the *C. leopardus* group, named for *Corydoras leopardus*. Since *C. leopardus* is a synonym of *C. julii*, this group is better named after the oldest known species belonging to it, *C. punctatus*, described as early as 1794 by Bloch.

This group is much less homogeneous than the two groups

---

1 In previous publications, the author has divided the species known to him into four groups. Even though he has been aware that numerous new species have not been classified, and that some, on closer inspection, appear to have been classified correctly, he resumes this classification here without modification. However, he has allowed a number of sub-species formerly recognized by him to be rescinded. A few notes regarding four groups of *Corydoras* species give some insight into the problems surrounding the systematic classification of *Corydoras*.

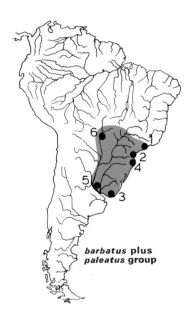

barbatus plus paleatus group

Illus. II-17. Distribution of the *Corydoras* groups, indicating the type localities of the best-known species. 1. *Corydoras barbatus*. 2. *macropterus*. 3. *paleatus*. 4. *garbei*. 5. *microps*. 6. *polystictus*. 7. *aeneus*. 8. *nattereri* 9a. *metae*. 9b. *melini*. 9c. *yersi*. 10. *arcuatus*. 11. *hastatus*. 12. *elegans*. 13. *punctatus*. 14. *julii*. 15. *reticulatus*. 16. *melanistius*.

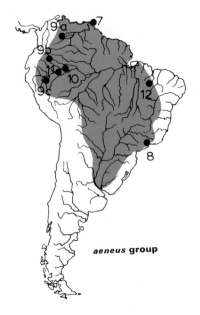

aeneus group

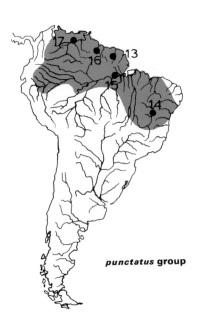

punctatus group

336

discussed above. Many species have been described which undoubtedly belong to this group and, technically (on grounds of useful systematic characteristics), can be differentiated either not at all or only with difficulty. Even the sub-species separated from each other by necessity have a tendency to merge, so this must be an IDEAL SPECIES. An ideal species is one that is composed of a great variety of populations having interlocking characteristics, locally substituting for each other, and all together making up a single, large population.

Obviously, this is bound to cause difficulties in naming the group. Each variety that deviates even slightly could be called a new species, —this has been done to a considerable extent—but this would not allow us a true picture of the relationship. Moreover, among a number of specimens caught at the same place and undoubtedly belonging to the same population, there are often specimens that vary from the others—such as the partial or entire lack of pigmentation in a spot that, in the others, is heavily loaded with pigment. Taken all together, study of the material and the literature has led to setting up the following classification. In this system, within the *C. punctatus* group, two smaller form series are distinguished, between either of which a distinct connection can be made with the ancestral forms of *C. barbatus* or *C. paleatus* groups.

Plate II-6. *Corydoras aeneus.*

Corydoras aeneus (Gill, 1858)
Aeneus Catfish
Bronze Catfish

Corydoras aeneus is a species that is growing continually more popular. Its distribution area stretches over the entire Guiana plateau and Trinidad. The many local varieties that are exported from that area furnished the basis for a great number of new names. It is not completely clear, due to the loss of much of the material, which aquarium fish really were *Corydoras aeneus,* and which belonged to another, though related, variety.

C. aeneus is one of the species that can attain a length of about 75 mm (3 inches). The males are somewhat smaller than the females. The general coloration is rust brown to greyish brown, depending on the place of origin, with an irregular, lengthwise stripe that is broad behind the gills, becomes narrower towards the tail, and is made up of spots flowing together. The root of the tail usually has a rather clear, vertical spot. The fins have neither spots nor dots; at most, they are but slightly tinted.

Corydoras arcuatus Elwyn, 1939
Skunk Corydoras
Tabatinga Catfish

Most currently available specimens of *Corydoras arcuatus* belong to the variety having a dark line curving from the corner of the mouth, along the back, to the underlobe of the tail fin. Aquarists may have noticed that the dark line is not of constant intensity and, particularly, that part of it between the eye and the dorsal fin is likely to fade, so that the fish looks more like *Corydoras myersi*. *C. arcuatus* can, however, always be definitely recognized by the total absence of a black, or even a dark, spot on the dorsal fin. Also striking is the yellow rim of the eye. Like other varieties, this species attains a total length of about 60 mm (2⅜ inches).

The coloration can certainly be called attractive, for the mouse-grey flanks have a green-gold sheen that is more or less brightly visible, depending on the light. Sometimes this is overcast with a rosy glow.

Plate II-7. *Corydoras arcuatus.*

Corydoras barbatus (Quoy & Gaimard, 1824)
Banded Corydoras

The native habitat of *Corydoras barbatus* stretches from Santos to close to Rio de Janeiro in the state of São Paulo, Brazil. Its length is about 85 mm (3⅜ inches).

The species is distinguished by hard, brushy, hair-fine, bony spines on the sides of the snout. This is less well developed, or completely absent, in the female. *C. barbatus* has a slimmer, longer shape than most *Corydoras* species. It should be kept at a temperature range of 20–25 °C (68–77 °F).

The basic coloration is golden brown with a blue-grey to dark blue-brown pattern. It is positively a bottom-dweller, sometimes burying itself completely in the mud.

Illus. II-18. Three stages in the development of *Corydoras bondi* **from the Sipaliwini Basin of Surinam.** *a* **is 25 mm (1 inch),** *b* **is 40 mm (1$\frac{19}{32}$ inches),** *c* **is 52 mm (2$\frac{1}{16}$ inches). The difference in pattern and its development in the larger specimens—especially that of the lengthwise stripe—is remarkable.**

Corydoras elegans **Steindachner, 1877**

Elegant Corydoras

This species has been known to European collectors since 1938. It is the only one of the larger-sized fishes that does not prefer to dwell on the bottom, but swims about in the middle layers of the water and rummages among the plants, similarly to *C. hastatus.*

The general coloration is olive brown with dark spots that melt together to form three more or less distinct, lengthwise stripes. There are some irregular spots on the dorsal fin. Its length is to about 60 mm (2⅜ inches).

Corydoras funnelli Fraser-Brunner, 1947

This variety can hardly be distinguished from *C. punctatus*. However, it does have a black iris in its eye and the spots on its head are less distinct, while the longitudinal stripe is more so. The caudal fin has five cross stripes.

Corydoras hastatus (Eigenmann & Eigenmann, 1888)
Pygmy Corydoras

This species is known in two places in Brazil—Villa Bella and Descalvados. It is not impossible, however, that these little *Corydoras* have a far wider distribution.

Unlike most of the other species, this variety does not take much to the bottom, but lives in the upper water levels among the plants, moving about like *Otocinclus*, for example, resting belly-up under the leaves. *C. hastatus* is an active and unusually attractive fish that grows no larger than about 35 mm (1⅜ inches). A deep black band ends at the root of the tail in a spot shaped like a lance-head. The edges of the band are milk white. The body and fins are spattered with fine, black dots.

Illus. II-19. *Corydoras griseus* Holly, 1940, from Guyana, a species or variety belonging to the group *potaroensis,* is regularly found in aquarists' tanks.

Plate II-9. *Corydoras julii.*

Corydoras julii Steindachner, 1906
Leopard Corydoras

Plate II-9 speaks for itself. The basic coloration of *C. julii* is very attractive—silver-grey with a blue-green lustre. The gill covers have a metallic sheen. The length is about 60 mm (2⅜ inches).

Corydoras longirostris Hoedeman, 1953
Long-Nosed Corydoras

This variety is native to the Amazon Basin, but the exact place of capture, unfortunately, is unknown. Although closely related to *C. melanistius*, *C. longirostris* shows a few marked differences, such as the seven cross stripes on the caudal fin. The spots on the body lie fairly regularly under each other, on the edges of the bony plates, and thus tend to form vertical more than longitudinal stripes. *C. longirostris* differs further in the remarkable length of its snout, while the dark band over the eye spreads considerably forward.

Because of this species' close relationship with other varieties, successful cross-breeding would be important.

Corydoras macropterus Regan, 1913
Big-Finned Corydoras
Large-Finned Corydoras

Although Regan did not mention this feature, the caudal fin of this species has cross stripes made up of short lines. Otherwise, it is much like *C. barbatus*. In full-grown specimens, the fins of the males are quite long—especially the dorsal and pectoral fins—from which comes the name *macropterus* (literally "big fin"). The design and coloration are the same as that of *C. barbatus*. Both fish grow to the same length and inhabit the same region. It might be useful to determine whether *C. macropterus* might not be males of a *C. barbatus* variety.

Plate II-10. *Corydoras melanistius.*

Corydoras melanistius Regan, 1912
Black Spotted Corydoras

Corydoras melanistius is native to the Guianas and to Venezuela to the west (in the Orinoco River Basin). It is possible that it will be found elsewhere, too, with or without more divergent forms. At first sight, the interesting collection from near Paramaribo and Bergendal in Surinam scarcely differs from the Guiana specimens. This possibly indicates a fairly recent migration into this area from the Amazon Basin.

Corydoras melini Lönnberg & Rendahl, 1930

This variety was at first assumed to be a sub-species of *Corydoras metae* (see Hoedeman, 1952 and later), but further investigation caused it to be considered, at least for the time being, as a separate species. Nonetheless, it undoubtedly belongs to the complex in which *Corydoras metae* has been classified.

Corydoras metae Eigenmann, 1914

Bandit Corydoras

Masked Corydoras

Corydoras metae can be clearly distinguished by the almost entirely black dorsal fin, and the black, curved band which does not run as far forward as the eye, as it does in *C. melini.*

Corydoras microps Eigenmann & Kennedy, 1903

Light-Spot Catfish

The basic coloration of this species is yellowish to olive brown, while the belly is yellow ochre. The body is covered with a number of large and small spots and dots, brownish blue to black, which fuse together into wavy bands down the middle of the flanks. *C. microps* grows to about 55 mm ($2\frac{3}{16}$ inches) long.

Plate II-12. *Corydoras myersi.*

Corydoras myersi Miranda-Ribeiro, 1942
Myers' Corydoras

On the one hand, *Corydoras myersi* is closely related to *C. aeneus*, from which it gets much of its beautiful, golden glow, and on the other hand, to *C. arcuatus*, from which it differs in only one respect: the intensely black band does not run all the way forward. *C. myersi*, a very attractive species, like *C. metae* and *C. aeneus*, is among the most brilliant *Corydoras* species. Like tiny *C. hastatus*, it swims about more in the upper water levels, showing little tendency to dwell on the bottom.

Plate II-13. *Corydoras nattereri.*

Corydoras nattereri Steindachner, 1877
Blue Corydoras

C. nattereri is related and very similar to *C. aeneus.* The basic coloration of this species is, however, more bluish, and there is a black spot on the foremost rays of the dorsal fin, and a much less distinct spot on the base of the adipose fin. The total length is about 60 mm (2⅜ inches).

Corydoras paleatus (Jenyns, 1842)

Peppered Corydoras

This fish, native to South America, is abundant in the Rio de la Plata and in the waters of the Brazilian states of Rio Grande do Sul and Santa Catharina.

C. paleatus is a typical fresh-water fish, which was brought to Europe (Paris) for the first time in 1880. It has since found its way into many home aquariums and is still a popular fish.

The body of this *Corydoras*, as it is with the rest of the species, is cone-shaped. The line of the head and back is arched. Towards the rear the fish is compressed laterally. This, like the flattened belly, indicates a life style as a bottom-dweller. The maximum length is 75 mm (3 inches). The mouth is small and completely under-positioned. The caudal fin is large and deeply forked, the upper fin lobe being somewhat larger and longer than the under one. All fins are well developed and pointed, and the foremost rays are the longer.

The general coloration is grey-green to olive green, with a sheen darkening towards the back to almost blue-black. The belly is a dirty

Plate II-14. *Corydoras paleatus.*

white with a soft, lilac tint. The back and flanks are spotted with many irregular dots and stripes of a dark (to navy blue) hue. The fins are also irregularly spotted and sometimes the small, blue-black spots are aligned and form stripes.

The sexes cannot be easily distinguished. The male is usually somewhat smaller and more slender than the female, and his pectoral fins are more pointed.

Any aquarium that is not too small is suitable for this pretty fish. The temperature should be maintained at 20 °C (68 °F), but it is not overly sensitive and can stand a temperature gradually dropping down to 15 °C (59 °F). It is even known to have survived temperatures hovering near the freezing point (0 °C or 32 °F), apparently without suffering harm. However, it is not advisable to put it to the test. High temperatures affect *C. paleatus* even less. If it feels any distress, it turns on the intestinal respiration system. This can be observed as it keeps shooting up to the surface for air in a typically noisy fashion that cannot be mistaken. At any rate, these temperature adaptations are mentioned only to show how well armoured, against a variety of circumstances, this armoured catfish is.

Like the rest of the *Corydoras* species, *C. paleatus* is omnivorous. As a scavenger, it is a veritable vacuum cleaner, sucking up everything. Once used to its surroundings, it begins to rummage about in the bottom of the aquarium, looking for something edible. White worms, tubifex worms, and gnat larvae that have burrowed into the bottom are quickly found and devoured. Otherwise, *C. paleatus* is quite peaceful and would let you "eat the cheese off its bread," as the saying goes, meaning that it would hardly stand up for itself. Often, the other aquarium fishes hang around while *C. paleatus* is grubbing for delicacies, and as soon as a choice tidbit is dug up, one darts forward and grabs it away right in front of *C. paleatus'* nose. Good-natured *C. paleatus* is never disturbed by this, but returns to his foraging with as much energy and hope as ever.

Corydoras punctatus (Bloch, 1794)

Spotted Catfish

The species is far more widely distributed than the literature makes it seem, since there are numerous varieties that should actually be classed as sub-species of *C. punctatus*. As Bloch's original type specimens have apparently been lost, and as his description and illustration are not quite clear as to precisely which variety he meant, material from Surinam was chosen for this book, as that is where Bloch got his specimens.

Nijssen & Isbrücker (1967), working with Surinamese material from Compagnie Creek, have recently selected a neotype. This species looks very much like *Corydoras wotroi* (see Plate II–19), but lacks the dark band over the eye, though it has a distinct, black spot on the dorsal fin, like *Corydoras reticulatus*. Lucky possessors of imports from Surinam can obtain a clear picture of *C. punctatus*' appearance from the illustrations of its related varieties, and will probably not confuse it with members of the other three groups (see page 335). All varieties of *C. punctatus* grow to about 55–60 mm ($1\frac{3}{16}$–$1\frac{3}{8}$ inches) long, the male being somewhat smaller than the female.

It is not known whether breeding of the *C. punctatus* group has been accomplished, but there should be no reason for this to be more difficult than it is with, say, the *C. aeneus* or *C. paleatus* groups.

Plate II-15. *Corydoras pygmaeus.*

Corydoras pygmaeus Knaack, 1966

The little fish in Plate II-15 clearly differs from *C. australe,* although, in many respects, it does resemble the type specimen. It is not known where the specimen in Plate II-15 came from. Its length is about 35 mm (1⅜ inches). The difference in the patterns of the two fish is clear, especially since *C. australe* has a much less intense total coloration.

According to Knaack (1966), *C. pygmaeus* should have been classed with the genus *Aspidoras,* according to the characteristics involved. In fact, examination of his *C. pygmaeus* material led him to announce that the genus *Aspidoras* should be regarded as a synonym for *Corydoras.*

***Corydoras rabauti* La Monte, 1941**

Dwarf Corydoras

Rabaut's Corydoras

Although it appeared in the United States, unnamed, in 1939, this tiny fish, which does not grow bigger than 30 mm ($1\frac{3}{16}$ inches), has probably not yet been introduced into Europe. The specimens described and illustrated under that name probably belong to the *C. metae* group. *C. rabauti* certainly is not the same as *C. myersi* (see Plate II–12), as Pinter suggested (1955).

Corydoras rabauti is a dwarf variety, distinguished by a salmon-orange basic coloration in front of the dorsal fin and over the head. There is a dark, blue-black stripe just in front of the eyes and a dark, triangular spot on the gill covers. An ink blue line runs around the body from a line between the first ray of the dorsal fin and the base of the pelvic fins to the root of the tail or a little short of it. In the last case, the dark part of the body runs out on the root of the tail in a narrow line that ends in two square, dark spots. That there is a relationship between this species and the *C. metae* group is evident because sometimes, the band around the body is lighter in coloration in the belly region, so that only an intensely-tinted stripe remains, running from the beginning of the dorsal fin, or somewhat farther forward (as in *C. myersi*), over the upper half of the body to the root of the tail. This dwarf variety is clearly totally different from the *C. metae* dwarf. That it is a dwarf variety has been confirmed by Francesca La Monte, who writes that she has bred specimens about 18 mm ($\frac{23}{32}$ inch) long, resulting in young that did not grow larger than 20 mm ($\frac{13}{16}$ inch).

Plate II-16. *Corydoras reticulatus.*

Corydoras reticulatus Fraser-Brunner, 1947
Network Catfish
Reticulated Corydoras

The white-edged black spot on the dorsal fin clearly distinguishes this variety from others. The specimen in Plate II–16 originated from a place that cannot be more closely pin-pointed than somewhere in the Amazon Basin (an extremely vague indication where such a vast region is concerned). Technically and as far as pattern is concerned,

Plate II-17. Deviant variety of *Corydoras reticulatus.* Note that the dark spot is missing from the dorsal fin and that there is different striping in the caudal fin. Could a sex characteristic be hidden here?

Illus. II-20. This close-up of the snout of *Corydoras reticulatus* shows very clearly the two paired nostrils and the mouth with its fleshy and rather short barbels.

the specimen in Plate II–17 corresponds completely with *C. reticulatus*, with the difference, however, that two black bands show up in the dorsal fin. Unfortunately, these cannot be clearly seen in the photograph. Although the fish pictured is probably not identical with *C. reticulatus*, it shall not, for the time being, be given a new name. Further material, however, may change this on the basis that it is an intermediate form, one of many local varieties of this group.

A great number of *Corydoras* species have been described, mainly on the grounds of differing patterns. The *C. reticulatus* in Plate II–17 on the one hand corresponds considerably with *Corydoras microps* (which, like others, has no stripes on the caudal fin), while, on the other hand, it is reminiscent of *Corydoras acutus*, which originates in Peru, in the upper region of the Amazon Basin.

Corydoras schultzei Holly, 1940
Schultze's Corydoras

This is obviously a variety of the *C. aeneus* group and should be cared for in the same way as the other members of that group.

355

Plate II-18. *Corydoras schwartzi.*

Corydoras schwartzi Rössel, 1963
Schwartz's Corydoras

The author believes that this species is related to *C. armatus* Günther.

Plate II-19. *Corydoras wotroi* is an acquisition from Surinam, described by Nijssen & Isbrücker (1967) as a new species.

Tribe Aspidoradini

Up to the present, only one genus with one species has been assigned to this group, *Aspidoras rochai*. It has not yet been kept in aquariums.

Genus *Aspidoras*

This group is differentiated from *Corydoras* and *Brochis* in that both left and right nuchal scutes meet at the back, instead of being separated by the outgrowing point of the occipital bone.

If Knaack (see under *Corydoras pygmaeus* on page 352) is correct, that this genus is synonymous with *Corydoras*, the whole genus will probably have to be discarded, and the species *Aspidoras rochai* will become a *Corydoras*.

Aspidoras rochai Von Ihering, 1907

Importation of this species would make this fish a welcome acquisition for the aquarist, because it has characteristics that could be a starting place for investigation into its special place in relationship to the Corydoradinae sub-family. Although a number of primitive traits are present, the round, diminished cranial foramen points to a higher development than *Corydoras* and *Brochis*, from which it certainly cannot be derived.

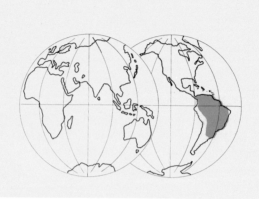

Illus. II-21. Distribution of the armoured catfish (Loricariidae).

Family Loricariidae

This is, in many respects, a remarkable family which is differentiated from practically all other families of fishes by the possession of an expandable iris-flap for control of light, which in construction and function, corresponds to the iris diaphragm in the eye of higher vertebrates.

This widespread family of catfishes lives exclusively in the South American territory shown on the map in Illus. II–21—from Panama in the north to Montevideo, Uruguay, in the south. It can be found in all kinds of environments—in stagnant pools and ponds, in slow- and swift-moving streams and rivers—up to about 3,000 m (9,840 feet) altitude. Most species live in running water in sandy or rocky surroundings, where they hide for most of the day in rocky clefts and come out towards sunset, when the sun has lost its strength.

These armoured catfishes are a specialized group well adapted to their environment. The name *lorica* means armour, and is given because the fish is armoured with bony scutes, no less ingeniously constructed than that of the medieval knights. Such armour is bound to hamper movement, but, to counteract this, these fish possess a body build of special design, as shown in Illus. II–35. Because of the clever way the "skin armour" is assembled, these fishes can manoeuvre with considerable ease without exposing the bare body. Although there are a number of natural groups in the family, all members have the same construction of four or five overlapping lateral and lateroventral rows of rather large, bony scutes, each of

358

which is set with a number of more or less large denticles. The head-shield is constructed differently in the various sub-families, and may serve as a means for telling one from another.

It is remarkable that the back is not covered with special, bony plates, but the plates on both sides come together on the back (as well as on the belly), leaving only a slit for protrusion of the dorsal and adipose fins. At the caudal peduncle, there are three or more extra bony plates on the back and the belly side, between those of the flanks.

A second characteristic, no less striking than the armour, is the fully under-positioned mouth. In running water, loricariids can attach themselves with their sucker-like mouths to plants or stones and, in the aquarium, to the glass panes. They can attach themselves so tightly, in fact, that it is impossible to pull them loose without harming them. Obviously, such a sucker is a valuable accessory in a strong current. By clinging to stones and other objects, they can rest between jumps that take them to another "mouth-hold" with a few strokes of the tail. Although they are not considered good swimmers, Loricariidae still make out better in rough water than many good swimmers that cannot withstand the current. Though they do not swim very much, they can move from place to place in a rapid, jerky fashion.

Obviously, these fishes do not take breathing water in through the mouth, as the mouth is usually holding on to something and is, therefore, sealed tight. A fish that has attached itself to the glass pane of an aquarium flutters its gills at a rapid rate that is twice the normal rate for breathing. This is caused by the water first being breathed in through the gill openings, then being breathed out again the same way —through the gill openings.

The mouth with its thick, fleshy lips is not protrusile. The upper lip bears a few barbels that are more or less strongly developed and, at the same time, partly grown together with the lip. The spines and brushy growths on the head are not barbels, although they do give the impression of being barbels. The jaws are set with hooked teeth, while the palate is devoid of them.

The gut, rolled into a spiral that takes up a large part of the body cavity, is very long, slender (typical of a plant eater) and, in some species, is plainly visible when the fish are sucked tightly to the glass pane of the aquarium. The adipose fin, if present, consists simply of a thin membrane supported by a spine.

Little is known about breeding the members of this family, but it has been determined, at least among a number of species, that a more or less exemplary brood care is undertaken by the male only. The eggs are deposited by the female on stones or other objects that have first been "grazed clean" by the male (or by both parents). As soon as the eggs are laid, the male fertilizes the eggs. He continues to remain by the spawn, sometimes covering it with his body and removing, with his thick lips, any troublesome impurity until the young hatch out. Supposedly, the male of certain species carries the eggs in the fold between his underlip and his throat until they hatch. Wherever this was observed, it was probably only a manner of transporting the eggs from one place to another, as has also been noted with many cichlids.

In addition to a difference in appearance of the sexes (see descriptions of the various species), and differences that can also be noted in the development of spines, brushes, and bony plates of the head armour, often, there also exists a remarkable difference in appearance and development of certain parts between the young and the adult members of the same species. In young specimens (Hypostominae), the dorsal fin is sometimes larger proportionately than in the adult. The opposite also occurs, and the dorsal fin continues to grow with age, as, for example, in *Pterygoplichthys* and many members of the sub-family Loricariinae. It is a family trait of Loricariidae that the pectoral fins continue to grow all the while the fish lives. Also, the length of the barbels depends on the age and species of the specimen. These are not sexual characteristics, nor are the great changes in coloration that sometimes appear. Many of the young possess four to six dark, vertical bands (occurring in many fishes) which fade more and more as the fish grows older. All in all, great changes may take place in the developmental period, which has resulted in confusion of the species and the introduction of many synonyms in the nomenclature.

Of the many genera included in this family, too few are known to aquarists. Loricariidae are attractive fishes in many respects—their coloration is exquisite—and they provide variation for the aquarium. It is entertaining to watch them as they go about their business. Their strange method of propagation is also well worth studying.

Plate II-20. *Panaque* species.

Sub-family Hypostominae*

*NOTE: The sub-family Hypostominae was formerly called Plecosto-minae, type genus *Plecostomus* Gronow, 1763. The names proposed by Gronow, however, do not follow the rules of nomenclature. *Plecostomus* was replaced by *Hypostomus* Lacépède, 1803, which changed the name of the sub-family at the same time.

This sub-family includes the following interesting genera: *Ancistrus, Hemiancistrus, Hypostomus, Pterygoplichthys,* and *Xenocara.* Species from a few other genera have occasionally been imported, but these then vanish without a trace, so the subject will not be pursued further here.

All members of this sub-family dwell in clear, running water, where they feed mainly on algae and other vegetable fare. However, an important part of their diet consists of plankton, along with small, crab-like creatures, and worms. In the aquarium, Hypostominae are pretty, peaceful fish, often of beautiful patterns and hues. They are well worth the attention paid them for the thorough care they provide for the brood.

Genus *Ancistrus*

Of the many species described under this genus, *Ancistrus oligospilus* is a welcome one in the home aquarium. It does not grow much longer than 10 cm (4 inches) in the aquarium, but it does grow larger in its natural habitat, the tributaries of the Middle Amazon.

Plate II-21. Belly-side of *Hemiancistrus pulcher.*

Illus. II-22. In certain parts of the Guiana Highlands, the layers rich in aluminum ore (bauxite) lie right at the surface. The peculiar red-brown coloration is so prevalent in the waters there that the fish living in it have effectively adapted their own coloration to it.

Genus *Hemiancistrus*

The remarks regarding *Ancistrus* are true for this genus as well. *Hemiancistrus schomburgki* is a species frequently imported from Surinam.

Plate II-22. A crystal-clear stream with a bottom of red stones is a habitat for, among others, various species of armoured catfish. *Corydoras aeneus* from that region is nearly orange-red with a greenish black iridescence in the dorsal region, while the protective coloration of the *Hemiancistrus* against a piece of bauxite ore speaks for itself.

Illus. II-23. A spot in the flood basin of the tropical forest edge (Surinam), which, as long as there is sufficient water, is a common haunt of *Corydoras* and *Hypostomus* species. There is an abundance of food for all kinds of fish.

Genus *Hypostomus*

This genus has contributed many popular aquarium fish, though it has been repeatedly and erroneously called *Plecostomus* (see note to Hypostominae on page 361).

Illus. II-24. Typical habitat of the armoured catfish (among others), directly above a rapids, in the Sipaliwini Basin, Surinam. Note the calm water, with beginning of rapids at the right. When high water comes, in the rainy season, it flows over the rocky area in the foreground.

Illus. II-25. *Hypostomus commersoni.* Above, side view of head, Illus. II-26, top view. Note the armour plates and the double nostrils with valves.

Hypostomus commersoni (Valenciennes, 1840)
Commerson's Suckermouth Catfish

The most striking difference between this fish and Loricariinae is the complete absence of bony plates on the abdomen. Although this fish grows to 40 cm (16 inches) in its natural habitat (the region of the

Illus. II-26.

Illus. II-27. *Hypostomus commersoni* is an eater of algae, like all its relatives. The armour plates are set with fine denticles, which gives the impression that the fish is covered with fine hair.

La Plata River and the Brazilian state of Rio Grande do Sul), it stays well below that in the aquarium. It has been repeatedly imported since 1893. Propagation is carried on in large aquariums, as it is with their related varieties.

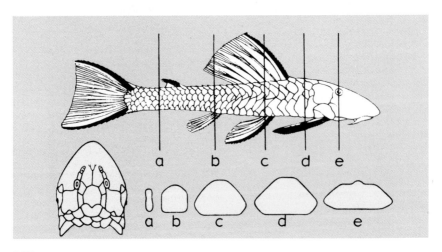

Plate II-22. *Hypostomus plecostomus.*

Hypostomus plecostomus (Linné, 1758)
Armardillo del Rio
"Plecostomus"
"Suckermouth" Catfish

The length of this fish is about 25 cm (10 inches), but smaller in the aquarium. It is a very attractive and popular species. If the tank is not too small, there is no worry about the fish tearing up the bottom. They like to have a few pieces of stone to lie on.

←

Illus. II-28. A sketch, including details, of a *Hypostomus*. The detail drawings from left to right show the arrangement of the bony plates on top of the head and cross-sections of the body and head, corresponding by letter to the lines crossing the body. The body structure of this entire family changes from head to tail from depressed (vertically flattened) to compressed (sideways flattened). The shape of the body is closely dependent upon the fish's manner of living and its habitat. On the one hand, it must have a rocky bottom with a broad, flat area where it can lie still and hold itself fast with the mouth. At the same time, the shape of the tail indicates the possibility of its being a good swimmer, especially when swimming against a strong current.

367

Plate II-23. *Hypostomus punctatus.*

Hypostomus punctatus (Valenciennes, 1840)
Spotted Suckermouth Catfish

The species *Hypostomus punctatus* has been imported quite often since 1928 from southeastern Brazil. In the past few years, it has begun to enjoy a revival of popularity. In the freedom of nature, it grows to 30 cm (12 inches) long. Sexual maturity is reached at 20 cm (8 inches).

Illus. II-29. **Head of** *Lasiancistrus maracaiboensis,* **viewed (left) from above and (right) from below. Here, too, the male has a flap lip covered with papillae.**

Plate II-24. *Xenocaria bufonia,* mouth, seen from below. The photo very clearly shows the lips, grown into a suction disc, and the papillae.

Genus *Xenocara*

The species *Xenocara bufonia, X. dolichoptera* and *X. latifrons* are the ones best known to aquarists. They are native to the Amazon Basin

Illus. II-30. *Xenocaria bufonia,* a close-up of the mouth, showing the two parts of the lower jaw, thickly set with fine, rasp-like teeth, which serve to scrape algae from stones.

370

and the Guianas. As these particularly lovely little fishes grow no longer than about 15 cm (6 inches), they are suitable for a home aquarium that is not very large.

The species included here—as well as *Ancistrus* and others— are commonly known as "bristle-nose" or "bushy face." The males especially, and in some species females, have a sense organ on the head, bristling with a number of remarkable projections. As the fish grows older, these develop into tentacles. Along with the barbels around the thick-lipped, under-positioned mouth, these projections adorn the fore part of the head. Among other things, their purpose is to sense the speed or strength of the current in their native habitat.

Plate II-25. *Xenocara bufonia.* In many respects, these catfish are attractive and very interesting fish. The taste-, smell-, and feel-organs are quite well developed. The strangely formed growths on the head are sense organs of touch, with which the fish feels its way about in murky waters. As it slips its sucking mouth over stones and the panes of the aquarium, this fish is reminiscent of slow-moving snails—as far as the mouth is concerned, of course—and it is continuously busy with the search for food. The iris flap over the eye, typical of this family, can be observed especially well in this photo and in Illus. II-30. Although the "eyelid" is immovable, it still serves a protective purpose.

Plate II-26. *Xenocara dolichoptera*, half-grown specimen.

Plate II-27. Belly-side of *Xenocara dolichoptera*.

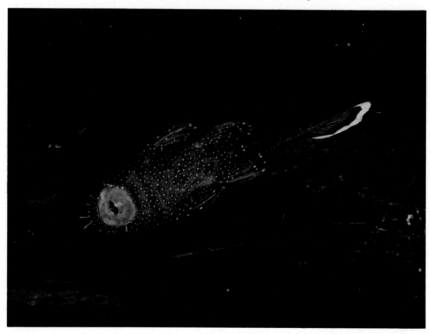

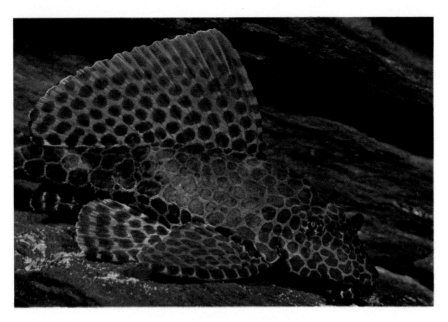

Plate II-28. *Pterygoplichthys gibbiceps.*

Illus. II-31. *Pterygoplichthys multiradiatus* Hancock, 1829.

Plate II-29. *Otocinclus flexilis.*

Sub-family Hypoptopominae

Of the six genera belonging to this sub-family, only several species of *Otocinclus* are known to aquarists.

Genus *Otocinclus*

The members of this genus are differentiated from previously-named members of the family because they have one or more pairs of bony plates on the sides that meet between the anal fin and the anus. They have a large ventral plate. The abdomen is flattened, but the body is much less depressed than in the sub-family Loricariinae.

Otocinclus flexilis Cope, 1894
Dwarf Sucker Catfish

This is a southern species, native to the La Plata River Basin and the Brazilian state Rio Grande do Sul. Along with the comments on related species with which more experience has been had, a simple reference to Plate II–29 will suffice.

374

Otocinclus vestitus Cope, 1871
Dwarf Sucker Catfish

This is the best-known and most frequently bred species of this fascinating genus. *Otocinclus vestitus* is known to come from south-eastern Brazil, near Santa Cruz and Rio de Janeiro. Experience from several other species indicates that it is probably more widespread than many other catfishes and armoured catfishes. It is not always a simple procedure to capture it in large numbers.

The body of this handsome little catfish is elongate, while the tail is compressed and the head depressed. The snout is blunt, rounded off, and the mouth completely sub-terminal. The maximum length is 60 mm (2⅜ inches). The dorsal fin begins about one third of the way from the eye to the caudal root and consists of one unramified, bony, though not spiny, ray and six weak, ramified fin rays. The anal fin has one unramified ray and five that are ramified. There is no adipose fin. Also, the paired fins have an unramified, hard ray provided with fine teeth or denticles on the fore edge. The entire body has an armour of small, bony plates; only the underside of the head remains uncovered. The general coloration is grey-brown with darker spots. A black band runs from the tip of the snout, over the eyes, to beyond the root of the tail. Both sexes show the same pattern and are difficult to tell apart. The females are presumably somewhat larger than the males, and, in any case, they have a thicker, rounder belly.

Otocinclus vestitus, like its near relatives, is found in more or less swiftly-running waters, an environment to which it is admirably adapted, in spite of its apparent inability to swim well. As it has no swim bladder, it cannot stand still, but it skips about from stone to plant to against the aquarium pane, and so on. The flat belly, the lips

Illus. II-32. *Otocinclus vestitus*.

grown out into a sucking disc, and the pelvic fins that serve as little hands, permit it to stick fast to any object it happens to land on. The busy activity of this little fish is a sight to be seen. If it feels at home in the tank and has enough oxygen and sunlight, it gives pleasure for a long time. It is not shy nor does it search for dark places to hide in. It is just as at home under artificial light or in the dimness of evening as in the daytime, when its aquarium is exposed to bright sunlight. It rests when it is dark, as other fishes do. It pays no attention to its companions in the aquarium and keeps itself busy cleaning algae off stones, plants, and the glass panes of the tank. The typical "rasp-mouth" moves quickly, while the creature is looking for still more places to "sucker onto" for a rest. It goes about its work in the oddest positions, even upside-down at the surface, when some tidbit to its liking—such as the common water skim, waterfleas, gnat larvae, or tubifex worms from the feeding session—floats up there. *Otocinclus vestitus* is essentially omnivorous, although plant-type fare (algae) is certainly the main dish on its menu, as may be concluded from the long, spiral gut. It makes only sparing use of intestinal respiration, even when little oxygen is present in the water. When it does come to the surface for air, it zips up and then back again to its starting point. Like other catfishes, this species is also very hardy and can stand a wide range of temperatures of 15–25 °C (59–77 °F) quite well. It is generally kept in water that is too warm for a running-water dweller, a condition that often brings with it a lowering of the water's oxygen content.

Breeding is fascinating and similar in many respects to that of the *Corydoras* species. The procedure differs here, however, in that fertilization takes place only after the eggs have been deposited in a certain place—on the aquarium pane, a stone or plant. No brood care, such as is undertaken by the *Loricaria* species, has been observed. The total number of eggs that can be laid varies widely; possibly, they are laid in several clutches. The author, Hoedeman, counted a clutch of 34 eggs, crystal-clear, slightly cream-tinted, truly ovoid in form, and piled in a thick heap.

Depending on the temperature and other factors, the eggs hatch after 50 to 100 hours. Very soon, the young ones dart about the tank, looking just like their elders. Even the under-positioned mouth immediately takes up the function of a sucker-disc.

***Otocinclus vittatus* Regan, 1904**

Striped Dwarf Sucker Catfish

This little fish from the Matto Grosso, Paraguay Basin, is similar in habits and characteristics to other members of the genus. The back is dark, the belly lighter and a dark longitudinal stripe extends from the tip of the snout through the eye to the caudal base and continues to the middle rays of the caudal fin.

Sub-family Loricariinae

This sub-family includes numerous genera and many species in South America. As an example for all the rest, the well known *Loricaria parva* is described below. Fans of this little fish will be particularly interested in the African relatives of this sub-family (see Amphiliidae on page 384).

Genus *Loricaria*

This is a very widespread genus, occurring all over South America— from Panama to Peru and from the Guianas to the Rio de la Plata. Of the dozens of species, *Loricaria parva* is most often bred in aquariums. *Loricaria lanceolata* and *Loricaria microlepidogaster* are often kept but never bred. The strangely shaped mouth has rasp-like teeth and the underlip is beset with numerous tiny bumps. In the male, this lip grows out into a very large flap. It has a special function in caring for the eggs, which is described under *Loricaria parva* on the next page.

Illus. II-33. Mouth opening of *Loricaria parva*, male. Note the broad, outgrown, lower lip with papillae and the denticles sticking out sideways from the head like bristles.

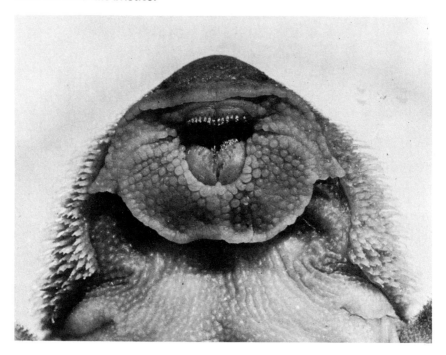

Illus. II-34. *Loricariichthys* is entirely different from *Loricaria*, even though it also has a broad flap of skin for an underlip. In the male's brood care, this flap serves in the protection and management of the spawn and the newly-hatched young.

Loricaria parva Boulenger, 1895
Whiptailed Catfish

In spite of its total length of about 75 mm (3 inches), the body is of such a slender shape that *L. parva* scarcely stands out in a medium-sized aquarium. The general coloration is beige to light brown with dark (to black) vertical bands and brown-black spots arranged in irregular stripes on the fins. As a typical bottom-dweller from rocky regions, *Loricaria parva* feeds mainly on algae. It uses its completely under-positioned mouth with rasp-like teeth to scrape algae from

379

Illus. II-35. Skin armour (only part of the caudal peduncle is shown) of a *Loricariichthys*. The difference is striking when compared with the double row of bony scutes of Callichthyidae (see page 318). Here are small scale-like bony plates, also provided with dermal denticles over the entire outer surface and rear edge. The transition of the armour median scales by way of the fulcra to the outer spines of the caudal fin is even more pronounced.

Illus. II-36. A typical view of *Loricariichthys*. Note the fragile dorsal fin rays (arrow).

plants and rocks. Its instinct for brood care is very strongly developed, a characteristic of the entire family. The relatively large, light brown eggs are deposited on a rock that has been thoroughly cleaned by joint action of the parents over a period of several days.

The female deposits four or five eggs at a time. Like the eggs of the rest of the family, these are very sticky, so that they adhere firmly wherever deposited. The male then pushes the female aside in order to fertilize the eggs. Soon, the female deposits another clutch of five eggs, and so on, until, in a few hours, about 50 to 60 eggs have been laid. Having finished her duty, the female withdraws, leaving the male to take over the care of the brood. This is quite similar to the parental care of the cichlids, but is even more intensely performed. If the aquarist were to push the little fellow away from his post by hand, he would try frantically to reach the eggs again and, succeeding, would cover them in a protective way with his head and breast (Friswold, 1949).

The male keeps watch over the eggs this way for 10 days, carefully cleaning away every slightest growth of fungus that might try to take hold. The young fish are about 10 mm ($\frac{3}{8}$ inch) long when they hatch out, and they hang on plants and rocks—perfect, miniature replicas of their parents, or rather, of the mother, for the head of the male broadens with age. Besides, the male has less of a belly than the female.

Illus. II-37. The head of *Loricariichthys brunneus* resembles the ancestral bony fishes, the ostracoderms and some placoderms. All the bony plates on the head, spines, and fin rays of the pectoral fins are set with fine denticles. Note the paired nostrils between the closely-set eyes on top of the flat head.

Plate II-30. *Farlowella acus.*

Plate II-31. *Farlowella gracilis.*

Sub-family Astroblepinae

Several species from genera of this sub-family would, if imported, have a good chance of becoming popular aquarium fish. This is a good hint for the dealer. The remarkable thing about this sub-family is that, although the members are armoured catfish, they have a bare skin which has lost the power to develop dermal scutes or plates.

Family Trichomycteridae

This family is closely related to and presumably deriving from the Loricariidae. Generally, these fishes are considered undesirable for home and public aquariums. However, the author, along with some aquarists, agrees that they are interesting fishes, some of which, especially certain *Pygidium* spp., are undeserving of the bad name. They are small and loach-like and are excellent scavengers when kept with fishes of approximately their size. They are being discussed here because of the very strange actions and the habitats of most of the species. In Chapter 6, more was said about these unusual fishes which live as parasites, more or less like lampreys, in the gill cavity of other fishes. Many species have a remarkable and unpleasant custom called "urinophilia" (see page 236), meaning entering urinary tracts. People bathing in the natural waters of South America must watch out for these intruders. The barbed hooks that arm the head of such a creature cannot be removed by any means other than surgery. Ichthyologically, however, they are interesting in many respects. As far as skull characteristics are concerned, they show a great similarity to the loaches (see Cobitidae, page 427).

Illus. II-38. Distribution of the Trichomycteridae.

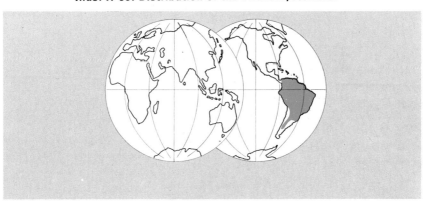

Plate II-32. *Phractura* species.

Family Amphiliidae

This African family is very closely related to the Loricariidae. Unfortunately, very little is known about how they react to being kept in the home aquarium. Nevertheless, a few very promising genera are named here, some of which, in any case, have been imported for aquarium purposes. These genera are: *Amphilius, Andersonia, Belono-glanis, Doumea, Paramphilius, Phractura,* and *Trachyglanis.*

Family Sisoridae

In the future, two Asiatic families will certainly be important for aquarists. These are the Amblycepitidae and the Sisoridae. An interesting species of the latter family—*Akysis variegatus*—already on the market, is a lovely orange-yellow-and-black striped species that grows to not much longer than 10 cm (4 inches).

Illus. II-39. *Akysis variegatus.*

Plate II-33. *Akysis variegatus,* a member of the Asian family Sisoridae.

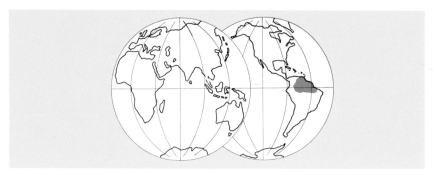

Family Aspredinidae

This is also a South American family of catfishes, which is just as remarkable as its relatives. Members are called "Frying-Pan Fish," a name that carries with it a mental picture of their strange body build. This is clearly shown in Illus. II–41 and II–42.

Although these fish are certainly not regular guests of the importers and dealers, it would be well worth the trouble to keep asking about them from time to time. Although Aspredinidae grow to a length of several decimetres (12 inches or more), an enormous tank is not necessary.

The two sub-families are Aspredininae and Bunocephalinae. A few species of the last-named sub-family have been imported, to the great satisfaction of many aquarists.

Illus. II-41. *Bunocephalus amaurus.*

Illus. II-42. *Bunocephalus amaurus* **from the Sipaliwini Basin in Surinam. This is a very striking armoured catfish, which for a long time, has been known to aquarists by the appropriate name of Banjo Catfish. How they happened to be called such a name is apparent from the photographs.**

Genus *Bunocephalus*

The species *Bunocephalus amaurus* is undoubtedly distributed over the whole Guiana plateau where it is quite abundant, along with several local varieties (sub-species). *Bunocephalus* spp. are commonly known as "Banjo Catfishes" because of their shape.

Hopefully, aquarists will try their luck with these fish, so that more will be known about them.

Family Helogenidae

This family contains a single genus with several species, of which *Helogenes marmoratus* is commercially available.

Genus *Helogenes*

Helogenes marmoratus Günther, 1863
Marbled Catfish

Helogenes marmoratus comes from Guyana and Surinam and probably from most of northeastern South America. As far as is known, the first aquarium specimens were introduced from Surinam in 1956. Until recently, this fish was known to be native to Guyana only, but in 1942 in Surinam, Geijskes caught the first specimens, which he preserved. The first official report from Surinam is by Boeseman (Leiden), dated 1952.

This is a very different type of catfish, classed in a separate family, for no relationship has yet been shown with other groups. Its length is about 80 mm ($3\frac{3}{16}$ inches). Although it looks and behaves in the strangest manner, the fish is extremely peaceful, lying still on one side to rest (seemingly a natural posture) for long periods.

The anal fin is very long, the dorsal and adipose fins extremely small. The general coloration is dark brown with lighter spots of a marbled, yellowish white. The caudal fin is much lighter in coloration than the rest of the fish; indeed, all the fins are lighter than the body.

Unfortunately, nothing can be said about breeding *Helogenes marmoratus*. Nothing in this field can be expected soon, either, considering the difficulty involved in breeding the group to which this little fish belongs.

A dark bottom soil, water temperature about 24 °C (75 °F), and all types of food materials contribute further to successful breeding of this interesting fish.

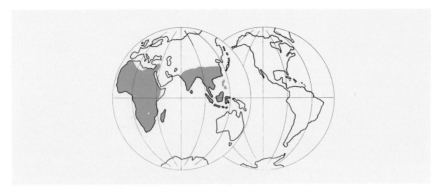

Illus. II-43. Distribution of the Clariidae.

Family Clariidae

For a comparatively small family, the Clariidae have rather a wide distribution. Insofar as suitable aquarium fishes are concerned, this family yields an interesting number of species belonging to the genera *Channallabes*, *Clarias*, *Heterobranchus*, *Gymnallabes*, and *Heteropneustes*. As far as is known, only *Heteropneustes fossilis* has been successfully bred in an aquarium. The best-known species is *Clarias batrachus*, but it is hoped that the popularity of species formerly in vogue will be revived.

Plate II-34. *Clarias batrachus*.

Illus. II-44. *Clarias batrachus.*

Clarias batrachus (Linné, 1758)
Walking Catfish

This is one of the relatively few creatures found well established in nature, in not only its normally pigmented, mud brown form but also in an albino form. The albino, with its pink, pigmentless skin and red eyes, is the form most popular as an aquarium fish.

Because of its ability to breath atmospheric air using its auxiliary breathing organ, *C. batrachus*, and others of the genus, can survive in water so foul that other fishes perish, and, with a wriggling motion aided by its powerful pectoral fins, it can propel its eel-like body overland at a respectable rate of speed, if necessary. A few years ago, in fact, this Walking Catfish received much publicity in Florida, when it left retaining ponds, where it was being held by tropical fish wholesalers, and became established in ditches and natural waterways. Because of its voracious appetite, it was feared that it might upset the ecological balance of such areas as the Everglades.

During land excursions or when removed from the water, the gill openings of *C. batrachus* are kept shut to prevent the gills and accessory breathing apparatus from drying out.

C. batrachus can live for many years in the aquarium and may reach 46 cm (18 inches) or more in length in a large tank.

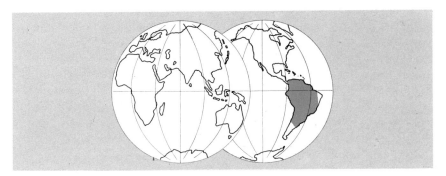

Family Doradidae

This is another South American family of catfish, two species of which are commonly found in aquariums. Many more species are known in the wild, most of which seem equally suitable for collectors. Perhaps more inclusive collections of these fishes will be seen on the market.

Acanthodoras spinosissimus Eigenmann & Eigenmann, 1888

Talking Catfish

This is a fish from the drainage basin of the Middle Amazon that is very common. It can attain a length of 150 mm (6 inches), but rarely

Plate II-35. *Acanthodoras spinosissimus.*

391

Illus. II-46. *Acanthodoras spinosissimus.*

grows longer than 100 mm (4 inches) in captivity. Since it was first introduced in 1920, it has been constantly available. As with the other members of this genus, little is known about its breeding habits. Perhaps it behaves as described in Hancock's report on the following species, *Amblydoras hancocki*, analogous to the breeding and parental care of the callichthyid genera, *Callichthys* and *Hoplosternum*.

Plate II-36. *Amblydoras hancocki.*

Amblydoras hancocki (Valenciennes, 1840)
Hancock's Amblydoras

A universally distributed species, *Amblydoras hancocki* is native to a region stretching from the lower Amazon to Peru, and in the Guianas. Its length is about 10 cm (4 inches) in the aquarium, and more than 15 cm (6 inches) in the wild. Hancock (1829) was first to set his field observations down on paper. He describes, among other things, the manner these fish have of building a "bubble nest" reinforced with pieces of plants at the surface. The eggs are laid in the nest which is thereafter guarded by the male. (See also page 147 on parental care.) Although this fish has been known for a long time to science, it was not until about 1950 that the first specimens of aquarium fish were imported. Results of breeding are not known, but this would be a good species to try one's luck on.

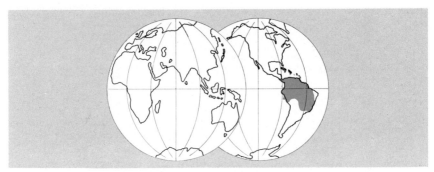

Illus. II-47. Distribution of the Auchenipteridae.

Family Auchenipteridae

South America, so rich in catfishes, also has numerous interesting species of this family. Among aquarists, however, only two species of the genus *Centromochlus* are known. Also promising are *Gephyromochlus* (Hoedeman, 1961, Bulletin Aquatic Biology), and *Trachycorystes*. Both are rather large fish, but their conduct qualifies them especially for larger aquariums.

Centromochlus aulopygius Kner, 1858
Midnight Catfish

This is one of the smallest species of auchenipterids with a maximum length to about 80 mm ($3\frac{3}{16}$ inches). It is native to the drainage basin north of the Amazon and as far as Venezuela.

Plate II-37. *Centromochlus aulopygius*.

Illus. II-48. *Centromochlus creutzbergi* from Surinam is an especially nice catfish, suitable for somewhat larger aquariums.

Centromochlus creutzbergi Boeseman, 1953

Little is known about this species. As it is small in size, it should be quite suitable for aquariums.

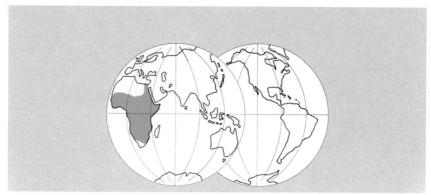

Family Mochokidae

Of the family Mochokidae, the genera *Acanthocleithron*, *Atopochilus*, *Chiloglanis*, *Euchilichthys*, *Microsynodontis*, *Mochokus* and *Synodontis* are known. From the last-named genus, a number of species are popular among aquarists.

Genus *Synodontis*

Of the dozens of species belonging in this genus, a number of interesting ones are regularly found on the market. Fortunately, this is a group about which more than usual can be said. In general, details regarding *Synodontis alberti* and *Synodontis angelicus* apply to all species. Swimming belly-up, a constant practice of *Synodontis nigriventris*, is typical of the whole family, though not practiced to the same extent.

Synodontis alberti Schilthuis, 1891

Synodontis alberti is native to the Congo Basin in Africa and Stanley Pool, Ubangi. As far as is known, it was first introduced in 1950.

Synodontis alberti is closely related to *S. nigriventris* and *S. angelicus*. After several years, it attains a total length of 160 mm (6¼ inches). The barbels at the upper lip can attain the same length as the body of the fish, which distinguishes it from its related species, as none have such long barbels. Illus. II–50 gives an excellent view of these long sense organs.

It is easy to see, in the aquarium, the important part played by these barbels in the life of these fish. First of all, they are important as "feelers"—organs of the sense of touch—while the small, ramified

Illus. II-50. *Synodontis alberti.*

barbels on the underlip serve to detect and choose food. As far as touch organs are concerned, *S. alberti* is well equipped, which is important as it appears that its eyesight is not as well developed as that of the two other similar species. This is more a creature of the dusk than *S. nigriventris* and *S. angelicus,* and its sensitivity to light is obviously greater. Although it tends to shun the light, it soon finds itself at home in a large tank. If the tank is provided with the necessary shelters, *S. alberti* can still be observed in daylight and even in sunlight. The aquarist can enjoy a wonderful show in the tank as it "vacuum cleans" the bottom, the glass panes, the plants and the rocks. It assumes every kind of position for this, and it appears that the swim bladder is so situated in the body that no position ever gives it trouble.

The basic coloration and pattern of this species is unlike that of *Synodontis angelicus,* being yellow-brown with large, irregular, dark, brownish black spots. The temperature should be 20–28 °C (68–82 °F).

Illus. II-51. *Synodontis angelicus.*

Synodontis angelicus Schilthuis, 1891

Black Clown Catfish

Polkadot African Catfish

This fish comes from the Congo Basin in Africa. *S. angelicus* attains a maximum length of 185 mm (7¼ inches), but only after several years, fortunately for the aquarist. Sometimes it does not grow this long at all in the aquarium. It is even possible that the imported specimens are of a sub-species that remains smaller than the prototype described.

The general coloration is dark brown to blackish over the entire body and fins. The belly (see Illus. II–51) is slightly lighter, unlike *S. nigriventris*. *S. angelicus* swims on its back quite easily, though its natural swimming posture appears to be belly downward. The body and fins are spotted with round to oval, yellow or yellowish white spots, which coalesce into bands on the fins and on the belly. Younger specimens possess fewer light spots, and very young specimens are almost entirely blackish brown.

With the exception of the pectorals, all of the fins are more or less rounded instead of pointed, as they are with many relatives of *S. angelicus*. The caudal fin is deeply forked. The under-positioned mouth is flanked by three pairs of barbels, the ones at the upper lip, unramified, being the longest. The two pairs at the underlip are ramified but not as much as in *S. nigriventris*.

The foremost, rigid spines of the pectoral fins make formidable

398

weapons. These spines are serrated or toothed with large thorny outgrowths on both the anterior and posterior edges. The dorsal fin spine has a smooth anterior margin in this species (the spine is sharply toothed posteriorly). When the fish spreads out these three spines, they act to hold the fish firmly in position. These spines, along with the heavily-armoured head, turn the fish into an impregnable fortress, properly respected by piratical fish. In this, *S. angelicus* is much like the well known little stickleback.

Although not commonly found in most aquariums, *S. angelicus* has still earned a certain popularity for itself and is truly interesting to study. The temperature should be 20–28 °C (68–82 °F).

Plate II-38. *Synodontis decorus.*

Plate II-39. *Synodontis flavitaeniatus.*

Synodontis flavitaeniatus Boulenger, 1919
Yellow-Striped Synodontis

This is a magnificently brilliant fish, from the Chiloango and the Congo Rivers of Africa, which grows to about 15 cm (6 inches).

Synodontis nigriventris David, 1936
African Upside-Down Catfish

S. nigriventris is native to the entire central Congo area. It is believed to have been first introduced into Europe in 1950, because before that time, it was not mentioned in either European or American aquarium journals.

This very interesting and attractive naked catfish grows no longer than 70 mm (2¾ inches). The remarkable thing about the species is that its members like to swim about on their backs, and for this reason, the belly, which is turned upward, is darker than the back, which is more lightly colored. With a number of the known species of *Synodontis*, back-swimming and resting belly-up is a common practice. They can turn over with the greatest of ease to go shuffling about the bottom, looking for something tasty.

The coloration of this species varies considerably and consists of a light brown background with white bands and stripes differing in

400

shape and varying in number. On the light background, in an equally changeable number and variety of shapes, are some roundish, blackish brown spots. No other colors are present, but the nuances in white, light brown and dark brownish black make the little creature an extremely attractive one.

The under-positioned mouth with its rasp-like little teeth has a pair of long barbels on the upper lip, while the lower lip has two pairs of short, ramified barbels. The adipose fin is low with a rather long base. See Plate II–40 for further details.

This species is, by preference, a bottom-dweller and hunts for food among waste and the rotting remains of plants. He uses his feelers, or barbels, to detect food particles among the rest of the junk. In doing so, he assumes every position imaginable. This is a positive indication that the fish is not a surface-dweller (which might also be assumed from its upside-down way of swimming). It prefers living close to the bottom, grazing on the underside of rocks, darting from place to place in search of organisms living in the dimness created by shelters intercepting strong light. It is not in any way selective about its food, and they seem to regard the bowels of dead fish especially as some kind of a special delicacy.

Like *Corydoras* from South America, this African catfish (which more or less represents practically all members of the group), is also nature's "vacuum cleaner," especially in the aquarium. It has never been found to dig up the thick layer of slime and peat dust on the bottom of the tank.

Although *S. nigriventris* has often been bred by amateurs, more precise data and breeding reports are awaited with interest. It seems to prefer the ceiling of a little cavity made up of rocks or a small flower pot as a place to stick its eggs.

Plate II-40. *Synodontis nigriventris* **in its normal, belly-up position.**

Illus. II-52. A striking position of *Synodontis nigromaculatus,* which it can hold for a long time while nibbling micro-organisms from a tree stump.

Synodontis nigromaculatus Boulenger, 1905
Black-Spotted Upside-Down Catfish

In spite of the fact that *S. nigromaculatus* can grow rather large, it takes a long time for the fish to achieve its maximum growth, about 200 mm (8 inches). It was imported in 1953 from the Upper Congo Basin (Bangweulu Lake). It is an attractive species, kept in the same manner as its relatives.

402

Illus. II-53. *Synodontis nigromaculatus* in a preferred position, half hidden behind a piece of rock.

Synodontis vittatus Boulenger, 1920
Striped Synodontis

This species also belongs to Congo imports of about 1952 and can, like *S. nigromaculatus*, reach a length of about 200 mm (8 inches). This fish has been massively imported from the type locality, Kisangani, and its surroundings. As in other varieties, the young specimens are the most attractive because the coloration pattern is plainer in the young than it is in older specimens. The basic coloration is brownish with dark (to black) stripes. The fins are yellowish, with seven black bands on the caudal fin and three more or less irregular bands over the dorsal fin. The first ray is grown out into a black thread.

Illus. II-54. The odd pattern of *Synodontis vittatus* shows up well in this old drawing.

403

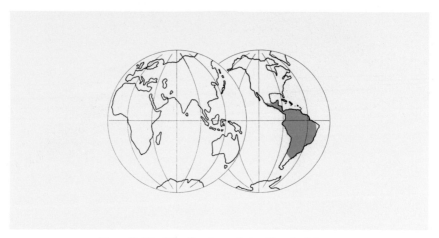

Illus. II-55. Distribution of the Pimelodidae.

Family Pimelodidae

Pimelodella gracilis **(Valenciennes, 1840)**

Graceful Catfish

Pimelodella gracilis is certainly one of the most attractive species of this family. It is generally native to the Orinoco and Amazon regions of South America as far south as La Plata. In the wild, it reaches a length of over 150 mm (6 inches), but sexual maturity in the aquarium is reached at a length of 100 mm (4 inches). As far as is known, no reports on breeding have yet been published.

Illus. II-56. *Pimelodus clarias* from Surinam.

Pimelodus clarias (Bloch, 1785)

This catfish enjoys a very large distribution area, from Panama throughout all of South America east of the Andes to Buenos Aires. The numerous local varieties are regularly imported. Practically every lot sent from South America contains a few young specimens that find their way to the aquariums of enthusiastic amateurs. Young specimens are very beautiful, lively and attractive, and extremely variable in coloration and pattern. When they get to be more than 100 mm (4 inches) long, they are no longer suitable for home aquariums, though they never become dangerous to their fellow aquarium dwellers.

No breeding information is available. The albino form generally available on the market might provide an idea or two for breeders, although this form may also have a natural origin. As so often happens, especially in Asian regions that used to be a source for many aquarium fish, it is possible that a clever exporter would breed *Pimelodus clarias* in ponds, or, at any rate, in its own habitat, thus maintaining a steady supply of sought-after species for the market.

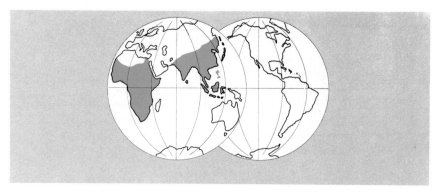

Illus. II-57. Distribution area of the Bagridae.

Family Bagridae

Several species of this family have found their way into home aquariums. Undoubtedly, the bagrids form an ancestral family of catfishes, and other families probably have been derived from them (more about this later). The relatively fragmentary knowledge that is available about such a comprehensive order of fresh-water fishes as catfishes, however, hardly permits unanimity of judgment among all those who have worked with them. The idea of assigning a great many sub-families to the large family of Siluridae has been abandoned, since doing so would only shift the problem to establishing another order of rank.

A remarkable point in the case of the undoubtedly primitive bagrids is that *Synodontis* (derived from the ancestral bagrids) shows a materially differentiated ossification of the skull, corresponding to *Clarias* and the Loricariidae which is not found in most (?) bagrids. In particular, the so-called post-temporal cranial bone of *Synodontis* is not attached to the skull by means of a layer of connective tissue, as it is with the bagrids and higher bony fishes. This situation corresponds to that of such primitive forms as Holostei.

Two sub-families of Bagridae are known—the African Bagrinae and the Asian Mystinae.

Sub-family Bagrinae

This sub-family includes genera spread out over the entire African continent, including the Nile Basin and excluding the region north of the Sahara. The drainage area of the Nile is also well populated with

406

many species. There are ten such genera: *Amarginops, Auchenoglanis, Bagrus, Chrysichthys, Clarotes, Gephyroglanis, Gnathobagrus, Notoglanidium, Parauchenoglanis,* and *Phyllonemus*. Rich fossil material from western Asia indicates that a direct connection must have existed between the two sub-families of Bagridae that are so distantly separated today. This connection can be readily established in a number of existing genera.

Genus *Auchenoglanis*

Since 1909, the species *Auchenoglanis occidentalis* has appeared regularly in the aquariums of some amateurs. For some unknown reason, however, it has never become particularly popular.

Genus *Parauchenoglanis*

Parauchenoglanis macrostoma has been imported since 1925 from the Congo and Ogowe River regions of Africa. Since it grows to about 24 cm (9⅜ inches), larger specimens would require a tank several metres (yards) long in order to feel at home. Young specimens—usually sold on the market—are particularly suitable for the home aquarium. They are beautifully patterned and rich in coloration.

Plate II-41. *Parauchenoglanis macrostoma.*

Illus. II-58. *Leiocassis poecilopterus,* closely related to the very similar *L. siamensis,* is another handsome Asian aquarium fish.

Sub-family Mystinae

Better known to aquarists are the Asian bagrids Mystinae, which include the following genera: *Bagrichthys, Bagroides, Leiocassis, Mystus, Peltobagrus, Pseudobagrus,* and *Rita.*

They are not problem fish in any way, although they have probably never been successfully bred in an aquarium. A remarkably rich variety of species of this sub-family inhabits the drainage basin of the Amur River in east Asia.

Genus *Leiocassis*

This genus has become especially popular because of its attractive species, *Leiocassis siamensis,* the Bumblebee Catfish. In addition, for amateurs with unheated aquariums and breeders with fish ponds, *Leiocassis braschnikowi* is an especially suitable species. Both are magnificent species. Importation of the first *Leiocassis* into Europe and America began about 1953 and it continues to hold its position of popularity.

Genus *Mystus*

This genus, which has been given many names, contains about 40 species, and is very common from Turkey to the south of China. Fossils of *Mystus* species from the Eocene have been found in Nigeria, Africa, and from the Pliocene in India (Siwalik Hills), so that it must have had a much wider distribution, unless the African fossils belong to the closely related genus, *Bagrus*. If not, then the evidence points to a migration of this group from Africa to southern Asia.

Mystus tengara (Hamilton, 1822)

This species, which can grow to about 100 mm (4 inches) long, is native to the marshes of northern India—to Assam and Madhya Pradesh.

It is often mistaken for *Mystus vittatus*, though *M. vittatus* can grow to twice the size of *M. tengara*. The most marked difference between the two is in the number of teeth along the inner side of the pectoral fin spines—namely, 8 to 10 in *M. tengara* as compared to 16 in *M. vittatus*. Besides, *M. tengara* is slightly higher, in relation to its length.

Although the photograph in Innes corresponds quite well with the real *M. tengara*, the barbels on the upper lip, which reach all the way to the anal fin (in the photograph) suggest that it is neither *M. tengara* nor *M. vittatus*, as both of these have barbels that do not grow beyond the pectoral fins.

Another difference between *M. tengara* and *M. vittatus* is the length of the median groove on the skull. In *M. tengara*, this extends as far as the occipital protrusion, while in *M. vittatus*, it does not.

Illus. II-59. *Mystus tengara* with the nose barbels so typical of this family.

Plate II-42. *Sorubim lima* is undoubtedly one of the most striking catfish with its feeler barbs standing out like spider legs.

Mystus vittatus (Bloch, 1797)
Striped Mystus

Mystus vittatus is very similar to *Mystus tengara*, but it grows to about 200 mm (8 inches) long. It is native to a widespread area in India, Burma, Thailand, and Ceylon. The sub-species *M. v. horai* comes from the Indus River near the city of Kalabagh in Pakistan.

Young specimens can be kept in aquariums, the same as *M. tengara*, but fully-grown fish create problems. The size at which they attain sexual maturity is not known.

Illus. II-60. Distribution of the Plotosidae.

Family Plotosidae

As shown in the map in Illus. II–60, this family has a remarkable distribution along the coastal waters of the entire Indian Ocean and part of the Pacific, as far as New Zealand. Obviously, the family is attracted to fresh water, for at spawning time, the fish seek the river deltas and deposit their eggs in water that is hardly even brackish. This has also been observed in other catfish genera, particularly in the family Siluridae. (Some aspects of the geographic distribution of these fish and the reasons for it were discussed in Chapter 2.)

From the family Plotosidae, which also includes a number of purely fresh-water varieties, comes the coastal variety *Plotosus anguillaris*.

Plotosus anguillaris Bloch, 1793

It is possible that the name of this fish will be changed to *Plotosus lineatus*, a name that is more descriptive, especially of the young. When dealing with a species whose life cycle is not exactly known, surprises can always be expected.

This eel-like, coastal catfish may grow as long as 30 cm (12 inches). Young specimens are often imported and can come from an environment of either fresh or salt (brackish) water. Ask the dealer about this when buying the fish. Young fish can become entirely accustomed to fresh water, if the proper procedure as described on page 269 is carefully carried out.

Plate II-43. A small school of young specimens of *Plotosus anguillaris*, in a salt-water aquarium.

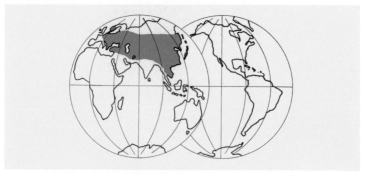

Illus. II-61. Distribution of the Siluridae.

Family Siluridae

Numerous imports of Siluridae over the past few years have provided a great deal more information about this family. It has a Eurasian distribution and is differentiated from all other catfishes by the possession of an unusually small dorsal fin, placed far forward, without spiny rays. In some varieties, the dorsal fin is entirely lacking. The family is divided into two sub-families, Silurinae and Kryptopterinae.

Sub-family Silurinae

To this sub-family belong the genera *Ompok*, *Parasilurus*, *Silurichthys*, *Siluroides*, *Silurus*, *Wallago*, and *Wallagonia*. Up to a short time ago, the largest fresh-water catfish, *Silurus glanis*, with a greatest known length of 367 cm (about 12 feet), had been found in the polders of the Netherlands. *Silurus glanis* is also known in eastern and central Europe and in western Asia. Compared to it, the well known Glass Catfish, *Ompok bimaculatus*, is just a dwarf, attaining a maximum length of 45 cm (17⅝ inches).

Illus. II-62. *Silurus glanis*, European fresh-water catfish.

412

Illus. II-63. *Ompok bimaculatus.*

Genus *Ompok*

A revised report on this genus was published by Hora (1936, Fishes of the genus *Callichrous* Hamilton). The genus consists of a large number of varieties which, however, can be classified in a rather small number of true species. The species *O. bimaculatus* has by far the widest distribution and is quite common everywhere.

Ompok bimaculatus (Bloch, 1794)
Two-Spot Glass Catfish

Ompok bimaculatus is kept as *Eutropiellus* (see page 415).

Plate II-44. *Malapterurus electricus,* with its thick and extremely sensitive lips, is certainly no beauty.

Family Malapteruridae

The two known species of this family are *Malapterurus electricus* and *M. microstoma* which are both attractive showpieces for public aquariums. They originate in tropical Africa. Much has been written about these remarkable fishes, even by the ancient Egyptians of 6,000 years ago, who portrayed *M. electricus* in easily recognizable wall paintings. It is probable that these Egyptians were impressed by the strong, electric field that this catfish was capable of generating around itself. (See, in Chapter 3, *Electrical Organs,* in connection with similar properties of other species.)

Family Schilbeidae

This family includes a considerable number of species in Africa and Asia that can be classed into two sub-families, the African Schilbeinae and the Asian Pangasiinae. The division is made on two grounds—geographical location and anatomical differences.

Sub-family Schilbeinae

The genera belonging to this sub-family are: *Eutropiellus, Eutropius, Irvineia, Parailia, Pareutropius, Physailia, Schilbe,* and *Siluranodon.* They differ from the closely related Silurinae, among others, in that they have a smaller number of rays in the pelvic fins. An exception—or perhaps a transitional variety—is *Irvineia,* which has more pelvic fin rays (typical of Silurinae), but is otherwise a purely schilbeid variety.

Many species have already been introduced into home aquariums, and a few enjoy steady popularity.

Genus *Eutropiellus*

The nomenclature of this genus has undergone many changes. In the literature, the names *Eutropiella, Entropiella,* and *Etropiella* have been used. The correct name, however, is *Eutropiellus.* The original name *Ansorgia,* given by Boulenger, was cancelled, since it had already been given to a butterfly (Lepidoptera). In 1933, the current names were adopted, but in 1935, Whitley, who was apparently unaware of the name change, proposed to substitute *Ansorgiichthys* for *Ansorgia.*

Eutropiellus is an *Eutropius* with fewer fin rays and without the frontal, lower-lip barbels, so that it is closest to the species *Eutropius liberiensis. Eutropiellus debauwi* is the only known species (with two sub-species) of the genus and automatically serves as the type species.

Illus. II-64. Distribution of the Schilbeidae.

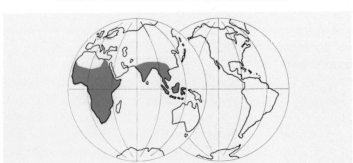

Plate II-45. *Eutropiellus debauwi.*

Eutropiellus debauwi (Boulenger, 1900)
African Striped Glass Catfish

There are two sub-species of *E. debauwi*—*E. debauwi debauwi* and *E. d. vittata*, both African. The first sub-species is native to the Congo Basin, the second inhabits the waters of Chiloango and the Batauri district in Cameroon, and the Ogowe River in Gabon.

E. debauwi attains a length of 100 mm (4 inches) or slightly more, yet it certainly belongs to one of the smaller species of the so-called Glass Catfish. In many respects, it resembles *Kryptopterus bicirrhus* or *Physailia pellucida.*

The general coloration is light brown or yellowish, sometimes with a blue-green sheen. A broad, intensely black stripe runs from the head to the base of the tail. A second, rather dark but not intensely black narrow band runs along the back and continues onto the upper lobe of the caudal fin. A third dark stripe runs along the belly, above the anal fin. The two foremost rays of the dorsal fin are darkly tinted, while the rest of the fins are transparent and almost invisible, which gives the impression that the dorsal fin consists only of a single thread.

Like other schilbeid and silurid catfishes, *Eutropiellus debauwi* should not be kept alone or in pairs in the aquarium. Preferably, allow four or five to live together, because alone, they waste away and hide most of the time. Moderate light is good for them. From time to time, they must be given live food. Being a tropical fish, they are best suited to a temperature range of 18–25 °C (64–77 °F). *E. debauwi* is not known to ever have been bred in captivity.

416

Genus *Physailia*

Physailia pellucida Boulenger, 1901

African Glass Catfish

Physailia pellucida is native to Africa, in the upper Nile region. Related varieties are classed as distinct species: *P. occidentalis* (Cape Lopez, Gabon) and *P. somalensis* (Somaliland). Once in a while, this fish can be found among imported lots, and, with proper care, they will live for years in the aquarium.

Typically, the dorsal fin is completely lacking. There is a small adipose fin well to the rear, and four pairs of fine, unramified barbels of about equal length. One pair sprouts from the upper lip, two pairs adorn the under lip, and one pair of nasal barbels project from the nostrils. The anal fin is very long, reaching the caudal fin, where the two are grown together. The caudal fin is forked. Both body and fins are transparent, allowing the vertebrae and ribs (the fishbone), as well as the swim bladder and other organs, to be clearly seen through the skin and flesh.

Physailia pellucida, which grows to about 90 mm (3½ inches), though definitely a catfish, is frequently considered to be related to the South American Gymnotidae or the African Notopteridae (knife fish). Actually, it is related to the African *Eutropius* species, which are also transparent, though less so than *Physailia pellucida*.

Although *P. pellucida* is not a popular fish, in the past few years a few

Illus. II-65. *Physailia pellucida.*

417

specimens have been imported and these have been thoroughly appreciated by aquarists.

It should be kept like other tropical fish, at a temperature about 23 °C (73 °F) in an aquarium that is not too small. It shuns direct sunlight but is not a twilight fish. It likes to spend its time among plant growth. Once it becomes used to its environment, it becomes frisky, especially at feeding time. It eats anything edible, but vegetable food is a must in its diet.

P. pellucida is inoffensive and will not molest even very small fishes, though newly-hatched fry are part of its food. Nothing is known about breeding it.

Genus *Schilbe*

Schilbe mystus (Linné, 1762)
Smoky Glass Catfish

This is a big catfish from the Nile River Basin—big for the home aquarium, at any rate, as it grows to a length of 35 cm (about 14 inches). The ancient Egyptians did not find it to their taste, either because it was too small or because its taste was bad. Nevertheless, the fish has been adopted by aquarium keepers ever since the 1930's, when it was first introduced. It is a species certainly well worth the trouble to observe closely; it is especially lively, not unattractively patterned, but not rich in coloration. As no report of successful breeding in the aquarium has been reported, it is a challenge to aquarists to lift the veil shrouding the mating of this and related species. In its native environment, *S. mystus* lives in marshy waters, and therefore it requires dark soil (no sand) in the aquarium, with petrified or hard wood and similar bric-a-brac.

Illus. II-66. *Schilbe mystus.*

Plate II-46. *Kryptopterus bicirrhus.*

Sub-family Pangasiinae

Only a few species of this sub-family are attractive enough for aquarium life. Among these, though, the following enjoy lasting popularity.

Genus *Kryptopterus*

In this genus a dozen or so species are known, of which only two are so far imported for the pleasure of aquarists—*K. bicirrhus* and *K. macrocephalus.*

Kryptopterus bicirrhus (Valenciennes, 1839)
Glass Catfish
This widely-distributed species was, for a long time, unknown in the Malay Peninsula. Hora & Gupta (1941) then described one from that region, so that its spread today runs unbroken through Java, Sumatra, the Malay Peninsula, Thailand and Borneo.

Illus. II-67. *Kryptopterus macrocephalus.*

Kryptopterus macrocephalus (Bleeker, 1858)
Big-Headed Glass Catfish

K. macrocephalus is native to Sumatra, Borneo and the Malay Peninsula. In the wild, it attains lengths of more than 200 mm (8 inches).

Both species should be kept like their nearest relatives. They are omnivorous; larger specimens may become rapacious and prey on smaller fish.

Order Cypriniformes

Research has led the author to believe that the group of carp-like fishes (Cypriniformes) should now be considered a separate order, distinguished from both the orders Siluriformes (see page 316) and Characiformes (see page 543). The three orders taken together form the super-order Ostariophysi.

Cypriniformes constitute one of the largest orders of true fresh-water fishes, with practically world-wide distribution. This order does not have members, however, in the Australian region east of the line between Borneo and the Celebes, in Madagascar, and in all of Central and South America. In the latter territory, it is replaced by the order Characiformes, which contributes even more species.

The Cypriniformes have a bony skeleton, with the first four vertebrae much different in shape from the others; they are often ankylosed (fused together) and form a support for a special series of bones that transmit pressure changes in the swim bladder to the auditory apparatus of the fish. This whole structure serves as a specialized sense organ and has been given the name Weberian apparatus (see page 133).

In the Cypriniformes, the shoulder girdle is attached to the skull, the pelvic fins are inserted ventrally, and the fin rays are soft. Often, the first two or three fin rays fuse into a false spine and sometimes, several such hard rays occur, always formed by the fusion and ossification of the segments of the forked, soft fin rays. These hard fin rays are quite different from the spines in the spiny-rayed forms of the higher orders.

Illus. II-68. Distribution of the carp-like fishes (Cypriniformes).

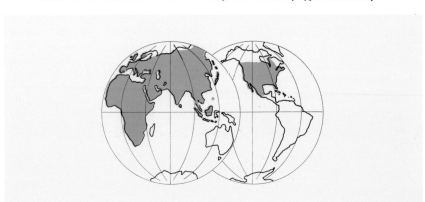

The body is generally, though not always, scaly, but the head is never covered with scales. The protrusile mouth usually has two or more barbels, although there may be none at all. The jaws are toothless, hence the old name, Eventognathi, given by Gill (1908) to denote that the normal teeth on the jaws have been replaced by so-called pharyngeal teeth, which have the same function. Unlike the Characiformes, which it resembles in many ways, Cypriniformes never has an adipose fin.

Carp-like fishes suck up their food. The gills shut tightly. producing a partial vacuum in the mouth cavity. Much water is sucked in with the food, but it is expelled later on. In doing so, most of the larger species make such a big fuss of eating that they are considered unsuitable for the home aquarium.

Sub-orders Cobitoidei and Cyprinoidei

The order Cypriniformes is sub-divided into two distinct sub-orders: the loaches (Cobitoidei), and the true carp-like fish (Cyprinoidei). Both groups consist of several families. The natural sequence (phylogenetic arrangement) of these families has long been a source of controversy, and, in a way, still is. Reasons for the sequence given below is more than a matter of appreciation. The order Cypriniformes connects with the ancestral siluriform stock through the loaches (Cobitoidei). Similar fishes among the Characiformes must be regarded as representing another assembly of fishes at the organization level of the loaches, Characidiidae.

Cobitoidei	Gyrinocheilidae	Hillstream fishes
	Homalopteridae	
	Gastromyzontidae	
	Cobitidae	Loaches
Cyprinoidei	Catostomidae	Suckers
	Cyprinidae	Carps and Minnows

Though it cannot be said that all these families have supplied aquarists with well known species, the blame falls largely on general ignorance about the species concerned, rather than on the species themselves.

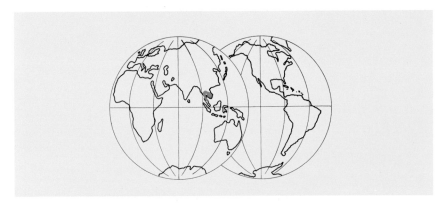

Illus. II-69. Distribution of the Gyrinocheilidae.

Family Gyrinocheilidae

The Gyrinocheilidae is a small family with a relatively restricted distribution. The members of this family, which comprise only one genus, are remarkable in a number of ways. Most characteristic is the respiratory apparatus, which resembles that of some South American catfishes (see pages 318 and 358). The gill cavity has a slit-like water outlet, covered by a flap of fleshy skin, and a round inlet above it. This structure enables them to breathe normally, even when the mouth aperture is occupied with a suction-hold on a rock; this results in a doubling of the respiration rate. Young fish still can take in breathing water through the mouth, but the adults seem to have lost this ability completely. When the young fish lie on a stone in their preferred position, with their head over the edge, and support themselves on their pectoral and pelvic fins, the flow of water and the rapid movement of the gill flaps is readily observable.

Genus *Gyrinocheilus*

Of the species in this family, only *Gyrinocheilus aymonieri* has found its way to the home aquarium.

Gyrinocheilus aymonieri (Tirant, 1883)

Chinese Algae-Eater

Sucking Loach

This loach from Southeast Asia, popular with aquarists, can grow to a length of more than 25 cm (10 inches) in its natural habitat. In the aquarium, however, it generally reaches sexual maturity at 15 cm (6 inches), and will not grow much larger. The reproduction cycle —mating and depositing of eggs—resembles that of the bottom-dwelling catfishes, and other loaches. This species has been successfully bred in captivity.

Plate II-47. *Gyrinocheilus aymonieri.*

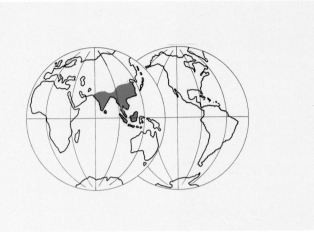

Family Homalopteridae

An Asiatic loach family, the Homalopteridae, is a typical inhabitant of swift highland and mountain streams. It is abundant throughout China, Burma, Thailand, the Malay Peninsula, and the islands of the Indonesian-Australian Archipelago, up to and including Java and Borneo. The best-known genera are *Balitora*, *Balitoropsis*, *Hemimyzon*, and *Homaloptera*.

Genus *Homaloptera*

This is, at present, the only homalopterid genus imported, from time to time, for aquariums. Many species of this genus swarm throughout the entire distribution area of the family Homalopteridae. Regular importation of the *Homaloptera* species would be greatly appreciated by many aquarists. All species, which never grow really big, would make suitable and interesting aquarium fishes.

Family Gastromyzontidae

This family has the same distribution area, and is sometimes considered a sub-family of the Homalopteridae (Gastromyzontinae). What was said about the genus *Gyrinocheilus* also applies, more or less, to the imported species of this family. They do not, however, have the same kind of sucking mouth. Instead, the sucking function is taken over by a remarkable structure of crosswise skin folds along the underside of the pectoral and pelvic fins. The fish dwells at the bottom of swift

425

Plate II-48. *Gastromyzon myersi.*

waters at high altitudes, hence its special sucking apparatus for combatting the force of the current. At all times, the mouth remains free. Some species are quite similar to catfishes of the families Sisoridae and Amblycepitidae, not only in their suction facilities, but especially in the construction of the enclosed air bladder (swim bladder). This latter constitutes a part of the hearing and transmitting apparatus (see Weberian apparatus, page 133).

Genus *Gastromyzon*

This is as widely-distributed a genus as *Homaloptera*, with numerous species from China to Borneo. The only species that is often kept by aquarists is *Gastromyzon myersi* (Plate II–48). It is worthwhile to try to obtain this little fish.

426

Family Cobitidae

This family is distributed throughout Europe and Asia, as well as in parts of east Africa. The Cobitidae are mostly bottom-dwellers and many of the species have adapted to life in swift-flowing mountain streams. They form a rather significant part of the fresh-water fauna of the western islands of the Indonesian-Australian Archipelago, though they do not appear anywhere in the Australian region itself.

The loach family, also known as bearded or spiny gudgeons, includes a number of generally small fishes with a more or less compressed body. The foremost part of the small head is depressed. The slimy skin is mostly covered with small, cycloid scales, which, however, may be lacking on certain parts of the body. In some cases, in fact, the scales are entirely absent.

The protrusile mouth is located on the underside of the snout. The mouth opening is surrounded by two to six pairs of barbels and the lips are thick. The most striking feature of the cobitids is their large, strong, and sometimes unusually long barbels. These are usually present in all carp-like fishes, but are sometimes difficult to find. These chin-, head- and nose-feelers aid in the search for food on the bottom, and always keep the fish in contact with the firmest part of his environment. Only a few species abandon the bottom for free swimming.

The close relationship between most species of Cobitidae and the carp-like fishes (Cyprinidae) is readily apparent from the structure of the Weberian apparatus. The cobitids do differ, however, from the

Illus. II-71. Distribution of the Cobitidae.

cyprinids in their small swim bladder, the anterior part of which is enclosed in a bony capsule, the posterior part being either very small or, simply, vestigial. The sensitivity of the cobitids to atmospheric changes is closely connected with their swim bladder and Weberian apparatus.

An interesting structure of the swim bladder (air bladder) is found in practically all loaches; here this bladder is divided into two sacs, which, during growth, become enclosed in bone (see Illus. II–74). The bony capsules are connected to the auditory organ by means of the chain of Weberian ossicles, the small bones extending from the dorsal wall of the air bladder to the region of the ears. The whole structure is similar in every respect to the corresponding apparatus in the original type of catfish.

Many loaches have the ability to spend long periods out of water, indicating the importance of intestinal respiration. During long periods of drought, for example, they bury themselves in the mud and survive without water. At the same time, they take in air, and relieve it of its oxygen in the intestine. Exhalation of the used air takes place through the anus.

Small, protruding rims ring the nostrils. The pelvic fins are very small and the anal fin is set back towards the tail. In some *Botia* and *Misgurnus* species there is a ridge formed by caudal fin rays, extending forward from the root of the caudal fin and the dorsal fin. A similar ridge is found on the ventral side, between the root of the caudal fin and the anal fin. The whole thing is reminiscent of a rather long fin seam, as found in the embryonic stages in most other fishes.

There are three sub-families of Cobitidae—Noemacheilinae, Botiinae, and Cobitinae—each of which yields several suitable aquarium fish. The Eurasian species can only be kept in unheated tanks. A number of species prevailing in warmer countries would do very well in tropical aquariums, if they were imported. This is especially true for the beautiful, brilliant small species of the genus *Botia*.

Illus. II-72. Creek near Ruurlo, the Netherlands, a typical biotope of European loaches.

Sub-family Noemacheilinae

Belonging to this sub-family is the Groundling, *Noemacheilus barbatulus*, which is very plentiful in Europe and Asia, the Asiatic *Noemacheilus selangoricus*, as well as the genera *Diplophysa* and *Adiposia*. *Adiposia* is extremely interesting, as this genus consists of the only loach known to possess a true adipose fin, a characteristic it shares with catfishes on the one hand and characins (especially the Characidiidae) on the other.

Genus *Noemacheilus*

Noemacheilus barbatulus (Linné, 1758)
Groundling or Stone Loach

This species, with its many sub-species, is found throughout Europe, except for northern Scotland, Norway, northern and central Sweden, and the Mediterranean region. It is also found in the Crimea and the Urals, as well as in Siberia, the Amur River in eastern Asia, and in Korea. The sub-species occur mainly in northern and central Asia. They live in clear lakes and running streams, preferably with stony bottoms.

429

The body of *Noemacheilus barbatulus* is long and the caudal section is vertically flattened (depressed). The fish grows to hardly more than 10 cm (4 inches) in the aquarium, but specimens caught in the natural state have measured as long as 15 cm (6 inches). The rather large head has a small ventrally directed mouth with a protrusile upper lip having two pairs of short and one pair of longer barbels. There are no barbels on the lower jaw.

Since the markings vary considerably, it is difficult to describe the coloration. The background is golden brown, tending, towards the back, to a darker olive green with some even darker blotches. The spots that cover the flanks are a mottled brownish and change to a creamy hue towards the belly. The lateral line is clearly visible as a continuous, white line, reaching from the gill covers to the caudal root.

The dorsal, caudal and pectoral fins are greyish, with dark spots and stripes. The anal fin is yellowish. The positions of the fins are characteristic of the entire sub-family. The small dorsal fin, located about in the middle of the straight back, has an oblique upper edge. The caudal fin is also small, but rounded. The tiny anal fin is inserted slightly behind the rear end of the dorsal fin, while the pelvic fins are located directly under the first part of the dorsal fin. The large pectoral fins are inserted laterally.

The sexes are extremely difficult to distinguish, and the only sure time to tell them apart is during the mating season (early April to late May), when the females carry their eggs between their pelvic fins. Intestinal respiration, so important to the loach family, plays no rôle with the Groundling.

Most books and periodicals do not have much good to say about this little fish. This seems to indicate that it is hard to keep *Noemacheilus barbatulus* in home aquariums and that it is not much fun to watch anyway. However, nothing is farther from the truth, provided that the fish is properly cared for and is given a suitable environment. The right treatment is essential for keeping and deriving pleasure from this cold-water fish. Most important, the water must be clear and fast-circulating, its temperature not exceeding 20 °C (68 °F). To maintain this temperature is probably the greatest difficulty, but with aeration and good water circulation, it can be kept below this mark, even in summer. On hot days, just add a few ice cubes.

As far as food is concerned, *Noemacheilus barbatulus* is certainly not a fussy eater. It consumes anything given to it, either fresh or dried, animal or vegetable.

The mating season occurs during April and May, when the eggs are deposited on stones and plants. A gravel bottom and a few larger stones scattered through the aquarium makes the fish feel at home.

Many sub-species of *Noemacheilus barbatulus* (Linné) are known: *Noemacheilus barbatulus barbatulus* (Linné), the European type; *N. b. vardarensis* Karaman, from Siberia (Vardar); *N. b. sturanyi* Steindachner, from Serbia and Albania; *N. b. caucasicus* Berg, from the Caspian Sea area; and *N. b. toni* (Dybowski), which appears in different forms, all from northern and central Asia.

A special feature is that the Groundling is bred in ponds in Bohemia (a province of Czechoslovakia) for its tasty flesh.

Noemacheilus selangoricus Duncker, 1904

This Asiatic species was first imported to America, and came from there to Europe. Its habits and shape are like those of the Groundling. The light yellow background coloration is covered by 10 to 12 very wide, dark brown bands, leaving only narrow stripes of the background visible. The dark stripes run over the back, but do not extend downward to the belly. The dorsal fin has three rows of dark spots. A pronounced blackish spot under the eye corresponds to the stripe in *Botia hymenophysa* and *Acanthophthalmus kuhlii*. For this reason, dealers used to sell this fish as a *Botia* species. It originates from Malaysia (Kuala Lumpur) and can grow to a length of 80 mm (about 3¼ inches).

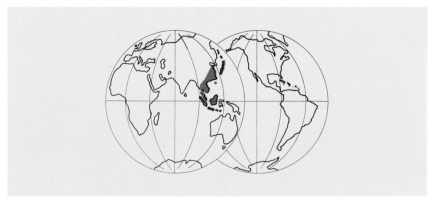

Illus. II-73. Distribution of the genus *Botia*.

Sub-family Botiinae

Genus *Botia*

Indigenous to the southeastern part of Asia and Japan, *Botia* also occurs on the islands of Sumatra, Java and Borneo.

Among the few Cobitidae appreciated by aquarists, *Botia* species occupy an important place and presently, several imported species have aroused aquarists' interest. These fish are more enjoyable than might be imagined, and all imported species have extremely attractive markings and coloration.

Botia has, like other cobitids, a spine near the eye—in this case, below it. This orbital spine is slightly moveable and can stick out from the head. Whether this spine has any purpose other than simply being a defence organ is unknown.

The body is covered with very small scales. The snout of *Botia macracantha* has eight barbels and *Botia hymenophysa* has six. Without exception, all these fishes resemble catfish, but can be easily distinguished from them by the completely scaled bodies. This feature developed in part because of their living in stagnant waters; for the same reason, they have large eyes.

Inhabitants of running water usually have small swim bladders and they cope with the current by living on the bottom. Species from stagnant waters, on the other hand, possess a very large swim bladder, which lies in close contact with the body wall. This swim bladder, as it developed in fresh-water fish, first of all serves a hydrostatic function—as an organ of equilibrium that keeps the fish upright and

432

enables it to remain at any chosen depth. The fish can leave such a position rapidly by making fin and tail movements and then, without effort, it can drift back to the original depth.

Temperatures in the aquarium should not range too high—18–24 °C (64–75 °F). The central ventrad location of the swim bladder—the same position it occupies in primitive forms—indicates that the bladder was originally a respiratory organ. If this is true, then the Cobitidae, in this case the members of this highly specialized genus, must belong to a rather recent fauna element, as other factors also seem to indicate.

Botia horae Smith, 1931
Skunk Loach

Young specimens of this species from Thailand strongly resemble young of *Botia modesta* because the young fish of both species have the same, striped markings. At all stages of development, though, *Botia horae* has an orange-brown coloration with an irregular dark (to black) band over the back running into a broad, vertical band at the end of the caudal peduncle, next to four, extremely narrow, dark cross bars on the flanks. The maximum total length of *B. horae* is about 100 mm (4 inches), whereas *B. modesta* can grow twice as long.

Plate II-49. *Botia horae.*

Plate II-50. *Botia hymenophysa.*

Botia hymenophysa Bleeker, 1852
Tiger Loach

Botia hymenophysa comes from Thailand, Malaysia, Singapore, Java, Sumatra and Borneo. Less well known than *B. macracantha*, this species has become available in small numbers, brought in from Singapore among other imports. The maximum total length is approximately 21 cm (about 8¼ inches)—smaller than *B. macracantha*. In aquariums, it grows to about 15 cm (6 inches).

The fish's basic coloration ranges from a beautiful pearl grey to yellowish, depending on the place of origin and the size of the fish. All have 11 to 13 brownish cross bands, set off with blue, on the body and three on the head, the first one running more or less horizontally down the long snout. The dorsal fin is orange-yellow with four blue cross bands. The caudal fin is yellowish green and also has four blue stripes. The other fins are bright yellow. This species should be kept in the same way as *B. macracantha*.

Plate II-51. *Botia lohachata.*

Botia lucasbahi Fowler, 1937

This fish has been imported regularly since 1955 from Thailand. The longest aquarium-length reached is about 75 mm (3 inches), suggesting that it is a small species, closely allied to *B. hymenophysa.* The specimens on which the description of this species was based were not longer than 73 mm (under 3 inches), whereas *B. hymenophysa* can easily grow to twice that length, even in the aquarium.

Plate II-52. *Botia lucasbahi.*

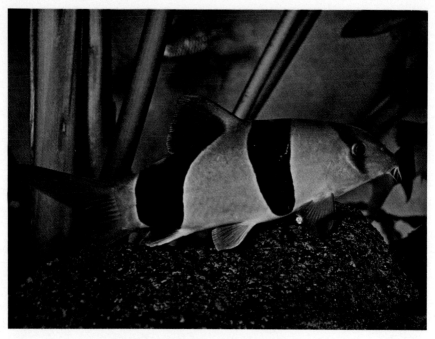

Plate II-53. *Botia macracantha.*

Botia macracantha (Bleeker, 1852)

Specimens of this species are often found among imports from the Indonesian-Australian Archipelago. Though they seldom grow to more than 15 cm (6 inches) in the aquarium, they grow to 20 cm (about 8 inches) in the natural state. Just the same, this is an excellent aquarium fish.

Although there may, at first sight, be doubt, *B. macracantha* is a true loach, obvious from its intestinal respiratory system with the gases escaping from the anus (for the most part, this is used atmospheric air). The European and Asiatic loaches (*Cobitis, Noemacheilus* and *Misgurnus*) exhale in the same manner.

The background coloration of *Botia macracantha* is light orange with three blue-black cross bands—the first through the eye, the second across the trunk, and the last across the caudal peduncle. The middle band lies just in front of the dorsal fin, while the band around the caudal reaches forward to the base of the last few rays of the dorsal fin, and ventrally extends as far as the anal fin. Plate II–53 is a clear picture of this fish. The ventral mouth has four pairs of barbels—two pairs on its upper lip, one pair placed forward on the lower jaw, and one more pair at the corners of the mouth.

436

Being a loach, this species might be expected to be a bottom-dweller, not given to much activity. Neither is true. Although it is, at first, rather shy, looking for hiding places, later on it does like to hang among the plants, supported by its fins in an upward-angled position. When moving about, it sometimes shows great speed, and darts about in the aquarium in its own characteristic oblique way, with tail held low. The beginning aquarist may at first worry when he notices the fish lying still for long periods—a phenomenon also found in the case of the catfish, *Helogenes marmoratus*. The fish appears to lie dead, either on the bottom, on its side, or, if a suitable rock is handy, on its back, belly up, a position also adopted by some *Synodontis* species. *Botia macracantha* practice these manoeuvres quite easily because of the very large swim bladder, the anterior part of which is enclosed in a bony capsule.

As with all loaches, this species keeps the aquarium free of algae, which it eats with gusto along with any bit of tasty refuse. When these or allied species are present in an aquarium, there is no worry about dead waterfleas. The fish gobble the fleas up in a hurry.

Presumably, the comparatively large size of this fish is one of the reasons why the species has never reproduced in an aquarium. As a tropical species, it requires a water temperature of about 24 °C (75 °F).

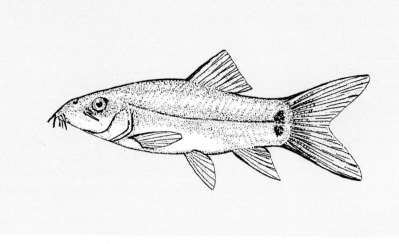

Illus. II-74. *Botia modesta.*

Botia modesta **Bleeker, 1865**
Red-Finned Loach
Yellow-Finned Loach

As is the case with many fishes that are spread over a large distribution area, this species varies greatly. The sub-species or population from Malaysia has only faint cross bands, but a prominent black band runs from the snout along the back onto the caudal peduncle, where it divides into two wide lateral bands which join again at the ventral side. Above the pectoral fins are a number of fine, irregular stripes, varying in number from four to ten, and a changeable number of black spots on the caudal fin.

A few specimens of this species were imported in 1949, and perhaps later, but have not, unfortunately, appeared since then. The maximum length for *B. modesta* is approximately 20 cm (8 inches), smaller in the aquarium. Depending on where the fish is found, the background coloration varies from blue-grey to greenish grey, or from yellow to pink, with a light yellow to white belly. Four or five blue-black to purple-brown cross bands of varying widths run over the body, alternating with narrower, darker bands. These secondary bands are absent in specimens longer than 80 mm ($3\frac{1}{4}$ inches). All the fins are yellow to orange, as is the iris of the eye.

438

***Botia sidthimunki* Klausewitz, 1959**

This is one of the species which stays small and reaches maturity at a total length of about 70 mm (about $2\frac{3}{4}$ inches). A great deal of interest will greet the first report of breeding of these beautifully brilliant and marked fish which are extremely suitable for a quiet aquarium.

***Botia striata* Rao, 1920**

Zebra Loach

This species, first imported in 1953, originates from Mysore (Thunga) in southern India. It grows to about 80 mm ($3\frac{1}{4}$ inches) without the caudal fin. It has particularly attractive coloration, and is undoubtedly one of the most beautiful species of this genus. On the yellow-green background, there are nine wide, darker, blackish green bands, like hoops around the body, alternating with bright yellow hoops. On the dark bands, which become fainter towards the ventral side of the fish, are narrow, white lines or a series of spots, which give the impression that the dark bands are in pairs. The head also possesses three double dark bands separated by a yellow streak and alternating with white bands running along it. The fins of *Botia striata*, which are nearly translucent, have three or four darker cross bands.

For the present, we may consider *B. striata* a distinct species. For a long time, some dealers sold *Noemacheilus selangoricus* under the names

Plate II-54. *Botia sidthimunki.*

Illus. II-75. Head of *Botia striata*. Compare markings with head of *Botia hymenophysa* (see Plate II-50).

Botia strigata and *B. striata*. *Noemacheilus selangoricus* plainly differs from *Botia striata*, especially in the shape of the body, which resembles that of Eurasian *Noemacheilus barbatulus*.

In a letter of April 28, 1955, Dr. Hora of Calcutta wrote the author about some characteristics of Kulkarni's new sub-species from Kolhapura, stressing the assumption that *B. striata* is a definite species which occurs with local populations next to the species *B. hymenophysa*. We will, for the time being, accept it as such, until proof is found in its variation range to justify considering it as a part of a super-population with a continuous distribution area. This will prove that the population from the Sunda Islands, no longer in contact with the true *B. hymenophysa* population on the mainland, will be the first to be classified as a distinct species.

To compare the color pattern and markings of *B. striata* and *B. hymenophysa*, refer to the photo of *Botia hymenophysa* on page 434.

What is known about *Botia striata* as an aquarium fish is poor, but nevertheless convincing that it could only be an asset for the hobbyist.

440

Sub-family Cobitinae

This sub-family can be divided into two tribes, the Cobitini comprising the genera *Misgurnus* and *Cobitis*, and Acanthopsini, including *Acanthopsis* and *Acanthophthalmus*. This Eurasian sub-family has a few forms in Ethiopia.

Genus *Cobitis*

Cobitis taenia Linné, 1758

Spotted Weatherfish

Spined Loach

Except for Norway and for Italy south of the Po River, this species inhabits all of Europe as well as a large part of Asia and North Africa. It is common in running and stagnant water and in fresh and slightly brackish waters with muddy bottoms.

Cobitis taenia grows to a maximum length of 140 mm (5½ inches), but seldom grows longer than 100 mm (4 inches) in the aquarium.

The entire body of this small loach is slightly compressed. Its back is brown with an edge of small, black spots. A row of shiny, brownish black spots runs along both flanks, and underneath, the chest and belly are light yellow. The upper lip has three pairs of equally long barbels. The small eyes are placed high in the head. Beneath each eye is a split spine which can be withdrawn into a skin fold. The sexes are similar in coloration and markings and, therefore, difficult to distinguish. The second ray of the pectoral fin of the males, however, is thicker than that of the females.

Because it likes to bury itself in the sand, *C. taenia* is, like the large loach, *Misgurnus fossilis*, not a very appealing aquarium fish.

Illus. II-76. *Cobitis taenia.*

Plate II-55. *Acanthophthalmus kuhli.*

Genus *Acanthophthalmus*

These eel-like loaches from tropical Asia show both a great individual and population diversity. This variability accounts for the many different names given to local forms, which together all form a single biological species.

Acanthophthalmus kuhlii (Valenciennes, 1846)

Coolie Loach

Kuhli Loach

Indonesian Loach

This species inhabits the regions of northeastern India, Bangladesh, Malaysia, Burma, and the Indonesian islands of Java, Sumatra, and Borneo.

It lives in ponds, canals, streams, and other waters having a muddy bottom. The first few specimens, brought to Europe in 1909, were immediately welcomed by aquarists. Several forms are distinguished, some of which have been classified as distinct species.

The body of this fish is eel-like, elongated and compressed only in the caudal region. It attains a maximum length of approximately 8 cm (a little over 3 inches). The dorsal fin is inserted rather far posteriorly on the back. The eyes, situated in the anterior part of the head, are covered by a transparent membrane. The mouth has

442

fleshy lips, with the lower lip divided in two. Altogether, three pairs of barbels are present. The oblique gill slit ends near the base of the pectoral fin. The body is covered with tiny scales; the head is naked.

The background coloration of this fish varies from reddish to orange, sometimes shot with mauve. The back is dark, with irregular, reddish brown to blackish brown, stripe-like markings which taper off towards the flanks. The belly is silver to pure white, but sometimes slightly pinkish. There is also a triangular brown mark at the base of the tail. The fins are transparent, and more or less without coloration. The dorsal and caudal fins only are decorated with a row of little brown dots. External sexual differences are not yet known, except that ripe females clearly show a swollen belly.

These fish require no great care. The bottom of the tank, however, must not be covered with sand, but with a peat layer in which the fish can burrow and scratch about as much as they please without fear of damaging the snout. Do not be afraid that this little fish will turn your aquarium into a mud bath. It can extract a tubifex or white worm from the bottom so neatly that you could not ask for improvement!

In winter, keep the water temperature at 22 °C (72 °F) and in the summer at about 25 °C (77 °F). It can withstand temperatures up to about 30 °C (85 °F), but it should not be kept permanently at this level.

The Kuhli Loach has a taste for every kind of living food, some of which it scratches right out of the bottom—it loves to hunt for small organisms. Because this loach is well known for ridding its surroundings of planaria, which may be parasitic, it is often kept in the community tank. It reproduces in the same manner as do many other bottom-dwellers. The female is recognizable by her enlarged, whitish belly which takes up three quarters of her total length. The eggs are sometimes visible through the ventral skin.

In mating, the fish intertwine with one another so that their sexual orifices approach each other. While the fish violently shake together, some eggs get deposited in a safe place—such as under a stone or between the roots of some aquatic plant. The furious movements of the parent fish create currents in the water that drive the eggs into the bottom layer. The parents sometimes eat some of the eggs, but, obviously, several eggs manage to escape their notice each time. Soon afterwards, a few larvae can be seen rummaging about in the peat layer. The young fish are dark (nearly black) all over, and the lighter bands that develop in adulthood are still very small. Little is known about this fish, largely because it does not appear much during daytime, but becomes active at sunset.

It would be a stimulating experience for seasoned breeders to try their luck with this fish. Since the various reports of its reproductive activities are contradictory, it would be interesting to ascertain whether it does build a bubble-nest. It is possible that various other species of *Acanthophthalmus* exist, and if this is so, it would explain the different mating procedures reported.

Illus. II-77. Posterior view of the two air bladder partitions, lateral to the vertebra, of the large European loach, *Misgurnus fossilis*. The embryonic connective tissue structure of the ossified capsules is clearly seen. Actual size, 12 × 15 mm (about $\frac{1}{2}$ × $\frac{5}{8}$ inch).

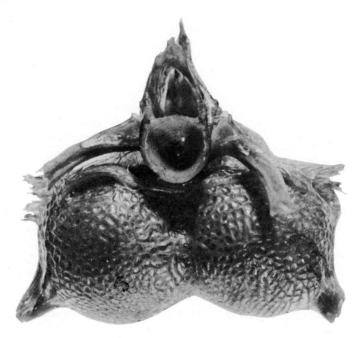

Illus. II-78. *Acanthopsis choirorhynchus.*

Genus *Acanthopsis*

This genus is restricted to the waters of Southeast Asia. The species belonging to the genus are characterized by a rather long, tapering head with high-set eyes. Only one species is found regularly among imported fishes.

Acanthopsis choirorhynchus (Bleeker)

This species is only seldom obtainable from regular dealers. Since it is a pleasurable fish, it is well worth the trouble of going after. It is sexually mature at a length of about 60 mm (2¾ inches), so that reproduction in the aquarium should be possible.

445

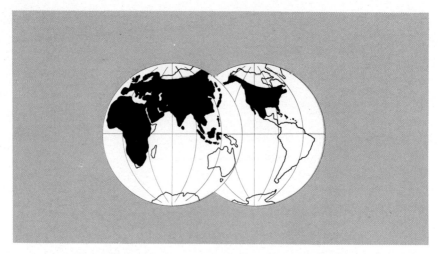

Sub-order Cyprinoidei

Except for the cold regions, Central and South America, Madagascar and the Australian continent, members of this group are found everywhere else in the world, in all kinds of waters. This almost universal distribution has had a definite effect on the appearance of these fishes and there is hardly a variation not represented in the group.

This sub-order is usually divided into two families: the Catostomidae and the Cyprinidae. We are interested more in the latter family which includes such popular fishes as the barbs, danios and rasboras. It is not surprising that scientists are in disagreement concerning the categorizing of this group. The diversity is so great, and the adaptations to environmental conditions so nearly limitless, that much work is yet to be done before a complete picture of the group can be set forth. It has been established that the roach-type fish represent an original stock from which other types have since evolved.

The earliest carp-like fish are undoubtedly the Catostomidae. This family is not particularly interesting to aquarists, but it is of great systematic significance. Presently, they seem to originate in China. At some time in the past, an offshoot must have crossed the Bering Straits to North America, because some members of this family are found also in North American waters. For the time being, simply

446

assume that the Catostomidae originated in old Gondwana—to be precise, in India, which, at early Cretaceous times, still formed a part of Gondwanaland.

The large family Cyprinidae, unusually rich in species of carp-like fishes, probably developed in China either from the Catostomidae or, at least, from a common ancestor. Not only are the Cyprinidae numerous in Asia, but also their specialization there is more advanced than it is anywhere else. Nowadays, it is more or less universally accepted that Cyprinidae first came to America in the Oligocene epoch, at the second time that a passable land-connection was created between Eurasia and North America.

Towards the end of the Cretaceous and the beginning of the Eocene, both the northern and the southern primordial land masses had approached each other so much that India was already in contact with present-day Asia. Africa, at the time, was separated from the still-largely-submerged Eurasian continent by a vast, shallow sea. (See the maps of the Cretaceous and Tertiary periods on page 59.)

The cyprinoids had thus settled in India. Even now, a distinct relationship to loaches can be observed in a number of indigenous species of carp-like fish. From the late Cretaceous and the early Eocene, carp-like fishes migrated from India into the new Asian area and China became the central area from which these fishes first spread and started to populate the rest of the world. They managed to reach America then by way of Europe, but they could not get to South America, the West Indian Archipelago, Australia, nor Madagascar. To this day, they have never penetrated these areas.

When Africa finally became linked to Asia by way of Arabia— roughly, towards the end of the Oligocene—it also inherited carp-like fish. Their take-over of the area was very slow, however, and the fishes there never showed a specialization like that in Asia. The probability is that there were three migrations from Central Asia; the first came about when the Catostomidae pushed through to North America at the beginning of the Eocene; the second took place towards Europe during the Eocene; and the third brought these fishes to Africa during the Oligocene.

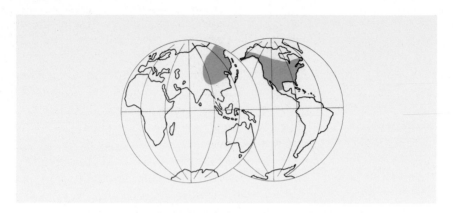

Illus. II-80. Distribution of the family Catostomidae.

Family Catostomidae

This family of carp-like fishes is known in America as the "suckers." It has numerous and richly varied members in America, but in China it contains only a few species, all belonging to the genus *Myxocyprinus*. They are deep-bodied, possessing a high dorsal fin, located far to the rear. They show their close relationship to the family Cyprinidae in many ways.

Family Cyprinidae

This family of carp, barbs and loaches is one of the largest families of fresh-water fishes. These fishes are distributed over the entire area of the sub-order Cyprinoidea, though nearly all the North American genera differ from the Eurasian and the African.

Four sub-families are distinguished here: the fresh-water gudgeons or Gobioinae, the carp and barbs of Cyprininae, the rasboras and the danios of the Rasborinae, and the loaches or Leuciscinae. Only the last three have so far become well known to aquarists, but it is likely that some species of Gobioinae will be suitable for the home aquarium, especially those imported from Asia, where they are numerous.

Sub-family Cyprininae

Although the hobby has been supplied with only a few genera from this sub-family, nearly all of these include many species. In fact, the yield of fish for the aquarium is rather high. Various imported species are not very popular because they grow too big for the home aquarium. You will find them regularly, however, in public aquariums.

Illus. II-81. Some main body forms within the group of carp-like fish from Eurasian waters. In general, they are distinguished from the tropical species which would be kept as aquarium fish mainly in size. 1. carp, to 50 cm (about 20 inches). 2. crucian carp, to 40 cm (about 16 inches). 3. tench, to 60 cm (about 24 inches). 4. barbel, to 50 cm. 5. river gudgeon, to 20 cm (8 inches). 6. bitterling, to 7 cm ($2\frac{3}{4}$ inches). 7. male bitterling. 8. bleak, to 15 cm (6 inches). 9. ide, to 50 cm (about 20 inches). 10. roach, to 30 cm (about 12 inches). 11. rudd, to 30 cm (12 inches).

449

Illus. II-82. *Balantiocheilus melanopterus.*

Genus *Balantiocheilus*

The only known species of this genus was distinguished from *Barbus* by Bleeker due to the different structure of the mouth and lips, and because of the lack of barbels.

Balantiocheilus melanopterus (Bleeker, 1851)
Silver "Shark"

This is a large species, which grows in Borneo up to 300 mm(about 12 inches) and in Thailand to about 200 mm (about 8 inches). Strikingly silver in shade, this fish has a dark band marking the outer edges of the dorsal, anal, and caudal fins. Therefore, in Thailand, it is called "The Burnt-Tailed Fish" (*pla hang mai*). The smaller specimens are quite suitable for the home aquarium. They should be treated like the other barbs.

450

Genus *Barbus*

For a long time, there has been some question about the proper generic name for some mainly Asiatic barbs, in case they should be separated from the old genus *Barbus*. Undoubtedly, a large number of these fish should no longer be classed under *Barbus*, because they vary too much from typical *Barbus*. Nevertheless, it is not just a question of whether or not to give another name to an arbitrary group of Asiatic species, as some writers have suggested.

There is a sufficient choice of names suggested for these barbs, but herein lies the difficulty: which name, indeed, is acceptable? If it were simply that the next name in chronological order should be taken—a method formerly used by some authors—then it would be *Puntius*. However, there is another side to the question. This concerns the type species involved (see page 205). At any rate, the species cannot be classified as *Puntius*—whether it still belongs in the old genus *Barbus* or not—as long as it is not properly determined which is the type species of that genus. The author of this genus, Hamilton, did not attribute a type species to *Puntius*. Today, such cases are anticipated by the International Rules of Zoological Nomenclature. Article 30 of these Rules deals with type species, and Section Ad of Article 30 applies directly to the case of *Puntius*: If there is among the original nominal species (those enumerated by Hamilton, under his *Puntius*) one which bears the generic name (*Puntius*) as a specific or sub-specific name, then this species (or sub-species, as it may be) *ipso facto* is to be considered the type species. This is the rule of "tautonomy" —literally, the rule of repetition. (A tautonym is a binomial name in which the generic and specific names are alike, such as *Puntius puntius*.)

Among the species listed by Hamilton under *Puntius* was the species *Puntius puntio*, which has already been taken by various writers as the definitive type species of *Puntius*. But, how far does tautonomy go? Taken literally, *puntio* is certainly not identical to *Puntius* and so should not apply here. Article 30 mentions in Section Bg the possibility of determining the type species from the next investigator who brings it up.

This is where another scientist, Pieter Bleeker, comes in. He had already assigned *Puntius sophore* as type species for *Puntius* in 1863. The problem was solved automatically, however, when it appeared that *Puntius puntio* was a "species inquirendum"—that is, a species with a dubious name about which further research is required.

However, even if the dubious species is ultimately re-instated, no such basis can ever be used for designation of a generic name. On such grounds, therefore, *B. puntio* must be discounted as a candidate for becoming the type species. *B. sophore*, then, comes into primary consideration, as it is a very well known and clearly outlined and described form.

Does this solve the whole problem? No. Even if it did, there would be no reason to classify all Southeast Asiatic barbs in the genus *Puntius*. They must remain within the limits of the genus as typified by *B. sophore*. It will take further study to determine which of the extant species should be so designated. Many of the popular aquarium barbs closely resemble *B. sophore*, but many differ from *B. sophore* just as much as *B. sophore* differs from the European barb, *Barbus barbus*.

It is certainly not the aquarist's job, without exhaustive research, to change a name to some other appellation that would not only be undesirable but would also be based on insufficient data. Let the name, for the time being, remain *Barbus*. If necessary, use the sub-generic name (*Puntius*) for *B. sophore* and its next of kin, *B. spilopterus* and *B. sophoroides*. If, in the future, *Barbus* splits up again, the process will have to go much further than simply a division into two genera.

Plate II-56. *Barbus arulius.*

Plate II-57. *Barbus chola.*

Barbus chola (Hamilton, 1822)
Swamp Barb
Chola Barb

Recent data show that this little fish is indigenous to all of India and Ceylon, where it inhabits the lowland waters. It grows to about 100 mm (4 inches). The background coloration is a silvery olive green with orange-yellow fins. The spot on the root of the tail is deep black, and the spot on the shoulder is present only in young specimens, but disappears when the fish grows longer than 30 mm ($1\frac{1}{4}$ inches). This nice little fish is comparable to its relatives and should be treated the same way they are. See *Barbus conchonius.*

Barbus conchonius (Hamilton, 1822)
Rosy Barb

Barbus conchonius originates in India, Burma and nearby countries. A few specimens were first taken to Europe in 1903. This lovely little fish seldom grows longer in the aquarium than 80 mm ($3\frac{1}{4}$ inches), and the males are a little smaller than the females. The robust body is flattened vertically, the back and belly are rounded off, and the body gradually tapers off to a spindle shape with a deeply forked tail and pointed caudal fins. The snout is short and has a medium-sized terminal mouth without barbs.

The background coloration is silvery, shot with pink. The large scales give it a net-like marking. Along the back, the coloration is a dark olive green, changing to reddish over the flanks and to whitish

453

Plate II-58. *Barbus conchonius.*

on the belly. The males are more brilliant than the females. The single fins especially are reddish with a black tip on the males but a softer, less-striking red on the females.

This species used to be one of the most often kept and one of the most preferred aquarium fishes. The reason for this was as much for the ease of keeping them as for the attraction of their beautiful markings and coloration. Any size aquarium is suitable, but a rectangular tank that allows plenty of room for swimming about is preferable. If the tank is spacious, well planted, and has some good hiding places, it is ideal for this fish. The plants should grow really thickly only along the sides of the tank. Place the aquarium where it will get sunlight from time to time, preferably in the morning. Normal water temperature is approximately 22 °C (72 °F). In the winter, although it must not go below 12 °C (54 °F), it must always be below 22 °C (72 °F).

As for food, this fish eats anything offered, but take care to ensure variety. It also likes to "graze" on the algae on plants and stones.

For breeding, put the male and female together into a spacious breeding tank having a temperature of 24–25 °C (75–77 °F). The courtship, which begins in the early spring, is sometimes quite violent, but it seldom degenerates into serious fighting. The female deposits about 20 large, crystal-clear, adhesive eggs in a place chosen by the male, who then fertilizes them. This procedure is repeated several times so that often several hundred eggs are deposited. Leggett (in "The Aquarist," Volume 33, January, 1968, page 30) published news about a successful crossing between *Barbus conchonius* and *Barbus nigrofasciatus*. Though several young hatched out and actually grew to adulthood, they were, as expected, sterile.

454

Barbus congicus Boulenger, 1899

Congo Barb

The fish in Illus. II–83 came from Zaïre (formerly the Democratic Republic of the Congo). The author was able to keep these for research purposes and studies show that this fish is identical to *Barbus congicus* but that it also shows all the characteristics which typify *B. pleuropholis.* Dr. Ethelwyn Trewavas suggested on a postcard to the author, dated October 24, 1953, that, from observations of young specimens, *B. pumilus* could be synonymous with *B. pleuropholis.* In fact, she stated the length for *B. pumilus* to be 26 mm (more than 1 inch), for *B. pleuropholis* 40 mm (over $1\frac{1}{2}$ inches), for *B. congicus* 75 mm (3 inches). After photographs had been taken by Timmerman, further studies of the specimens of *B. congicus* revealed that they attained a length of 62 and 65 mm ($2\frac{7}{16}$ and $2\frac{9}{16}$ inches), the female being slightly smaller.

Further examination after the death of the specimens, and comparison with other information from different localities, revealed that not only was Dr. Trewavas right and that *B. pumilus* were actually young *B. pleuropholis,* but at the same time both were the young of the 75-mm (3-inch) long *Barbus congicus.* Variation in the

Illus. II-83. *Barbus congicus.*

number of scales and the length of the fish are undoubtedly attributable to local differences.

A species which we must, therefore, call *Barbus congicus* inhabits an area stretching from southern Sudan (White Nile) to the Congo Basin, downstream from Stanley Falls.

It is striking how this very small barb resembles the well known Sumatran *Barbus oligolepis*. In some scientists' opinion, close relationship to *B. oligolepis* should not be excluded simply because of a geographical discontinuity in the distribution. Even the background coloration and the coloration of the fins show a strong resemblance. In both species, the background coloration is brownish with an olive green back and a light belly. The dorsal, anal, and caudal fins are a beautiful orange-red. As in *B. oligolepis*, the large scales of *B. congicus* are edged with a deep red to a rust. The pelvic fins are also deep red to rust, while the pectoral fins are without coloration.

One closely related African fish is *Barbus pseudognathodon* Boulenger, 1915, from Mweru Lake (Zaïre, formerly the Democratic Republic of the Congo, above Stanley Falls).

Experienced breeders should not have difficulty with the reproduction of this fish. The occurrence of the fish over a very large area indicates that it is not a "tricky" species in this regard. Quite a small species in the larger barbel genre, this little fish is a definite asset to collectors.

Barbus cumingi Günther, 1868
Cuming's Barb

This little fish from Ceylon belongs to the smaller species, since it only attains a length of 55 mm (2¼ inches). Comparison with *B. nigrofasciatus* from the lowland waters of Ceylon is of interest. *B. cumingi's* environment, mountain waters that run faster than lowland waters, has caused it to become a more active swimmer. Such activity can also be observed in the aquarium. The statement that these two species are found together is correct only insofar as both are native to Ceylon, because they exist in totally different environments. When setting up a regional aquarium, therefore, we cannot simply decide to include species from Ceylon, regardless of their original environment. Although Ceylon is an island, the biotopes there differ enormously. *Barbus cumingi* may, however, be found in companionship with *Barbus titteya*.

Little is known about the reproduction of *B. cumingi*. However, in an environment in which *B. titteya* feels enough at home to reproduce,

Plate II-59. *Barbus cumingi.*

this fish should respond in a similar manner.

The background coloration of *B. cumingi* is silvery with yellow, with shiny spots on the back and head. There is an oblong, vertical, black patch close behind the gill flaps and a second smaller, and also vertical, patch directly above the last rays of the anal fin. The fins are orange to deep yellow, the dorsal and pelvic fins being a darker orange. The dorsal fin has two rows of black spots and a black dot on the first ray.

Illus. II-84. *Barbus eugrammus.*

Barbus eugrammus (Silas, 1956)
"Barbus fasciatus"
Striped Barb

This fish is found universally in both running and stagnant waters of Southeast Asia—Malaysia, Sumatra, Bangka and Borneo—though it is not very well known by collectors. The first importation of such fish into Holland took place in 1935.

This *Barbus* is another of the larger species and can attain a length of 120 mm (about $4\frac{3}{4}$ inches), though even in a very large aquarium of 1,600 gallon capacity, they do not grow much longer than 80 mm ($3\frac{1}{4}$ inches). *B. eugrammus* is an extremely lively species, especially the young specimens, whose conduct and longitudinal stripes are similar to the danios. *B. eugrammus*, apparently more of a swimmer than most of its relatives, is also more inclined to frequent the middle depths of the aquarium.

The body is rather long, drawn out, and vertically flattened. The snout is somewhat more sharply pointed than that of its relatives, and the mouth is terminal. Illus. II–84 gives a good, over-all picture of the outward characteristics.

There are usually two pairs of well developed barbels on the snout. *Barbus lineatus* from Malaysia (Selangor-Muar River), described by Duncker, has no barbels and differs slightly in other ways from *B.*

458

eugrammus, but otherwise is so similar that we can consider it identical— a so-called "local variety," as Duncker calls it.

The background coloration of *B. eugrammus* varies from rust-brown to yellow-brown or grey-brown, easing off to a lighter tone towards the belly. Five or six dark brown to black stripes run lengthwise along the body, from head to tail. One runs down the side, from the gill flap to the root of the tail. Above this are two clearly marked stripes and a third which is less striking, but, in general, still clearly visible. It goes no farther than under the dorsal fin. Under the central stripe, there is usually only one clear stripe from the edge of the gill flap, extending as far·as a little to the rear of the last ray of the anal fin. Sometimes a narrow stripe is fairly visible along the belly, from the base of the pelvic fin to the anus.

In bright light, the scales on the flanks have a metallic green sheen. The fins are yellowish grey to a translucent pink. The caudal fin is mostly pink to a light, reddish brown. The sexes are easy to recognize because the females are much more robust and rounder than the slightly smaller males. During the mating season, the male is somewhat more brightly tinted than the female.

Barbus everetti Boulenger, 1894
Clown Barb

Barbus everetti comes from Southeast Asia—Malaysia, Singapore, Borneo and Bunguran Island.

This species, which, along with *Barbus lateristriga,* *B. binotatus* and *B. semifasciolatus,* is one of the larger *Barbus* species, and can grow to about 115 mm (about $4\frac{1}{2}$ inches) long. The body proportions, fin placement and markings are shown in Illus. II–85. The markings, and to some extent the coloration of young specimens, especially, bear a striking resemblance to many other barbs. In 1916, Weber & De Beaufort said that there is even a possibility that *B. everetti* is a cross between *Barbus lateristriga* and *B. tetrazona.* It is also possible that the species *B. dunckeri* is identical to *B. everetti.*

Care and breeding of *Barbus semifasciolatus* applies to this species as well (see page 477). However, more space for *B. everetti* is preferable. The aquarium should be placed in the sun, be thickly planted in parts, have a good, thick layer of humus on the bottom, preferably with algae growing on it, and have a few good-sized rocks placed here and there.

459

Illus. II-85. *Barbus everetti*.

Suitable plants are *Cryptocoryne, Aponogeton, Hydrilla verticillata, Najas,* but not *Myriophyllum* if you want the aquarium to look nice.

Barbus everetti is a peaceful fish, which likes to browse all day long in the typical manner of the barbs and always manages to find something edible. Sometimes it plunges an inch or so into the bottom of the tank and comes up thrashing and gasping, but clutching a tubifex worm. A well-established aquarium in which the bottom is "heavy" accommodates this little digger quite well. There is not too much disturbance of the humus layer and the fish is a delight even to the most particular aquarist.

When the time is ripe, hundreds of quite large eggs are deposited, usually after the male has submitted the female to a fairly impassioned courtship session. If the aquarium is too small, too thinly planted, and has an unsuitable layer covering the bottom, most of the eggs usually fall prey to the parent fish, who love to eat them (see page 147 for a discussion of parents eating their own eggs). If some eggs survive this voracity by adhering to plants—such as bunches of thread algae, *Nitella* or *Chara*—the first young will appear after about 50 hours. The young are seldom seen at this stage, however, as they go at once and hide themselves among the roots, thread algae, and so forth, on the bottom. After a few weeks, but still alert to danger, the young fish start rummaging about on the bottom, in imitation of their parents. Before a month has gone by, the bands distinguishing the adult fish can be observed.

The temperature limits of the water for *B. everetti* range from 18–28 °C (64–82 °F). The water should preferably be neutral or slightly acid in pH (replace evaporated water with clean rain water). The fish can stand occasional lower temperatures, down to 15 °C (59 °F), but only if the change is not too sudden.

Barbus filamentosus (Valenciennes, 1844)
"Mahecola"

This recently imported fish (1952) at first had no name, but later was circulated under the name *Barbus mahecola*. It is evident, from the literature on this fish, that the name *B. mahecola* is synonymous with *B. filamentosus* and that the species was simply described, by the same writer in the same work, under two different names.

It comes from southern India, from Kanara in the south, along the west coast, and from the Travancore Hills. It also occurs in Ceylon (Hora, 1942, and Deraniyagala, 1952). According to Deraniyagala, it can also be found in Burma. It is abundant in all kinds of moderately running and stagnant waters. The females, ready for spawning from January to July, frequent the quiet river bends that are rich in vegetation or pools where mating takes place.

The great variation in some characteristics of *B. filamentosus*— particularly, the development of the barbels, which is probably connected with the place of origin—is remarkable. Day, who also described this species under two names, was well aware of their similarity and suggests that *B. filamentosus*' lack of barbels is the most important point of difference. However, he also writes, "*B. mahecola*, with its two barbels, is very similar to *B. filamentosus*, without barbels."

Examination of a number of specimens showed that some of these barbels are especially small in those fish from high altitudes (the Travancore Hills). In the fish of the lower-lying areas of Kanara and the Nilgiris, the barbels are larger, and *B. mahecola* is more prevalent. Towards Madras, however, this species is scarce or totally absent, and the *B. filamentosus* predominates. The question then arises as to whether there are indeed two separate species, or, simply, two separate transitional stages.

Day had already noted the differences and similarities between these fish. *B. filamentosus* grows to about 150 mm (6 inches), though other smaller forms are known, depending on the place of origin. Ceylonese members of this species have been observed 110 mm (about 4½ inches) long. In spite of these slight differences, this fish is still considered as one of the larger barbs. In other aspects, it is comparable to *B. lateristriga, B. everetti, B. gelius, B. dorsalis* and *B. melanampyx.* A number of filament-like rays, which give the name *B. filamentosus,* grow out from the dorsal fin, mainly in the males. One striking peculiarity, which can be seen in other species as well, is the great difference in the markings between the young specimens and the adult fish. This makes it quite clear that *B. filamentosus* belongs to the group of "transverse striped" species. The spots on the bodies of the adults below the first rays of the dorsal fin, above the anal fin, and on the root of the tail, are the remains of the broad, vertical bands that crossed the body during youth. There is a dark line on the base of the tail and the tips of the forks of the caudal fin and of the dorsal fin are also dark. The background coloration is greenish; the back is olive green. The belly is white to yellowish green, while the throat, belly and anterior part of the flanks are sometimes salmon-pink in the males.

The caudal fin has white dots with a darker edge underneath, the remainder of the fin being a deep orange that fades to a lighter shade towards the base. During the mating season, the larger males get rows of wart-like growths on the snout, a characteristic of many barbs.

Although this species has probably not yet reproduced in the aquarium, it can be treated in exactly the same way as *Barbus everetti* and *B. lateristriga.*

Plate II-60. *Barbus gelius.*

Barbus gelius (Hamilton, 1822)
Dwarf Barb
Golden Dwarf Barb

This little fish comes from central India (the Ganjam district of Orissa), Assam, and Bangladesh, where it is found in moderately running waters, always in small shoals among the river-bank vegetation. According to Hora (1940), it occurs where there is a muddy bottom, sand or pebbles.

This barb belongs to the smaller species and grows to about 40 mm (a little over 1½ inches). The females are sometimes larger. As this fish is closely related to *Barbus phutunio*, refer to page 474 for further details.

The background coloration of *Barbus gelius* is an almost translucent olive green, changing to silver-white on the belly. Depending on the circumstances, the whole body may be shot with a rather striking, golden sheen. In males, sometimes there is a beautiful, copper-red stripe running from the head to the caudal fin, which often becomes intense red. The whole scheme of coloration is set off nicely by the dark spots that show up so well in Plate II–60. Except for the reddish caudal fin, the fins are soft yellow.

Not only do the females grow somewhat larger than the males, they are also deeper, having a broader belly, and not as bright. The copper-red, lengthwise stripe is less pronounced in appearance.

These fish should be kept in an aquarium provided with plenty of vegetation. For the water, 18–22 °C (64–72 °F) is plenty warm, but

463

the temperature should, preferably, not be constant. Small fluctuations between day and night temperatures are desirable.

Reproduction is accompanied by a very lively courtship, during which hundreds of eggs are deposited. The very small, yellowish eggs are adhesive and stick to the leaves on which they are deposited. The next day, the first young hatch out. If the aquarium is not too small, the parent fish may be allowed to remain with their eggs. Unlike many other barbs, these fish have no tendency to eat their own eggs, because their entire menu consists of vegetation and the small animals that are fed to them. After the second day, the young should be well supplied with ditch-water infusoria. Make sure there are plenty of the protozoans, as the parent fish will feed from these, too.

Barbus holotaenia Boulenger, 1904

Since 1913, this African barb has appeared regularly among the imports from the Congo region. It grows to approximately 120 mm (about 4¾ inches). It is a challenge to breeders to try their luck at breeding this very attractive fish, because so far, it has apparently not been bred in captivity.

Barbus lateristriga Valenciennes, 1842

Spanner Barb

T Barb

This fish is very common in clear streams, small rivers and pools in Southeast Asia, Malaysia, Sumatra, Bangka, Billiton, Java, and Borneo. With its close relative, *Barbus everetti*, this species belongs to the largest barbs imported for aquariums. In the natural state, it grows to 200 mm (about 8 inches), but 100 mm (4 inches) in the aquarium is about the limit. Even at that length, the fish is adult and can reproduce.

The background coloration is olive green to brownish green, the sides are reddish with a golden sheen, and the belly in the females is orange-red to whitish. Most striking in the markings are the two, broad, vertical bands and the horizontal band on the tail. The shape of these bands varies a great deal, depending on the place of origin. The normal black of the bands is also liable to vary. The fins are a beautiful orange-red to blood red, with the exception of the pectoral fins which are without coloration. In larger specimens, the fins have a bluish border—*not* a distinguishing mark of the sexes, as some tend to think. The sexes are quite easy to recognize by the somewhat less intense coloration and the more obviously rounded belly of the female.

This extremely lively species requires an aquarium with plenty of room to dart about, and with dense vegetation along the sides. Imported fish are very shy to start with, and *Barbus lateristriga* hardly ever let themselves be seen. A great many related fish are equally shy, especially well known *B. semifasciolatus*, which resembles *B. lateristriga* in much of its pattern of conduct. A turf bottom is recommended for the aquarium to make the fish feel at home. The sooner they feel at home, the sooner they show off their beautiful coloration.

For food, although they consume anything that is offered, the diet should actually consist mainly of living organisms. The desirable water temperature is 18–25 °C (64–77 °F). It is not necessary to raise the temperature for breeding if it usually ranges from 23–25 °C (73–77 °F).

After an energetic chase by the male, which begins when the first rays of sun penetrate the aquarium, both fish disappear, side by side, into the tangle of plants. The eggs are strewn about, preferably in shallow water. Like most barbs, the parents are predatory and they will devour every egg they can reach, unless these manage to sift down into a thick layer of thread algae (or something similar) on the bottom. Mating is repeated several times until several hundred eggs have been deposited.

When mating appears to be finished, the fish hang about, exhausted, among the plants. At this stage, it is a good idea to remove and transfer them to a quiet, roomy aquarium. They prefer not to be in the company of fish that are too active at this time, as it disturbs them too much.

The young hatch out within two days and bury themselves at once in the layer of turf so that they are seldom seen until they are a week old. Be patient. Just now, they should be given very fine food—infusoria and *Bosmina* (crustaceans) are good. Later on, change the diet to finely sieved waterfleas and finely chopped worms, such as white worms and tubifex. The older fish, of course, will be well fed if given white worms and other palatable fare. Variation in the menu for both old and young is desirable. If well fed, the young fish grow rapidly. After a little more than a month, the characteristic markings become visible.

This species and *B. everetti* and *B. dunckeri* are closely related. A thorough examination would probably show that they all belong to a single species which is broken up into a number of geographical sub-species. *Barbus lateristriga*, which has the largest distribution, can be taken as the root form, while *B. everetti* and *B. dunckeri*, if not themselves identical, are derivatives of it.

Barbus macrops Boulenger, 1911

Although it has been thought that this fish belonged in several other genera, for the present, allow it to keep the name *Barbus*. It has two pairs of barbels, although in the specimens examined, these were reduced to rudimentary whiskers. Therefore, according to old ideas, the name *Barbodes* would be considered appropriate. The genus *Labeobarbus*, among others, is also characterized in this way. See pages 451–452 about the question of *Barbus* or *Puntius*.

This little barb from Portuguese Guinea grows to a length of 65 mm (over 2½ inches) and is certainly one of the more attractive *Barbus* species. It is one of the few African barbs still found among collectors since World War II, though it apparently has not been used for breeding. The background coloration is yellowish to olive green on the back, whitish on the belly, and a well defined black band runs from the upper lip to the root of the tail. In many ways, this fish resembles its South Asian relatives, *Osteochilus vittatus*, *Epalzeorhynchus kalopterus*, and *Garra taeniata* (see pages 498, 492 and 494), which have also been imported. The most obvious differences, besides the fact that these species grow three times bigger than *B. macrops*, are the smaller eyes and the black band continuing to the caudal fin in *O. vittatus*. *Barbus deserti* from the Niger Basin is also closely related, but differs mainly in that the black band runs back to the caudal fin.

Illus. II-86. *Barbus macrops.*

Plate II-61. *Barbus nigrofasciatus.*

Barbus nigrofasciatus Günther, 1868
Purple-Headed Barb
Black Ruby Barb

Barbus nigrofasciatus occurs in the densely vegetated, slow running waters of southern Ceylon. At certain spots in these waters, the fish seem to find things which are needed but which are not present elsewhere. It is only in these certain places that *B. nigrofasciatus* is found in large numbers.

The body, characteristic of many barbs, is rather deep and more or less vertically flattened, depending on the age of the specimen. The fish runs to about 60 mm in length (about 2½ inches). The head is small in proportion to the body, has a pointed snout and a large, upward-slanting mouth. The fins are all well developed and the caudal fin is deeply forked. The whole body, as well as the base of the dorsal fin, is covered with large, cycloidal scales. The background coloration is olive green to greyish yellow, the area of the back is moss green, and the belly whitish. Each individual scale is set off with a silver sheen.

Four blackish, vertical stripes run down the flanks. The intensity of these varies with the emotional state of the fish. The dorsal fin of the male is brownish black to purplish black. This fish gets its popular names from its magnificent, purple-red head. This intense coloration

467

occurs only in the males; the females are less vivid. The dorsal fin of the female is yellowish to almost no coloration, while the rest of the fins, in both sexes, vary from pale to transparent.

Caring for this beautiful barb should not be difficult. It needs a large aquarium in which it can swim to its heart's content. Do not place the aquarium where it is too light or in direct sunlight, and put dense vegetation along the sides. Plants, such as *Cryptocoryne*, are recommended for the bottom, as the darker the bottom, the better it is for the fish and the more it feels at ease. The normal water temperature is 24–25 °C (75–77 °F). In the autumn, this can be slowly brought down to about 20 °C (68 °F) and left at that level for the duration of the winter.

In the natural state, especially in southwestern Ceylon, the fish lives in rivers and creeks in the lowlands. The water there is muddy and cloudy and sometimes, when close to the sea, brackish. The daytime temperature is about 28 °C (82 °F); at night, it drops a few degrees. The bottom is very dark and is covered with a regular forest of *Cryptocoryne* species. In these low-lying plains, water temperature drops as low as 18 °C (64 °F) and rises to approximately 36 °C (96 °F) at the highest. In the dry season, the rivers draw back from the banks of their wide beds; in the wet monsoon season, they swell back over them and the fish then feast on the multitude of insects inhabiting the flooded area.

The aquarium temperature may be raised slightly for breeding, but no higher than 26–28 °C (79–82 °F). Breeding these fish is as simple as caring for them. Arrange the breeding tank with thick clumps of finely-leaved plants, and plant the bottom with such plants as *Eleocharis acicularis*. The parent fish are extremely predatory and, given half a chance, they will not miss devouring a single egg. When choosing a pair of fish for breeding, it is a good idea to make sure beforehand that both fish are showing symptoms of the desire to mate. Otherwise, when placed in a tank together, they may attack each other.

A good breeding pair is a joy to watch. As soon as the male is transferred into the breeding tank, he starts his advances. Holding himself at an angle, he rests his fins by folding them together along his body. The show is on, for now it is possible to fully admire the magnificent hues which the male fish can display. The vertical stripes disappear. The tail section turns dull grey with a red sheen; the areas of the head and breast take on a dark, purple-red coloration. The male tries to hustle the female into the thick vegetation and, if he has his way, the female only has to endure very little, for the eggs are deposited very quickly. Both fish disappear together among the vegetation, pressed together side by side, fins spread wide and shaking violently. Deposition of eggs can take several hours, after which the female, usually exhausted, hauls herself off to a handy corner and begins munching on the eggs intently.

Right now someone must intervene, unless sufficient care has been taken to assure that a large portion of the eggs has fallen where the parents cannot get at them. Do not allow the male to chase the female too much once she has rid herself of her eggs. At any rate, it is better to separate the fish, removing both parents from the tank, unless it is a very big one with unusually dense vegetation. In this case, the young fish have a place to hide and can avoid the cannibalistic appetites of both their parents.

The adhesive eggs are preferably laid in the upper half of the tank, deposited on fine-leaved plants or among the roots of large, floating plants, such as *Ceratopteris* and *Pistia*. After about a day (24 to 30 hours), depending on the temperature and other circumstances, the young hatch out. They hang on to the plants and to the glass sides of the tank, looking like crystal-clear little balls with almost invisible tails. Food now fed to them must be as fine as dust, accompanied by ditch-water infusoria. Infusoria alone is usually not enough.

Depending on the temperature and the food, the larvae speedily grow up. After a week, the form is less compressed, and a few days later, the black eyes become visible. Then the fry go hunting, frisking at first along the bottom, then growing bolder and daring to swim to higher levels. Keep on feeding dust-fine food and infusoria for another week; then, shift to sieved daphnia, cyclops or brine shrimp. *B. nigrofasciatus* is not at all fussy about its food—it will eat anything, living or dried. Within a month, coloration begins to appear and the largest fish is already more than 10 mm ($\frac{3}{8}$ inch) long.

Sometimes, the first breeding does not succeed—that is, the first laying of eggs by either young or old fish. The eggs may still hatch out, but the offspring soon die. A rest period of a few weeks and some good food can prepare the parents for another attempt at breeding. Do not put fish that do not get along well together in the same breeding tank. The result will only be disappointing.

A crossing with *Barbus conchonius* has been successful.

Barbus oligolepis (Bleeker, 1853)

Checkerboard Barb (U.S.)

Chequer Barb (England)

Sumatra Barb

This fish commonly runs in shoals in the fresh waters of Sumatra in Indonesia. It was imported into Europe for the first time in 1925. The background coloration is red-brown to dark brown, the back being darker and the belly lighter. There is an olive green to mother-of-pearl sheen over the whole body. In the males, this appears pinkish, and is mainly along the back and the belly. Generally, each of the scales on the upper half of the body has a bluish to black shining mark with a black border which causes net-like markings over the flanks. The base of the single fins is dark red-brown, lightening towards the edge. The dorsal, anal and pelvic fins are set off by a border which ranges from blue to black. Where the males show a pink coloration, the females tend towards more of a beige, and only the dorsal fin has a dark border.

During the mating season, the males are vividly brilliant and the black borders and markings show up in sharp contrast. The females are less-strikingly brilliant. They are predominantly olive green to greenish brown and, where the males are red-brown, the females are beige.

Plate II-62. *Barbus oligolepis.*

Where the males are black, the females are brownish. The golden yellow flanks of the females have three to six irregular markings. These are also prominent on all the young fish, but fade on the males slowly as they grow up.

Its small size and beautiful coloration make this little barb welcome in the home aquarium. It needs lots of vegetation with fine-leaved plants. It is best to plant the bottom with *Cryptocoryne*, which darkens the tone of the bottom, and results in darker, more vivid coloration of the fish. A dark bottom is, in fact, recommended for all *Barbus* species. Do not let the water temperature drop below 20 °C (68 °F). During the mating season, raise it gradually to 24–26 °C (75–79 °F). It is important that these fish do not go through the winter at a temperature above 20 °C. If the winter temperature is too high, the fish will not be in good condition for the next breeding season and breeding will only result in disappointment.

The total number of eggs laid varies from 100 to 300. The first young emerge after one and a half days (35 to 40 hours), looking like little splinters of glass hanging on the plants and the sides of the tank. After two or three days, when the yolk sac has been used up, the quickest new fish start trying to swim. They are very clumsy at first, but soon get the hang of it, inspect their territory thoroughly and busily chase infusoria. The young are brought up in the usual way—feed them ditch-water infusoria.

Here again environment influences the conduct of the fish. Sometimes the eggs are laid just as other barbs and danios lay them—that is, they are laid freely. This is what usually happens when four males and four females are put together into the breeding tank. The eggs fall between the plants and down on the bottom in such a way that their adhesive capacity has little effect. Sometimes, however, a single couple in a small tank with a thick bottom layer of humus deposits from two to eight eggs at a time on the plants. Here, the adhesive quality of the eggs is clearly demonstrated.

In these cases, the young hatch out during the second day, but bury themselves at once in the humus, and do not re-appear until they are a week old.

A good point about this *Barbus* is that, unlike many of its relatives, it does not tear up the humus bottom and make the water cloudy and dirty. It does, of course, indulge the *Barbus* predilection for rummaging about in the bottom of the tank, but it does so without upsetting the clarity of the water.

Barbus oligolepis prefers a habitat of moderately running water, choked with dense vegetation, although it is also found in clear, standing water. Towards the low-lying plains, this fish becomes less common and decreases somewhat in size.

Specimens caught outside Sumatra differ slightly from the Sumatran fish, the background coloration being slightly darker. In the Sumatran highlands, water temperature ranges from 19–25 °C (66–77 °F). On the lower plains, the average is higher, 22–27 °C (72–81 °F). In Malaysia and Singapore, where most of the imported specimens come from, temperatures ranging from 21–27 °C (70–81 °F) have been recorded. These are obviously normal temperature ranges, not in any way extreme, for *Barbus oligolepis*.

As already noted under *Barbus congicus*, it is possible that *B. oligolepis* forms a natural group with a few other species, including the African *B. congicus*, and that these species possibly even represent a completely new genus. This is also the reason that the generic name *Puntius* cannot simply replace *Barbus* for all the Southeast Asia species.

Plate II-64. *Barbus pentazona johorensis.*

Barbus pentazona johorensis Duncker, 1904
Six-Banded Barb

This species from Sumatra belongs to the barbs with cross stripes. Together with *B. rhombocellatus*, it forms the *B. pentazona* group, closely related to the *B. tetrazona* group, to which *B. tetrazona*, *B. partipentazona*, and *B. anchisporus* forms belong.

The groups can be distinguished from each other because the *B. pentazona* group has no black spot or stripe on the dorsal fin, though this is present in the *B. tetrazona* group. The cross bands are outlined with a light shade in the former and are not outlined at all in the latter. There is no band running through the eye in *B. pentazona*, except in *B.p. johorensis*, whereas this band is present in the *B. tetrazona* group. In general, the coloration of the *B. tetrazona* forms are somewhat brighter and redder than in the *B. pentazona* forms, where they are more brown.

Barbus pentazona johorensis is a beautiful fish that gives the aquarist no trouble. At the same time, it is easier to breed than, for example, *Barbus tetrazona.*

Illus. II-87. *Barbus phutunio.*

Barbus phutunio (Hamilton, 1822)

It is usually stated that this fish comes from India, Ceylon, and Bangladesh. However, according to Deraniyagala, *Barbus phutunio* specimens attributed to Ceylon actually belong to the species *Barbus cumingi*. According to Hora's documentation of the fauna in Central and Southern India, *Barbus phutunio* does not occur there either, but is, evidently, replaced in that region by a closely related species, *Barbus gelius*. This leaves only northern India and Bangladesh as the distribution area for *B. phutunio*. The systematic standards are not yet fixed, however, and it is not known whether or not a number of forms should be distinguished. Many species have more or less the same markings and coloration and are practically ·identical in fin ray count and scale formation. They do differ, though, in the number of barbels and in the development of a lateral line, which may be either complete, vague, or only rudimentary. These characteristics, however, are of only relative value for systematization, and it is hoped that, after a proper revision of the assembled data, a natural grouping will emerge.

The basic markings of B. *phutunio* are two dark and two light cross bands. The first dark band runs from the back to the middle of the pectoral fins; the second from the back to the base of the anal fin. The first light band runs downward from the foremost dorsal fin ray, and the second from the last of the dorsal fin rays. There is also a dark band in the dorsal fin and around the base of the tail. All these bands—especially the light ones—stand out in contrast to a brownish background and slowly disappear as the fish approach adulthood. Eventually, only two clear patches remain on the middle of the flanks, one on the tail, just above the root of the posterior anal fin ray, and the other above the root of the pectoral fins. The fins are yellowish, the dorsal and anal fins having orange tips. The dorsal fin also has a dark border and a row of dark spots, decreasing in size from front to back, forming a kind of stripe.

Barbus rhombocellatus Koumans, 1950

This fish from Borneo has probably never been imported as an aquarium fish. An illustration of the fish is shown here (Illus. II–88), but refer to Plate II–64 of *Barbus pentazona johorensis* for the coloration and markings, from which *B. rhombocellatus* differs only in detail. The most noticeable difference is that *B. p. johorensis* has a stripe running through the eye, while *B. rhombocellatus* does not.

Illus. II-88. *Barbus rhombocellatus.*

475

Plate II-65. *Barbus semifasciolatus.*

Barbus semifasciolatus **Günther, 1868**
China Barb
Gold Barb
Half-Banded Barb
Schubert's Barb

This fish is found in Southeast China, from Hong Kong to the island of Hainan, in all kinds of quiet, fresh waters, irrigation reservoirs, and rice fields. Since 1909, it has been universally known and appreciated as an aquarium fish. This very beautiful barb belongs, along with *Barbus everetti* and *B. fasciatus*, to the larger species. The males—seldom larger than 80 mm (3¼ inches)—are usually noticeably smaller than the females, which grow to around 100 mm (4 inches).

The coloration is extremely variable, as are the stripes. The vertical stripes may be broken up into spots, or they may be almost entirely absent. Although the intensity of shades and markings hardly differ at all between the sexes, the females are easy to recognize, as they are plumper and larger.

476

Although it belongs to the larger type of barb, *Barbus semifasciolatus* is satisfied with a less spacious aquarium than some other species. Of course, it would be at home in a large tank, but it is just as happy in one no more than 24 inches long, well planted with *Cryptocoryne*, *Hydrilla*, *Najas*, *Ceratopteris*, and with a bottom of thick humus.

Except in the mating season, *Barbus semifasciolatus* is a quiet swimmer, always on the lookout for something to eat. During courtship and mating, it develops such a capacity for speed that it could justifiably be called tempestuous. However, the fish never goes so far as to damage itself or its partner, and, in the end, remains as peaceful and tolerant as it usually is. It is certainly a good idea to cover the aquarium during the mating season, since the fish repeatedly jump out of the water and fall back in again with a splash.

In the course of laying her eggs, the female darts in and out among the weeds, leaving 10 to 30 eggs behind with each trip. The male follows her closely and fertilizes the deposited eggs at once.

If the aquarium is large enough and there is a big enough supply of food, it is not necessary to remove the parent fish after the eggs are laid, although, of course, they will manage to do away with some of the eggs. If the young hatch out after about a day and a half, there is

Plate II-66. *Barbus bariloides* **is an import from Angola which, in coloration and markings, is similar to** *Barbus semifasciolatus.*

no further cause for worry, as the parent fish very seldom attack their young.

From 50 to 400 eggs are laid in one mating period, depending on various factors, and, by the second day, the larvac may be seen hanging on the plants, tank wall and stones. By the third day, the earliest fish hatched are already swimming with the remains of the yolk sac still attached. They grow fast and, after a week, will certainly be in shape to dine on sieved waterfleas.

"*Barbus schuberti*" is a name sometimes used for a xanthoristic (golden) form first bred by Thomas Schubert in America. It is now accepted that *B. schuberti* is merely a different coloration of *B. semifasciolatus*.

Barbus sophore (Hamilton, 1822)

This species is distributed over a wide area, including India (but not Ceylon), Bangladesh, Burma and Thailand. *B. sophore* is subject to a broad variation in marking as well as in the development of the barbels and the lateral line, resulting in a confusion of names. This was clarified by Chaudhuri in 1916 (see under Hora, 1941) and since 1940, the name *Barbus sophore* has been recognized by Hora.

The barbels are not always absent as they are with *B. stigma*. (Earlier classifications referred to *Barbus sophore* as *Barbus stigma*.) In groups of fishes caught in different places, there are some barbels present, varying from rudimentary ones to two pairs of very small ones.

Hora (1940) gives some interesting facts about the environment of these fish. First, he lists a number of species found together in the same water, a village pond in Singpur, India, full of water lilies and *Elodea*, a species of *Scrophularia* with thorns and blue flowers in one corner, and reeds of Cyperaceae species. Here, he caught *Brachydanio rerio*, *Rasbora daniconia*, and *Barbus sophore*. A "jheel"—a kind of pool—at Nagri on the Raipur Forest Tramway in India, in December, 1939, yielded more specimens. The pool, located between the rice fields, was supplied only with rain water, having no connection whatever with a stream or river. Weeds of all kinds grew in the pool—*Potamogeton*, *Elodea*, *Trapa spinosa*, lilies—and along its banks grew all kinds of grasses and thread algae. The fish caught included *Brachydanio rerio*, *Esomus danricus*, *Barbus ticto*, two species of *Ophicephalus* and *Nandus nandus*. He also gives a number of examples of the vegetation found at different places of capture—an important note for collectors. Also in December, 1939, at a bend in the Mahanadi River in India, 5 km (about 3 miles) from Sihawa, just before its confluence with the Balka Nallah River, along muddy bottoms and at places that were sandy with pebbles and without vegetation, he caught *Chela laubuca, Barilius bendelisis, Brachydanio rerio, Esomus danricus, Rasbora daniconia, Barbus gelius, Barbus guganio, Barbus ticto, Noemacheilus botia, Noemacheilus denisoni, Mystus tengara, Ophicephalus punctatus.*

Barbus sophore does not appear in this deep water without vegetation, but it can be found in all pools, lakes and waters that have thickly growing grasses and reeds along the banks, water lilies, *Potamogeton, Cyperus,* or thread algae in ankle-deep water 200 mm (about 8 inches). Occasionally, larger specimens are found in deeper water.

The background coloration of *B. sophore* is a brownish green to olive green, lighter on the belly, with two round spots, one on the root of the dorsal fin, and one at the base of the tail. The anal and pectoral fins are blood red (slightly more orange in the female) during the mating season. At other times, the coloration is slightly less vivid. The length can be up to approximately 150 mm (6 inches). Depending on the place of origin, however, it is usually smaller than this. Aquarium-bred specimens grow to a good 80 mm (3¼ inches).

Barbus tetrazona (Bleeker, 1855)
Tiger Barb

The general habitat of *Barbus tetrazona* is the Shan States of Burma, South Viet-Nam, Malaysia, Thailand, Sumatra and Borneo, mainly in still or moderately running lowland waters, swamps, ditches, canals, other shallow waters with overhanging banks and/or dense vegetation, and in jungle waters. They always inhabit areas with a thick humus layer on the bottom.

The background coloration is bright pink to yellowish, with a metallic sheen. The back is a darker gold-brown and the belly whitish. The four blackish green, vertical bands run, as a rule, right round the body, though one or more, usually the second, can be shorter.

Along the root of the dorsal fin is a blackish green band. The snout, dorsal fin, anal fin, and pelvic fins are, depending on the environment, a beautiful bright red, running from yellowish to no coloration along the edges. The anal and pectoral fins are also without coloration, perhaps a little darker on the rays. Often, the third band extends from the tail base down upon the anal fin. The scales have brownish edges which show up as a net-like marking over the flanks.

The sexes are not easy to distinguish—certainly not from the intensity of the coloration or markings. They can only be differentiated

Plate II-67. *Barbus tetrazona tetrazona.*

with any certainty in specimens at least 40 mm (over 1½ inches) long by the higher and broader shape of the females who are ready for spawning. This little fish is sometimes still considered difficult and capricious. It is often written of them that they suddenly stand on their head and, with no further sign of discomfort, sink dead to the bottom. This generally happens in "clean" aquariums with a nicely siphoned-off bottom that is strongly light-reflecting. Aquarists possessing a tank with a dark bottom in a quiet location, not too brightly lit except for occasional sun rays, and supplied with good vegetation, will not experience such freakish action from this fish and will be able to enjoy its company for many years.

A good bottom layer of humus (in the form of peat dust) puts the fish at ease immediately. Feed it regularly with ditch-water infusoria. Put these fish preferably in a roomy tank that is not too high, is moderately populated with quiet fish, and is thickly planted in some places. The average temperature should be 22–24 °C (72–75 °F).

If possible, do not transfer *Barbus tetrazona* to a new environment for breeding. It is preferable to remove all the other fish from the tank in which they grew up. In some circumstances, certain fish may be left with the breeding pair. When the arrangements have been made, leave them alone. If you do transfer them to a breeding tank without taking the necessary precautions, they are usually quite upset and nothing comes to pass.

After a courtship that is usually short, the eggs are laid in the normal way, among thick plants, three or four at a time, over a space of a few hours—a total of about 500 eggs. Plenty of food during and after the mating period is necessary. The small, light, yellowish brown eggs are usually not very adhesive and some of them soon sink to the humus bottom.

It is not really necessary to raise the temperature for breeding. In fact, the temperature must not exceed 26 °C (79 °F), unless this is by natural summer warmth. In a large tank, the parents can be left with their unhatched brood and later on with the live young, although they will, of course, eat some of them.

After 24 hours, the first young are visible on the plants and tank walls, where they are left, undisturbed, by the parent fish. At this time, both parents and young must be supplied with plenty of food. In a large tank, all will flourish quickly.

The natural waters in which these fish are found are characterized by their pH value of 6 to 7 (apparently not important, since the pH value can fluctuate greatly within a few hours), by a cloudy yellow coloration, muddiness, 1.1 mg of carbon dioxide per liter (1 liter = 1.057 liquid quarts), 3.6 mg of manganese per liter, and a hardness of 2.4° (quite soft).

There are, as has been shown, various differences of opinion concerning nomenclature. Here, the question is whether two species— *B. tetrazona* and *B. partipentazona*—that exist so closely together and differ from each other so slightly are, in fact, distinctly different. Consider them as two sub-species, differing from each other as follows:

B. tetrazona partipentazona (Fowler, 1934)

This fish is from Southeast Asia and Malaysia. The variation in coloration from Malaysia, described by Duncker in 1904, is identical to *B. t. partipentazona*. This sub-species differs from *B. t. tetrazona* because it has only 9 to 10 teeth on the last, hard dorsal fin ray. The third vertical band, distinctly separate from the band on the dorsal fin, sometimes runs over upon the body, and ends in a point. The background is more yellowish than *B. tetrazona*. There are 21 to 23 scales lengthwise.

B. tetrazona tetrazona (Bleeker, 1855)

This fish is from Sumatra and Borneo and is characterized by a reddish, rather than a yellowish, background. It has approximately 18 teeth on the last bony ray of the dorsal fin. The third vertical band is connected, or almost connected, to the band (patch) on the dorsal fin. There are 20 to 21 scales lengthwise.

482

Illus. II-89. *Barbus ticto.*

Barbus ticto (Hamilton, 1822)

The habitat of *Barbus ticto* is Southeast Asia—from Ceylon through India over the whole Ganges Delta, into Burma and Thailand. Illus. II–89 shows the basic form of this beautiful barb which varies greatly, depending on the place of origin. These variations are so great that, when only two of the most extreme forms were known, they were described as two separate species. The discovery of a number of variations showed that there was actually only one species involved. The fish was imported for the first time in 1903 (*B. ticto ticto*) and the local Burmese form was introduced to collector's circles about 1925.

It is worth noting that in the natural state, the length of normal, fully-grown specimens varies from about 50 to 100 mm (2 to 4 inches), depending on the area where they live. They occur not only in the warm, coastal areas, but also in the high mountain regions where the temperature is about 12 °C (54 °F). Described here are the two best-known sub-species imported by dealers from time to time.

Barbus ticto stoliczkae (Day, 1869)

This form differs from the following one by having only two single and eight forked rays in the dorsal fin, 23 to 25 scales, 8 to 10 scales in

483

front of the dorsal fin, and the lateral line runs over seven or more scales to the whole length of the fish.

Markings are approximately as shown in Illus. II–89, except that in the males, the dorsal fin is different—blood red. In addition, the first ray is black, and in the middle of the fin is another arc-shaped mark or dot of black. There are also many little black dots and stripes on the fin membrane. Compare this barb with *Barbus conchonius*, *B. everetti*, and other large relatives.

Reproduction takes place in the same way for all these species. Also, both *ticto* forms can stand temperatures down to about 15 °C (59 °F) or even lower. The best temperature, however, is about 22 °C (72 °F), at which point the fish should spontaneously lay eggs.

Barbus ticto ticto (Hamilton, 1822)

The dorsal fin has three single and eight forked rays; the anal fin has two single and five forked rays. There are 23 to 26 rows of scales lengthwise, and 11 to 12 rows between the dorsal and anal fins. On the back, in front of the dorsal fin, 10 or 11 scales are placed in an even row. The lateral line is incomplete and goes only as far as six or eight scales. This form is much like the specimen of *Barbus ticto* in Illus. II–89, both in coloration and in markings.

Plate II-68. *Barbus titteya.*

Barbus titteya (Deraniyagala, 1929)
Cherry Barb

Quite common in the stagnant, shallow, lowland waters of Ceylon, *Barbus titteya* has been known in collecting circles only since 1936.

This little barb, about 55 mm ($2\frac{1}{4}$ inches) long, is one of the most beautiful fishes suitable for the aquarium. The coloration shows up well in Plate II-68. Sometimes, particularly in the mating season, the dark edges on the dorsal, anal, and pelvic fins become more pronounced in the male.

The sexes are not always easy to distinguish. Usually, the female is not as shiny or as vivid as the male. Yellow-pink predominates. The belly area is usually whitish and larger than the male's. This barb does not like bright light and requires a roomy aquarium with thick vegetation. Cover the bottom with a good layer of turf (humus). Place the tank so that occasionally an hour or so of morning sunlight can penetrate the thick plants.

The natural habitat of these fish is shallow, usually stagnant water at the foot of a hilly landscape—where the lowlands are flooded in the rainy season—sometimes surrounded by high, granite rocks. Daytime water temperature: range from 26–30 °C (79–86 °F) and sometimes higher. At night, it falls to about 24 °C (75 °F). The habitat is populated by numerous *Barbus*, *Rasbora*, *Danio* and *Aplocheilus* species,

485

choked with luxuriant vegetation, and beset with millions of insects hovering above the water. The loamy bottom is covered with regular forests of *Cryptocoryne*. Of course, there are also various anabantoids in these waters.

Although some of the genera and groups mentioned here venture into the brackish, or somewhat brackish, coastal waters, *Barbus titteya* occurs only where the lowland waters are fresh. The temperatures are rather high as, after all, Ceylon has a purely tropical climate with a high rate of rainfall in the high, mountain areas. The average "winter" temperature does not fall below 23 °C (73 °F), although lower temperatures can occur temporarily in some places.

After violent trembling when the male presses the female against or between the plants, one or two (seldom more) eggs are deposited. The rather small, somewhat yellowish brown eggs adhere to the plants or fall to the bottom. The laying continues at longer or shorter intervals for several hours a day. In one day, not more than about 20 eggs are laid. Ten eggs are considered a good day's work. In this way, about 50 eggs can be expected in the course of the spawning season. After a few weeks, another mating period begins if the fish have had sufficient rest and food in the meantime. It is advisable to bring pairs of fish together, but not several males with one female or vice versa. The males will be too irritated with one another to pay attention to the females.

The young hatch out the following day in a temperature of about 26 °C (79 °F). They are difficult to see, unless they hang on the sides of the tank. After the second day, as soon as they start to swim, they again disappear from sight and you might possibly think that the breeding has been unsuccessful. In about a week, the young grow to 10 mm ($\frac{3}{8}$ inch) long and can be seen on the bottom, busily searching for food. Raising them to adulthood is not difficult.

This *Barbus* can also be bred in the open air. A good place is a warmly situated pool, shadowy and not too deep, but with a good-sized surface area. Do not put the fish out before mid-summer, of course, and preferably only one couple at a time. By the end of summer or the beginning of autumn, if all goes well, the pond will be alive with innumerable young fish thriving on a diet of insect larvae.

Barbus titteya is one of the many forms of the *Barbus* genus that differs to some extent from many aspects of its related species. Some authorities believe that these differences are large enough to justify establishing a new genus (or, at least, a new sub-genus) for them to be classified under. Unfortunately, the *Barbus* genus comprises many species from an enormous distribution area. Therefore, a revision of the systematization of the whole group is necessary before any divergent species can be separated from it. Such a revision, necessitating the study of hundreds of forms over a period of years, is not likely to come about very quickly. So, for the time being, do not worry about any official changes in the existing names.

This *Barbus* species illustrates again how careless the captors and importers can be concerning the place of origin of the fish they handle. When this fish first appeared among collectors in 1936, nothing was known about its habitat or from what region it came. There was not even a decided opinion as to what country it came from. Comparison of a few dead specimens with the collection at the Natural History Museum in London, however, quickly cleared up the identity of the species. If it had, indeed, been a new species, much greater difficulties would have been encountered. It is obvious, then, that captors and importers can do a great deal more for the hobby, as well as the science, than merely importing the fish.

Illus. II-90. *Barbus vittatus.*

Barbus vittatus (Day, 1865)

This fish is known to come only from India and Ceylon—evidently imported from there into the Maldive Islands. Reports of its presence in Southeast Asia have not been confirmed and should be considered doubtful.

B. vittatus is quite a small species, about 40 mm (a little over 1½ inches) long, not counting the caudal fin. The background is a silvery green. The back is olive brown with a blue, metallic sheen, especially in the region of the belly. A yellowish green band runs lengthwise from just above the gill flaps to the root of the tail. The fins are yellow to orange, the dorsal fin having a broad, dark stripe from the root of the fifth or sixth ray, upward to the point of the first single ray. It has a regular spot on the base of the tail and a dark patch by the anus. These characteristics will always be enough to permit recognition of this rather variable species. This is a nice little fish in every way, and it presents no breeding problems. It thrives best in a temperature of 20–30 °C (68–86 °F), and should be kept and cared for like its relatives.

Caecobarbus geertsi Boulenger, 1921
Blind Barb

This cave-inhabiting barb from the Lower Congo (caves near Thysville) is a most interesting import. It lives in underground water systems in absolute darkness. Consequently, the eyes fail to develop very early in the existence of the fish (see also *Anoptichthys jordani* on page 633). The skin is without pigment, looks like human flesh in coloration, and supplies an attractive variation in the aquarium. *Caecobarbus geertsi* is a quiet fish, in no way handicapped by being unable to see.

It would be interesting to breed this fish to see if the young in any of successive generations did develop normal eyesight if kept under regularly lighted conditions. It would be possible from this to deduce how the fish originated.

Illus. II-91. The typical biotope of *Caecobarbus geertsi*.

Carassius auratus (Linné, 1758)
Goldfish

An enormous amount of material has been written about the Goldfish—so much, in fact, that readers, particularly those who keep Goldfish in garden ponds, are referred to it for details. However, something should be said here about the great variation possibilities of this fish. The indigenous Chinese Golden Carp, *Carassius auratus*, has been cultivated for centuries in stock ponds as an important food source.

The ability of this fish to develop a strong, yellowish red coloration under certain circumstances has resulted in careful selection and breeding to develop this, and breeders have succeeded in producing shades ranging to blood red. The bodies and fins can also be dealt with in selective breeding. Breeders (the Japanese, especially) have been successful in developing a wide range of extraordinary forms, for which international breeding and coloration standards have been drawn up, the same way they have for canaries. The Guppy (see *Poecilia reticulatas*, on page 910) has slowly attracted similar interest, so that there are now breeding standards for it, too. Of course, whether you

Plate II-69. A magnificently developed Veil-Tail Goldfish, *Carassius auratus* var.

Illus. II-92. Five of the best-known Goldfish variations. 1. comet tail, the most ordinary form, usually with considerably lengthened fins. 2. the shubunkin, a bred variety in which the body is developed normally and the caudal, anal and ventral fins are lengthened. 3. telescope veil-tail, with large, goggling eyes, lengthened fins and double caudal fin. 4. egg fish, with an egg-shaped body, double caudal fin and dorsal fin absent, the fins are not particularly lengthened. 5. lion head fish, an egg fish with morbid growths on the head. Dozens of forms have been bred from these basic varieties, while hues—such as silver, gold, orange, crimson and black—can also play a rôle in the over-all results.

approve of this kind of breeding or not, it is certainly interesting to be able to study the possible changes in coloration and body form.

VARIATIONS OF GOLDFISH

Illus. II–92 shows the various products of selective breeding. In most cases, the fish have difficulty moving about, as they are more showpieces than practical animals. They would certainly not last long in the natural state. Nevertheless, it is interesting to note that in the course of breeding, some young fish always grow up as normal Goldfish—in the nature of an hereditary throwback. As long as the weather does not turn to freezing, it is possible to breed these Goldfish in an outdoor pond.

Plate II-70. *Epalzeorhynchus kalopterus.*

Genus Epalzeorhynchus

Two species of *Epalzeorhynchus* arrive from time to time with other imported fishes. The inferior mouth opening is remindful of a shark's mouth.

Epalzeorhynchus kalopterus (Bleeker, 1850)
Flying Fox

This fish is found in the Indonesian Archipelago—Sumatra (Palembang, Lahat, Bantang, Hari River, Djambi River), Borneo (Kapuas River, Sintang, Pontianak, Sebruang, Sibau, Kahajan River, Banjarmasin), and in parts of Thailand. It is only occasionally imported, usually together with other cyprinids. The species grows rather large, to about 150 mm (6 inches), and this is probably the reason that it is not often seen. The characteristic inferior mouth and the forward-pointing, sickle-shaped marking on the dorsal fin make the fish recognizable at once. A broad, black band runs from the snout to the base of the tail, and continues on the caudal fin. The stripe is less intense on the snout (in front of the eye).

The background coloration depends on the place of origin and changes from red-brown to yellowish, turning to silver-white on the belly, with a yellow or pink sheen.

492

Usually, little or nothing is known about fishes imported as seldom as this one. However, it should be treated in the same way as the larger barbs, such as *Barbus lateristriga*. It eats everything, and, as a typical inhabitant of the lower water levels, the inferior location of the mouth is ideally suited to foraging on the bottom. Peace-loving and quiet, *Epalzeorhynchus kalopterus* can be kept in the same aquarium with smaller fishes without danger to the latter, if the tank is large enough.

Epalzeorhynchus siamensis Smith, 1931
Siamese Flying Fox

This species differs from *Epalzeorhynchus kalopterus* in that it lacks black tips on the fin rays in the dorsal, pelvic and anal fins. The maximum length is 14 cm (about 5½ inches). This fish, especially the young specimens, looks a great deal like *Barbus macrops, Garra taeniata,* and *Osteochilus vittatus.*

Illus. II-93. *Garra* species.

Genus *Garra*

This very common genus is found in Africa, Syria, Arabia, India, Ceylon, Burma, Thailand, and Borneo. The only species now imported is *Garra taeniata*.

Garra taeniata Smith, 1931

Stone-Lapping Fish

Garra taeniata grows to 15 cm (6 inches), but is already sexually mature by the time it is 8 cm (3¼ inches) long. In the natural state, it occurs in company with *Epalzeorhynchus siamensis*, which it greatly resembles. The most important difference, other than in markings and coloration, is that *Garra's* lips are grown together in such a way as to form a suction disc. *Epalzeorhynchus* does not possess this. It is a quiet fish, happy to rummage for food in the company of other barbs.

Illus. II-94. *Garra taeniata.*

Genus *Labeo*

Labeo is a very important genus, with a large number of species. These are distributed over all of Africa, through the Middle East to southern Asia and the large Sunda Islands. *Labeo's* closest relatives are *Barbus* and *Varicorhinus*, but it can be distinguished from them by the inferior mouth and well developed lips which have practically grown into a suction organ. The teeth, which none of the cyprinoids possess, have as a substitute a sharp, horny ridge that functions as a cutting machine. Because most *Labeo* spp. are quite large, they are not usually appealing to aquarists, even though they are sometimes very attractive.

The species described below, all recent imports, have attracted some interest. Very little is known about these fishes.

Labeo bicolor Smith, 1931
Red-Tailed Black "Shark"

Velvet black, except for its magnificent, orange-red caudal fin, this fish grows to 12 cm (about 5 inches).

At 70 mm (2¾ inches) long, this fish is already sexually mature and starts to reproduce. It can certainly be called a splendid aquarium fish that attracts immediate attention. It should be kept as other carps; it is quiet and unpredatory, and can be kept in the same tank with other Asiatic fishes. Not unjustifiably, this fish is popular as a suitable and attractive aquarium fish.

Plate II-71. *Labeo bicolor.*

Plate II-72. *Labeo (Morulius) chrysophekadion.*

Labeo (Morulius) chrysophekadion (Bleeker, 1850)
Black Shark

This species from Southeast Asia and the large Sunda Islands grows to about 60 cm (nearly 24 inches), and, when mature, is only suitable for public aquariums.

The beautiful, velvety-black coloration of this fish, without sheen, is its main attraction. Young specimens can be kept in the same way as barbs. Older fish show a golden sheen on the caudal fin, reminiscent of their close relative, *Labeo bicolor.*

Plate II-73. *Labeo variegatus.*

Illus. II-95. *Labeo weeksi.*

Labeo weeksi Boulenger, 1909

This fish from the Congo grows to about 225 mm (about 9 inches). Its size distinguishes it from the much larger *Labeo lineatus* which grows up to 650 mm (25½ inches). Specimens of the same size from both species can be differentiated by the sickle-shaped dorsal fin of *L. weeksi*. In *L. lineatus*, this fin is rounded.

The background is yellow-gold with six to eight brown-red to almost black, lengthwise stripes in young specimens.

Illus. II-96. *Osteochilus vittatus.*

Genus *Osteochilus*

This is a very common genus, inhabiting the quiet waters of Southeast Asia, Sumatra, Java and Borneo. Medium-sized barb-like fish, these comprise a number of species extremely suitable for the aquarium.

Osteochilus vittatus (Valenciennes, 1842)

This species is also found together with *Garra taeniata* and *Epalzeorhynchus* species. Although they can grow to 25 cm (10 inches) or more in the natural state, they are already sexually mature by the time they reach 6 cm (2½ inches) long. Up to this length, and perhaps even to a bit longer, they are entirely suitable for the home aquarium.

Sub-family Rasborinae

This group consists mostly of small fish occurring in large numbers in all kinds of quiet and slowly running waters in Southeast Asia and the nearby archipelago islands. The sub-family is divided into two tribes, the danios (Danionini) and the rasboras and fly-barbel (Rasborini). These tribes are recognizable by the number of forked fin rays in the anal fin, 10 or more in the danios, and 5 to 8 in the rasboras.

Tribe Danionini

As shown in the map below, representatives of this tribe can be found in South and Southeast Asia—India, Burma, Ceylon, Sumatra—and a part of China. The danios are mainly restricted to the waters of India and Ceylon, northwards to the Himalayas and eastwards to the north of Burma. The *Brachydanio* species occur from the east coast of India to Thailand, Malaysia and Sumatra.

Danionini are generally small, slim fish, living in shoals in stagnant, slow and moderately running waters. The body is somewhat vertically flattened, though the belly is always rounded and never sharply pointed.

Fish belonging to this group are exceptionally well suited to the home aquarium, not only because they are small, but because they are lively and playful and love to swim. Moreover, their striking coloration and markings make them visually attractive.

Illus. II-97. Distribution of the Danionini.

One negative quality, which manifests itself only during breeding, is their greediness for eggs. Breeding itself generally causes little or no difficulty. If the breeding tanks are set up properly, little trouble will be experienced from this fish's desire to gobble up its eggs.

Plantings in the tanks containing danio-like fishes of this tribe from India and Africa should, if possible, be from these parts of the world. Clumps of finely-leaved *Myriophyllum*, *Nitella*, and *Chara* are suitable. The tank should preferably be placed so that, from time to time, morning sunlight can penetrate into it. There should be plenty of light and a dark bottom and background so that the beautiful coloration of the fish, which it only shows when it feels quite at home with its surroundings, can be displayed to its best advantage.

Genus *Brachydanio*

Since 1916, many new species have been brought to light, which, in part, constitute links between *Danio* and *Brachydanio*. However, for the present, these will be referred to as *Brachydanio*, a genus first described in detail by the two Dutchmen, Professor Max Weber and Professor L. F. de Beaufort, in 1916. The body resembles *Danio*, though smaller. The lateral line is either incomplete or totally absent. There are only 7 to 9 forked, weak fin rays in the dorsal fin; the anal fin has 12 to 16. The small mouth opening slants upward and does not extend as far as under the eye, as it does in *Barilius*.

Brachydanio albolineatus (Blyth, 1860)

Golden Danio

Pearl Danio

This fish comes from southern Asia—Thailand, Burma, Sumatra and Malaysia—where it lives in slow and fast-running rivers and streams, to quite far up in the highlands. According to Nicholas (1952), it is also found in Ceylon.

This fish is a fast, active swimmer, with a long, stretched-out, spindle-shaped body which is vertically flattened mainly in the tail region. The belly is rounded. The length is approximately 55 mm ($2\frac{1}{4}$ inches). In the natural state, the length for specimens from Thailand is 42 mm ($1\frac{3}{4}$ inches), and from Burma, 50 mm (2 inches). Lengths up to 60 mm ($2\frac{1}{2}$ inches) are not unusual in the aquarium.

Plate II-74. *Brachydanio albolineatus.*

This fish, like its relatives, loves to live in shoals, or schools of fish. Six or eight specimens should be kept together in the aquarium. Normally, and if kept under the right conditions, with the surroundings well lit, *Brachydanio albolineatus* is a fish that will not be still for a moment. Occasionally, however, when there are no related fast swimmers close by, it will remain still among the plants on the surface. This is a sure sign that something is wrong. It does not feel at home in a small tank, and under such circumstances, do not expect it to show its normal activity. The same breeding rules apply as for *Brachydanio rerio*, which is also a fish that likes to mate in a little—or even a lot—of sunlight, preferably with a number of males and females together.

Plate II-75. *Brachydanio kerri.*

Brachydanio kerri Smith, 1931

This is a splendid little danio that grows to a maximum of 50 mm (2 inches) long. In conduct and markings, it falls between *Danio aequipinnatus* and *Brachydanio albolineatus*. It is a very attractive species, of which a number of specimens should be kept together in the same tank.

Brachydanio nigrofasciatus (Day, 1869)

Dwarf Danio

Spotted Danio

Brachydanio nigrofasciatus is found in Southeast Asia in practically all lowland waters. Known to collectors since about 1911, it was not until after 1925 that it was kept more or less regularly. It is neither as well known, nor as popular, as *Brachydanio rerio* and *B. albolineatus*. Practically identical in build with both of these popular *Brachydanio* species, this fish remains smaller and hardly ever grows longer than 45 mm ($1\frac{13}{16}$ inches).

The little danio has very attractive markings. The back region is shiny, dark, olive brown to blue-green, with a net-like marking created by the dark-edged scales. The belly is soft pink to whitish or yellow; in the males, it is sometimes a light orange. A band of three stripes

502

runs from the gill flaps to the root of the tail, made up of a gold to brownish stripe bordered on both sides by deep blue stripes, the lowest one of which is the most striking.

The lower half of the body is a similar deep blue and also has a more or less regular line made up of dots or dashes. Similar little stripes or dots can be found on the anal fin, while on the caudal fin there are a number of blue dots or spots which sometimes become connected. The dorsal, anal, and pectoral fins have a whitish border with a fading, bluish band next to it.

Generally speaking, this fish is not as easy to keep as its close relatives. Do not keep the temperature too high—about 16–22 °C (61–72 °F)—and this little danio will be a rewarding little fish for your aquarium. It can be treated in the same way as *Brachydanio rerio*.

The number of eggs laid in one period can amount to approximately 300. When females of this species are crossed with males from *B. albolineatus* or *B. rerio*, very attractive—but sterile—specimens result. This fish has also been crossed artificially by wiping the eggs with the sperm (Merckens & Spoelstra, 1952).

Plate II-76. *Brachydanio nigrofasciatus.*

Plate II-77. *Brachydanio rerio.*

Brachydanio rerio (Hamilton, 1822)
Zebra Danio
Zebra Fish

B. rerio is found in India—along the east coast from Calcutta to to Masulipatam—in Burma and in nearby countries in stagnant waters, in flooded rice fields, in streams, and in small and large rivers. A number of specimens were brought to Europe for the first time in 1905, where they were soon taken up in the aquariums of collectors. *Brachydanio rerio* is still appreciated, and magazine articles concerning it are constantly appearing. It grows to a maximum of 60 mm (about 2⅜ inches). The flanks are shiny blue with four yellowish to yellow-brown (golden) stripes down the body, from the gill flaps to the end of the caudal fin. The anal fin, also blue with three yellowish cross stripes, is completely edged with white. The pectoral and pelvic fins are without coloration and transparent. The base of the dorsal fin is an olive-yellow, darkening above until it turns blue. It is also edged with white. There are two pairs of barbels on the upper jaw. The iris of the eye is reddish with a golden sheen. The gill flaps are blue and have a number of irregular, golden spots and stripes for decoration. If the fish are not too young, the sexes are easy to tell apart. The female's belly is more rounded and whiter than the male's, which is, instead, very slim. It is pure myth, despite what some scientists maintain, that the sexes can be distinguished by the intensity of the yellow in the lengthwise stripes.

Do not let the temperature fall below 15 °C (59 °F) or rise above 26 °C (79 °F) for breeding. Normally, this lively and delightful fish should be kept at a temperature of 20–22 °C (68–72 °F). The breeding tank (or the community tank) should be well planted with fine-leaved plants, but leave plenty of room for swimming. A long, not-too-high tank is recommended for a shoal of these little fish. They live happily together with related fishes.

Brachydanio rerio prefers dark surroundings, so do not leave the bottom bare, with only sand of light coloration, but plant it with *Cryptocoryne.* Daytime lighting must not be too bright, and under no circumstances should the light shine horizontally through the tank. The light must always enter the water from above. Cover the surface of the tank with floating plants. This will make the fish feel that it is in its proper element, and it will reward you by sparkling with beautiful shades of blue and golden yellow. Heed all of these suggestions for surroundings to bring out the best in these fish.

The breeding temperature should be no more than a few degrees higher than normal. For breeding, take only those specimens which show their readiness for breeding by the dark, golden yellow of their lengthwise stripes. Specimens with light yellow or white stripes are unsuitable for breeding. The parent fish should be very well fed for a few months beforehand to ensure good, strong, young fish.

Egg-laying takes place, preferably, in a tank with fine-leaved plants, so that the sun can reach in, but there are also areas of shadow. Subdued sunlight is desirable for a successful mating.

If you watch carefully, you see an individual female chase after a male—or even after several males. The males then shoot into the weeds, showing off their most beautiful coloration. They press themselves against the females and disappear, shaking, into the vegetation, where they immediately fertilize the eggs expelled by the females. Sometimes the male helps the female emit the eggs by wrapping his tail around her body. The total number of eggs deposited is quite large. When the young start to appear, after about a day and a half at a temperature of approximately 25 °C (77 °F), the tank walls are crawling with them. On the second day, great numbers of young are everywhere, looking like dark splinters of glass, hanging on the tank walls, plants and stones, slowly using up their yolk sacs.

The parent fish, which should have been removed after fertilization has taken place, will be ready for another breeding in about two months, if they are well fed. After three days, the young fish, at first so helpless, will be swimming about in shoals on the surface, filling their little bellies with infusoria.

The main difficulty with breeding this fish—and many of its related species—is the voracity of the parent fish for their eggs. As soon as the brood has hatched out, though, they leave it alone. If you do not want to remove the parent fish (and it is not absolutely necessary to do so), see that most of the eggs find a safe hiding place. Very dense vegetation of finely-leaved plants and a bottom covering of *Eleocharis acicularis* are best for this. The breeding yield will be smaller, of course, because some of the eggs always fall prey to the parent fish. A mating pair that has already laid eggs once before is easier to encourage to reproduce than a new pair.

The author once had an interesting experience with this fish. He put three females in a runner—a long tank about $100 \times 30 \times 30$ cm (3 feet $\times$ 1 foot $\times$ 1 foot)—to collect their eggs. The tank was not especially set up for breeding, as the intent was only to gather the eggs. There was a thick clump of thread algae in the tank and plenty of food was supplied. When the females had visibly completed their task—the egg-laying took a whole week—they were returned to the community tank.

The author then emptied and cleaned the runner, since he wanted to start breeding Fire Neons. He put the plants, including the clump of thread algae upon which a large number of eggs had been deposited (he thought by now the eggs were all gone), out on a large dish. Unable to continue the work that afternoon and evening, he returned the following day and removed the bottom material from the tank, then cleaned it and rinsed it again. Part of the removable matrix bottom, which held most of the sand, was thoroughly cleaned. Then, the old matrix bottom was replaced in the tank, covered with the washed layer, and filled up with new sand.

On the evening of the second day, the tank was filled with water. The wet plants, which had remained on the dish at a room temperature of 5 °C (41 °F), were returned to the tank on the morning of the third day. The water temperature was then 16 °C (61 °F). The tank was further set up for breeding Fire Neons and the temperature was raised to 22 °C (72 °F). On the evening of the third day, the breeding pair went into the tank and at 4 o'clock in the afternoon of the fourth day, there were young hanging on the glass walls of the tank. Not knowing

Plate II-78. *Brachydanio rerio frankei.*

what the actual result had been, the author removed the Fire Neons.

In brief, the tiny fish that appeared were young *B. rerio.* The conclusion drawn from this is that the eggs of *Brachydanio rerio* (and possibly of other species as well) can take a lot of punishment and still survive. They had spent three days at a very low temperature with practically no water, but, of course, plenty of oxygen. All this merely delayed the process of development, and the young fish grew up normally.

Genus *Danio*

The members of this genus differ mainly from *Brachydanio* by having a longer base to the dorsal fin and a more flattened body. Of the many *Danio* species that have been written about, only a few are known among collectors. The first choice, of course, has been for old faithful "malabaricus," *Danio aequipinnatus. D. devario* and *D. regina* are species imported later, but seldom seen. Of these two, *D. devario* is the more popular.

Danio aequipinnatus (MacClelland, 1838)
"Danio malabaricus"
Giant Danio
Malabar Danio

This fish is quite common in clear, stagnant and running waters along the Malabar coast in India and in Ceylon. A specimen was brought to Europe in 1909, and later on, many more were imported. In the aquarium, it grows to about 12 cm (4¾ inches), but in the natural state, to about 20 cm (8 inches), though these sizes are exceptions.

The mouth has two pair of barbels, although the barbels on the upper jaw are usually missing. The background coloration is greyish brown or olive brown. The back is steel blue to bluish green, with silver near the head, and a light pink on the belly. Three to four steel blue stripes run along the flanks, separated by lines of gold. There are also gold stripes and spots on the head and the gill flaps. The sexes are easy to tell apart by the slimmer, more attractive appearance of the male, and the "stuffed" belly of the females.

These fish should be kept and fed in the same way as other species. However, the aquarium should be larger. The summer temperature is kept at 22–24 °C (72–75 °F), and a little higher during breeding (maximum 26 °C or 79 °F). In winter, suitable temperatures range from 18–20 °C (64–68 °F).

In spite of its large measurements, this fish can be kept with other, smaller species. An extremely peaceful fellow, it is very tolerant of other fishes in its environment. It very much appreciates a little morning sunlight in its tank.

The manner of fertilizing the eggs is characteristic of *Danio*. During mating, the male pushes himself against the female and brings his anal fin, which he has rolled up into a kind of a bag, under the female's anus. The eggs are caught in this bag and are fertilized at once. The male then scatters the fertilized eggs among the plants.

The number of eggs per mating is small—only 5 to 20—though a total of several hundred eggs can be laid. The eggs are clear as glass, not adhesive, and measure about 1 mm (.04 inch) in diameter.

About two days after the eggs have been laid, the first young fish appear. Depending on various factors, however, it can take as long as a week before the last egg has hatched out. Temperature is not the least of these factors.

This *Danio* is known for its incredible speed, noticeably faster than that of other species. It is practically impossible to remove this fish from the tank without creating a great deal of disorder, unless you take its flight direction into account and capture it between the net and the receiving jar (fish trap).

Danio devario (Hamilton, 1822)

This fish, first imported into Europe about 1938, comes from Pakistan and northern India—from Sind to Assam. It shows a close affinity in shape, coloration and markings to *Danio aequipinnatus*, but it is much shorter and more thick-set in build. The barbels are rudimentary or entirely missing and the scales are smaller—the count is 42 to 48 lengthwise, as opposed to 32 to 38 for *D. aequipinnatus*, even though the latter has a longer body. *D. devario* grows to about 100 mm (4 inches) long. The females are slightly less vivid than the males, though the males are plainly deeper in body size.

The background is silver-green, darker on the back. The flanks have three blue stripes, separated by yellow. There are also three or four cross stripes on the anterior half of the body, behind the gill flaps, as in *D. aequipinnatus*. The central stripe on the tail area is visible in Illus. II–98. Note how this continues upon the upper fork of the caudal fin and shadows it. With this very large dorsal fin (17 to 20 rays) and the equally large anal fin (15 to 19 rays), this species is doubtless closely related to the Danionini root. In this respect (as well as in a number of other characteristics), it seems to be more closely associated with the bitterling-like fishes (Rhodeinae) than with the Rasborinae.

Up to a point, the reproductive conduct of the danios and the bitterlings is closely related, though the bitterlings have reached a high degree of specialization towards sharing a community of interests with fresh-water mussels.

Genus *Daniops*

In build, this genus stands between *Danio* and *Brachydanio*, with a complete lateral line and only eight dorsal fin rays.

As far as is known, *Daniops myersi* has not yet been imported from Thailand.

Illus. II-98. *Danio devario.*

510

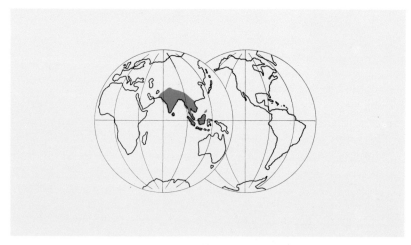

Illus. II-99. Distribution of Rasborini.

Tribe Rasborini

Three genera well known to collectors belong to this group:
1. No barbels present; anal fin with only 5 forked rays . . . genus *Rasbora*
2. Barbels present; 5 to 8 forked anal-fin rays
   A. Small mouth opening; long barbels; 5 forked anal-fin rays . . . genus *Esomus*
   B. Large mouth opening; not long but well developed barbels; 6 to 8 forked anal-fin rays . . . genus *Luciosoma*

Genus *Esomus*

This genus comes from Southeast Asia, the Indonesian Archipelago, Singapore, India, Ceylon and the Nicobar Islands.

Esomus danricus (Hamilton, 1822)
Flying Barb

According to Smith, this species does not occur in Thailand, and the specimens found there belong to *Esomus metallicus* Ahl. It is very common in all types of water, even in hot springs. When necessary, it spends the dry season buried in mud, a sign of its hardiness.

E. danricus has a slim, elongated and slightly flattened body. Its length extends up to 125 mm (5 inches). The whole build is indicative of a quick swimmer from the upper water levels. The placing of the fins enables this fish to bend and turn with incredible speed. The head is small and pointed, and the terminal mouth, pointing upwards, can be opened very wide. The lower jaw is slightly undershot. The snout has a pair of short, thick barbels extending beyond the eyes and a second pair of long, filamentous, upper-jaw barbels that reach as far as, or even farther than, the pelvic fins.

The dorsal fin is placed far to the rear and the anal fin begins about under the dorsal fin. The pectoral fins are large, the first rays being elongated and running out to a thread-like point. This feature can also be found in the smaller pelvic fins in good specimens. The large pectoral fins enable this fish to make leaps in the air. It is from these rather small jumps out of the water that the name "flying barb" originates, because the fish does not really fly. After a relatively short dash forward, this fish springs out of the water and hops over the surface, helped by the pectoral fins. On the way, it snaps at insects, which, in the natural state, form an important part of the diet. Only recently imported fish try this jumping manoeuvre in the aquarium. Therefore, a cover is needed on the tank to keep the fish within bounds, and, after bumping this a few times, it learns not to jump any more. Of course, a high cover or other special arrangement can be provided so that it does not hurt itself, and it can then also continue the jumping practice.

An arrangement of this kind is certainly a good idea, if you want to watch the natural activity of this fish. To start with, the cover should be high—at least 15 cm (6 inches) above the surface of the water—so that some flying insects may be released under it. It is amazing how quickly the fish spots its prey and starts chasing the flies with attractive little leaps. To keep it from hurting itself, cover all sharp edges with strips of rubber and see that there are floating weeds in the tank, to give the flies some place to settle.

The background of *Esomus danricus* is brownish green to olive with a mother-of-pearl sheen. The back is speckled with a lot of small, dark dots. The flanks are a characteristic purplish red to reddish brown with a silvery sheen, especially when sunlight falls on it. From the eye to the root of the tail runs a wide, black to brownish black stripe, which in good specimens (males) is on the upper side and bordered by a shining, gold stripe. The fins are orangish to yellow-brown; the pelvic fins are reddish. Here, too, the females can be recognized mainly by their plumper build and somewhat larger size. The males are slim. Catching this fish with a net or jar trap can be difficult, unless the trial is made at dusk or in a dim light, when the fish is a little less active and, presumably, cannot see as well. It is practically impossible to catch it in bright light, especially for nervous aquarists who soon create chaos in the tank while attempting to capture the fish.

Breeding is not much more difficult than with other rasboras and barbs. However, because *E. danricus* loves sunlight, the best results are in an aquarium that is located in the sunlight.

An extremely lively and swift courtship precedes the equally fast mating. Then, both fish disappear, side by side, trembling with emotion, into the fine vegetation. Some 15 to 40 eggs are laid—or rather, "sprayed out"—each time. After this, as if to reciprocate for the "help" given her by the male in the egg-laying, the female puts her snout against his belly to activate him to spray his sperm. This, of course, is not visible. This procedure is repeated at fairly short intervals until about 300 small, transparent eggs have been deposited. These hatch out within 24 hours.

Although an occasional egg is consumed by the fish, *E. danricus* are not so predatory as most of their relatives, and it is seldom necessary to remove them after mating, if they are given enough food. During mating, both fish are gorgeous in coloration, especially the male in his "wedding garb," which delights every keeper. His whole tail is a splendid, shining, rust-red, while, at the same time, all the other colorations and markings are also displayed at their best.

Illus. II-100. *Esomus lineatus.*

Esomus lineatus Ahl, 1925

This is a beautifully-marked species from the Ganges Delta and the Calcutta region. They are kept the same as their relative fish. They grow up to 60 mm (2½ inches) long.

Esomus malayensis Ahl, 1924
Malayan Flying Barb

This species from Malaysia should be kept in the same manner as *Esomus danricus.* It is a colorful species which has a characteristic round spot on the tail. The back and flanks are golden yellow with a metallic, blue sheen. It has orange fins and grows to about 100 mm (4 inches).

Esomus metallicus Ahl, 1924

This fish comes from Southeast Asia and should be kept like *E. danricus.*

Illus. II-101. *Esomus metallicus.*

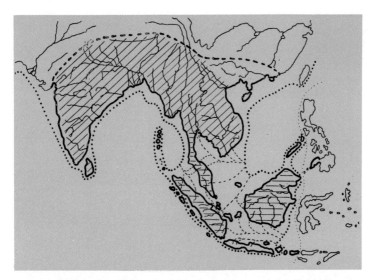

Illus. II-102. The distribution of the genus *Rasbora*, is indicated by the thick line and the thick broken line. The thick dotted line approximately indicates the border of the continental shelf, the dividing line with the deep sea. The light broken lines indicate historical river beds. The light dotted line is the zoogeographical division between Indonesia and the Australian Archipelago. The slanting hatched lines indicate the distribution of the *R. daniconia* complex, and horizontal hatching that of the *R. einthovenii* complex.

Genus *Rasbora*

A very important study by Brittan of the *Rasbora* genus shows what forms are true species and how they are related to one another. This publication is of interest to scientists and aquarists, as it works out the distribution routes and provides data on environment.

Brittan differentiates eight complexes of *Rasbora* forms, but he is unable to unravel the relationships between the following well known species: *R. heteromorpha, R. kalochroma, R. maculata* and *R. reticulata.*

Plate II-80. *Rasbora borapetensis.*

Rasbora borapetensis **Smith, 1934**
Black-Lined Rasbora
Borapet Rasbora
Red-Tailed Rasbora
This lovely little species—it grows to about 45 mm (about 1¾ inches) —occurs in small groups. It is very suitable for smaller aquariums.

Rasbora daniconia **(Hamilton, 1822)**
This species is universally distributed throughout Southeast Asia, except for Malaysia. There are, in fact, two allopatric groups: the *R. daniconia* complex and the *R. einthovenii* complex. These forms are very similar to each other, though they are geographically exclusive. (See map on page 515.) The *R. daniconia* complex comprises only three separate forms (species)—*R. daniconia* (with sub-species, *R. d. daniconia* and *R. d. labiosa*), *R. caveri* and *R. kobonensis*. As a group, they differ from the *R. einthovenii* complex by having 14 scales around the tail base, as opposed to only 12 in *R. einthovenii* and its relatives.

Plate II–80 gives a good picture of the habitat of *Rasbora daniconia*, though the black stripe from behind the eye to the tail base does not show up clearly. The characteristic Ceylonese form has a heavy black stripe covering almost two rows of scales. The Indian forms have a fainter, lengthwise stripe. There is considerable local variation in the intensity of the stripe.

The background is silvery with an olive-yellow tint; the belly is silver-white. The black stripe is edged on both sides with a light, silvery line. The fins are yellowish, and there is a narrow, black line just above the base of the anal fin (this is visible in the lower fish in Plate II–80). They can grow to about 100 mm (4 inches), though they are usually smaller.

Reproduction takes place as with related fish, the eggs being deposited among fine-leaved growth. The only way to distinguish between the sexes is by the shape of the body. The males are slim; the females are deeper.

The distribution of the two complexes, *R. daniconia* and *R. einthovenii*, requires further explanation. The map on page 515 shows the two regions by shading and also, clearly, how the two groups replace each other. They overlap, but do not mix, only in the Malay Peninsula. According to Brittan, this overlap concerns a very old group that inhabited the whole area in the Pleistocene period, the distribution of which is shown on the map—from western India to the southern part of the Philippines, from South Viet-Nam to Java. This area (bounded

Plate II-81. *Rasbora daniconia.*

by the thick dotted line on the map) was then land and the rivers also ran their natural courses towards the sea. Their probable courses in the area which is now below the surface of the sea is shown by broken lines. Evidently, Malaysia and Sumatra were joined together by the same river system, while Sumatra and Borneo were similarly connected. There was, presumably, even a connection between all three areas— Malaysia, Sumatra, and Borneo—by means of one river system. That Java was not connected to these other regions can easily be deduced from the elements of fauna existing there. It is true that *Rasbora* specimens are found in Java, just as they are in the southern Philippines, but these forms must be viewed as very old and primitive, coming into existence earlier than other forms which no longer had the opportunity to reach these later-isolated areas.

Interestingly, *Rasbora daniconia* occurs on the Andaman Islands, where it is the only representative of the cyprinoids. It is probable, therefore, that these islands were formerly connected to the other areas where this species occurs. No carp-like fishes are known at all on the Nicobars.

Rasbora dorsiocellata Duncker, 1904
Eye-Spot Rasbora

A rather small species from Malaysia and Sumatra, *Rasbora dorsiocellata* is characterized by an almost round, black spot on the dorsal fin. The maximum length is about 45 mm (1¾ inches), not counting the caudal fin. *R. dorsiocellata* thrives best, like other typical *Rasbora*, when it is kept in groups.

Plate II-82. *Rasbora dorsiocellata.*

Illus. II-103. *Rasbora einthovenii.*

Rasbora einthovenii (Bleeker, 1851)

Einthoven's Rasbora

Brittan (1954) classified the species *R. einthovenii, R. cephalotaenia, R. jacobsoni,* and *R. tubbi* as belonging to the *R. einthovenii* complex. (See also page 516.)

Plate II-83. *Microrasbora rubescens.*

Rasbora heteromorpha Duncker, 1904
Harlequin Rasbora
Red Rasbora

This fish inhabits stagnant and running lowland waters of Southeast Asia, Malaysia, Singapore (in ponds in the Botanical Gardens) and eastern Sumatra. It was first imported into Europe in 1906. The two forms now accepted by collectors are both imported from Singapore and hardly differ at all, though their total coloration makes them identifiable. Both appeared in 1932 or even earlier. Plate II–84 shows one form, which can be somewhat redder all over, while the second form is more reddish brown and, instead of an orange iris, it has a light pink one.

Examined specimens of both forms, that had been preserved in formalin and alcohol, were clearly distinguishable because the first form becomes a darker, brownish coloration than the second. However, no other points of difference were discovered, except that the lateral line in the first specimen extended over nine scales.

The difference between the sexes, which, with many fishes, is always difficult to determine, is easily seen in *Rasbora heteromorpha* from the time that they reach a length of 25 mm (1 inch). The females are

Plate II-84. *Rasbora heteromorpha.*

characterized by a slightly deeper body, a more deeply curved line to the belly, a small bulge at the level of the anus, and a broader, fatter belly. The males are recognizable by a light stripe on the back, which shines golden yellow when lit from above, and which runs above the conical-shaped patch. This stripe, noticeably less pronounced in the females, is, in some cases, completely faded out. In order to find out how much the conical patch could be used in determining sex, 22 specimens were examined. Of these, 14 had an inferior point running forward on the patch. These proved to be nine males and five females. The eight specimens having a patch with the base of the cone straight across, or which bulged out forward, were all females. Of these 22 specimens, three—two females and one male—possessed a patch in which the upper corner continued slightly forward.

During the course of this experiment, it appeared that *Rasbora heteromorpha* belongs to the group of fishes in which bisexuality is common. Among the nine males, four specimens had visible, rudimentary ovaries. This was more the case in the half-grown males (24 to 27 mm or 1 to 1⅛ inches) than in the larger specimens (35 to 36 mm or about 1⅜ inches).

Both sexes can attain a maximum length of 42 mm (about 1¾ inches) in the aquarium. In the natural state, specimens measuring more than 38 mm (about 1½ inches) have seldom been caught. Following is a summary of the factual material on *Rasbora heteromorpha*, gathered at different times by different writers.

The veil of secrecy that has been hanging over this little fish for more than 30 years has now been lifted. *Rasbora heteromorpha* is now ranked with those fishes that are not too difficult to care for or breed. They are similar to *Barbus tetrazona*, and like a similar environment.

THE NATURAL ENVIRONMENT

These *Rasbora* appear to inhabit two types of water, both in the low-lying plains. These are the moderate to swiftly flowing jungle streams (speed of flow 10–65 cm or ⅜–1½ inches per second) and the swamps and floodlands connected with them. The water is usually clear, sometimes polluted with organic substances without coloration, or with humus material and slightly yellow with traces of iron. Unfortunately, given details vary a great deal.

TEMPERATURE

Ramsperger (1935) records, for Johore (in Malaysia) and Sumatra, temperatures between 20 and 30 °C (68–86 °F)—that is, 20 °C in the

521

shadowy streams and 24–25 °C (75–77 °F) in the open lowland swamps and flood areas.

Ladiges (1939) gives, as the average annual temperature in the same kind of waters, 25–27 °C (77–81 °F). In May, the warmest month, he registered 27.4 °C (81.3 °F) as the average temperature in Palembang (in southeastern Sumatra). At the other end of the scale, in January, the coldest month, he still found an average of 26.6 °C (79.9 °F). The daily temperature fluctuations are important throughout this area, amounting to as much as 6.5 °C (41.7 °F). Of course, the heavy rainfall makes a lot of difference to the temperature and to the pH value of the water.

Marsack (1948) recorded temperatures between 25 and 29 °C (77–84 °F) in Johore, Malaysia, in April, which was the warmest period.

ACIDITY

The writers mentioned have also recorded great differences in the pH value of the water, though many of these, presumably, can be attributed to divergent circumstances—time of year, before or after rainy season, inaccurate analyses of water samples performed on the spot or elsewhere. It has been proved that the pH value in the aquarium, though not without importance, plays a smaller rôle than was at first thought. After a heavy rainfall, the acidity of the water is greatly reduced (rain water is neutral, having a pH of 7). The acidity value drops to zero at pH 7, above which the numerical pH indication refers to alkalinity. The pH value of 7, precisely in the middle, is neither acid nor alkaline, therefore neutral. The pH value recorded by Ramsperger for Johore (pH 6.8) shows the influence of rain water and therefore will be higher than the pH value mentioned by other writers. Ladiges records a pH value of 6 to 6.15 (measured later). Marsack probably gives the most accurate record, though this is only for the month of April. This was pH 5.3 to 5.9. In one place, after a heavy rainfall, he measured a pH value of 6.9. Massola records everywhere a pH value of 6.8 (1939).

RATE OF FLOW, DEPTH, AND HARDNESS

The rate of flow of the water in streams is between 10 and 65 cm per second ($\frac{3}{8}$ inch and $1\frac{1}{2}$ inches per second). According to Marsack, the depth in the streams varies between 30 and 50 cm (12 and 20 inches), while Ladiges records stream widths of 200 to 300 cm (7 to 10 feet) and depths up to 100 cm (40 inches). The bottoms were usually of gravel as fine as grains of rice (red sandstone) and humus (mud). The only place where there is not much humus is in shallow areas where the current flows faster. Traces of iron found in the water (0.003 to 0.025 per cent), together with the humus substances, give the water a light yellow look.

CHALK AND CHLORINE LEVELS

The total titrate hardness amounts to 1.0° to 2.4°, German DH. The water, therefore, is extremely soft. The chlorine level is practically nil everywhere.

VEGETATION

Vegetation is scarce in these waters. The genus *Cryptocoryne* is the most common, represented by the following species: *Cryptocoryne purpurea, C. griffithi, C. cordata, C. johorensis* and *C. ciliata.* The plants cover large areas of the muddy bottom with a very dense matting of roots that can be 15 cm (6 inches) or more thick. *Blyxa* or *Oryzetorum* (probably *Blyxa echinosperma*), a *Vallisneria*-type plant, are present in the water, along with a plant having fine, grass-like leaves. Towards the banks, rich swamp and jungle vegetation flourish, often hanging down upon the surface and offering a welcome hiding place for many fishes.

POPULATION

Along with *Rasbora heteromorpha,* many other species live in these waters. Almost all the fishes caught here can be considered suitable

Plate II-85. *Rasbora heteromorpha espei* Meinken, 1967.

aquarium fishes, so far as size, coloration and markings are concerned. They include: *Barbus binotatus, B. dorsimaculatus, B. belinka, B. maculatus, B. eugrammus, B. tetrazona,* and *B. lateristriga; Rasbora argyrotaenia, R. daniconia, R. dorsiocellata, R. elegans,* and *R. trilineata; Acanthopsis choirorhynchus; Botia hymenophysa; Hemiramphus cantoris; Hemirhamphodon pogonognathus; Dermogenys pusillus; Chanda* species; *Betta taeniata; Luciocephalus pulcher; Sphaerichthys osphromenoides; Trichogaster leeri, T. trichopterus,* and *T. pectoralis; Anabas testudineus; Channa* species; *Nandus nebulosis; Osteochilus hasselti; Chela laubuca; Brachydanio albolineatus.*

Young *Rasbora* were found in every stage of development, up to 18 mm ($\frac{3}{4}$ inch) long in the shallow, stagnant backwaters thickly overgrown with needle-fine grass and thread algae.

Rasbora heteromorpha was also found swimming in groups of three, with other species, at a depth of about 15 cm (6 inches) below the surface.

An aquarium set up in accordance with the above data will be a regional aquarium well suited for study purposes. The best kind of tank for this would measure about a metre (yard) long, as wide as possible—50 cm (20 inches) or more—and about 30 cm (12 inches) high. In one corner, make room for a small swamp area. Power filters will provide the desired current, and these can be set up in one or two corners. A good humus bottom, planted with *Cryptocoryne* species, preferably a broad-leaved species, completes the environment.

FOOD

After examination of the stomach contents, it was determined that small midge larvae constitute the main dish of *Rasbora heteromorpha.*

BREEDING PERIOD

As nearly all stages of development, up to the full-grown fish, were present in April (Marsack, 1948), the conclusion is that the season of reproduction for this *Rasbora* is at least several months. It is not impossible that it could reproduce on and off throughout most of the year—any given specimen, of course, having rest periods between the mating sessions. Reproduction (breeding), then, is not accompanied by insuperable difficulties. From the data gathered by the researchers named, it seems that it is not yet clear where, in the natural environment, the eggs are deposited—in running or stagnant water, or in areas of moderate or dense vegetation. Taking into account the preference this fish has in the aquarium for depositing its eggs where the aquarium growth is thickest, it is probably true that, in the natural state, the eggs are also deposited in dense vegetation.

524

The most important part of mating, egg-laying, has by now already been observed by many collectors. In general, the following procedure will be observed, with more or less variation. During courtship, the males swim above the females. The courtship is even more interesting when more than one couple is present. Whether this is a natural occurrence, as is the case with roaches, is not known, but the result of putting two or more pairs together is always amazing.

After a preparatory period that is sometimes extremely long, the females search for the underside of *Cryptocoryne* leaves or similar vegetation. By rubbing the oviduct several times against the leaf, they presumably stimulate themselves until they are in condition to lay their eggs. If a male comes along at that moment, the real laying begins, usually quietly, though sometimes violently. With her belly still turned upwards, the female slides along under the leaf, while the male, below her, winds himself over the back of the female and fertilizes the eggs as soon as they come out of the oviduct and adhere to the leaf.

The eggs are always laid in the morning hours. The number laid during a mating period varies from just a few to about 20. The mating sessions can follow one after the other for hours, so that a single female may lay as many as 300 eggs. A large number of eggs usually fall to the bottom and, if they are fertilized, and if nothing happens to them, they will hatch out normally.

The eating of the eggs by the parent fish can be quite complete, but this is usually the result of an incorrectly set-up aquarium. The parent fish should be removed, though reasonable results can be obtained even without doing this. The activity provided by an aquarium populated by both the old and the young is far more enjoyable than that of only a single generation.

One hundred per cent of the eggs laid can never be viable, and specimens die at various stages of their development—a completely natural phenomenon. The end result, the number of fish yielded, often appears rather small in the eyes of collectors and breeders. A yield of 30 specimens from one *Rasbora heteromorpha* pair is a successful brood, worth far more than a large number of inferior specimens induced to hatch out by artificial means.

These, and many other fishes, go into raptures if an artificial rainfall visits the aquarium occasionally. The preference is for rain water, which can be sprinkled over the surface from a sprinkler.

Plate II-86. *Rasbora kalochroma.*

Rasbora kalochroma (Bleeker, 1850)

This species, which can grow to 90 mm (3½ inches), greatly resembles *Rasbora maculata*. It is, however, a true species, not synonymous with *R. maculata* (see description of *R. maculata* below). It does not appear very often and seems not to have been bred very much. However, those who observed *R. kalochroma* in the aquarium will certainly want to obtain the species. It should be cared for the same as its related species. Mating is carried on in small shoals.

Rasbora lateristriata (Van Hasselt, 1823)

This is one of the large *Rasbora* species that grows to about 120 mm (4¾ inches) and which inhabits running waters up to an altitude of about 3,750 feet. It is very common in Malaysia, Java, Sumatra and Borneo. Temperatures should be between 18 and 24 °C (64–75 °F). Treat *R. lateristriata* like its other large relatives. A number of local forms are known—for example, *Rasbora elegans* and *Rasbora trifasciata*.

Rasbora maculata Duncker, 1904
Dwarf Rasbora
Spotted Rasbora

This species is fairly common everywhere in Southeast Asia, the Indonesian Archipelago and Singapore. *Rasbora maculata* run in shoals

526

in stagnant and moderately running water. They inhabit open air waters, shallow and swampy, with a thick, muddy bottom dense with water plants, such as *Cryptocoryne* species. They also inhabit creeks and other jungle waters which themselves contain little vegetation, but which have dense, overhanging bank vegetation. They live there mainly in company with *Barbus*, other *Rasbora* and *Brachydanio* species.

The inhabited waters are often cloudy and yellowish, somewhat acid with a pH value of 6.3 and a hardness of 0.5–2.5°. Later writers considered *Rasbora maculata* as young *Rasbora kalochroma* (Bleeker, 1850). This mistake was corrected by breeders when it became obvious that *R. maculata* specimens of 25 mm (1 inch), that gave no indication of ever growing bigger than 25 mm, could reproduce. *Rasbora kalochroma*, however, can grow to 90 mm (about 3½ inches).

Although these two species are undoubtedly closely related (they also have practically the same distribution), it has been established that they are two distinct species, even though they do resemble one another in coloration and markings. *Rasbora maculata* is one of the most attractive fish of the *Rasbora* genus. At the same time, it is one of the smallest of aquarium fishes. The body is typical of *Rasbora*, elongated and slightly flattened. The terminal mouth points distinctly upward. All the fins are well developed.

Plate II-87. *Rasbora lateristriata elegans.*

The background is orange-red, the back darker. The belly is light orange to golden yellow. A light, blue-green sheen shimmers over the whole fish. The fin rays are also reddish, sometimes with dark, purple-red dots or spots. The first rays of the dorsal and anal fins are blackish to dark purple-brown. There is a large, egg-shaped black spot in the middle of the flanks, below the first dorsal-fin ray. There are also a number of smaller, differently shaped blackish spots scattered over the body.

Again, the sexes are rather difficult to distinguish. If fully grown, the females are somewhat larger and much broader and rounder in the belly than the very slim males. Also, the females may be recognized by their slightly less vivid coloration and the lighter belly. Keeping the natural environment in mind, set up the tank with a humus bottom (a good layer of peat moss) and plant it with *Cryptocoryne*, *Limnophila*, *Hydrilla* and floating water ferns, as well as rooted ferns of the *Ceratopteris* genus. The water temperature range should be 22–26 °C (72–79 °F), but it is allowed to rise by the heat of the sun. Follow the same reproduction procedure as for the related species.

Rasbora meinkeni De Beaufort, 1931
Meinken's Rasbora

In 1928, the first few specimens of *R. meinkeni* were imported from Sumatra, its native locale. The body is slim, elongated and vertically flattened. The male grows to approximately 55 mm ($2\frac{1}{4}$ inches) and the female to a maximum of 65 mm (about $2\frac{1}{2}$ inches). The snout is short and the mouth points upwards. The background is shining yellow, the back area is olive green to brownish, and the belly varies from pale yellow to white. A black stripe runs lengthwise from the gill flaps to the end of the tail. Above this black stripe is an equally wide, golden area, bordered on either side by a row of shining, blue scales.

The anterior part of the body and the head shine bluish green when light falls on them. The large scales of the belly area are dark-edged. The dorsal and caudal fins are light brown, with darker fin rays and a light blue border. The pelvic and anal fins are light brown; the pectoral fins are without coloration and transparent. The sexes are recognized chiefly by their difference in size and by the fatter, rounder belly of the female. Both sexes are practically identical in coloration and markings.

Rasbora meinkeni does not require much in the way of care and is best kept in a large, spacious aquarium. Here it shows up to its best advantage, especially when light shines on it, against a dark bottom vegetation of *Cryptocoryne* species and dense weeds along the sides. Take care to provide a good, open area for swimming. The water temperature in winter should be 18 °C (64 °F), and in summer, about 20 °C (68 °F). Raise this to 24 °C (75 °F) during breeding. In order to breed strong, young fish, it is advisable for the parent fish to spend the winter at a low temperature. The breeding aquarium should not be too small—say, 40 × 25 × 25 cm (16 × 10 × 10 inches). To minimize the number of eggs eaten by the parents, plant the tank with *Eleocharis*, *Myriophyllum*, *Nitella*, and clumps of thread algae. The eggs are usually laid in the early morning after a lengthy courtship and much pretense at mating. It is advisable to put the female into the tank in the evening, alone at first—at least for a few hours. If sunny weather is expected on the following morning, then the male should also be put in the night before with the female.

With the first rays of the sun, many tiny, yellowish eggs are deposited among the clumps of weed. When all the eggs are laid, and this can be seen by the appearance of the female's belly, the parent fish should be transferred to another tank. Then, reduce the water level in the breeding tank to about 15 cm (6 inches) in depth. After 24 to 30 hours at a temperature of 23–25 °C (73–77 °F), the earliest of the young fish to hatch are seen as tiny little stripes or glass splinters on the plants, stones and tank walls. At this stage, check carefully for un-hatched and possibly mouldy eggs. If necessary, remove them. To complete the procedure after most of the young fish have hatched out, introduce a few aquarium snails into the breeding tank. In a very short time, they will hunt out the mouldy eggs and eat them. As the snails also find good eggs a tasty morsel, never introduce them into the breeding tank at an earlier stage. After at least two days, you will find the young fish swimming freely about. The parent fish can be used again for breeding after a rest period of about a month.

Plate II-88. *Rasbora maculata.*

Illus. II-104. *Rasbora pauciperforata.*

Rasbora pauciperforata Weber & De Beaufort, 1916
Red-Striped Rasbora

The *R. pauciperforata* complex, as conceived by Brittan, consists of the species *R. pauciperforata, R. taeniata, R. beauforti, R. chrysotaenia, R. vegae, R. borapetensis* and *R. urophthalma.* To these he adds, provisionally, the species *R. palustris* and *R. semilineata.* The complex is distributed through Malaysia, Borneo and Sumatra. They are small species having a maximum total length of about 65 mm (2½ inches). The lateral line is very reduced and there are 12 scales around the root of the tail. The coloration consists of a silvery background with a dark, lengthwise stripe, bordered on the upper edge by a shining, metallic stripe, which is copper-red to gold in *R. pauciperforata.*

Rasbora pauciperforata belongs with *R. heteromorpha* as the most beautiful species of their genus. It is also an exemplary aquarium fish. The coloration and markings in both sexes are identical, though the females can be easily recognized by their deeper body and rounder belly. Although they can be kept without too much difficulty, they have not yet been bred in the aquarium, so that the imported fish simply die out without reproducing. This difficulty had also arisen with other species, such as *R. heteromorpha,* though this fish is now bred quite regularly. It is to be expected, therefore, that the same thing will happen in the case of *R. pauciperforata.*

Rasbora taeniata Ahl, 1922
Black-Striped Rasbora

This species grows to about 80 mm (3¼ inches) and, although not known everywhere, it is one of the most attractive and suitable *Rasbora* that have been imported up to now. Care for them the same as their related species.

Rasbora trilineata Steindachner, 1870
Scissor Fish
Scissortail Rasbora

The habitat of *R. trilineata* is the Indonesian Archipelago, including Sumatra, Borneo, and Burma and Thailand.

The body is elongated, flattened vertically, and the fish possesses well developed fins. It is obviously a fast swimmer from open waters. Its length is 150 mm (6 inches), and longer in the islands region, while the maximum length for Thailand is about 60 mm (2⅜ inches). The terminal mouth is moderately large and slants slightly upwards.

The large caudal fin, the most attractive and striking feature of this fish, gives the fish the name of "Scissor Fish." The fin is deeply forked, and the two lobes are extremely mobile. They perform a semblance of cutting movements. It is thought that only "large" *Rasbora trilineata—*

Plate II-89. *Rasbora taeniata.*

Plate II-90. *Rasbora trilineata* **from Sumatra** *(R. caudimaculata).*

ones that grow into really giant fish—are known among collectors. Aquarium specimens more than 16 cm long (about 6¼ inches) are known but other smaller forms have been described that are fully grown by the time they reach 6 cm (2⅜ inches).

The background of the larger forms from Sumatra and Borneo is shining silver to soft, metallic blue. The back is brownish, the belly yellowish white. A dark to blackish brown stripe, which runs from the gill flaps, along the root of the tail, to the end of the short, middle caudal fin ray, is usually pronounced in tone only from the dorsal fin to the tail. The stripe is widest and most vivid at the root of the tail, and usually extends into a vivid spot at this point. An equally dark (to black) line runs, in both sexes, along the base of the anal fin. The striking tail lobes are without coloration and range from transparent to pale yellow at the root. Next on the tail lobes is a milk white cross stripe, and then a black band or spot, which varies in shape and tone and which sometimes (as in *R. calliura* Boulenger) extends to the points of the lobes of the caudal fin. Normally, the extreme tips of the lobes again turn milk white to shiny blue.

The dorsal, anal and pelvic fins are a light reddish brown. The pectoral fins are without coloration and transparent. Plate II–90 makes it unnecessary to describe this fish further, even though there are some differences between local forms.

The small form, presumably only a geographical variation, comes from Thailand and differs slightly in coloration and markings. The general impression is that it is slightly darker, more greenish, and the scales at the central point show a grey spot. The lengthwise stripe is more pronounced and shows up better on the anterior part of the body. The stripe at the base of the anal fin, already described in the larger form, is present on both sides of the body and also runs back to the anal fin, under the tail and through to the caudal fin. There is also a similar black line on the back, in front of and behind the dorsal fin. The membranes of the dorsal, anal and pelvic fins are transparent, decorated with small, dark dots. The fin rays are greenish yellow.

The sexes can only be recognized by the rounder, broader belly of the somewhat larger and deeper females.

Because this species is a very active swimmer, do not keep it in too small an aquarium. Otherwise, it may be kept in the same manner as related species. Specimens of the larger type are usually sexually mature and ready for breeding when they get to be 6 cm (2⅜ inches) long. The temperature range is 18–28 °C (64–82 °F).

Mating begins suddenly, without any noticeable, preparatory courtship. The eggs are "strewn" among the plants and, because they are not very adhesive, a large percentage of them falls to the bottom. This is not, however, detrimental to their hatching. The young fish hatch out within 24 hours and the fry are swimming about by the third day.

Rasbora trilineata is a fast swimmer which comes from slightly acid water that is poor in chalk (pH 6 to 6.8), has a thick humus bottom and vegetation consisting predominantly of water ferns and *Cryptocoryne* species. It lives in company with *Rasbora heteromorpha*, and the other species which live in the same environment as *R. heteromorpha*.

Plate II-91. *Rasbora urophthalma.*

Rasbora urophthalma Ahl, 1922

Along with *R. dorsiocellata* and *R. maculata*, this species is one of the dwarf rasboras, attaining a maximum total length of 30 mm (1¼ inches). It should be kept in groups of four or more, in company with smaller fish. It is a very attractive species. The fish mate spontaneously and prefer to lay their eggs among fine-leaved plants. The nests are usually not large. The young hatch out on the third or fourth day and grow up quickly and easily.

Rasbora vaterifloris Deraniyagala, 1930
Ceylonese Dwarf Rasbora
Pearly Rasbora

This is a small species from Ceylon that grows to a maximum of about 40 mm (about 1⅝ inches) long. In contrast with most other species, it has a less elongated body and is not as thick vertically as *Rasbora heteromorpha.* (This is one of the characteristics upon which Brittan bases the sub-genus *Rasboroides.*) This species has been regularly imported since 1936.

Plate II-92. *Rasbora vaterifloris.*

Sub-family Leuciscinae

This is a very old group of carp-like fishes, perhaps the oldest found over the total distribution area of the family. It may be surprising to hear that these roach-like fishes, as far as is known, are still the greatest stumbling block for systematists, undoubtedly because they produce bastard lines so easily. Only a few from this group may be considered aquarium fishes, and the choice is very small indeed for the heated aquarium. Many tropical species that are attractive in shape and coloration should be imported to restore the balance between Leuciscinae and the excessive number of small, imported characins.

Tribe Leuciscini

Most of the approximately 40 genera comprising this tribe of minnows in the United States have several quite lovely species. Many species referred to as "Minnows" are also known as "Dace," "Chub" and "Shiner." The name "Minnow" is sometimes even applied to species from quite different families and orders (toothcarps, for example).

The most well known to aquarists are: *Notropis* spp., such as the beautiful Red Shiner and Redfin Shiner, *N. lutrensis* and *N. umbratilis*, the Spot-tail Shiner, *N. venustus*, and the Common Shiner, *N. cornutus*; *Notemigonus*, with its single species, the Golden Shiner, *N. chrysoleucas*; *Pimephales*, with the Fathead Minnow, *P. promelas* and the Bullhead Minnow, *P. vigilax*; and the beautiful Black-nosed and Red-belly Daces of the genera *Rhinichthys* and *Chrosomus*. The rivers and streams of North America contain numerous small minnows and other fishes which are suitable for keeping in the aquarium, and interest in them by aquarists is increasing rapidly.

Other well known American minnows include the Fallfish, *Semotilus corporalis*, which reaches as much as 46 cm (18 inches) and 3 pounds weight, the Creek Chub, *Semotilus atromaculatus*, which reaches 25 cm (10 inches), and the Squawfishes of the genus *Ptychocheilus*, including the largest American minnow, *P. lucius*, which reaches almost $1\frac{1}{2}$ m (5 feet) in length. These are obviously not aquarium fishes.

Plate II-93. *Tanichthys albonubes.*

Genus *Tanichthys*

Tanichthys albonubes Lin, 1932

Chinese or Canton Danio

White Cloud

White Cloud Mountain Fish

This fish is common in the Canton area of China (White Cloud Mountain). It lives in stagnant and running water, mountain streams and similar bodies of water. The first specimens appeared in Europe in 1939.

In 1932, the Chinese explorer Tan—from whom the genus takes its name *Tanichthys* ("Tan's fish")—discovered this fish on one of his expeditions in the Canton region, to White Cloud Mountain. A detailed, scientific description by the head of the fishing research station at Canton, S. Y. Lin (Lin-Shu-Yen) soon appeared in the Lingnan Science Journal (1932): "New Cyprinid Fish from White Cloud Mountain, Canton." He published an illustration in the same journal in 1935, accompanying an article entitled: "Contribution to a Study of Cyprinids from Kwangtung and its Provinces."

Dr. Eastman of Montreal acquired a few specimens from Canton and sent a pair to William T. Innes in Philadelphia. This little fish conquered Europe via America, where it is now a much appreciated guest among collectors.

In many aspects, this fish with its splendid markings and beautiful coloration is reminiscent of the Hong Kong danio (*Hemigrammocypris lini* Weitzman & Chan, 1966), which it greatly resembles. The popular names are actually misleading, as neither the Canton nor the Hong Kong Danio is a real danio. However, the contention that this fish should not be kept in the same tank with danios because of a natural antipathy they have for each other is, in some opinions, a myth.

The body of *Tanichthys albonubes* is elongated and grows to a maximum of 40 mm (over 1½ inches). The snout points upward, is small, and has a small mouth aperture. The lower jaw is slightly undershot. The dorsal fin begins in the posterior half of the body, at about two thirds of the distance from the snout to the root of the tail. The caudal fin is forked. The anal fin starts directly below the fourth dorsal-fin ray and its base is longer than that of the dorsal fin. The pelvic and pectoral fins and the single fins are of normal size.

Behind the greyish brown background is a net-like marking, caused by the dark-edged scales. The whole body is covered with small, cycloid scales. From the point of the snout to the root of the tail runs a band consisting of three narrow lines. The upper line is a shining, rosy-gold, the middle line is greenish and the lower line bluish black. Depending on how the light falls on them—especially sunlight—a wonderful mixture of red-copper shows up, along with all shades of green and blue, shot with silver and gold. The stripe ends in a dark patch at the root of the tail. Dorsal and anal fins have more or less the same coloration—yellow at the base and the remainder a light red to no coloration—and are transparent, with an edging of yellowish red to greenish blue.

The caudal fin consists of three zones, the two outer ones being pale yellow to no coloration. The extreme tips of the tail lobes are sometimes edged with a milky white. In direct light, especially sunlight, the eye is light green. In such light, the beauty of the coloration shows up best. The females are usually slightly less vivid and do not have the bright red in their fins. The sexes are easy to identify only during the mating period (May to October), when the belly of the female is rounder and the roe is sometimes very obvious.

Young specimens at first sparkle with wonderful coloration and markings. Up to a certain age, they can be compared to the much admired Neon Tetra and, according to some enthusiasts, are not outshone by them. Unfortunately, the fish lose their brilliant coloration fairly quickly, though not entirely, after a few months. They can, however, still be called extremely beautiful and vivid (especially the males). Indeed, the coloration is actually kept in reserve for the mating season and special occasions.

Innes is justified in writing that this fish is the Guppy among the egg-layers. Eggs are laid at a temperature between 15 and 30 °C (59–86 °F), and with such ease and speed that it is a joy to behold. Apart from the beautiful coloration and markings (there is more life in these fish than even in the neon fish), they are extremely tolerant and lively in their play. They are, therefore, suitable for the community aquarium. A shoal of these little Chinese fish among the danios and rasboras is extremely attractive. As can be seen from their natural environment, these fish can withstand temperatures near freezing. Immediately after being in these cold temperatures, it is ready for breeding. Of course, a change in temperature must take place gradually.

Therefore, they can be kept in cold, sub-tropical, or tropical conditions. A not-too-high temperature is recommended for breeding. During the preceding winter, keep the fish in a tank at a temperature of about 15 °C (59 °F) to assure stronger progeny. At higher temperatures, the chance is that the brood will be larger, but the real enthusiast would rather have strong fish, beautiful in shape and markings.

The courtship is not so boisterous. The males do not chase after the females, but appear calm about the whole affair. After trembling heavily, the female distributes a few extremely tiny eggs at a time and these remain hanging on the fine-leaved plants. *Myriophyllum* is very suitable, but the eggs will also be deposited in thick clumps of *Heteranthera zosteraefolia*. The size of the breeding tank and the depth of the water are not important. Just as good results have been achieved with one couple in a small, low tank (25 × 35 × 35 cm or 10 × 14 × 14 inches) at a temperature of 18–20 °C (64–68 °F) as in a large tank, measuring 50 × 55 × 80 cm (20 × 22 × 31½ inches), at a temperature of 13–15 °C (55–59 °F), with two couples present. No eggs have been observed being eaten by the parent fish—at any rate, not to such an extent as to make it necessary to remove the parent fish. In lower temperatures, of course, eggs take longer to hatch than at higher temperatures. From 24 hours to a few days are generally required. The newly hatched fish are 4 mm ($\frac{3}{16}$ inch) long and hang on the tank walls and plants like splinters of glass. The two eyes are clearly visible. The shape of the body changes rapidly, and then the whole body becomes transparent. They grow quickly, if well fed. These fish do not eat very much at one time, but they do enjoy small quantities of food at frequent intervals. Bear this in mind when establishing a feeding routine.

That this little fish has a rather special position among the "tropical" fish can be attributed not only to the interest that every new species awakens in the aquarium keeper, but also to the fact that it is not exclusively a tropical fish, but is also a sub-tropical and, almost, a cold water fish. It can survive in water temperatures ranging from 0–30 °C (32–86 °F).

Although the literature in regard to importing and breeding states that aquarium specimens do not grow longer than 3 cm ($1\frac{1}{4}$ inches), this is not always true. Having learned from experience that this little fish can well withstand low temperatures and presumably suffers no ill effects but even delights in a current of cool water, the author has, for some years, been breeding this fish in a small, outdoor pond from June to September. The observation was made that it is crazy about running water. While the pond was filling up from the garden hose (pond water, temperature 16 °C (61 °F); tap water, temperature 12 °C (54 °F)), it leaped about and tried to climb the "waterfall," which was splashing on the sloping, stone walls of the pond, as though it really enjoyed such sport. It was, presumably, not merely curiosity that made it act in such a manner.

The results of breeding in this pond were above the usual length expectations. No food was given during the whole period, but the pond contained enough waterfleas and larvae from all kinds of insects for them to subsist on.

Plate II-94. *Rhodeus amarus.*

Rhodeus amarus (Linné, 1758)
Bitterling

The reason for going a little more deeply into a species not truly tropical is to witness a rather special care of the brood. Without *Rhodeus amarus*, the picture would be incomplete. The bitterlings—not only the indigenous, European *Rhodeus amarus*, but also the American and Asiatic species—demonstrate an almost lost specialization in the biology of reproduction. This fish is able to reproduce only in co-operation with certain fresh-water mussels.

The European species *R. amarus* inhabits the whole continent with the exception of the British Isles and the Scandinavian countries. It occurs eastwards as far as Asia, where the genus is represented by another species. In all these areas, the painter's mussel (*Unio pictorum*) or, sometimes, other species of the mussel family, Unionidae, can also be found. It usually lives in stagnant and moderately running waters.

Although this is a species for a cold or unheated aquarium, the Bitterling is not to be outdone by other aquarium fishes in the way of coloration and attractive shape. Plate II–94 shows this clearly enough. Their close relationship to the deeply built danios is obvious; their specialization must be extremely old.

540

In the spring, from April to June, the male Bitterling, in wedding garb, goes in search of the fresh-water mussel, the future home of its progeny. In the manner of other nest-builders, the Bitterling remains in the vicinity of the mussel and chases any other fishes from what he considers his private territory. In quiet moments, he flutters his fins, thus stimulating the mussel to open its shell. The mature female, recognizable by an ovipositor 3 to 4 cm ($1\frac{1}{4}$ to $1\frac{1}{2}$ inches) long, gets involved at this point. By means of the long ovipositor, the eggs are placed one by one into the mussel's breathing tube. This is followed immediately by an ejaculation of sperm from the male. This is taken in with the mussel's breathing water, to fertilize the eggs lying between the mussel's gills.

Eggs are laid in this way at shorter or longer intervals, until all the eggs have been expelled by the female and taken up by one or more mussels. This form of symbiosis is useful for both parties. For the fish, a safe hiding place is ensured for the eggs, but the mussel larvae are also sure of a fairly large distribution. How is this accomplished?

Twenty or thirty days after the eggs were laid, the larvae, already grown to 6 to 8 mm ($\frac{1}{4}$ to $\frac{3}{8}$ inch), leave the safe shelter of the mussel shell over a period of a few days. It is not entirely a voluntary departure, either, for the mussel, irritated by the prickling of the Bitterling larvae, spits out some of its annoying guests with its breathing water.

The service rendered by the Bitterling larvae in return for their keep is distribution of the mussel progeny. The mussel larvae are extremely small and attach themselves with tiny little hooks and adhesive threads to the young Bitterlings. They are thus taken outside the mother mussel's body and are further cared for by being allowed to feed on their host without harming it at all. After a few weeks, the mussel larvae let go of the young Bitterlings and live independently on the bottom, wherever they happen to find themselves.

It is quite possible to breed Bitterling in the aquarium and, thus, to have the opportunity to witness this very interesting method of reproduction and the brood symbiosis. It is possible to catch or buy both the fish and the mussels. At least two mussels should occupy the breeding tank along with the Bitterling pair. Swan mussels (*Anodonta cygnea*) can be used instead of painter's mussels.

When setting up a tank for this breeding process, it is advisable to provide suitable vegetation, a good layer of river sand, and, of course, the mussels. If the tank is placed in a sunny place, there will soon be enough food, in the way of micro-organisms, for the mussels. When these settle to the bottom, the time is ripe for introducing the Bitterling couple into the tank.

It is of historical interest to mention the discovery of this brood symbiosis. In 1787, eggs, presumably from a fish, were found in fresh-water mussels by Cavolini. This was later confirmed by Dollinger (1818), Kuster (1839) and by Vogt (1848), though none of them realized the significance of the discovery. In 1857, Kraus described the phenomenon of the long ovipositor, also without realizing its purpose. Only in 1869 and by close observation did Noll see the connection between the Bitterling and the fresh-water mussel. The truth was finally demonstrated by Schott (1870), when he managed to rear Bitterlings from mussels collected outside.

Order Characiformes

The distribution map in Illus. II–105 indicates the area now inhabited by members of this order. There is little or no indication that this area has not always been the maximum area inhabited by this group. Up to present times, there have presumably been obstacles preventing these fishes from penetrating any farther than is shown on the map. In recent times, there must have been a small migration to the southern United States, and there is also the possibility that their occurrence in East Africa, the Nile region, has taken place in sub-recent times.

As an order, the Characiformes form a more or less homogeneous whole, in that they differ in a number of characteristics from both of the other orders within the Ostariophysi, the Siluriformes and the Cypriniformes. They have a normal covering of scales (some Gymnotidae have no scales) in common with the Cypriniformes and they have an adipose fin (which is missing, however, in a few exceptional cases) in common with the Siluriformes. Although the characins can be classified as one basic type, they can adopt extremely divergent forms and their life cycles can also differ greatly. Think, for example, of the fragile, slim Nannostomini and the plump, predatory piranhas. In every case, they differ from the other two orders by having no barbels and no capacity for protruding the mouth.

The jaws are often set with teeth, and there are often four upper pharyngeal bones (seldom less). The lower pharyngeal bones are nor-

Illus. II-105. Distribution of the characins.

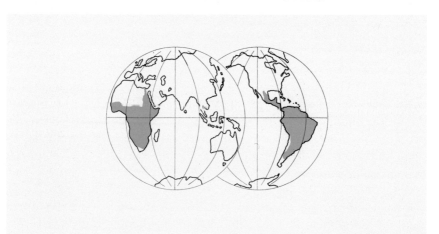

mal, not sickle-shaped, sometimes set with small, thread-like teeth. The gill flaps are complete. The fin rays, never spiny, are sometimes in one piece, slightly ossified, and are usually forked, mobile and weak. Undoubtedly, the closest relative of the characins (in the strict sense), the Gymnotidae, or knife fishes, has not yet been satisfactorily placed within the system. The current view is that they are degenerated characoids. The author is inclined to regard them as a very old branch of this order, similar to the catfish in many characteristics, which went their own specialized way long ago. On these grounds, he classes them, with others, in a number of families which, together, form the sub-order Gymnotoidea.

DEVELOPMENT

This order was already represented on earth by a few very primitive forms at the beginning of the Cretaceous period. It is in the southern hemisphere, which had been tearing itself into continents for a long time, that the earliest forms, the most primitive Characoidea, appeared. Their entire development took place in fresh water.

Table I–4 shows that this order sprang from a strongly differentiated group of fishes at the beginning of the Cretaceous period. In order to picture the circumstances prevailing at that time, which is necessary for a correct understanding of the recent distribution, it is necessary to know how the earth looked during this Cretaceous period. The face of the world was a great deal different than it is now. There is reason to believe that this order had its birthplace in the extensive fresh-water areas of the land masses of Africa and South America, which were still joined together at the time of the Cretaceous. Characiformes do not occur in Madagascar because at the time they were migrating eastward from their place of origin (which is still happening, to a limited extent)—this island was already separated from the African mainland by salt water.

In South America, the Characiformes have never gone farther south than roughly the latitude of Buenos Aires. This also explains why these fishes did not penetrate to Australia and Madagascar via the Antarctic mainland. An ultimate separation of these parts from the southern continents can, therefore, well have taken place during or after the Pliocene. During this period, the northern and southern primordial continents came closer and closer together, though South America still had no dry land connection with North America. Thus, the Characidae were unable to get through to this part of the world until, after the Pliocene, the link between North and South America—

that is, Central America—came into being. Because of the further penetration northwards of the gymnotoids, a greater age can be attributed to this group. It is possible, however, that a rôle is played here by other factors.

It is certainly no simple matter to establish a link of descent between the Ostariophysi and the other two orders. It is, however, clear that the link is probably with the catfishes and loaches and certainly not with the carp-like fishes. It is, indeed, possible that this order has no monophyletic (single root) origin. There may have been several different lines of evolution, right up to the development of the families now joined together.

In spite of objections, there are a number of factors that point towards a certain kinship between some Characiformes and the mudfish (Amiiformes). The mudfish certainly are not the direct ancestors of the characins, though the striking eye of these fish resembles in detail the eye of the catfish in general. This is, perhaps, one of the important points calling for further research.

The differentiation of families—of which only one occurs both in Africa and in South America—points towards a youngish group, which, in the author's opinion, definitely began to flourish only after the beginning of the Cretaceous period. This was especially so in South America, where they had no competition from carp-like fish.

Sub-order Gymnotoidei

Although this is an extremely interesting group of fishes, up to now only a few have become known to aquarists. One of the most remarkable characteristics of these fishes, in which they are like the Osteoglossidae and Notopteridae, is the way they achieve forward movement by means of the extremely long, rippling anal fin that runs the full length of the belly and tail. Another oddity is that the anal opening is displaced far forward, in front of the first anal ray, under the pectoral fins. The anus continues to function when the fishes have buried themselves completely, tail and body, in the bottom mud. In a well set-up aquarium, this burying will not create an enormous mud puddle; the fish do this calmly and cleanly.

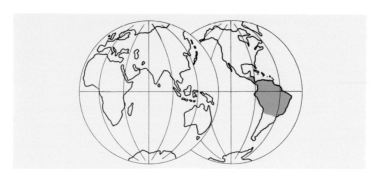

Illus. II-106. Distribution of the Gymnotoidea.

Family Gymnotidae

This family, in the limited sense considered here, includes two sub-families (which many authorities place in two separate families, Gymnotidae and Electrophoridae), totalling only three species, and for the aquarist is probably of less interest than the two other families.

We distinguish the sub-family Electrophorinae, its only species being the ill-famed electric eel, *Electrophorus electricus*, and the sub-family Gymnotinae, with the genus *Gymnotus*.

Genus *Gymnotus*

For a long time, the "Carapo" was considered the only species of this genus. In 1962, the author studied a collection of material from Surinam and found a second species, which he named *Gymnotus anguillaris*. (*Gymnotus coropinae*, also described by Hoedeman in 1962, proved to be synonymous with *G. anguillaris*.) Another species, *G. coatesi*, has also been described.

Illus. II-107. *Gymnotus carapo*.

Illus. II-108. *Gymnotus anguillaris.*

Gymnotus anguillaris Hoedeman, 1962
Banded Knife Fish
Eel Knife Fish

Supposedly, this species generally occurs with *G. carapo*. It would be desirable for importers to try bringing them in. Although the original description was based on specimens from Surinam, this fish is undoubtedly common in a great deal of South America. *G. anguillaris* remains rather small, has a strongly eel-shaped body and a forward-sloping pattern of broad, dark and narrow white stripes on the posterior part of the body and the tail. The height of the body is considerably less than that of *G. carapo*.

Family Rhamphichthyidae

This is not only an interesting family but, at the same time, one that has already produced various species for the aquarium, all of which have already achieved a certain amount of popularity. This family includes the genera: *Eigenmannia, Gymnorhamphichthys, Hypopomus, Hypopygus, Parupygus, Rhamphichthys, Steatogenys* and *Sternopygus*.

Genus *Eigenmannia*

This genus includes only two species (perhaps three), *E. macrops* and *E. virescens*, the first appearing to be restricted to Guyana, the second occurring as far south as the La Plata region.

Eigenmannia virescens Valenciennes, 1847
Glass Knife Fish

Even at this late date, not much is known about this fish. The most striking thing about it is its way of swimming, which is normally controlled by the waving movements of its long anal fin; it swims backwards and forwards with the greatest of ease, without bending its tail or body. Only when the fish is frightened into swimming quickly

Plate II-96. *Eigenmannia virescens.*

Illus. II-109. Young specimen of *Hypopomus artedii.*

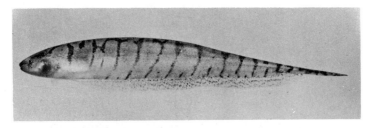

Illus. II-110. Young specimen of *Hypopomus beebei.*

does the body take on the waving motion. This species is an attractive golden brown, patterned with greenish brown.

Genus *Hypopomus*

Two species of this genus have been imported, both rather small (to about 10 cm or 4 inches), *H. artedii* (Kaup, 1856), from the Guianas, Amazon River and Paraná in Brazil, and *H. beebei* Schultz, 1944, from the Guianas.

Genus *Hypopygus*

Hypopygus lepturus Hoedeman, 1962

This is a small, attractive species which, hopefully, will be imported.

Illus. II-111. *Parupygus savannensis.*

Genus *Parupygus*

Parupygus savannensis **Hoedeman, 1962**

This is an especially beautiful species, with a seemingly great length of about 20 cm (8 inches), yet it is suitable for a tank that is not too small. The somewhat eel-shaped body makes the length unobjectionable.

Parupygus litaniensis **Hoedeman, 1962**

This species is closely related to the preceding species and like it, is about 20 cm (8 inches) long.

Genus *Steatogenys*

Steatogenys elegans **(Steindachner, 1880)**

Hopefully, this species will be imported for the benefit of aquarists.

Illus. II-112. *Steatogenys elegans* from Surinam *(surinamense).*

Plate II-97. *Sternopygus macrurus.*

Genus *Sternopygus*

Sternopygus macrurus (Bloch ed. Schneider, 1785)

Long-Tailed Knife Fish

Like all remaining members of this family, *Sternopygus macrurus* are dwellers of the open stretches, savannahs (where they commonly occur in ditches), canals, and artificial waterways of plantations. Although they can grow to about 40 cm (16 inches), young specimens make fine aquarium residents.

Little is known of the method of reproduction of these gymnotids. Recent research has indicated that during the breeding season males stake out territories which they hold during periods when they ordinarily would be moving to open water to feed. They can be differentiated from females of the same species by differences in the electric signal. Since these differences only occur in the breeding season, they seem to be part of the reproductive activity. It is assumed—since young have been found among the larger imported specimens—that they are perhaps live-bearing. Is there an experienced breeder who can supply a positive answer?

Sub-order Characoidei

As characoids (sometimes called characins) are, perhaps, the most important group of fishes for aquarists, they have also been coming more and more to the attention of scientists. The direct result of this is that the system of kinship is always being reviewed. Of the four clearly-defined families now distinguished, the Characidiidae is perhaps the most interesting, as far as its derivation is concerned. Next in interest are the families Erythrinidae, Characidae, and Citharinidae. It is presumed, incidentally, that one family developed only after the geological separation of Africa and South America, the Citharinidae.

Family Characidiidae

These fishes differ in so many important characteristics from the Erythrinidae, on the one hand, and the Characidae, on the other, that it is justified to classify them in a distinct family. This point of difference has already been pointed out (Hoedeman, 1950), and later on, research and other authors have affirmed this opinion.

Two sub-families are distinguished—the Characidiinae and the Crenuchinae. The first sub-family especially demonstrates many similarities to loaches, and when we are looking for a connection with the other Ostariophysi, we may find it here.

Sub-family Characidiinae

A number of genera, brought together in this sub-family, are undoubtedly similar in a number of characteristics to the primitive tribal members of the order Characiformes, and also show a relationship to loaches and catfishes, on the one hand, and to carp-like fishes, on the other. The recently created genus *Klausewitzia* also belongs here. It is an interesting group of fishes which certainly demands closer investigation and then will probably provide an introduction to some remarkable conclusions.

Genus *Characidium*

This genus, possessing numerous varieties, has in some un-explainable way escaped the attention of aquarists. Perhaps it is not so unexplainable, because their life style is such that the fishermen do not find it easy to catch them in any number, a reason they are seldom found in import shipments. During the past few years, however, they have appeared on the market from time to time and have been welcomed by experts with great enthusiasm. In a remarkable way, one species has been able to maintain itself down through the years, and this species also crops up regularly. It is a species that is less emphatically a bottom-dweller.

Characidium fasciatum Reinhardt, 1866
Darter Characin

Characidium fasciatum is an enjoyable aquarium fish, a welcome completion to the regional aquarium in which the bottom-dwelling varieties are in the minority. Although this species is basically less typical than most relatives of its genus, it is still in the lowest water levels that it stays continuously. Most *Characidium* species bury themselves in the sand regularly; *C. fasciatum* does this but seldom and never completely. It attains a length of about 60 mm (2⅜ inches), although this can vary according to the place of origin. Mainly, it is a species having an enormously wide distribution (practically the entire Amazon and Orinoco River Basins, Paraguay and Rio São Francisco in Brazil), which is also expressed in the pattern as well as in the many local varieties that have been described. In general, the basic coloration is brownish to olive green, with a dark (to black) lengthwise band, which mostly breaks up into a number of fragments, in agreement with the number of cross stripes exhibited, usually in their youth, but which are also sometimes seen on adult specimens.

Reproduction takes place about the same way it does among *Neolebias ansorgei*, close to the bottom. Numerous eggs are laid in plant clumps; they hatch out in two days and the young quickly grow up. A diet of predominantly animal food is desirable.

Illus. II-113. *Characidium fasciatum.*

Sub-family Crenuchinae

An interesting discovery was made that *Crenuchus* (as well as *Poecilocharax*) differs in numerous characteristics from the other groups of characins. Indeed, Hoedeman's assertion in 1950 (Amsterdam Naturalist) which supposed that *Crenuchus* held a distinctly separate place in the system, was affirmed, leaning in the direction of certain affinities with both the other orders (Siluriformes and Cypriniformes) of the Ostariophysi. This sub-family, and the Characidiinae, are probably best considered as relicts of old races which possessed characteristics typical of catfishes as well as loaches.

It is quite likely that soon more will be heard about these groups from the scientific side.

Crenuchus spilurus Günther, 1863
Sailfin Characin

Crenuchus spilurus comes from Guyana, the middle of the Amazon Basin, and Surinam. It has been known though not so popular as an aquarium fish since 1913. The specimens very recently imported from Surinam possibly represent a separate form, to which in any case, however, the following will apply. Its length runs to about 60 mm (2¾ inches).

The basic coloration is brownish yellow to red-brown above the lateral line. Every scale is dark-edged, which causes the net-like pattern so typical of numerous species. A copper red to gleaming gold stripe runs from the gill covers to under the root of the tail. The iris of the eye is bright red. A rather large, more or less round, black spot is usually quite visible on the lower half of the tail, right by the base of the caudal fin. The fins are soft yellow to slightly violet, the dorsal and anal fins tinted with dark, orange-red spots, especially in the male. A very small adipose fin is present to show that *Crenuchus spilurus* is a characin and not a cichlid, as was assumed at one time.

This last, completely incorrect supposition is just as incorrect as the assertion that this very agreeable fish is a predator or plant destroyer. It is unjust that *C. spilurus* still does not enjoy great popularity, because it is a species that must be constantly imported since it cannot be re-bred in great numbers.

Trustworthy data on the manner of reproduction have not yet been found, but it is hoped that breeders will succeed with the recent imports from Surinam to win this lovely fish over to a lasting stay in the hobby.

In the aquarium, it likes to stay somewhat aloof and seek out calm places. In addition to all kinds of live animal food, sufficient vegetable fare must also be provided.

A temperature of about 25 °C (77 °F) appears better than a higher or lower temperature, although *C. spilurus* are not distinctly sensitive to gradual fluctuations.

Family Citharinidae

Although the comparatively small family Citharinidae provides aquarists with some very interesting species of African characins (in many respects outdone by the African members of the family Characidae), the family still gets too little attention from enthusiasts. Only a few species have become known—*Neolebias ansorgei* and *Nannaethiops unitaeniatus* and *N. tritaeniatus*. These species greatly resemble the Nannostomini, their activities being quite similar. Occasionally, a specimen belonging to the *Citharinus* species is found by collectors. Numerous other members of this family have escaped notice. This is because, of course, they were hardly ever imported, while dozens of American characins are imported in large quantities. There are two sub-families of Citharinidae—Citharininae and Distichodontinae. For the time being, only a few members of the last-mentioned sub-family will be considered.

Sub-family Distichodontinae

From this sub-family, the tribe Nannaethiopini and the two genera *Neolebias* and *Nannaethiops* are of special interest.

Illus. II-114. Distribution of the family Citharinidae.

Tribe Nannaethiopini

Both genera of Nannaethiopini come from tropical West Africa, though *Nannaethiops* has a wider distribution including central tropical Africa. They are similar to their South American relatives, the Nannostomini, which they also resemble in their activities. They live in shallow, densely grown areas of moderately running waters, as well as in pools and ponds. They exist mainly on insect larvae. They like to hold themselves up among fine-leaved plants, always keeping to the edge of the open water. The females prefer this more than the males. The best temperature range is 22–26 °C (72–79 °F). The beautiful tones of coloration show up best against a dark bottom and background. The females, which are noticeably deeper, larger and fatter, are slightly less vivid than the males. Also, in the species possessing a phosphorescent stripe, this is less of a red-gold in the female. One remarkable feature is that the scales are set with fine, little teeth, which are reminiscent of the ctenoid (comb-like) scales of the perch-like fish.

Genus *Nannaethiops*

Two species of this genus have become known among collectors, *N. unitaeniatus* and *N. tritaeniatus*. The last should not be confused with *Neolebias lineatus*.

Nannaethiops is a genus inhabiting practically all of tropical Africa. It closely resembles the South American Nannostomini, with the markings and coloration sometimes almost identical. *Nannaethiops*, however, have a slightly deeper build and are a little more thick-set in shape. In regard to environment, life style and reproduction, these fish are also comparable to the South American characins.

Nannaethiops tritaeniatus Boulenger, 1913

This Congo characin differs from *N. unitaeniatus* in that it has three dark bands running lengthwise, separated by light, almost white, lines. Other than this, the description of *N. unitaeniatus* is applicable here, too.

Nannaethiops unitaeniatus Günther, 1871

This species occurs in the White Nile region, southern Sudan, in the little rivers in Ghana, in Nigeria, Cameroon, Gabon and the Congo Basin. It grows to about 60 mm (2⅜ inches). The background is olive brown, with a dark to black stripe running lengthwise on the body. There are usually also dark tips to the lobes of the caudal fin. A silvery white stripe runs along above the dark band. The belly is pale yellow. Above the end of the anal fin is a tiny adipose fin.

N. unitaeniatus inhabits all types of water, but it likes sunny spots best. Keep this in mind when setting up the aquarium for these fish and place it where there is often sunshine.

In regard to further care and reproduction, what has been written about the South American tetras (see page 617) also applies here. An approximate total of 200 or more eggs is deposited in each mating period, and these hatch out within two days.

Plate II-98. *Nannaethiops unitaeniatus,* **male.**

Plate II-99. *Nannaethiops unitaeniatus,* female.

Genus *Neolebias*

Breeding this genus is the same as for *Nannaethiops*, though it differs in appearance from *Nannaethiops* by not having any scales on the caudal fin. The upper jaw has no teeth. The five *Neolebias* species known to the aquarium world can be differentiated as follows:

1. Less than 40 scales in longitudinal series
   A. Dorsal fin with 7–8 fin rays; one dark, lengthwise band
      a. Vertical 9, lengthwise 29–32 scales . . . *ansorgei*
      b. Vertical 10, lengthwise 32–36 scales . . . *unifasciatus*
   B. Dorsal fin with 9–12 forked fin rays; 2 or 3 dark, lengthwise bands
      a. 9 rows of scales; 3 lengthwise bands . . . *trilineatus*
      b. 10 rows of scales; 2 dark, lengthwise bands . . . *landgrafi*
2. 40–43 scales lengthwise and 12–13 vertical; dorsal fin has 11–12 forked fin rays . . . *spilotaenia*

Neolebias ansorgei Boulenger, 1912

This fish comes from the swamps of the lower Congo Basin, Angola, and perhaps Cameroon. It is a typical dweller of the lower water levels, though not on the bottom.

As a representative of the Citharinidae, which are the equivalent of the South American family Characidae, this is a very attractive little fish. Plate II–100 shows that this is not an exaggeration. In addition to having a splendid coloration, this fish moves about and acts very attractively, and coupled with its small size and great adaptability, makes an ideal aquarium fish. It is not a difficult fish to keep if the aquarium is set up as described for the other swamp inhabitants— *Hemigrammus* or *Hyphessobrycon* species—from South America.

The coloration is brownish, changing from olive green to yellowish on the belly, with a quite broad, dark brown to black band from the head to the root of the tail (not continuing upon the caudal fin). The band is separated from this fin by a narrow, vertical, whitish line. Next to this is a vertical black stripe on the base of the caudal fin. The foremost ray of the anal fin begins exactly below the last ray of the dorsal fin. There is no adipose fin. Dorsal, anal and caudal fins range from brownish to an orange-red or crimson, with an occasional appearance of black pigment. The females are a little deeper and broader than the males and usually are less vivid. The sexes are difficult to recognize when the fish are not fully grown. Adult females are fairly obvious with their rounded shape, and the males usually are somewhat more vivid.

Reproduction is heralded by a violent, rollicking courtship. The actual mating, during which a few eggs at a time are deposited among the plants, also takes place with the boisterousness of the South American tetras. The most suitable temperature for these fish is about 24 °C (75 °F), and this should not be raised for breeding. It is a good idea to let the temperature cool down a few degrees at night if it can rise again, gradually, in the morning. After a refreshing "shower of rain," imitated with rain water from a sprinkling can, mating starts spontaneously.

A remarkable feature of this fish is that each one establishes a territory of its own if two or more specimens are kept together. While paying short visits to their companions, they display their most beautiful coloration, putting on a splendid spectacle for the enthusiastic collector.

The length is up to about 35 mm ($1\frac{3}{8}$ inches). In spite of their small size, however, a spacious aquarium is best for these fish. Keep some areas open, with a sandy bottom and bits of red stone, and other places planted with thick clumps of *Myriophyllum*. A totally dark background shows off the coloration to best advantage, though, in fact, the coloration will show up well regardless of the background, if the fish are healthy and at ease in their surroundings. Sunlight may be allowed to shine into the tank, but avoid artificial light that is too bright.

Neolebias landgrafi Ahl, 1928

For a long time, it was thought that this fish was identical to *N. ansorgei*. Although Ahl had made some mistakes in his description, it appeared that *N. landgrafi* was, in fact, a true species, closely related to *N. unifasciatus*. In a recent review by Poll & Gosse, 1963, *N. landgrafi* was again placed in synonymity with *N. ansorgei*, but aquarists who ever keep both in a tank will be able to tell the striking difference.

N. landgrafi grows to about 30 mm (1¼ inches) and is indigenous to Cameroon. The coloration is reddish brown, almost the same as *N. ansorgei*, though in this fish, the dark, lengthwise stripe runs out upon the caudal fin. The tips of the caudal fin lobes are also dark.

There is a light, bluish cross stripe on the root of the tail. The middle fins are wine red with a generous sprinkling of black pigment. These characteristics show clearly enough how this fish differs from *N. ansorgei*. There is also no adipose fin in this species.

Neolebias spilotaenia Boulenger, 1912

This species resembles *N. unifasciatus*, and grows to a length of about 33 mm (1 5/16 inches). It comes from the Lower Congo Basin. It has a very small adipose fin and is the only *Neolebias* species that has a diagonally cut-off dorsal fin. Otherwise, it is practically identical in coloration to *N. unifasciatus*. The dark, lengthwise band continues to the end of the middle caudal fin rays. There is a black patch on the dorsal fin which runs over the entire length of the first forked ray and becomes smaller toward the rear. It disappears completely at the base of the seventh ray.

Neolebias trilineatus Boulenger, 1899

This fish is an old friend of many collectors. Unlike both the above species, an adipose fin can be present, though in many cases it hardly shows. Although somewhat lighter, the coloration is again brownish but with three dark, lengthwise bands. Between the uppermost and middle bands runs a red-golden phosphorescent stripe. The fins vary from no coloration to a very light reddish without cells of black pigment. The length is about 30 mm (1¼ inches). In this species, too, the female can be more robust, less vivid, and above all, recognizable by the deeper, broader build of the body.

Neolebias unifasciatus Steindachner, 1894

This fish is slightly more elongated than the above-mentioned species and is known from Liberia to the Congo. Again the coloration is predominantly brown with slightly more red in it than *N. ansorgei* has. A dark brown to black stripe runs lengthwise, is narrower than on *N. ansorgei* and runs out upon the caudal fin. It is bordered on its upper side by an almost equally wide stripe of shining orange-gold. Here, too, the fins are bright red with quite a few black pigment cells, especially along the edges. There is no adipose fin. The length runs to about 42 mm (1⅝ inches).

562

Tribe Distichodontini
Genus *Distichodus*

Distichodus antonii Schilthuis, 1891

This is a very beautiful characoid from the Congo area. Unfortunately, like most members of its genus, it grows to enormous size and is then unsuitable for the home aquarium. However, it takes a few years for them to reach maximum size (up to about 500 mm or 20 inches).

The background is a lovely reddish brown with 10 to 14 blackish cross bands. The base of the adipose fin is bright red, set off by a black edge and separated from the red by a milk white line.

D. antonii is a quiet, sociable swimmer, subsisting mainly on vegetable food. Because it has to be about 25 cm (10 inches) long before it is sexually mature, nothing is known about its reproduction. This is, therefore, a fish which continually dies off and has to be imported again.

Illus. II-115. *Distichodus affinis.*

Plate II-101. *Distichodus lusosso.*

Distichodus lusosso Schilthuis, 1891

This beautiful African characin resembles *D. antonii* in markings and coloration, but it has only seven vertical bands. In addition, *D. lusosso* has a remarkably elongated snout which it thrusts here and there among the stones, in search of food. It is one of the most suitable African species and, together with the above-mentioned species, it is certainly a rewarding fish for larger aquariums.

Family Erythrinidae

The theory that *Erythrinus*-type fish are not the ancestral stock of other characins, but the small, widely differentiated tetras, the tribe Cheirodontini are, is based on studies by Eigenmann, Rowntree, Cockerell, Gregory & Conrad, and others.

Sagemehl (1884 and later), however, thought that *Erythrinus*-type fish, which possess many primitive characteristics, as well as scales which resemble those of the cyprinids, should be taken as a starting point.

Rowntree (1903, 1906), after studying the erythrinids, concluded that there can be no relationship with Amiiformes—such as was supposed by Sagemehl. Cockerell (1912, 1913) studied the scales of the African and American characins and, thus, gave considerable support to the investigation into the development of these fishes. Gregory (1933) concurs with Sagemehl in his conception of the origin of the erythrinids. Gregory & Conrad (1938) present a collective study and a usable natural system which at present, it is true, is not in every respect acceptable. They do, though, reverse the idea that the erythrinids may be as primitive as Sagemehl supposed.

Finally, contributions have been presented by numerous authors, all of whom expand our insight into the development of this group, however much they may appear to contradict each other.

Not the least important publication, certainly, is the report of Meinken's investigation (1931) into the development of the tail fin among several species of characins, to which science, up to that time, had not paid much attention.

As usual in such studies, *all* the authors are correct up to a point. Continuing to build on collected factual material, faulty conclusions or conclusions not in agreement with other facts are drawn which obviously place the authors immovably against one another. Without any pretense of asserting that *the* solution has been found, the author of this book is of the opinion that all workers in this division are right *up to a certain point.*

Very recent study of material on the characinoid fishes has focussed on Sagemehl's pronouncement. It is now asumed that the Erythrinidae form a separate stock that developed parallel to the other characins. The caudal fin research of Meinken, from which it appears that a difference exists embryologically between the Erythrinidae and Characidae families, has provided important support of this view.

However, for the time being, though there is little factual material supporting this, this combination of acceptable data leads to the conclusion that the groups summed up above certainly form a natural unit. Undoubtedly, this assemblage also will be modified or will have genera or groups added to it, perhaps causing the natural unit to expand as well.

Nonetheless, all the species investigated by Meinken (1931) fall into this assemblage, though he started with a quite different assumption of relationships.

Erythrinidae differ from the other characins principally because they were formerly considered as belonging to genera among the Characidae, due to the structure of the skull and the rest of the skeleton, the structure of the scales, and—so far as investigated—the embryonic development, which is of the so-called *Lepisosteus* type, meaning a development of the embryonic tail (fin)—as in *Lepisosteus*—in which the extremity of the spinal column continues on in the lance-shaped, archaic tail fin, which, at that point, is divided by a notch.

Sub-family Erythrininae

Of this sub-family, numerous species are well liked and often kept as aquarium fishes. The remaining varieties are less well known or less attractive; they represent such great predators as *Erythrinus* and *Piabucina*.

Tribe Pyrrhulinini

At present, three genera are included in this tribe, all characterized by the longer, upper caudal fin lobe. Although certainly no parallel can be drawn from this characteristic alone, note that this same, lengthened, upper caudal fin lobe is found in Lepisosteiformes and even in the caudal fin of *Amia*. The species that was especially common and well liked 20 years ago, *Copeina guttata*, shown in Plate II–102, is a true large species, which, even in a medium-sized aquarium, shows to its full advantage due to its especially beautiful, pastel coloration and calmness. *Copella arnoldi* has especially attracted the attention of hobbyists by reason of its reproductive biology. The *Pyrrhulina* species are somewhat less common.

There are about 25 described species or varieties in this tribe, and in chronological order, these are: *filamentosa* from Surinam; *melanostoma* from Pebas, Rio Maranon, Peru; *laeta* from the Peruvian Amazon; *semifasciata, brevis* and *nattereri* from the estuary of the Rio Negro, Brazil; *guttata* from the vicinity of Obidos, Brazil; *argyrops* from the vicinity of Pebas, Peru; *maxima* from Tabatinga, Brazil; *australe* from Arroyo Trementina, Mato Grosso, Brazil; *vittata* from Obidos, Brazil; *arnoldi,* from Venezuela; *callolepis* from the Amazon (?, no closer indication); *eigenmanni* from Para near the mouth of the Amazon River, Brazil; *carsevennensis* from Carsevenne, French Guiana; *metae* from Barrigona, Rio Meta, Venezuela; *lugubris* from the same place; *osgoodi* from Nazareth, Peru; *beni* from Ivon, Rio Beni, Bolivia; *obermuelleri* from Iquitos, Peruvian Amazon; *rachoviana* from Rosario, Uruguay; *compta* from Sao Gabriel, Rio Negro, southern Brazil; *eleanorae* from Contamana, Rio Ucayali, Peru; *nigrofasciata* from the Peruvian Amazon (?); and *stoli* from the Maroni River system, Surinam.

Of all these varieties, at least three clearly belong to one of the two current genera, *filamentosa* in *Pyrrhulina,* of which the type species is *P. argyrops,* and *guttata,* which is the type species of the closely related genus *Copeina.*

In 1956, Myers established the genus *Copella* for the remaining species.

Genus *Copeina*

The discussion given under *Copella arnoldi* can be applied equally to *Copeina* species and to *Pyrrhulina,* with the understanding that with *Copella,* egg-laying and parental care are unique, while among the other known species they are carried on in the usual way.

Plate II-102. *Copeina guttata.*

Copeina guttata (Steindachner, 1875)
Red-Spotted Copeina

This species from South America inhabits the central area of the Amazon Basin and Rio Negro in northern Brazil. It was imported for the first time in 1910.

Copeina guttata is one of the larger characin species, attaining a maximum length of 150 mm (6 inches), though in nature, as well as in the aquarium, it is sexually mature at 70 mm (about 3 inches) and can also be full grown at that size. At the same time, this is a fish that grows slowly for a long time, even in a rather moderate-size aquarium. For a long time, it was thought that *C. guttata* was an exception, for it should grow larger in the aquarium than in natural surroundings. Upon closer observation, this appeared to be incorrect, especially when specimens of maximum length were caught.

The body structure, placement of the fins, and the coloration show up quite well in Plate II–102, so that it is not necessary to go into details. A remarkable feature is the difference in size between the two caudal fin lobes. In this species, the upper lobe is clearly bigger and more powerfully developed than the lower. The lateral line organ is entirely absent.

An adipose fin is absent in specimens having an over-all length of more than 3 cm (1$\frac{3}{16}$ inches). However, among young specimens, in the place where an adipose fin occurs in related species, there is a thread-like appendage (urostyle) which quickly disappears again.

The sexes can be told apart while still quite young, although the dark (to black) spot in the dorsal fin among young specimens of both sexes is rather pronounced. The red dots on the scales, however, show up clearly only on the young males. Among larger and full-grown specimens, the dark spot in the dorsal fin of the males almost or completely disappears, but among females it remains readily visible. The scales of the males in the middle, just in the place where the scales are covered by those lying beside them, have bright, carmine red dots.

Since *C. guttata* is a dweller of more or less flowing waters, a certain amount of circulation of the aquarium water is very desirable, though not necessary. This fish should preferably be kept in a low, roomy (long) aquarium with a steeply sloping bottom, or a bottom which may descend in terraces. Consider that *Copeina guttata* is a formidable jumper and must not be restrained by a low lid or by a thick growth of vegetation on the surface of the water. Still, its jumping out must be avoided by covering the tank with a high hood.

Plant with marsh plants if desired. Further, set up the tank with plants that are, preferably, heavily clumped and not spread out too much, a couple of fine pieces of stone and some sandy spots.

The temperature range runs from about 15–30 °C (59–86 °F). A sunny spot for the tank is recommended, for *C. guttata* likes a lot of light. These factors must also be taken into consideration as much as possible in the community aquarium. This species certainly does not make heavy demands, nor is it predatory and, thus, it can even be kept in the same tank with very small species.

When the mating season begins, which takes place when the couple pretends to mate, but is not really doing so, then there is a real show, such as is seldom observed. Depending on the circumstances, the action is initiated by either the male or the female. As a rule, the action instituted by the female is quite remarkable, especially if she is bigger than the male, which is usually the case when the fish are the same age. Tempestuously, she literally wades into the male, who initially is not much interested in her attentions and hastily flees to the plants. She sets forth tirelessly to follow after him, until finally he chooses the wisest course and gives up.

Closely watched from a distance by the female, he begins to construct the "house," a furrow or hole in the sand. Indeed, sometimes, he cleans a stone for the eggs to be laid upon, yet that is only in exceptional cases.

Twisting his belly about in the sand, he makes a hole 5 to 6 cm (2 to $2\frac{3}{8}$ inches) across and from 1 to $1\frac{1}{2}$ cm ($\frac{3}{8}$ to $\frac{5}{8}$ inch) deep, mostly right beside a clump of plants. With his ventral and pectoral fins, he shoves part of the sand over the edge of the hole so that a kind of little rampart is erected around it. The female sometimes assists the male in the final construction of the future nest. If this is necessary, the male then fetches the female and the real mating begins. Bodies bent, both fish swim after each other for a few seconds above the round hole, forming a living, moving circle. Then the female stretches herself out, her snout turned a bit upwards, while the male presses himself closely against her, his snout pointing upwards. He folds all his fins, especially the anal fin, over in her direction, holding her while doing so, as firmly as possible.

With gently shaking movements, the female issues about 25 eggs. These are picked up in the rolled-up anal fin of the male, where they are immediately fertilized. Then both fish relax; the female swims away, while the male allows the eggs to fall into the hole. The male goes at once after the female and brings her back to a position above the hole. This can be repeated several hours later, until, for large specimens, about 1,000 eggs have been laid.

After mating, the female disappears among the plants and is no longer followed by the male. She is literally white from "emotion."

The small (about $\frac{1}{2}$ mm or $\frac{1}{50}$ inch across), yellowish eggs lie in a heap in the hole and are carefully fanned by the male. For two days, he busily cares for the spawn. From time to time, he interrupts the fanning to take a few eggs into his mouth and clean them with chewing movements. He then spits them back into the hole. During the second day, the eggs turn white and seem to be mouldy. If we look at them with a magnifying glass, we notice, however, that the embryo in the white egg is moving, and not long thereafter, the first young emerge free of their egg shells. Quickly, then, there is much teeming and swarming in the hole that is a delight to watch.

A day later, all the larvae can be seen hanging on the panes and the plants, living off their little yolk sacs. As they undertake their first attempts at swimming, the time comes for them to hunt for completely suitable food. Rather than feed an infusoria culture from lettuce leaves and such, strain ditch water through fine muslin, or squeeze wads of algae, and so forth. Later on, a switch can be made to pressed mosquito larvae, white worms, tubifex worms, and such.

Only in a very large aquarium will a reasonable number of young develop further. When they are about a month old, the young show a typical pattern differing entirely from that of their parents, a yellowish and grey-brown zebra pattern, which again changes after a few weeks into the well known, soft pastel tints of the parents.

In spite of the size which this characid species can attain after the first year, *C. guttata* is a splendid and extremely suitable fish for larger aquariums. In deep aquariums, they practically always stay in the upper water levels while they prefer a lower depth of water (for example, 30 cm or 12 inches) for reproduction.

As far as food for the adult is concerned, *C. guttata* is an extremely easy fish to keep. In addition to all known kinds of live food, it gladly accepts shredded meat, fish, mussel, and the like.

Plate II-103. *Copella arnoldi.*

Genus *Copella*

This genus was mainly set up because the long species, up to now included in it, are clearly different in technical characteristics, as well as in biology, from the robust species of *Copeina*. On the other hand, the species of the genera *Copella* and *Pyrrhulina* are difficult to distinguish from each other.

Copella arnoldi (Regan, 1912)
(formerly known as *Copeina arnoldi*)
Splashing Salmlet
Spotted Characin
Spraying Characin

This fish, widely kept for a long time, has a broad distribution area which extends over practically the entire Brazilian Amazon region and, it appears, into Surinam and possibly also into the other two Guianas. This very distribution is the cause of the numerous names under which this species has received recognition in scientific as well as hobbyist circles. The confusion with the genus *Pyrrhulina* has not yet been completely or satisfactorily resolved. The recently imported

572

specimens from Surinam represent a sub-species, which not only in some technical characteristics, but also in coloration and pattern, deviates from the formerly known *Copella* species.

C. arnoldi is an ornamental, long, slim fish that can reach a length of about 80 mm ($3\frac{3}{16}$ inches). A very large female may grow to not less than 100 mm (4 inches) without, and 140 mm (5$\frac{9}{16}$ inches) with, the caudal fin. This is an exception, because it appears, from considerable scientific material, that the females are smaller than the males.

The sexes are always very clearly distinguished by the bright coloration and strongly developed and outgrown fins of the males. In both sexes, all fins are well developed and the upper lobe of the caudal fin is considerably larger than the lower, especially among the males.

The basic coloration is, depending on the region of origin, olive brown to dark reddish brown, light towards the abdomen (females are less distinct in coloration). The scales are darkly edged, causing the well known, net-like pattern. In accordance with the lighting, *C. arnoldi* gleams with an alternate blue-green to violet, with a distinct spot of glistening gold on the gill covers. From the lower jaw through the eye and over the gill covers (continuing more or less distance in the various sub-species) runs a deep black stripe, which can continue more weakly towards the back. The fins are yellowish to dark orange or brownish red. The base of the dorsal fin is white as milk and close above it is a small, round to larger triangular black spot. The tip is orange-red, while the foremost rays are usually an intense black. The ventral and anal fins have a red tip and a black edge, and the caudal fin is bright red above and below.

C. arnoldi has a reproductive biology that is unique in its kind. Undoubtedly, this "brood care" will be of great classificatory value and can give indications of the correct proportion of relationship. We are already familiar with the brood care of many species. With one species, it is an "obviously conscious and efficient nest-building"; with another species, it is an establishment of the female organism itself (egg-live-bearing) for the preservation of the young, while with *C. arnoldi*, the continued existence of the species must be guaranteed by how far out of reach the spawn is placed—out of reach of the parents themselves (?) and whatever enemies may be near. Here, "enemies" does not necessarily mean predators. Practically every fish eats eggs and young fry.

Brood care consists here of laying the eggs out of water. Among these fish, the ability to remain out of water by hanging on with their fins is highly developed (it is perhaps less known that many other fishes can do the same thing). Use is made of this ability in the mating season. After the male has hunted up a suitable place (he observes this place from all sides and sometimes makes a few "test jumps"), he invites the female and together they jump towards the chosen place, and hang on tight. Then, the female releases a jelly-like mass containing dozens of eggs, which adhere to the surface and which are immediately fertilized by the male.

This laying process takes at most 20 seconds. It is remarkable that a second laying always takes place alongside the first, such that one layer of jelly does not lie over the other. If the space is large enough, a total of more than 200 eggs can be laid. The most beautiful and natural way, of course, is when the fish lay their eggs on plants above water (leaves of floating plants) or upon stones. If such an opportunity is not available—or if they do not like it if it is—they then lay the eggs on vertical or horizontal glass panes (on the underside, of course) with equal ease.

Still, the male's job is not finished, for to prevent the spawn from drying out, he keeps it wet in a unique and extremely effective way. By powerful movements of his caudal fin, in which the large upper lobe performs yeoman service, he splashes drops of water upon the mass of eggs. He repeats the splashing with surprising regularity every 15 to 20 minutes, two to three days running, until the young burst out of the egg capsules and glide into the water, seeking refuge.

During the first three to seven days, not much is seen of the fry, unless they are visible hanging to the panes or water plants. After three to ten days, the young, sometimes rather strongly differing in development, swim freely about at the surface. Then they like to seek out each other's company and swim about in a little school. Bring them up on infusoria and fine-strained waterfleas. After about ten days, they will eat large food without difficulty.

It goes without saying that this fish, which likes to jump out, requires a not-too-small and especially well covered aquarium. The temperature should be about 24 °C (75 °F), and there should be dark bottom soil and thick growth in places. C. arnoldi likes a corner with a few floating plants in it to which it can retire from time to time. Moreover, it does not make many demands, and certainly not with respect to feeding. In addition to the usual kinds of live food, it will also accept dried food (if offered sparingly and separately from other food).

This is a fish which, since its first importation into Germany in 1905,

Plate II-104. *Copella callolepis.*

has not only kept its place, but has continually gained popularity as an aquarium fish, and rightly so. It is a beautiful fish, peaceful and interesting to watch, especially during the mating time described above. In all respects an extremely suitable aquarium dweller, this species reproduces readily and without difficulty. Undoubtedly, this has affirmed its popularity, and is the reason it has been able to keep its place.

Genus *Pyrrhulina*

All described *Pyrrhulina* species have become known in hobbyist circles, although the type species *P. filamentosa* and *Copella arnoldi* are certainly the best known and are also more commonly bred.

Pyrrhulina brevis Steindachner, 1875

This species is known to hail from the Amazon Basin and the Rio Negro in Brazil. It attains a length of about 80 mm ($3\frac{3}{16}$ inches). The basic coloration is bluish, turning lighter towards the belly, the head more rosy. The fins are orange to orange-red, more yellowish in the female. The well accentuated, dark stripes in the pattern, the spot in the dorsal fin, and the edging of the anal and ventral fins can be a very deep black. The back exhibits a beautiful brownish green to greenish brown sheen. The flanks are decorated with about four rows of very large, carmine red dots. In general, it comes very close to *P. rachoviana*.

Pyrrhulina brevis should be kept the same as *Copella arnoldi* (see page 572), although it is generally a less active species. Nothing is known of breeding results.

Plate II-105. *Pyrrhulina filamentosa.*

Illus. II-116. *Pyrrhulina laeta.*

Pyrrhulina laeta (Cope, 1872)
Half-Banded Pyrrhulina

This species, hailing from the upper Amazon and Peru, is quite similar to *P. nigrofasciata* and *P. rachoviana*. It is very possible that in the course of time these three species will be brought together into one species. *P. laeta* has perhaps already been imported as an aquarium fish, without its having been recognized as such. Like all the other varieties of this genus, it is a very attractive fish, and will certainly do well in the aquarium.

Pyrrhulina melanostoma (Cope, 1872)
Black Mouth Pyrrhulina

This is a rather frequently occurring species which is becoming continually better known as *P. semifasciata*. It is distributed from the Amazon River and the state of Paraná in Brazil and Ecuador to Colombia and the Guianas. It should be kept like *P. rachoviana*. Nothing is known about breeding it.

Pyrrhulina metae (Eigenmann, 1914)

Closer study of various samples of *Pyrrhulina* and *Copeina* has brought a change in current opinions concerning these genera. Although two groups can undoubtedly be distinguished within the Pyrrhulinini, the boundaries of these genera are different than is generally supposed. The one or two rows of teeth in the upper jaw are not the most important characteristic, but the genus characteristics lie elsewhere.

Pyrrhulina rachoviana Myers, 1926
Fanning Characin
Rachow's Pyrrhulina

This species, a southern variety from the La Plata River region of Uruguay, is quite similar to *P. brevis*, but in this case the head is more stumpy looking. The dark stripe running from the snout continues through to the rear, changing into a darker coloration flowing out upon the caudal fin.

The fish lays its eggs on plants, but seems to prefer certain broad-leaf varieties. If it does not like the plants available, it then makes ready a place on the bottom for the spawn.

From 50 to 200 eggs are laid per mating period, and these are watched over and fanned by the male. After the first day, all the eggs will have fallen to the bottom, where, within the second day, the young emerge and hang by threads from plants or stones (or panes).

The water should not be too deep, with a temperature of 18–25 °C (64–77 °F). The parents must be removed from a small tank or from one where the plants offer little shelter for the young.

Pyrrhulina vittata Regan, 1912
Striped Pyrrhulina

This especially attractive and very suitable aquarium fish exhibits a number of characteristics of its relatives—the comparatively small size (about 70 mm or 2¾ inches), the soft pastel tints of its cousin *Copeina guttata* and the ornamental swimming movements of a *Pyrrhulina filamentosa*.

The basic coloration, as can be seen in Plate II–106, is a very soft blue-green, the back somewhat brownish, the belly rosy. In the mating season, the belly region of the male often turns a deep, flaming red. The fins are blue-grey or practically transparent, gradually turning to a soft rose as the size increases, turning again to yellowish red or bright red in the mating season. Young specimens show the spot characteristic of the group in the dorsal fin, but this spot disappears, as it does in *Copeina guttata*, practically entirely in the older fish. It remains visible longer in the female. In many respects, *P. vittata* strongly resembles *Copeina guttata*, which has resulted in doubt concerning the characteristics of the genus, since these two varieties are classified in two separate genera. Biologically considered, they are certainly most closely related. Further study of *P. vittata* in the aquarium, particularly its reproductive biology, is of great importance. Perhaps it behaves like *C. guttata*, yet maybe too it does not. So far as is known, only a single report has appeared concerning it (Van Dijck, 1956), which observed that mating was carried on about as described for *Copeina guttata*, except that the eggs were not laid in a hole or trench, but on a leaf. The eggs, possessing no adhesive in *P. vittata*, fall off the leaf as the male fans them, so that this manner of laying must be assumed to be abnormal.

In a note on Van Dijck's article, Van den Nieuwenhuizen remarks that fanning the eggs, which had indeed been laid on a leaf, was carried out more vigorously than among the cichlids, for example.

Although *P. vittata* has already been bred for a long time, still little is known about the actual procedure of reproduction.

Finally, it must be noted that doubt was cast on the correct name for this fish at first sight of the photo. It appeared hardly possible that a variety so closely related to *Copeina guttata* had been placed in the genus *Pyrrhulina*. It is, however, clear, as already noted, that the correct definition of these two genera is not a matter of a few days' work. A revision must be undertaken, which will take maybe a year or perhaps longer. Because the fish in Plate II–106 agree in detail with Regan's description of *vittata*, there is certainly no objection to using this

579

Plate II-106. *Pyrrhulina vittata.*

name, preferably, for the time being, in combination with the genus name *Pyrrhulina*.

Tribe Erythrinini

Often, very young Erythrinini specimens are brought in with import shipments. Then, they are indeed attractive little fish, but in a few weeks they have, for the most part, already grown up into dangerous predators, and are thus unattractive for most aquarists.

The most commonly occurring and best known species are: *Hoplerythrinus unitaeniatus* (Spix, 1829), *Hoplias malabaricus* (Bloch, 1794), and *Pseuderythrinus rosapinnis* Hoedeman, 1950.

Pseuderythrinus rosapinnis Hoedeman, 1950

This fish comes from Surinam, in the vicinity of Paramaribo. In 1950, this species was classified in the new genus, *Pseuderythrinus*, based on a specimen imported in March, 1949, which had been brought in from Surinam in a shipment of aquarium fishes. Numerous, especially young, specimens were imported from Surinam from November, 1951, to March, 1952.

Together with *Hoplias malabaricus, Hoplias macrophthalmus, Hoplerythrinus unitaeniatus* and *Erythrinus erythrinus,* this species forms a small group of tropical "pike," which are not normally kept in an aquarium. There are, however, always hobbyists (happily) who like to indulge in keeping lesser known varieties. They are never disappointed in their expectations, so far as this species is concerned. It is thus assumed that *Pseuderythrinus rosapinnis* is a "pike type." This fish does not hunt, as do the perch, for example, but lies in wait for its prey.

The specimen described here was first kept in an aquarium belonging to Mr. Van Boordt so that he could make a water-color painting of this beautiful fish.

The fish was then 105 mm (4$\frac{1}{8}$ inches) long and devoured before the author's eyes a 40 mm (1$\frac{5}{8}$ inches) long, female *Xiphophorus (Platypoecilus) maculatus,* as if it were no more than a fly. Catching the prey took place the same as if the specimen were a pike, the victim disappearing tail first. Warned by this observation, the author placed the predator in an aquarium with only a large (70 mm or 2$\frac{3}{4}$ inch) dwarf catfish (*Ictalurus nebulosus*) which, with its large head, would certainly run no danger of going the way of the female *X. maculatus.* Under the circumstances, it was given nothing suitable to eat, until it was served a fine portion of tubifex. Reacting as usual to every movement of the water, the predator shot forward, but lost all interest when it discovered what the food was. However, the dwarf catfish quickly came closer with pendulum-like movements, but before it could catch a single one of the little worms, it was seized by the rapacious predator.

The result was that only the hind quarters of the catfish—contrary to custom—were eaten, and the head, which was indeed too hard and too big, was left over. Of course, it was not a very refreshing show, but it did clearly demonstrate that fish, too, deviate from a certain norm, if the circumstances require it.

That *Pseuderythrinus* poses no threat to larger fish may become apparent in due course. Meanwhile, the fish was fed regularly on frogs, flies, other insects, earthworms, and such. The ordinary small food—such as tubifex, white worms, *Daphnia*, and the like—was not accepted. Its mouth is not made to accept such food, which also explains how the piranha can swim about in the midst of a school of guppies in the Artis aquarium (Amsterdam) without eating these small fish. Its mouth is set up only for "tearing" flesh—the flesh of larger fish.

In the course of time, this *Pseuderythrinus rosapinnis* was transferred to a larger tank in which there was an *Aequidens portalegrensis* couple and a *Hemichromis bimaculatus* couple. Before that, these cichlids had been giving each other a hard time, each apparently wishing to build a nest. They were about 100 to 130 mm (4 to 5⅛ inches) long and it seemed very improbable that the predator would fall upon these large, high fish. Nor did anything of the kind happen. However, the intruder was attacked with the combined strength of the cichlids (the two species had concluded a cease-fire), so that there was practically not even a fin left on its body. The poor fish was then freed from its hard-pressed position, and, astonishingly enough, its fins grew back completely in 10 days.

Of course, there is little to say about breeding this fish, as only a single specimen was available. Also, the related varieties (see above) which have indeed been kept, are equally unknown in regard to their reproductive activities. As far as temperature goes, it appears that even a drop to about 15 °C (59 °F) (at which point all action and reaction seems to cease) has no detrimental effect, provided, of course, that the change is effected gradually over a period of time. The fish should, however, normally be kept at 20–25 °C (68–77 °F). Feed with anything available, as long as it is alive. Waterfleas alone are not enough.

On the head are found the canals and pores that enable the fish to be aware of the least and smallest movement in the water. This system of pores and canals is connected with the well known lateral line organ and is very strongly developed. Every pore is connected to the outer world, in this case to the water, and internally passes on to the brain the slightest vibration, by means of an extremely fine net of nerve fibres. The transfer of these vibrations to the nervous system of the brain is not yet fully understood. Perhaps still other stimuli play a part in it.

The presence of this system, in practically all aquarium fishes in a more or less developed stage, explains much of their conduct, although a thorough investigation may yet bring to light the fine details involved.

Sub-family Hemiodontinae

This sub-family, called Hemiodontinae after the genus *Hemiodus*, includes the genera and tribes as described by previous authors, excluding the Characidiini (see Hoedeman, 1950) as well as *Paradon* and its relatives, which apparently do not belong in this sub-family.

The members of this sub-family are practically without exception aquarium fishes, and a considerable number of species are kept in aquariums. (NOTE: Most authors, including Berg, list this as a separate family, Hemiodontidae.)

Tribe Nannostomini

The members of this group occur in South America—the Guiana countries westwards to Colombia (the Orinoco River) and the Rio San Francisco along the Andes in Argentina.

NOTE: Some authors (Greenwood, Rosen, Weitzman and Myers) place this group in the family Lebiasinidae.

This group includes exclusively slim varieties of fishes that are more or less long and drawn out and moderately compressed. The height of the body runs about a third to a fifth of its length. The snout is usually pointed and the mouth is small and nonprotrusive, end-positioned. The jaws are set with firmly positioned, small, conical teeth that are either notched or equipped with fine points. The teeth in the upper jaw (premaxillary) and the lower jaw (dentary) are arranged in a single row.

The foremost opening in the top of the skull (the frontal fontanelle) is grown over; the rearmost, if present, is extremely small. An adipose fin is present, rudimentary, or entirely missing. Whether or not an adipose fin is present appears not to be of systematic value, as formerly suggested by some authors. In *Nannostomus marginatus*, for example, as well as in *Nannobrycon eques*, and even in specimens from the same nest, the adipose fin can be either present or absent. In young specimens up to about a month old with a length up to about 15 mm ($\frac{5}{8}$ inch), a tiny "spinelet," the so-called "urostyle," which is composed of the endmost tail vertebrae, can be found in front of the future caudal fin. Later on, this spinelet disappears and is included in the already further developed caudal fin. Notable among young specimens of Nannostomini is the way they move forward by means of the skin-fold around the urostyle. Not until later, when the caudal fin is rather large, does it take over the function of an organ of movement.

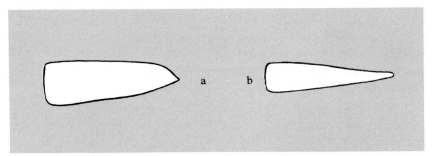

Illus. II-117. Swim bladder of a. *Nannostomus*, and of b. *Nannobrycon*, the latter being markedly thinner in the posterior end (right), thus giving less upward pressure, accounting for the typical angled position.

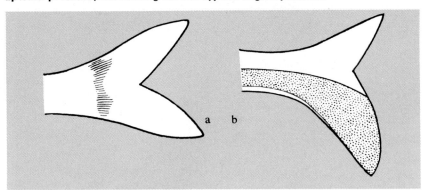

Illus. II-118. Caudal fin of a. *Nannostomus*, with equal lobes and practically without pigment cells (melanophores) and b. *Nannobrycon*, with enlarged lower lobe and numerous melanophores.

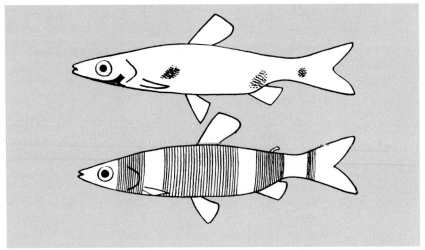

Illus. II-119. The extremes in the nocturnal markings of *Nannostomus beckfordi* and *N. trifasciatus*.

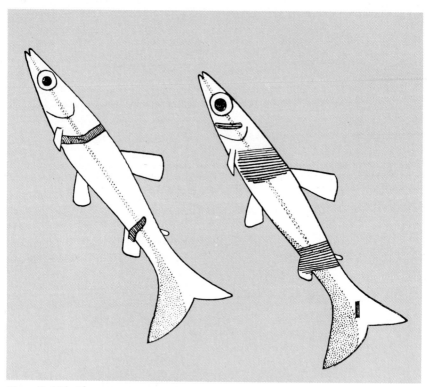

Illus. II-120. The extremes in the nocturnal markings of *Nannobrycon eques* in its typical, slanting swimming position.

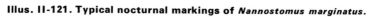

Illus. II-121. Typical nocturnal markings of *Nannostomus marginatus.*

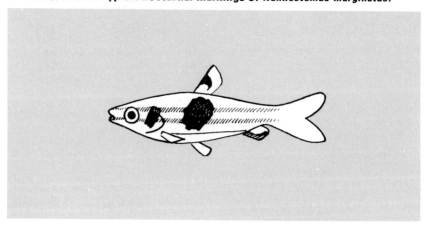

In his article, "Observations of the Nannostomidi," Van den Nieuwenhuizen describes those so suitable and always pretty species belonging to the three already-mentioned genera (see Hoedeman, 1954). He describes their mating and the differentiation of the sexes, on which point many questions still seem unanswered. Recognition of the sexes, however, is not simple, especially since those believed to be males sometimes appear more as females (or to have been females), for it also seems, among Nannostomini, that conspicuous male characteristics continue to exist among those later becoming female. The ice blue edging of the ventral fins, a male characteristic (the males also have some ice blue in the first rays of the anal fin), occurs in the larger females. Some of these females, upon examination, still possess remains of male sex organs. Sex change thus occurs in this group, also.

THE NOCTURNAL PATTERN OF THE NANNOSTOMINI

We shall devote some attention to the peculiar pattern which the Nannostomini exhibit under certain circumstances. Illus. II–117 to Illus. II–121 provide an idea of this pattern which appears as soon as the aquarium lighting is turned off, or as soon as the sun sets and no artificial light is turned on.

If artificial light is available and is turned on some time after the sun sets (the tank thus having stood in the dark for a short time), the night pattern can be observed quite well. Among the species *Nannostomus beckfordi* (syn. *N. anomalus*) and *N. trifasciatus*, the dark lengthwise pattern disappears and its place is taken by a cross pattern, of which the extremes are shown in Illus. II–119. In the case of *Nannostomus marginatus*, this is usually no more nor less than in Illus. II–121, while *Nannobrycon eques* (Illus. II–120) shows variation.

If the light is turned on suddenly in the dark, then the fish becomes frightened and reacts to it in various ways. Sometimes it shoots wildly away (a defence against harm) and disappears among the plants. Other times, it may remain fixed in place, but in every case, the normal day pattern slowly re-appears after a short time. It may show this pattern in full light, which is an indication that it does not feel at ease, that it is frightened, startled, or sick.

Genus *Nannobrycon*

This genus is clearly distinguished from the remaining Nannostomini by its angled swimming posture and the characteristics named below.

Several "species" have been described in the course of time, which, however, as well as can be shown, all belong to one true, if indeed variable, species, *Nannobrycon eques*. There are, however, terms present for distinguishing at least two varieties.

Nannobrycon eques (Steindachner, 1876)

This fish is found in stagnant or slowly flowing waters with reed- or grass-grown banks in South America—in the Amazon Basin, Rio Negro, and the Guianas. It was introduced into Europe for the first time at Hamburg in 1910, and since then has been imported from time to time.

Nannobrycon always exhibits the more or less pike-like body hanging at an angle. It is strongly compressed only in the tail.

The pointed snout has only a small, end-positioned mouth. Further structure and placement of the fins are clearly shown in Plate II–107.

Plate II-107.
Nannobrycon eques eques.

Plate II-108. *Nannobrycon eques ocellatus.*

The lower caudal fin lobe is considerably larger than the upper, respectively with 14 and 9 fin rays. The small difference in coloration between the sexes is present in the redder lower lobe of the caudal fin and the red anal fin, and possibly in the over-all, somewhat more distinct coloration of the male. The male is, at the same time, somewhat slimmer than the female and grows to a maximum length of 48 mm (about $1\frac{7}{8}$ inches), while the female can grow to 54 mm (about $2\frac{1}{8}$ inches). The dorsal, ventral and pectoral fins vary from being without coloration to being light rose, and are transparent. The upper lobe of the caudal fin is equally transparent, or somewhat greyish among the males. The porcelain white dot on the lower lobe of the caudal fin is sometimes more and sometimes less apparent.

This fish should not be kept in aquariums that are too high, long or wide, but rather more medium in measurements, thickly planted around the sides, and provided with floating plants. The lighting should not be too bright, although a few rays from the sun are always welcome. The water must be soft, with a pH value of between 5.2 and 7, preferably about 6. The temperature should be 22–26 °C (72–79 °F).

All suitable food animals, if not too large for their small mouths, are

589

gladly accepted by *N. eques.* In this regard, it is certainly not a choosy fish.

Reproduction is carried on in the calm manner that typifies the entire life of this stately fish. Although they put on a show of surprising speed from time to time, the male approaches the female at the time of mating rather calmly and they swim at a certain angle to each other, with the male at an angle above the female, snout to snout, in so-called horseback fashion. The eggs are rather large and are laid three or four at a time among the fine-leaved plants, or on the underside of coarse-leaved plants, sometimes also among the floating plants, in any case usually close to the surface. The total number of eggs per period may reach 100 to 150. The young hatch out on the third day, sometimes within 50 hours, and are not difficult to raise.

Here, too, the peculiar nocturnal or dusk pattern occurs.

Plate II-109. *Nannobrycon eques unifasciatus.*

Plate II-110. *Nannostomus beckfordi.*

Genus *Nannostomus*

Of the entire sub-family, this is perhaps the best-known and best-liked genus, and it includes several little ornamental tropical fishes. In 1953, among a shipment of fish from Surinam, an entirely new species was found (*N. bifasciatus*), described on page 595 and illustrated in Plate II–111.

Distinguishing the genus *Nannobrycon* from *Nannostomus* is based, in part, on a very remarkable characteristic with which every aquarist was familiar, yet which had not actually been officially noted. It was a matter of the angled rest and swimming position of *Nannobrycon*, which is caused, in the first place, by the shape of the rear part of the swim bladder. At the same time, the caudal fin has adapted to the angled position, as a result of which the lower lobe of the caudal fin possesses more rays, and is larger, than the upper lobe.

Nannostomus beckfordi Günther, 1872

Nannostomus beckfordi inhabits South America—the Amazon Basin, Rio Negro and possibly also Guyana (formerly British Guiana). A few specimens were imported into Europe for the first time in 1911, and since then this little fish has become a welcome guest on the hobbyist scene.

591

This ornamental characin, about 40 mm (1⅝ inches) long, has a slim, moderately rounded figure, round on the belly side. Both dorsal and anal fins have a short base; the first is located about in the middle of the back. An adipose fin is absent, to which this *Nannostomus* is indebted for its old name *N. anomalus* (deviating). On the upper part of the root of the tail (farther towards the back than where an adipose fin would normally be located), the young fish, of about a week old, exhibit a sharp outgrowth similar to a small spine. This growth is the urostyle, which is almost as long as the topmost fin ray of the caudal fin. After about two months, this little spine disappears again.

For such a small fish, the scales covering the body of *N. beckfordi* are rather large. On the flanks, the scales are pierced by a lateral line organ. The vertically compressed and pointed snout has a small, end-positioned mouth and nostrils positioned quite close together. The skull and the rear part of the head are flat and possess no covering of scales. The caudal fin is forked and the two caudal fin lobes are somewhat sharply pointed. All the fins are well developed.

The basic coloration is, as Plate II–110 clearly shows, yellowish brown, turning, towards the back, into a brownish red and, towards the belly, from brown to yellowish. The throat and belly areas are whitish. Over the entire body, from the point of the snout to the root of the tail, runs a reddish yellow-green gleaming band, which is accompanied on the underside by a dark brown to black stripe. The net-like pattern over the entire body is caused by the dark edging of the scales. The large, lively eyes are black with a golden yellow iris. The ventral fins are sometimes a soft rose red with blue dots, the other fins being transparent and practically without coloration, with the exception of the caudal fin which, especially among the males, is sometimes bright red on the underside. Also, the lengthwise stripe of the male is bordered on the upper edge by a bright red band. Although the sexes are difficult to distinguish from each other, sometimes the males can be clearly recognized by the more highly developed anal fin, of which the first four rays are broader and more branched than those of the female, which are cut off further, compared to the rounded anal fin of the male.

Except that this fish requires a good deal of warmth (not below 22 °C or 72 °F), it is not especially demanding. *Nannostomus beckfordi* is a nice little fish for community and family aquariums. When kept with strange and large fish, however, it remains shy and does not show up to its best advantage. Also, in a tank that is too small (minimum contents should be about 15 litres or about 4 gallons per specimen), *N. beckfordi* does not feel at ease, a state of mind that clearly shows up in the loss of practically all coloration at the time of day when it is normally lively and lovely. For food, provide mainly live food, alternating kinds. In case of need, resort to dried animal food, which will not, however, be happily accepted, especially not if it has not been softened in water beforehand.

Although not easy to accomplish, breeding at a temperature of 25–28 °C (77–82 °F) presents a very interesting show for the real hobbyist. This is recommended only for the advanced aquarist. Patience and experience at having conducted other breedings are indispensable, as are insight and the necessary precautions with temperature and water composition. Note especially that not just any male and female may form a suitable breeding system, but once a couple has been formed, the whole process sometimes meets with unusual success.

The number of eggs laid each time seldom count more than about 20. They are mainly and preferably laid among the thick clumps of fine-leaved plants. To be certain that the comparatively small number of eggs is not nibbled at by the parents, the parents should be removed from the breeding tank *immediately* after laying, when they are tired out and resting on the bottom. During the process, be especially careful that the temperature and constitution of the water do not vary. The eggs hatch in two to five days and raising the young begins. They grow quickly on a good, rich diet of infusoria and after a week can be put on a "waterflea hunt."

From time to time, these tender, lovely little fish betray their predatory nature. If you watch them regularly and carefully, you may observe that they will ignore the most delicious food particles for the eggs of other fishes or even for their own eggs—at least, if they get a chance at them. Even with their sharp snout and small mouth opening, *N. beckfordi* can catch and swallow a week-old fry of live-bearing fishes. Although often considered as shy, timorous fish, they do sometimes make one think of a pike as they stand motionless among the plants, with their fins violently vibrating. Yet they can be kept in the same aquarium with other fishes of about their own size and much pleasure can be experienced from them.

In the wild, *N. beckfordi* lives in rather shallow, calm waters, cut off from the main current by sand banks, among profusely thick plant growth where the principal floating plant is the *Salvinia brasiliensis*, in company with its nearest relatives, *Poecilobrycon* and *Nannobrycon* species, the peculiar *Gymnotus carapo* and *Electrophorus electricus*, as well as various Siluriformes (catfishes), such as *Bunocephalus chamaizelus*. In addition to the so-called savannah creeks, *Nannostomus beckfordi* is also found in many jungle creeks, in company with hatchet fishes (Gasteropelecini), *Hemigrammus* and again *Poecilobrycon* and *Nannobrycon* species. They are never found in water that is wholly open, but always in areas protected by water- and marsh-plants or bank growth.

Whether Meinken's *Nannostomus aripirangensis* may be taken strictly as a synonym of *N. beckfordi* or not, or can better be considered a subspecies, has been left an open question for lack of scientific material. However, the differences are such that, for the time being, certainly the relationship of *N. aripirangensis* as a local variety of *N. beckfordi* should willingly be introduced. Available material about *N. beckfordi* shows such wide variation that the variety *N. aripirangensis* could well fall within it. This concept, of course, is not a law and anybody can and may differ from this opinion. Classification is now largely based on the opinions of the compilers of the different groups. That the different varieties of *N. beckfordi* will not cross successfully is not enough basis not to consider them members of a common species. Many species include local varieties which do not or no longer mutually recognize each other as potential mating partners.

Nannostomus bifasciatus Hoedeman, 1953
Two-Lined Pencil Fish

This species comes from Surinam, in the vicinity of Berg and Dal. It was imported through Blijdorp, the Rotterdam Zoo (the Netherlands), in March, 1952. This species is an important and splendid acquisition for the hobby and, at the same time, is of much significance to science. Like its nearest relatives, *Nannostomus beckfordi* and *Nannostomus trifasciatus*, it reaches a length of about 40 mm (1⅝ inches). He who does not look beneath the surface will probably be confused by the similarity in pattern of the lower caudal fin lobe, which is indeed a great deal like that of *Nannobrycon eques*. Whatever the relationship with the genera *Poecilobrycon* and *Nannobrycon* may be, it appears, nevertheless, clearly to be a *Nannostomus*.

The basic coloration of *Nannostomus bifasciatus* is whitish to gleaming silver, with a rosy golden sheen. From the lower jaw, through the eye, to the tail root, then flowing out along the rays of the lower caudal fin lobe runs an intensely black band. If an imaginary line is drawn from the tip of the snout to the middle of the tail root, then it appears as if the half of the fish above the line is the negative of the half below it. Among the females only, the belly region may be somewhat more sturdily built, but this comparison does not entirely hold true.

The fins of *N. bifasciatus* are without coloration and transparent, except for the lower lobe of the caudal fin with the black out-flowing of the lengthwise band and the ice blue tips of the ventral fins, especially in the male. Sometimes a soft red appears on the base of the caudal fin, as it does among other *Nannostomus* species. A red-gold line runs from the point of the snout on the division of the white-and-black lengthwise band to about under the dorsal fin.

In spite of its lack of coloration, only white and black in various nuances and a little red-gold, *N. bifasciatus* is one of the most attractive nannostomins and a very welcome addition to the hobby. Reproduction is carried on in the same way as among its close relatives.

How important the discovery of a new species is may appear in the conclusions drawn from the data which a number of dead specimens can provide, in addition to a study of the living fish.

Up to a short time ago, the genus *Nannostomus* was considered the most original (most primitive) of the three now known genera of the tribe Nannostomini—*Poecilobrycon, Nannostomus* and *Nannobrycon*. *N. bifasciatus*, however, not only takes a place among these three genera, but it also connects *Poecilobrycon* with *Nannostomus* and *Nannobrycon*. This is not only expressed in the pattern, but at the same time in the technical characteristics—the number of scales, fin rays, the state of the teeth, the form and structure of the swim bladder, and so on.

Plate II-111. *Nannostomus bifasciatus.*

Plate II-112. *Nannostomus ocellatus.*

Nannostomus espei (Meinken, 1956)

This fish looks like the other varieties of *Poecilobrycon* and *Nannostomus,* but with about five cross stripes running slantingly forward on the under half of the body. These stripes occupy the same place where, in other varieties, the peculiar night pattern appears.

Although it may indeed seem that we have here an unknown variety, the author's report is hardly accounted for by the form in which the description and nomenclature are presented. (NOTE: At the time Meinken's paper was published, Böhlke's paper describing the same species was on press. Böhlke, however, described the fish as a *Nannostomus* species and revised his paper to retain Meinken's specific name, but not his generic name (*Poecilobrycon*). This considerably more detailed paper certainly substantiates the validity of this fish as a new species.)

Plate II-113. *Nannostomus espei.*

Plate II-114. *Nannostomus marginatus.*

Nannostomus marginatus Eigenmann, 1909
Marginatus Pencil Fish

This species is also found in South America—in the lower reaches of the Amazon and in the Guianas. Like its relatives, it is a fish from calm, shallow waters. It has been known in hobbyist circles since 1928, but since it was hardly ever re-bred, it always died out again. At the present time, *N. marginatus* is being bred successfully by many aquarists and will certainly continue to become more popular.

Those hobbyists who consider this fish the most beautiful of the tribe are undoubtedly right. *Nannostomus marginatus* grows no longer than 30 mm $(1\frac{3}{16}$ inches) without the caudal fin. The shape of the body is somewhat more thick-set, hence a little higher, than in *N. beckfordi* and *N. trifasciatus*. It is very closely related to the latter and is quite similar to it in coloration and pattern. The most important point of difference—in addition, naturally, to the shape, fin rays and number of scales—is the black border to the anal fin, which is absent in *Nannostomus trifasciatus*.

A form and coloration description in addition to Plate II–114 are superfluous, so that only the sexual characteristics will be pointed out—the red dots above the middlemost, dark lengthwise stripe on the males, which also occur in *N. trifasciatus*. The first rays of the dorsal fin are always quite clearly black, much more so than in *N. trifasciatus*. These fish are kept the same as their related species in a somewhat sun-lit, roomy, but not too large, and well planted aquarium with a considerable open space. Plant *Riccia, Salvinia* and, in larger tanks, some floating *Ceratopteris* varieties or *Eichhornia crassipes*, because *N. marginatus* like to rest among the roots of floating plants and also prefer to lay their eggs among them.

Although *N. marginatus* have already been kept in hobbyists' aquariums for dozens of years, up to a short time ago, practically no sign of re-breeding was seen. Yet, breeding is no more difficult than with *Nannostomus beckfordi* or the other Nannostomini. The number of eggs laid per period, however, is rather small, a maximum of 100. The temperature limits are 18–26 °C (64–79 °F). At temperatures below 20 °C (68 °F), if constant, *N. marginatus* do not feel very well, which shows up clearly in their conduct. At 22 °C (72 °F) or a little warmer, they are, however, very active and lay eggs spontaneously, even in community aquariums. The eggs are very small and cream-tinted. Hatching of the young and raising them is the same as described for the other *Nannostomus* varieties.

Contrary to the common opinion that Nannostomini are very sensitive to the hardness and acidity of the water, this is the case much less than may actually be expected. They feel well and very much at home and the young grow up in neutral water, or water of slight acid or alkaline content (pH 6.5 to 7.5) with a hardness of about 13.5. At a hardness of 9 and more, however, hatching of the eggs seems to be slowed down too much. Of course, still more factors can have a rôle in this.

Although *N. marginatus* likes to have a little sun in the aquarium (hence the advice for a lightly sunny aquarium location), it is desirable that there also be places that are completely dark. Bright light is harmful to the eggs and also, at first, the young prefer the shadows.

Nannostomus trifasciatus Steindachner, 1876
Three-Lined Pencil Fish

This species also comes from South America—the Amazon Basin and Rio Negro, from Guyana (British Guiana), and apparently also from Surinam and French Guiana. It has been kept in hobbyists' aquariums at intervals since 1912.

A species that grows to about 40 mm (1⅝ inches) long, *N. trifasciatus* has a body shape quite a bit similar to *Nannostomus beckfordi*. It is distinguished from this species, however, by the larger number of scales in the lengthwise direction.

Plate II-115. *Nannostomus trifasciatus.*

The basic coloration is silvery to purplish brown, and is very variable. The belly is whitish, the back darker. Over the body run three dark bands. The middle one runs from the lower jaw, through the eye and to the underside of the root of the tail where it runs out into a more or less blurred spot. The same happens with the upper stripe, which runs from the uppermost edge of the gill cover to the upper side of the tail root. The third stripe runs from just behind the pectoral fins, is usually somewhat less distinct in appearance, and ends anteriorly in a dark spot at the base of the anal fin. Above the uppermost stripe, in the dark back area, a fourth stripe, which is very irregular and consists of a number of dots and short stripes, is usually found. The coloration is the same as for *N. marginatus*, except that *N. trifasciatus* lacks the black edging to the anal fin. Distinguishing the sexes is very simple for an expert, and the layman can always rely on the stippled red line that is located on the middle dark stripe of the males, between the rear edge of the gill cover and the start of the dorsal fin.

With the exception of the caudal and pectoral fins, which are without coloration to very light blue, the fins are reddish, turning from porcelain white to bluish at the back, near the top. The foremost rays or the undermost points of the ventral fins are bright blue in fine young and old specimens of both sexes.

This species is best kept in an aquarium with its nearest relatives and smaller species. The aquarium should be roomy, yet not too large, and placed in a somewhat sunny location.

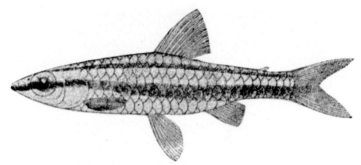

Illus. II-122. *Poecilobrycon digrammus.*

Genus *Poecilobrycon*

This genus, with two species, *P. harrisoni* and *P. digrammus*, is characterized by a long, stretched-out body, rather long snout, adipose fin behind the end of the anal fin, and two caudal fin lobes of the same shape.

At least one of the two species, namely *P. harrisoni*, has been imported and kept in aquariums.

Poecilobrycon digrammus Fowler, 1913

This variety can hardly be distinguished from *P. harrisoni*. Up to now, it has not been imported.

Poecilobrycon harrisoni Eigenmann, 1909

Harrison's Pencil Fish

This nannostomin compares very well with its related species (*Nannobrycon* and *Nannostomus* species). Refer to them for details.

Plate II-116. *Poecilobrycon harrisoni.*

Tribe Hemiodontini

The genera *Anisitsia, Hemiodus* and *Pterohemiodus* are included in this tribe.

Only *Hemiodus* has, up to now, yielded a species which could be considered an aquarium fish.

Not only do a number of species imported since 1954 belong in this group, but at the same time there appeared a welcome revision of the group (see Böhlke, 1955), of great importance to the scientific placement of the species and no less important to aquarists.

Illus. II-123. Sketches of coloration patterns.

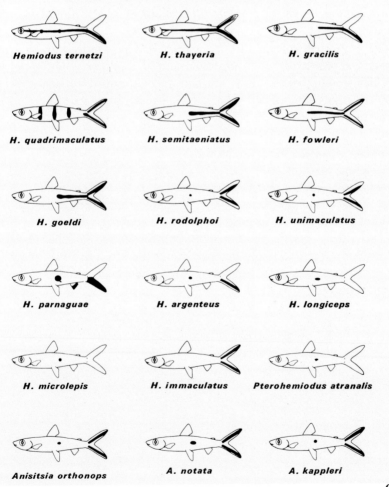

Hemiodus ternetzi   *H. thayeria*   *H. gracilis*

H. quadrimaculatus   *H. semitaeniatus*   *H. fowleri*

H. goeldi   *H. rodolphoi*   *H. unimaculatus*

H. parnaguae   *H. argenteus*   *H. longiceps*

H. microlepis   *H. immaculatus*   *Pterohemiodus atranalis*

Anisitsia orthonops   *A. notata*   *A. kappleri*

Genus *Hemiodus*

This genus is represented by numerous species in the Amazon Basin. In Böhlke's revision, attention was first paid to the coloration pattern of the various species. Although there is a different pattern for each variety, there is also clearly a basic pattern that is a foundation from which a development can be derived.

Two known species—*H. ternetzi* and *H. thayeria*—possess this basic pattern, which consists of a dark stripe that runs from the eye to the root of the tail and then bends down into the lower lobe of the caudal fin. In the lengthwise stripe are two black spots, one opposite the tip of the pectoral fins, a second opposite the tip of the ventral fins. The last spot especially is always found in the various species. A spreading of the pigment, weaker than elsewhere, is found, moreover, in the upper lobe of the caudal fin of *H. thayeria*. This pigment is also found in other species.

The imported species are *H. gracilis, H. quadrimaculatus, H. semitaeniatus, H. unimaculatus, H. argenteus,* and *H. microlepis.* Böhlke did not consider to what extent these are true species, and it appears that the problem is not yet solved, especially because of the variability of the different varieties.

Hemiodus argenteus Pellegrin, 1908
Silver Hemiodus

So far as is known, *Hemiodus argenteus* comes from Venezuela, but the catch location on the Para River, Surinam, is not certain.

What is true for all imported specimens may also be applied here; still, practically nothing is known about most of the species or varieties, although they undoubtedly belong among the attractive fish which, in many aspects, may be compared with the much smaller growing Nannostomini.

Sub-family Anostominae

This is a well defined group of South American characins, of which a number of species are of significance to the aquarist. Six tribes are distinguished, of which five possess a few species suitable as aquarium fish.

Genus *Anostomus*

Of the five described species, only two are known to hobbyists.

Anostomus anostomus (Linné, 1766)

Striped Anostomus

In South America, this fish is found in the Guianas and the Amazon Basin, in moderately running water and quiet river bends under the bank (among growths of reeds and grass).

It was first imported to Hamburg in 1924 by Eimeke, and after that, many times—and numerous specimens. Imported specimens have also been recently received.

Anostomus anostomus is an attractive fish, even though it grows rather large. It may attain a length of 136 mm (5⅜ inches) in both sexes. Nevertheless, it is a very suitable species for somewhat larger community tanks. It has a vibrant pattern, is lively and is very tolerant. It often shows off with its peculiar "head stand." It is fond of resting often among the plants and also of looking for food on the bottom, and at these times its position is like that of *Nannobrycon eques*, but with the head down, as also exhibited by *Chilodus punctatus*. It can easily assume this position because its swim bladder runs far to the rear and is not as wide at the front, compared to most of its relatives. The lateral line organ is complete and well developed.

The basic coloration of *Anostomus anostomus* is golden yellow with a metallic gleam. Three black, lengthwise bands can be seen, the middle one being widest and most intense. The bases of the dorsal, anal and caudal fins are blood red to carmine. Fine examples are often, especially on the tail, suffused with a soft red. The sexes are practically the same in shape and pattern, except that the red on the females is somewhat weaker and their bellies are rounder. The males can have a "sucked in" stomach, which often gives the impression that they are sick. However, this is in no way disturbing in young specimens provided that the line of the abdomen shows no inward curve but is almost straight.

Real pleasure can be had from this species if the fish are kept in a

Plate II-117. *Anostomus anostomus.*

very roomy aquarium, 100 cm (39¼ inches) or more in length. They require a thick edge planting, for, although this fish is not shy, it likes to rest among the plants where it is concealed, with its head slanting downward.

A temperature between 22–26 °C (72–79 °F) appears to be the most suitable, preferably about 24 °C (75 °F). The fish is then at its liveliest and the attractive pattern is shown off to best advantage.

A. anostomus will accept all kinds of food, though worm-like creatures have the most attraction for it. While certainly not predatory, it scorns young fishes no more than its relatives, the Nannostomini, do. Even just-born fry of live-bearers are often considered suitable food. Nevertheless, they can be kept with even very small species without trouble.

Grobe describes the aggressive conduct which this species sometimes takes against its aquarium companions without, however, its being dangerous or predatory. When looking for food on the bottom, *A. anostomus* assumes a vertical position (which is also assumed whenever it stops to rest) and as soon as something is suspected of being edible, the fish turns over with its belly up and roots into the ground and among the stones with its upper lip and nose.

604

A rather large species, certainly one of the most beautiful and suitable for the home aquarium, *A. anostomus* fully deserves a thorough study. For, although it is one of the species long known to science, practically nothing is known about *A. anostomus'* living habits. Breeding results are also still unknown.

Anostomus trimaculatus, the Three-spotted Anostomus, is to be kept in the same way as this species.

Anostomus taeniatus, the Banded Anostomus, was imported for a number of years. It is also a "head stander," exhibiting a pattern of conduct quite similar to that of *Chilodus punctatus*, and the lengthwise stripe is also the same. It lacks the small spots on the scales, however (see page 607).

Plate II-118. *Anostomus trimaculatus.*

Plate II-119. *Abramites hypselonotus.*

Genus *Abramites*

Abramites hypselonotus (Günther, 1868)
Small-Headed Abramites
Striped Head Stander

Abramites hypselonotus hails from the lower Amazon and is represented in the Guianas (at least in Surinam) by a sub-species.

Both sexes attain a length of a good 65 mm ($2\frac{9}{16}$ inches) (not including the caudal fin) and are especially suited for a tank that is not too small, because of their particular life style. The angled swimming and resting position are the most striking features of this fish. Standing among the plants, where they prefer to hide, they always keep their heads down; while swimming, the position is at a somewhat lesser angle.

Although the coloration is limited to a sprinkling of black and white with all the combinations of grey in between, *A. hypselonotus* is a very attractive fish.

The female, shown in Plate II–119, has more bands in her pattern than the male and she can be especially recognized by the dark border to the anal fin.

This species is claimed to be a desperate plant-eater, which ruins any tank vegetation. As far as further particulars are concerned, the best reference can be made to *Chilodus punctatus*, to which *Abramites hypselonotus* is quite similar in habit. So far as is known, *A. hypselonotus* has never been successfully bred in captivity.

Genus *Chilodus*

Chilodus punctatus Müller & Troschel, 1844

Head Stander

Spotted Head Stander

This species inhabits the northern part of South America. Known to aquarists for many years and always kept with pleasure, this fish exhibits a remarkable swimming position from which is derived its name, "the head stander." This name, like many other popular names, can in fact be applied not only to this species, but also to related species, such as, for example, *Abramites hypselonotus*, which take on the same peculiar posture.

The basic coloration of *Chilodus punctatus* is light brownish to olive brown, the sides gleaming silver with a net-like pattern from the dark edges to the scales. The various local varieties (sub-species and varieties) also have different patterns, in which a more or less wide, black band runs from the head to the root of the tail (in both sexes), or is dispersed into a row of spots or dots. The net-like pattern may be concentrated into blackish spots on the scales, while a black spot of variable tone (or several small spots) is present in the dorsal fin.

Since *Chilodus punctatus* dwells among the bank growth in clear

Plate II-120. *Chilodus punctatus.*

607

water, the aquarium should be set up similarly. Keep the temperature between 18 and 26 °C (64–79 °F). In general, *C. punctatus* should be kept like the Nannostomini, taking into account that the specialty on their menu consists of small food creatures and algae.

Feigs discussed the reproduction of this exceptional fish in detail, and although his report does not describe a first breeding, it is certainly the most detailed of any so far published.

Genus *Curimatopsis*

Up to now, only two species have been described, *C. macrolepis* and *C. saladensis*, both of which can be classified as very suitable, though rather robust, aquarium fish. They are quite similar to *Curimatus spilurus* mentioned above.

Curimatopsis macrolepis Steindachner, 1876

Large-Scaled Curimatopsis

A species that usually alternates in numerous catches with *Curimatus spilurus*, from which (see Plate II–122) it appears to differ very little. It is striking that, in the material from Surinam (vicinity of Berlijn), this species was much more abundant (in March) than *Curimatus spilurus*, while according to Eigenmann (1912: 261) in a collection from Rockstone (Essequibo River, Guyana), only 16 specimens of *Curimatopsis macrolepis* were found among 323 *Curimatus spilurus*.

The Surinamese variety deviates in detail from the earlier described varieties of *Curimatopsis macrolepis* only slightly and will probably appear to be a sub-species that has not yet been described.

Curimatopsis saladensis Meinken, 1933

This species attains a length of about 60 mm (2⅜ inches) and is the only one of this tribe for whom breeding results have been described (Meinken). In this respect, *C. saladensis* can be well likened to *Hemigrammus unilineatus*, which is one of the larger tetras.

Plate II-122. *Curimatopsis macrolepis.*

Genus *Curimatus*

This genus includes dozens of species, a number of which have been kept by aquarists for a long time. They generally occur in all kinds of calm water in practically every part of South America. The species are all easily recognizable by the absence of teeth as well as by the absence of scales on the caudal fin, and by a complete lateral line organ. *Curimatus spilurus* and *Curimatus argenteus* especially have been kept in aquariums.

Curimatus spilurus Günther, 1864

This species has a distribution that covers practically the entire habitat of the genus. Recent imports from Surinam have brought a very attractive sub-species of this fish into the tanks of happy hobbyists.

A maximum length of about 80 mm ($3\frac{3}{16}$ inches) is attained by both sexes, which are distinguished principally by the somewhat duller coloration and the rounder belly of the females.

The basic coloration is predominantly silverish with a soft, olive-yellow gleam and a deep black spot on the tail root, which either runs off forward a little but not out upon the caudal fin rays as with *Curimatopsis*, or is hardly visible. Under certain circumstances, an almost milk white band which runs from the upper edge of the gill covers to the black tail spot is visible. In habits, this fish can be likened to *Moenkhausia oligolepis*, for example, or to related, larger species. It requires a large aquarium with substantial edge planting and a sunny location. Keep the temperature between 18 and 25 °C (64–77 °F).

Curimatus spilurus is certainly a fish that needs company and is better kept in a small school rather than as a single couple. As lively and even boisterous as it is, these factors must certainly be taken into consideration. It eats practically anything and, in this regard, do not forget that vegetable foods must form an important part of its diet.

So far as is known, this fish has not yet been bred.

Plate II-123. *Leporinus arcus.*

Genus *Leporinus*

This is one of the most difficult genera of the entire family, about which many are far from being in agreement. In hobbyist circles, sporadic specimens (usually one at a time) are known from import shipments, without our being able to trace down the species we were dealing with.

In a short time, a revision is expected. For the few aquarists possessing representatives of this genus, a reference in general to, among others, *Chilodus punctatus* is enough.

The *Leporinus* species are formidable jumpers, which must properly be taken into consideration. So far as is known, it has not been bred.

Leporinus arcus Eigenmann, 1912

Arched Leporinus

The fish in Illus. II–123 comes from Surinam, probably from the vicinity of Zanderij Airfield (near Bosbivak?) and is quite similar in many characteristics to the *L. arcus* of Eigenmann, so that it seems reasonable that it should be provisionally described under this name. The genus *Leporinus*, however, needs thorough revision.

611

There is practically nothing to say about this species, because only a few specimens were imported alive, all of which are probably dead by now. The basic coloration is beige with a green glow over the back and flanks above the dark brown, lengthwise stripe, which in the caudal fin turns into a brown film. The underpart of the caudal fin is darker and, in fact, is a continuation of a faint stripe running from the pectoral fins, along the abdomen, out to the root of the tail. The imported specimens were about 60 mm ($2\frac{3}{8}$ inches) long, while a few dead specimens received later on measured 87, 94 and 105 mm ($3\frac{7}{16}$, $3\frac{11}{16}$ and $4\frac{1}{8}$ inches). It must, therefore, be concluded that this variety may attain a length of about 100 mm (4 inches) or a little more, a length also known for the *L. arcus* from Guyana.

Plate II-124. *Leporinus friderici.*

Leporinus friderici (Bloch, 1795)
Frideric's Leporinus

This species, with its wide distribution, was the first one from Surinam to be described. It reaches a length of about 35 cm (13¾ inches) and for this reason does not belong among the most preferred aquarium fish. Nevertheless, young specimens are very beautiful, the pattern of spots being much more strongly developed than in older specimens.

After revision of the genus *Leporinus*, a great number of species will be added together, a few will perhaps be added to other genera (mostly new ones), while especially the spotted *L. maculatus*, *L. granti* and *L. alternus* will probably have to be considered as one exceptionally variable species, its name being *L. friderici*. This is the oldest suitable name for this group, and this is also the reason for calling this species *L. friderici* here, notwithstanding the fact that it could also be attributed to a *L. maculatus* population.

Family Characidae

Although up to now probably a heterogeneous group, here all the remaining characin fishes are brought together into a number of sub-families, at least, all those not belonging to the families treated heretofore: the Erythrinidae, Characidiidae, and Citharinidae. The sub-families are: Cheirodontinae (with tribes Aphyocharacini and Cheirodontini); Alestinae (a sub-family of African characins); Tetragonopterinae (with tribes Tetragonopterini and Stethaprionini); Characinae (with tribes Characinini, Bryconini and Glandulocaudini); Gasteropelecinae; Hepsetinae, and Serrasalminae. Some of the more important groups will be discussed here in more detail.

Sub-family Cheirodontinae

The Cheirodontinae form an especially large group of small fishes, with dozens of genera and many hundreds of species, and they have been considered for a long time as the original characins. In spite of their enormous spread and locally massive occurrence, the members of this sub-family have not yielded such a large number of aquarium fish as the Tetragonopterinae (tetras). The most important characteristic dividing these two sub-families is the presence of only a single series of teeth on the premaxillary (front part of the upper jaw) as in the Cheirodontinae, as against two or more (among Tetragonopterinae). This basis appears at once to be completely insufficient and unnatural. There are certainly a number of very rational characteristics that can be brought out which justify a division into two or more groups, but for the time being let us maintain the current division.

Two tribes can certainly be distinguished within the Cheirodontinae, the Cheirodontini and the Aphyocharacini, both of which exhibit an affinity for the various members of the family Characidiidae. Moreover, the same is also true for a number of varieties from the sub-family Tetragonopterinae. Once we have found reliable characteristics for classification, then perhaps the division of the Characidae will look a great deal different.

Tribe Aphyocharacini

Among hobbyists, only two genera with only one single species each have become more or less known, *Aphyocharax* and *Prionobrama*.

Genus *Aphyocharax*

This is a genus of miniature herring, with a silvery body and fins of yellow, orange, pink, salmon or red.

Aphyocharax alburnus (Günther, 1869)
Gold-Crowned Aphyocharax

This is a fish that grows to about 50 mm (2 inches) long and may be compared in every aspect to the popular and well known *Aphyocharax rubropinnis*.

Aphyocharax rubropinnis Pappenheim, 1921
Bloodfin

This fish inhabits the drainage basin of the Rio de la Plata and the Paraná River (vicinity of Rosario) in Argentina. It was first imported in 1906.

It is a slim, minnow-like fish which attains a maximum length of 55 mm ($2\frac{3}{16}$ inches). Were an adipose fin not present, it could easily be taken for a relative of the rasbora-type fish. It is a silvery fish, whose great attractiveness comes from its blood red fins. The silver of the body can, however, depending on the angle of the light, vary from yellowish to light violet or light green. The lengthwise stripe visible from time to time, which runs from the upper edge of the gill cover to about under the dorsal fin, is varying metallic blue. The iris of the rather large

Plate II-125. *Aphyocharax rubropinnis.*

eye is golden yellow with a green glitter. As already said, the fins are blood red with the exception of the ventral fins, which have no coloration and are transparent. The adipose fin is dull whitish to grey-green. A metallic green spot ornaments the gill covers. The sexes may be differentiated only in the larger specimens by the more boldly developed and somewhat larger, broader females. Tiny hooks invisible to the naked eye, as in many of its relatives, are present on the anal fin of the males, which cause them to get hung up in the net. Again it is the same as in the case of similar fish: Never take them from the water with a dip net. They may, however, be caught with a dip net, so long as the ring of the net remains above water and the fish is removed from the net by hand; otherwise, a bell trap should be used.

Like many rasboras, danios and other minnow-like fishes, *Aphyocharax rubropinnis* is a dweller of the edge regions of open waters—that is, it lives on the edge of bank vegetation in running water, always in large groups or schools of hundreds of specimens together.

Mating also takes place in the same way as with other minnow-like fishes. At set times, the mature fish set forth in larger or smaller groups towards the shallow marshes which have watery connections with their customary haunts. The average water temperature in the rivers and creeks is about 18 °C, from 15–20 °C (64 °F, from 59–68 °F). In the marshes, however, this can rise above 20 °C (68 °F). During mating here, thousands of eggs are laid in a (relatively) very limited area. Naturally, many of the eggs fall prey to the parents themselves and to other enemies, yet a considerable quantity of them always manage to develop so that the species can maintain itself and develop further.

How best to arrive at a satisfactory breeding result may be deduced from the above-mentioned natural circumstances. Soft water with a pH value of 7 or thereabouts is certainly recommended, as well as, if marsh conditions cannot be imitated, plenty of thread algae to offer some protection to the eggs against the predatory instincts of the parents.

Plenty of swimming room, an hour or so of sunlight per day, predominantly animal food (ditch infusoria) and a soft alga in a well covered aquarium (they are jumpers)—these are about all the demands *Aphyocharax rubropinnis* makes.

The hatching and development of the young is only a matter of enough room and enough infusoria. After they have come out of their eggs, they subsist for three or four days on the yolk sac and then they can be started out immediately on the hunt for infusoria.

Tribe Cheirodontini

To this group belong the most primitive characins, only a single one of which exceeds a length of 80 mm (3 $\frac{3}{16}$ inches), *Leptagoniates*.

For the time being, the following genera are of interest to aquarists, of which a few species have already been kept in aquariums. These are: *Cheirodon, Paracheirodon, Phoxinopsis*, and *Leptagoniates*. Still other genera from this group have been imported, but suitable data concerning them are scarce, so that a discussion is hardly sensible until re-imports can be studied.

Genus *Cheirodon*

A large number of species is described under this genus name. Of these, only two have become a little known in hobbyist circles; other species have been placed in other genera, or recognized as sub-species. *Cheirodon* is exclusively from South America.

After Géry was able to determine that the formerly known *Hyphessobrycon innesi*, the Neon Tetra, was not a *Hyphessobrycon* but a *Cheirodon*, a great change took place in the nomenclature of many formerly trust-worthy aquarium fish.

An interesting publication (Stallknecht, 1965, Aquarien Terrarien) gives a review of the mating pattern of a number of characins. Perhaps this pattern will have classificatory value.

Cheirodon axelrodi Schultz, 1956
Cardinal Tetra

The well known Cardinal Tetra is related to the also widely known Neon Tetra, *Paracheirodon innesi*, and differs from it, in addition to a number of technical details, by the red band which runs forward and out upon the head.

Apparently several collections of this fish were imported from South America and reached the hands of prominent ichthyologists and aquarists. Ladiges, early in 1953, received a letter from Dr. Sioli, in which the latter reported a Neon Tetra from the upper reaches of the Rio Negro, Brazil. The preserved material is, according to Ladiges (1956), identical with the Cardinal Tetra. Dr. Sioli, not recognizing it as a new species, and referring to it as a Neon Tetra, probably dissuaded others from looking further into the matter. Dr. Herbert R. Axelrod, however, also collected specimens of this fish and was the first

617

Plate II-126. *Cheirodon axelrodi.*

to recognize it as being different from the Neon Tetra and, therefore, a species new to science.

It is interesting that two fishes that resemble each other so much are placed in different genera. Actually *Hyphessobrycon innesi* has been placed in a third genus, *Paracheirodon*, by Dr. Jacques Géry who has described a third "Neon Tetra" which superficially resembles the other two but differs on some technical points of anatomy. Since the resemblance was so great, he chose to name his new species *Hyphessobrycon simulans* (Géry, *Tropical Fish Hobbyist*, April, 1963). There are at least three species of tetras, *Cheirodon axelrodi*, *Paracheirodon innesi*, and *Hyphessobrycon simulans*, with the neon blue stripe and red band below it (at least posteriorly).

The Neon Tetra hails from the western Brazilian part of the Amazon Basin, the Cardinal Tetra from the region of the Rio Negro, according to Myers and Weitzman, and from Porto Velho, Brazil and Colombia, according to Schultz and Axelrod. Usually, when two populations of fishes are living in contact with one another and they do not inter-breed under natural conditions, they are said to be distinct species. When these groups of fishes are separated geographically it becomes more difficult to prove whether they are separate species or merely sub-species of the same species. The question remains open and the decision is, or should be, left to competent ichthyologists who have a good knowledge of the group of fishes being treated. It appears that the "Neon Tetra" group falls into this latter category.

The aquarium hobby has turned up a good number of new species of fishes and its contributions on observations of living fishes help to solve the many problems of ichthyology. The Cardinal Tetra is one of the many discoveries directly traceable to these aquarium studies.

Cheirodon interruptus (Jenyns, 1842)

This species hails from the southeastern part of Brazil (Porto Alegre) and Uruguay (Montevideo and the Uruguay River Basin). It grows to a length of about 60 mm (2⅜ inches) in both sexes.

Cheirodon interruptus should be kept in a well lighted aquarium, with a temperature of 15–25 °C (59–77 °F). In other respects, it is similar to the other tetras (for example, *Hemigrammus* and *Hyphessobrycon* species). Of the large number of eggs laid among the plants, many fall to the bottom and must be protected from the predatory instinct of the parents. The young hatch out on the second day.

Cheirodon piaba Lütken, 1874

This species comes from the Amazon River and Ceara in Brazil and from the Paraguay River.

Its length reaches about 45 mm (1$\frac{25}{32}$ inches), and it is similar to the foregoing species. The basic coloration is brownish green or otherwise, depending on the place of origin. The fins are yellowish and transparent; the base of the caudal fin is reddish.

Genus *Paracheirodon*

Paracheirodon innesi (Myers, 1936)

Neon Tetra

This species comes from South America—the Amazon Basin, the westernmost part of Brazil, a part of northern Peru, Ecuador and Bolivia. It is found in the upper reaches of the rivers, in water with little or no plant growth, in the flood regions of the jungle, with thick bank growth. It was first brought to Europe in 1936.

As is sometimes the case with certain species, all kinds of marvelous tales circulated about *Paracheirodon innesi*. Although it has a very striking appearance and requires a special environment, it is just another fish like its relatives and not at all mysterious, if we go to the trouble of determining how it ought to be kept.

The basic coloration is silver-grey with a soft, metallic gleam and sometimes a rosy glow. The famous "neon stripe" runs from the mouth over the eye and along the upper half of the body to approximately between the dorsal fin and the caudal fin, turning, depending on the circumstances, into a blue-green, iridescent band. If the fish swims directly towards us, the eyes appear to light up like the headlights of a car. Beneath the length of this glowing stripe, on the tail, appears a strongly contrasting, bright red, yet not luminous, stripe, which extends from behind the ventral fins to the under edge of the body, ending at the root of the tail. The back, above the luminous stripe, is dark, the belly yellowish white to soft rose, sometimes with a light blue tint. The fins are almost without coloration and transparent.

Both sexes are equally beautiful, with the same intensity of coloration, though the females are somewhat higher and wider and, in adult specimens, the belly is prominently thick.

Considering the circumstances under which these fish are found in nature, the conclusion is that it is best to keep them in a completely different manner than is usually the case. It seems best, therefore, to first discuss the natural circumstances of their environment.

Here is a bird's-eye view of the journey described by the Frenchman, Auguste Rabaut, the discoverer, in 1936. (The fish was indeed already known to the native population before that and possibly also to others, yet no publications regarding it appeared.) He left France in February and a month later set foot on the shore in Manaos, the huge seaport located about 1,600 km (1,000 miles) inland, on the left (northern) bank of the still huger Amazon River. Another 1,600 km of the distance were covered by boat, to a point close to the Colombian border, after which the party continued on foot to penetrate the almost unknown region. Sometimes they were able to further the journey by canoe, until they reached the Putumayo River, which rises in Colombia and pours its water over the border of Brazil (after becoming the Içá River) into the Amazon. Hiking trips were made from a camp through a region which, up to then, had never been trod by a white man. There, the first Neons were caught—in small jungle creeks and flooded areas with thick humus bottoms, thick layers of dead leaves, in areas abundant with fallen jungle giants lying in waters where there was not a single growing plant! The water depth varied between 25 and 100 cm (10 to 40 inches) and the temperatures from 20–21 °C (68–70 °F), not higher.

To the foregoing, enlightening description the following must be added. The water in which the Neons live has the following typical composition: The pH value fluctuates between 6.2 and 6.8 (mostly 6.6); the water is odorless, yellowish, slightly turbid, poor in dissolved materials; per litre, there are 6.0 mg chlorine, 0.4 mg latent carbonic acid and practically no free carbon dioxide; the titrated hardness is 1.0. Other jungle waters have similar compositions.

It should be clear to everyone that there is only one correct way to set up an aquarium for Neons. Plants are really not suitable, but a little thread algae may be included to bring a little life to the tank. If a large aquarium is used, you can, to satisfy your own personal likes, plant a part of the tank with some fine-leaved plants. The natural environment can be imitated by providing some small branches—oak or birch— which will take care of the acid content requirement. Add a bottom layer of humus, or imitate it with water-logged peat-moss and a few stones. A ceiling of floating plants or bent-over *Myriophyllum* can sufficiently temper the light so that even a few rays of sunlight will not disturb the natural setting. However, a great deal of light must not be allowed to stream through the vertical panes, but, at best, light should come from the top down. In spite of the nearly twilight-dark, the neon bands glow at their best and, if you like, if the tank is not being used for breeding, you can provide this fish with the company of other fish living under similar circumstances, such as *Hemigrammus ocellifer, Hyphessobrycon callistus, Hyphessobrycon heterorhabdus, Hyphessobrycon rosaceus,* and *Hyphessobrycon erythrozonus.*

The natural period of reproduction falls from December to the start

621

of April, from which *Paracheirodon innesi* seldom deviates, even in captivity. Egg-laying in the wild probably takes place among finely divided clumps of roots or algae, considering the preference this fish has for *Myriophyllum*. Laying occurs as among related species and a total of 100 to 200 eggs are issued and fertilized immediately by the male. Eggs that start out looking a little turbid turn glass-clear in a few minutes; they are extra sticky and remain firmly attached to the plants. After only 24 to 30 hours, the young hatch out of the eggs and dive immediately into the humus layer. They are usually not seen again for several days, when they start to make timid attempts at swimming movements. The coloration is then a very light, yellowish brown and, about five weeks later, the red stripe begins to appear. When they are two months old and about 10 mm ($\frac{7}{16}$ inch) long, the neon stripe also appears.

Mischances in breeding are undoubtedly due to an incorrect set-up and, consequently, among other things, alkaline water (pH above 7), too much light and too high a temperature. The temperature must not be more than 20–22 °C (68–72 °F) and a slight, nightly cooling off to a little under 20 °C (68 °F) can be beneficial. The eggs will not mildew if treated as advised. The sand bottom should never be kept scrupulously clean—that is never found in nature! Use a peat filter because water flowing through peat-moss becomes acid and brown-tinted. Although we have gone on rather expansively here about *Paracheirodon innesi* and its environment, there is still another interesting particular.

The first specimens brought to Paris by Auguste Rabaut were delivered directly to a large breeder and then on to the hobbyists. Several specimens were sent to the well known hobbyist and publisher, W. T. Innes of Philadelphia, and a number went to Hamburg, where they were soon re-bred. A shipment from Hamburg via the zeppelin "Hindenburg" in 1936 suffered, on the way, a temperature drop to about the freezing point. Most other fish were killed off, but the Neon apparently suffered no harm, for all specimens arrived alive.

Genus *Phoxinopsis*

Phoxinopsis typicus Regan, 1907

This fish comes from the vicinity of Rio de Janeiro. The maximum length is 27 mm (1 1/16 inch), and it should be kept the same as *Aphyocharax rubropinnis* (see page 615); the temperature should be 20–25 °C (68–77 °F).

The basic coloration is brownish with a dark brown, lengthwise stripe from the edge of the gill cover to the root of the tail, and with a second stripe along the base of the anal fin, sometimes running forward to the base of the pectoral fins. The median fins are yellow-red. Here, too, the anal fin of the males is hollowed out considerably; the fourth, fifth and sixth frontal rays are lengthened. There is no adipose fin.

Plate II-126A. *Paracheirodon innesi.*

623

Sub-family Alestinae

This sub-family includes the so-called African tetras, of which, unfortunately, only a few species have become known in hobbyist circles. They are such attractive fish, however, that a desire for more imports is expected. Several genera of this group are now represented among aquarium fish and a review of these genera is in order. For the time being, of importance to us are the genera *Alestopetersius, Arnoldichthys, Bryconalestes, Micralestes* and *Phenacogrammus*.

A discussion of *Alestes nurse* (Franke, 1966, Aquarien Terrarien) gives some interesting particulars in regard to this large characin, while Beck (1967, Aquarien Terrarien) published some information on its cousin *Alestes emberii*.

Illus. II-124. *Alestopetersius hilgendorfi.*

Genus *Alestopetersius*

Alestopetersius hilgendorfi (Boulenger, 1899)

This species grows to about 100 mm (4 inches), but nevertheless, belongs among the gladly welcomed imports, although it is, unfortunately, seldom offered. Since nothing has become known about the reproduction of this species, it is constantly disappearing from the tanks of hobbyists. Considering its living conditions, which are similar to those of the South American tetras, it should not be too difficult to breed. What is said in regard to *Phenacogrammus interruptus* (see page 630) can certainly be applied to this species.

A. hilgendorfi, with its sub-species, inhabits the far-reaching Congo Basin. *A. h. hilgendorfi* comes from the upper reaches of the drainage basin, *A. h. grandi* from Rochefoucauld, Ubangi, and *A. h. kribensis* from Kribi, Cameroon.

The basic coloration is the same as that of *Micralestes acutidens* and the pattern is quite similar. *A. hilgendorfi*, however, is slightly larger and also has a clear shoulder spot (right behind the gill covers). Furthermore, the tip of the dorsal fin, which has lengthened fin rays, is dark in *A. hilgendorfi*.

Genus *Arnoldichthys*

Arnoldichthys spilopterus (Boulenger, 1909)

Arnold's Red-Eyed Characin

This fish is found in West Africa—from Lagos to the Niger estuary in Nigeria—principally in the coastal region where it may live in company with its close relative *Micralestes acutidens*. It attains a length of 80 mm ($3\frac{3}{16}$ inches).

This member of the African tetras can be immediately distinguished from all its relatives by its peculiar scale pattern. The scales on the upper half of the body are significantly larger than those on the lower half. The more or less current popular name now in use refers to the splendid, red iris of the eye. The body is stretched out and laterally compressed. From the eye to the root of the tail runs a black, lengthwise band, bounded on the upper side by a practically indescribable combination of blue-green to olive green, metallically glittering scales, under which is a belly region of gleaming gold. When the light is at a certain angle, the black lengthwise band is set off on the upper side by a narrow, luminous stripe of strongly contrasting coloration. The shape and placement of the fins are outstandingly illustrated in Plate II–127, and the characteristic large black spot in the dorsal fin shows up quite clearly. The adipose fin is without coloration, shading to light rose, while the remaining fins are yellowish. In addition, there is a dark pattern in the anal fin of the male, made up of light and darker yellow. In the female, this fin is almost uniform in coloration but with a black spot on the base of the last rays, which can also be well seen in Plate II–127 (upper specimen). Also, two light stripes can be observed in the caudal fin, the upper as a lengthening of the upper light stripe on the body, and the lower under the dark, lengthwise band. Often, the middle rays of the caudal fin are also somewhat darker (blackish) as a dispersion of the lengthwise stripe.

In addition to the already-noted differences, the females are easy to recognize by their somewhat higher and wider shape. An often cited point of difference is the stronger inward bend of the anal fin in the male, but this does not appear to be a typical characteristic; at the most, this fin in the male is somewhat rounder in front.

This beautiful fish should be kept in a roomy aquarium, not too thickly populated, at a temperature of 22–30 °C (72–86 °F), normally about 25 °C (77 °F).

Arnoldichthys spilopterus is an extremely tolerant fish and certainly not at all predatory, although its comparatively large size might lead one

Plate II-127. *Arnoldichthys spilopterus.*

to surmise otherwise. It even leaves the smallest species alone, as long as there is sufficient suitable food available, of course. It eats literally everything that even slightly comes to its attention. It must be kept in mind, however, that the menu must be composed, to a large extent, of vegetable food, in the form of soft algae (on overgrown stones, for example) or some leaf greens from time to time.

Unfortunately, nothing is yet known about breeding *A. spilopterus*. It would be desirable to collect detailed data on its life in the natural environment in order to breed this beautiful characin.

Genus *Bryconalestes*

The varieties belonging to this genus, of which two are known among hobbyists, are distinguished from the members of the genus *Alestes* (to which unknown, rather large fish belong) by their attractive coloration and interesting activities, which are both very similar to those of the South American tetras.

Bryconalestes longipinnis (Günther, 1864)

African Long-Finned Tetra

This beautiful characin inhabits the waters of West Africa. The typical form (*B. l. longipinnis*) lives in the region from Sierra Leone to the Congo—in the Niger and Congo River basins—while a second variety (*B. l. chaperi*) occurs only in the lower reaches of the Niger Basin.

Both varieties belong to the larger characins (up to 100 mm or 4 inches long), and require a large aquarium, open swimming space, a sunny location, and moderately thick edge planting.

The basic coloration is olive green to yellow-green; the dorsal fin is red at the base; the caudal fin is red; and the remaining fins are practically without coloration. A dark band (turning to black) runs towards the tail as far as the end of the middlemost caudal fin rays.

Bryconalestes longipinnis is a typical school fish and a small group of these splendid characins require a good-sized tank. At lengths above 60 mm (2⅜ inches), the sexes can be distinguished by the more intense coloration of the males and the larger abdomen of the females. Mating takes place quickly after a very long courtship, and the eggs are laid among the thick edge planting, during which the couple, shaking and pressed close against each other, tumble about. Depending on the water and temperature, the eggs hatch after four to six days; the larvae look like splinters of glass, but grow up rapidly upon being fed foods consisting of the finest particles.

Illus. II-125. *Bryconalestes longipinnis.*

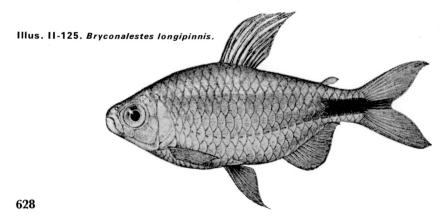

Plate II-128. *Micralestes acutidens.*

Genus *Micralestes*

This genus includes a number of the smaller species from this group of African tetras and is sub-divided into two sub-genera, *M. (Micralestes)*, with type species *M. (M.) acutidens*, and *M. (Rhabdalestes)*, with type species *M. (R.) tangensis* (Hoedeman, 1951).

Micralestes acutidens (Peters, 1852)

This undoubtedly especially attractive fish inhabits, with its subspecies, a very large region, from the Nile and Lake Chad through Nigeria to the drainage basin of the Zambezi River. It is very common in the Congo Basin.

Micralestes acutidens can be compared with its South American relatives from the tetra group. It attains a length of about 60 mm ($2\frac{3}{8}$ inches) in both sexes.

The basic coloration is silvery with a yellow tone, olive brown towards the back. The lengthwise stripe is only rarely dark-tinted, yet always easily observed, the blackish pattern showing up clearly on the tail. In the male, the lengthwise stripe runs through the middlemost caudal fin rays as a black band. In both sexes, but particularly in the male, these rays are more or less lengthened, which gives the impression of three lobes. The dorsal fin and sometimes also the anal fin have somewhat lengthened fin rays, also principally in male specimens.

Plate II-129. *Phenacogrammus interruptus.*

Genus *Phenacogrammus*

Phenacogrammus interruptus (Boulenger, 1899)

(Also known as *Micralestes interruptus* Boulenger, 1899)

Congo Tetra

This near relative of the well known South American tetras inhabits the Congo Basin. It attains a length of about 80 mm ($3\frac{3}{16}$ inches), somewhat less for the females. Laterally, the body is rather substantially compressed.

The basic coloration is silvery with a blue-green, metallic sheen. On the flanks above the lateral line (the lateral line organ is incomplete) runs a copper to red-brown band from the gill cover to the adipose fin. The back is dark, the belly yellow-green. The fins, greyish yellow to light pink and edged with white, are quite distinct in larger males. The total effect of the very attractive coloration is principally created by light refraction and much less by coloration cells. This is also the reason for the continually varying magnificence under the influence of light.

The shape and placement of the fins show clearly in Plate II–129. The specimens illustrated are males, distinguished by their peculiarly shaped anal fin, the longer dorsal fin rays and the far more lengthened middlemost rays of the caudal fin. These rays run out into one or two black points, while the whole fin is set off with milk white lines.

This species should be kept the same way as its South American relatives, with the understanding that it likes a sunny location. The water should preferably be somewhat acid (pH 6 to 7), and not too high a lime content (5 to 6 degrees), and a temperature of 20–25 °C (68–77 °F).

Mating usually takes place in sunlight. The eggs are laid close to the bottom, and if this takes place among the plants, they usually fall to the bottom because they have little or no adhesive quality. The parents cannot be considered egg eaters, although, of course, they may be violent to the spawn. A total of 500 eggs can be laid, which hatch out in 5 to 7 days, which contrasts sharply with their American relatives, whose eggs hatch much more quickly. It is, of course, possible that the slow hatching (as has been reported by various breeders) has a different cause and is not directly a natural phenomenon.

Sub-family Tetragonopterinae

This is one of the most extensive and species-rich groups of characins, from which comes about 50 per cent of all kept aquarium fishes. We shall, for the time being, distinguish two tribes—Tetragonopterini and Stethaprionini.

Tribe Tetragonopterini

It is almost impossible to imagine the great number of varieties in this group, the so-called tetras. It is perhaps striking that continually over 50 per cent of all the fish caught in South America belong among the tetras, while a large part of the remainder are derived from them.

This undoubtedly original group is continuously in a stage of expansion and in the midst of development of form. In fact, aside from a few already very specialized species, the core still includes uncountable forms with many possibilities of variation, which have caused much brain-racking among the scientists working with this group, and actually with not very satisfying results. The distribution and nature of the development especially had to be discovered, if scientists wanted to arrive at any kind of understanding of the whole. Eigenmann and practically all those following him who are concerned with the tetras consider the genus *Astyanax* as the focal species, perhaps along with the hardly-separable genus *Moenkhausia*, both derived from Cheirodontini.

This group includes the following genera, most of which are well known among aquarists: *Anoptichthys, Astyanax, Creagrutus, Ctenobrycon, Gymnocorymbus, Hasemania, Hemigrammus, Hyphessobrycon, Moenkhausia, Pristella, Thayeria* and many others, among which are included numerous new genera, and a large number of newly-imported species. However, as long as these are not better known, a discussion here, for the time being, is not necessary. Most of the species conduct themselves much like their closest relatives and create no problems in the aquarium.

Genus *Anoptichthys*

This is an extremely remarkable genus with only one species, comparable to, among others, the blind, cave-dwelling barb, *Caecobarbus geertsi*. *Anoptichthys* clearly demonstrates that every biotope is potentially habitable as long as adaptation has progressed sufficiently.

Anoptichthys jordani Hubbs & Innes, 1936
Blind Cave Characin
Blind Cave Tetra

This species comes from Mexico—from San Luis Potosí, the southwestern part of the drainage basin that receives its water from the Rio Tampaon (Rio Pánuco drainage basin), at the inlet to the Rio Coy. (Numerous other cave locations have since been discovered, indicating a quite extensive range.) It was imported by C. Basil Jordan, a dealer in aquarium fish in Dallas, Texas, in 1936. Due to its being blind and to its peculiar activities, *A. jordani* probably attracts considerable interest.

It grows to a length of about 70 mm (2¾ inches). Outwardly (technically), it can hardly be distinguished from related species of the genus *Astyanax* (to which this species also belongs, except that its great specialization caused it to be included in a separate genus; some authorities do place this fish in the genus *Astyanax*, from which it definitely evolved), but it can be recognized at once by its coloration, or better, by its lack of coloration, and the closed eye sockets. (Its coloration, without pigment, is mainly determined by the blood gleaming through the skin.)

To give some idea of the natural environment of this exceptional fish, here is a brief version of the tale told by its discoverers. This account is from a letter received by Jordan from an unidentified collector who entered the cave with four Indian companions.

It is very difficult to realize how impressive are the caves that have been formed in the habitat of this fish in Mexico described above. After having walked about 1 kilometre (6/10ths of a mile) through narrow caverns, blocked here and there by fallen boulders, the men came into a space large enough to contain a cathedral, entirely covered with stalactites and stalagmites. The whole area was lighted in a fantastic manner. Finally, the men came to the first pool where it was clear, by the great number of bones, that not only men but also animals had become lost. It is still a place dreaded by the Indians. In order to avoid losing themselves in the caves, the men marked the way with chalk. After many difficulties, and slipping and sliding, they squeezed,

Illus. II-126. *Anoptichthys jordani.*

with trouble, through narrow openings, past several pools of great depth, and in these pools 100 specimens of *Anoptichthys jordani* were caught.

Of these 100 specimens, 75 were sent to Jordan, and all of them arrived alive in Dallas. They seemed not difficult to keep. They accepted all kinds of food, and shortly after their arrival, he was successful at breeding them.

One might expect that this fish needs a special aquarium. However, this is not entirely correct. By nature, *A. jordani* requires an aquarium located practically in the dark, without any plant growth (except perhaps some algae), water that is heavy with lime, and a rather high temperature (this was not included but may be deduced from their sensitivity to "speckling" at low temperatures). Although we may assume that the temperature in the caves is somewhat lower than in open water in the outside world, the water in the caves could very possibly be 18–20 °C (64–68 °F), a temperature at which they obviously feel most at ease. Nonetheless, it appears that a high temperature—even as high as 30 °C (86 °F)—has no noticeably injurious effect.

Of course, as was not expected, this new fish showed itself to be unusually suitable for the aquarium. It reproduced spontaneously without difficulty and adapted itself with the greatest of ease to practically every thinkable aquarium condition.

Aquarists and laymen sometimes in the beginning feel compassion for this blind fish, but its activity soon blurs this feeling. *A. jordani* is not shy and quite certainly allows no one to "eat the cheese from its bread," as the saying goes; it mates in a completely normal manner and with equal pleasure eats its own eggs up, as many of its relatives do. It seldom swims up against anything or collides with other *A. jordani* (and then never seriously), not even in completely strange surroundings. For this, it is equipped with a lateral line and head-pore organ that works to perfection. The striking "wagging" or "waving" way of swimming is clearly necessary in order to give this lateral line organ every opportunity to perform its function.

The development of this organ is so far advanced that no food problem exists, understanding, of course, that live food creatures as well as all other food materials are not only sensed by these feel- and smell(?)-organs, but are also consumed with pleasure. *A. jordani* is certainly greedy, and least of all choosey. When it is placed in the company of other species, however, there is no fear that those species will be added to *A. jordani's* fare.

It is also remarkable how living food creatures are closed in upon and seized. *A. jordani* only has trouble with a few, such as the erratically wriggling larvae of the *Tendipes* gnat (commonly known as the bloodworm, an excellent and common live food) and the jumping larvae of the *Corethra* gnat. Outside the feeding time, to call it such, this fish is constantly in search of food among the plants (if there are plants present in the tank) and among the stones on the bottom. Everything is tested for edibility, but, again, it is certainly not choosey.

Reproduction has been adapted to its blindness, but scarcely differs from that of related species. The two sexes seek contact, find each other, and mate "in the open field," at which time the eggs fall to the bottom after they have been fertilized by the male, who at the start presses himself for some time against the female. Then, direct contact lessens, although the female keeps on for some time with her egg-laying. The sperm of the male is apparently very active and extremely tenacious, for even the eggs laid in this final manner by the female alone are fertilized.

If the known precautions have not been taken, then most of the eggs fall prey to the parents. The eggs hatch out after 2 to 4 days, depending on the hardness and temperature of the water and possibly on other factors. After about a week, the young are seen swimming about. Bringing them up is easy and is accomplished in the usual way.

Do not consider this species a "garbage disposal unit," but give it, as well as the other fishes, what is its due, and it will be not only a beautiful object of study for a long time, but also a gladly welcome inhabitant of your aquarium.

As already stated, this species is very closely related to the genus *Astyanax*. In the waters of Mexico, in the Rio Pánuco drainage basin, lives only one species of characin, *Astyanax mexicanus*, which, without doubt, is the original form of *Anoptichthys*. Surprising and certainly not simple to explain is the fact that though *Astyanax mexicanus* has a custom of staying in caves, it does not have either a strongly or even normally developed lateral line organ. Young as well as male specimens of *Anoptichthys* have a layer of pigment on the tail root, where the well known, diamond-shaped spot develops on *Astyanax*. This pigment later disappears from *Anoptichthys*, as does that which was originally present near the eyes, very small though it may be. In the growing fish, the eye sockets are filled entirely with a fatty tissue that extends out over the snout and possesses sensory organs.

Genus *Astyanax*

Of the known characins, this genus has indeed the widest distribution—from the vicinity of Buenos Aires in the southern part of South America to the southern part of North America, where it has penetrated into Texas. It is, indeed, one of the genera (if not *the* genus) having the greatest number of varieties. In that regard, it is perhaps somewhat strange that only a very few species have become known among hobbyists. This can be partly blamed on the size of many of the varieties, and partly on the relatively simple appearance and shape (basically, *Astyanax* is a silvery fish that has only a few dark spots or stripes). It is a fast, frisky fish that stays in open, sun-lit water and may be compared with, for example, the better known tetras, such as *Hemigrammus unilineatus* and *Pristella riddlei*.

Reproduction takes place in the same way as with most characins, and raising the fry is not difficult. Important to these species is a generous amount of vegetable food in addition to the usual diet of waterfleas, mosquito larvae, etc.

Plate II-130. *Astyanax* **species.**

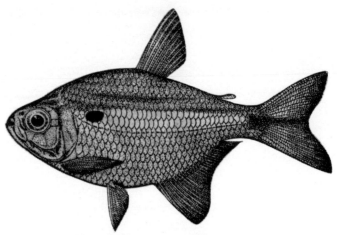

Illus. II-127. *Astyanax bimaculatus.*

Astyanax bimaculatus (Linné, 1758)
Two-Spotted Astyanax

This species inhabits practically all the large and small waters of South America, from Venezuela to Buenos Aires and from the eastern Atlantic coast to the Andes. Hence, it is certainly not strange that many dozens of varieties occur, all of which belong to this species. The shape of the fish is entirely dependent on the place of origin. Characteristic of all, however, are the two spots from which it gets its name, *bimaculatus.* Most varieties attain a length of about 120 mm ($4\frac{3}{4}$ inches) or a little more, but usually remain a little smaller in the aquarium. They must be kept in a very large aquarium to be shown off to best advantage.

The basic coloration is silver-bronze with an olive green to green-bronze back. The nearly round shoulder spot—distinct in most varieties, less distinct in others—is black, like the horizontal, lens-shaped tail spot, which disperses somewhat on the root of the tail.

Astyanax fasciatus (Cuvier, 1819)
Banded Astyanax

This species, with at least eight sub-species, inhabits the same extensive region as *Astyanax bimaculatus*. It differs from the latter in the more or less clear forward run of the caudal fin spot, which develops into a dark band (*fasciatus*). As a species, *A. fasciatus* grows a little smaller than *A. bimaculatus*.

Astyanax mexicanus (Filippi, 1853)
Mexican Tetra

This species also hardly differs from *A. bimaculatus*. This is the most northerly penetrating characin, which inhabits practically all of Mexico and Texas as far as the drainage basin of the Rio Grande.

It is distinguished from *A. bimaculatus* by a number of technical characteristics, by the almost complete absence of the shoulder spot, and by a light, silvery white band between the gill cover and the root of the tail. Moreover, the basic coloration is lighter, more of a silvery olive.

As the original form of the peculiar, cave-dwelling *Anoptichthys jordani*, this species is of interest to aquarists. It is, moreover, a suitable aquarium fish which attains a maximum length of 80 mm ($3\frac{3}{16}$ inches).

Astyanax potaroensis Eigenmann, 1909

From imported aquarium specimens, it seems that this specimen occurs in Surinam. Other scientifically collected specimens from Surinam, resembling *A. potaroensis*, have, however, been identified as *A. abramoides*.

All in all, *A. potaroensis* is a really beautiful tetra, silvery with a blue-green sheen and an olive green back. A light silver stripe with a golden sheen runs from the upper edge of the gill opening back into the black spot on the caudal fin; this and all other fins are reddish with black frontal rays. The dorsal fin in the male has a deep black spot. No reports have appeared on reproduction, but this must run parallel with that of related varieties (*A. potaroensis* may be compared to the *Moenkhausia* species and many *Hemigrammus* and *Hyphessobrycon* species). The length reaches about 50 mm (2 inches) without the caudal fin.

Boehlkea fredcochui (Gery, 1966)

Boehlkea fredcochui originates in the upper Amazon River and Loreto and Yacu, Brazil. Originally introduced under the name *Microbrycon fredcochui*, this pretty little characin is about 45 mm ($1\frac{13}{16}$ inches) long. The background is a metallic bluish to purplish, with translucent fins, and lacking the often-occurring characin shoulder spot. The tips of caudal and adipose fins are milk white. *B. fredcochui* looks much like several species of *Aphyocharax, Hemibrycon* or *Knodus*, and should be kept under similar conditions (see *Aphyocharax rubropinnis* on page 615).

Since this is a social fish, you should keep at least four together so they feel comfortable.

Genus *Creagrutus*

This genus differs from *Astyanax* mainly in the short anal fin and the structure of the jaws. It is represented by a number of species in northern South America and the hub of its distribution lies in Colombia.

Creagrutus beni Eigenmann, 1911

Gold Banded Characin

This species also comes from South America—Venezuela, in the vicinity of Lake Valencia and the small rivers that spring up in the Cordillera range; also in Colombia; Ecuador (Rio Putumayo); Peru (Rio Marañón, Rio Ucayalli); Brazil (the upper reaches of the Amazon Basin and the lower reaches of the Rio Tocantins); and Bolivia (Rio Beni, whence the name was taken). From this distribution, it may be deduced that this fish also occurs in the regions lying between the named places; however, this fact has not been established. A few specimens were imported for the first time in 1932.

The body of *Creagrutus beni* is less thick-set than in most tetras, the forepart hardly at all, and the tail strongly compressed laterally. The length may be 30 to 80 mm ($1\frac{3}{16}$ to $3\frac{3}{16}$ inches), but the fish known to aquarists seldom reach a length of more than 45 mm ($1\frac{13}{16}$ inches). This considerable difference in size is explained as follows: The best known catch location is Lake Valencia in Venezuela. The fish coming from there attain a length of about 40 mm ($1\frac{9}{16}$ inches) or less. The coloration and pattern of this tiny race is more beautiful than those of the larger fish, which are more southerly in environment and differ very little in pattern. These larger fish attain a maximum length of 80 mm ($3\frac{3}{16}$ inches). However, nothing is known about the importation of these larger fish.

In proportion to the body, the head is rather small. The mouth is striking in appearance due to the out-thrust upper jaw and the thick lower lip.

The basic coloration of *C. beni* is yellow-brown to olive green, the back light brown, the belly a soft, silvery brown with a violet lustre. The lengthwise stripe is golden with a red sheen and divides under the beginning of the dorsal fin into two narrower bands, between which, broadening towards the tail, is a brownish black stripe. The shoulder spot is equally brownish black. The dorsal and anal fins are reddish with a triangular black spot. The lower caudal fin lobe is reddish to yellow. The ventral and pectoral fins are sometimes less vivid, but usually a bright, yellowish red. *Creagrutus beni* is an exception, for the females are more beautiful than the males. Regardless, however, there is no satisfactory means of determining the sexes. At the same time, the females are somewhat more robust and, especially in the belly, are clearly rounder than the males.

Preferably give this fish a brightly-lit aquarium, containing at least 25 to 30 litres (about 6 to 8 gallons, U.S.). Plant with *Myriophyllum* and *Heteranthera*, etc. The water temperature should be 20–24 °C (68–75 °F), a little higher for breeding, 24–26 °C (75–79 °F). The water in the breeding tank should not be deeper than about 20 cm (8 inches).

This fish possesses a kind of internal place of fertilization. During the chase, the female is fertilized by the male, probably receiving internally the spermatozoa emitted by the males (not to be confused with the internal fertilization of live-bearing fish). After fertilization and as the first eggs are laid, the female continually chases the male away, so it is better to transfer him to another tank. The eggs are laid among fine-leaved plants, after which the female should also be removed. The eggs hatch out after about a day, at a temperature of about 25 °C (77 °F), and after three days the young are already able to go off hunting infusoria by themselves. In hobbyist circles, this fish has made a name for itself as, among others, a destroyer of planarians (flatworms).

This really sociable and active fish is quite suitable for the community aquarium, where it mainly keeps to the bottommost water levels and shows itself off well among other tetras and other fish of about its own size.

Genus *Ctenobrycon*

This genus lives in the bright, open waters of the Amazon Basin, the Guianas in the north and as far as the southern region of the Rio Parnaíba in Brazil.

These little characins, quite striking with their ctenoid (rough) scales, have been represented in aquarist circles by only a single species since 1912. However, it is very possible that several *Ctenobrycon* species have been kept under the name *spilurus*.

Ctenobrycon spilurus (Valenciennes, 1859)
Silver Tetra

This beautiful characin inhabits Venezuela and the Guianas and has been regularly imported since 1924 in small numbers. The specimens that have been coming from Surinam in the past few years were found among *Rivulus, Poecilia, Hemigrammus* and *Hyphessobrycon* species. They are quite similar to *Moenkhausia* or *Astyanax* species, but the most important characteristic distinguishing this fish from all its relatives are the ctenoid (so-called toothed or rough) scales, which are not normally found in this order, but are typical of perch-like fish. The basic coloration of *Ctenobrycon spilurus* is silvery white with an olive green sheen. Two dark spots are, moreover, the only pattern—that is, a black spot on the tail root and a vague, but sometimes distinct, nearly round, shoulder spot. A milk white line, sometimes appearing iridescent green, runs forward from the root of the tail.

In spite of its very simple, almost sober, exterior, *C. spilurus* is a particularly attractive fish, provided it is kept in small groups of at least six specimens, in a good-sized aquarium with a large, open swimming space into which a little sunlight can penetrate from time to time. While the fish darts about, the scales glitter like little diamonds.

Both sexes attain a length of 65 mm ($2\frac{9}{16}$ inches), but are nonetheless quite suitable company for all kinds of smaller fish. They enliven the aquarium greatly, but are plant eaters if they are not given sufficient vegetable food.

Reproduction is carried on the same as with related species, and although as many as 2,000 eggs can be laid, the predatory nature of the parents is so great that only timely intervention can save even part of them.

Raising the young is not difficult.

Genus *Gymnocorymbus*

This genus, of which two species are known—possibly only geographical sub-species—is distinguished from the other tetras mainly by its deeper body shape. In this respect, *Gymnocorymbus* strongly resembles the *Moenkhausia* species in one of the stages of progression towards the forms which eventually became the Serrasalminae.

Gymnocorymbus ternetzi (Boulenger, 1895)

Blackamoor

Black Tetra

Black Widow (U.K.)

Butterfly Tetra

Petticoat Tetra

This fish comes from South America—Paraguay, Brazil and Bolivia—the drainage basins of the Amazon, Rio Paraguay, Rio Pilcomayo, Rio Guaporé, Rio Mamoré, Rio Beni, Rio Madeira, Rio Tapajos, Rio Negro and Lake Rogoa, in shaded, mostly shallow waters and flood regions.

This always gladly welcomed characin is a striking object in the aquarium, as long as it is in good condition. The body is high, a maximum of 56 mm ($2\frac{7}{32}$ inches) long. As a rule, the males are a little smaller. The dorsal and anal fins begin about half way between the eye and the root of the tail. The dorsal fin has a very short base and the anal fin a long one. The frontal fin rays in both these fins are considerably longer than those following. In the anal fin, the length of the fin rays falls off gradually and the fin curves outwards. The snout is directed upwards with a moderately large mouth opening. The large pectoral fins reach far back beyond the bases of the ventral fins. The ventral fins extend just to the anal fin.

The basic coloration is light brown to gleaming silver-green, the back olive green, turning to white towards the belly. Across the shoulders run the two familiar shoulder spots found on many tetras. The entire after part of the body, to just beyond the root of the tail, is velvet black, usually more intense than the also black shoulder spots. If the fish are in good condition, the black is very intense, as it shows up especially in young specimens. The black often turns pale in older specimens. The caudal fin and the paired fins are without coloration and transparent.

It is not difficult to distinguish the sexes among individuals of about the same age, which have grown up normally. In addition to the fact that the males are somewhat smaller and slimmer than the females, the

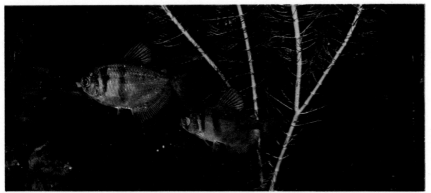

Plate II-132. *Gymnocorymbus ternetzi.*

latter, when seen from above or from the front, are clearly broader in the region of the belly and the body cavity shows up round by transmitted light, while that of the male comes to a sharp point.

Like its related species, *Gymnocorymbus ternetzi* requires a large aquarium, clear water, and a thick growth of plants along the walls, thus leaving plenty of swimming space in the middle. The darker the background and bottom of the tank, the more at ease the fish feels, as compensation for which they regale us with a continuous show of their most intense coloration and pattern. A single ray of sunlight can do no harm, but there must be an abundance of shadowy spots. As far as food is concerned, it is a fish that makes few demands in spite of its more or less predatory appearance (though it is not so in the least), and thus can be well likened to the Red Rio or Flame Tetra (*Hyphessobrycon flammeus*).

On the whole, *G. ternetzi* is not as particularly sensitive to low temperatures as has been thought. It should normally be kept at a temperature of 20–23 °C (68–73 °F). This temperature must be raised for breeding. The reproduction period, as for most characins from its distribution area, falls from December to March, but it can be bred in other months.

Egg-laying is the same as among the related species. The eggs hatch after about 24 hours and the tiny larvae are soon able to swim about freely in search of food. They are immediately able to swallow good-sized pieces, which results in rapid growth.

Little is known with certainty about the importation of this fish, but it has been determined that the first specimens, as aquarium fish, were in the hands of North American hobbyists about 1934.

645

Genus *Hasemania*

This genus is distinguished from *Hyphessobrycon* solely by its lack of an adipose fin. Like the already mentioned characteristic of scales on the caudal peduncle, differentiating *Hemigrammus* from *Hyphessobrycon*, perhaps the absence or presence of an adipose fin is a characteristic that can be independently made use of in the identification of several varieties.

Hasemania melanura Ellis, 1911

This fish comes from the Rio Iguacu in southeastern Brazil.

An unfortunate confusion of names has arisen, by which this fish is commonly taken for *Hasemania marginata* of Meinken (1938). However, Meinken's *H. marginata* is apparently nothing more than a local variety of *H. melanura*.

The total length of *H. melanura* amounts to about 50 mm (2 inches). The shape of the body and the pattern, as well as the attractive coloration of the males, show up clearly in Plate II–133. The females are a little smaller and somewhat heavier in the body, while they are less reddish and more on the grey side.

Although not imported for the first time until 1937, in a few years this fish has not only completely conquered the hearts of many aquarists, but also has earned a special place for itself among characins, in part due to its attractive coloration, which it shows off completely, especially in sunlight, as the fish "play" with each other. On the other hand, *H. melanura* is an extremely lively little fish, tolerant of other species. The remarkable angled position, which the fish often take on during "play," may disturb the beginner aquarist, if he is not well acquainted with the species, because these fish act as some fish do who are suffering from a swim bladder disease. Closer examination quickly shows the angled position to be an expression of pure love of life aimed at a species companion, male or female, some distance away.

During mating *H. melanura* is as busy as or even busier in its movements than at other times. If the reproductive period is interrupted, then this play continues and can go on for many weeks. At intervals, the rather small, greyish eggs are laid among fine-leaved plants or algae in the manner of most other Tetragonopterini. This species usually reproduces more spontaneously in the aquarium than most other related species. The most suitable temperature is about 24 °C (75 °F), but they can stand sensible temperature variations very well. The eggs hatch out within 36 hours and the young are then

Plate II-133. *Hasemania melanura.*

extremely small, dark in coloration and, if the tank is set up with a dark bottom, they remain invisible for the first 10 days. For this reason, it is desirable to be very careful and patient, for no sooner than about two weeks can we expect to catch sight of their first serious attempts at swimming. Do not become disheartened if you do not see anything right away.

Genus *Hemigrammus*

This genus, set up as a sub-genus of *Poecilurichthys*, quickly became one of the most important ones to aquarists. Together with *Hyphessobrycon*, it now forms the largest group of South American tetras already imported as aquarium fish.

Like the many aquarists who have been asking themselves for a long time whether certain varieties belong to a given genus or some other, ichthyologists are still in doubt about the subject. However, it is quite clear at present that the division of a group of as closely related varieties as *Hemigrammus* and *Hyphessobrycon* species, solely and mainly by whether or not there are scales on the caudal peduncle, is in no way a natural division. Undoubtedly, very close relatives are presently included in two or even more different genera, while many less related varieties are placed next to each other.

It is known that in America (Böhlke, Weitzman) and in France (Géry) scientists are determined to bring clarity among the tetras. It is unfortunate that new species, or rather, new species names, are continuously being created without sufficient reason. From the viewpoint of classification, the naming of the most popular aquarium fish still continues to be chaotic.

Hemigrammus armstrongi Schultz & Axelrod, 1955
Golden Tetra

Again a new tetra was named and the already much too long array of species names enriched with another one. The reference here to species names and not species is intentional, because it has become quite clear that there is really only a small number of true, typical species— not dozens, as the number of available names might make one suppose. Just how great is the variability of these fishes is well known by aquarists; it is a recent group, created, as it were, as a result of a kind of explosion of varieties. Characteristics of specific value in other groups are of no importance here, so that new distinguishing characteristics must be found. That part of the lateral line organ situated on the head, for example, appears to be important. It consists of a number of tiny tubes which, by means of pores on the surface of the skin, are in contact with the water. The orientation of these tiny canals and the number and location of the pores appear to be important for classification, aside from other differences between many *Hemigrammus* and *Hyphessobrycon* varieties.

The above may clearly illustrate why the naming of new tetras before

648

Plate II-134. *Hemigrammus armstrongi.*

the group as a whole has been thoroughly examined can hardly be justified. Such an examination must involve the nature of classification as well as biological considerations, taking into account that preserved samples without live specimens available afterwards can never provide a good picture of the situation.

Hemigrammus caudovittatus **Ahl, 1924**

Buenos Aires Tetra

Diamond Spot Characin

This species hails from southern South America—from northeast Argentina (Rio Paraná and tributaries) to Buenos Aires. It was first imported into Europe in 1922.

This is one of the larger species of the genus *Hemigrammus* with a length to about 100 mm (4 inches). The body is somewhat longer than in most of its relatives. A three-toned tail root—black, yellow and red—was the reason this fish was named Belgian Flag Characin, a name which formerly and more appropriately was applied to *Hyphessobrycon heterorhabdus*. Depending on the circumstances, the total coloration of *Hemigrammus caudovittatus* can be very dark and the back even brownish green to purplish brown. The fins sometimes appear less red than shown in Plate II–135, and from time to time a so-called shoulder spot appears behind the gill covers.

The sexes may be told apart only in adult specimens, as is the case with most characins; the females are then a little deeper in the body and, when seen from above, appear broader in the belly.

The Diamond Spot Characin is a very easy to keep fish, although

Plate II-135. *Hemigrammus caudovittatus.*

it seems, at present, to be unpopular because some specimens (really only "some" specimens which come from unplanted tanks), if given too little vegetable food, can seriously damage aquarial plant growth. This is unfortunate, as it is not reasonable that *H. caudovittatus* should become "extinct" among aquarists because of this, as has happened with many other species.

The temperature range runs from 10–30 °C (50–86 °F). It should be kept at 18–22 °C (64–72 °F), but the fish can withstand a temporary drop in temperature unusually well. The mating season (October to January) is independent of the temperature. They will just as cheerfully lay their eggs and hatch them out at 18 °C (64 °F) as at 24 °C (75 °F). Usually, the larger female has the upper hand, but as soon as she has persuaded the male to care for the offspring, he takes command, if he has not been too badly damaged by his spouse, which can, indeed, occur. The eggs, which can be laid in large numbers (up to about 600), although only slightly sticky, mostly remain hanging among the fine-leaved plants. In most cases it is not necessary to take the parents away from the eggs after laying is done, provided that beforehand and during the breeding period they have been well fed. A nest of 200 eggs is always easy to bring up. Never try to attain *more* by means of higher temperatures.

Plate II-136. *Hemigrammus erythrozonus.*

Hemigrammus erythrozonus Durbin, 1909

Fire Neon

Glowlight Tetra

This South American species comes from the Guianas, the Amazon Basin, Rio São Francisco and Rio Paraguay.

Fraser-Brunner has raised a question in regard to this fish, known by the name *Hyphessobrycon gracilis* since its importation into America, which cannot be considered entirely answered. Perhaps there are several varieties possessing the typical stripe of the Fire Neon. The not entirely finished investigation of aquarium material by Hoedeman brought to light that the characteristic for the genus *Hemigrammus* (that is, scales on the caudal fin) does not hold true for this species. It is also difficult to determine to which of the two genera this species might belong. Some of the investigated specimens, which without doubt all represented the same species, had a caudal fin without scales (genus *Hyphessobrycon*), a large number (17 of the 42) stood just on the edge between the two species and genera—that is, with two rows of scales just past the root of the tail—while 16 specimens showed a normally scaled caudal fin (genus *Hemigrammus*).

Any deviation in the shape of the body from the Neon Tetra is not worth mentioning, and most of what was said with reference to that fish can be applied to this one as well (see *Paracheirodon innesi*). The length in both sexes is about 45 mm (1$\frac{13}{16}$ inches).

The basic coloration of *Hemigrammus erythrozonus* is grey-brown, more or less distinctly varying according to circumstances. The specimens which, so far as can be traced, have been imported into the Netherlands and re-bred, however, have never been sea-green. A very distinct, red-gold, iridescent stripe runs down the middle of the tail, continues, though somewhat less distinctly, forward over the body cavity and ends with strong luminosity in the upper edge of the iris of the eye. This red stripe runs on past the root of the tail and flows out over half the caudal fin. Not iridescent but similarly hued is the base part of the frontal rays of the dorsal fin. All other fins are without coloration and transparent, except that the extremities of the frontal rays and the lower lobe of the caudal fin have a porcelain white border or stripe which, in fine specimens, can blend into a beautiful ice blue.

Larger live specimens usually also have an additional dark pattern on the root of the tail, on either side of the iridescent stripe, on the head, above the eye, in the tips of the dorsal and anal fins, and on the gill covers.

Hemigrammus erythrozonus is a strong little fish that reproduces even more quickly and spontaneously than *Paracheirodon innesi*. A clear differentiation between the sexes is not present here, though the experienced hobbyist usually possesses the necessary "feeling" for recognizing the males, which are slimmer than the females. Fine-leaved plants are preferred, although the eggs are only slightly adhesive, so that a large part of the up to 300 eggs which can be laid fall to the bottom. However, this should not cause the eggs to mildew. Neutral, lime-poor, chlorine-free water (for example, rain water that has been left standing in a planted tank for a week), at a temperature between 20 and 26° C (68–79 °F), is very suitable.

Plate II-137. *Hemigrammus ocellifer.*

Hemigrammus ocellifer (Steindachner, 1882)
Head-and-Tail-Light Tetra

In South America, this species is commonly distributed throughout the entire Amazon drainage basin and the Guianas. It lives in all kinds of waters and under sometimes strongly varying conditions, together with Nannostomini, *Pyrrhulina, Loricaria,* various Cichlidae, and *Dormitator gymnocephalus.*

It was first imported in 1910 and since that time has been welcomed into the aquariums of hobbyists.

The basic coloration of gleaming silver-green, traced over with a net-like pattern by the dark-edged scales, varies strongly according to circumstances as does the intensity of the dark, lengthwise stripe. This lengthwise stripe runs out in a diamond-shaped spot onto the root of the tail, with a golden yellow spatter above the diamond.

In the aquarium, it is obvious why this fish has been named "Head-and-Tail-Light Tetra": the upper half of the iris is red, the lower half golden, and the eye shines brightly with reflected light. The bright, golden yellow area above the caudal or tail spot, like the eye, is also reflective. The over-all impression of a school of these fish in a not-too-brightly-lit aquarium with some reflected illumination is that each fish is carrying a tiny light at each end.

The sexes are not so difficult to tell apart, mainly by the broader and deeper shape of the females. The crosswise stripe occurring in the male over the first five or six fin rays of the anal fin (see Plate II–137) is no positive characteristic. Although it does not occur in the female, it is also absent in many male specimens. When it is present, however, we know that we are dealing with a male. Moreover, the fins of the male are usually somewhat more sharply pointed. The temperature should be 18–28 °C (64–82 °F). Thick plant growth in the tank is recommended, as is protection against light falling in from the side during the mating period.

Hemigrammus pulcher Ladiges, 1938
Pretty Tetra
Pulcher Tetra

This splendid tetra has won more of the field in the past several years and can certainly be considered as one of the most popular species. It comes from South America—the Amazon Basin between Tabatinga (Brazil) and Iquitos (Peru).

Hemigrammus pulcher is a rather stumpily built species which in both sexes can attain a length of about 45 mm ($1\frac{13}{16}$ inches). Its basic coloration is dark grey with a golden gleam. The back can exhibit a

Plate II-138. *Hemigrammus pulcher.*

glittering, purplish glow, reducing towards the belly and resolving into reddish to a soft, yellowish gleam. The tail and the tail root have a deep black, band-shaped spot, bordered by a luminous, golden yellow spot on the upper side, in front of the tail root. The iris of the eye is bright red on the upper edge.

The dorsal fin has reddish spots, the anal fin and the ventral fins are lemon yellow and translucent, and the pectoral fins are almost without coloration. The caudal fin is a weak yellow, while the small adipose fin is black at the base.

The sexes are a little more clearly distinguished than in most of the related species, principally because the frontal rays of the anal fin are milk white in the male, but without coloration in the female. Also, the caudal fin of the male is usually somewhat larger, a little more deeply bifurcated, and the frontal rays are somewhat longer than those of the female. The females can always be recognized by the distinctly broader and rounder belly.

Although *Hemigrammus pulcher* is one of the newer characin species, it was not until 1938 that it was introduced to hobbyists and not until 1939 that it received any kind of recognition. Still, specimens have already been bred in the aquarium. It requires an environment the same as that of most related species (*Hemigrammus ocellifer, H. unilineatus,* etc.) and not too high a temperature, best at 18–23 °C (64–73 °F). Thick edge planting and moderate light coming mainly from above, a dark background and bottom are recommended.

Although about 600 eggs can be laid per mating session, *H. pulcher* is not usually so productive because it seldom spawns more than once per season. This is possibly only a first impression which better acquaintance with this lovely fish would qualify as not entirely correct.

In the Peruvian Amazon, this species lives together with, among others, *Paracheirodon innesi, Hyphessobrycon peruvianus* and *H. loretoensis,* in addition to representatives of the genus *Bario,* not entirely unknown to aquarists, and numerous other characins, such as: *Nannobrycon eques; Characidium steindachneri; Psectrogaster amazonicus; Curimatella alburna* and *C. meyeri; Leporinus bimaculatus, L. holostictus* and *L. striatus.* From the catfish species, the following also occur in this region: *Ageneiosus ucayalensis; Hypophthalmus edentatus; Callichthys callichthys; Hoplosternum littorale, H. thoracatum; Corydoras aeneus, C. eques; Hypostomus emarginatus; Panaque dentex; Loricaria maculata* and many others—species which, for the greater part, are still unknown among aquarists.

Plate II-139. *Hemigrammus rhodostomus.*

Hemigrammus rhodostomus Ahl, 1924
Red-Nosed Tetra
Rummy-Nose Tetra

This unusually attractive little fish from the lower and central reaches of the Amazon Basin was introduced in 1924. For a long time, nothing more was seen or heard of it, until it cropped up again in America in 1933. It soon disappeared once more and did not appear again in America until after 1945 and in the Netherlands until about 1948.

Few hobbyists have kept this species yet, because breeding does not seem to want to succeed. Some hobbyists, however, have succeeded in bringing up a small brood.

The fish can grow to a total length of 50 mm (2 inches). The basic coloration is olive-yellow with a black, long drawn-out, diamond-shaped spot on the root of the tail, white caudal fin lobes with a black cross band on each lobe. The snout can be blood red.

H. rhodostomus should be kept the same as most of its relatives, several specimens together or possibly with some closest relatives. This is necessary for their well-being. They then delight in darting through the tank, showing off the most beautiful hues. (Another very similar species, *Petitella georgiae*, has a less distinct tail pattern and the red coloration only covers the upper part of the head. See next page.)

Plate II-140. *Hemigrammus unilineatus.*

Hemigrammus unilineatus Gill, 1858
One-Lined Tetra

This species hails from Trinidad and northern South America, where it is a numerously occurring species always found in large groups (schools).

H. unilineatus is one of the larger tetras, and bears a superficial resemblance to *Pristella riddlei*, yet is somewhat less brilliant in coloration. It formerly became very popular, but has been more and more crowded out by the more vivid species.

Plate II-141. *Petitella georgiae.*

Genus *Hyphessobrycon*

Hyphessobrycon is distinguished from *Hemigrammus* mainly by the absence of scales on the caudal fin. It is not yet certain, however, that the absence of scales on the caudal fin is a characteristic on the basis of which the many species (at present *Hyphessobrycon*) can be brought together.

Hyphessobrycon callistus (Boulenger, 1900)

Callistus Tetra

This species comes from the drainage basin of the Rio Paraguay in the Mato Grosso of Brazil; Paraguay (sub-species *H. c. callistus*); Guyana (sub-species *H. c. minor*); the Amazon; Rio Guaporé; and the upper reaches of the Rio Paraguay Basin (sub-species *H. c. serpae*); the upper reaches of the Amazon (sub-species *H. c. copelandi*); Amazon, Obidos, Bentos (sub-species *H. c. bentosi*). The variety illustrated in Plate II–142 was imported for the first time in 1933 (?).

As may appear from the foregoing, this species breaks down into five sub-species, of which *H. callistus callistus* and *H. c. serpae* are known to aquarists.

Plate II-142. *Hyphessobrycon callistus.*

Hyphessobrycon callistus bentosi Durbin, 1908
Bentosi Tetra

It can be deduced from Durbin's description that this variety is more or less a transitional form to the *H. rosaceus* varieties. The most important characteristic that divides the two groups—the shoulder spot—is always moderately developed, not distinctly black, but brownish in *H. c. bentosi*. In other details, *H. c. bentosi* and *H. rosaceus* resemble each other to such a degree that it is practically impossible for them really to be two true species. Closer investigation will bring a solution, with the inevitable consequence that the current name *H. rosaceus* will have to be dropped. The maximum length is 38 mm (1½ inches).

Breeding is carried on the same as with *Hyphessobrycon rosaceus*, with the difference that bright light (the sun) must be screened off, especially after the eggs are laid. As usual in breeding, quiet is also an important factor.

It may be assumed that all described *H. callistus* varieties have the same requirements, although in a strict sense, this holds true only for the variety known as "Minor" (*H. c. callistus*). In any case, the other imported fish, *H. c. serpae*, can also be co-ordinated with this.

Lime-poor, neutral (fresh) water at a temperature of about 25 °C (77 °F) is desirable. In most cases, the eggs are laid high up among the plants, part of them sticking tight, the others falling to the bottom. The total number of eggs laid per period amounts to about 500. With each mating, the female sprinkles 10 or so eggs about, a procedure that continues for several days on end with pauses of a quarter hour to several hours. The parents can be rather predatory.

The eggs hatch very quickly, so, if the eggs are laid in the morning, the young can even hatch out by evening. The young are dark in coloration and not until after a few weeks, sometimes a little sooner, do we see them scavenging through the tank in search of food. The smallest food particles are required during the first few days. Ditch infusoria is excellent.

Hyphessobrycon callistus callistus (Boulenger, 1900)
Minor Tetra

This is the variety known up to now as "Minor." The dorsal fin is entirely black with never more than a narrow, white base. The extreme tip of the frontal rays is milk white. The anal fin clearly has a black border, the frontal rays are from entirely to half black, the base is reddish in either case. The black shoulder spot is well developed.

Hyphessobrycon callistus copelandi Durbin, 1908
Copeland's Tetra

It is probable that this variety has not yet been imported. It is quite similar to the original form (*H. callistus*) but may be outwardly distinguished by the milk white frontal rays of the pectoral and ventral fins and the dark streak down the back. The shoulder spot is rather large, but vanishes from older specimens. The length is about 42 mm (1$\frac{11}{16}$ inches).

Hyphessobrycon callistus minor Durbin, 1909

This variety reaches a maximum length of 25 mm (1 inch), without the caudal fin. The shoulder spot is very small.

Hyphessobrycon callistus serpae Durbin, 1908
Serpae Tetra

This variety differs very little from *H. callistus* and mainly then in coloration. Basically it is more pink with iridescent blue edges to the scales, which results in the body having a purplish lilac glow. The shoulder spot is moderately large, irregular, somewhat lengthened ventrally (as shown in Plate II–142), especially clear in young and half-grown specimens. The spot is often very weak or has disappeared entirely in older specimens. In this connection, perhaps *H. rosaceus* is no more than a sub-species of *H. callistus*, as it appears to be.

In *H. c. serpae*, the frontal rays of the dorsal and anal fins sometimes grow out to a considerable extent, as is also the case with *H. rosaceus*, which, however, is very clearly distinguished by the complete absence (also in youthful specimens) of the black shoulder spot. *H. c. serpae* attains a maximum length of 45 mm (1$\frac{13}{16}$ inches), without the caudal fin.

Plate II-143. *Hyphessobrycon eos.*

Hyphessobrycon eos Durbin, 1909
Dawn Tetra

This fish, at first known to come only from Guyana, after 1952 was regularly imported into Europe from the vicinity of the Surinamese airport, Zanderij.

Hyphessobrycon eos is one of the numerous tetras in which South America is so rich. Although perhaps not belonging to the most beautiful species, this rather small fish (about 45 mm or $1\frac{13}{16}$ inches) should certainly not be despised as an acquisition to the hobby.

Even though the greater part of available material shows only 9 (several show 10) rays in the dorsal fin and only 30 to 32 scales in the lengthwise direction (in type material, respectively 11 and 33 or 34), it is not difficult to recognize this species. Contrary to the type material from Guyana, where the fins are reddish (sometimes orange-red), the Surinamese material is clearly orange to deep yellow in the fins. The black spot on the base of the caudal fin runs somewhat out upon the outermost rays; the lengthwise stripe is quite weakly developed. The gill covers and snout are yellow, the body silvery with a yellow glow.

Keep *H. eos* like its relatives at a temperature of 20–25 °C (68–77 °F).

Hyphessobrycon flammeus Myers, 1924
Flame Tetra
Red Rio

H. flammeus comes from the vicinity of Rio de Janeiro. It was first imported in 1920 and since then has become an aquarium fish that is known and loved everywhere.

Differentiation of the sexes is founded on a broad, black border to the anal fin of the male, this border being either completely absent in the female or simply narrower and lighter in tone. The region of the belly is thicker and rounder in the female, which makes them deeper in the body than the slimmer males. The maximum length is 43 mm (1$\frac{11}{16}$ inches).

This characin is often kept too warm. Hailing from sub-tropical districts, where it can temporarily become quite hot, this fish does require a temperature of 18–22 °C (64–72 °F). The aquarium must be set up with fine-leaved plants and a thick, dark bottom soil of humus with thread algae. The tank is preferably placed so that, from time to time, some sunlight can penetrate from above through the thick growth. *H. flammeus* likes the company of others of its and related species, so that several such sets should be kept together. It also

Illus. II-128. *Hyphessobrycon flammeus.*

prefers to reproduce in groups. Courtship is violent and a delight to the observer. When kept under the right conditions, *H. flammeus* is a very productive fish. It is not necessary to put several males in with one female as has been advised for breeding; it is better to have two or three couples together in a roomy, but not too high, aquarium.

Reproduction, hatching out of the young and the growing up of the young fry, are not difficult if the fish are assured of a quiet location. A total of about 500 eggs can be laid per period. The eggs hatch out in 45 hours, after which the young hang from plants and panes and dare their first attempts at swimming on the second day.

All kinds of live food are gladly accepted—*H. flammeus* does consume dried animal food, but that should, nevertheless, only be given as an exception.

Hyphessobrycon georgettae Géry, 1961

Georgette's Tetra

This dwarf tetra discovered by the well known fish dealer Pijpers (Paramaribo, Surinam) became one of the most popular species shortly after its importation began. *H. georgettae* apparently grows no larger than about 18 mm ($\frac{3}{4}$ inch). The striking, salmon-red coloration seems to glow from every part of the body and is equally intense all over. Moreover, there is a black, oblong spot in the dorsal fin, a pair of very narrow, dark lines run across the flanks in a lengthwise direction, and there are accumulations of dark pigment on the gill covers, on the

Illus. II-129. The savannah of southern Surinam, where the biotope of *Hyphessobrycon georgettae* was found.

Illus. II-130. The biotope of *Hyphessobrycon georgettae* **(see also the detailed catch report on page 255).**

frontal rays of the anal fin and in some pattern in the caudal fin. In various characteristics, it is quite similar to the "Minor."

A temperature of 25 °C (77 °F) seems to be important to the well-being of this fish, which then shows off its finest coloration.

Illus. II-131. *Hyphessobrycon georgettae.*

Plate II-144. *Hyphessobrycon griemi.*

Hyphessobrycon griemi Hoedeman, 1957
Gold Spotted Rio

This splendid acquisition to the hobby was imported in 1956 by Aquarium Hamburg from southeastern Brazil, the region whence also come the two other species of this group, *H. bifasciatus* and *H. flammeus*. *H. griemi* is similar in most characteristics to both of these species, but the basic coloration is more golden to copper-red. Moreover, it is to be kept like its nearest relatives; its reproduction, which has been completely successful in the aquarium, is also similar to that of its relatives.

Hyphessobrycon heterorhabdus (Ulrey, 1895)
Belgian Flag Characin

This species inhabits the lower reaches of the Amazon and its tributaries, Rio Para and Rio Tocantins. This fish was first imported into Germany in 1910. Aquarium-raised specimens reached Holland in 1934. After 1945, regular imports were arriving in the Netherlands from Surinam, which also yielded Dutch re-breeding.

666

The basic coloration is brownish silver-grey. The flanks are decorated with a distinct, three-toned, end-long band—from above to below, carmine red, yellow and deep black—from which it gets the name of Belgian Flag Characin.

The back is dark olive brown, the belly silver-white, gleaming. The fins are almost without coloration and are transparent. Seen by transmitted light, the body cavity of the female shows up as rounded, while the male's is pointed.

The water temperature must be at least 20 °C (68 °F), preferably a little higher. At a normal temperature of 24 °C (75 °F), which is not allowed to drop below 22 °C (72 °F) in the fall, *H. heterorhabdus* will be continually at its best in showing off its coloration.

Breed this fish at 25–28 °C (77–82 °F) for good results; a roomy breeding tank is recommended. The plant growth in regular and breeding aquariums should be thick, composed of fine-leaved plants. A dark bottom and dark back wall, and top light or light falling downwards on the surface of the water are desirable.

A total of several hundred eggs (these are small and glass-clear) are laid on plants and other objects. The first young hatch out after two days. The parents, and especially the young fish, are very sensitive to temperature fluctuations, as well as to changes in the environment and the composition of the water.

Plate II-145. *Hyphessobrycon heterorhabdus*.

Hyphessobrycon peruvianus Ladiges, 1938
Peruvian Tetra

This fish hails from the Peruvian Amazon, from the vicinity of Loreto. The name Tetra of Loreto or Loreto Tetra is already commonly known and is now quite current in hobbyist circles. This is not only too bad, but also misleading, because another species hailing from the same region has the scientific name *Hyphessobrycon loretoensis* and has a more cogent claim to this popular name. Peruvian Tetra would be more suitable for this little fish, although both popular names are potentially applicable to a large number of tetras from that part of the Amazon.

The fish being treated here is certainly a jewel. It falls in the group of small tetras, together with the species of the genus *Hasemania*, and the smaller members of the genera *Hemigrammus* and *Hyphessobrycon*. It reaches a length of about 30 mm ($1\frac{3}{16}$ inches) without the caudal fin. Sometimes a more or less distinct, milk white line may be observed on the tail, just above the dark band, while the fins also exhibit milk white tips. The iris of the eye is golden yellow, the upper edge reddish.

Closely related to the Neon Tetra, *Paracheirodon innesi*, this fish is kept in the same way and is certainly bred in the same manner.

So far as is known, breeding reports have not yet been published.

Hyphessobrycon pulchripinnis Ahl, 1937
Lemon Tetra

Although *H. pulchripinnis* hails from the vicinity of Para (Brazil), the correct catch location is dubious. Imported into Germany in 1937, this species did not arrive in the Netherlands until 1947. Since then, more and more specimens are being found among hobbyists.

Plate II–146 gives an excellent picture of this splendid fish, which is gradually making a firm place for itself among the characins. By its soft tints, which are still distinct, it takes a place out in front of its numerous, attractive relatives. It is similar in all respects to the other *Hyphessobrycon* and *Hemigrammus* species. All external characteristics are clearly shown in Plate II–146, except that older specimens exhibit a black edge along the forked rays of the caudal fin, which is typical for this species. The pectoral and ventral fins are transparent. The females are somewhat darker (a little redder) than the slimmer males. The maximum length is 42 mm (about $1\frac{43}{64}$ inches).

Keep the temperature at 18–24 °C (64–75 °F). *H. pulchripinnis* likes a tank with thick edge-planting, a few floating plants (*Riccia, Salvinia*),

Plate II-146. *Hyphessobrycon pulchripinnis.*

and a location that receives some sunlight (especially in the morning hours).

This species can be well compared at breeding to the Red Rio (*Hyphessobrycon flammeus*). It is a very productive fish and offers a boisterous courtship to watch. Depending on the temperature, the eggs hatch out after 30 to 50 hours.

Hyphessobrycon rosaceus Durbin, 1909
Rosaceus
Rosy Tetra

With certainty, this species is known only in the drainage basin of the Surinam River, in the vicinity of Paramaribo, and in the Amazon Basin. The length of the males is a maximum 45 mm (1 $\frac{13}{16}$ inches), of the females, a little less. The snout is short with a large, upward-turned mouth opening. The large dorsal fin, in the males running in a sharp curve, is placed rather far forward.

The basic coloration of these unusually beautiful little fish is soft red with a silvery sheen and an olive green glow over the entire body. The back and upper part of the head are carmine red to reddish brown. The dorsal fin is black with whitish fin rays and a milk white frontal edge. The remaining fins are light reddish with a slight green sheen and bright red spots. In addition to the differences already mentioned, the males can be clearly distinguished from the females by their more robust build and larger fins, at least as soon as they have attained a length of about 25 mm (1 inch).

Hyphessobrycon rosaceus is an ornamental fish, extremely peaceful but

Illus. II-132. *Hyphessobrycon rosaceus.*

Plate II-147. *Hyphessobrycon roberti.*

very lively. The community aquarium will be enriched to the utmost with a pair of these attractive and high-spirited fish.

For breeding, take a not too small tank in the spring and plant it well with *Myriophyllum, Heteranthera zosteraefolia* and *Vallisneria.* Bring the temperature up gradually, by sunlight if possible, to 25–26 °C (77–79 °F), but not higher, to avoid exhaustion. Egg-laying then takes place, preferably where sunlight can penetrate among the clumps of plant growth. The courtship that follows is certainly worth the trouble of watching. In his most beautiful suit, the male "dances" around his chosen one, now left, now right, always showing off the most sparkling coloration, which at that time only is seen in all its glory. During the mating, however, both fish tend to lose some of their coloration.

The eggs are finally laid, light yellow to yellow-brown, and not even a millimetre (0.04 inch) in diameter. While shaking violently, the parents press their bodies close against each other and the eggs rain down. When you feel that the eggs have all been laid—it is indeed a question of feeling—then do your best to remove the parents. Be patient.

As a rule, the young can be spotted after two days, but only with difficulty. They are extremely small, and that they may not be visible does not mean that they are not there. Many a brood has gone down the drain owing to the owner's impatience. Sometimes after even five days the eggs are still hatching and not for a week or more later can the first young be seen frisking about. Although small breeding results are often mentioned, 500 to 600 eggs can be laid and, thus, more than 500 progeny in a single brood are possible. A brood of 100 fry who will thrive is, however, considered a very decent result.

Reproduction of this species, unlike that of its closest relatives—even the Neon Tetra—is a difficult operation, so much so that Sibbes calls it Problem Fish No. 2. Although the author's personal experience has been otherwise, this may perhaps be ascribed to the way the aquarium was set up, and perhaps to the dimensions of the aquarium. Transferring breeding groups to the breeding tanks is certainly a mistake; better the opposite, a removal of the other fishes from the large tank at the onset of mating. But, this must not degenerate into a chase after the other fishes, for then the breeders would certainly be more disturbed than if they had been transferred into a breeding tank. If the water from all the tanks circulates through all aquariums—a combination show-tank/breeding-tank might deserve consideration—then a cautious transfer of *H. rosaceus* is possible (in the evening hours, by twilight) without the breeding fish being retarded. Establishment of the aquarium with a turf-dust soil is always good for these picturesque fishes and much better than filtering over peat with sand.

H. rosaceus does not mate in schools, as Sibbes supposes, although it is clearly a school fish. The mating activity, however, is wholly established on the formation of couples and, thus, is a higher grade of reproductive biology than primitive mating in schools, as is practiced by the minnow-like fishes (such as various rasboras). Naturally, this does not mean that several specimens together will not give good results, but a carefully chosen couple (out of a small band) will, by exercise of judgment and sufficient fore care by the owner, certainly give equally good results. Enough space and a more or less shallow part with a thick growth are certainly necessary in order to arrive at reasonable results.

Plate II-148. *Hyphessobrycon rubrostigma,* fully developed male.

Hyphessobrycon rubrostigma Hoedeman, 1956
(probably identical with *Hyphessobrycon erythrostigma* Fowler, 1943)
Bleeding Heart Tetra
Blood Spot Tetra

In characteristics and conduct, *H. rubrostigma* is quite similar to its related species and varieties from the *Hyphessobrycon callistus* group.

Hyphessobrycon scholzei Ahl, 1937
Black-Banded Characin

In South America, this fish is found in an Amazon estuary, in the vicinity of Para, Brazil.

This species can attain a maximum length of 65 mm ($2\frac{9}{16}$ inches), a length which is not quickly, or, in general, not ever, reached in the aquarium. Nevertheless, smaller fish can already be fully grown and mature sexually without the "quality" of the fish being lessened. Even in the wild, adult specimens are found that have not attained full growth by reason of circumstances, and yet they are splendid in all respects.

Although *H. scholzei* shows few tones, the distinct black band, which runs out into a diamond-shaped spot on the root of the tail, is so attractive on the silvery gleaming body that the Black-Banded Characin is certainly going to be one of the very popular aquarium fishes. Above the black band very beautiful specimens exhibit another light, whitish to golden green gleaming line, more or less strongly contrasting with the usually darker, net-like pattern decorating the back.

The sexes are easy to tell apart, though not by means of the white or porcelain-like to ice blue frontal fin rays of the anal fin, but more by the higher build and broader belly of the females.

In general, what has been said about, among others, *Hyphessobrycon heterorhabdus, Pristella riddlei* and relatives from the same region, applies equally well to *Hyphessobrycon scholzei*. As a dweller of mostly shadowy waters, it withstands strong temperature variations very well, only, however, if they occur gradually. At temperatures of about 12 °C (54 °F), the first clear signs of discomfort are noticed, although it can start laying eggs at about 16 °C (61 °F), if conditions are contributory. A more suitable temperature lies between 18 and 22 °C (64–72 °F).

For mating, *H. scholzei* likes to be in company with its own kind, so preferably keep several couples together in a roomy aquarium. A very thick plant growth of fine-leaved varieties or bundles of algae is

Plate II-149. *Hyphessobrycon scholzei.*

Plate II-150. *Hyphessobrycon vilmae.*

well liked by *H. scholzei* for laying its moderately adhesive eggs on. In the usually rather boisterous mating, the males lose practically all coloration and pattern from the body; the fins, which usually are without coloration and transparent, become somewhat darker. The coloration of the females remains the same as outside the mating season.

About 100 to 500 eggs can very easily be laid per period by a single couple. The eggs hatch out, depending on the temperature, after 30 to 50 hours. There are no difficulties attached to raising the brood and they grow up very quickly. A requirement is thick growth along the sides, and floating plants to temper the bright illumination. A dark background as well as a bottom soil overgrown with thread algae (or otherwise darkened) is greatly appreciated by both parents and young.

Plate II-151. *Serrasalmus nattereri.*

Plate II-152. *Micobrycon cochui.*

Plate II-153. *Nematobrycon palmeri.*

Plate II-154. *Metynnis roosevelti.*

Genus *Megalamphodus*

Although the genus *Megalamphodus* has already been noised about for more than 50 years in scientific publications, these Phantom Tetras were not seen in hobbyists' aquariums until several years ago. In many respects, they are classified among the tetras, especially those of the *Hyphessobrycon callistus* group, and should be kept as those are.

Megalamphodus megalopterus Eigenmann, 1912

Black Phantom Tetra

The Black Phantom is a handsome Brazilian import which is ideal for an aquarium containing other small fishes of similar size and nature. It is active and hardy, but peaceful, and reaches a length of slightly more than 4 cm (1½ inches). The body is dusky, almost blackish, silvery towards the belly and has a prominent shoulder spot. The caudal fin is blackish.

The sexes are easily distinguished in mature fish, since the male has a longer and more prominent dorsal fin. The anal fin of the male is also larger and darker. Both anal and adipose fins are redder on the female. Spawning is carried on in typical tetra fashion—adhesive eggs are scattered in plant thickets or bundles of plants. The eggs hatch in a little over a day. Eggs are reportedly light-sensitive and susceptible to fungus.

Plate II-155. A recent import, referred to on the market as "Roberti," is probably a *Megalamphodus* species.

Megalamphodus sweglesi Géry, 1961

Red Phantom Tetra

The Red Phantom Tetra was discovered near Leticia, Colombia, in 1960 and was described by Géry as a new species in 1961. Like its relative, *M. megalopterus*, it is a small, typical tetra which in many ways is similar to some of the *Hyphessobrycon* spp. It is active and peaceful and is best kept in schools.

The body is a translucent, reddish brown with a prominent black shoulder blotch. The fins are reddish brown, the dorsal with a black or dark spot which may vary in intensity. Mature fish can be easily sexed by the longer dorsal fin of the male.

Feeding and other requirements are the same as for other similar tetras.

Genus *Moenkhausia*

The genus *Moenkhausia* is, in addition to *Astyanax*, one of the most interesting genera of tetras, not so much for aquarists as for the study of the characins. A large number of species and varieties has been assembled in the genus on the basis of, among other things, the straight lateral line. It is obviously a rather heterogeneous genus, yet the extremes in form very clearly blend into each other. Directly derived from *Moenkhausia* are, among others, the Stethaprionini, which lead in a straight line towards the Serrasalminae.

The members of this genus have the hub of their distribution in the Guianas and Amazonas region, but also occur more to the south, as far as Paraguay. The few forms being kept in aquariums hail from the Guiana Highlands.

Moenkhausia oligolepis (Günther, 1864)

Glass Tetra

Hailing from the Amazon Basin and the Guiana Highlands, this is a fish that has enjoyed great popularity for a long time. It had disappeared entirely from hobbyists' aquariums, but about 1951 cropped up again. Imports from Surinam again populate the tanks of many hobbyists, and so far as can be checked up on, the Surinamese form is more beautiful than the fish we formerly had from Guyana or the Amazon Basin. This beauty is not only because of the coloration of *M. oligolepis*, as can be seen in Plate II–156, but especially because *M. oligolepis* is a variety that obviously does not attain the dimensions of its relatives from the other districts. Where these related fish are 100 mm (4 inches) and longer, the Surinamese form is probably not much larger than about 60 mm (2⅜ inches), without the caudal fin. Although this is still a proper size for an aquarium fish, it is a very gratifying and tranquil swimmer, which especially in schools is a true acquisition for the hobby.

In its life style *M. oligolepis* does not differ from the already discussed *Hemigrammus* species and may be compared to it in all respects. Also, reproduction takes place as described, for example, for *Hemigrammus caudovittatus* or *H. pulcher*. However, a prerequisite is a very roomy aquarium with edge planting and a little sunlight. The temperature should be 20–25 °C (68–77 °F).

Moenkhausia pittieri Eigenmann, 1920

Diamond Characin

Diamond Tetra

This species comes from Venezuela—from Lake Valencia and its

Plate II-156. *Moenkhausia oligolepis.*

Plate II-157. *Moenkhausia sanctae filomenae.*

681

surroundings, Rio Chiriquito and Rio Bue. It has been a commonly kept species since 1933, and is still viewed with high regard by numerous hobbyists.

A characin of high build, appreciably compressed laterally, *M. pittieri* can attain a length of about 65 mm ($2\frac{9}{16}$ inches). The basic coloration is silver-grey with a very strong, alternating glow of light purplish to soft green. The scales have a splendid golden sheen, which, in direct light from above as a varying number of scales are lighted, gives off a glitter like a diamond—hence the popular name of this species.

The fins are very large and, especially in the male, the dorsal and anal fins can take on formidable measurements. The dorsal fin grows out in a large sickle-shape, of which the extreme point on the outside can reach the caudal fin.

Keep *M. pittieri* like the other tetras, preferably in a roomy aquarium at a temperature about 24 °C (75 °F). Preferably, keep several specimens of this species together, and they will put on a surprisingly beautiful show in a well planted tank into which the sunlight penetrates.

Reproduction is as with its relatives. *M. pittieri* is an egg-eater, thus a thick growth of fine-leaved plants is required. The young hatch out after 50 hours and are not difficult to bring up. Feed the young ditch infusoria, and later strained waterfleas, cyclops, etc. A good spawning can yield several hundred specimens.

Plate II-158. *Moenkhausia pittieri.*

Genus *Pristella*

This genus, to which only two species belong—*P. riddlei* and *P. aubynei*—differs from *Hemigrammus* only in that its upper jaw is completely set with teeth. *Pristella* is very common in the coastal regions of the Guiana Highlands to the drainage basin of the Orinoco River.

Pristella riddlei (Meek, 1907)
Pristella

X-Ray Fish (U.K.)

This species inhabits the northerly part of South America—Venezuela, the Guianas, and the lower reaches of the Amazon. A number of specimens were first brought to Europe in 1924.

The basic coloration is silver-grey, and the body is transparent with a soft, light brown to yellowish sheen. The pattern of spots is very striking—a shoulder spot, a large spot in the dorsal fin, one in the anal fin and one in the ventral fins, all dark brownish to deep black. The dorsal and anal fins are lemon yellow on the base with white dots; the caudal fin has a soft red sheen. The sexes are quite clearly distinguished, as the dark, translucent area of the belly in the male is

683

pointed, in the female rounded. Therefore, the males are generally slimmer and smaller than the females, a characteristic mark, however, only in completely full-grown specimens. During the mating season, the females have a clearly rounder belly. Also, the red in the tail is brighter in the male than the female; otherwise, the pattern of coloration in both sexes is the same.

Pristella riddlei is a fish that gives a great deal of pleasure to hobbyists, and can be called one of the most beautiful tetras. It requires a water temperature of at least 22 °C (72 °F), but is most at ease at a temperature of about 24 °C (75 °F), as well as at its most beautiful in coloration and pattern. There is a commercially-bred albino version available.

A roomy breeding tank, a sunny location, a sufficiently large, open swimming space and good, thick plant growth along the walls are necessary for good results. Egg-laying takes place as among its related species. About 250 to 500 small, glass-clear eggs are laid. The young hatch out on the second or third day and at first are very small, puny little creatures, extremely sensitive to changes in their surroundings.

This very lively fish, which has a special preference for clear water, was originally considered a variety of *Hemigrammus unilineatus*. It is very popular among hobbyists, which is no surprise, for it is lively, extremely tolerant, and in the community aquarium a welcome guest who cheers the whole place with its particular coloration. It should be kept among members of its own species and other fishes of about the same size, in an aquarium having many fine-leaved plants.

Plate II-160. *Thayeria boehlkei.*

Genus *Thayeria*

This genus is distinguished from *Hemigrammus* and related fishes such as *Nannobrycon* and *Nannostomus*, by the larger and heavier lower caudal fin lobe, the shape of the swim bladder and angled position of the fish in the water because of it.

Thayeria boehlkei Weitzman, 1957
Boehlke's Penguin Fish

This South American species comes from the Amazon region near Obidos, Brazil.

Since its importation in 1935, this little characin, which hangs at an angle in the water, has been drawing a constantly growing share of admirers because of its graceful movements and interesting actions. The shape of its body is a great deal like that of the Black-Banded Characin (*Hyphessobrycon scholzei*), but is, however, stretched out a little longer. The caudal fin is partly covered with scales. The length of both sexes attains a maximum of 82 mm ($3\frac{1}{4}$ inches).

The basic coloration is silvery with a brassy yellow sheen and a black,

685

lengthwise stripe. The band, running from the edge of the gill cover over the root of the tail and into the lower caudal fin lobe, is coal black, bordered on the flanks and underside by a line of gleaming gold. According to conditions, the back can be yellow-brown with green in it, the belly whitish with a red-violet sheen. At the base of the frontal rays of the dorsal fin, the coloration is orange-red to yellow, which can also be present in the upper lobe of the caudal fin. The frontal rays of the anal fin are white; beyond this, the fin is without coloration or light yellow.

Thayeria boehlkei is kept like its related species, but in an aquarium that is much more thickly planted with fine-leaved plants. Moderate light and a temperature between 20 and 25 °C (68–77 °F) are recommended. Reproduction takes place as with other Tetragonopterini, at least as violently. The eggs (10 to 15 per mating) are laid close to the surface among *Myriophyllum* or *Riccia*, but usually fall to the bottom as they are not very adhesive. In view of *Thayeria boehlkei's* preference for laying at the surface, it is recommended that the water stands high in the tank, or that a terrace be made. They also appreciate a dark soil bottom, like practically all their relatives, against which they look much better. Bright light apparently damages both the eggs and the young; therefore, allow, at the most, only a few rays of sunlight to fall into the tank from above. The yellow-brown eggs hatch out very quickly, and usually the first young are already swimming about a day after the laying. If the light has been sufficiently screened off, they like to stay at the surface; otherwise they remain at the bottom. A good mating pair is very productive and per mating period (which can extend over 5 to 8 weeks) can produce 2,000 eggs. In a correctly set-up aquarium, the young grow quickly and within a month start to show the black band. The remarkable angled position of this fish, which is also found in other species of this family (without their being closely related), such as *Hemiodus, Nannobrycon,* and others, is caused by muscle tissue and structure of the caudal fin which makes the rear half of the body heavier. When the fish swims in a forward direction, the body is usually horizontal, and it swims upwards in a line that is parallel to the line of the lower caudal fin lobe. This species has the greatest elevation when hanging still in the water and the stripe in the caudal fin points straight downward.

The shape of the swim bladder also gives the body the elevation peculiar to this species.

Illus. II-133. *Thayeria obliqua.*

Thayeria obliqua Eigenmann, 1908
Penguin Fish

Weitzman has shown in a publication (1957) that up to the time of that publication, most specimens current among aquarists were not *Thayeria obliqua,* but the new species *Thayeria boehlkei.* At present, both species are current.

Illus. II-134. *Poptella orbicularis.*

Tribe Stethaprionini

This is perhaps a completely artificial group of tetras, which is distinguished from the high-built Tetragonopterini by a forward-lying spine in front of the dorsal fin. As a whole, however, this group forms the link between the Cheirodontinae, Tetragonopterinae and the Serrasalminae.

Up to now, only one species has been imported—a very attractive aquarium fish—which has not the slightest indication of any relationship to Serrasalminae.

Genus *Poptella*

Up to now, only one species of this genus is known.

***Poptella orbicularis* (Valenciennes, 1849)**

Disc Characin

This South American characin comes from the Amazon Basin, as well as from Peru to Brazil and the Guianas. Recent imports from Surinam belong to this species, but perhaps to a deviant sub-species from those of the Amazon Basin.

According to its place of origin, this little fish attains a size of about 50 mm to 100 mm (2 to 4 inches), without the caudal fin. Although this seems rather large, the form is such that even full-grown specimens, because of their strongly compressed body, are not disturbing in

688

community aquariums, as long as the tank is large enough. The sexes can be clearly recognized, both by the larger dimensions of the female and by the intensely black frontal rays of the anal fin of the male.

The basic coloration of the Surinamese specimens, which enliven the community aquarium a great deal with their activities, is simply silver, and, depending on the angle of light and conditions, either highly glittering or matt. It gradually turns to olive towards the back, sometimes olive green, sometimes more brownish, and some scales glisten a bright golden yellow. The fish, of course, must be in completely good condition for these splendid manifestations to show up, which naturally is true for all other fishes in tanks, as well.

In addition to simple and some distinct coloration, the only other hue present is the already-mentioned black of the frontal rays of the anal fin in the male. In a few specimens, however, the species-characteristic shoulder stripes can occasionally be seen. These two shoulder spots, which distinguish this species from the very closely related *Moenkhausia bondi*—they are difficult to tell apart by eye—are more clearly present on specimens from the Amazon Basin. In *Moenkhausia bondi*, which in addition to the technical characteristics differs by only one rather round shoulder spot, the anal fin does not have black rays, nor does it have any lengthened fin rays.

This fish, even though it can grow rather large, is certainly going to occupy a permanent place among aquarium fishes, and can be likened to various *Hemigrammus* or *Moenkhausia* species, which have a similar lively and mobile nature. *Poptella orbicularis* dwells in open water, just under the banks where it can hide among the plant growth. When frightened, it quickly flees and in the aquarium seeks safety behind plants and in places that are more shadow-filled. Soon, however, it pops up again and darts about in the more brightly lit, open part of the tank. It gladly seeks out company of its own kind, so it is recommended to keep several specimens together. It is remarkable to see a small group standing still and all dancing in the same tempo, in a manner that can, it is true, be seen in other tetras, yet is conspicuously *Poptella's* own. The dance (as the fish are standing still) is brought about by moving the pectoral fins towards each other.

This species was re-bred in large numbers in 1952 in Rotterdam.

Poptella orbicularis is certainly not any more predatory than the other characins of this group so there is no objection to keeping it together with other fishes which normally occur in its company, such as the various Nannostomini, *Hemigrammus* species, Gasteropelecini, *Corydoras* species, and others.

Tribe Gasteropelecini

The map in Illus. II–135 shows the distribution area of the fishes belonging to this group. In the wild, they are found in marshes, submerged or flooded regions, in ditches, brooks, small and large rivers. As a rule, they are close beneath the surface where they like to lie among marsh and water plants.

The hatchet fishes are distinguished from all the remaining members of the family by the remarkably deepened belly. In fact, not less than a fourth of the total weight of the fish is included in these muscles. These fishes are thus able to make long, gliding flights over the water, made easy by the extremely compressed sideways, almost axe-sharp "prow." Of course, they do not really fly by moving their "wings" up and down in the air (nor, to be sure, does any other kind of a "flying fish").

It is decidedly unfortunate that we seldom get to see this "flying" in the aquarium, for even though the fish might try it at first, they soon get so roughly treated by the limited space that, if they do not damage themselves severely and die, they never try it again.

In 1937, Hoedeman had several specimens (*Carnegiella strigata*) to care for and, luckily, a large aquarium—150 cm (about 5 feet) long.

As a precaution, the tank edges above the water surface were cushioned with curtain material held clear by sponge rubber, which was gratefully made use of during the first few days. The fish learned quite quickly, however (and they all seemed not so susceptible to fright), that only limited space was available. Readers who plan to purchase some of these fishes if they get a chance are certainly advised to rig up some similar kind of precautionary measure.

Illus. II-135. Distribution of the Gasteropelecini.

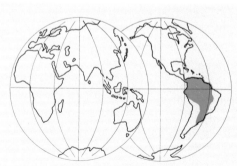

Illus. II-136. Top and front views of a hatchet fish. Note the pectoral fins grown out to great length.

Genus *Carnegiella*

A total of three species, *Carnegiella myersi, C. marthae,* and *C. strigata,* of which only the last is commonly known and represented by not less than five sub-species, are included in this genus.

Illus. II-137. This man is wading through the pool while the air buzzes with the flight of insects. Here dozens of little hatchet fish fled over the water plants. This is a typical biotope for these insect-eaters.

Carnegiella strigata (Günther, 1864)
Marbled Hatchet Fish

In the Guianas, and the central and lower reaches of the Amazon drainage basin, *Carnegiella strigata* is especially found in quantity in the jungle streams. In 1912, a few specimens were taken into Europe for the first time and later were repeatedly imported.

The basic coloration is brownish to golden yellow with a silver sheen; the back is more or less dark green with black dots of varying sizes. The flanks are covered with a pattern of spots of a typical pink to brown, changing to light blue. A pair of dark stripes may be seen on the sides of the head; from the gill covers to the caudal fin runs a black lateral line, bordered on the upper side by a gleaming silver stripe. From the edge of the belly run three irregular, dark blue to brownish black stripes angling forward and backward across the body. The streak lying above the anal fin is also blackish. The fins are light greenish and transparent. The caudal fin is clearly green. External sexual characteristics are unknown. This unusually shaped and ornamental fish requires a well planted aquarium with clear water at a temperature of 24–30 °C (75–86 °F). It is very tolerant and can be kept without danger among all species of fishes of about the same size. In any case, it is advisable to have a large aquarium at its disposal, considerable sunlight, and plants that grow up to the surface of the water. Food is no problem. In addition to waterfleas, even large ones, *C. strigata* willingly eats white worms and mosquito larvae, as well as dried food floating on the surface, gnats, flies, and other small insects.

Sometimes even white worms that have sunk to the bottom will be retrieved by a fish standing in a vertical position. Even though it is an enjoyable and much kept little aquarium fish, nothing at all is known of the results of breeding.

Contrary to the silvery *Gasteropelecus, Carnegiella strigata* is not a pronounced surface dweller. Apparently, it prefers to lie among the plants, without being shy, however. That does not mean that it spends all its time among the plants and is seldom seen; to the contrary, it is a very mobile and playful species.

The males put on a lot of sham fights among themselves, but never do any serious damage.

Carnegiella, a graceful, elegant fish, was named for Miss Margaret Carnegie.

Genus *Gasteropelecus*

According to the latest views, this genus includes only two true species, *Gasteropelecus sternicla*, a variety that has been known since 1758 through Linné (Linnaeus), and *Gasteropelecus maculatus.*

Gasteropelecus sternicla (Linné, 1758)
Silver Hatchet Fish

Several sub-species, which formerly were often taken for "true" species, are presently distinguished. There are at least three varieties, which differ only slightly externally, but which anatomically form clear, geographical sub-species. One of them has been known for a long time as *Pterodiscus levis.*

As a pronounced dweller of the more open water (in contrast to *Carnegiella strigata*), *G. sternicla*'s coloration is not very conspicuous and thus the fish is adapted to an environment having little or no plant growth. Here, it lives directly below the surface, and seen from above, with the dark, lengthwise stripe, it seems to be an ordinary fish. Not until it has been taken from the water, or has been closely watched through the front pane of an aquarium, is it noticeable that the shape

694

of the body deviates considerably from normal. This is caused by the extensively outgrown "crow's bill bones" (coracoid process) which have been folded to give them greater stiffness. The purpose of this is to let the fish shoot through and over the water with the speed of an arrow, on the one hand to escape from its enemies, and on the other, and perhaps mainly, to enable it to hunt flying insects above the water, which form the main dish of its menu. The marvelously shaped crow's bill bones serve, at the same time, for attachment of the strongly developed muscles actuating the pectoral fins. The large pectoral fins move with lightning speed, and they pedal the fish across the surface of the water, while only the rearmost part remains under the surface. If the speed becomes great enough, the fish is lifted completely out of the water and makes a gliding flight, sometimes up to many metres (yards) long.

The species *Gasteropelecus maculatus* with its three sub-species has somewhat more pigment and exhibits a few irregular black spots on the flanks.

Illus. II-138. Skeleton of *Thoracocharax securis.* The enormously developed pair of crow's-bill bones (coracoid processes) can be clearly seen.

Genus *Thoracocharax*

Under this generic name, three forms have been named— *T. securis, T. stellatus,* and *T. eigenmanni.* From their distribution pattern, scattered throughout the Amazon region, it seems likely that several other forms may still be discovered. They may, however, all turn out to be local varieties of a single species.

Orders Polypteriformes to Esociformes

In Table I–4 on page 34, which tries to represent the developmental history of fish, the bony fishes (item 21) are divided first into three orders that together form the super-order Ostariophysi (item 21a) and a number of orders (items 25 to 33) directly related to them, and second into the remaining orders of bony fishes (item 21b), subdivided into Holostei and Teleostei.

Although the orders in items 25 to 33 include a comparatively small number of imported aquarium fish, it will still be of value to go into further detail concerning them. The orders included here are as follows: Polypteriformes (item 25), Osteoglossiformes (item 26), Notopteriformes (item 27), Mormyriformes (item 28), Elopiformes (item 29), Anguilliformes (item 30), Clupeiformes (item 31), Salmoniformes (item 32), and Esociformes (item 33). Although the mutual connection and the relationship are by no means clear, these groups are distinguished, by numerous characteristics, from the other bony fishes, Holostei and Teleostei (sensu stricto), and have a more

Plate II-163. *Apteronotus albifrons.*

or less clear connection with the Ostariophysi (item 21a), orders Siluriformes (item 22), Cypriniformes (item 23) and Characiformes (item 24).

On the basis of a less strongly ossified axial skeleton in a number of families, and the apparently entirely different type of scalation (ganoid scales), a number of these orders are generally referred to as the super-order Chondrostei. This group comprises a few well known fossil orders (for instance, the Palaeonisciformes) and the recent orders Acipenseriformes (sturgeons) and Polypteriformes (polypterids). Their relation to the armoured catfishes, however, appears to be based on a number of characteristics which influenced the decision to include them in the present classification.

The orders given no further consideration here are the Elopiformes (tarpons and related large marine fishes), Anguilliformes (eels), Clupeiformes (herring), and the Salmoniformes (salmon), as well as the Esociformes (pike), important food fishes, none of which have any significance for aquarists as aquarium fishes.

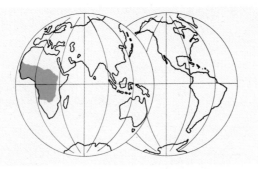

Illus. II-139. Distribution of the Polypteridae.

Order Polypteriformes

This is a very old group that has existed on earth since the Triassic period. Even today, only two genera are known, both from Africa. The dorsal fin is remarkable in that it consists of a number of flag-shaped growths on the fin rays, each one separate from the following one. Fossil scales have been found in the Upper Eocene strata in Egypt. The scales are diamond-shaped, covered with a glazed coating and provided with fine, tiny teeth. The order includes only one family with two genera.

Family Polypteridae

The two still existing genera, *Polypterus* and *Calamoichthys*, inhabit the fresh waters of Africa.

Genus *Polypterus*

This genus is characterized by two or more forked rays on the dorsal fin spines. Ventral fins are present, in contrast to the genus *Calamoichthys*, which lacks them; the caudal fin is symmetrical; and the pectoral fins have a thickened lobe-like base covered with small scales. The body is snake-like.

Young polypterids (larval stage) betray a close relationship with some Amphibia and exhibit a remarkable metamorphosis. At first, they have external gills, feather-like outgrowths on the edge of the gill covers, above the regular gill opening. Even when the fishes are 20 cm (8 inches) long, these external gills remain, fully developed, as clearly shown in Illus. II–140. Beyond this stage of development of the larvae, however, the external gills are gradually resorbed.

Plate II-164. *Polypterus delhezi.*

Plate II-165. *Polypterus palmas.*

Plate II-166. *Polypterus ornatipinnis.*

Closely related to the lungfishes, the polypterids are also able to breathe with the aid of their air (swim) bladder and by doing so can remain out of water for some time. A primitive characteristic in fish is a well developed spiral valve in the end of the intestine, a remainder of which is present in the polypterids. On the other hand, this spiral intestine has completely disappeared from all higher, bony fishes.

Polypterus bichir from the Nile, the best known species, grows to not less than 150 cm (5 feet) long.

Illus. II-140. Larva of *Polypterus lapradei.*

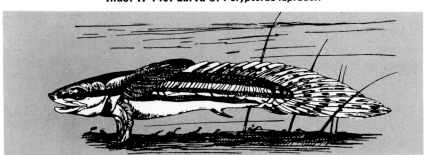

701

Genus *Calamoichthys*

This genus differs from *Polypterus* in that it has an extremely eel-like form, no ventral fins, and only one forked ray on the dorsal fin spines.

Calamoichthys calabaricus (J. A. Smith, 1865)
Reed Fish

Snake Fish

This, the only known species of this genus, inhabits mud banks in the estuaries of West African rivers, from Nigeria to Cameroon. Although by origin a typical fresh-water fish, it is often found in brackish, coastal waters.

Calamoichthys calabaricus is a very striking, but not attractive, fish with a brownish back, yellow to orange belly, and fins practically without coloration. The total length, however, is not less than 37 cm ($14\frac{1}{2}$ inches), and though it is certainly not a commonly known fish, it is indeed considered special by aquarists. It is clear that the dimensions of the aquarium should be proportionally large. The temperature should be 20–26 °C (68–79 °F) and more. Nothing is known about their propagation, at least, not with certainty. It is known that the females have fewer rays in the anal fin (9 to 12) than the males (12 to 14). In the male, the anal fin is transformed during the mating season and broad, sac-like folds of skin appear between the rays. Since developed eggs have been found in preserved females, it may be concluded that some kind of internal fertilization takes place. Intestinal respiration is the same as with *Polypterus*. All types of food are appropriate.

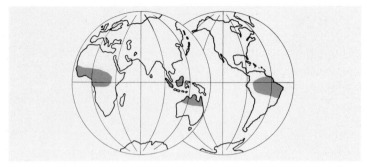

Order Osteoglossiformes

Presently included in this order are the families Plethodontidae (known only from Cretaceous fossils from Europe and North America), Arapaimidae, Osteoglossidae and Heterodontidae (which some authorities include in one family, Osteoglossidae), which together form the sub-order Osteoglossoidei. They are all very large fishes which, in their native lands, inhabit the large rivers and are a sought-after food. They are not suitable for the aquarium, but from time to time,

Illus. II-142. *Osteoglossum bicirrhosum,* young specimen.

Plate II-167. *Osteoglossum albifrons.*

smaller specimens may be seen in public aquariums. However, the order is of further interest to us particularly because of the second sub-order, Pantodontoidei.

Sub-order Pantodontoidei

Only one family with a single known species comprises this sub-order, which is closely related to the Osteoglossidae.

Illus. II-143. Distribution of the Pantodontoidei.

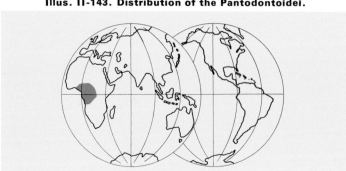

Plate II-168. *Pantodon buchholzi.*

Family Pantodontidae

Pantodon buchholzi **Peters, 1876**

Butterfly Fish

This decidedly fresh-water fish is from tropical Africa—the rivers draining into the Atlantic from the Niger to the Congo. *Pantodon buchholzi* prefers a temperature of about 25° C (77 °F). It accepts as food all living insects and their larvae (even big cockroaches), worms and the like, provided they are floating on the surface.

As it does not often dive down to retrieve sinking food, it is decidedly a surface fish which skims the surface in a long gliding flight, using its unusually large pectoral fins for wings.

The mating procedure is very interesting. A chase by the male precedes the egg-laying. During the preliminaries to the actual mating act, he rides "horseback" on the female. They swim about like this for some time, after which the male slips down alongside the female's tail.

Egg-laying takes place quietly among the plants, the female remaining dead still, the male by her side, holding her tightly with his fins. The further course of mating needs more study, as does the number of eggs that are laid and their further developmental history. It is known that the eggs hatch after about a week.

The male (Plate II–168) has a peculiarly formed anal fin, while the rest of the fins are somewhat more substantially developed than in the female.

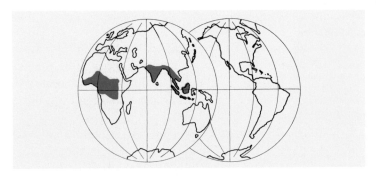

Illus. II-144. Distribution of the Notopteriformes.

Order Notopteriformes

This is a small order with a number of interesting species for the aquarist. Of the two families, Hiodontidae and Notopteridae, only the latter is of interest to us. Their relationship to the Mormyriformes order is plausible.

Family Notopteridae

Both known genera of this family are significant to aquarists, although representatives are, at present, not commonly known and appreciated, but are considered more as special fishes.

Genus *Notopterus*

These so-called knife fishes are held in the greatest esteem by aquarists, in spite of their strange appearance.

Notopterus is represented by one species in Africa and three species in Asia, of which only the African species is known in European aquarist circles. Both *Notopterus notopterus* and *Notopterus chitala* are occasionally seen in America.

Notopterus afer Günther, 1868
African Featherfin

The lateral compression of the body of *Notopterus afer* is extreme. It has a very, very small dorsal fin at about three eighths the distance from the snout to the end of the tail. A low anal fin runs from the pectorals to the point of the tail, with no clear division from the caudal fin.

This fish is a rather timid crepuscular or twilight-active fish. Its coloration is dark olive brown with blackish marbling. The temperature should be about 25 °C (77 °F). It eats all kinds of large and small live food animals.

This amazingly-shaped fish has a laterally compressed, club-shaped body, from which it gets the name "knife fish," a name that is also used for the entirely unrelated Gymnotidae.

Among the featherfins, the anal and caudal fins are grown together with a total of not less than 110 to 130 fin rays. This fin, running the full length of the fish, is its means of movement through the water.

Plate II-170. *Notopterus chitala.*

Body waves pass along the length of the fin, causing the fish to move either forward or backward, depending on the direction of the fin movement. The waving can be increased to the point where considerable speed through the water is attained. The backward swimming, which is also seen in *Gymnotus carapo*, for example, and in various catfishes—*Kryptopterus, Physailia, Ompok*, etc.—is so immeasurably better developed among these fishes that no other fish with a normally-shaped anatomy can equal them.

Like the three Asiatic species, *Notopterus afer* has a small dorsal fin of six or seven rays, located in the middle of the back. This is the "featherfin" from which the fish gets its scientific name, *Notopterus* (*noto* means feather and *pterus* means fin), and its common name. *Xenomystus nigri* (see page 711) has no dorsal fin. The nostrils are, as in *Phractolaemus ansorgei*, provided with a kind of tentacle. The head and body are covered with very fine, cycloid (smooth) scales. The belly, just in front of the anal fin, has a saw-tooth edge, consisting of about 40 small spines.

The basic coloration can vary considerably in accordance with the catch location, yet it is mainly greenish brown with a darker, marbled pattern.

As a dweller of practically stagnant waters, thickly begrown with vegetation, *Notopterus afer* prefers a quiet aquarium, arranged accordingly. As for temperature, it should be about 25° C (77 °F) or higher. Literally anything will serve as food, as long as it is living animal matter, waterfleas, tubifex, mosquito larvae, insects, earthworms, snails, young fish, and even rather large fish. From this, it may be obvious that care is required in keeping this fish in a community aquarium. It is an interesting fish, which, unfortunately, gets to be rather large (to about 500 mm or nearly 20 inches), but only after a rather long time.

Just like several other fishes from the primitive groups of teleosts, they possess a lung-like swim bladder which serves as a kind of labyrinth for taking in air directly from the atmosphere

Illus. II-145. *Notopterus notopterus.*

Notopterus notopterus (Pallas, 1780)

This species is common to practically all the waters of Southeast Asia and in various parts of its distribution area may reach a length of 600 mm (nearly 24 inches). However, the usually recorded maximum length of 35 cm (about 14 inches) for specimens from the Indonesian Archipelago is usually not exceeded in most parts of its distribution area. Nevertheless, it is certainly not a very popular fish, because of these measurements, and also because it is difficult to breed in home aquariums, since it must have reached a length of 200 mm (8 inches) or more before being sexually mature.

Young specimens still show a primitive pattern, consisting of about 30 irregularly-sized cross stripes or bands that give it a marbled appearance, similar to that of the young of the *N. afer* from Africa. At a length of about 100 mm (4 inches), the dark stripes flow together and become partially blurred, and the fish is more or less even in coloration all over. Just above the anal fin is a series of large black ocelli ringed in silver. The number of ocelli varies according to the locality.

This species varies from place to place, yet it is easily recognizable by its short upper jaw, which does not run farther back than directly under the leading edge of the eye, unlike the other species, *N. afer* and *N. chitala*, in which the typically herring-like structure of the mouth is readily noticeable, and the upper jaw runs far back and beyond the eye.

Genus *Xenomystus*

***Xenomystus nigri* Günther, 1863**

African Knife Fish

(erroneously called Black Knife Fish since "nigri" is a reference to the Niger River)

Although smaller than *Notopterus afer*, this species may attain a respectable length of about 300 mm (about 12 inches) when it gets older. It has no dorsal fin at all, but unlike the genus *Notopterus*, it does have ventral fins. The basic coloration is yellow-green, blue-green, or brownish green, with a number of darker, lengthwise stripes and no marbling. During the mating season, a purplish brown striping dominates, and the whole fish can take on this coloration. Otherwise, what was said about *Notopterus* applies equally well here. Regarding reproduction, nothing is known other than that the eggs lie loose in the body cavity, for there is no oviduct. Whatever external sex characteristics *Xenomystus nigri* may possess are still unknown.

Plate II-171. *Xenomystus nigri.*

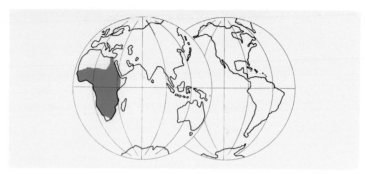

Illus. II-146. Distribution of the Mormyriformes.

Order Mormyriformes

This order is undoubtedly one of the best differentiated of all the groups of bony fishes, by its possession of, in comparison with all other vertebrates, a very large cerebellum. Only two families are distinguished.

Family Gymnarchidae

This family comes from tropical Africa, north of the equator. The single known species, *Gymnarchus niloticus* Cuvier, 1829, can reach a length of more than a metre (39¼ inches).

This is an eel-like fish with a very long dorsal fin, which runs from the head to the point of the tail. The anal fin, caudal fin and ventral fins are absent. It has a swim bladder.

Family Mormyridae

This family comes from the Nile and the fresh waters of tropical Africa. Up to now, ten genera have been described (Boulenger), most having numerous species. Only a few species from the genera *Marcusenius* and *Gnathonemus* have, up to now, become more or less known in aquarist circles.

Genus *Marcusenius*

These fishes have a great variety of shapes, but all are characterized by having the dorsal and anal fins set far back and vertically in line with each other, a rather long and thin tail and an oddly shaped snout, which is sometimes a kind of parrot beak or pig snout. These are decidedly fresh-water fishes that live in slow-moving or stagnant waters.

Illus. II-147. *Marcusenius nigripinnis.*

The temperature should be 22–30 °C (72–86 °F). Ply them with live food animals taken from the bottom. Nothing definite is known about either reproduction or sexual characteristics.

Although fairly large species are known, the smaller, preponderantly dusk-loving fishes are quite suitable for the aquarium.

Genus *Gnathonemus*

This genus is distinguished from *Marcusenius*, among others, by its end-positioned mouth (more or less under-positioned in *Marcusenius*). Remaining data for this genus are the same as described for *Marcusenius*.

It is indeed desirable for more attention to be paid to these species.

Plate II-172. *Gnathonemus schilthuisiae.*

Illus. II-148. *Phractolaemus ansorgei.*

Order Clupeiformes

This widespread order, very important to evolution, includes all herring-like fishes and their relatives which can be thought of as having developed from the primitive herring. The Leptolepidae, primitive, though now extinct, herring-like fishes, represent the main evolutionary line from which not only all other clupeids developed, but which were also the ancestors of the spiny-finned, or perch-like fish.

Naturally, our interest as aquarists is not directed towards the herring as such; however, among the families classified with them also belongs the family Phractolaemidae. Included is a remarkable species that has managed to reach the aquarium.

Genus *Phractolaemus*

This genus is clearly related to the primitive, herring-like fishes, and not to the Osteoglossidae, which was Boulenger's original opinion. Only one species is known at the present time.

Phractolaemus ansorgei **Boulenger, 1909**
African Mud Fish
Fossil Fish

This, again, is a fish which, although interesting and rare, is only occasionally imported from Africa.

It is a dweller of mud banks and the shady shores of the West African rivers—the Niger, for example—and the drainage basin of the upper Congo. The temperature range is from 24–30 °C (75–86 °F).

This fish lives on all kinds of edibles that it gleans from the mud with its outward-folding, trunk-like mouth. Nothing is yet known about its reproduction. Its length is to about 150 mm (6 inches).

Super-order Holostei

This name is still commonly used for a number of orders, including various groups, known only as fossils, with a degenerated axial skeleton, next to the Teleostei (see items 36 to 47 on page 29). The Holostei differentiated from the main stem of bony fishes during the Permian Era (see Table 1—4 on page 34), and is still represented in present-day fauna with two orders. Also, these fishes are more interesting than suitable for home aquariums, although they are indeed sometimes seen in public aquariums. Both orders have been subjected to intensive study and a great deal of writing has been done on the build and finer structures of these fish. On one hand, the Amiiformes have been branded as the ancestral group of the toothcarps, while, on the other hand, this possible relationship has been denied. An old conception of Huxley, who placed the catfishes in his system in such a position that the Ostariophysi, as well as the Amiiformes and Lepisosteiformes, could have originated from them, was fiercely contested, mainly by Regan. Closer investigation, however, points more and more in the direction of Huxley's interpretation.

Order Amiiformes

From this order of fresh-water fishes—that was undoubtedly glorious in former times—now only a single species is known to be living. It will certainly remain a puzzle why just one species has survived its competition. Fossil amiids have been found from the Lower Eocene in Europe and the Middle Eocene in North America of a species which was identical to or very closely related to the single, still-living species from the mud flats of the Great Lakes region, the Mississippi drainage basin, Texas, and Florida in North America. There is only one family, Amiidae, with one species, *Amia calva*.

Order Lepisosteiformes

This order, too, is represented among the current fauna of North and Central America by a single family with only one genus. Plate II–173 gives a good idea of the kind of fishes they are, the so-called garpikes. Fossil finds indicate that its former distribution area was considerably greater than today's, for, in addition to Europe (Upper Cretaceous to Lower Eocene strata), its remains have been found in the Eocene strata of India, and in North America from the Middle Eocene strata up until today. Still, only a few varieties have survived

Illus. II-149. Recent distribution of Lepisosteiformes. The red spots indicate fossil finds of *Lepisosteus*.

into the present, and it appears that these will continue to preserve their place among American fauna for some time. They are decided predators which, in time, will bring fish life into such a dangerous position that controversy will surely result, and traps, especially, will be recommended as the most efficient method of catching them (in order to reduce their population).

Small specimens have occasionally been kept in aquariums, more as curiosities than as aquarium fishes, which they really are not.

Plate II-173. Head of *Lepisosteus tristoechus*.

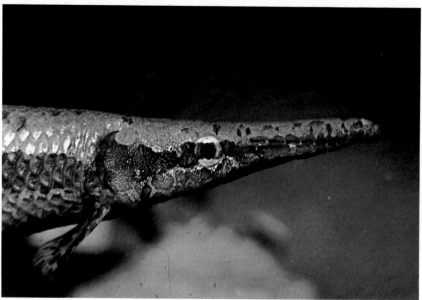

Super-order Teleostei
Orders Mugiliformes to Cyprinodontiformes

The orders included in this system (see Table I–3) are brought in for completeness and are only of partial interest to aquarists. For discussion, only Mugiliformes (item 36), Beloniformes (item 40) and Cyprinodontiformes (item 41) will be considered.

Order Mugiliformes

This order, the so-called "ear-of-grain" fishes or silversides, also erroneously called pike-perch, includes a small number of groups, usually classified in three families. They populate all the seas in temperate and tropical districts. A number of varieties, however, are restricted to coastal waters and a part of them migrate over into fresh water only for spawning. These are the species that interest us here, all belonging to the sub-order Mugiloidea, which separates into two families, the Mugilidae and the Atherinidae.

Family Mugilidae

The genera *Agonostomus* and *Mugil* furnish a few species from fresh or brackish coastal regions for the aquarium fish trade (*Mugil oligolepis*, a very common species near the Indian Ocean, and *Agonostomus monticola*), though they have never become popular. *Pseudomugil signifer* is a very common fresh-water fish in Northern Australia, which, according to available data, is similar to the very well known *Telmatherina ladigesi*. Perhaps the importers will succeed in procuring a few species from Australia. It looks as if the species native to that region are well worth the trouble, and, according to most ichthyologists, are in no way "primary fresh-water fishes."

Family Atherinidae

This family separates into two sub-families, the Nannatherininae—which are distinguished from the Atherininae by their low-set, practically symmetrical pectoral fins and dorsal fins that run together, unseparated. The Atherininae have two distinctly separate dorsal fins.

Sub-family Atherininae

This sub-family is characterized by unsymmetrical pectoral fins which are not set low, an anal fin with only one spine, and dorsal fins which are separated.

This sub-family can be divided into four or five tribes, of which only two are interesting: the Atherinini and the Melanotaeniini.

Tribe Atherinini

To this group belongs, among others, the genus *Telmatherina*. The other genera are, for the time being, of little or no significance.

Genus *Telmatherina*

This genus appears to be limited in its distribution to the Matana and Towuti Lakes on Celebes Island. From this distribution, it may be concluded that the genus may perhaps be considered a relict of a rather recent date.

Telmatherina ladigesi Ahl, 1936
Celebes Rainbow Fish

This fish is native to the hinterland beyond Macassar in Celebes. It reaches a length of about 60 mm (2⅜ inches), not including the caudal fin; the females are somewhat smaller.

Illus. II-150. *Telmatherina ladigesi.*

The basic coloration is dirty yellow to olive green with silvery, glittering scales on its flanks. A striking, light bluish green stripe runs from the middle of the body to the root of the tail, where it merges with a blackish spot which continues along the outermost rays of the fin. The foremost rays of the dorsal and anal fins are just as dark, to black, and on the males are partially unattached to the fin membrane and have a milk white tip. This gives the fish rather a dilapidated look, which has a certain amount of charm, augmented in the mating season by the flapping fin rays. In addition to the striking dorsal fin, which lies directly above the anal fin and is actually the second dorsal fin—as occurs with all representatives of this order (Mugiliformes)—there is still a less outstanding, smaller, first dorsal fin, which often lies flat on the fish's back. The fins are a faded yellow-green to clear lemon yellow. The pectoral fins are transparent. The caudal fin, particularly in the males, shows some white dots at the extreme ends of the caudal fin lobes.

Give this fish an aquarium in a sunny place, with not too high a temperature (about 25 °C or 77 °F) and a water hardness of 6 to 15° DH, which seems necessary. The addition of a little sea water also seems to be required, although, considering the origin of this fish in the fresh-water lakes of the highlands of Macassar, this is unexplainable.

Planting the tank with fine-leaved plants is recommended. Mating and further stages of reproduction take place without much difficulty if these preliminaries are taken care of. The eggs hatch out in about two weeks, whereupon the youngsters are brought up in the usual manner on infusoria, later being fed the smallest living food. Within six months, the young are sexually mature and their total length measures about 50 mm (2 inches).

Tribe Melanotaeniini

To this group belongs the genus *Melanotaenia,* as well as the genus *Pseudomugil,* which, however, will not be discussed for the time being, until varieties belonging to it are again imported.

Genus *Melanotaenia*

This genus, with a small number of species, is distributed among the fresh waters of Australia, New Guinea, and the Aru Islands and is generally regarded as having developed from related genera with a marine distribution.

Up to now, two species have been imported as aquarium fish, *M. maccullochi* and *M. nigrans.*

Melanotaenia maccullochi Ogilby, 1915
Black-Lined Rainbow Fish
Dwarf Rainbow Fish

The members of this genus, like the others considered to belong to the order of Mugiliformes, are dwellers of the coastal waters and

Plate II-174. *Bedotia geayi.*

720

Plate II-175. *Melanotaenia maccullochi.*

are commonly found in the fresh-water estuaries of rivers. That is how this species lives in northeastern Australia, in the Barron River in Queensland, where it attains a total length of about 55 mm (2$\frac{3}{16}$ inches).

The basic coloration is brownish silver, normally with eight rows of dark, reddish brown spots on the scales, one above the other, which, above the middle, have more intense coloration than on the belly side. There are a few brown spots on the bases of the dorsal and anal fins, usually arranged in two rows. The fins are soft yellow to no coloration, with a reddish edge. The foremost dorsal fin is somewhat yellower and the red of the edge is more intense; the foremost rays are a dark red-brown. On and behind the gill covers are a variable number of yellow and ice blue spots.

These fast swimmers require a correspondingly spacious aquarium (the tank should be a metre or a yard long), planted only along the walls with a good-sized open space within. The temperature should be 20–25 °C (68–77 °F). Breeding is quite easy, and the numerous little eggs hatch out in two weeks (after 8 to 11 days). The course of development within the egg is easily observed among these mugilids, owing to the rather thin and transparent egg wall.

Plate II-176. *Melanotaenia nigrans.*

Melanotaenia nigrans (Richardson, 1843)
Australian Rainbow Fish
Red-Tailed Rainbow Fish

There is hardly anything to say about this species, except that it is about twice as big as *M. maccullochi* and that it has not been popular at all. It is, in fact, a rather undesirable species, because of its large size and the consequent swimming requirements. Also, its coloration is not very attractive.

Order Beloniformes

Gill (1872) gave the name Synentognathi to this group of fishes, on the basis of the typical structure of the mouth. The lowermost pharyngeal bones are grown entirely together (in Greek *syn* means together; *entos* means within; *gnathos* means jaw).

Regan (1911) worked the systematics out further, based on the structure of the axial skeleton and the skull.

Because many members of this order are true marine fishes, they are distributed over the entire globe, but especially in the warmer waters. As an order, then, Beloniformes is cosmopolitan.

A number of species from this group—those species that we are most concerned with—are mostly small dwellers of the brackish and fresh waters of the tropics and sub-tropics. The garpike-like fishes have soft-rayed fins and a long, thin body. The swim bladder has no open connection with the alimentary canal; thus, the fish are physoclists. The lateral line organ is usually well developed and runs the entire length of the body along the bottom. In a few species, however, it is rudimentary or entirely absent. The name given by Müller (1844) refers to the fused pharyngeal bones.

The fins, which possess no spiny rays, do have, however, one or more unforked rays. The ventral fins are located on the belly and have six rays, unconnected to the pectoral girdle. The dorsal fin is placed very far to the rear, often wholly or partially opposite the anal fin. The caudal fin always has 13 forked rays. The pectoral fins are usually set high.

The body is covered with cycloid (smooth) scales. The arrangement of these scales in the forepart of the body deviates from the normal (a number of species), because the free (or unfastened) edge lies not to the rear but to the front. At the place where the scales laid forward meet those laid backward are one or more of the so-called reflecting scales covering the junction. Because these reflecting scales are easily shed, loss of the scale covering quickly follows (especially in dead specimens). The intestine is short and straight, which indicates that Beloniformes live on animal food, although many species like a thread of soft alga now and then.

These garpike-like fishes are true surface dwellers which eat practically entirely land- and air-borne creatures (insects, spiders, worms, and such), and, moreover, plankton in the broadest sense. So far, they have not been observed very much.

As an order, Beloniformes are closely related to the Cyprinodontiformes and Percopsiformes. The three orders taken together should probably be regarded as stemming from a common form, belonging to the Clupeiformes probably about the Cretaceous period.

The most acceptable division of Beloniformes is into two sub-orders, the Scombresocoidei and the Exocoetoidei. However, in connection with the idea that has already been brought forth many times, that fresh-water dwellers should be considered more original forms, the order will be reversed here, placing the latter first. This does not mean, however, that Scombresocoidei must have been derived from the Exocoetoidei. It appears far more probable that the correct explanation is a common ancestral form. On these grounds, it appears that re-classification of the named sub-orders into orders is inevitable.

Indications of a progressive reduction of the lengthened jaws, especially in the Hemiramphidae, are found in an obvious series of transitional forms and probably even in the length of the under jaw (that is set with teeth), the section opposite which there is no upper jaw. Only the Hemiramphidae family interests us for the time being.

Family Hemiramphidae

Considered at first as belonging to the family of flying fish (Exocoetidae) as the sub-family Hemiramphinae, as distinguished by Gill, these fish were classified by Günther (1866) into one family, next to the Exocoetidae.

These fishes inhabit all kinds of tropical and sub-tropical waters, streams, rivers, pools, ponds, marshes, brackish coastal waters, and also occur in salt waters near coral reefs. Many species inhabit the numerous islands in the Indian and South Pacific Oceans. The Asiatic species are the best known and have been represented since the Eocene.

The hemiramphids form a natural group of very interesting fishes, most closely related to the Belonidae (needlefishes) on one hand, and to the Exocoetidae (flying fishes) on the other. It is generally thought that the Exocoetidae derive from the Hemiramphidae, although here again a common ancestral form is more in agreement with the history of its development.

The most notable characteristics are the beak-shaped, lengthened lower jaw and the small upper jaw fused together with the inter-maxillary bone. On either side of the beak is usually a horizontally-projecting fold of skin. The end of the beak is sometimes bent downwards in a hook shape; other species have a small knob on the end, or a piece of skin or other tissue growth. The mouth is upper-positioned, a feature that shows up well in young specimens, while in the just-born, the mouth is still sometimes almost end-positioned. The intermaxillary bone and that part of the lower jaw lying under it are set with identical, small, usually triple-pointed teeth. The hard palate and the tongue have no teeth. A number of varieties have teeth on the extended part of the lower jaw, to the downward-bent tip. The beak-shaped lower jaw is connected immovably to the skull and only the upper jaw (with the intermaxillary bone) can be bent upward. The gill openings are wide, the lamellae (thin plates composing the gills) remain unfused with the ISTHMUS (the connecting structure between the two gill openings on the underside of the fish), and the gill arches are long.

The body of Hemiramphidae is very slender and long and laterally compressed in the tail section, yet sometimes it is more or less cylinder-shaped. The entire body is covered with rather large (sometimes small, however) cycloid (smooth) scales. The lateral line runs very low, through the second or third row of scales from the bottom to behind the anal fin, and turns somewhat upwards, and ends at the tail-root. A lengthwise stripe, generally a very fine, dark line, runs over the whole body from the base of the pectoral fins to the root of the tail.

The dorsal fin, as well as the anal fin, lies quite far to the rear. Both fins, along with the shape of the caudal fin, are considered important characteristics of classification. The ventral fins are very small to almost rudimentary and lie in front of, in, or behind the middle of the body length. This, however, does not seem to be of any value as a classificatory characteristic. The pectoral fins are usually placed very high, the long base either more or less vertical or sloping to the rear. In general, the caudal fin of marine genera is deeply forked, the lower lobe being somewhat larger than the upper. Among fresh-water species, the caudal fin is more rounded. Most of the species described are small to very small, not more than 15 cm (6 inches) long, although a few (marine in particular) can reach a total length of more than 45 cm (about 18 inches). The number of vertebrae is 48 to 63.

The fresh-water, and many brackish-water, species live mainly on insects, spiders, and so on, while algae, seaweed and plankton provide the main diet of the marine species.

That a place is made here for a short discussion of the living habits of these fishes is because of the uniformity in this regard of numerous members of this family. Although until the present time only a few species have been imported, it is just as well to go more deeply into

725

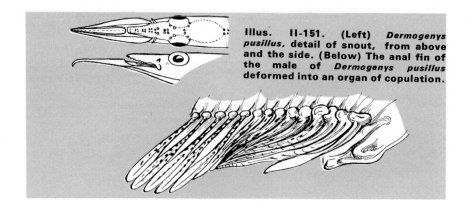

Illus. II-151. (Left) *Dermogenys pusillus,* detail of snout, from above and the side. (Below) The anal fin of the male of *Dermogenys pusillus* deformed into an organ of copulation.

this, because undoubtedly (hopefully) more hemiramphids will very quickly be imported for the aquarium.

Even though data concerning the life of hemiramphids in the wild is very scarce, there is already so much to be learned from the various reports concerning them that a good understanding of their living habits, and consequently of how they should be kept in captivity, is possible. The discussion below deals directly with the commonly known *Dermogenys pusillus,* yet it can, in large part, certainly be adapted to the remaining species.

The half-beak, *Dermogenys pusillus,* is found in pools, ponds, marshes, rivers and streams with a moderate current, in rice paddies and in certain districts under the native pile-dwellings. These are, of course, regions teeming with mosquitoes, flies, spiders, and so forth. These, along with worms and the larvae of various insects, form the basic diet of the half-beak. The water is shallow there, for only by exception would food be taken up from water layers below about 10 cm (4 inches) beneath the surface. Although it can swallow relatively large insects and spiders, it does not seem to consider young fishes as food, a fact which can be established in the aquarium. This, of course, is not to say that it never consumes a fish larva.

It likes to lurk among reed growth sticking out of the water along the banks and between rocks heavily grown with algae, dead trees, posts (under pile dwellings), etc. The strangely shaped "beak" is an especially suitable adaptation, for as soon as a creature of prey alights upon the surface, it shoots towards its prey with upper jaw lifted, and is always successful. As has been observed, the half-beaks are better mosquito eradicators than guppies and other toothcarps, which are planted especially for mosquito control. Toothcarps restrict themselves mainly to larvae, while the half-beaks attack the evil at its source by devouring the egg-laying females. In addition to the capture of insects that descend to the surface, the half-beak also hunts down insects flying above the surface, and always successfully. The streamlined shape, the placement of the pectoral fins, and the ability to see out of the water enables *Dermogenys pusillus* to hunt while gliding over the water.

When setting up an aquarium for these fish, the height is of lesser importance (keep it as low as possible, a marsh tank) than the surface, which is the most important aspect. Plants that grow high and sway over the water are not desirable; even less so is a thick covering of floating plants. A corner with some reeds or grass-like plants sticking out above the water (rice, too) is ideal. A high terrarium cover, partly of glass and partly (one side) of fly-screen is necessary to keep the food-animals from escaping. In addition to mosquitoes and other such animals, an easily set-up fruit-fly culture (*Drosophila*) will be very beneficial.

CLASSIFICATION AND REVIEW OF THE GENERA

Because this family, in comparison with many others, is still relatively little known, and undoubtedly many dozens of species still await discovery, a classification which approaches the natural relationship as closely as possible is a risky undertaking.

The species of hemiramphids known and described at the present time can be classified into several genera and a number of natural groups, of which, however, none is derived directly from any of the others. A division into smaller groups also leads, then, to the splitting of the family into groups of one or two genera, sometimes even with only one or a few species. Each addition of new species will give a better insight into the relationships, to which the aquarium hobby can perhaps contribute, as it did with the toothcarps.

Fowler (1934) gives a not very satisfactory classification, discussed in more detail later on, which was followed by Meinken (1936), among others.

Illus. II-152. Embryos of *Dermogenys pusillus*.

Fowler's sub-family Euleptorhamphinae is considered a separate family, next to the Hemiramphidae. The basis for the following classification is the work of Erna Mohr, and rests primarily on reproductive biology (and embryology). It concerns a series which, in the course of reproductive development, can be compared, in a certain sense, with the Cyprinodontiformes. In respect to the Poecilioidea, an excellent verification for this classification has been found (Hubbs, 1924) in the structure of the so-called gonopodium—there seems to be a relationship between the two concerning the respective progressive development of an ordinary anal fin into a specialized breeding apparatus. Among the hemiramphids, a certain fusion of the anal fin rays of the males, which also plays a part in mating, may be observed in a number of genera. However, other genera are lacking such a transformation. The indicated series is:

1. True egg-laying with external fertilization.
2. Egg-laying with internal fertilization.
3. Egg live-bearing (ovoviviparous) (internal fertilization).
4. True live-bearing (viviparous) (internal fertilization).

Although genera can be classified with certainty in three out of the four named stages of development (particularly, Stages 1, 3 and 4), and probably also in Stage 2, there are still a great number of transitional forms, discovery of which will probably take place in the future.

The classificational value of the "egg-laying" characteristic is substantially strengthened by two other characteristics, which are perhaps of equal value—the forked caudal fin and, at the nostrils, the absence of barbels, such as those which appear on all other members of this family.

There is certainly reason behind a division into two groups. The first group will just be indicated as "egg-laying." In this category belong the genera *Hemiramphus, Arrhamphus* and *Zenarchopterus*. The genus *Zenarchopterus* probably includes a number of varieties which should have been placed in the second category (that is, with internal fertilization). The hemiramphids, all of which are considered viviparous by many authors, appear to be only partially so (Mohr, 1926 and 1936), making the concept "viviparous" generally too broad.

In the case of *Hemirhamphodon* and *Dermogenys*, the eggs develop fully in the ovary and remain, until just before birth, rolled up in the egg membrane. The membranes emerge directly after the young are born,

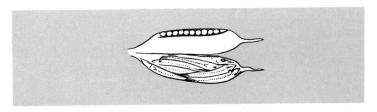

Illus. II-153. Laid open "womb" of *Nomorhamphus hageni.* The lower half with 20 mm ($\frac{13}{16}$ inch) long young (note the extended position), and the upper half showing the string of eggs.

or are already so dissipated that they are re-absorbed. A uterus as such is completely lacking and the eggs, developed in the ovary, maintain the same size after they are fertilized.

With *Nomorhamphus*, reproduction is carried on differently. Next to an ovary (divided into two strands), a paired uterus is present. Both uteri possess an ovary strand that lies against the side wall. In this case, too, the eggs are fertilized in the ovary, partially develop there, and finally release still undeveloped young into the uterus. The egg capsules are re-absorbed, while the uterus walls give off a fluid nutrient, which is absorbed by the unborn young, first through the entire body surface, then later through the mouth opening. The uterus, which has six to eight embryos in each half, continues to swell up during the embryonic process. As soon as the young have been born, never more than 16 at a time, a number of eggs again come into the uterus, which have meantime been kept in the ovary as sperm-fertilized and partially developed eggs.

In *Nomorhamphus*, too, as in *Dermogenys pusillus*, the sperm are stored in a cavity in the ovary wall, to be used when the time is ripe.

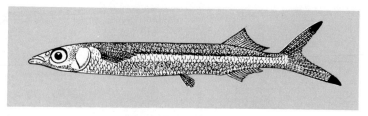

Illus. II-154. *Arrhamphus brevis.*

Sub-family Hemiramphinae

Genus *Arrhamphus*

This genus is found from the South China Sea (Philippines, Sulu Islands, Palawan), Riouw Archipelago (Bintan), Borneo, Celebes, the east coast of Australia, and possibly New Zealand, in fresh and salt water, mainly along the coasts and coral reefs.

Arrhamphus is a deviant from the other members of the Hemiramphidae family, since the lower jaw is not lengthened into a beak shape. This is, however, the most important difference, especially with *Hemiramphus*, which is the closest relative of this genus.

In *Arrhamphus*, the dorsal fin commences in advance of the anal fin. The first rays of all fins are the longest.

Up to now, two species have been described—*A. sclerolepis* Günther, 1866, and *A. brevis* (Seale, 1909). Until the present, none have been imported alive as aquarium fish, although they would probably be quite suitable for that purpose.

Genus *Hemiramphus*

The name of this genus, written *Hemi-Ramphus* by Cuvier in his description, was later changed, incorrectly, by Voigt (1832) to *Hemirhamphus*.

The attempts of various authors to split this genus up into sub-genera or several true genera encountered difficulties due to a whole series of transitional forms. Without better and less variable characteristics than positioning of the ventral fins with respect to the anal fin and the length of the lower jaw, such sub-dividing is hardly possible.

This genus has more species than any other genus of the family, and, at the same time, includes the largest varieties.

Besides a large number of species measuring between 8 and 15 cm

$(3\frac{3}{16}$ and 6 inches), this genus also includes varieties that can reach a length of more than 35 cm (about 14 inches). The latter are sought after by native fishermen and are sold on the market. Contrary to the usually not-so-prized relative, the European garfish, the flesh of the tropical hemiramphids is white, firm, and very tasty. Since they live in shoals, the harvest is usually abundant and not difficult to reap.

All species of the genus *Hemiramphus* are built like the one in Illus. II–155, their mutual differences being slight, and then mainly by different measurements of the bodily parts and in the number of scales and fin rays. The coloration pattern can vary more or less considerably, and quite as much within the species as between the species. Still, the basic coloration is always predominantly silver-grey with a metallic sheen. The true marine varieties are especially characterized by a very dark back.

The body of *Hemiramphus* is cylindrical, long and slender, and more or less laterally compressed. The fore half of the body, among the females, is usually higher and wider than that of the males. The caudal fin is deeply forked. The forward edge of the dorsal fin lies in front of the anal fin. The foremost rays of all fins are the longest.

None of the several dozen species of this genus are imported alive, although they, like *Arrhamphus*, would certainly be very suitable as aquarium fishes.

Although well founded facts on the distribution of *Hemiramphus* are scarce and anything but complete, it is probable that the distribution area extends out over the Pacific Ocean. Occurrence in the Atlantic Ocean is not excluded.

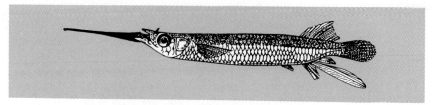

Sub-family Zenarchopterinae

Only the genus *Zenarchopterus* belongs to this sub-family, since no conclusive basis for division of the genus has been found. There are, nevertheless, forms which certainly do differ from the general type.

Genus *Zenarchopterus*

Zenarchopterus inhabits the whole region of the east coast of Africa, Madagascar, as far as the western Pacific Ocean (Hong Kong, Micronesia, Polynesia, New Guinea, the Philippines, Australia), in all waters for hundreds of kilometres inland, in rivers that are 300–400 metres (980–1,320 feet) above sea level, and in the salt waters of the coral regions. Together with the sub-family Zenarchopterinae, the Hemiramphinae represent the egg-laying Hemiramphidae. *Zenarchopterus* is clearly distinguished from these by its rounded and never-cleft or forked caudal fin. Again, *Zenarchopterus* also includes a large number of species that could be called suitable aquarium fish.

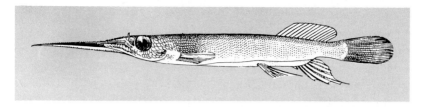

Sub-family Hemirhamphodontinae

The genus *Hemirhamphodon* is very closely related to *Zenarchopterus*, which should warrant its allocation to the sub-family Zenarchopterinae, in which case, however, it should be in a separate tribe. In the author's opinion, the collective differences are amply sufficient for Hemirhamphodontinae to be an individual sub-family itself, which better reflects the proportion of relationship. This is done here, in spite of the fact that only a single genus with but two species is described.

Genus *Hemirhamphodon*

Hemirhamphodon is found in Singapore and the Indonesian islands of Sumatra, Bangka, Belitong, Borneo, and Halmahera, in slightly brackish and fresh water.

The clearest characteristic distinguishing the two species of this genus from the other members of the family is the low placement of the pectoral fins, below the middle line of the body. Also, a clear difference is the way the lengthened lower jaw of *Hemirhamphodon* is set with tiny teeth, although a slight growth of teeth on the lengthened lower jaw of *Zenarchopterus* spp. may also be observed.

Sub-family Dermogenyinae

Dermogenys and *Nomorhamphus* were brought together in one sub-family by Fowler. Their previously indicated characteristics differ so much, however, that they really deserve to be kept as two separate groups, regardless of the fact that so few species are known.

Genus *Dermogenys*

This genus has also been considered a sub-genus of *Hemir(h)amphus*. Mohr (1936) gives as authors of this genus Kuhl & Van Hasselt, 1822. This name was indeed introduced for the first time in that year by these men, but it was not correctly published.

Dermogenys is found in India (according to Herre, 1944), the Malay Peninsula, Singapore, Burma, Thailand, the Philippines, Borneo, Sumatra, Java and Celebes, in all kinds of waters, including brackish coastal waters but not salt water. (See also the following discussion of the species imported as aquarium fishes.)

The genus *Dermogenys*, together with *Nomorhamphus*, differs from the other hemiramphids by the major dorsal fin being smaller and set farther to the rear. The first ray of the dorsal fin is set behind the first ray of the anal fin. In males, the anal fin can have undergone a change of form. In most literature, the anal fin is described as a reproductive organ and the fish are considered live-bearing. As already set forth, *Dermogenys* is ovoviviparous (egg live-bearing) and has, indeed, a method of internal fertilization, at least among the species known in aquarist circles.

Plate II-177. *Dermogenys pusillus,* albino variety.

Dermogenys pusillus Van Hasselt, 1823
Half-Beak
Wrestling Half-Beak

This species is found in the southern Philippines, Borneo, Java, Sumatra, Singapore, the Malay Peninsula, Burma and Thailand, in all kinds of fresh waters, for more than 100 km (over 62 miles) inland, and also in moderately brackish coastal waters, but not in salt water. It has been imported occasionally since 1905. A limited number of specimens, females for the most part, are now being steadily brought in from Singapore.

The shape of the body is shown quite well in Plate II–177. The fish grows to a maximum length of 80 mm ($3\frac{5}{32}$ inches). The males are somewhat smaller and slimmer than the females.

As will be seen later on, the fish imported under the name *Dermogenys pusillus* (also as *Dermogenys sumatranus*) are all of one species which, however, is broken up into a number of sub-species, or so-called geographical races. This is exhibited especially by the coloration and pattern.

The varieties that had been known in aquarist circles before 1940 had either a brownish or a blue-green basic coloration. The specimens

735

imported into The Netherlands during 1949 were more silvery. The latter variety will be described here in more detail.

Over the whole, silvery to light blue-green (depending on the lighting), sometimes brightly glistening body length, runs a dark stripe as far as the root of the tail. The base of the pectoral fins is just as dark. Underneath the length of the beak-shaped lower jaw runs a very dark (to black) stripe as far as the tip, set off by a red line in fine, male specimens.

The bases of the dorsal and anal fins (especially in the male) are orange-red, changing more to yellowish towards the outer edge. Doubtless, the earlier imported varieties are more attractive, although from this lesser endowed variety emanates an ever-present charm in its high-spirited bearing and its strange way of life.

In an aquarium that has been set up in accordance with the discussion of the environment of the family Hemiramphidae, though somewhat shy at first, this fish will provide a great deal of pleasure for its owners as soon as it has become accustomed to its surroundings.

If we take the trouble, from time to time, to let loose a few mosquitoes or smaller flies (such as fruit flies) under the aquarium cover, then this fish is right in its element. However, it will also gladly accept the usual live food, such as tubifex, white worms, mosquito larvae (both white and black), waterfleas and all kinds of food creatures. It is a good idea to put it into a tank that is not too high (maximum height, for example, 40 cm or 16 inches), since it seldom captures food deeper than 25 cm (10 inches) below the surface. If the aquarium does not get a little sunlight from time to time, the fish should be given small portions of soft algae to keep it in condition.

Keep the temperature at about 25–28 °C (77–82 °F), but at night, you can drop it to about 20 °C (68 °F), without injuring the fish.

Reproduction is just as interesting as the fish itself. The courtship is usually quiet, but can also take place in a violent manner, especially if several pairs are put into the aquarium together. This never causes trouble and is, in fact, recommended, as the mating play then becomes even more interesting.

By butting against the female's sexual opening with its bill, the male stimulates her into taking up the ejected sperm. While she continues to swim along with him, the male brings his oddly-shaped anal fin (which has the first eight rays directed sharply backwards) to the female's sexual opening, at which time the transfer of sperm takes place. The sperm is absorbed by the female into the ovary wall, using part of it for the fertilization of a number of eggs. After 3 to 5 weeks (at a low temperature, it can take longer), the first young are born.

Dependent on various factors (age of the female, temperature and feeding), a maximum of 30 young are born at a time, yet litters of 5 to 12 individuals are quite normal. About a month later, without a repeat fertilization by the male, still another group of young is born. The process is, thus, a productive one.

At birth, the young are about 10 mm ($\frac{3}{8}$ inch) long and immediately start eating small food creatures. The micro-worms commonly fed are gladly eaten by both young and old. If the aquarium in which the fish are kept is sufficiently spacious, for the size of the surface plays a principal rôle, then heavy feeding causes the young to grow up speedily, and within two months, the males can be recognized by the modified anal fin.

Imported specimens of *Dermogenys pusillus*, like many other aquarium fishes, are very timid. With this species, this can lead to damaging or even the breaking-off of the lower jaw. Although the jaw is regenerated in the course of time, it does not repeat the original shape. It is best, therefore, to provide thick growth around the sides of the tank, especially at the surface and on the side where the light falls, to allow algae to grow thickly or to screen the light.

The addition of sea water or kitchen salt to the aquarium water, which used to be recommended, is no longer considered desirable.

The fish can be calmed down sooner by regularly casting mosquitoes on the surface for them and by giving them as much peace as possible (without too much light) in the first months.

The birth of young lacking vitality, as also occurs among the toothcarps, is usually the consequence of unsuitable feeding and too low a temperature.

Although the half-beaks can polish off fairly large-sized insects, as well as other food animals, they do not eat their own young or those of other fishes, if these have reached a length of more than 10 mm ($\frac{3}{8}$ inch). Naturally, this is only if there is enough of the right kind of food. *Dermogenys pusillus* is an aquarium fish about which little is yet known. This is not only the consequence of a small number being imported, for they reproduce abundantly without difficulty, but also and especially because most aquarists are more on the lookout for gorgeous coloration than for something that is truly interesting and wonderful.

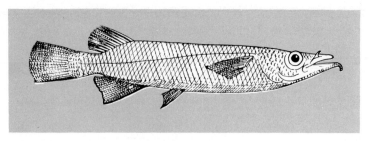

Illus. II-158. *Nomorhamphus celebensis.*

Sub-family Nomorhamphinae

On the basis of previously named characteristics (of true live-bearers), the genus *Nomorhamphus* is discussed here as a separate sub-family.

Genus *Nomorhamphus*

Nomorhamphus is native to Celebes, Indonesia, where it lives in fresh water. Its body is laterally compressed and the lower jaw is only slightly lengthened, with the tip bent downward and ending in a fleshy flap. The forward edge of the dorsal fin is behind that of the anal fin; the pectoral fins are set high on the body. Nasal barbels are present. The intermaxillary bone forms a triangular plate, set with a row of fine teeth. There is a similar row of teeth on the lower jaw. The body is covered with fairly large scales. The lateral line runs very low and faint, without an edging of scales.

Order Cyprinodontiformes

Toothcarps occur in all geographic areas, with the exception of Australia—in North, Central and South America, Africa and Madagascar, Arabia, Iran, India, Indonesia and Japan. The distribution points to a westerly origin, since they do not occur in the region of Australia.

The genus *Aplocheilus* is especially common in Indonesia. In the Poso and Lindu Lakes in Celebes a few species occur which deviate strongly in bodily structure, and this makes it necessary to accommodate them in a separate order (Phallostethiformes).

In addition to being found in all fresh waters in their distribution area, Cyprinodontiformes are often found in brackish and even in salt water.

ORIGIN OF THE TOOTHCARPS

Every consideration regarding the origin of this order remains rather speculative. Actual points of contact with representatives of other orders have not yet been discovered. However, something more is known about their development and distribution over the world, although in that regard, too, every consideration is speculative.

It is a certainty that the toothcarps were already present in the early Oligocene period. In early times, a great, watery region stretched out along the entire equator. If the situation actually was such, numerous questions are simply answered, especially concerning the distribution and relationship of the species, which, though obviously closely related, today live far separated from each other. In southern Europe only a few representatives of Cyprinodontiformes are still living. In Spain and Corfu (Greece), the sub-family Cyprinodontinae is still represented by the genus *Valencia*, a genus that apparently should be regarded as a remnant of the ancestral group.

Suppose that the place of origin is assumed to be what shall provisionally be called the Mediterranean Basin, which, in the Cretaceous period (at the end of the Mesozoic), looked about as it still appears on the map. The fossil finds, which are shown in Illus. II–159, allow the slenderest connection, but in either case they do lie within the recent distribution area. It is probably not too risky to accept the fact that the first toothcarps—at least, the fishes that these first toothcarps developed from—made their entry on the world scene towards the end of the Cretaceous or beginning of the Eocene.

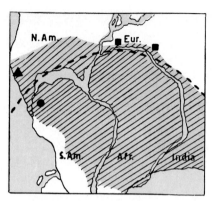

Illus. II-159. Sketch of the dispersal of toothcarps at the beginning of their development (see hatched area). The continental shelves at that time had not yet drifted apart. ▲ Site of fossil *Parafundulus* in Miocene layers; ■ *Prolebias* from the Oligocene and Miocene; ● *Carrionellus* from the early Tertiary. The arched, broken line represents the Equator.

The Cyprinodontidae of the Old World are less well represented than those of the New World, yet the genera included in the tribe Aphaniini live in a more expansive region than their nearest American relatives, which is to say, from North Africa and Spain to India.

An obstacle in the form of salt water (of course, fresh water contains some salt, too) was not insurmountable. The oldest Cyprinodontinae, as well as the Rivulinae, could thus move westward and take possession of North America. The remaining groups and families of this order must be derived from the Fundulini.

RECENT DISTRIBUTION

Before discussing the groups, there is still something to be said regarding recent distribution. Why do they occur in that region and not outside it? As far as the northern boundary is concerned, it can be agreed that temperature is the determining factor—the northern boundary concurs approximately with the 15 °C (59 °F) annual isotherm. In southern Arabia, the sandy desert has, up until today, prevented toothcarps from establishing themselves there. Australia was cut off from the remaining region by some obstacle at the same time that the distribution of these fishes was spreading out in that direction. The lack of toothcarps in southern South America is also because of the 15 °C (59 °F) annual isotherm, which again forms the boundary there. The complex of questions about this group of fishes is far from being as simple as presented here.

The toothcarps, as their name indicates, differ from the carp by having teeth in the jaws and palate, but were formerly included among the carp-like fishes. Later research, however, has justified placing them closer to the spiny-finned fishes.

The fishes belonging to Cyprinodontiformes are characterized by soft-rayed fins and the lack of an open connection between the alimentary canal and the swim bladder. The connection that exists between the alimentary canal and the swim bladder is lost soon after birth and then disappears completely or ceases to function. Barbels and the lateral line organ are totally absent. The lowermost pharyngeal bones are not fused together. Furthermore, they are usually small fishes— from less than 20 mm ($\frac{13}{16}$ inch) long to seldom larger than 100 mm (4 inches)—often showing a very striking difference between the sexes.

Cyprinodontiformes are especially suitable for home aquariums and are represented in at least one of the community tanks of every aquarist. Often, aquarists take care to put them in breeding tanks to assure numerous progeny. It is undoubtedly the toothcarps that have been important contributors towards lifting the aquarium fish hobby to the high level it now occupies. It is regretted that so many species have been unpopular with aquarists for such a long time. The special and often very costly imported fishes often squeeze out the cheaper ones, such as the toothcarps, which are no less pretty and are certainly quite as important objects of study.

Illus. II-160. Distribution of the Aphaniini in the Mediterranean Basin. + Aphanius, ▲ Tellia and ● Anatolichthys.

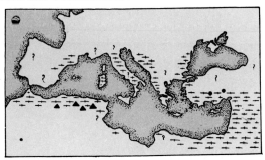

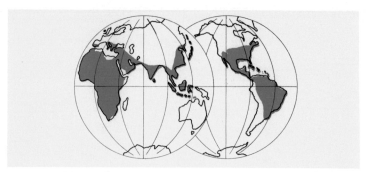

Illus. II-161. Distribution of the toothcarps, Cyprinodontiformes.

At first, the toothcarps, as well as the fishes belonging to the Amblyopsoidei, were accommodated in the family Cyprinodontidae. This family could not at first fit into any existing order, so that it was finally made a separate order, Cyprinodontiformes, which was certainly the correct thing to do, proved by the more accurate scientific data available today. To the sub-order Amblyopsoidei, with a single family, Amblyopsidae, belong a few genera of cave-dwelling fishes, mainly blind cave fishes (genera *Amblyopsis*, *Chologaster*, *Troglichthys* and *Typhlichthys*) from the middle and eastern parts of North America. Although they are very interesting, they appear not suitable as aquarium fishes—at least, none has yet been so kept.

The second sub-order, Cyprinodontoidei, is, however, one of the most important providers of aquarium fishes, as to it belong all the egg-laying and live-bearing toothcarps which have actually made the hobby so popular.

As has been discussed, various systems have been introduced at different times in order to achieve a natural form of classification. On the basis of a noticeable difference in reproduction (mating biology), egg-laying toothcarps are first of all separated from the live-bearers, into two super-families, respectively, Cyprinidontoidea and Poecilioidea. However, further research has made it clear that the live-bearing fishes in no way form a natural, monophyletic (having one common ancestor) group, but that probably various families are derived from an egg-laying ancestral form. Although research about this will continue for a long time, the system following hereafter is based upon so many characteristics that it approaches the natural development of the group as a whole with probable accuracy.

742

In spite of the fact that live-bearing fishes in various places and times have been known to derive from an egg-laying variety, the named divisions are being provisionally maintained here for practical reasons. We shall thus draw the dividing line between egg-layers on the one side and the live-bearers on the other.

FRONTAL SCALATION

In the research and working up of a large collection of toothcarps, principally *Rivulus* from Central and South America, it occurred to the author that on the head of *Rivulus* was a pattern of enlarged scales which was not only quite regular, but also constant and varying from group to group. From further research among other groups of tooth-carps (a total of several thousand specimens from about 60 species were examined), it soon became apparent that the pattern was a very useful and extremely easy-to-handle determination characteristic. For an idea of the pattern and the placement of the scales, see Illus. II–162.

In order to be able to work with this pattern characteristic, it was necessary to codify it. Quite by accident, a point of departure was easily found in *Rivulus* specimens, because there is always one centrally-located scale, mostly covered by those around it. This scale was taken as the point of departure and called scale *a* of the pattern. Moving clockwise, the surrounding scales were coded *b, c, d, e* and *f*. The symmetrical counterparts of the scales lying to the side were called

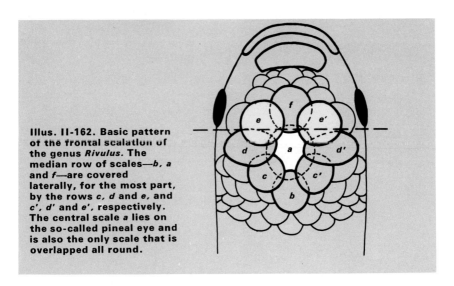

Illus. II-162. Basic pattern of the frontal scalation of the genus *Rivulus*. The median row of scales—*b, a* and *f*—are covered laterally, for the most part, by the rows *c, d* and *e,* and *c', d'* and *e',* respectively. The central scale *a* lies on the so-called pineal eye and is also the only scale that is overlapped all round.

c', d' and e'. It was all quite simple at first, until it was noticed that sometimes extra scales were present in the pattern, and also that, in other genera, there was no central scale a. It therefore became desirable to fix a position for this central scale, in respect to a fixed point, which was found on a straight line between the rear edges of the eye sockets. The central scale a always lies either entirely or for the most part behind this line. Further work verified that this determination was both tenable and usable.

In addition to the identification of groups and even genera and species, it appeared further that sometimes irregularities were found in the pattern, at least with certainty in *Rivulus*, by cross-breeding, whether this came about naturally or artificially.

Super-family Cyprinodontoidea

Distribution of the egg-laying toothcarps (often known as killies or killifishes) is identical to that of the entire order. These fish are found in all waters—in rivers, streams, fish ponds, pools and marshes—in fresh, brackish and salt waters.

The egg-laying toothcarps all possess a long, thin, often cylindrical body; the frontal part is more or less vertical; the tail area is laterally compressed. The dorsal and anal fins are placed far to the rear. The gorgeous coloration and endless shapes of the fins are strikingly beautiful. Cyprinodontoidea are, without exception, veritable jewels of exotic ornamental fish which are unsuitable for the community aquarium only because of a predatory inclination. Their predatory instincts, however, are never so highly developed as to render them totally unsuitable for all aquariums. All species are warmth-loving; only a few North American and European species can be kept at lower temperatures.

Reproduction is carried on calmly, although it can be tempestuous, in which case the surface-dwellers lay their eggs among fine-leaved plants and preferably on the roots of floating plants (*Ceratopteris cornuta, Pistia stratiotes*) or among thick clumps of *Riccia fluitans*. The laying is often nothing more than the casting off of sex products. A few bottom-dwelling species use their pectoral fins to fan the eggs under the humus layer which covers the bottom of the breeding tank and sometimes also in other aquariums where toothcarps are kept. The development of the eggs takes a long time, often from two to more than five or six weeks. After they are hatched, however, the young grow very quickly, helped immeasurably by their gluttony and speedy digestion. Two families are distinguished here, Cyprinodontidae and Orestiatidae, of which only the first is discussed in further detail, because no suitable aquarium fishes are known to belong to the latter.

Family Cyprinodontidae

All parts of the world, with the exception of Australia, are inhabited by this family. Its greatest development is reached in the two Americas and in Africa.

Cyprinodontidae are small fishes with a long body that is round to laterally compressed and sometimes slightly stumpy, covered with rather large scales. The head is often flattened—especially in surface dwellers —and at least partially scaled. In many species, a so-called pineal-eye is easily observed. The mouth is end-positioned and usually directed upward, small or moderately large, outward folding or otherwise. The jaws are equipped with one or several rows of triple-pointed or conical, incisor-like teeth on the vomer (often, because of its shape, called the ploughshare bone). There are never teeth on the palate.

The ventral fins have six to seven rays. The gill LAMELLAE (thin plates composing the gills) are free of the isthmus and more or less mutually connected.

The Cyprinodontidae are egg-laying fishes. The anal fin of the males does not undergo deformation as it does with the *Poecilia,* and hence there are no shortened and hardened rays.

In some species, however, the anal fin of the males is thickly set with tiny spines, or a few rays are longer than those of the female. Among some *Fundulus* types, the oviduct of the female is lengthened, in this way somewhat approaching the live-bearing fish. Meanwhile, *Profundulus* is the only genus which, in structure and organic arrangement, is closest to the remaining (live-bearing and other egg-laying) toothcarps, which must, in turn, be considered as deriving from *Profundulus,* or as being very closely related to it.

It has already been brought out that the members of this family are egg-layers—oviparous. However, one difference can be established —their care of the spawn—in comparison with most of the carp-like fishes, which are all also egg-layers.

Of the fishes that have appeared since the Cretaceous, the family Cyprinodontidae is the first group to have developed a more or less efficient brood care, or better, spawn care.

The peculiar environment of the smaller water dwellers in those turbulent times preceding the late Eocene undoubtedly led up to this specialization and was possibly even the whole cause behind the very existence of this variety-rich group.

About the time of the Cretaceous-Eocene, the continental land mass was characterized by a practically complete absence of the waters that are so numerous today, and for that reason was unsuitable for a heavy fish population. The majority of members of the Cyprinodontidae are adapted to running water and they are, in general, good swimmers. In the aquarium, these species are more often seen standing still in the water, or hanging directly below the surface, like the pike, than found swimming actively or restlessly, like most carp-like fishes.

The species living on a preponderantly vegetable fare and having a long intestine (*Cyprinodon* and *Jordanella*) act more like carp-like fishes, and when they are not resting quietly among the plants, they are quietly going about the business of looking for something edible. In the wild, these Cyprinodontidae are found in calm, practically stagnant waters, in the quiet bends of the rivers, in lakes, marshes, pools, flood areas, springs, and so on. A large number of these waters are subject to periodic drought and consequent destruction of the fish that dwelled there. Rather than seek salvation in running waters, a solution is found in reproduction and the product of reproduction, the eggs. The most primitive varieties are typically bottom-layers and, in various ways (see *Aphyosemion* and *Cynolebias* on pages 768 and 796), place their eggs in certain positions between the roots of plants or under the bottom layer of mud. In this way, the eggs are protected against the fierce sun when drought visits the habitat. The eggs themselves can remain out of water for a long time without losing their ability to germinate, and it even appears likely that a seasonal drying of the eggs contributes to their further development, as long as water (the first rains) re-appears.

In the same genus, we can find one species which is a bottom-layer, and the eggs are thus protected in a special way, while another species lays its eggs among the plants or even at the surface among floating plants. The latter usually live in waters that are not so heavily exposed to periodic drought.

Mating is generally carried on quite calmly, mostly preceded, however, by a more or less violent courtship. The number of eggs laid each time is often small, but the mating sessions are repeated over long periods. Often, a nest of young provides only a few specimens of the same size. The period of development of the egg is usually long, from one to eight weeks or longer. In other words, it takes from a week to two months for the first young to show up.

DIVISION AND REVIEW OF THE FAMILY

This family, which is so important to aquarists, has in recent decades acquired a steadily growing recognition among scientific as well as hobbyist circles. An important part of this must be ascribed to the aquarist himself, who gave the first species to appear such a fine reception that the importers and the explorers were encouraged by it. New species are continually being found and will continue to be found, all of them jewels of form and gorgeous coloration. Obviously, classification had to keep pace with the constantly growing number of, for the most part, still unknown species. As already said, if there was only one family in 1866 in which all kinds of toothcarps were included,

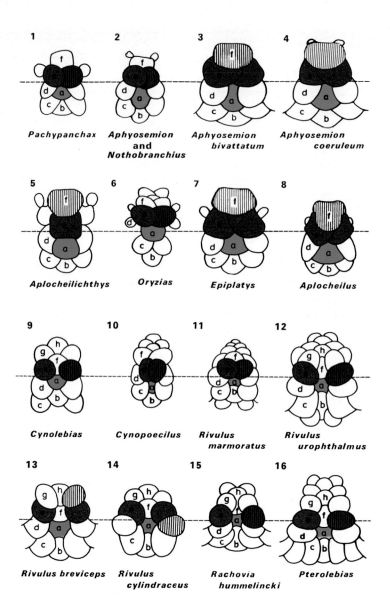

1 **Pachypanchax**

2 **Aphyosemion**
and
Nothobranchius

3 **Aphyosemion**
bivattatum

4 **Aphyosemion**
coeruleum

5 **Aplocheilichthys**

6 **Oryzias**

7 **Epiplatys**

8 **Aplocheilus**

9 **Cynolebias**

10 **Cynopoecilus**

11 **Rivulus**
marmoratus

12 **Rivulus**
urophthalmus

13 **Rivulus breviceps**

14 **Rivulus**
cylindraceus

15 **Rachovia**
hummelincki

16 **Pterolebias**

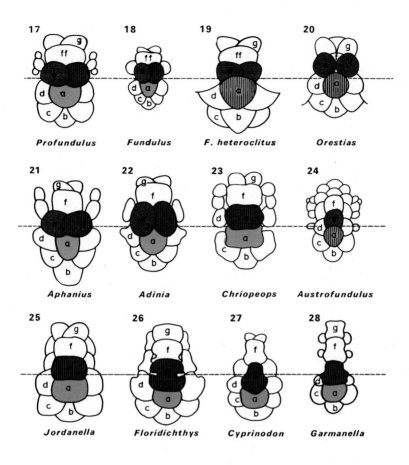

17 Profundulus	18 Fundulus	19 F. heteroclitus	20 Orestias
21 Aphanius	22 Adinia	23 Chriopeops	24 Austrofundulus
25 Jordanella	26 Floridichthys	27 Cyprinodon	28 Garmanella

(Chart continued on page 866.)

Illus. II-163. Pattern of frontal scalation for all known genera of the sub-family Rivulinae. The relationship of the patterns is clear, especially in comparison with those of the Cyprinodontinae and Fundulinae.

the following years brought the necessity for more accurate division, so that by now the system looks as it appears here.

The sub-family Orestiatinae Myers, 1931 (Orestiinae Regan, 1911) is considered a separate family here, the Orestiatidae, even though, up to now, only one genus, *Orestias*, has been distinguished. This family, the Orestiidae, like the Poecilioidea, derives from the genus *Profundulus*. As far as is known, no suitable aquarium fishes belong to the Orestiatidae.

The probable relationship between the various sub-families and tribes, which is certainly not based solely on the frontal scalation, is shown in Illus. II–163. The drawings of the scale pattern may aid in recognition of new varieties, when these show up, and their classification among the already imported (known) species. The following division is maintained here: The most inclusive group is probably the family Cyprinodontidae, which is split into three sub-families, namely, Rivulinae, Aplocheilichthyinae, and Cyprinodontinae; next is the already-named Orestiatidae with the genus *Orestias*; then, *Profundulus*, connecting with the families of live-bearers (see Poecilioidea).

No further interpretation of the scale patterns will be given here, except to point out that they are arranged according to a number of clear lines of development. The *ee'* scales are, moreover, tinted red, because throughout the whole order these obviously occupy the most important place. The central scale *a* is tinted green.

Sub-family Rivulinae

With newer insight, this sub-family is set up for a number of genera, which are certainly not derived from the Fundulinae s.s., but which lead back to the ancestral stem of the order.

The genera that are important to aquarists are included in three tribes, namely, Aplocheilini (with *Aphyosemion, Nothobranchius, Aplocheilus, Epiplatys* and *Pachypanchax*); Cynolebiatini (with *Cynolebias* and the more or less dubious genus, *Cynopoecilus*); and Rivulini (with the American genera *Rachovia, Rivulus, Pterolebias,* and *Trigonectes*).

Tribe Aplocheilini

On the basis of a number of characteristics, including the frontal scalation pattern, *Aphyosemion* and *Nothobranchius*, in addition to *Aplocheilus, Epiplatys,* and *Pachypanchax*, are also classified in this tribe. These are all African genera, but *Aplocheilus* also hails from Southeast Asia.

750

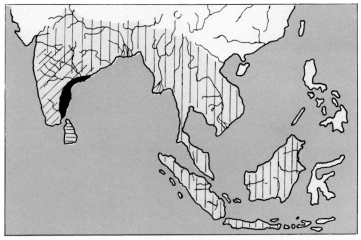

Illus. II-164. Distribution of the genus *Aplocheilus:* ■ *A. blocki,* ══ *A. lineatus dayi,* //// *A. lineatus lineatus,* |||| *A. panchax.*

Genus *Aplocheilus*

From the species belonging to this genus, the following are imported as aquarium fish: *Aplocheilus blocki* Arnold, the smallest species, native to Madras, India; *Aplocheilus lineatus* with two sub-species, *A. l. lineatus* and *A. l. dayi*; and *Aplocheilus panchax*, which will be discussed here in further detail.

Aplocheilus blocki was not named in the recent *Atlas* of Deraniyagala, but it is mentioned, however, by Innes (1949, 10th edition: page 297), as coming from Ceylon.

Plate II-178. *Aplocheilus blocki.*

Aplocheilus blocki **Arnold, 1911**

Dwarf Panchax

Green Panchax

This fine fish hails from Madras, India. It is small (about 45 mm or $1\frac{5}{8}$ inches) and is distributed along the Coromandel Coast, but not on Ceylon.

The basic coloration is olive green with a metallic sheen, with six rows of red spots, fins of grey-green to dirty yellow, which also have rows of little red spots and an orange-yellow edge along the dorsal and anal fins in the males. Care and breeding are like the other species.

Aplocheilus panchax (Hamilton, 1822)
Panchax

This species comes from India, Thailand, Burma, the Malay Peninsula and Indonesia. Generally, it is found in the lowlands and coastal waters, yet locally, too, in mountain streams.

From the shape of this fish, it can be seen at once that it is a surface dweller. The body is long and thin, the head and forepart of the back flattened, and the snout is laterally flattened, which gives this fish a pike-like look. This genus is distinguished from the genus *Oryzias* by its forward-projecting upper jaw. The ploughshare bone (vomer) is set with teeth. The small dorsal fin begins above the last rays of the anal fin. The physical differences of the sexes are slight, limited to a somewhat less vivid fin pattern on the female, which also exhibits a thicker belly region, somewhat lighter in coloration than that of the male. Both sexes can attain a length of about 80 mm (3⅛ inches).

Two varieties or geographic races are described, namely, *A. p. mattei*, with a bluish abdomen, olive green body, orange dorsal fin, lemon yellow anal fin, grey-green caudal fin, and an orange border along the anal and caudal fins and *A. p. lutescens*, with a greenish brown body, light green belly, indigo spotted scales, and median fins with a sulphur yellow edge.

Plate II-179. *Aplocheilus panchax.*

Like most of its relatives, the panchax belong to the less demanding species which reproduce quietly, even in company with other fishes. Although they occur in brackish water, the addition of sea water or salt to the aquarium water is unnecessary. They prefer fine-leaved plants and floating plants (*Riccia, Salvinia, Ceratopteris*), as well as a little sunlight, falling into the aquarium from above. They crave exclusively living food, without, however, any special preference, including insects of all kinds, as well as their larvae. Keep the temperature about 18–25 °C (64–77 °F).

The eggs (10 to 60 eggs per spawning, a total of 200 eggs per period) are laid among floating plants or elsewhere, directly under the surface, on plants or on stones. Mating continues in the same way as with related surface fish, while the eggs, depending on the circumstances, hatch out in from 20 to 30 days. The young grow up quickly and, by the time they are 15 mm ($\frac{5}{8}$ inch) long, all have a dark spot on the dorsal fin. This disappears from some of the males when they reach a length of 25–30 mm ($1–1\frac{3}{16}$ inch). There are also males, however, who continue to bear traces of the childhood spot.

Aplocheilus panchax is an old-time aquarium dweller, which has occupied a place in the scheme of things since 1899. In its natural surroundings, it lives in company with *Barbus* species, and in some places with *Etroplus maculatus, Oryzias,* etc.

Genus *Epiplatys*

This is a genus with many species and varieties in Africa. A respectable number of species has been imported in the course of time, although most of these have since vanished from the tanks. An important part of recent import shipments has been composed of new varieties (new to science as well), as will be shown in the following pages, so that the original number of species is again in force.

Of the species which are being imported today, only the following are current among hobbyists, listed in chronological order of their first description: *E. sexfasciatus* (type locality indicated by number 1 and distribution area indicated on the map in Illus. II–165 by slanting, hatched lines), *E. fasciolatus* (2), *E. senegalensis* (3), *E. marnoi* (4 and horizontal hatching), *E. chaperi* (vertical hatching), *E. singa* (5), *E. chevalieri* (6), *E. decorsii* (7), *E. macrostigma* (8), *E. striatus* (9), *E. dageti* and *E. sheljuzhkoi* (10). Because of the very broad distribution of the type species of this genus, *Epiplatys sexfasciatus*, this species might also be considered ancestral to a great number of forms. The form *E. multifasciatus* Boulenger, 1913, from the central Congo River outlets and the Sankuru River is considered a local variety of *E. sexfasciatus*, while the variety *E. nigricans* from the Welle (Uele) river of central Africa, can prevail as a sub-species of *Epiplatys chevalieri* (*E. c. nigricans*). The variety *E. chaperi olbrechtsi* Poll, 1941, from the vicinity of Nuon, Liberia, is considered a sub-species of *Epiplatys fasciolatus*. How the relationships of the known species to each other are inter-associated has still to be brought out.

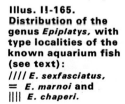

Illus. II-165.
Distribution of the genus *Epiplatys*, with type localities of the known aquarium fish (see text):
//// *E. sexfasciatus*,
= *E. marnoi* and
|||| *E. chaperi*.

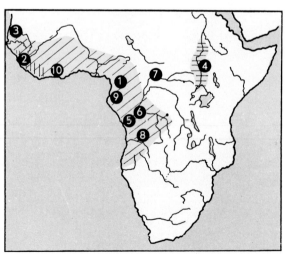

755

Epiplatys chaperi (Sauvage, 1882)
Chaperi
Fire-Mouth Killie

Epiplatys chaperi comes from Africa—the tropical west coast—Sierra Leone, Liberia, and the Ivory Coast, as far as Ghana. It is found in shallow, fresh-water ponds, but not very commonly. The fish was first imported by Siggelkow-Hamburg in 1908 and was rather commonly bred.

This very attractive surface-dweller has an elongated body that is more or less cylindrical. The head and part of the back are flattened; the tail is laterally compressed. The snout is turned upward and has a rather large mouth. It reaches a maximum length of 65 mm ($2\frac{9}{16}$ inches). In the males, all the fins are more or less sharply pointed, but they are rounded in the females. The anal fin is larger than the dorsal fin and begins a little farther forward.

The basic coloration is olive brown with a very distinct scale pattern in various tones. The scales on the back are edged with reddish black,

Plate II-180. *Epiplatys annulatus.*

Plate II-181. *Epiplatys bifasciatus.*

those on the flanks are blue-green with a black edge. About five cross stripes of brownish black do not cross the back entirely, but come together from either side on the belly. The anal and caudal fins are edged all around in the same tone. The underside of the head and part of the breast are deep red, the same coloration that may appear in tiny spots on the fins. The underside of the eye is also red, the upper edge green. The cream-yellow to yellowish brown tint of the fins can sometimes, depending on the angle of the light, turn into a soft blue.

As a typical dweller of shallow pools and a somewhat less decided surface dweller than the other *Epiplatys* species, *Epiplatys chaperi* requires a roomy, but not necessarily high, aquarium. A good layer of humus on the bottom, plantings of *Myriophyllum, Eleocharis acicularus, Nitella* and *Charax* in small clumps and a rather thick layer of *Riccia* and other floating plants on the surface are also recommended. The aquarium should be placed so that it receives considerable sunlight. The temperature should be 16–26 °C (61–79 °F) with a nightly cooling of a few degrees. If the fish are at ease in their surroundings, they will not delay mating when summer comes. During the mating period,

757

which can last for several months, extra food should be supplied, inasmuch as *E. chaperi* frequently eats its own eggs. If the aquarium is roomy enough—for example, 120×60×30 cm (48×24×12 inches) length-width-height—there is no need to worry about egg-eating.

About 100 young can be reared without any problem from the various matings. The eggs are laid at the surface among *Riccia* or something similar and are rather large (about 1 mm or .04 inch) and transparent. The young that hatch out in one to two weeks are not difficult to raise and immediately start to eat large quantities of dust-fine food. They grow quickly in smaller tanks; many a brother or sister from a later spawning falls prey to the earlier-born young. A sharp watch should be kept because of this and, if necessary, those young fish that are too big should be moved to another tank. Like most of its relatives, this species also eats mainly animal food, but it is not particular about what kind.

Because this toothcarp reproduces comparatively easily, take care to use only· beautiful and well developed specimens for breeding.

This fish degenerates quickly and does not grow to normal size in an aquarium that is too small. In such cases, its coloration, too, is a lot less beautiful than it normally is.

Epiplatys chevalieri (Pellegrin, 1904)
Chevalier's Epiplatys

This handsome Congo import reaches a length of about 60 mm (2⅜ inches). This species is so clearly an *Epiplatys* that classifying it in the genus *Aphyosemion* is beyond comprehension. It is somewhat more comprehensible when it gets mixed up with the related species *Epiplatys macrostigma* (with which it is often confused in literature) and *Epiplatys sheljuzhkoi*. Not excluded is the possibility that *E. macrostigma*, distributed along the coast, is the ancestral form of a number of varieties from the region farther upstream. None of these closely related species is found in company with others of their group; instead, they substitute for each other locally. *E. chevalieri* has a greenish to olive green basic coloration, dark back, and lighter belly; the sides are decorated with rows of carmine red spots which angle somewhat downwards towards the rear and, especially the two bottommost rows, more or less merge into an irregular stripe on the tail. Plate II–182 gives a clear picture of this. The fins are yellowish, lighter in the females, also with red spots or stripes. The dorsal and anal fins are edged a deep, carmine red, and the outermost edge of the caudal fin is set off in the same way with red. Among females during the mating season, the bottom rows of red spots merge and turn a bluish black, while the back turns a

Plate II-182. *Epiplatys chevalieri.*

yellowish blue clay coloration. The female's iridescent green glow disappears in the mating season. This species does not seem to be an egg-eater in particular and the young, according to the publications of breeders, are safe from their parents. It is probable, however, that this fish will exhibit its predatory nature under certain circumstances, so be aware of the possibility of its rapacity and act accordingly. Keep this species like its relatives; certainly, do not add salt to the water, considering that it is a dweller of distinctly fresh water.

Plate II-183. *Epiplatys dageti.*

Epiplatys dageti Poll, 1953
Daget's Epiplatys

Among an import shipment from the Ivory Coast, the birthplace of the well known and long kept *Epiplatys chaperi*, was found a variety close to *E. chaperi*, which, from Poll's research, apparently represented a species not yet described. Research of old aquarium material shows that this new species, *E. dageti*, has already been kept for a long time in aquarist circles. Although it could be shown to be different, it seems understandable that up to now hobbyists have taken it for the same species as *E. chaperi*. Amplified material will also probably demonstrate that here again we have a local variety of *E. chaperi*. The deep orange of *E. chaperi* is more yellowish here, and the edges of the male's anal and caudal fins have a great deal less black pigmentation than in *E. chaperi*. As for the rest of the details, they are the same for both.

Epiplatys duboisi Poll, 1953
Dubois' Epiplatys
(In 1967, Clausen placed this fish in a new monotypic genus, *Aphyoplatys*. Accordingly, he says, the correct name should be *Aphyoplatys duboisi* (Poll, 1953).)

This lovely fish comes from the Congo region, in the vicinity of Kinshasa, from a small creek with a light current near N'Dolo, and up to now is the smallest of the described species of this genus. Both sexes reach a total length of only 35 mm (1⅜ inches). Because Plate II–184 shows the form and coloration quite well, they will not be considered further here.

E. duboisi appears to be a typical school fish that does not feel at home in an aquarium by itself, and only in a group of eight or more does it display a multi-toned liveliness which would delight any hobbyist.

The eggs are laid in the usual way among and on the plants or roots, but only a few at a time. The larvae appear within two weeks and at first hide among the necessarily thick plant growth. Because *E. duboisi* remains such a small fish, it seems as if the young do not grow up quickly. In a few months, however, the sexes can be easily told apart. After about four months, they are full grown.

Plate II-184. *Epiplatys duboisi.*

Of course, the natural environment must be imitated as closely as possible in the aquarium, so thick clumps of vegetation should be planted along the edges of the tank. The water must be clear, and for many fishes, should stream through the tank in such a manner as to substitute for the weak current of a creek. This contributes to the well-being of many fishes, and, in almost every instance, is neglected by the hobbyist, particularly if there is no provision in the tank for creating such a current. Stagnant water has a completely different effect from running water on the fishes and this will have to be taken into consideration when the breeding tank is prepared. On the other hand, many fishes, including *E. duboisi*, prefer to leave the running water and migrate to pools and ponds for reproduction. There is much about this that still needs research, especially since even a fish that reproduces in the aquarium is not necessarily pleased with its surroundings.

Epiplatys fasciolatus (Günther, 1866)
Banded Epiplatys
This fish is found in Africa—in the coastal lagoons of tropical West Africa, from Sierra Leone east to the upper Nile—exclusively in fresh, marshy waters. It has been imported many times since 1911.

This toothcarp is one of the larger species, with a maximum length of 80 mm ($3\frac{1}{8}$ inches). The body is somewhat more laterally compressed than in most of its relatives.

The coloration is rather variable and *E. fasciolatus* can, according to how it feels, be a darker purplish to dark olive green. Both sexes are very attractive, although the male is even more so because of the extra decorative effect of the fins and the more intense coloration. Behind the dorsal fin—on the tail—sometimes appear about eight or nine dark, vertical bands.

As for the aquarium set-up, the water must be exclusively fresh, and the addition of salt to make the water somewhat brackish—as usually recommended—is, on the whole, not advisable. Breeding gives disappointing results when salt is added. It is completely correct that the natural habitat—the shallow, coastal marshes—are flooded from time to time by the sea. Certain waters are thus constantly more or less (changeably) brackish. However, this species is not found there, but only in those coastal waters that seldom come into contact with salt water. Like its relatives, *E. fasciolatus* has a great ability for adaptation. The small, water-filled places in the jungle, in which *Epiplatys* mainly lives, have a thick bottom cover of dead vegetable matter and the water reaction is slightly acid to neutral (between pH 6 and 7), although this varies with circumstances.

The suggested temperature range is 20–30 °C (68–86 °F). During the breeding season, it should be 25 °C (77 °F). Only live animal food can keep this fish in good condition.

The pike-like body structure betrays its predatory nature. Indeed, *E. fasciolatus* is, in a certain sense, a predator, but it is not a "killer fish," as it used to be considered. Only small fishes fall prey to it, as it is quite peaceable towards larger fishes and can, therefore, safely be kept with other species from its habitat.

Thick plantings, as well as floating plants covering the surface, are recommended.

Parents and young are both typical dwellers of the upper layers of water, just below the surface. Courtship can be violent, or it can take place quietly. The eggs are laid in the thick clumps of vegetation, are clear as glass (if fertilized, but they quickly become cloudy if not fertilized) and stick firmly to the plants. Here also direct sunlight can cause damage. The long reproductive period causes the young of various spawnings, which hatch out in about two weeks, to be disproportionate in size. The smaller fish, hatched later, can be harmed by the larger ones. Very large, thickly planted tanks are therefore recommended. Otherwise, dip out the larger specimens.

Epiplatys macrostigma (Boulenger, 1911)
Big-Spot Epiplatys
Large-Spotted Epiplatys

This species, hailing from the coastal region of West Africa (Congo to Chiloango), achieves a length of about 60 mm ($2\frac{3}{8}$ inches), and so is the same size as *Epiplatys chevalieri*. The basic coloration, however, is less green, but olive brown, yellowish white towards the belly and brown on the back. A blue-green glow with light iridescence plays over the whole body, which is further decorated with rows of blood red spots, which give an especially beautiful effect against the basic greenish brown coloration. The fins are blue-green with carmine red spots and stripes. The caudal fin, especially, is heavily pigmented with red spots and stripes. As for the rest, what has been said for *E. chevalieri* and its relatives is equally valid here, though reports on this species declare it to be an out and out predator and even its own eggs and young are not safe near it. The eggs are more numerous and considerably smaller than those of *E. chevalieri*.

Epiplatys marnoi (Steindachner, 1881)

As far as known, this fish is being described for the first time as an aquarium import. According to the notes accompanying the preserved material, it is said to come from the upper part of the Congo Basin. Although it was not known that this species came from the Congo region, it is certainly not impossible, especially since it is a variety that is in total technical agreement with the description of *E. marnoi* from Bahr-el-Jebel (the White Nile). But in spite of that, it appears to be a local variety.

The basic coloration is a soft olive brown, darker on the back, lighter on the belly. Along the lower side of the body runs a broad, dark brown to purplish band, which consists of eight to ten spots. These spots are the remains of cross striping which is either only vaguely visible or is entirely assimilated into the spots. Distributed over the body, especially in the vicinity of the gill covers, are red or carmine spots. Red is scarce in the fins, which themselves are lilac to bluish purple, with a dark red edge to the anal and ventral fins. This is a very beautiful fish that certainly, considering the researched material, belongs among the smaller fishes; it grows to about 45 mm (1¾ inches) in length. As far as is known, this species has not yet been bred.

Epiplatys sheljuzhkoi (Poll, 1953)

This fish has been imported several times in the past few years and is generally adopted by hobbyists, in spite of its obvious characteristics of the true *Epiplatys,* the real surface-dweller. It can lie at the surface

Illus. II-166. *Epiplatys sheljuzhkoi.*

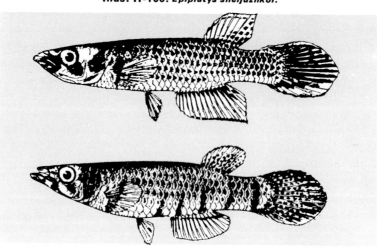

Plate II-185. *Epiplatys sheljuzhkoi.*

for a long time, literally without moving a fin, lying in wait for insects which, in the wild (and therefore in the aquarium as well), compose its main diet.

This species grows not much larger than *Epiplatys chevalieri* and *Epiplatys macrostigma*, but has a considerably stronger build. Again, the basic coloration is brownish, less green, and the rows of spots are more rust brown than really red. Both sexes, especially the adult females, exhibit somewhat angling cross bands or stripes on the tail and right behind the gill covers. The fins are yellowish with a bright yellow spot on the lower lobe of the caudal fin in the adult males. The fins show hardly any reddish pigment, and the dots and spots so typical of the two species mentioned earlier are usually not visible.

Plate II-186. *Pachypanchax homalonotus.*

Genus *Pachypanchax*

The various species formerly classified in the genus *Haplochilus* or *Panchax*, native to the Seychelles and Madagascar, were united by Myers in the genus *Pachypanchax* and are characterized by details which are hardly important here. Only the scale-covered caudal fin will be mentioned, which distinguishes it from all other African toothcarp species. The known species are *P. playfairi*, *P. homalonotus*, *P. nuchimaculatus*, and *P. sakaramyi*.

All species compare well with the members of the related genera *Epiplatys* and *Aplocheilus*.

Plate II-187. *Pachypanchax playfairi.*

Pachypanchax playfairi (Günther, 1866)
Playfair's Panchax

That sex changes can also occur among other species of fishes than the classical case of *Xiphophorus helleri* (see page 889) has been set forth many times. Wolfsheimer now discusses a similar case of sex change among these egg-laying toothcarps and actually provides a photograph of three specimens one above another, a normal male and female and a female that has turned into a male.

It would be useful and interesting for breeders to pay more attention to this change. Many breeding failures with a supposed pair of fish can perhaps be ascribed to a similar cause!

Genus *Aphyosemion*

One of the genera of great interest for aquarists is surely *Aphyosemion*, and rightly so. There are few genera of fish that can provide so much pleasure for their owners and which are so attractive in coloration and conduct as the members of this group. As is often the case with similar genera that are highly attractive to both dealer and breeder, confusing information gets published, and later on this becomes quite difficult to correct.

Although he has worked continuously since 1947 at further reviews of the dozens of *Aphyosemion* species described, the author always comes to the conclusion that too little is known about the fishes themselves to enable a logical, or more natural, classification to be made.

Of course, the research will continue, but for the moment it is useful to put forth a few points, so that hobbyists can possibly contribute to the solution of the problem. Starting with some accurate data and limiting the discussion to only a small number of the dozens of described species, it can already be clearly determined that a division of the group into three sub-genera, as recommended by Myers (1933) on grounds of morphological and anatomical characteristics, agrees in principle with a division based on the biology of these fishes, especially taking ecological and ethnological factors into consideration.

A very clear distinction exists between the species which do and those which do not lay their eggs in the bottom, as well as between the respective incubation periods of the eggs. The species which are presently rather commonly known among aquarists—*A. australe, A. bivittatum, A. calliurum, A. christyi, A. coeruleum, A. cognatum, A. gardneri, A. loennbergi, A. petersi, A. sjoestedti,* and *A. walkeri*—all have from 8 to 16 dorsal rays. (The fish known as *A. coeruleum,* the Blue Gularis, is known as *A. sjoestedti* to some aquarists and the fish known as *A. sjoestedti,* the Golden Pheasant, is, instead, *Roloffia occidentalis.*)

It can also be seen, on the basis of more modern biological characteristics, that two groups cannot be clearly distinguished, since, for example, a few species considered as bottom-layers are called plant-layers by some breeders. Whether this is indeed a question of two kinds of reproductive biology in the same species or variety, or whether the determining characteristics have been doubtfully described, is a point for present study. It is a positive fact that, in broad terms, the two groups, *Aphyosemion* (*Aphyosemion*) and *Aphyosemion* (*Fundulopanchax*) are differentiated in egg incubation, which runs about 10 to 15 days for the

Plate II-188. *Roloffia occidentalis.*

first group and about 30 to 40 days for the second. Some varieties belonging to the sub-genus *Aphyosemion*, as a group also referred to as the *calliurum* group, are *A. australe, A. calliurum, A. cognatum* and *A. christyi*, besides a great number of varieties which can partly be included here but are unknown to such an extent that they cannot be considered for the time being. Considering that all four of the above-named species inhabit another region, and also that they concur in their biology as well as in other characteristics, the inclination is to speak of one variable species having a number of local varieties. More-over, specimens have been found in the available material which are obviously cross-breeds of *A. australe* and possibly *A. calliurum*. A decision concerning the division of local *Aphyosemion* varieties should, then, be possible, were it not that many more forms have been described about which little is known and for which there is no further material available. For the moment, therefore, it is more understand-able to maintain the current names for the various forms, but to add them to the *A. calliurum* complex.

The name *Fundulopanchax* was introduced by Myers (1924), and later

(1933) was reduced to a sub-genus of *Aphyosemion* for the species *A. arnoldi, A. batesi, A. beauforti, A. bitaeniatum, A. bivittatum, A. coeruleum, A. filamentosum, A. gardneri, A. gulare, A. loennbergi, A. multicolor, A. pappenheimi, A. riggenbachi, A. rubrostictum, A. splendidum, A. splendopleuris, A. spurelli* and *A. zimmeri*. Later on, a number of varieties were added to these—namely, *A. unistrigatum* and *A. fallax*.

Although all these varieties concur a great deal with each other morphologically and anatomically, in the eyes of aquarists, some deviate considerably in looks and life style (reproductive biology, etc.) from most members of the group. This becomes strikingly apparent, for example, in the case of *A. bivittatum* and *A. coeruleum,* two well known aquarium fishes, which are totally different in their essential characteristics. The impression is, therefore, that Myers' division is a forced one and anything but natural. Therefore, groups will be narrowed down here, distinguishing the complexes which biologically belong together, and limiting the discussion to those varieties that have been imported as aquarium fishes and with which necessary experience has been had.

The genus *Aphyosemion* inhabits special waters, which entirely or almost entirely dry up in the dry season, only to turn again into pools and streams with the onset of the rainy season. In Africa, principally at the mouths of the Congo and the flood areas along the west coast from whence these fish come, are many such ponds and streamlets.

It is clear that there is a great difference in the constitution of the water just before drying up and just after the first rains have fallen. The reproduction period falls just before and after the dry season; that is to say, egg-laying by the true bottom-laying species takes place in very shallow water, the eggs being deposited in the mud bottom (see also the discussion under *Aphyosemion coeruleum* on page 782 and the related *Cynolebias* species on page 796). After the first rains have fallen and the dried-out mud gradually soaks it up, the eggs hatch.

For the aquarium, a soft water that is slightly acidic—having a pH of about 6—is ideal; recommended for this is rain water filtered through peat moss, or an aquarium with a peat bottom filled with rain water. It is necessary to return the water level to normal after the eggs have been laid; adding soft rain water after a few days is beneficial for the development of the eggs, which soon hatch.

The species that are not bottom-layers should be treated as other egg-layers whose eggs are more or less adhesive.

A point deserving notice is the capacity of *Aphyosemion* for jumping, because it likes to seek out higher places, just as *Rivulus* does. If there is a small marsh present, or a somewhat dry terrace laid out, then that is the place it prefers to be. It lies on the mud, completely out of the water, or on a stone, and suns itself peacefully, and only its gill covers are seen to move slowly, but without letting air escape through them. Breathing is conducted entirely through the mouth opening.

Of the many species which have been described of *Aphyosemion*, a number are well liked by aquarists, partly because of their gorgeous coloration and partly because of their interesting conduct.

THE *A. calliurum* COMPLEX

For the time being, the varieties *A. australe, A. calliurum, A. cognatum* and *A. christyi* will be summarized below. Observe that this complex is, therefore, not identical with Myers' sub-genus *Aphyosemion*, for to this belong still other varieties, such as *A. elegans, A. lujae, A. meinkeni*, etc.

What characterizes these representatives of the *A. calliurum* complex? In the first place, the females of all these fishes can barely, if at all, be told apart, and there is a question as to whether the males of any given species can, either. In each case, however, the males of different species are so different from each other that they can easily be told apart, which accounts for the many names that have been applied to them. It is clear, then, that variation is in no way a criterion for accurate identification of species.

These species are further characterized by a short incubation period of their eggs—from a few days to two weeks, depending on the temperature—while about 10 to 12 days appears to be normal. Quick hatching of the eggs (the author himself has noted the lapse of only two days between laying and the observing of young) can be caused by a low temperature. This seems strange, yet it has appeared that after fertilization, a fully ripe egg develops more quickly than a ripe egg more or less forced by high temperatures. Perhaps other factors also play a rôle here. In any case, *A. australe* appears to be a species whose eggs develop quickly, compared to the other species. Of course, the hatching of eggs over a long period is a consequence of the laying period, which can also stretch out over a period of days. The rather adhesive eggs of the fishes in the *A. calliurum* complex are laid on plants, preferably on floating plants, just under the surface. Information about some of the species named here laying eggs *in* the bottom must be provisionally ascribed to an incorrect determination of these varieties.

The varieties combined in this complex are predominantly smaller than the gularis-like fishes (*A. coeruleum*, etc.). Because they, by reason of many characteristics, fall in between the sub-genus *Aphyosemion* (fall into the *A. calliurum* complex) and the gularis-type fishes, they form a clearly outlined natural group which, among other things, has an incubation period of 10 to 15 days. A notable point of difference with the *A. calliurum* group is, moreover, that the females are characterized by two more or less distinct lengthwise stripes. These alone distinguish *A. bivittatum*-type females from *A. calliurum*-type females. The males have the same two stripes and the dorsal fin is usually somewhat bigger, because it has more rays.

As far as reproductive biology is concerned, *A. bivittatum* members differ from fishes in the *A. calliurum* group because they lay their eggs very close to the bottom, yet still among the plants (clumps of algae and fine-leaved vegetation). That matings sometimes seem odd procedurally suggests that *A. bivittatum*-type fishes are exceptions that are observed everywhere, yet this should certainly not be considered the normal, natural way. It can indeed be said that in conduct, the *A. bivittatum* group concurs with the members of the *A. calliurum* group, except that, in the case of *A. bivittatum*, there is an apparent tendency to lay eggs closer to the bottom.

Those species or varieties which belong to the *A. bivittatum* complex are: *A. bivittatum*, *A. hollyi*, *A. loennbergi*, *A. multicolor*, *A. splendopleuris*. Whether conceived as local varieties of *A. bivittatum* or not, these are certainly not to be considered as true species unto themselves.

THE *A. gulare* COMPLEX

In the first place, the fishes included under the sub-genus name *Fundulopanchax* (type *Fundulus coerulea*=*Aphyosemion coeruleum*), are distinguished from the remaining members of the genus *Aphyosemion* by their substantially larger body bulk and their broader head. The characteristic pointed out by Myers for distinguishing the species is the placement of the dorsal fin, in front of, above, or even behind the beginning of the anal fin. This, however, does not coincide with concepts of a natural grouping, because the same thing is found in *A. bivittatum*, which is clearly more closely related to the *A. calliurum* group. Yet, on this basis, Myers and his followers classify *A. bivittatum* in the *Fundulopanchax* group.

The *A. gulare* complex is thus identical with Myers' *Fundulopanchax*,

Plate II-189. *Aphyosemion arnoldi.*

without, however, the *A. bivittatum* complex and minus *A. sjoestedti*, for which the sub-genus *Callopanchax* was set up later on.

Of more interest to the aquarist is the reproductive biology of these larger *Aphyosemion* species, the Blue Gularis being foremost.

The *A. gulare* complex includes the following varieties: *A. gulare*, *A. sjoestedti, A. arnoldi, A. walkeri* and *A. gardneri*—all of which have been imported as aquarium fishes—and a number (included under *Fundulopanchax*) which have not been imported, or at any rate are not well known. Perhaps *A. fallax*, which also belongs in this complex, has been imported a number of times.

The *A. gulare* group is conspicuous by reason of its robust appearance. More important to aquarists is the knowledge that all these forms are bottom-layers as described for *A. coeruleum*. An exception which may form a link with the other groups is *A. arnoldi*, which not only lays its eggs in the bottom but also, according to pertinent publications, in clumps of algae and similar places. That the same species practices two different methods of egg-laying appears improbable. Further research reveals, however, that perhaps an incorrect determination has been made, the more so since *A. arnoldi* is the smallest of these larger species and, thus, stands closer to the other groups.

The incubation period of the eggs in this group runs from 30 to 40 days.

Plate II-190. *Roloffia geryi.*

In summary:
1. Smaller varieties, incubation period up to about 12 days
    A. Females without distinct, lengthwise stripes, surface-layers . . . *A. calliurum* complex
    B. Females with two distinct, lengthwise stripes, plant-layers close to the bottom . . . *A. bivittatum* complex
2. Larger varieties, incubation period more than two weeks, bottom-layers
    A. Incubation period from 30 to 40 days . . . *A. gulare* complex
    B. Incubation period from 60 to over 100 days . . . *A. sjoestedti* complex

Some years ago, an attempt was made to place the various larger species in the genus *Roloffia*, without, however, seriously considering several important features. For the time being, until a more thorough study is available, the generic name *Aphyosemion* will be used, since there are so many species and forms that link the various complexes recognized here.

Aphyosemion australe (Rachow, 1921)

Cape Lopez

Lyretail

Lyretailed Panchax

This fish hails from Cape Lopez in West Africa. In the wild, it lives in very shallow brook-tributaries and ponds, and in marshy grassland, where it prefers to dwell among clumps of grass hanging down into the water.

Formerly, a number of different species were designated by the name *A. australe*. This can be blamed mostly on their great similarity to the various *Aphyosemion* species. This was especially so if they had not been kept correctly and, as a consequence, did not display their full array of gorgeous coloration. For a long time, this species has been confused with *Aphyosemion cameronensis* Boulenger, especially in English and American aquarist circles.

This species attains a maximum length of 70 mm (2¾ inches). The females are somewhat smaller. Plate II–192 gives a good impression of the glittering coloration of this very suitable aquarium fish. The female is less distinctly toned and patterned and also has no lengthened fin rays, as the male has, but has all rounded fins.

It is very important that this fish be kept in slightly acid water (pH 5.7 to 7). The aquarium set-up should preferably be a roomy but low tank (for example: 25 cm high (10 inches), 40 cm wide (16 inches) and 60 cm long (24 inches)). On the bottom put a layer of humus (sand really has no place here), plant with *Fontinalis*, *Najas minor* and

Plate II-191. *Roloffia liberiensis.*

775

other smaller species, and place a few rocks overgrown with thread algae, and *Riccia* on the surface.

The temperature must not be allowed to rise too high, in no case above 25 °C (77 °F), and it appears that a nightly drop in temperature is desirable though not needed to keep the fish in good health. Breed at 22–25 °C (72–77 °F). Winter over at 18–20 °C (64–68 °F), preferably with no bottom heating.

Mouldiness and failure of the eggs to hatch can largely be ascribed to the following factors: If the pair to be bred are fed too many white worms shortly before mating, this will often be harmful to reproduction. A pH of 7 or higher, as well as too high a temperature, will slow down or prevent proper development of the eggs, after they have been laid. Too much sun is not desirable and the absence of a humus layer in which the newly-hatched young can bury themselves are important points which should not be overlooked.

The eggs, laid 50 to 200 at a time, preferably among floating plants or similar, hatch out on the second day. They may not, however, depending on various factors, hatch until 6 to 10 days have passed (most breeders agree that eggs usually hatch between 10 and 16 days,

Plate II-192. *Aphyosemion australe.*

12 to 14 being average), although this does not vary as much as it does in other species of this genus.

Cross-breeds of *Aphyosemion australe* with related species have been described, which indicates once again that many species are very closely related to each other, and in due time, perhaps, will turn out to be only sub-species, races or varieties of a single species. It is notable, as a matter of fact, that all the fishes of this genus described as species inhabit individual regions of their own and are seldom, if ever, found in each other's company, even though the catch locations may be separated from each other by only a few dozen metres.

Aphyosemion bivittatum (Lönnberg, 1895)
Aphiosemion
Red Lyretail

A splendid representative of the genus *Aphyosemion* which is attracting more and more interest, *Aphyosemion bivittatum* hails from the typically *Aphyosemion* waters of Cameroon and Nigeria.

This species, which can grow to a length of 65 mm ($2\frac{9}{16}$ inches) is already an old timer—that is to say, it is one of two sub-species known among aquarists since 1910—and is bred in fairly reasonable numbers.

The basic coloration is a beautiful red-brown, turning to light green towards the tail, and with a greenish sheen on the back. The purplish red dots on the scales contrast beautifully with the green; sometimes violet from the edges of the scales merges into a network design.

The fins are greenish at the base, red towards the outside, with a nearly black lower edge to the anal fin, and deep carmine red towards the outside. The dorsal fin varies in coloration with carmine to violet stripes and spots and a black outer edge. On the base of the caudal fin appears a round lilac to purplish red spot, running out forward into two dark bands, the upper one approximately above the middle of the sides, the lower one along the base of the anal fin, along the underside of the eye to the point of the lower jaw.

The coloration gradations are, moreover, such that only a real-life photograph could give a completely correct view of them, and then only of a certain variety, for there are several sub-species that have already been described, each of which would require a plate of its own to give a fair impression of the whole species.

As a typical representative of the *Aphyosemion* group that does not lay its eggs in the bottom, *A. bivittatum* may be seen looking for a good spawning place among the plants, though rather close to the bottom.

Plate II-193. *Aphyosemion bivittatum.*

A suitable temperature again is about 24 °C (75 °F); a little lower or higher has little effect on the breeding results, which, in most cases, may be called satisfactory. The water, however, should be poor in lime (soft). A hardness less than 8° DH is necessary.

Plate II-194. *Aphyosemion bualanum.*

Aphyosemion calliurum (Boulenger, 1911)
Calliurum

Aphyosemion calliurum has been found many times on the west coast of Africa—in Liberia, the Ivory Coast, the Gold Coast, Nigeria and Cameroon, the flood region of the Congo and its tributaries. The first specimens were brought into Europe in 1908.

The body of this beautiful fish is slim, cylindrical, the tail section strongly flattened on the sides. The length measures about 60 mm (2⅜ inches) for the male, about 55 mm (2 3/16 inches) for the female. The head is somewhat flattened on top. The snout is broad and short, the mouth small and turned upwards. The fins of the male are unusually beautiful in coloration and design and very striking in their ornamental shape. The basic coloration of the body is blue-green, changing to dark, olive green on the back. Directly behind the greenish luminous gill covers are four bright red, irregularly shaped, horizontal stripes which continue into the just as red, but less distinct, side stripe composed of tiny dots and little lines. The rear of the body is decorated with irregular cross stripes that appear sometimes more and sometimes less distinct. The dorsal fin, placed far to the rear, consists of three zones. The foremost zone is milky white, behind it is a zone of deep, red-brown, while most of the fin is yellowish brown with small, violet spots. The caudal fin consists of two parts, each a mirror-image of the other. The outermost fin rays are lengthened, as are the middle ones. The outermost edges are again milky white enclosing on both sides a purplish red zone. The central division is a beautiful, light blue-green, again with many small, violet spots. The anal and pelvic fins are, like the dorsal fin, divided into three zones; the anal fin is large, but the ventral fins are small. The females are easy to recognize, first by their being soberly clad, compared to the gorgeous coloration of the males; second, in sexually ripe specimens, by the clearly visible, brownish eggs showing through the belly region. The fins are also much less strikingly shaped and are yellowish.

Aphyosemion christyi (Boulenger, 1920)

This fish, too, is found in the typical *Aphyosemion* waters of the Congo region and, as shown by available data, has a very broad distribution area.

The first specimens that went to aquarists in Belgium were imported in 1947 and 1948. Since then, many more have been imported.

At first, this import went under the name of *Aphyosemion singa,*

779

which appears to be an incorrect designation. The *Haplochilus singa* of Boulenger (1899) is, however, an *Epiplatys*.

As far as coloration is concerned, the formerly applied specific name, *castaneum*, was pointedly chosen, for the basic coloration of *A. christyi* is a beautiful chestnut brown on a beige background, with a sky-blue tint over the fore part of the body. The belly is yellowish.

The gill covers and cheeks are a strongly iridescent blue-green. On the caudal fin are two ochre yellow bands which, towards the front, join with the soft ochre yellow of the tail.

Spread over the body in more or less irregular lines are a very substantially varying number of bright red to carmine dots. The iridescent, blue-green spots on the gill covers often merge into irregular, wreath-like little lines.

The light to ochre yellow dorsal fin exhibits a dark red edge with a number of irregularly sprinkled, blood red spots in the middle, and with the milky white, lengthened after-rays so typical of many of the related *Aphyosemion* varieties. The anal fin is yellow-green at the base, turning darker towards the edge, often into a beautiful red. There are also a number of bright red spots on the anal fin.

For breeding, refer to the discussion of *Aphyosemion australe* and *Aphyosemion coeruleum* and their relatives, with the understanding that, according to Meder (1952), that *A. christyi* lays its eggs in fine-leaved

Plate II-196. *Aphyosemion calabaricus.*

plants. Whether this takes place normally, or whether it is a question of adaptation to circumstances, is not at this moment precisely clear. If a marshy area is provided in the aquarium, it is possible that *A. christyi* belongs to those species, as with most *Rivulus* varieties, that prefer to lay their eggs above water, or in the mud bottom. Further study of this fish will help to decide whether *A. christyi* represents two groups in the wild—the bottom- (marsh) layers and the free- (plant) layers.

The eggs of *A. christyi* are clear as glass and obviously less sensitive to light than those of the "true" bottom-layers. They hatch out (without a dry period) within two weeks.

Plate II-197. *Aphyosemion fallax.*

Aphyosemion coeruleum (Boulenger, 1915)
Blue Gularis

This fish is very common in slowly running and stagnant waters, thickly grown with vegetation, in Cameroon and the Niger delta.

This splendid fish reaches a length of more than 100 mm (4 inches) (the females somewhat smaller). The body is cylindrical, long and slim, the head vertical, the tail compressed sideways. The fins are impressive in shape and patterning, especially among the males, where the three-toned caudal fin first attracts attention. Plate II–198 is clear enough, insofar as the color is concerned, that a further detailed description is unnecessary.

In addition to a basic brownish red coloration, yellow, green, blue and bright red are worked together into a glittering combination, which can vary considerably according to the age of the fish, the state of its feelings, and the time of year. The smaller females are, in general, less striking, yet the various hues are still quite bold.

In the matter of breeding, opinions are inclined to differ. All aquarists who have ever been lucky enough to take care of this fish are in agreement that the first requirement is a roomy and well planted aquarium facing south or southeast. A quantity of floating plants is also indispensable. For the well-being of this fish in a community aquarium, these requirements must be satisfied or things will go wrong. It is better if it is not put into the usual kind of community aquarium but, instead, with species companions or other fishes which live under similar circumstances. It must have a hiding place to get away from light that is too bright. Moreover, it is peaceable near fish larger than it is, but when near smaller and younger fishes, it quickly betrays its predatory nature. A bottom soil without sand is desirable, though not necessary so long as there is a place provided where the fish can give rein to its desires. The aquarium must not be stirred up into a mud puddle, and will not be, so long as there are no species present, such as *Barbus*, which quickly turn the tank into a mudhole.

As far as food is concerned, *A. coeruleum* eats anything that lives and moves if it is small enough to swallow whole, but care and moderation must be exercised in serving it. Considerable variation in the menu is desirable, keeping in mind that any food scorned must be dipped out of the aquarium at once, because the fish will not care further about it.

By the beginning of winter, the breeding tank must be prepared, with peat dust if at all possible, and placed so that the main light falls into the tank from above, thus allowing little or no light through the

Plate II-198. *Aphyosemion coeruleum.*

vertical panes. Top light is indeed the best. Sunlight, too, is desirable for adequate water vegetation and floating plants. It is best to choose a wide but low tank about 20–25 cm (8–10 inches) high. Slowly bring the temperature up to about 22 °C (72 °F) and as soon as there is a little sunlight, the violent courtship begins, conducted mainly by the male, but with some allurement by the female. It can easily happen that the male starts knocking his mate about to such a degree that you must intervene, so watch carefully. Very near the bottom and pressed closely together, the male tries to hug the female to him with his anal and dorsal fins, and the female emits her glass-clear, tiny eggs. The eggs are fertilized and then washed into the peat layer with powerful fanning of the fins. In this manner, several dozen eggs can be laid every day.

The duration of mating can be several weeks, during which about 100 to 200 eggs are laid. Success follows, especially if not too many of the eggs turn mouldy.

After these matings, which are sometimes interrupted by the exhaustion of one or both of the fish, keep a good watch and interfere if necessary. Do not begrudge the fish a few weeks rest, preferably in two separate tanks. Take care now that no direct sunlight penetrates the eggs. The fish, in most cases, have already taken measures against this eventuality by burying the eggs some distance under the sand or peat bottom.

The temperature remains about 20 °C (68 °F). Higher temperatures are bad for the fish and can even slow down the development of the eggs. The tank should be shielded on all sides against strong daylight; leave only the top open to the light, at the same time taking care that not too much light is able to enter.

If the first young have hatched out within a month, then gradually start increasing the light, but still guarding against the penetration of bright sunlight too deeply into the tank.

When just out of their eggs, the little *A. coeruleum* are only about 1 mm (.04 inch) long and very difficult to see. Do not be too quick to believe that the breeding has failed. The best thing to do, after a month, is to provide infusoria and after about 5 or 6 weeks, feed the fish fine-sieved live food. *A. coeruleum* grow quickly and eat astonishingly large amounts. A month after hatching, they can have passed the 2-cm ($\frac{13}{16}$-inch) mark in length. After a few more weeks, the yellow stripe in the caudal fin of the males appears in many of the fish. The beautiful shape of the fins does not come until later. A mistake that many used to make was to use these fish too soon for breeding, since they are sexually mature in only about three months. Not until they are at least 80 mm ($3\frac{1}{8}$ inches) long (after about six months) should the progeny be used for breeding.

A. coeruleum are strong fish and will provide many years of pleasure if attention is paid to the preceding information. These fish certainly do not belong among the so-called annual fishes like *Cynolebias* which, upon completion of the life cycle—egg–young–adult–reproduction–eggs—die within a year. Although *A. coeruleum* bear up well under temperature fluctuations, they are very sensitive to sudden changes in the composition of the water. Therefore, do not ever transfer the fish directly from one tank into another.

Plate II-199. *Aphyosemion cognatum.*

Aphyosemion cognatum Meinken, 1951

This rather recent Congo import belongs to the group of *Aphyosemion* species which, at present, are commonly known as the *A. calliurum* group. This group includes the *Aphyosemion* species that lay eggs with an incubation period of about two weeks. As far as the aquarium layout and reproduction are concerned, refer to these individual species.

Although there is no certainty that Plate II–199 actually shows *A. cognatum*, and considering that no material on it has yet been investigated, it seems that the fish maintained by Timmerman should indeed be classified under *A. cognatum*. This is, then, already a variety clearly distinguished from the related *A. calliurum* group species.

The hues correspond, although they are less distinct, with those of the *A. calliurum* group, although, here again, the females are less attractive and somewhat grey. The basic coloration of the males is light olive brown with a reddish glow in the mating season. Those in good condition (if full grown) are sometimes lavender. The gill covers are blue-green with irregular, bright, carmine red spots and stripes. The darker spots on the body and fins are also carmine red. The carmine red dots or spots on the scales can merge into more or less distinct lengthwise or crosswise stripes. The fins are orange-yellow with carmine red edge, sometimes bordered with a light blue edge.

A very attractive acquisition for the tank, *A. cognatum* will surely, now that it has been re-bred in considerable measure, be widely dispersed.

Plate II-200. *Aphyosemion labarrei.*

Plate II-201. *Aphyosemion petersi.*

786

Plate II-202. *Aphyosemion austr-ale,* red or gold variety. Sometimes called *Aphyosemion australe hjerreseni.*

Plate II-203. *Aphyosemion filamentosum.*

Aphyosemion gardneri (Boulenger, 1911)
Blue Aphyosemion (variety)
Gardner's Aphyosemion

This is an especially lovely toothcarp from Togo, Africa, that is not yet generally known by aquarists. This is partly because only a few specimens have been imported, and, further, because the few imported specimens have not been easy to persuade to reproduce, possibly a consequence of their being in the hands of less experienced breeders. It does not seem logical that this species, which corresponds so much with its relatives, should be more difficult to breed. Its environment is like that of the other *Aphyosemion* species.

Older males have lengthened fin rays on the anal and caudal fins, which give them a strange but very attractive look. The basic coloration is beige brown with a light blue sheen; the body, head and fins are decorated with purplish red spots and stripes. In the fins, light blue and yellow mingle with each other. The iris of the eye is an iridescent blue-green. Moreover, the small ventral fins are remarkable with a bright red stripe along the edge, which, however, is not present in all specimens (and only in the males when present), so that perhaps this may be a local variation.

Plate II-204. *Aphyosemion gardneri.*

Plate II-205. *Aphyosemion nigerianum,* male, blue variety.

In addition to a noticeable difference in coloration, as with its relatives, the females are substantially smaller (about 32 mm or 1¼ inches), while the males grow to about 60 mm (2⅜ inches), including the fins.

The eggs are not laid on the bottom, but very close to it, among the plants. The young hatch out of the eggs within two weeks.

Plate II-206. *Aphyosemion nigerianum,* male, yellow variety.

Aphyosemion gulare (Boulenger, 1901)
Yellow Gularis

Except for its coloration and slightly smaller size (up to about 8 cm or 3 inches), this species is almost identical with Boulenger's *A. coeruleum*. *A. coeruleum* and *A. gulare* inhabit the same area and must be considered sibling species or probably sub-species of a greatly varying population.

Aphyosemion sjoestedti (Lönnberg, 1895)
Golden Pheasant

This species, which is erroneously sometimes taken for one of the gularis forms, is quite different in several respects, particularly in how it behaves, its courting activity and the incubation time of the eggs, which lasts almost twice as long as for the gularis forms. When kept together with its relatives, in fact, *A. sjoestedti* is without doubt a true and distinct species.

Since, however, the area of distribution partly overlaps that of the gularis forms in Cameroon, there is always a possibility of natural hybridization, but this has still be to fully researched and sorted out by specialists.

Plate II-207. *Aphyosemion spurelli.*

Plate II-208. *Aphyosemion striatum.*

Plate II-209. *Aphyosemion walkeri.*

Plate II-210. *Aphyosemion* (? cross-breed).

Genus *Nothobranchius*

This African genus corresponds closely to the South American genus *Cynolebias*.

Nothobranchius guentheri (Pfeffer, 1893)

Carmine Nothobranchius

This fish hails from East Africa—from Mombasa, Kenya, to the Pangani River and the island of Zanzibar. As a consequence of the widespread confusion of names regarding the African toothcarps there is not complete certainty as to the identity of this species. Many of the described *Nothobranchius* species are probably synonymous with this one.

As relatives of *Aphyosemion coeruleum*, the members of the genus *Nothobranchius* are distinguished, in part, by the higher, somewhat more laterally compressed body and the always rounded fins. Insofar as care is concerned, refer to the discussion of *Aphyosemion coeruleum* on page 782. It seems more beneficial to maintain a lower average temperature—for example, a daytime temperature of about 22 °C (72 °F) and a nighttime temperature that gradually drops to about 18 °C (64 °F).

The eggs are laid on the bottom in about the same way as with *Aphyosemion coeruleum*. By fanning the eggs with his fins, the male forces them under the upper (mud) layer of the bottom. In this, the

793

Plate II-212. *Nothobranchius brieni.*

reproduction procedure is almost the same as in the *Cynolebias* species, and covering the eggs with a layer of mud certainly has the same purpose (in the wild, at least, when the dry season comes on)—of preventing the eggs from drying out completely and from losing their germinating ability. A moderately acid environment (pH 6–6.5) is necessary for the eggs to develop. The bottom layer (peat dust) must be at least 3 cm ($1\frac{3}{16}$ inches) thick. Moreover, the tank should be placed so that, at

Plate II-213. *Nothobranchius melanospilus.*

Plate II-214. *Nothobranchius kuhntae.*

some time during the day, the sunlight can penetrate for a few hours.

That this fish has a short life is indeed in accordance with nature. However, this does not mean that it cannot live for a somewhat longer time in the aquarium. As far as is known, however, two full years is the longest period, and by then it has long since lost all of its glory and gorgeous coloration. In nature, the old fish die, for the most part, as a result of the dry season—hence shortly after the eggs are laid.

Plate II-215. *Nothobranchius palmquisti.*

Tribe Cynolebiatini

The members of this tribe are so-called annual fish. The pattern of scales on the head differs particularly from Rivulini by the loose, rear edge of scale *a*, the same as with the Aplocheilini (see page 750). In their remaining characteristics, they very closely approach the various *Rivulus* complexes, while their life cycle again corresponds with that of *Aphyosemion* and *Nothobranchius*.

Genus *Cynolebias*

Although several species have been described, only one species is well known in aquarist circles. A short time ago, a second species, *C. nigripinnis*, appeared.

A number of fish received from a hobbyist died en route, but were still well preserved. It was a South American shipment, and closer examination of the fish showed that a few of them looked a lot like *Cynolebias*. They appeared to be *C. splendens*, and thus, in addition to *C. bellottii* and *C. nigripinnis*, the third species was on the way to hobbyists. After that, nothing more was seen or heard of this fish—even whether it had found its way into the hands of any hobbyist.

Plate II-216. *Cynolebias whitei.*

In 1942, Myers discussed briefly the Cyprinodontidae family and at the same time said a few words about *Cynolebias* and *Cynopoecilus*. Up to then, the following species had been described: *Cynolebias adloffi, Cynolebias bellottii* and *Cynolebias wolterstorffi* and *Cynopoecilus melanotaenia*. On the basis of rather comprehensive material—fresh from Rio de Janeiro—that yielded the new forms *Cynolebias constanciae, C. whitei, C. opalescens, C. zingiberinus, C. minimus* and *C. splendens,* Myers expressed doubt whether *Cynopoecilus* as a genus could be retained next to *Cynolebias.* The most important characteristic differentiating these two genera—widely separated ventral fins—according to Myers no longer holds true. There are thus transitions. Now, in accordance with modern concepts, it is impossible for two genera to be differentiated by means of the same characteristic. Yet that does not remove the fact that the habitat of *Cynopoecilus melanotaenia* differs substantially from that of the *Cynolebias* varieties. Even this would subsequently appear to indicate that the two genera are not divisible; yet this does happen, though on different grounds.

Of two species, *Cynolebias bellottii* and *C. nigripinnis,* it is now known with almost absolute certainty how reproduction is carried on. (Observations from nature have been noted only for *C. bellottii.*)

However, nothing is known about the type species of this genus, *Cynolebias porosus.* The generic name *Cynolebias* can, of course, only be maintained for *bellottii* and *nigripinnis* if *Cynolebias porosus* is indeed also a bottom-laying annual fish.

Another point concerns *Cynopoecilus melanotaenia,* which has also been classified by Myers under *Cynolebias.* Only on the basis of the great difference in reproductive biology (*C. melanotaenia* is, assuming that these statements are correct, a surface-dweller which lays its eggs in the same manner as described under *Aphyosemion* for the *calliurum* group) is there the inclination to let this genus exist, at least until more is known about it.

Of all the new species described by Myers (1942), nothing was known about reproduction until the article mentioned was published under the title *Cynolebias* (*Cynopoecilus*) *splendens* Myers. (This method of citing suggests that Myers has perhaps classified it as a sub-genus *Cynopoecilus,* though this is incorrect, as may be gathered from the preceding.)

The two species well known at present, *Cynolebias bellottii* and *Cynolebias nigripinnis,* require an incubation period of 40 to 60 days or somewhat longer and the requirement for *C. splendens* is for the same length of time, during which the eggs lie buried in the almost dry bottom. It is only upon such grounds as this that the species *splendens*, as Myers suggests, may be allotted to *Cynolebias* and not to *Cynopoecilus*.

Cynolebias bellottii Steindachner, 1881

Argentine Pearl Fish

This fish is found in South America—the flood basin of the Rio de la Plata, the pampas surrounding Buenos Aires, the brackish estuarial waters of the La Plata and Rio Brancas in Argentina. It has been regularly imported by German breeders since 1906.

Unlike the closely related *Rivulus* species, *Cynolebias* is characterized by a rather high body that is laterally compressed. Its length is about 70 mm (2¾ inches). The mouth is large, semi-top-positioned; the jaws are set with teeth. The dorsal and anal fins are almost the same size and have long bases. Those of the male, especially, are large, and may be almost twice as long as those of the female. The caudal fin is rounded and, like the pectoral fins, well developed. The ventral fins, situated on the belly, are small.

The sexes are very easily distinguished, by the rounder belly and somewhat higher body of the females, and by the noticeably longer dorsal and anal fins of the males (male, dorsal fins, 21–24 rays, anal fins, 26–30 rays; females, dorsal fins, 16–19 rays, anal fins, 22–26 rays). Moreover, the male is bluish, although this is quite variable; the female is greenish brown and muddy, with dark brown spots and stripes. Both sexes have a curved stripe over the eye. Because, in addition to the basic coloration, still different tints of metallic silver to reddish brown can appear, a detailed description of the coloration is difficult to make.

This sub-tropical species likes a roomy, preferably long but low aquarium in a sunny location. It gets along well in an unheated aquarium as long as the temperature does not drop below 8 °C (46.4 °F). *Cynolebias bellottii* is one of the unusually suitable fish for the real hobbyist, and can give a great deal of pleasure. One requirement, as for many related species, is that in addition to a more or less sharp difference between day and night temperatures (water exposed to the sun), a "cold" period should precede the mating season to ensure successful breeding.

Although it comes from the southern hemisphere, this fish relatively easily acclimates to the shift in seasons, since, at the time of northern summer, it is wintertime in its native land.

Good, well fed specimens will begin to prepare for breeding in early spring (March), as soon as the winter water temperature (8–15 °C; 46–59 °F) increases under the spring sun.

798

If the fish are about the same size and at least 60 mm (2⅜ inches) long, the female quickly responds to the attentions of the male and begins a rather calm breeding session, which can last for several weeks on end. If the fish are not mature, or if either one is not yet "ready," then serious injury can result and it is best to separate them.

If everything goes well, the little fish dart about after each other, the male in the lead, constantly thrusting his head into the humus bottom, the female right after him. They generally seek out the shallowest places, so be sure that there is sufficient slope to the bottom, so that part of it may even be dry (marshy).

Afterwards and for several days, egg-laying takes place, and then the courtship begins anew, usually very early in the morning, as soon as the sun shines into the tank. With his snout, the male roots out tiny holes in the humus bottom, whereupon the female comes up beside him and they squeeze themselves together, accompanied by a violent trembling of both fish. A single egg is then deposited in one of the holes. The performance continues this way until about 100 eggs have been deposited in the bottom over a period of several weeks. Then, the parents go on without paying any more attention to their recent efforts, and soon, the feeling is that the breeding has miscarried. Patience and discretion are primary requirements, for, as is true with most egg-laying toothcarps, considerable time passes before the eggs hatch out. From eggs laid in the period between March 12 to May 2, for example, the young came forth in September of that year—about four months after laying. Because of the long laying period, it is clear that the young will show a great difference in size. This is no reason to dip out the parents and the larger young, as, in comparison with their own related species, *C. bellottii* seem to be only slightly predatory in nature. It is obvious that they must be constantly well fed, mainly with live food. Crustaceans and mosquito larvae are especially well liked. The addition of one drop of codliver oil is desirable.

The preferred temperatures noted during the first very successful breeding were: For mating, 10 15 °C (50–59 °F) from January to the beginning of March, the night-time temperature usually being a few degrees lower, and after that, during the laying period from March 12 to the beginning of May, 14–18 °C (57–64 °F). The first young appeared at the end of April—just five weeks after laying—at temperatures of 12–18 °C (54–64 °F). From April to August, the temperature fluctuated between 12–22 °C (54–72 °F), and in the sun, sometimes took a sudden jump up to 26–28 °C (79–82 °F), without annoying the fish in the least. From the approximately 100 eggs that were laid, 37 specimens grew up into fine, beautiful fish. The water level was from 0 to 28 cm (0 to 11 inches) high, vegetation was principally *Myriophyllum* and *Ludwigia*, in addition some *Vallisneria* and a lot of thread algae. If you leave the tank alone, success is assured. The young grow up very quickly and in two months will already have grown to 50 mm (2 inches) long.

Cynolebias bellottii is one of those fish species that knows how to adapt to its environment and is not even afraid of brackish water. In the La Plata flood basin, it inhabits literally every little water hole, down to the tiniest rain puddles that sometimes dry up under a few hours of hot sun. The temperatures measured in the wild (Ladiges, 1939) vary from 0–40 °C (32–104 °F) from winter nights to summer midday. A clear reason has been found why this fish customarily hides its eggs under the bottom, since it has been shown that completely dried out pools, without any connection with any other waters, are again populated with young fish shortly after a considerable rainstorm. The eggs are apparently protected enough by the thin layer of mud, so that they can develop later and re-populate the ponds.

In company with *Cynolebias bellottii*, are often found various Loricariidae, such as representatives of the genera *Hypostomus, Xenocara* and *Otocinclus*; various Cichlidae, such as *Cichlasoma facetum* and *Geophagus brasiliensis*; and, of the toothcarps, *Jenynsia lineata* and *Cnesterodon decemmaculatus*.

Cynolebias nigripinnis Regan, 1912
Black-Finned Pearl Fish

After the discussion of the related *Cynolebias bellottii*, a reference to *C. nigripinnis* is sufficient. This is a somewhat smaller species than *C. bellottii*. The coloration is predominantly purplish blue with whitish dots; the fins are almost black.

Plate II-217. *Cynolebias nigripinnis.*

Plate II-218. *Cynolebias nigripinnis*, male with two females.

Genus *Cynopoecilus*

This genus differs from *Cynolebias* mainly in a number of anatomical characteristics, and the reproductive biology is also variant. Up to now, two species have been imported, *C. melanotaenia* and *C. splendens*.

Cynopoecilus splendens (Myers, 1942)

This fish, which comes from the vicinity of Petropolis, Brazil, grows, according to the original description, to a length of 22.5 mm ($\frac{7}{8}$ inch), not counting the caudal fin. The height of the body goes 4.5 times into the body length (less caudal fin), thus, the fish is considerably slimmer in shape than *Cynolebias bellottii* and even slimmer than *Cynolebias nigripinnis*. The basic coloration is methyl or bright green with narrow, bright, light red bands; the head is red with green spots. The red cross stripes, but not the green ones, run out upon the bases of the dorsal and anal fins and merge with the massive red of these fins; the dorsal fin has a green border, and there is a green border to the upper part of the red caudal fin; the paired fins are yellowish. The preserved material shows somewhat more clearly the striped pattern, which consists of about 14 cross bands with light, narrower spaces between; one male specimen shows curved stripes on the caudal fin.

Plate II-219. *Cynopoecilus melanotaenia.*

802

The fins do not stand out far, but have rather broad bases; the dorsal and anal fins are sharply pointed; the caudal fin is rounded.

Living specimens with a total length of 40 mm ($1\frac{9}{16}$ inches) look like *Rivulus* with beautiful, lengthened dorsal and anal fins; the basic coloration is emerald green with dark, wine red cross stripes, which run on out into the fins; and the iris of the eye is a brilliant, light green. Nothing is said about the females. Reproduction takes place in the manner of the bottom-laying species of the genus *Aphyosemion*, but not as it is done among the related *Cynolebias* species, which bury themselves in the bottom. Schroeter mentions the laying of the eggs above the bottom, then the pushing of them down into the bottom material (compare with *Aphyosemion coeruleum*).

This first report on the breeding and life style of *C. splendens* is of great importance. A good thing now would be for several experienced breeders to publish their experiences with this species. It might be established for certain whether there actually is a difference in the method of reproduction—as compared to the related species, *Cynolebias bellottii* and *C. nigripinnis*. If this difference is limited to the mating couple's burrowing or not burrowing into the bottom, it becomes a question of circumstantial detail. There appears to be no reason for classification in the genus *Cynopoecilus*, especially since the well known *Cynopoecilus melanotaenia* (formerly kept and studied by aquarists, at least), according to statements made about it, is not a bottom-layer but a surface-layer.

Tribe Rivulini

Genus *Rivulus*

This is a widely distributed genus found in South America and on the Caribbean islands, with the greatest variety of forms in the Guiana Highlands. According to conventional norms, about 40 or more species are distinguished. An extensive study, however, made it clear that there are probably a very small number of biological species with numerous local varieties which interbreed at the edges of their individual biotopes. The previously discussed frontal scalation (see page 748) provided the decision to introduce the following groupings.

The first group, characterized by scale *ee'* lying wholly on top, is called the oldest species, the *R. marmoratus* group. The second group, characterized by scale *dd'* lying wholly on top, is next to the oldest group, and is called the *R. cylindraceus* group. The third has pair *gg'* on top and is called the *R. breviceps* group. This grouping is certainly not based only on the frontal scalation, but also on conventional characteristics.

The various patterns are named for the scales lying on top, respectively, *e*-type, *d*-type, and *c*-type patterns.

THE *R. marmoratus* GROUP

As a group characterized by *e*-type frontal scalation, the *R. marmoratus* group is divided into three complexes, distinguished from each other as indicated below:

1. In front of the dorsal fin, as far as the head scales, 32 to 39 scales . . . *R. marmoratus* complex
2. In front of the dorsal fin, only 27 to 30 scales; the caudal fin among males usually without white or black edges; practically the same among females
    A. Dorsal fin with 8 to 11, anal fin with 11 to 16 rays; length in front of the dorsal fin 70 to 75 per cent of body length less caudal fin . . . *R. isthmensis* complex
    B. Dorsal fin with 6 to 8, anal fin with 11 to 13 fin rays; length in front of the dorsal fin 76 to 82 per cent . . . *R. urophthalmus* complex

THE *R. marmoratus* COMPLEX

On grounds of usable characteristics, this complex is composed of the species *Rivulus marmoratus*, *R. waimacui*, *R. myersi*, and *R. ocellatus*. The distribution is remarkable and gives the impression that the

804

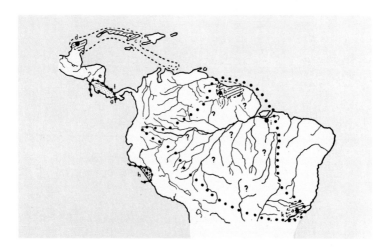

Illus. II-167. Distribution of the *Rivulus marmoratus* group, indicating the type localities. //// *R. marmoratus* complex, with a. *R. ocellatus*. c. *R. marmoratus* and d. *R. myersi*. ===== *R. isthmensis* complex, with e. *R. isthmensis*. f. *R. volcanus*. g. *R. hildebrandi*. h. *R. peruanus*. and ... *R. urophthalmus* complex, with i. *R. urophthalmus*. j. *R. lanceolatus*. k. *R. santensis*.

Caribbean islands might have been a part of the South American mainland. The discontinuous distribution of this complex can be blamed on man's ignorance of the varieties occupying the regions between. It is accepted that we are dealing with relicts, relicts of a group which, in ancient times, had a substantially greater distribution. It is, moreover, clear that the *R. marmoratus* form is a very old one.

It is, perhaps, interesting to hear that the species which for many years has been known among aquarists as the Cuban rivulus, *Rivulus cylindraceus*, has not by any means always been this species. Long ago, Poey described two species from Cuba, *R. cylindraceus* and *R. marmoratus*, which were lumped together by Garman (1895) and considered the same species. Recently, Rivas (1945) showed that these two species, considered as one since 1895, actually represented two different forms. Investigating material originating with aquarists, this author also found that there were two species. On the one hand, the difference is not a large one, but, on the other, close investigation shows it up very clearly. It appears, for example, that the two species cannot be cross-bred. In the first place, there is again that difference of frontal scalation, *R. marmoratus* being of the *e*-type and *R. cylindraceus* of the *d*-type, and other characteristics as indicated in the table on the next page.

R. marmoratus
Frontal scalation *e*-type, lengthwise 47 to 50, vertically 11 to 12 scales; Body with distinct, marbled pattern; Lengthwise stripe indistinct; Eye spot at root of tail in both sexes;
Often light edge to the median fins.

R. cylindraceus
Frontal scalation *d*-type, lengthwise about 36, vertically 9 to 10 scales; A dark band from head to root of tail, no marbling; Eye spot on root of tail only in young and females;
Median fins, especially of males, have black border.

THE *R. isthmensis* COMPLEX

This complex includes the species *R. isthmensis, R. volcanus, R. hildebrandi* and *R. peruanus,* and has a startling distribution. It is not yet completely clear whether any of the other forms living in the region lying between South America and the Caribbean islands could belong to this group. However, it looks at present as if the rising of the Andes Mountain range in this case split a continuously distributed group into two parts.

THE *R. urophthalmus* COMPLEX

Of more importance to aquarists is the *R. urophthalmus* complex, to which belong at least three species or varieties that are known aquarium fishes—*R. urophthalmus, R. santensis,* and *R. xanthonotus.* Further classified with these are the varieties *R. stagnatus* and *R. lanceolatus,* often incorrectly considered identical to *R. urophthalmus.* As far as distribution is concerned, this group has practically the same habitat as the *R. breviceps* group—the Amazon flood basin, the Guiana Highlands, and the vicinity of Rio de Janeiro.

As indicated by material from Surinam, populations of *R. urophthalmus* probably cross-breed with populations of *R. holmiae* (at least representatives of the *R. micropus* complex). It would be useful if hobbyists would test this and then give some attention to, among other things, the frontal scalation of the results of cross-breeding. In such a case, typical scalation representing a stage between these two groups has been found. Moreover, the other characteristics were of a binary nature, so that the fish could not be ascribed to one group nor the other, although everything about them indicated that they still were members of one of the two complexes concerned.

On grounds of frontal scalation, as well as other characteristics, it

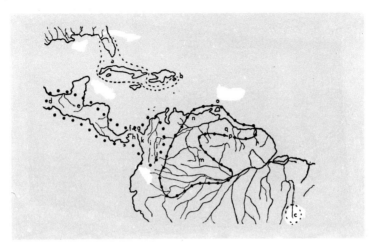

Illus. II-168. Distribution of the *Rivulus cylindraceus* group, with type localities.
——— *R. cylindraceus* complex, a. *R. cylindraceus.* b. *R. heyei.* c. *R. zygonectes.*
... *R. elegans* complex, d. *R. t. tenuis.* e. *R. t. godmani.* f. *R. b. brunneus.*
g. *R. b. chucunaque.* h. *R. montium.* i. *R. e. elegans.* j. *R. e. milesi.* k. *R. leucurus.*
l. *magdalenae.* and —•— *R. micropus* complex. m. *R. micropus.* n. *R. bondi.*
o. *R. harti.* p. *R. holmiae* and q. *R. mazaruni.*

is clear that the genera *Rachovia* and *Pterolebias* evolved from ancestors of the *R. urophthalmus* complex.

THE *R. cylindraceus* GROUP

Just like the *R. marmoratus* group, this group is also sub-divided into three complexes—the *R. cylindraceus* complex, the *R. elegans* complex, and the *R. micropus* complex. All three are characterized by *d*-type frontal scalation, but are mutually distinguished as indicated below.

1. A dark band from snout to caudal fin, no other dark, lengthwise stripes; eyespot on the root of the tail only in young and females . . . *R. cylindraceus* complex

2. A number of dark, lengthwise stripes; caudal fin of males usually with dark mid-section, light edges; in the female, this fin often has a dark outer edge

A. 23 to 25 scales in front of the dorsal fin . . . *R. elegans* complex

B. 26 to 35 scales in front of the dorsal fin . . . *R. micropus* complex

THE *R. cylindraceus* COMPLEX

For the present, the species *Rivulus cylindraceus,* *R. heyei,* and *R. zygonectes* are included in this complex. However, it is not at all certain that *R. zygonectes* really belongs here, yet in view of the many charac-

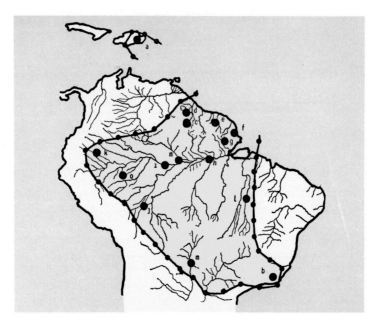

Illus. II-169. Distribution —•— of the *Rivulus breviceps* complex indicating the type localities ● of a. *R. roloffi.* b. *R. dorni.* c. *R. frenatus.* d. *R. breviceps.* e. *R. agilae.* f. *R. geayi.* g. *R. dibaphus.* h. *R. ornatus.* i. *R. strigatus.* j. *R. beniensis.* k. *R. taeniatus.* l. *R. compactus.* m. *R. punctatus.* n. *R. obscurus* and o. *R. atratus.*

teristics that correspond to *R. cylindraceus*, it is provisionally accepted, in spite of the very discontinuous distribution that this complex has. Too little is still known about the regions lying in between South America and the Caribbean islands to be certain that there are no further relicts of this group there.

THE *R. micropus* COMPLEX

Of the five known species belonging to this complex, only two have become known in aquarist circles—namely, *Rivulus harti* and its close relative, *Rivulus holmiae*. The species *R. bondi, R. mazaruni,* and *R. micropus* have probably not yet been imported. All species, which perhaps later will be included in a single species, *R. micropus*, are related to *R. elegans*.

THE *R. breviceps* GROUP

The species belonging to this group are, among other things, characterized by a *g*-type frontal scalation. The described species are *R. breviceps* as the leader, *R. agilae, R. brasiliensis, R. compactus, R. benien-*

sis, R. frenatus, R. roloffi, R. dorni, R. geayi, R. dibaphus, R. ornatus, R. strigatus, R. taeniatus, R. obscurus, R. punctatus and *R. atratus.* Up to now, only *R. agilae* has become known in hobbyist circles.

The map in Illus. II–169 indicates the region inhabited by the members of this group, and, moreover, the type-locality of each. With the exception of *Rivulus roloffi*, which is found in Haiti, this group inhabits the far-reaching flood basin of the Amazon and the southern part of Brazil (Mato Grosso and the vicinity of Rio de Janeiro).

In addition to their frontal scalation, the members of this group are distinguished by the absence of an eye spot on the root of the tail in both sexes; their small size, the maximum length being about 50 mm (2 inches), not counting the caudal fin; rather large scales, hence a small scale-count in the lengthwise direction; a number of dark, vertical stripes, predominantly on the tail, especially in young specimens; and usually a very clear difference between the sexes, particularly in the patterning of the caudal fin.

Plate II-220. *Rivulus agilae.*

***Rivulus agilae* Hoedeman, 1954**

This fish hails from Surinam, between Agila on the Surinam River and Berlijn on the Para River, in a small, rocky stream. It is an exceptionally attractive *Rivulus* which in every way rivals the most beautiful *Aphyosemion.* Moreover, it is a truly small species, which, as it appears from preserved material, grows to a length of not more than 55 mm ($2\frac{3}{16}$ inches), not counting the caudal fin. It can further be noted that it is most closely related to *Rivulus breviceps* of Guyana, which is also found in Surinam, and to *Rivulus geayi* of French Guiana. More thorough investigation will perhaps make it clear that these varieties from the Guiana Highlands are local varieties of a single species. The material available, however, is not enough to allow such a conclusion. Besides these, other close relatives are *Rivulus dibaphus* and *R. ornatus* from the Amazon flood basin.

The remarkable difference in patterning of the caudal fin can be seen in Plate II–220.

***Rivulus cylindraceus* Poey, 1861**

Brown Rivulus

Cuban Rivulus

Green Rivulus

This fish is native to Cuba and, according to Fowler, is also known in Florida. The fish was not imported into Europe until about 1929 and, in spite of the difficult period of 1940–45, it is one of the few *Rivulus* types still commonly met with today among hobbyists.

Rivulus cylindraceus is the generic type of an out and out *Rivulus*, with its long, thin, cylindrical body. This fish can reach a length of about 55 mm (2$\frac{3}{16}$ inches); the females are often somewhat larger and sturdier. The very end of the tail is slightly compressed sideways and the head is slightly flattened down. The typical dorsal fin, located far to the rear, is, like the other fins, rounded. Only among the males do the dorsal and anal fins have a somewhat pointed rear edge. The short, rounded snout has a clearly upward-directed mouth opening, from which aquarists conclude that *R. cylindraceus* is a dweller of the upper waters, just below the surface.

The basic coloration is brownish to orange-brown, with green spots. From the mouth and over the eye to the root of the tail runs a handsome, more or less distinct, but irregular, purplish brown stripe. Under it, the coloration is yellowish grey to orange-red. On the tail, directly under the stripe, are a number of scattered, bright red dots. The dorsal side is darker than the belly, yet generally lighter than the lengthwise stripe.

The eye is black with a gleaming yellow edge. Right behind the gill cover on each side is a bright blue spot that is strikingly distinct.

Youthful specimens of both sexes possess, on the upper edge just in front of the root of the tail, the so-called black eye spot, which gradually disappears from the growing males and among the females becomes steadily more intense. With the exception of the pectoral fins, which are without coloration, the fins are a soft yellow, becoming orange in handsome, full-grown specimens.

The older they are, the more the males' dorsal, anal and caudal fins are decorated with little red dots and lines; the dorsal and caudal fins, moreover, have a blue border, on the upper edge, which is edged on the bottom with a black line.

This *Rivulus* is really one of the few species that give their owners full pleasure. It may not perhaps be so brilliant in coloration and patterning, yet, so far as water, food and temperature are concerned, it is not demanding. It is best kept in a tank that is not too small, planted with *Ludwigia*, *Myriophyllum*, and so on. It enjoys some floating plants and will rummage about among them, looking for water insects and the like. The water temperature should range between 18 and 26 °C (64–79 °F), depending on the time of year, although it can stand lower temperatures at times, without quick transition, of course, down to about 15 °C (59 °F). It prefers a varied diet of living animal food, and, though it cannot be called greedy or gluttonous, it can easily polish off good-sized chunks.

811

R. cylindraceus is really an attractive fish whose aquarium companions should not be too active, or it will quickly vanish among the plants. In a separate tank, it makes good use of the available swimming room and is then very lively, yet sometimes hangs motionless for minutes on end, "without stirring a fin," in a corner, among the plants and rocks.

Breeding is quite a simple process and, therefore, it is incomprehensible that this *Rivulus* does not enjoy greater popularity. Unbeknownst is unbeloved. At 22–24 °C (72–75 °F) or a little higher (but not too high—at least, not constantly) the courtship begins, sometimes boisterously, other times more quietly. The male invites the female to follow him through the clumps of plants which he has chosen by swimming along under her belly. (Sometimes she chooses.) If there is a second male in the tank, the first male shoots right after him, but without being able to touch him, and then shoots back again to his chosen bride. The play continues until the weaker sex, still attracted by the male, who is seldom rough about it, goes with her mate among the plants and, while shaking violently, lays her eggs, usually close to the bottom. The eggs look like tiny grains of sand, a little sticky and yellowish brown. The number can vary, according to the age of the female, feeding, etc., yet *R. cylindraceus* is, in general, very productive. The young appear after 10 to 14 days, but sometimes not until five weeks have passed, and are not difficult to raise. Before the first batch of eggs has hatched, the parents are busy on a second. They seldom eat the eggs (if well fed) and the young are also safe from their parents.

Illus. II-170. *Rivulus harti.*

Rivulus harti (Boulenger, 1890)
Giant Rivulus
Hart's Rivulus

Rivulus harti is a dweller of the lowland waters of Venezuela, and the islands of Margarita and Trinidad. It occurs no farther eastward than Trinidad, and the specimens under this name that have been reported on from Surinam belong to *Rivulus holmiae*, which substitutes locally for *R. harti* in Guyana and Surinam. This species differs extremely little from *R. holmiae*, but principally in the somewhat thick-set body, the somewhat larger eye, and smaller number of scales. It is probable that in the future *R. holmiae* will be considered a local variety of *R. harti*, and perhaps, indeed, both are local varieties of *R. micropus*. In the review on page 808, the very close relationship of the members of the *R. micropus* complex is indicated. Yet, because material on all species was not sufficiently available, it seemed more sensible, for the time being, not to turn the old names into synonyms, or to reduce species to sub-species.

For aquarists to delve further into what variety they are dealing with, it is desirable to know the region from which the fish comes. If this cannot be followed up on, it is perhaps most sensible to indicate all the varieties as *R. micropus* super-species. For an idea of how *R. harti* looks, refer to the picture of *R. holmiae* in Plate II–221.

Rivulus holmiae Eigenmann, 1909

As already mentioned under *Rivulus harti,* this "species" substitutes for *R. harti* in Guyana and Surinam and perhaps also in French Guiana, from whence it has not yet been reported on.

R. holmiae is a splendid, slender fish that sports about considerably near the surface, yet not so much as the *Aplocheilus* and *Epiplatys* species do at times. Larger specimens are somewhat predatory, but they really belong among fishes of higher body shape and species of the same size.

The basic coloration is brownish beige with light blue, lengthwise bands on which (on each scale) is a row of red dots—a total of eight, one above the other—which is less distinct in the belly region. The tail is somewhat darker, as is the mid-section of the caudal fin among males. This fin is set off below, and usually also above, with a black and white border. Among females, the caudal fin has about the same coloration as the body and there are several vertical rows of dots on the fin membrane. The same pattern is found in the other fins, also in the male, and often his dorsal and anal fins are bordered with black. In the young and the females, an eye spot or ocellus surrounded by lighter coloration is found on the root of the tail.

Plate II-221. *Rivulus holmiae.*

Plate II-222. *Rivulus milesi.*

R. holmiae is a lively and easy-to-keep fish which can also be bred without difficulty. It requires not too high a temperature of about 18–24 °C (64–75 °F), and an adequate current in the water. It is very productive, omnivorous, and a little predatory where small and young fishes are concerned.

Plate II-223. *Rivulus urophthalmus.*

Rivulus urophthalmus **Günther, 1866**

Golden Rivulus

Green Rivulus

This species inhabits flowing waters in the Guianas and in Brazil, as far as São Paulo, and also occurs in the flood basin of the Orinoco, the Amazon and its tributaries. In 1905, the first specimens were brought into Germany from Maranhão, Brazil, whence the breeding products came into the possession of hobbyists in the Netherlands. Since then, many more have been imported.

The true *Rivulus* grows to a maximum length of 60 mm (2⅜ inches). The back is flat as far back as the dorsal fin (surface-dweller). The tail is flattened in from the sides. The caudal fin is circular. The base of the anal fin is more than twice as long as that of the dorsal fin. The pectoral fins reach precisely to the anal opening.

The basic coloration is olive brown, the flanks a little darker. The caudal, anal and dorsal fins are stippled with red. The females have a dark brown to deep black eye spot just in front of the base of the caudal fin. The spot is edged with yellowish white.

A rather roomy, not too high aquarium is best for keeping this species in. Plant it with thick clumps of fine-leaved plants. In the

816

community aquarium, *R. urophthalmus* is very tolerant of other fishes and is truly ornamental among other shapes of fish. However, there must be a good layer of floating plants; it likes to hang out among them and sometimes even climbs partly out of the water upon a large, floating leaf. Although a preference for living animal food has been observed, it will also accept dried animal food. The water should be at a low level for breeding, 10–15 cm (4–6 inches). After a lengthy introduction, a tumultuous courtship takes place, which can sometimes last as long as 10 or 12 days. During this time, the eggs are laid among the fine-leaved plants or the *Riccia*. If plenty of food is provided, the parents will eat neither the eggs nor the young which hatch out after 14 days. Because of the difference in age of the young, since the first are born 10 to 12 days sooner than the others, after the first few weeks, fish of considerably varying size are seen swimming about, requiring provision of both infusoria and dust-fine food. The breeding temperature should be held at about 26 °C (79 °F). Normal temperature in the aquarium is 22–24 °C (72–75 °F). *R. urophthalmus* can be allowed to winter over at 22 °C (72 °F); lower temperatures, in time, however, are fatal.

It often happens that the male is too violent and the female is too lustily pursued. The sensible thing to do, then, is to provide the male with another female, or, if need be, with two more, among whom he can divide his passion.

Contrary to many other *Rivulus* species, *R. urophthalmus* likes to swim about and keep in motion. Sometimes, it is even pugnacious. Because it is a surface fish that likes to leave the water from time to time, the aquarium must be kept well covered, not only to keep the fish from leaping out, but also to keep the temperature of the water and of the air above it from differing too much. This *Rivulus* is an especially suitable inhabitant for the marsh aquarium.

Among the many imported specimens, golden yellow varieties are repeatedly found, from which breeders have bred the well known and beloved red variety. The basic coloration of this variety is more golden than red, although sometimes especially beautiful reddish specimens are found among them. The rows of dots are bright red; the fins are golden yellow or lemon yellow. The females of this variety of coloration, contrary to those of the normal *R. urophthalmus*, are somewhat lighter than the males. This red variety is sold on the market as *Rivulus harti*, but this is actually a case of mistaken identity.

It is typical of the red variety that a completely normal first generation can be bred without difficulty, with lovely, well developed young. Contrary to the normal variety, whose first generation of young can usually be bred again, breeding a second generation from the red variety seldom succeeds. Moreover, if young are produced, they turn out to be nothing but miserable, skinny creatures, which obviously have degenerated owing to some circumstance or other. The first sound generation must thus be bred with the usual yellow partner, in order to have at least part of the young develop into beautiful red ones. The cause of this degeneration is probably from overpigmentation and hormone activity, as is also found in many completely sterile hybrids of the ovoviviparous (live bearing) toothcarps. There is much here to be investigated and possibly the researcher will succeed in tracing down and eliminating the true cause of the disadvantageous results that accompany cross-breeding of the red varieties.

Although the subject is considered hackneyed by some aquarists and breeders, it is recommended that aquarists pay some attention to this yellow *Rivulus* and its red variety, especially where there is an opportunity to keep it in a special, low aquarium with a marshy area, marsh growth, floating plants, and a terrarium cover. It is truly a splendid sight to see *R. urophthalmus* basking in the sun from time to time, resting on a little piece of dry land, on a large, floating leaf, or on a small rock. Lying about like that, it is so much at ease that it will not dive under, even if touched with a finger.

To treat *R. urophthalmus* to a delicious tidbit, turn loose some kind of live insect or spider under the cover, whereupon it executes nimble leaps and starts hunting it down.

Rivulus xanthonotus Ahl, 1926
Yellow Rivulus

This species, found in the Amazon flood basin, is possibly only a sub-species of *Rivulus urophthalmus*. It attains a length of about 75 mm (3 inches) in both sexes. The basic coloration is yellowish, the back more reddish, and there are a number of irregular cross bands running halfway down the sides, merging with each other on the back. The bands are red-brown, flowing towards the belly. The belly and throat are reddish. On the gill covers are a lot of dark brown spots. The scales on the sides each have a red dot and these provide a striking accent to the attractive coloration pattern. The mouth is bordered with light red. The fins are greenish yellow, the ventral fins have a little ice blue. The female again exhibits the typical black dot at the top of the tail root. The median fins have rows of red dots, and in the male the dorsal fin and sometimes the anal fin have a dark edge.

In regard to breeding, comments are the same as for *Rivulus urophthalmus* (see page 817). *R. xanthonotus* is, however, a species that is much more active and freedom-loving than most of its relatives, which are not as intolerant as *R. xanthonotus* is. It is still certainly a species that can be characterized as especially attractive and suitable for the aquarium.

Unfortunately, it seems that this species has been imported only once (so far as is known); still, specimens of this fish may be found from time to time among imports of *R. urophthalmus*. This appears especially likely since the author, in 1937, found three such imported specimens, captured along with some related varieties, while the first actual import dates from 1924.

Genus *Pterolebias*

This genus, which is closely related to and could be derived from the genus *Rivulus*, was considered a rivulin with "long fins" (*longipinnis*). For a long time, only this single species was known from Santarém, Brazil, and the Lower Amazon. In the past few years, however, two new species have been imported and described and must be considered welcome acquisitions for the hobby. The four species which we know at present are: *P. longipinnis, P. zonatus, P. peruensis* and *P. bockermanni*. They are native to Venezuela (*P. zonatus*, Orinoco Basin), the Peruvian Amazon (*P. peruensis*, the eastern part of Loreto province), and Brazil (*P. bockermanni*, from the Rio Guajara-Mirim, Guapore, Brazil).

Pterolebias bockermanni Travassos, 1955

Travassos gave the species name of this fish two different spellings, and also spelled the name of the collector in two different ways, all within seven pages in the same publication. In the first instance, it was given: Sr. Werner Bockerman as collector, then the name *Pterolebias bokermanni* sp.n., next Bokermann, but not once was the name given as Bockermann, a rather common German name. The name should be written with *ck* and *nn*.

This species is known only from a scientific collection and has not been imported alive for the aquarium trade, neither in Europe nor America. The reproduction of the original drawing in Illus. II–17.1 shows the most important characteristics with sufficient clarity. Its total length is about 70 mm (2¾ inches); not counting the caudal fin, the length is about 50 mm (2 inches). There are no bands across the body.

Illus. II-171. *Pterolebias bockermanni.*

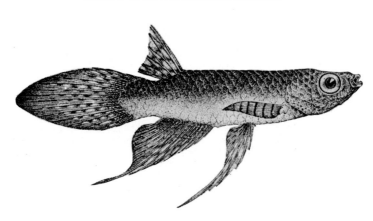

Plate II-224. *Pterolebias longipinnis.*

Pterolebias longipinnis Garman, 1895
Longfin
Longfin Killie
Longfin Pterolebias

This species attains a length of about 60 mm (2⅜ inches), without the caudal fin, in both sexes. The caudal fin of the male can grow to a length of more than 30 mm (1 3/16 inches). When the fish reaches a length of about 50 mm (2 inches), it becomes sexually mature.

The basic coloration is olive brown with bright yellow, metallically gleaming spots which become more intense as the fish grows up, and naturally, show up better on the males than on the females.

Angling across the body and tail run dark bands. A clear, copper-red eye spot, located behind the gill covers at the height of the pectoral fins, is less distinct in the female. The fins are dark wine red with brownish black spots, often placed in rows; in the anal fin, these are only on the last fin ray and show up only weakly in the female.

P. longipinnis is one of the so-called "annual" fishes. As far as their reproductive cycle is concerned, these fish can be compared with the members of the related genus *Cynolebias*. For further particulars, especially since not many details regarding this species are known, refer to the description of the *Cynolebias* species on page 796. Breeding results are not entirely known, either.

Plate II-225. *Pterolebias peruensis.*

Pterolebias peruensis Myers
Peruvian Longfin
Peruvian Pterolebias

This fish reaches a length, not counting the caudal fin, of about 50 mm (2 inches), the female being a little smaller. The basic coloration is brownish with metallic green cross bands and dark stripes in the dorsal, anal and caudal fins. For further particulars, see Plate II–225. *P. peruensis* is a very remarkable fish, which is quite a bit similar to *P. longipinnis.*

Pterolebias zonatus Myers

This species differs from *P. longipinnis,* among others, in the vertical striping on the sides—11 narrow bands on the brownish background. Nothing further worthy of information is known about this species which, so far as is known, has not been imported alive.

Sub-family Aplocheilichthyinae

This sub-family includes the genera *Aplocheilichthys, Plataplochilus, Cynopanchax, Hypsopanchax, Platypanchax* and *Procatopus,* all from Africa. As a group, these fishes differ from their related representatives of the family Cyprinodontidae, among other things, by the very high position of the pectoral fins and the rather long snout which projects far beyond the eyes. (In other words, this sub-family has a large, preorbital distance.) It is distinguished from the Oryziatini by its protruding mouth. The beginning of the dorsal fin is always behind the line of the foremost anal fin rays.

Plate II-226. *Procatopus aberrans.*

Plate II-227. *Aplocheilichthys macrophthalmus.*

Genus *Aplocheilichthys*

This genus, of which only a few species are known to aquarists, counts about 20 species, all predominantly small or very small fishes. *A. macrophthalmus* is a typical representative found in hobbyists' aquariums.

Aplocheilichthys macrophthalmus Meinken, 1932
Lampeye

This little fish hails from Nigeria and attains a total length of 55 mm (2 3/16 inches). Reproductive procedure is equivalent to that of the *Aphyosemion bivittatum* group. A total of up to 100 eggs are laid per mating period, which can last for several days. Note that the fishes of this genus not only systematically, but also biologically, appear to form a link between the Oryziatini and the remaining Cyprinodontidae. The expelled eggs remain hanging on a little bundle of slime-threads (these are very short but elastic) from the belly of the female after they are fertilized. Afterward, these clusters of 10 to 12 eggs each rub off among the fine-leaved plants, after which the mating continues. Thus, the eggs do not hang on the female's belly for a long time as with the *Oryzias,* but for a short time only. The eggs are relatively quite large and hatch out after about a week.

Plate II-228. *Aplocheilichthys flavipinnis.*

Plate II-229. *Aplocheilichthys pumilus.*

Plate II-230. *Aplocheilichthys spilauchen.*

Aplocheilichthys myersi Poll, 1952
Myers' Lampeye

Certainly one of the prettiest toothcarps from Africa, *A. myersi* is quite similar to the slender *Cynopoecilus* species. As it is a typical surface fish which also lays its eggs in the uppermost water layers, take care to provide plenty of floating plants with roots hanging down into the water.

Plate II-231. *Aplocheilichthys katangae.*

Tribe Oryziatini

This tribe includes only a few genera with a distribution from Japan and Central China southward to the Celebes and Timor and westward into southern India (see the map in Illus. II–172).

The tribe Oryziatini is distinguished from related tribes by the non-projecting upper jaw and the high-positioned pectoral fins.

Up to now, only two species have become fairly generally known among aquarists—*Oryzias latipes* and *Oryzias javanicus*—while the remaining species, which are usually ascribed to the species *O. celebensis* and *O. melastigma*, have not yet been imported.

The Oryziatini, or rice fishes, do not belong to the especially vivid and picturesque species of the toothcarp order, yet their method of reproduction is so interesting that they were once kept by hobbyists and they will continue to be sought after. In spite of their plain appearance, they certainly attract attention in most aquariums, especially in sunlight. Depending on their place of origin, they should be kept in aquariums at temperatures between 18 and 28 °C (64–82 °F). None of the species, regardless of origin, is very sensitive where temperature is concerned. They make few or no demands on the aquarium water, which can be rather hard or possibly even brackish, as well as fresh and lacking in lime or possessing a high pH value. Also, reproduction and development of the young is hardly affected, if at all, by different environments.

Genus *Oryzias*

This is the only genus in this tribe and to it four species are ascribed. Since their unique method of reproduction (also found only

Illus. II-172. Distribution of the tribe *Oryziatini*.

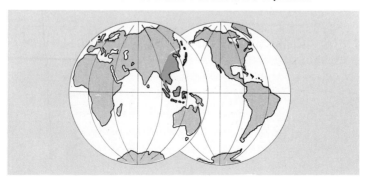

in a far separated genus of this family, the Cuban toothcarp, *Cubanichthys cubensis*), is the same for all four species, a summarization follows here.

Oryzias species are especially dwellers of the rice paddies, hence their name rice fishes (they are also called "medaka"). They are met with in all kinds of waters, but not, however, where the current is strong. They choose open water into which sunlight can penetrate.

Mating takes place near sundown or later—that is, courtship begins when the sun is low—and at twilight the eggs are expelled and the male fertilizes them. These fertilized eggs are especially sticky and each is equipped with an elastic thread. The clump of eggs hangs like a cluster of grapes from the anal opening of the female and, in the wild, they seem to remain there for some time (females have been caught at varying times of day with the cluster of eggs still hanging from the belly). In the aquarium, this usually lasts a few hours, and before the following day's sun begins to give off a tolerable degree of warmth, the eggs are laid by the female, in groups or singly, on rice stems or water plants. It can thus be clearly observed that places that are not in the direct rays of the sun or the beams of the lamps (in the aquarium) are always sought out.

The eggs develop rather slowly and not until after at least two weeks, sometimes not for a month (this is dependent on all kinds of factors, such as temperature, constitution of the water, origin and species), do the first larvae have a chance to break through their egg shells and take off for open water. They then live on their yolk sacs for only a short time. Usually, by the second day they are already hunting for food. During this period, sunlight and codliver-oil food (dry animal food dipped in a drop of codliver oil) are necessary to avoid a shortage of vitamins.

To discuss the tank set-up further is unnecessary, since what constitutes the natural environment of this fish has been brought out. It will be possible for every hobbyist to set up his own tank in accordance with these requirements, which are in fact, very slight—merely sunlight.

Plate II-232. *Oryzias javanicus.*

Oryzias javanicus (Bleeker, 1854)
Javanese Rice Fish

As the name indicates, this species hails from Java; it also occurs at Lombok, Singapore and Malacca on the Malay Peninsula.

The specimens that have been recognized in hobbyist circles are usually of this species, although *Oryzias latipes* also seems to have been imported (*O. latipes* has been kept in and imported into North America for some time).

Oryzias javanicus attains a length of about 40 mm ($1\frac{9}{16}$ inches) and generally is a little less grey and thus somewhat more attractive in coloration than *O. latipes*. The rather monotonous basic coloration is enlivened by a blue-violet gloss. A narrow, black stripe runs from just behind the base of the pectoral fins to out upon the tail root where it spreads out into a dark spot. Also, the bases of dorsal and anal fins are darkly tinted.

The male anal fin in fine, large specimens shows a "ravelling" out of the edge like the African characin *Phenacogrammus interruptus*. The median fins, in both sexes, are set off with a border varying from milk white to ice blue.

Illus. II-173. *Oryzias latipes.*

Oryzias latipes (Schlegel, 1850)
Japanese Rice Fish
Medaka

Oryzias latipes is the Japanese representative of this genus, and is common in Japan among the rice paddies, in pools and ponds and slow-flowing water. It reaches a length of about 40 mm ($1\frac{9}{16}$ inches) and is indeed the most attractive species of this genus. The basic coloration is silverish with a blue gleam; the flanks are olive green to brownish and the transparent fins, usually without coloration, can sometimes be orange-yellow. A very attractive, yellowish form, variety "auratus," which has a predominantly orange-red coloration, has been described. This is obviously a result of selective breeding by the Japanese, who in this regard have earned recognition with many species of fish.

Oryzias melastigma (McClelland, 1839)

This fish comes from India and Ceylon and is a very common inhabitant of the rice paddies. The aquarium should be set up to imitate its natural environment. It attains a length of about 45 mm (1¾ inches). The females can grow a little larger. The basic coloration is again a simple grey; the fins often are a green to orange-yellow. Over the body and the caudal fin runs a branching, dark band, as with *O. celebensis*, its nearest relative.

This close relationship of two species from the same genus is, of course, nothing special. Compared with the species from the region lying in between, however, these two are more closely related, although their respective habitats are located on the opposite-most edges of the distribution area of the genus. The whole order of toothcarps is, on the grounds of zoögeographic considerations, indeed of great importance. The relationship here not only leads to the conclusion that this is an old genus, but also that the species probably developed in India and spread out from there.

Sub-family Cyprinodontinae

Of the three tribes, Aphaniini, Cyprinodontini, and Fundulini, only the first occurs in Europe, Asia and Africa, while of Fundulini, only one comes from Europe—the little known genus *Valencia*, from Spain. The other representatives come from the Americas (compare the maps in Illus. II–161 and Illus. II–176). Technically, the Aphaniini and the Cyprinodontini can hardly be separated, and their relationship is thus very close, which supposes a splitting-up in relatively early geological times. As far as the pattern of frontal scalation is concerned (compare numbers 17, 18, 19, 21–28 in Illus. II–163), it appears by this that the Aphaniini (see number 21, *Aphanius*) form a splitting off from the stem close to *Pachypanchax*, with connections, on one side, to Cyprinodontini and, on the other, to Fundulini (via number 17, *Profundulus*).

Tribe Aphaniini

The Aphaniini form a group of toothcarps that, unfortunately, is still little known among hobbyists. This is too bad, since these species are far more easily kept than the American relatives, which are far more popular.

The reason for the lack of popularity of these south European species is not known, though it has been determined that it is not a question of their being less attractive or that they are difficult to keep. Perhaps they will some day conquer the hearts of aquarists, for they would undoubtedly be a fine acquisition for the hobby.

Included in this tribe are the genera *Aphanius, Aphaniops* and *Anatolichthys*.

These genera are mainly distinguished in appearance by the more elongated, cylindrical body shape of the Cyprinodontini.

Genus *Anatolichthys*

Anatolichthys burdurensis Aksiray, 1948

This species is rather common in the brackish and fresh waters of Burdur Lake, Turkey. It concurs with the following species in many respects, but deviates from it, among other ways, by having a deeper body, shorter tail stem or caudal peduncle, smaller ventral fins, the dorsal fin set farther towards the back, and a shorter total length with a maximum about 36 mm ($1\frac{7}{16}$ inches). Also, the coloration of both sexes is somewhat less outstanding than is the case with *A. splendens*.

According to the investigators and authors of these new species, they are all (especially this species and *A. transgrediens*) very suitable aquarium fishes, which, though they do possess, to a degree, the less tolerant habits of their American cousins, can still be kept well with other fishes.

Anatolichthys splendens Kosswig & Sözer, 1945

This genus, which was discovered and described in 1945, has made important contributions to our knowledge concerning the European toothcarps. A phenomenon that also appears elsewhere—namely, body scaling reduced to the minimum—had not, up to then, been observed in toothcarps.

The genus *Anatolichthys* is most closely related to *Aphanius* but *Aphanius* is distinguished principally by the larger number of scales in the lengthwise direction (insofar as the scales have developed, at least)

Illus. II-174. *Anatolichthys splendens.*

and the almost free placement of the scales (hardly covering each other, if at all).

Anatolichthys splendens grows to a maximum length of about 50 mm (2 inches). It was caught in a mountain lake rich in benthonic (bottom) life consisting of *Asellus*, chironomids, gammarids, and planaria. In spite of the elevation of the lake (1,300 m or 4,263 feet), the temperature was sufficiently high to make life possible for this toothcarp (the temperature was not given in the publication, but must have been at least 15 °C (59 °F)). This species was kept in good condition in the aquariums of the University of Istanbul so long as the water was clear and rich in oxygen. At 24 °C (75 °F), the eggs hatched out after 12 days. The coloration is gleaming silver, the back darker, with 8 to 14 dark cross bands which, in the female, disperse into irregular spots. The fins are yellow with dark to black bands, the pectoral fins are without coloration. On the whole, this fish is variable in its appearance.

Genus *Aphaniops*

This genus is distinguished from *Aphanius*, among others, by the smaller number of rays in the dorsal fin (only 8 or 9, as against 10 to 14 in *Aphanius*), and the absence of an anal skin sac around the foremost rays of the anal fin, as occurs in *Aphanius*.

Aphaniops dispar (Rüppell, 1828)

It was only determined a short time ago that the habitat of this species did not extend into southern Europe, as sometimes had been indicated. *A. dispar* lives in coastal and inland waters of northern India, Iran, Arabia, Ethiopia, Israel, Jordan, and appears, since the opening of the Suez Canal, to have penetrated for the first time into the region of the Mediterranean.

Aphaniops dispar is a *Cyprinodon*-like fish with a somewhat longer, slimmer body. The rather large dorsal and anal fins of the male are located behind the middle line of the length of the body; the dorsal fin begins a little in front of the foremost rays of the anal fin. In the female, these fins are arranged in the same way but are sensibly smaller in size.

The males are spattered with bright blue flecks on a yellowish grey background. The fins are golden yellow, and the caudal fin is also decorated with two to four vertical, black bands. The female is dun-toned, darker than the male, with a varying number of blackish, vertical stripes across the body.

On the basis of the sometimes extremely varying patterning, a number of local varieties are distinguished. Basically, each more or less isolated region has its own typical variety. The total length runs to about 80 mm ($3\frac{3}{16}$ inches). The females grow a little larger than the males. They are very active, very swift fish.

Genus *Aphanius*

Of the three genera belonging to the tribe Aphaniini, this one is best known among aquarists. Many authors continue to classify it under *Cyprinodon*, from which, however, it is clearly distinguished by the longer, lower shape of the body, the placement of the ventral fins clearly in front of the first ray of the dorsal fin, and the maximum of 30 scales lengthwise.

All species of this genus known up to now are undoubtedly very suitable for the aquarium, although a number of species have not yet been imported. The species still unknown among aquarists will possibly have certain environmental requirements for keeping, since a number are from special waters. According to the nature of the catch locations, *Aphanius* inhabits fresh, brackish or salt waters. In the final instance, it is not so much a sea-dweller as an inhabitant of waters left over from the primordial waters, formerly part of the Tethys Sea, that have a fairly high salt content.

In general, the early species imported liked a light, preferably sunny location, and a temperature between 10 and 30 °C (42–86 °F), ideally about 20 °C (68 °F). Thus, they can also be very well kept in an unheated aquarium at room temperature. As far as measurements are concerned, they can be accommodated in a tank having a capacity of at least 50 litres (13.2 gallons), a size quite suitable for a single couple. A thick, in-place planting, liberal clumps of thread algae and a bottom of humus are also indispensable for these species.

The eggs are large in proportion to the size of the fish and are laid uniformly, usually among the thick clumps of plants or algae. If the fish are fed well and appropriately, very little trouble will occur with egg-eating, especially if the tank is roomy. *Aphanius* species can be kept together with members of their own species and other fishes of their own size without difficulty. Also, the young fish, which hatch out after about a week, are usually safe from any possible gluttony of their parents. The hatching of the eggs is, however, dependent on a number of factors. The constitution of the water and the temperature play important rôles. A number of eggs (usually from later layings rather than the earlier ones) may open up after only three or four days and the young come out, while others may take several weeks. Patience is required here as with many African and South American relatives.

Up to about 10 years ago, only a few *Aphanius* species were known. Recent investigations have enlarged the number of varieties to several dozen.

Aphanius apodus (Gervais, 1853)

This fish is native to Algeria, to the region around Tell, to the south of Constantine, the high plateaus of the Atlas Mountains and the warm springs near Batna. It only grows to 60 mm (2⅜ inches) long and obviously must be considered a suitable aquarium fish, but it has remained up to now completely unknown among aquarists. Hopefully, in time, we shall be able to admire this fish at closer range. The male is olive green with dark cross bands and red and blue dots spattered over the body. The females are, again, less striking and have spots in place of cross bands.

The name *apodus* (literally, legless) refers to the absence of ventral fins. However, this is an insufficient reason to maintain a separate genus, *Tellia*, so that today, the latter is classified with *Aphanius*.

Aphanius chantrei (Gaillard, 1895)

In contrast to the more warmth-loving species—*A. sophiae* and *A. cypris*—this is a species which seeks out high altitudes and, in Turkey, has spread westward, transforming into numerous local varieties.

All varieties of *A. chantrei* may be clearly differentiated from the other species by the rounded caudal fin and the very small ventral fins. The pattern of both sexes, though again quite variable, looks as it does in Illus. II–175. The coloration is silver with dark stripes having a golden yellow sheen with red and blue spots scattered over the body; the females are more dull-looking in pattern than the males. *A. chantrei* is undoubtedly a suitable and attractive fish for the aquarium, yet so far,

Illus. II-175. *Aphanius chantrei.*

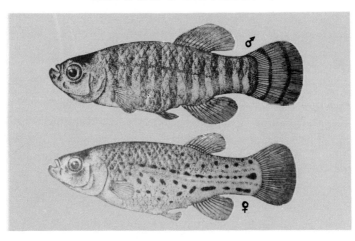

837

too little attention has been paid to it and there is, of course, too little known about it. Importation of this and related species from the Balkans is highly recommended. Many difficulties occurring with imports from outside Europe should not be experienced with this fish.

The variety in Illus. II–175 is *A. chantrei chantrei* (Gaillard, 1895) from Karpuzatan. In addition, *A. c. venustus* Kosswig & Sözer, 1945, from Lake Tuz, Turkey, has been described, along with *A. c. maeandricus* Aksiray, 1948, from the vicinity of Dinar, Civril and Karakuye (Turkey); *A. c. litoralis* Aksiray, 1948, from near Tefennis and Burdur; *A. c. parvus* Aksiray, 1948, also from the vicinity of Tefennis. A further number of sub-species from this vicinity have also been described. The maximum length is about 35 mm (1⅜ inches).

Aphanius fasciatus (Valenciennes, 1821)

This is the most widely distributed species of the genus. It occurs from Italy and Sardinia to the Near East and northern Africa.

The length reaches a maximum of about 60 mm (2⅜ inches). The females become larger than the males and are distinguished by their less distinct pattern and smaller fins. From related species, *A. fasciatus* is distinguished by the 10 to 13 rays in the dorsal fin and a single dark band in the caudal fin of the males, which, however, can be entirely absent. The coloration is olive-grey to dark olive green, the belly whitish, the fins yellow. About 10 to 15 dark (to black) bands cross the body, which in the males are broader than the lighter spaces between the stripes. The stripes are narrower in the female and run not so far towards the belly as they do in the males. According to the place of origin, *A. fasciatus* is a variable species, which, on closer study, can certainly be divided into numerous sub-species.

Aphanius iberus (Valenciennes, 1846)

This species comes from the Iberian peninsula (near Barcelona and Seville) and northwest Africa. It remains noticeably smaller (50 mm or 2 inches) than the previously mentioned species and differs, further, in pattern. The silver-grey background is broken by about 14 to 20 light blue cross bands. In the female, these bands disperse into two or more spots lying one under the other.

This species is quite variable in pattern, depending on the place of origin, and a number of local varieties can be distinguished.

Aphanius sophiae (Heckel, 1843)

This species, which has been divided into a large number of sub-species, inhabits the region from Iran to Turkey. It is sensitive to lower temperatures and must be kept at a temperature of at least 15 °C (59 °F), preferably a little higher.

This species differs from *A. chantrei* and *A. iberus* by its olive brown background coloration on which the light blue to white dots stand out distinctly. Hobbyists call *A. sophiae* the most attractive representative of its genus, although here, too, the female is less richly endowed than the male. The fins are bluish with light, pearly dots, as on the body.

This is a species that occurs commonly in numerous local varieties in fresh and brackish waters. Further details would be the same as already expressed for the other *Aphanius* species. The bringing up of the young is no more difficult than for the American toothcarps and in many respects they may be compared with the better known *Jordanella floridae* or *Cyprinodon variegatus*. The length is to about 65 mm ($2\frac{9}{16}$ inches). The males are smaller than the females. From the vicinity of Antalya, Turkey, comes *Aphanius sophiae mentoides* Aksiray, 1948, and from near Konya, also in Turkey, comes *Aphanius sophiae similis* Aksiray, 1948.

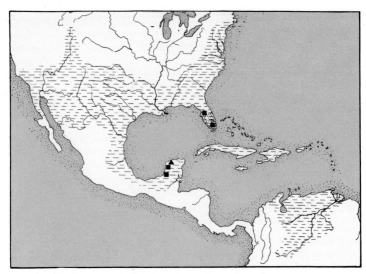

Illus. II-176. Distribution of the Cyprinodontini in the region near the Gulf of Mexico. – – – *Cyprinodon,* /// *Jordanella,* ▲ *Garmanella* and ■ *Floridichthys.*

Tribe Cyprinodontini

Of the sub-family Cyprinodontinae, this tribe includes the species that have already earned necessary recognition among aquarist circles. Although *Cyprinodon variegatus* used to be kept in aquariums by hobbyists, at present, *Jordanella floridae* is more commonly represented in the various tanks.

In contrast to the Aphaniini, which inhabit Europe, Asia and Africa, the Cyprinodontini are found exclusively in the Americas, with the hub of their distribution in the region near the Gulf of Mexico. In addition to the districts where water is plentiful—where *Bacopa amplexicaulis* is native—the Cyprinodontini also live in the marshy area of Florida (the Everglades), in California, and along the whole length of the Colorado River and its tributaries, in creeks and ponds, in the widespread Mississippi delta, in Alabama, Georgia, Texas, along the Atlantic coast of Mexico and Yucatán, from the islands of Cuba, Hispaniola (Haiti and the Dominican Republic), Jamaica, Puerto Rico, and in South America in the estuarial waters and flood plain of the Orinoco River, Venezuela.

In addition to fresh waters in the indicated regions of habitation, species of *Cyprinodon, Floridichthys* and *Garmanella* are found in brackish water and perhaps even in the open sea. *Cyprinodon* has also taken over

840

some of the scant waters of Death Valley, California, as well as desert springs and salt ponds.

The Cyprinodontini, which includes the genera *Cyprinodon, Jordanella, Garmanella* and *Floridichthys*, differ in looks from the Aphaniini by the more thick-set, higher shape of the body.

Genus *Cyprinodon*

This genus is best represented in the Everglades of Florida, but still inhabits, in addition, the entire remaining distribution area of the tribe. From its activities, body structure and pattern, it can be understood that the members of this genus are found mainly in stagnant or only moderately flowing waters.

The natural environment of most of the representatives of this genus is certainly of special interest—the marshes of Florida, which have been made passable by drainage canals. A short description of the Everglades will certainly interest aquarists.

This watery region, the Everglades, equal to about half the size of the Netherlands, is passable only for flat-bottomed, air-propeller-driven boats which are continually used by the Floridians, the state

Illus. II-177. A watery region with dry-land vegetation, such as the Florida Everglades, is found in many places round the world. Seldom, however, is there such an abundance of fish as there is in the Everglades.

Illus. II-178. Herons skim the very shallow water, the habitat of the toothcarps. The white stork puts in a very rare appearance in this region.

Illus. II-179. At the edge of the deeper water in the immense Everglades, pelicans and frigate birds have their hunting grounds. A pelican makes an accurate dive into the water to catch a fish. At the last moment, it folds its wings backward and stretches out its neck.

842

rangers, and naturalists. The average water depth is not even a quarter of a metre (10 inches), and the water is thickly grown practically everywhere with reeds.

The most fantastic flowers and birds are seen there. Somewhat drier little islands over-grown with jungle growth are populated by herons and water hens (coots). A little higher up, in the tangle of woods, the wood ibis and the water turkey nest. On another sandbar is a flock of terns and stilt-legged avocets which, like the previously-named birds, live practically exclusively on the fish that are present in the shallow water. Naturally, other birds, which subsist more on the animal life than on fish, also live there.

Among the mammals, besides the puma, are the fish otter and the porpoise, the rare sea cow or manatee. Of course, other animal groups are well represented and the abundant plants make a feasible living-, breeding- and hiding-place for the various animals.

Of course, our concern is with the fishes that live in these Everglades and mainly, in fact, with the Cyprinodontini. The genera *Cyprinodon*, *Jordanella* and *Floridichthys* are quite common there. All species and varieties have a thick-set body structure and are quite variable in many respects, which has again led to confusion in nomenclature. Across the body usually run one or more clearly outstanding cross bands. There is usually also a band on the edge of the caudal fin. The males, larger than the females in some species, usually have a higher shape to the body. The females usually have a dark spot on the last rays of the dorsal fin, the same spot being present in both sexes while they are young, as with many Rivulini.

Cyprinodon variegatus Lacépède, 1803
Sheepshead Killie

This toothcarp is often encountered along the east coast of North America (sub-species *C. variegatus variegatus*), in fresh as well as brackish and even in salt water.

Sub-species are known from Yucatán, Mexico, *C. v. artifrons* Hubbs, 1936; from the Bahama Islands, *C. v. baconi* Breder, 1932; from the West Indies and Venezuela, *C. v. dearborni* Meek, 1909; from Jamaica, *C. v. jamaicensis* Fowler, 1939; and from Florida, *C. v. hubbsi* Carr, 1936.

This fish, of which the variety *Cyprinodon variegatus variegatus* Lacépède is especially well known to aquarists, reaches a maximum length of 58 mm ($2\frac{5}{16}$ inches) in the male and about 80 mm ($3\frac{1}{8}$ inches) in the female. The body is somewhat laterally compressed, the snout is rather short, with a moderately large, upward-directed mouth.

The basic coloration is olive green to brownish with a lighter belly. From the back over the sides run 6 to 10 stripes, identical in coloration. The dorsal and caudal fins are rather large and are bordered by a dark band. The female lacks these dark edges, yet possesses in place of them a rather large, dark spot among the rearmost rays of the dorsal fin. This spot is also found in the young of both sexes. The entire body has a metallic sheen, the flanks near the belly sometimes have an orange glitter, which, towards the rear, merges into blue-green to dark blue. Also, the front edges of the dorsal and anal fins are orange, while these fins are more bluish towards the back. On the whole, the female is somewhat faded looking, the fins being yellowish.

Illus. II-180. *Cyprinodon variegatus.*

Cyprinodon variegatus is quite easy to keep, making few demands. It does, however, require a roomy, thickly planted tank and some sunlight. Specimens just imported are often somewhat shy. Also, as far as food is concerned, *C. variegatus* is easy to satisfy, and will accept any kind of fish food. The addition of sea water (or sea salt) to the aquarium water during the breeding season (spring—April to June) is necessary only with specimens certain to have come from a coastal region. Usually, in breeding for a second generation, the addition of salt is in no way required. The temperatures at which this fish is most most comfortable range between 10 and 30 °C (50–86 °F). *C. variegatus* is extremely suitable for keeping indoors in an unheated aquarium, yet at the same time, it is a very suitable inhabitant of garden ponds where, for half the year, it feels quite at home and assures numerous offspring. Take it outdoors in spring (April) and bring it back inside again in autumn (October). The eggs are usually laid on the plants, just under the surface. The young hatch out in about a week, and within four months are already mature, if they have had plenty of space at their disposal.

Genus *Floridichthys*

Floridichthys is most closely related to the genera *Jordanella* and *Cyprinodon*. This genus is distinguished especially by the unscaled snout, by two scales placed one behind the other between the ventral fins, and by the stem of the tail being rather broad and the same size over its entire length.

Floridichthys carpio (Günther, 1866)

As expressed in the name, this species is an inhabitant of Florida. Two other geographic varieties of this species also occur in Yucatán, Mexico, so there are actually three sub-species. From this distribution, it appears once again that there is a concurrence and relationship of the fauna of the Florida peninsula with that of the Yucatán peninsula.

In aquarium-keeping, *Floridichthys carpio* sspp. are treated in every respect like *Jordanella* or *Cyprinodon*. Blue, yellow and red form the predominant coloration of *Jordanella* as well as of the genus *Floridichthys*. The length of *F. carpio* is to 70 mm (2¾ inches).

Genus *Garmanella*

Like *Floridichthys*, which has only one known species up to now, *Garmanella* is distinguished from its related genera by the considerably longer dorsal fin, which has 15 to 17 rays. The base runs to almost half the entire length of the back.

Garmanella pulchra Hubbs, 1936

This fish, which only grows to about 40 mm (1⅝ inches) long, lives in fresh and brackish water near Progreso, Yucatán. Except for the low but very long dorsal fin, it resembles *Jordanella* a great deal. The males, however, are slimmer than the females, while among *Jordanella*, the females are slimmer than the males. Also, the eye spot in the dorsal fin, so characteristic of many Cyprinodontini, is absent in young *G. pulchra* as well as in the females.

Genus *Jordanella*

Up to now, this genus is only known to come from Florida and Yucatán (*J. floridae*). Myers has noted (*Copeia*, 1940) that it appears to have been present for some time in Borneo (imported?).

Jordanella floridae Goode & Bean, 1879

American Flag Fish

Flag Fish

As its name indicates, this little toothcarp hails from Florida. It is known, moreover, in Yucatán, Mexico. Imported into Europe for the first time in 1914, it has since then, from time to time, enjoyed a position of importance among aquarists.

The little fish has a length of about 50 mm (2 inches). The females remain a little smaller. The body is somewhat laterally compressed and rather high.

The head is rather flat on top, the snout is short with a medium-sized, top-positioned mouth. The entire body is covered with large scales. The basic coloration is brownish olive green. The sides of the

Plate II-233. *Jordanella floridae*.

male are varied in coloration, going from the dark black through the red, green, blue and golden silvery gleaming flanks over into the light, silvery belly. The dorsal, caudal and anal fins are large and their bases are dotted with several rows of small, red spots. The females are somewhat less vivid, so that they have a greyer appearance.

This fish, which has been sadly misjudged by many aquarists, can quickly be made to feel at home. It prefers the smallest tank, as long as there is plenty of plant growth present and the tank has a sunny location. It eats everything (omnivorous) and should especially be fed vegetable material, such as algae and pieces of dead plants. It also gladly accepts all kinds of living and dried food animals. The temperature at which it feels at its best is about 20 °C (68 °F)—not between 24 and 30 °C (75–86 °F), as often indicated in the literature. Only during the breeding season is the temperature allowed to rise to about 25 °C (77 °F), not higher. At that temperature, a lively court-ship takes place that can last for as long as a week. The eggs, about 60 of them in all, are laid on plants. (Sometimes, however, the eggs are laid in a nest-like depression on the bottom.) The parents do not have to be removed. The young hatch out after five to eight days. After about two weeks, they should be transferred to a tank thickly grown with algae, where they will grow quickly and mature in about three months.

Jordanella floridae is rather timid. Therefore, avoid approaching the tank suddenly or tapping against the panes. During the mating season, the males are very intolerant, so it is best to transfer them to a separate tank just before that time. Except for the mating season, however, the males can be kept without danger in the community aquarium with other fishes of the same size. It is a lovely fish which no one would be sorry to include among their fishes.

Tribe Fundulini

The genera composing this group are distinguished from the Cyprinodontini by their sharply pointed, incisor-like teeth, conical in shape, and always-present parietal (skull) bone. Moreover, they are distinguished principally by the longer, more drawn out body of the the toothcarps. There are numerous known species that have already been kept for dozens of years by many aquarists. In general, Fundulini are picturesque fishes, not large, lively, often peculiar and interesting in their living habits and, practically without exception, easy to breed.

Genus *Chriopeops*

This genus is distinguished from *Fundulus* mainly by the teeth being placed in two rows—not in a band as in *Fundulus*, nor in one row, as in *Lucania*. Only one species is known.

Chriopeops goodei (Jordan, 1879)
Bluefin Killie

This species is found in Florida—Jacksonville (St. Johns River), Gainesville (Bivens Arm), De Leon Springs, Lake Butler, Lake Monroe, Welaka Swamps, and the Everglades—in slowly flowing and stagnant waters, lakes and marshes. It is very abundant in schools.

Here, too, Plate II–234 gives a very good idea of this attractive fish. It is a typical, *Fundulus*-type fish, with, however, more of a spindle-shaped body. Its maximum length is about 60 mm ($2\frac{3}{8}$ inches) in aquariums, but in most cases, it is seldom more than 50 mm (2 inches). A cross-section of the body is oval-shaped. The height (of the body) amounts to about one fourth the length from the snout to the root of the tail. The dorsal fin begins just halfway along this length. The anal fin begins a little farther to the rear. The snout is rounded, and the mouth end-positioned, with the mouth opening directed upward.

The natural habitat of this species includes the predominantly stagnant, marshy waters of Florida. *Chriopeops goodei* does not occur in the equally marshy but more brackish coastal waters, but exclusively in the pure, fresh waters which, because of humic acid, have a pH of about 6.3.

An important point which must be taken into account is the variable temperature of this region. It ranges from nearly tropical in the summer to very cold in the winter—that is from about 5 to 25 °C (41–77 °F). This little toothcarp is thus best kept in an unheated tank at room temperature, together with species that share its natural habitat,

Plate II-234. *Chriopeops goodei.*

such as *Fundulus chrysotus, Elassoma evergladei, Jordanella floridae,* and others.

Cover the bottom with a substantial layer of humus and plant it with *Myriophyllum, Najas,* etc. Feed *C. goodei* principally insects and insect larvae, also various worms and crustaceans (*Daphnia* and *Cyclops*).

Courtship, as with its relatives, is sometimes carried on rather tempestuously. The eggs are laid in the upper water layers, on and among the fine-leaved greenery. Two to five eggs result from each mating, which can be carried on daily for several weeks on end. The yellowish brown eggs are rather large (about 2 mm or 0.08 inch in diameter) and stick to the plants by means of short slime-threads. Depending on the temperature, the eggs hatch out after a week or 10 days. At temperatures above 23–24 °C (73–75 °F) most of the eggs remain unfertilized (the optimum temperature for the sperm seems to be about 18–19 °C or 64–66 °F).

This fish is also suitable for outdoor aquariums and small fish ponds, where the aquarist is better able to imitate the natural environment. Although *C. goodei* likes to play in the sunshine, plenty of shady places must also be provided.

The young grow up very quickly and after five to six weeks, the red tail of the male can be seen in process of development.

Like many *Fundulus* types, *C. goodei* is sensitive to changes in the constitution of the water. Hence, never transfer it directly from one tank to another. It cannot withstand fresh water from the water mains as well as it can a tank filled up with rain water.

Genus *Fundulus*

Of this genus, which is represented in North America by a large number of species, only a few species are, unfortunately, known in aquarist circles. Among these is the well known Gold-Eyed Fundulus, *Fundulus chrysotus*, which has been included for a long time among the most popular species of toothcarps. Sadly enough, this is no longer the case, and it appears less and less, or, on the whole, not at all, in private aquariums. Various, more richly hued relatives have taken its place, yet it is desirable that once again there be imports of this genus.

The body of *Fundulus* is more or less cylindrical, the males a little more thick-set than the females and, at the same time, somewhat richer in coloration. The dorsal fin is always located behind the first ray of the anal fin. The head is broad and a little flattened. The mouth is end-positioned and both jaws are equally thrust forward, but only the intermaxillary bone is somewhat protrusive. The jaws are set with rows of conical teeth. The fins are ordinarily small and rounded; the dorsal and anal fins are placed far to the rear. As far as reproduction is concerned, refer to the description of *F. chrysotus* below. If deviant factors or circumstances play a rôle, these will be mentioned in the discussion of the individual species concerned.

In regard to the area of distribution, different *Fundulus* species inhabiting the coastal stretches are found in brackish and even in sea water.

Fundulus chrysotus (Günther, 1866)
Golden-Eared Killie
Gold-Eyed Fundulus
Gold-Eyed Killie

This species inhabits the southern states of the United States—Texas, Arkansas, Missouri, Tennessee, South Carolina, Georgia, Florida, Alabama and Mississippi. In 1904, it was brought for the first time into Europe (Germany) as an aquarium fish. A dweller of the coastal reaches, where it lives in very shallow waters, it is especially numerous in Florida.

This fish reaches a maximum length of 70 mm ($2\frac{3}{4}$ inches), has a light olive green coloration with a metallic blue gleam. Over the flanks run rows of bright red dots, while the gill covers are spattered with luminous, green spots. The iris of the eye in the male is golden, in the female, dark. Except for the ventral and pectoral fins, which are without coloration, all the fins are lemon yellow. The females are brownish and

851

The picture on page 852 is incorrect. Please moisten this gummed replacement of <u>Fundulus chrysotus</u> and paste over the incorrect picture.

Plate II-235. *Fundulus chrysotus.*

have a smaller dorsal and anal fin. A black-spotted (melanistic) variety was reported by aquarists in North America in 1922.

As an aquarium fish par excellence, *F. chrysotus* makes few or no demands in its care or environment (aquarium or fish ponds), as long as the area is not too small and thickly populated. *F. chrysotus* lives mainly on little worms and insects (larvae).

The temperature, of course, depends on the place from which the imports come, but ranges between 18 and 30 °C (64–86 °F). They have outstanding resistance to lower temperatures, especially in the fish pond where there is usually a larger quantity of water than in the home aquariums. However, they can seldom withstand temperatures below about 12° C (54 °F) for very long.

Reproduction takes place in the manner of other toothcarps and after a sometimes lengthy and rather tumultuous courtship, up to about 200 eggs (often less) are laid among the plants, preferably close to the surface in shallow places (in the fish pond, it prefers the marshy area where the water stands only a few centimetres deep).

F. chrysotus is certainly not an egg-eater, like the carp-like fishes. Bringing up the young in the fish pond is no trouble; in the aquarium, however, a lot of (ditch) infusoria must be present at all times, if the fish are to hunt waterfleas and the like. The water plants to be considered for decorating the environment are primarily species of *Myriophyllum*, water thyme (American riverweed or *Podostemon*), *Najas*, iris, and the like. Avoid covering areas with floating plants. Note particularly that the genus *Fundulus*, presently populating only North and Central America, did not penetrate into those areas until recent times and, in fact, is not a part of the original fauna. In Florida, this fish, together with its nearest relatives—*Jordanella floridae, Chriopeops goodei*, and the like—forms an important source of food for the large colonies of birds which inhabit the Everglades.

It is strange and sad that, of the numerous other *Fundulus* species, no others have ever been kept or, if they have, only sporadically. Still, a few will be named that would certainly be worth the trouble.

Fundulus cingulatus Valenciennes, 1846
Banded Killie or Killifish
Redfin Killie or Killifish

This species is found in North America—from North and South Carolina to Texas. Its length is to 80 mm ($3\frac{1}{8}$ inches). In coloration and pattern, *F. cingulatus* is quite similar to *F. chrysotus*. Its back is olive brown, its flanks silver-blue, its belly yellowish, its under-jaw edged with red, the iris of the eye silver-yellow, the gill covers golden green with red dots. The scales, especially in the middle of the flanks, each have a red dot, forming, on the aftermost part of the body, about 15 cross stripes. *F. cingulatus* is a rather variable species. The fins are yellowish to deep red, and the ventral and anal fins have a black border.

Illus. II-181. *Fundulus heteroclitus.*

Fundulus heteroclitus (Linné, 1766)
Zebra Killie

This species inhabits a widespread region: Eastern North America, from Canada to Mexico and the Bermuda Islands, in fresh, brackish and even in salt water. It is extremely variable in appearance, in accordance with the place of origin. The many synonyms have been raised to sub-species, each of which has its own typical habitat. Keep *F. heteroclitus* in the same way as its relatives, with the understanding that the brackish-water varieties require an equivalent addition of salt water to their environment. *Najas* species of plants which occur abundantly in these districts, can withstand a considerable addition of salt. Plant mainly *Najas marina, Najas guadalupensis, Najas flexilis, Najas gracillima* and *Ruppia maritima.*

Fundulus majalis (Walbaum, 1792)
Striped Killie or Killifish

As a result of the quantity of patterns (shown in Illus. II–182) which this species displays in the course of its development, it has, over the years, been given numerous names by numerous authors. However, all these names are not strictly synonyms of *F. majalis*, since it is quite clearly a species that includes many varieties, depending on the region it lives in (the district of origin). A number of sub-species will undoubtedly be distinguished, each of which, at present, bears one of the synonymous names.

This fish has almost the same home territory as *F. heteroclitus* and also occurs in brackish and salt water. It is quite common.

The young fish have a lengthwise stripe, composed of irregular, brownish black spots, which gradually dissolves into a number of

Illus. II-182. Various stages of development of both sexes of *Fundulus majalis*, which gives a very good picture of the extraordinary difference in the appearance of young, half-grown, and full-grown males and females. 1, 3, 5 and 6 are male, and 2, 4, 7 and 8 are female specimens.

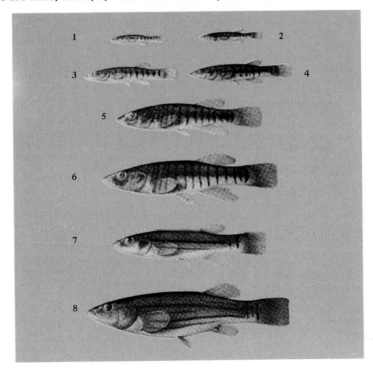

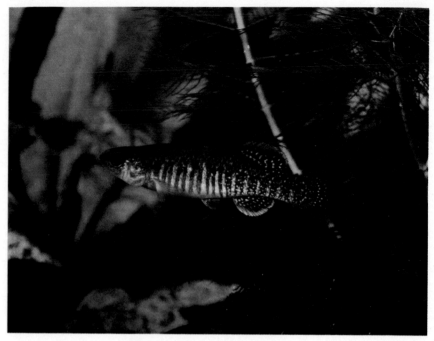

Plate II-236. *Fundulus majalis.*

vertical lines. The males, which are noticeably smaller (to about 12 cm or 4¾ inches) than the females (to about 15 cm or 6 inches), retain this pattern of vertical stripes and the horizontal line remains faintly visible. The females possess an intense, horizontal stripe, with one or two weaker lines above and below, ending on the root of the tail in several vertical lines.

The basic coloration is yellow-green, the back is dark olive green, the belly yellow to orange.

Genus *Leptolucania*

Only one species belongs to this genus, *Leptolucania ommata*, which is distinguished from its relatives by several characteristics. The dorsal fin is located far to the rear, the characteristic of surface-dwellers, such as *Rivulus*. A genital sac, such as possessed by *Fundulus*, however, is absent in *Rivulus*.

Leptolucania ommata (Jordan, 1855)
Swamp Killie

This species hails from some of the southern states of the United States—southern Georgia to Florida—from marshes and other exclusively fresh waters.

A very attractive, small, *Fundulus*-type fish, *L. ommata* reaches a length of 35 mm (1⅜ inches) in the male and 40 mm (1 9/16 inches) in the female. It should be kept like its nearest relatives from the same district.

On a light brown basic coloration with a blue sheen runs a dark brown band (substantially lighter in adult males), sometimes with about eight cross bands in the male. The dark spots have light edges. The fins are yellowish to orange. The outer part of the anal fin is reddish with a black tip.

Genus *Profundulus*

This is a rather unknown genus with only one species that has been found only once in an amateur aquarium. For the other species, the details are the same as for *Profundulus punctatus*.

Profundulus punctatus (Günther, 1866)
Spotted Profundulus

As described by De Vet (1948), full-grown specimens with a length to about 100 mm (4 inches) can turn out rather unsociable. This fish should be kept only in larger aquariums among fishes that are not too small. It comes from Central America (Guatemala) and should, correspondingly, be kept at a temperature between 20 and 28 °C (68–82 °F). It is a dweller of the upper water layers, although not such an out and out surface-dweller as the Aplocheilini. The eggs are laid spontaneously and in great numbers among fine-leaved plants, close to the surface. The fry hatch out after about a week or a little longer, and the bright yellow young are easy to raise.

This species is so important because it is accepted as a vestige of the forms from which all the other groups of toothcarps, including the live-bearing species, originated. This concept is supported not only by the body structure but also by the distribution of this fish.

Aquarists also know about *P. labialis* (Günther, 1866), *P. oaxacae* (Meek, 1902) from Mexico (Oaxaca); *P. candalarius* Hubbs, 1924, from Guatemala (Candalaria, near the Mexican border), and *P. hildebrandi* Miller, 1950, from Mexico (San Cristobal de las Casas, Chiapas). The similarity in appearance to the genus *Umbra* (the Dogfish or Mud Minnow) will, in the future, probably appear more significant than merely a superficial resemblance. Possibly, even a link between this order and the Clupeiformes (the herring-like fishes) will be found.

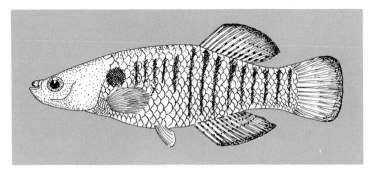

Genus *Valencia*

This genus hails from the Mediterranean Sea region (Spain and Corfu), and is most closely related to *Profundulus*. It is difficult to determine whether or not more than one species exists and for that reason, only the type species will be discussed.

Valencia hispanica (Valenciennes, 1846)
Spanish Toothcarp

This species shows a clear difference between the sexes. Not only is the female bigger (about 80 mm or $3\frac{1}{8}$ inches) than the male (about 60 mm or $2\frac{3}{8}$ inches), but in the female, the typical pattern of the male, with the vertical bands on the tail stem, is absent or only vaguely indicated. The coloration is olive green, dark on the back, lighter towards the belly. The vertical bands of the male are dark brown, 10 to 12 in number.

As far as care and breeding are concerned, the details are the same as for *Profundulus*. It withstands low temperatures very well, as much as you might expect of a sub-tropical species. Temperature as low as 5 °C (41 °F) only makes it listless. The best temperature is about 18 °C (64 °F), so that it is an especially suitable species to keep outdoors during the summer months.

Like *Profundulus*, *V. hispanica* is a fish which, from time to time, literally must be given room. They sometimes fly at each other to give a sound "thrashing," only later, fin in fin, to slip away into the clumps of vegetation. Sometimes, only the male is unfriendly towards the female. If, in the course of time, her consort gains the upper hand, an extremely interesting exhibition, a kind of marriage offer, then follows. The glass-clear eggs, which take on a dull, yellowish coloration after a few hours, hatch out in about one to two weeks.

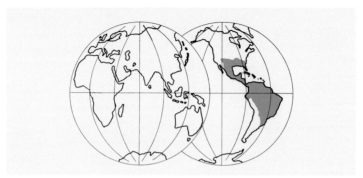

Super-family Poecilioidea

The ovoviviparous (literally egg-live-bearing) toothcarps are native to the warm regions of North, Central and South America, as shown on the map in Illus. II–184. Like oviparous (egg-laying) toothcarps, they are found in rivers, lakes, marshes, pools and puddles, even in the smallest pondlets left behind by floods, which dry up in the dry season. In this way, the dry season causes the death of millions of lovely fish each year.

The body of these toothcarps is elongated, more or less thick-set, and laterally compressed. The entire body, sometimes even including part of the fin bases, is covered with scales. Sexual dimorphism is particularly conspicuous in these fishes, not only because mature males are much more vivid than the females, but also because of the so-called GONOPODIUM, the male copulatory organ which directs sperm capsules towards the female genital opening. (More about the gonopodium later.)

In addition to a number of external differences which distinguish the males from the females, there are also a few internal ones. For instance, a number of vertebrae in front of the tail section in the males, underneath the dorsal fin, have a kind of elongated bony ray. To these are attached the vigorous muscles that operate the gonopodium. It is in this connection with the growth of this organ that a sexless fish becomes male—the so-called change of sex, or reversal, frequently observed in ovoviviparous fish. The elongated vertebrae divide the swim bladder of these fishes into two parts.

By now we are used to the idea of young fishes being born alive in the aquarium, and give the miracle no further thought. It is still something to marvel at, yet there is little cause for wonder, after all. This is a natural occurrence, even though it used to be considered a privilege of mammals alone. Although the organization of viviparous creatures—those that bring forth their young alive into the world—and the manner in which the young are born alive are not the same in every instance, live birth occurs in almost all groups of the animal kingdom. Some unicellular organisms at the lowest level of development have a similar way of reproducing, as do some kinds of snails, sharks and other animals. Among fish, Poecilioidea are by no means the only viviparous ones, for the half-beak genera, *Dermogenys* and *Hemiramphus*, are also live-bearers.

Poecilioidea are ovoviviparous and viviparous. The difference is considerable, but can be clarified in a few words. Higher mammals are purely viviparous—that is, the fertilized eggs remain stored in the mother's body and are fed directly from the blood stream of the maternal organism, incorporated into the mother's circulatory system, thus implying a vital connection between mother and baby. There is no egg-shell at the time of birth, so the babies are literally brought forth alive. In the case of most ovoviviparous toothcarps, reproduction takes place much as it does with egg-laying fishes (the babies also come into the world alive and fully developed), the difference being that the male sperm is brought into the body of the female, and thus internal fertilization of the eggs takes place before they are laid. The egg, which has a well developed shell, develops within the body of the mother but *without* feeding on her vital fluids, and is not incorporated into her circulatory system. At the moment of birth, the shell bursts at the slightest pressure, either inside or just outside the mother's body; thus, the baby is born alive, but from an egg. For nourishment, the developing embryo consumes the contents of the yolk sac, in exactly the same way as the larvae of egg-laying fishes do. The great difference is that egg-layers do so outside the maternal body, where they are exposed to all the risks of a hostile environment.

As soon as the young leave the mother's body, they swim away. At that moment, they are comparable to the larvae of egg layers when they set out to hunt food on their own. There seems to be no inkling of relationship between the fry and their mother, such as is so obvious in mammals. An exception are the Goodeidae, a truly viviparous family, about which more will be said on page 867.

Obviously, fertilization is different in these ovoviviparous fish than in egg-layers. In order to perform internal fertilization, the males are provided with a copulatory organ, called the gonopodium, which is

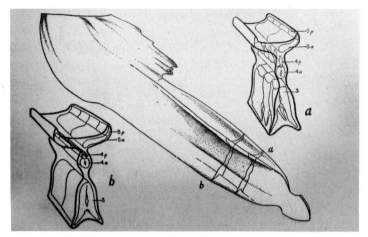

Illus. II-185. Stereogram of a gonopodium of *Xiphophorus* sp. with the cross-sections indicated at a. and b. See also Illus. II-194 on page 898.

one of the distinguishing sexual characteristics. The gonopodium in these fishes develops from the first few rays of the anal fin. The manner of growth is characteristic for different families, and this will be discussed more thoroughly in considering the various families themselves.

The sperm is conveyed to the female in small capsules of spermatozoa alongside of or through the gonopodium (depending on its structure). The female can store the spermatozoa for a very long time; in fact, some species continue to produce young over a long period after a single fertilization.

Nature provided these fishes with a reproductive system that would amply compensate for the countless dangers to which the small fish are exposed. Live-bearers, native to still or moderately flowing waters in tropical or sub-tropical climates, which, in the dry season, are deprived of fresh water from rivers or rain water, accommodate themselves to a considerable periodic drying of their natural environment. As the females can, after a single mating, continue to give birth throughout the whole season, the survival of the species is, to a certain extent, assured.

What actually goes on in the various habitats of these fishes? The females stay, for the most part, in shallow pools, while the males prefer deeper water with a faster current. The fry are most often born in pools and puddles isolated from the main stream during the dry season. Such seclusion provides them with a measure of comparative safety from their natural enemies. By the time the rains arrive, just about all the fry have reached sexual maturity, at which time they mate. Thereafter, the males migrate to the deeper, free-flowing waters through channels opened up by the rains. The fertilized females stay in the quiet, safer waters. Thus, nature provides a two-fold precaution for the preservation of the species: fertilization inside the maternal body and the instinct to seek safe, sheltered water for the bringing forth of the young.

As a rule, the process of fertilization takes place as follows. During the mating season—which in the freedom of nature is shorter than in the aquarium—the male releases a hormone called COPULINE into the water. Copuline has a curious effect on the females—at least, on those females that have not been fertilized before. It causes them to take on an elevated position in the water, heads up at about a 20° angle. They either stand still or swim about. In this position, it is much easier for the males to approach them for the purpose of fertilization. Investigation (Jaski, 1939) showed this to be true for the Guppy (*Poecilia reticulata*), and later it was found that most of these live-bearers behave in the same way.

For fertilization, the gonopodium of the male is swung sideways, or sometimes in front, and the sperm is deposited *on* the body of the female. No proper kind of copulation takes place, as has been assumed. In other words, the male organ does not introduce the sperm *into* the body of the female, but the sperm capsules are expelled from the gonopodium towards the female genital opening. This has also been observed (Breder & Coates, 1935) in the Guppy. The spermatozoa (the motile gametes in the sperm) clump together to form clusters called spermatophores in the seed duct. Thousands of seed cells are contained in these spermatophores, cohered by means of a proteinaceous substance which is later dissolved in the female oviduct to release part of the seed cells. These then fertilize the eggs. Thus, the males have no active part in the actual fertilization; the female takes care of the entire process.

When breeding ovoviviparous fish, it is desirable to keep the sexes apart as much as possible (which is what happens in the wild as well), and then to bring together several females with only a single male. This also seems to be the normal thing in nature, for relatively more females than males are found there. Curiously enough, in the aquarium, sometimes there is an entire brood of males only, without so much as a single female. It is not known how this occurs, nor whether it also happens in the wild.

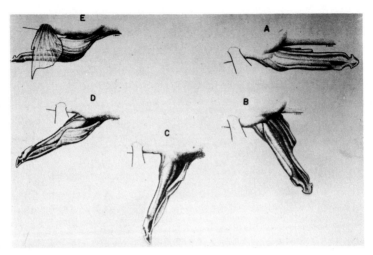

Illus. II-186. Five phases *(A* through *E)* in the swinging forward of the gonopodium of a swordtail *(Xiphophorus)* just before copulation.

Now for a close look at how the gonopodium works—certainly not as a copulative organ but, instead, more like the barrel of a gun. The barrel is formed from outgrown rays of the anal fin and is cocked and ready to fire when it is turned frontwards, together with the pelvic fins. The genital exit lies between the bases of the pelvic fins and the gonopodium (the anal fin), and from it emerges one or more seed balls to be pushed to the tip of the gonopodium. This takes place with lightning speed, so that it is not possible to see whether the discharged seed ball actually strikes the target.

What goes on in "virgin" females that have not previously been fertilized? Mature virgin females, when exposed to the effect of the hormone copuline become, as it were, high—that is, they undergo a reaction of extreme excitation. The reaction lasts for a period of four days to a week, depending on the water's temperature and on the age of the female. At about the middle of the period, when the females swim in the most elevated position, chances for a successful target-shoot with the spermatophores are best. This is a condition worth being remembered by breeders.

When the spermatophore has penetrated into the oviduct, gradually and according to the demand, a part of the enveloping substance is dissolved by a fluid separated from the wall of the oviduct. In this manner, a number of spermatozoa are freed of the spermatophore to fertilize a number of eggs. These remain in the wall of the ovary sac

864

until they are ripe. When about to hatch, they descend into the oviduct, from which the young emerge. Parturition usually takes a few hours, but, under certain circumstances, it can go on for several days. The number of young at a birth differs from species to species and may be anywhere from 4 to 100. The number, of course, may be influenced by the mother's age, the tank's temperature and the quality and quantity of food in the period preceding mating, as well as other factors.

Inspection of the map in Illus. II–184 showing the distribution of Poecilioidea and comparison with that of their egg-laying cousins shows that they are restricted to a relatively small area, the Americas only. It seems correct to conclude, therefore, that this is a fairly recent group that never was more widely distributed.

Like the egg-laying species, or even more so, these toothcarps are eminently suited to the aquarium. Because of their often lively coloration, their briskness, and their peaceful nature, they can be kept along with most other species. For the beginning aquarist, they are an easy group to start with, for they require only simple care. Even breeding is easy and often surprisingly successful. Still, Poecilioidea are not directly qualified as "guinea pigs" for the beginner, for breeding them requires at least as much insight as it does for other fishes. Breeding in a hit-or-miss manner can cause loss and destruction of many lovely fishes.

CLASSIFICATION AND SURVEY OF THE FAMILIES

Live-bearing toothcarps are classified according to their structure and organization. The difference in the structure of the gonopodium is actually the only clearly visible characteristic. Hence, in the table below, the form of the gonopodium was adopted as a criterion.

The four families have been familiar to aquarists for a long time, and the Poeciliidae in particular have contributed a veritable treasure chest of pretty specimens.

1. The gonopodium is formed by part of the anal fin only
    A. The gonopodium has an extremely simple structure. It consists of the six foremost anal fin rays, shortened and hardened, separated from the remaining rays . . . family Goodeidae
    B. The gonopodium is built up of the third, fourth, and fifth anal fin rays. During growth, the anal fin shifts towards the head . . . family Poeciliidae

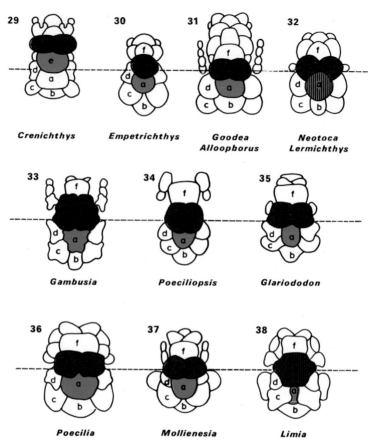

Illus. II-187. The frontal scalation of some live-bearing toothcarps. The comparatively slight variation in the pattern may indicate that live-bearers as a group are rather young—in any case, more recent than the egg-laying toothcarps. On the other hand, there are indications that the super-family Poecilioidea is a polyphyletic group, derived from more than one ancestral egg-laying family. Chart continued from Illus. II-163.

2. The whole anal fin is grown out to form a tubular, copulatory organ, not shifted towards the head

    A. The gonopodium is not scaly, eyes normal . . . family Jenynsiidae

    B. Gonopodium scaly, eyes horizontally divided into two parts . . . family Anablepidae

Recent research shows that the families can be classified according to more natural criteria, considering differences in the gonopodium of minor significance. For the time being, the more familiar classification will be adhered to.

Family Goodeidae

The fish included in this family were, up to 1902, classed in various other toothcarp families. Based on their teeth and the length of their guts, they were divided into plant-eaters and meat-eaters. Meek (1902) was the first ichthyologist to classify a number of species of the family Poeciliidae into a sub-family, Goodeinae, based on characteristics of reproduction. Regan (1907, 1911) elaborated the collected data and classified them in the sub-family Characodontinae. However, his system was again based on the dental structure of the fish, which does not hold true. In 1939, Hubbs & Turner set up a new natural system based on peculiar forms of the reproductive organs (trophotaeniae or rectal protuberances; ovary and gut protrusion of the embryos). These traits had been studied earlier by Turner (1932) and by Mendoza (1937).

At this time the family includes a fairly large number of species, divided into four sub-families. Although specimens are few and rarely get into the home aquarium, it may be useful to review them briefly.

The habitat of these fishes is restricted to part of Mexico, comprising the peculiar, so-called region of solar transition between the Tropic of Cancer (point of the summer solstice) and the 18th parallel of latitude: Rio Grande de Santiago, Rio Lerma, Lago de Chapala, Rio Verde (San Luis Potosí), Valle de Mexico, Quitzeo.

The sub-families are: Ataeniobiinae Hubbs & Turner, 1939 (with the only genus *Ataeniobius*); Goodeinae Jordan, 1880 (with the genera *Allotoca, Alloophorus, Xenotoca, Chapalichthys, Goodea, Allodontichthys, Neophorus, Xenoophorus,* and *Zoogeneticus*); Characodontinae Regan, 1907 (with the genus *Characodon*); Girardinichthyinae Hubbs & Turner, 1939 (comprising the genera *Balsadichthys, Girardinichthys, Ilyodon, Lermichthys, Neotoca, Ollentodon,* and *Skiffia*).

Sub-family Ataeniobiinae

A genus belonging to this sub-family is believed to be an ancestral variety which differs from the rest of the family by the absence of rectal protuberances in the embryo. Instead, the embryonic fin folds are conspicuous, and the yolk sac is larger than in other members of the family.

The only known species is *Ataeniobius toweri* (Meek, 1904), native to Rio Verde in San Luis Potosí, Mexico. Its length is about 50 mm (2 inches). Not yet introduced, this species seems to be promising for fans and importers.

Sub-family Goodeinae

Together with the sub-families Characodontinae and Girardinich-thyinae, Goodeinae are distinguished from Ataeniobiinae by the growth of rectal protuberances in the embryos. They are live-bearing fishes and scientists are inclined to compare the rectal protuberances to the placenta in mammals, for they serve the same purpose. Consequently, the yolk sac of the embryo is less developed, for it is nourished by the mother during part of the gestation period. The protuberances pene-trate the tissue of the ovary wall.

The species of Goodeinae described, among others, are: *Alloophorus robustus* (Bean, 1892), from Rio Grande de Santiago, length up to 125 mm (5 inches); *Allotoca dugesii* (Bean, 1887), from Rio Lerma, length 50 mm (2 inches); *Xenotoca variata* (Bean, 1887), plateau and lowland tributaries of the Rio Grande de Santiago and Rio Panuco, length 70 mm (2¾ inches); *Goodea gracilis* Hubbs & Turner, 1939, Rio Santa Maria, length 55 mm (2¼ inches); *Goodea atripinnis* (Jordan, 1880), small waters of the Rio Grande de Santiago, length 50 mm (2 inches); *Allodontichthys zonistius* (Hubbs, 1932), coastal area of Colima, length 50 mm (2 inches); *Neophorus diazi* (Meek, 1902), Rio Lerma, Valle de Mexico, length 50 mm (2 inches); *Xenoophorus captivus* (Hubbs, 1924), Rio Panuco near Jesus Maria, 45 mm (1¾ inches); *Zoogeneticus quitzeoenesis* (Bean, 1898), Rio Grande de Santiago near Chapala and Quitzeo, length 50 mm (2 inches).

Sub-family Characodontinae

This sub-family consists of a single genus with only one species, *Characodon lateralis* Günther, 1866. It lives isolated from its relatives in the basin of the Rio Mezquital. Its length is about 60 mm (2⅜ inches).

Sub-family Girardinichthyinae

This sub-family has the most developed trophotaeniae and the smallest yolk sac in the embryonic stage. Some species are: *Balsadichthys whitei* (Meek, 1904), Rio Cuautla, Morelos (Rio Balsas), in pools and rivulets not deeper than 60 cm (23½ inches), length about 50 mm (2 inches); *Girardinichthys innominatus* (Bleeker, 1860), Valle de Mexico, length about 50 mm (2 inches); *Ilyodon furcidens* (Jordan & Gilbert, 1882), Colima, Jalisco, and clear, shallow, flowing water, length about 85 mm (3⅜ inches); *Lermichthys multiradiatus* (Meek, 1904), Lago de Lerma, length about 45 mm (1¾ inches);

Neotoca bilineata (Bean, 1887), for a long time known to aquarists under the name *Skiffia bilineata*, sometimes kept in aquariums with *Goodea atripinnis*, inhabits practically the whole family habitat, length about 60 mm (2⅜ inches); *Skiffia lermae* and *Skiffia variegata* Meek, 1902, from Lago de Patzcuaro, Michoacan, and from Celaya, respectively.

Family Poeciliidae

This family, originally found in Central America and the islands of the West Indies, has migrated northwards into the southern part of North America and southwards as far as Rio La Plata in South America.

The appearance of a few species (*Poecilia* and *Gambusia* spp.) in Europe and Asia is not due to natural distribution. To fight malaria, man has successfully imported these small toothcarps into marshy lands to destroy the larvae of mosquitoes. As this distribution is man-made rather than natural, it shall not be considered further.

As mentioned before, the criterion upon which classification is based is the structure of the copulatory organ of the males, the gonopodium. This and the lack of occipital knobs distinguish members of this family from all other species.

The gonopodium, which develops rather late in the males' life cycle, is mainly made up of the third, fourth and fifth anal fin rays. During the development, the anal fin as well as the anal and genital openings shift forward. Before this occurs, the fishes display no distinguishing characteristics of sex, but during the process of maturation, the appearance of the male fish undergoes a complete change. He becomes more slender, the fins grow out and their coloration becomes more intense until he is markedly different in appearance from the females who are almost colorless. This is a very good example of sexual dimorphism.

Strictly speaking, the biology of reproduction of the Poeciliidae is slightly different from that of the other live-bearing families, Goodeidae and Jenynsiidae. With the aid of the gonopodium, the male sperm is introduced in clusters (spermatophores) into the genital opening of the female. In this family, the gonopodium is not a true elongation of the sperm duct, for the latter opens freely in front of the base of this tubular copulatory organ.

The spermatophores are channelled along, or through, these tubes with the aid of the typically deformed pelvic fins. The process is also helped along by the tiny denticles and hooks at the tip of the gonopodium, which assure solid contact with the female. The gonopodium can be moved freely in all directions, unlike, for instance, the similar organ of the Jenynsiidae.

Should one or more sperm clusters manage to penetrate into the oviduct of the female—not always with her consent and co-operation—then the envelope is dissolved by a substance released automatically from the oviduct. The spermatozoa thus set free are attracted by certain substances secreted by the female, so that they migrate spontaneously into cavities inside the wall of the oviduct, where they are stored until their services are needed.

In the connective-tissue lining of the ovary, an indefinite number of eggs are fertilized by the stored sperm. The eggs develop in place, much like the spawn of egg-laying species, which develop amid plants or in the upper layers of mud on the bottom. They are provided only with the oxygen they require. Thus, in the maternal body, the embryos are not nourished by the mother, but simply consume the contents of the yolk sac. Shortly before birth, mature eggs shift to the far end of the oviduct, where they hatch. At short intervals, they then emerge from the mother's body, head or tail first. The egg-shells follow the same route, provided that they have not yet been resorbed. Under certain conditions of temperature, water composition, and so on, the young fish may be born while still in the egg capsule. Generally, however, they discard the envelope immediately.

In the case of several species, the "stored" sperm remains viable for a considerable time, so that the female can give birth to several "litters" without having to go through the mating process again.

CLASSIFICATION AND SURVEY OF SUB-FAMILIES

The following system has, with a few modifications, been adopted from Hubbs (1924), who completed and, where necessary, adjusted the survey of Regan (1913). Although the groups can be distinguished by other criteria, this system is based primarily on the structure of the gonopodium.

The family is divided into five sub-families, which will be discussed individually, for they all concern the aquarist.

Though the families differ widely in size, each belongs to a natural unit. It must therefore be assumed that they developed separately from a common stem. There seem to be no links connecting the sub-families. Usually a sixth sub-family—the Tomeurinae—is added. These, however, are not viviparous, but are egg-layers and should be classified as belonging to the super-family Cyprinodontoidea. Possibly, they are the descendants of certain highly developed egg-layers, for fertilization occurs within the maternal body, as with the Poecilioidea, with the aid of a bizarre, long gonopodium.

1. Underside of caudal peduncle rounded
    A. Gonopodium rays are level; they form no tube or gutter
        a. Jaws firmly connected (except in *Girardinus*); pelvic fins similar in both sexes . . . sub-family Gambusiinae
        b. Pelvic fins of the males are larger and deformed . . . sub-family Poeciliinae
    B. Rays of gonopodium form a small tube on the right side.
        a. Cycloid scales; pectoral fins normal . . . sub-family Poeciliopsinae
        b. Ctenoid (rough-edged) scales; right pectoral fin, of male, with grasper . . . sub-family Xenodexiinae
2. Underside of caudal peduncle keel-shaped, sharp; short gonopodium with the tip enclosed in a prepuce-like bladder . . . sub-family Alfarinae

Sub-family Gambusiinae

This sub-family, in particular the tribe Heterandriini, is considered to be ancestral to the remainder of live-bearing toothcarps. In many respects, it is an interesting group. For years, aquarists have been fond of various species as ornamental fish. Moreover, some species are valuable as destroyers of mosquito larvae, and, for combating disease, have been successfully introduced into infested marshland. The five tribes recognized are: Heterandriini, Quintanini, Gambusiini, Girardiniini, and Cnesterodontini.

Tribe Heterandriini

As shown on the map in Illus. II–188, these fishes are native to the southeast portion of North America (the Carolinas and Florida) and to Central America down to the northwestern part of South America (Colombia and Ecuador). They are not present, however, in the Caribbean islands.

They are found in low coastal areas (the Canal Zone) in marshes, pools, etc., and in higher altitude waters up to elevations of about 1,200 m (about 4,000 feet). Temperature ranges from 14 to 26 °C (57–79 °F) throughout the year. In shallow, stagnant pools, however, the temperature may rise to as high as 30 °C (86 °F) during the day.

With the exception, perhaps, of *Pseudoxiphophorus*, all Heterandriini are tiny fishes, very well suited for the aquarium. There are a great many varieties within a given species, due undoubtedly to local ecological conditions in the various kinds of water in which they live fairly isolated lives. The small size of these viviparous fishes enables them

Illus. II-188. Habitat of the Heterandriini.

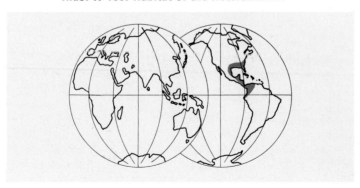

to escape all kinds of difficulties and so assures the survival of species and tribe. Cross-breeding does not seem to occur in the wild, partly because each species population inhabits its own rather isolated niche. Even where they co-exist with other species, they seem to prefer mating with their own kind. Cross-breeding in the aquarium can succeed only under very special conditions and is, therefore, rare.

Genus *Heterandria*

This genus is closely related to *Gambusia* and *Priapichthys*. Only a single species is known.

Heterandria formosa Agassiz, 1853
Dwarf Live-Bearer
Mosquito Fish

Native to North America, from North Carolina to Florida, *Heterandria formosa* is found in swift flowing rivers and stagnant pools, in lowland rivulets, brooklets, pools, field drains and marshes. Since 1914, when it was introduced to Europe, it has been regularly bred in aquariums and is still a popular fish for lovers of small-sized species.

This live-bearing toothcarp is one of the smallest vertebrates. Males have a total length of about 18 mm (¾ inch), and females 35 mm (1⅜ inches), again, a pronounced sexual dimorphism. The body is elongated with the tail slightly compressed. In relation to the body, the

Plate II-237. *Heterandria formosa.*

head is rather small, with big eyes. The dorsal fin is located rather far to the rear, more so with females than with mature males. The caudal fin is well developed and rounded; the anal fin of females is slightly larger than the dorsal fin, and the first rays are elongated, so that it appears pointed. The pelvic fins are small and pointed; the pectoral fins large and rounded. The anal fin of the male grows into a very long gonopodium (about half the total body length), situated rather forward, under the pectoral fins, together with the well developed and somewhat deformed pelvic fins. There are 28 to 30 scales in the lateral line. The general coloration is gold-brown to ochre-gold. The back is darker than the belly, which is almost a light, golden yellow. A fairly broad, irregular black-brown band runs from the eye to the caudal root, with 6 to 10 intersecting, vertical stripes of the same tone. In young fish, the vertical stripes are more conspicuous than the horizontal one, but in the mature males, these cross bars fade away and are replaced by the broad lateral band.

The fins are golden yellow with dark fin rays. At the base of the dorsal fin and of the anal fin there is a dark, brown-black spot, trimmed along the outer edge with an orange-red and red-brown border.

Though the coloration is not spectacular, the fish is a most attractive one and its easy association with other fishes makes it an asset to the community aquarium.

Although it is counted among the real tropical fish, *Heterandria formosa* is actually more at home in sub-tropical regions. Therefore, the ideal temperature in the home aquarium should be 20–25 °C (68–77 °F). The limits of temperature are 15 °C (59 °F) at the coldest to 26 °C (79 °F) at the warmest. The aquarium should be placed in sunlight, with the water not too deep, a thick vegetation of thin-leaved species, and the bottom covered with a layer of peat. Under such conditions, a great deal of pleasure is created by these little pets.

Heterandria formosa is less prolific than its close relatives; still, in one mating season, a female can produce some 40 or more offspring from a single fertilization. The young are born one to three at a time at temperatures between 16 and 22 °C (61–72 °F), at intervals of 20 to 30 hours. Immediately after birth, the fry are as active as the young of the Guppy. Although they are tiny, they are quite capable of defending themselves when the need arises, which is amusing to watch. Several males in a tank constantly engage in a sham fight, spreading out all their fins to impress the adversary. This is an entertaining fish to own. It feeds on anything at all suitable to be consumed.

Genus *Pseudoxiphophorus*

This genus is closely related to *Heterandria* and *Priapichthys*. Here, also, only a single species is known.

Pseudoxiphophorus bimaculatus Heckel, 1848
False Swordtail
Pseudo-Swordtail

This fish is native to the region extending from Central Mexico to Honduras. The four sub-species inhabit zones of the higher mountain rivers in eastern Mexico, down to lower-lying, somewhat warmer waters near Veracruz, Mexico, to Tehuantepec, Guatemala and Honduras. It is a very pretty toothcarp, remindful of *Xiphophorus helleri*—hence the name—yet with substantial differences.

The body is long and laterally compressed. Four sub-species—which merge into each other—can be distinguished. The prettiest one, which has been regularly in the trade since 1909, is the sub-species *Pseudoxiphophorus bimaculatus taeniatus*, to be discussed here.

The dorsal fin is well developed and rounded, with a rather long base. It begins about half way between the snout and caudal root. The anal fin of females begins under the fifth ray of the dorsal fin; the gonopodium begins in front of the dorsal fin.

The general coloration of *P. bimaculatus taeniatus* is olive green, the back dark green to brownish green, the belly silvery. The conspicuous reticular aspect (network pattern) is due to the dark, almost black edges of the scales. The scales have a metallic green sheen, while a gleam of blue-green characterizes the gill covers and the abdomen in front of the ventral fins. There is a striking, orange-red spot on the gill cover. The dorsal fin of the male is greenish yellow with red-brown membrane, dotted with rows of fine, dark spots; the edge is brown-black. Behind the gill cover and on the caudal root there is a dark, blackish brown spot, hence the specific name *bimaculatus*—meaning two-spot. In larger specimens, these two spots, the first one in particular, may vanish, leaving only an irregular dark stripe between the first and the second spot, caused by the melting together of the dark scale-rims.

The caudal fin is without coloration to light bluish. In bigger fine specimens, the clear, red spot in front sometimes runs through to the base of the tail. The edge is somewhat darker, sometimes bluish, and the undermost rays are lengthened a little, looking like a primordial "sword," as is seen fully-developed in the genus *Xiphophorus*. The pectoral and ventral fins are without coloration to light blue.

The females are more modestly tinted—the anal fin is yellowish to orange; the gestation spot is clearly visible. They attain a size of about 85 mm (3⅜ inches), while the males rarely grow longer than 45 mm (1¾ inches). There is thus a noticeable sexual dimorphism. The young bear the typical, vertical stripes of all Heterandriini, more marked near the head than on the tail. The two large spots persist for a long time. Remarkable are the relatively large dorsal and anal fins in proportion to the body of the young.

Genus *Priapella*

In addition to the well known species *Priapella bonita*, a second species has been introduced, *Priapella intermedia*.

Priapella bonita (Meek, 1904)

The home of *Priapella bonita* is in Mexico, in the tributaries of the Rio Papaloapan, up to considerable altitudes. This small fish can live in any water, as long as it is a few centimetres (about one inch) deep.

The body is built much like that of *Heterandria formosa*, which it closely resembles. Females can attain a length of 70 mm (2¾ inches); males about 35 mm (1⅜ inches).

The dorsal fin begins a little beyond the half-way point between the mouth and the caudal root. Dorsal and caudal fins are rounded; anal, pectoral and ventral fins have somewhat lengthened anterior rays. The anal fin of the males is shifted forward and is grown into a fairly long gonopodium that is markedly different from that of other Heterandriini. The anal fin of females begins slightly in front of the dorsal fin and, just above the first rays, the gestation spot can be seen. The mouth is terminal, directed strongly upwards; the mouth-opening is rather large. The jaws are set with small, conical teeth.

The general coloration of *Priapella bonita* is grey-green, the fins yellowish to olive-yellow. The back is green-brown, shaded very dark or dotted with dark spots. The ventral part is lighter, to yellow-grey. In the proper light, the flanks reflect a lovely, sea-green gloss.

The handsome but fairly simple coloration is enlivened by a very thin, dark, brown-black line running from gill cover to tail stem. The scale edges, especially on the flanks, are sometimes quite dark, giving a pretty, reticular (net-like) pattern.

The rays of the dorsal, caudal and anal fins are decorated with dark spots and stripes. In some fine specimens, the outer edge of dorsal and caudal fins has a dark border.

On the whole, the story of *Heterandria formosa* (page 874) holds true for this fish as well. This simple but very attractive fish requires a sunny —though not necessarily large—aquarium with rich vegetation. Animal food along with plants is necessary for sound development. Waterfleas, mosquito larvae, tubifex, white worms, and so forth, are the principal dietary requirements, together with algae, which is usually abundant in sunny aquariums. The temperature should be 20–26 °C (68–79 °F).

The number of offspring during a mating period varies according to the age and size of the female, and may be anywhere between 15 and 40. Parturition seems to be easily accomplished, for the young come out quite fast, one after the other, which is not so with *Heterandria formosa.*

Tribe Quintanini

Only a single species of Quintanini is known. It is closely related to *Gambusia* and probably originated from the same heterandrid ancestral stock.

Genus *Quintana*

Quintana atrizona Hubbs, 1934

Quintana atrizona is found in Cuba—Pinar de Rio Habana and Isla de Pinos. Reports of its occurrence in eastern Cuba (Baracoa) are doubtful, and at any rate, have not been officially confirmed.

The structure of *Quintana's* gonopodium differs from that of the related Gambusiinae to such an extent that no very close relationship between the two can be claimed. If we consider this genus (or tribe) as an entity, then it must be regarded to have evolved from the tribe Heterandriini, from a form from which *Gambusia* (*Gambusia*) also originated, as a certain resemblance with *Gambusia* (*Gambusia*) *affinis affinis* is found in the structure of the fifth gonopodium ray.

The body is elongated, laterally compressed. The male does not attain a length beyond 27 mm ($1\frac{1}{16}$ inches), and the female grows to about 50 mm (2 inches). The mouth is terminal, directed strongly upwards; the lower jaw protrudes slightly. In spite of such a mouth shape, its habitat is in the middle water layers rather than at the surface.

The general coloration of *Quintana atrizona* is a soft, olive-yellow turning to silvery yellow towards the abdomen. The entire body—except for the female abdomen—is finely reticulate. Head and snout are dark, the tail behind the body cavity is diaphanous in a backlight, so that the spinal column is clearly visible.

A more or less accentuated line runs from the gill cover to the caudal root, crossed by three to nine similarly varying, vertical stripes. The dorsal fin is orange to yellow, with a black or dark edge and, especially in the male, with a black root. The anal fin of the female is like the dorsal fin, but somewhat paler. The gonopodium is pigmented black between the rays. The caudal fin is a lemon tone and so are the paired fins, but a little paler, sometimes with a light blue tinge.

Q. atrizona should be kept like its relatives, in a sunny aquarium, with thick, fine-leaved vegetation, and a temperature of 20–25 °C (68–77 °F). In addition to algae (plants or stones overgrown with algae), its preferred food includes tiny, living organisms.

This fish is less prolific than the related species. It seldom produces more than 30 young at a time. The young reach sexual maturity in about four months. Parturition of the relatively tiny young is apparently an easy matter.

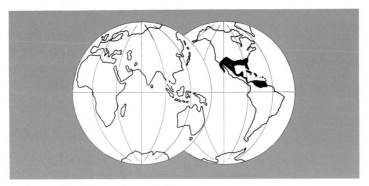

Illus. II-189. Habitat of the Gambusiini.

Tribe Gambusiini

As shown on the map in Illus. II–189, this group is native to the southern tier of North America (from Virginia, the Carolinas, Georgia, and Florida on one side to New Mexico on the other). It also lives in the West Indies and along the east coast of Central America, southward as far as the Panama Canal, where it inhabits fresh water as well as brackish coastal waters.

There are some 22 species in the group, not more than four of which have gained popularity with aquarists. One of them is *Gambusia affinis*, the first known viviparous fish, known since about 1900. It has acquired a reputation for being a help to man in fighting malaria.

The structure of the body and the gonopodium, as well as the geographic distribution, indicate close relationship to the Heterandriini, from which the Gambusiini presumably derive.

Genus *Gambusia*

The genus *Gambusia* is spread over the whole area shown on the map (Illus. II–189). Twenty species have been distinguished, but differences from *Gambusia affinis* are slight. In general, all members of the entire genus are, for live-bearing toothcarps, extremely gluttonous.

Hubbs (1926, pp. 21–26) divides the genus *Gambusia* into four subgenera, each of which includes a number of species, as follows:

• *Gambusia* (*Heterophallina*) *vittata, G.* (*H.*) *regani,* and *G.* (*H.*) *panuco;*
• *Gambusia* (*Gambusia*) *senilis, G.* (*G.*) *nobilis, G.* (*G.*) *affinis, G.* (*G.*) *nicaraguensis, G.* (*G.*) *melapleura, G.* (*G.*) *punctata, G.* (*G.*) *caymanensis, G.* (*G.*) *wrayi, G.* (*G.*) *gracilior, G.* (*G.*) *dominicensis, G.* (*G.*) *oligosticta,* and *G.* (*G.*) *puncticulata;*
• *Gambusia* (*Arthrophallus*) *patruelis;* and
• *Gambusia* (*Schizophallus*) *holbrooki.*

Gambusia affinis (Baird & Girard, 1854)
Common Mosquito Fish

At least two sub-species of *Gambusia affinis* are distinguished, both of which will be discussed.

The males present a broad variety of spotted design, so that the plain, blank ones are seldom kept in aquariums. In the wild, melanism (the concentration of blackish brown pigment cells in the skin) is a regular feature of the male, so that in every population one or two dark-spotted males can be found. These are preferentially selected by the trade, under the name *Gambusia holbrooki.* Melanism is extremely rare in females, but such specimens have been produced through selective breeding.

The view that *Gambusia affinis* is the blank species and *G. holbrooki* the spotted one does not hold, for there are spotted males in both species, which differ from each other by other criteria.

Gambusia have a well deserved reputation for exterminating mosquito larvae and have been utilized over the entire world for fighting malaria, mostly with success. The temperature range may be 5–38 °C (41–100 °F).

Gambusia affinis affinis (Baird & Girard, 1854)
Common Mosquito Fish

Native to North America, this fish is found in lowland waters from Alabama to southern Illinois and from the coastal areas of Texas as far as Tampico and Mexico.

882

The fish is a lively sort, with a length of about 30 mm ($1\frac{3}{16}$ inches) for males and up to 65 mm ($2\frac{9}{16}$ inches) for females. The general description of the genus applies to it in every respect, but this sub-species has seven ramified rays in the dorsal fin. The third ray of the anal fin of the male (the gonopodium) is not ramified. These features are contrary to those of the second sub-species. Normally, both forms have a greyish tint, with a metallic sheen. Most specimens in the trade are decorated with irregular black spots over the entire body and fins, in both males and females.

Gambusia affinis holbrooki (Girard, 1859)
Holbrook's Mosquito Fish

This fish is native to the lowland waters from the coast of Delaware down to Florida and Alabama. It resembles *G. affinis affinis*, except that it has eight ramified dorsal fin rays and a ramified third ray in the gonopodium.

Genus *Belonesox*

The genus *Belonesox* constitutes a single species, with several sub-species, all native to Central America.

Belonesox belizanus Kner, 1860
Pike Live-Bearer
Viviparous Dwarf Pike

Belonesox belizanus is native to the fresh and brackish coastal waters between Veracruz, Mexico, and northern Nicaragua—including British Honduras, Guatemala and Honduras. It has been in the trade since 1909 without, however, attaining any great popularity.

Belonesox is a striking exception among the many live-bearing tooth-carps, as none of the others shows such "pike-like" activity. Some of its relatives are rather rapacious (*Pseudoxiphophorus* and *Gambusia* spp.) but they are contented with spawn and young fry, generally. *Belonesox*, however, would attack any mature, small fish, so that in the wild it seems to take up the rôle of its northern "godfather," the pike, which is also true of *Aplocheilus* in the Indonesian Archipelago and *Epiplatys* in Africa. A likeness is demonstrated even in the elongated body that is compressed only near the tail end, the long head with the beak-like jaws set with sharp teeth, the large, mobile eyes, and the arrangement of the fins. One of the giants among the live-bearing toothcarps, males of this species attain a length of about 100 mm (4 inches), while the females grow to about 175 mm (about 7 inches). Even longer specimens are found in the wild.

The general coloration of *Belonesox belizanus* is olive green to grey-brown, with a dark, spotted design, varying according to the geographic location. At the base of the tail, the males have a clearly outlined, ocellar spot, which is somewhat less distinct in the females. The coloration is not what would be called attractive. The fins are transparent, almost without coloration, slightly yellowish, with a narrow, dark edge. Sometimes, depending on the origin and other circumstances, a pale pink shade can be observed.

A large, long aquarium and a regular supply of live food fish promote the welfare of this fish. The best food for the fully grown fish is all kinds of small fishes, up to about 50 mm (2 inches) long. If necessary, dead animal food may be served (meat, mussels), though the fish may be reluctant to accept it. Normal aquarium food (mosquito larvae, tubifex, etc.) is consumed only by the young specimens. In its native surroundings, this fish is used to stagnant fresh water and brackish

Illus. II-190. *Belonesox belizanus.*

water, so the water in the aquarium need not be too fresh. Keep the temperature between 20 and 30 °C (68–86 °F).

If a couple is made to feel comfortable, the aquarist is likely to be surprised at regular intervals with a good number of offspring. If the vegetation in the tank is right, including floating plants, there is little risk of the young being devoured by their parents. Mature females are capable of bearing as many as 100 offspring per mating season. The young are by no means helpless and they grow up fast.

By preference, mature fish live a solitary existence—like the pike— amidst thick vegetation. If a school of small fish chances to swim by, they rush out of hiding and gobble their bellies full.

The young live together in schools, feeding on fry, insects, and other, similar prey.

Genus *Heterophallus*

According to its body build and the structure of its gonopodium, this genus must be regarded as the most primitive and least specialized of the group. It shares many features with the Heterandriini and the Girardinini (*Glaridichthys*). Within the group, it is closely related to *Gambusia panuco, G. regani* and *G. vittata*, and, to some extent, also to typical *Belonesox belizanus.*

Tribe Girardiniini

This small group comprises the genera *Toxus*, *Glaridichthys*, and *Girardinus*, only the last of which is known to aquarists.

Genus *Girardinus*

A single species is known to ichthyologists as well as to aquarists.

Girardinus metallicus (Poey, 1855)
Metallic Live-Bearer

Native to Cuba, *Girardinus metallicus* was first introduced into Europe in 1863. The body is laterally compressed, the head slightly flattened. The snout is broad and rather short, with the gape directed upwards. Males attain a length of about 50 mm (2 inches), females up to 80 mm (3½ inches). This is the sole representative of the genus discovered to date, and is distinguished from other genera by a two-pronged gonopodium which is comparatively long.

The general coloration is olive green to yellowish grey, with an exquisite metallic sheen. The back is dark brownish, the abdomen whitish. Along the flanks are a number of sickle-shaped silver stripes or bands against a dark ground. Both sexes have a black dot or spot on the dorsal fin, at the base of the last rays.

Although this fish is less well known among breeders than some other live-bearers, it is a desirable fish to keep, for its sociable nature recommends it for the community aquarium. It may be kept with smaller fry without risk. The temperature should range between 20 and 26 °C (68–79 °F), with exposure to sunlight, and a diet of mixed vegetable and animal food.

Reproduction is the same as with other live-bearers. Although this fish is far less prolific than the guppy, about 50 offspring can be expected in a single mating season. The young mature fast and are sexually ripe within three months.

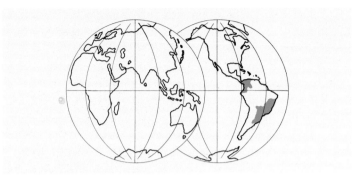

Illus. II-191. Remarkable distribution, on both sides of the Amazon Basin, of the Cnesterodontini.

Tribe Cnesterodontini

This group has a rather peculiar distribution, as the map in Illus. II–191 shows.

Belonging to the group are the genera *Darienichthys, Diphyacantha, Cnesterodon, Phalloceros* and *Phallotorynus*. Of these, only *Phalloceros* is more or less well known to aquarists. The others might be an asset to the aquarium if they were made available.

Genus *Phalloceros*

From this genus, only a single species has been described.

Phalloceros caudimaculatus (Hensel, 1868)

Phalloceros caudimaculatus comes from South America, from Brazil to Argentina, from Rio de Janeiro to the La Plata, in coastal regions, and in mountain creeks where the minimum temperature ranges to about 5 °C (41 °F).

Illus. II-192. *Phalloceros caudimaculatus reticulatus.*

The first specimens were imported into Europe in 1938 as the first available forms of live-bearing toothcarps for the aquarium, and they have been made available from time to time ever since. The first spotted variety was imported in 1905 from the area of Rio de Janeiro.

The body is long and moderately compressed, mostly towards the tail. The head is rather pointed and flattened; the mouth is terminal, directed upwards, and cannot be folded outward very much. The lower jaw protrudes. The upper and lower jaws are each set with two rows of small teeth. The length of the male runs to about 37 mm ($1\frac{1}{2}$ inches), and the female to about 60 mm ($2\frac{1}{2}$ inches). The dorsal fin begins about half way between the rim of the gill cover and the base of the tail. The caudal fin is large and rounded; the caudal peduncle—especially in males—is comparatively high. The anal fin of the female is located entirely forward of the dorsal fin. In the male, the gonopodium is shifted against the pelvic fins. All fins in both sexes are rounded.

The general coloration of the main population is a brownish grey with a darker back and yellowish to red-brown on the belly. The top of the head is very dark, the flanks have a silvery, yellow shimmer, altogether variable as the direction of the light changes. A more or less distinct black band runs from the gill covers to the caudal stem, often visible only behind the pectoral fins. At the level of the dorsal fin, there is a lens-shaped, dark or black spot crossing it. This spot is generally rimmed with golden yellow. Young fish show several of these spots, mostly at the tail end. The dorsal, caudal, and anal fins are tinted yellow to light red-brown, sometimes without coloration, like the paired fins. The dorsal fin, particularly in males, has a conspicuous black edge.

The spotted variety, *P. c. reticulatus* Köhler, 1905, shown in Illus. II–192, came from Rio de Janeiro.

Another variety caught near Santos (Brazil), and Entre Rios, Raiz da Serra, and Mogy Guassu (Argentina), *P. c. immaculatus* Hykes, 1938, has none of the distinct, lens-shaped spots, but has instead a number of faintly outlined, vertical stripes, or none at all. A random yellowish variety, the so-called Golden Gambusia, known as var. *aurata* Stoye, 1935, was bred under certain circumstances in an aquarium and should not be mistaken for the golden *Gambusia nobilis*.

Sub-family Poeciliinae

The tribes Pamphoriini, Xiphophorini, and Poeciliini are classed in the sub-family. Of these, only the last two concern us.

Tribe Xiphophorini
Genus *Xiphophorus*

For the time being, seven species are known, three of which are familiar to aquarists. These are: *Xiphophorus (Platypoecilus) couchianus*, *X. (P.) maculatus*, *X. (P.) variatus*, *X. (P.) xiphidium; Xiphophorus (Xiphophorus) helleri*, *X. (X.) montezumae* and *X. (X.) pygmaeus*.

Xiphophorus (Xiphophorus) helleri Heckel, 1848
Green Swordtail
Mexican Swordtail

This fish inhabits Central America—the rivers emptying into the Gulf of Mexico, southern Mexico to Guatemala and British Honduras. It was first imported into Europe via Hamburg for collectors. It has been a popular aquarium fish ever since.

The shape of *Xiphophorus (Xiphophorus) helleri* is very much like that of its close relatives of the sub-genus *Platypoecilus*, with the body more elongated. The fish is so well known that with Plate II–202 further comment seems superfluous.

To describe the coloration of the Green Swordtail is extremely difficult, for a pure variety can hardly be found any more. Plate II–202 shows its most common form, which most closely resembles the original, imported variety.

VARIATIONS AND SUB-SPECIES

A variety of *X. helleri*—or possibly a good sub-species of it—is known as var. *rachovi (Xiphophorus helleri rachovi* Regan). It has a crescent-shaped spot or two dots on the body of the tail. For the rest, it is in every way like the Green Swordtail in Plate II–238.

Xiphophorus jalapae Meek (*X. helleri jalapae*) must be regarded as a geographic sub-species. It is less markedly vivid, paler, with two rows of red dots at the base of the dorsal fin and a black line along the mouth opening. It has several varieties.

Xiphophorus helleri strigatus Regan, known as *X. h.* var. *strigatus*, has three or four red, zigzag lines instead of just one or two, and a variable number of dark, vertical bands.

To decide whether one is dealing with a true species, with a sub-species, or with varieties or natural hybrids, would require extensive

889

investigation. This species varies more or less also in the wild as a result of isolation, environment, and other circumstances.

Because of the close relationship of the sub-genera X. (*Xiphophorus*) and X. (*Platypoecilus*), cross-breeding was successfully achieved. Countless hybrids resulted, some of which were surprisingly good, but most of them were sadly disappointing.

Whether or not the aquarist has misgivings about cross-breeding, there is no denying that, some 35 years ago, the Red Swordtail which resulted became a well known and much liked variety. Undoubtedly, it is at least as graceful as the Green Swordtail, and breeders find the fierce red pleasing to the eye.

The Red Swordtail is a cross between a red X. *maculatus* (male or female) and the opposite sex of the green X. *helleri*. It is noteworthy that the X. (*Xiphophorus*) shape is dominant over that of the X. (*Platypoecilus*), so that all male offspring have the elongated swordtail shape. On the other hand, the coloration of X. (*Platypoecilus*) prevails over that of X. (*Xiphophorus*). Albino hybrids are very much in vogue.

For geneticists, X. (*Xiphophorus*) *helleri* and X. (*Platypoecilus*) *maculatus* hybrids are readily available and are desirable objects for study.

The well known "Black" Swordtail is a cross between X. *helleri* and the "Mirror Platy" (a variety of X. *maculatus*), which is bred in countless varieties, depending on the variability of the parent fishes.

Not only are coloration and spot patterns varied, but also the length of the caudal lobe, the sword of the males. The so-called "montezuma" hybrids are very popular and known by all kinds of names to aquarists. They should not be confused with *Xiphophorus montezumae*, a true species.

PIGMENTATION AND CANCER

A pigmentation often observed with hybrids, which gives rise to cancerous tissue (similar to melanoma in man), has been the object of diverse studies. The American geneticist Gordon discovered two types of black pigment cells in X. (*Platypoecilus*), a small one underlying the general grey tints, and a large one causing the intense black pattern.

These large, black pigment cells, if inherited by cross-fertilization, cause uninhibited growth in the swordtail, very much like cancerous tumors. The disease is well known to breeders. It occurs in the fins (appearing mostly as over-pigmentation) of, for instance, the so-called

Plate II-238. *Xiphophorus (Xiphophorus) helleri*, green variety.

Berlin or Hamburg hybrids, as well as in the cells of the tail and body. Sometimes the growths on the fins can be simply clipped off and the fins will continue to grow normally.

It is interesting to note that Heckel gives this fish the name *Xiphophorus* (the name literally means "sword-bearer") because of the sword-shaped gonopodium and not for the sword-shaped lengthening of the lower lobe of the caudal fin, as it is usually interpreted. Apparently, it was the first time Heckel had observed this peculiar organ of the live-bearing toothcarps.

Plate II-239. *Xiphophorus (Xiphophorus) helleri*, red variety (dominant cross-breed with a red *Platypoecilus*).

Plate II-240. *Xiphophorus maculatus.*

Xiphophorus (Platypoecilus) maculatus (Günther, 1866)

This fish is native to Mexico, where it populates the pools and creeks of tropical jungles near the states of Veracruz and Oaxaca. As many as 150 different designs can be observed in the species. Comparatively few of them have been tagged with popular names, such as the Moon Platy (bearing a crescent-shaped, black spot on the stem of the tail), the One-Spot and Two-Spot Platy (with one or two black dots on the caudal root), the Comet Platy (with a black band running along upper and lower edges of the tail fin), from which descended the popular Wagtail (with black rays in the dorsal, anal, caudal, and ventral fins), which, in turn, brought forth the Black-Bottom Wagtail (fins completely black, with sometimes even the entire caudal portion pigmented intense black).

All these hybrids, some of which are illustrated, should be kept like their relatives. They are pretty fish that would ornament any show aquarium.

Plate II-241. *Xiphophorus (Platypoecilus) maculatus,* cross-breed.

Plate II-242. *Xiphophorus (Platypoecilus) maculatus,* Mirror Platy with black fin rays.

Xiphophorus (Xiphophorus) pygmaeus Hubbs & Gordon, 1943
Pygmy Swordtail

As can be seen from the sketch of the biotope in Illus. II–193, this fish resides among coastal vegetation, just below the surface of rivers but not in the depths of the current. It is thus related to varieties occurring in pools in flood areas, isolated and rarely venturing into the open current. Through genetic development, a dwarf variety was produced. As *Xiphophorus* and *Platypoecilus* hybrids are sometimes also dwarfs, and as they share many of the characteristic traits of *X.* (*X.*) *pygmaeus*, it may be wondered whether the two are related. An important feature that can be seen at once is that *X.* (*X.*) *pygmaeus* usually has 10 dorsal fin rays as compared to 11 to 15 in other varieties. Another typical trait is the very short sword. This, however, can also be found in the larger species. It would be interesting if amateurs could investigate, through selective breeding, whether or not a *X.* (*X.*) *pygmaeus* genome was active in the natural or experimental hybrids, which might account for the introduction of the species in an unorthodox manner.

The natural specimens attain lengths up to about 45 mm (about 1¾ inches). The general coloration is golden yellow with metallic blue. A deep black stripe runs from the lower jaw through the eye, as far as the base of the tail. There are two less distinct black lines on the upper half of the flanks, and a black band on the underside of the tail, beginning at the last ray of the anal fin (or gonopodium in the male). The dorsal and caudal fins of the male are edged in black and have a black band close to the base of the dorsal fin.

Geographically, the Rio Axtla in Mexico (as described by Gordon, 1954) is of considerable interest. A brief summary of his report will no doubt be of value for keepers of geographic tanks. In this rather small area, *Astyanax mexicanus, Gambusia, Pseudoxiphophorus,* and *Xiphophorus* have their habitat. The report was prepared in the dry season (April, 1932), so that a number of other species that normally keep them company must have departed. In the first pool, in a rocky environment, *X. montezumae* and *X. variatus* (with red tail) were caught. In following years, the same species were found in similar habitats. Gordon then derived the following conclusion:

Xiphophorus occurs only in the lowlands; *X. montezumae* inhabits deeper pools of the shallow flood area of the rivers, and *X. pygmaeus* dwells in the deep part of the open river—up to 2.5 m (8 feet)—among ribbon-like water plants such as *Vallisneria*. Obviously, the three species

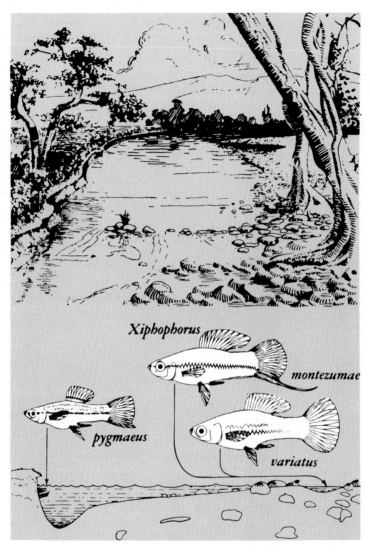

Illus. II-193. Sketch of the biotope (in Rio Axtla, Mexico), indicating the micro-biotopes of three true species of *Xiphophorus*.

are thrown together as a result of weather and floods, but Gordon asserts that this is only a random association which does not last. His investigation of a large body of scientific material did not reveal any hybrids. In the laboratory, however, *X. pygmaeus* crossed readily with all related species.

Plate II-243. *Xiphophorus (Platypoecilus) variatus* Mirror Platy with veil dorsal fin.

Plate II-244. *Xiphophorus (Platypoecilus) variatus,* Berliner hybrid.

Plate II-245. *Xiphophorus (Platypoecilus) maculatus,* original variety.

Xiphophorus (Platypoecilus) variatus (Meek, 1904)

This fish is native to Mexico, to the eastern states along the Rio Grande as far as Tehuantepec, to the tributaries of the Rio Grande, Rio Conchos, Rio Salado, Rio Soto la Marina, Rio Pánuco, Rio Axtla, and Rio Papaloapan. It is sometimes confused with *Xiphophorus maculatus* and its varieties. It was first introduced in 1931.

Males as well as females grow to about 7.5 to 8 cm (3 to $3\frac{1}{4}$ inches). In captivity, however, they do not grow larger than 6.5 cm ($2\frac{9}{16}$ inches), unless the tank is a very large one. The size, therefore, is a safe distinguishing mark from *X. maculatus,* where the females are not larger than about 6 cm ($2\frac{3}{8}$ inches) and the males about 4 cm ($1\frac{9}{16}$ inches). The young males of *X. (P.) variatus* can be recognized early in life by their sex marks. Their anal fin grows deformed and shifts forward. There is a black spot that appears in males in front of the vent, in the place where the gravid spot appears in females. Coloration and design show great variation as is indicated by the name. Variations include blue, red, black or marigold bodies, red or yellow tails, yellow dorsals and various amounts of spotting on the body and fins plus any combination of the above characteristics. This renders

897

the males of the species some of the prettiest aquarium fish among the ovoviviparous toothcarps. The females are plain in both coloration and design, as with the guppy (*Poecilia reticulata*). The general coloration is olive green to grey-brown, with a purple sheen over the back. A zig-zag line runs from the gill cover to the base of the tail.

This attractive fish does best in a show aquarium. The tank should be provided with a dark bottom, and if possible, it should have stones (sandstone), and should be densely planted in part with vegetation of various types. The normal temperature is 20–23 °C (68–73 °F). The fish can stand lower temperatures for short periods very well; even at 15 °C (59 °F), it shows no signs of discomfort. Nevertheless, it must not be kept permanently at so low a temperature.

In the wild, it lives in shallow pools left behind by floods, where the water is anything but clear. Rather, it is muddy and dark, teeming with frog tadpoles. *Xiphophorus montezumae* keeps company here with *X. variatus* and both eat their bellies full of gnat larvae and tadpoles. In these pools, day-time and night-time temperatures vary over a wide range. In the daylight hours, tropical sunlight penetrates directly to the surface of the pool. The fish produces young in the pools, but these, for the most part, are doomed to an early death, for the pools eventually dry up. The main body of this species, therefore, is found, after the onset of the dry season, in the withdrawing rivers.

Strangely enough, the largest specimens are not found in rivers, as might be expected, but in the pools. In the confinement of the aquarium, this species remains small. The reason for this is likely to be found in the quiet life afforded by the pools, where it does not have to exert itself swimming against a current.

Illus. II-194. Skeleton of the gonopodium (deformed anal fin) of *Xiphophorus variatus*. Figures 1-9 stand for, respectively, the anal fin rays from front to back, from which it appears that only rays 3, 4 and 5 take part in formation of the gonopodium.

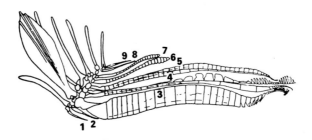

Breeding fine fish requires patient and judicious selection. Lengths of 7–8 cm ($2\frac{3}{4}$–$3\frac{3}{16}$ inches) are hardly known to the amateur breeder, yet that length does not indicate a giant form but the normal, natural size of this fish.

Breeding is simple and the females are very prolific, but not quite so much as the Guppy. The young males develop their coloration only in the following year, if born in the summer, as they do in the wild. If they gain coloration early—within three to five months after birth—they will seldom grow big. In any case, the lively coloration of the father does not fully develop before 7 to 10 months of age. At that time, they are sexually mature and can be used for breeding. In any case, a male that has not yet gained its full coloration should never be taken for breeding.

The fish is a peaceable one, but sometimes the males will fight each other, and some females also have a habit of biting. It is better to isolate these anti-social specimens—at any rate, do not keep them in the company of fishes of the same or smaller size. The breeding temperature ranges from 24 to 28 °C (75–82 °F), or slightly higher for short periods. If parturition is slow, the addition of fresh water at the same temperature as that in the tank usually gets things moving.

What do they feed on? Mainly vegetable food—algae, for example, but all kinds of dried or live food, vegetable or animal, are also welcome. If the aquarium gets sunlight from time to time, some algae will always grow on the rocks.

The variety of coloration and patterns of this fish must be explained by the fact that, in the wild, different races occur. Roughly, one race has males with an olive green general coloration and a dark, lengthwise stripe; another race shows dark brown spots and dots on the olive green to lemon yellow ground coloration. A third form has a yellow-brown coloration mottled with dark brown.

From one male (as the one in Plate II–243) and a normal female, a brood has been obtained in which all the males were exactly alike, except for some slight variation in the pattern. On further breeding, no significant variation was observed through three generations. Apparently, the first female carried the same genetic properties as the male, as a result of which no significant alterations occurred in 214 specimens of offspring in four generations. The only difference was that the males kept growing bigger and visibly more beautiful.

The males attained lengths up to 72 mm ($2\frac{27}{32}$ inches) and the females even more. Obviously, the affair concerned only a single race. Mating

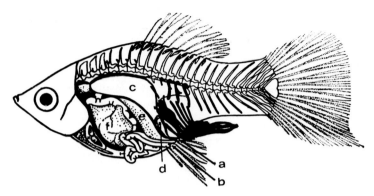

Illus. II-195. Sketch of the live-bearing toothcarp *Xiphophorus xiphidium*, dissected to show the position of the organs. a. sexual opening (urogenital opening) corresponding to the "gonopodium". b. anal opening. c. swim bladder. d. urinary bladder. e. testis. f. liver.

between *X. (P.) variatus* and other *Xiphophorus* species yields perfect fertility. This confirms the assumption that, in spite of many differences, all known varieties should be considered as members of a common species, divided into sub-species, races and varieties. The differences between the sub-species and races are not sharply enough defined to substantiate the current tendency towards classification into many species. In the aquarium as well as in the wild, numerous inbetween varieties occur.

If *X. maculatus* genes are introduced into a *X. (P.) variatus* stem, it will be directly noted that a number of male offspring remain far smaller than the females. This seems to be typical of *X. maculatus*. Obviously, a great deal here remains to be investigated, and we have not yet heard the last of it.

Tribe Poeciliini

To this tribe belong the genera *Poecilia, Micropoecilia, Parapoecilia, Lebistes* (*?*), *Allopoecilia, Molliensia,* and *Limia.* Except for *Parapoecilia* and *Allopoecilia,* all these fishes are well known to aquarists for one or more species. According to most recent views, all genera in this group should be synonymous with *Poecilia.* Since this lumping together of these genera is increasingly more accepted among aquarists (although not by the author), the Guppy, *Lebistes reticulatus,* is called *Poecilia reticulata* here. No other change of name has been made in this book. The controversy is briefly discussed in the Introduction.

Genus *Limia*

Six species have been described: *L. caudofasciata, L. heterandria, L. melanogaster, L. nigrofasciata, L. ornata,* and *L. vittata.* Three of them—discussed below—are well known to breeders. The others have been imported but were later forgotten. It would not be a bad idea to resume importation of *Limia nigrofasciata* and *L. vittata.*

Limia heterandria (Regan, 1913)
Dwarf or Haitian Toothcarp

Regan (1913) erroneously gave the natural habitat of *Limia heterandria* as La Guaira, Venezuela, a point that has been hard to clarify. The species is, however, found only in Hispaniola (Haiti and the Dominican Republic). The first import to Europe dates back to 1908.

The long, slender body is slightly compressed. Females attain lengths up to 45 mm (1⅝ inches), males a maximum of 30 mm (1 3/16 inches). In the male, the dorsal fin begins half way between the mouth and the base of the tail. In the female, it starts a little farther back. The dorsal and caudal fins are rounded. The anal fin of females and the pectoral and pelvic fins of both sexes have slightly elongated fin rays. The anal fin of the male is shifted forward and is grown into a gonopodium. The ventral fins have also been deformed to help out during copulation. The anal fin of the female begins at the same level as the dorsal fin.

The general coloration is yellowish, but in fully grown, fine specimens, it is rather on the orange side. The back is brownish grey and the abdomen yellow. In fine male specimens, the orange shade of the ventral portion does not develop until 7 to 10 months after birth. The dark, lengthwise band is best seen between the dorsal fin and the base of the tail, but in mature males it can be seen running over upon the gill covers. It can be faint in females. Under the dorsal fin, two to four crescent- or lens-shaped dark spots cross the lengthwise band. The fins are yellowish, in the males more vividly tinted than in the females. The latter show a black spot above the base of the dorsal fin, and above the anal fin, a rather small, very dark gestation spot.

The dorsal fin of males is much darker yellow to orange-red, and has two black, horizontal stripes running through the whole fin. Sexual dimorphism is very pronounced. The young take on coloration very early, and all have a very dark dorsal fin. Like most of its relatives, this graceful, lively fish requires a sunny aquarium with dense vegetation and a dark bottom. Temperatures should range between 20 and 28 °C (68—82 °F). Cooler temperature overnight is apparently preferred, but not below 18 °C (64 °F).

Limia heterandria is not a picky eater, but a varied diet is best. A female can produce a brood of 25 to 50 young per mating period, so that the species is very prolific, though less so than the Guppy. The young are obviously not as strong as young Guppies, but can fend for themselves while growing rather slowly.

Limia melanogaster (Günther, 1866)

Limia melanogaster is native to the West Indies, to small creeks in the northeastern region of Jamaica. It was first known to American breeders in 1933 and was introduced into Europe by German breeders in 1935.

The long, stretched-out body is laterally but moderately compressed. The males grow to about 4.5 cm ($1\frac{3}{4}$ inches), the females to about 6 cm ($2\frac{3}{8}$ inches) at the most. The small mouth opens upward. The fins are not large, but are well developed. The dorsal fin begins half way between the gill cover and the base of the tail. The anal fin of the female begins vertically under the dorsal fin; the gonopodium of mature males is located close up to the pelvic fins, which are in line underneath the pectoral fins. The caudal fin is rounded.

The general coloration is dark olive green to brown-green. In the full-grown fish, this is shot with a metallic sheen. Six to eight dark brown to black, vertical stripes bent backwards and edged with silver decorate the flanks. The fins are yellowish. The dorsal and caudal fin of the male are black-edged, and half way down the dorsal fin of both sexes is a sickle-shaped stripe made up of tiny spots. The stripe is broader towards the front side. Mature females bear a conspicuous gravid spot that is unusually large. Mature males show a black, over-flowing spot on the tail section, which runs under the tail as far as the gonopodium.

Illus. II-196. *Limia melanogaster,* **male.**

Limia melanogaster requires warm temperatures and should be kept at 22–24 °C (72–75 °F). In the breeding season, keep it even warmer. Depending on the age and size of the female, broods of 20 to 50 are produced. The young reach sexual maturity at three months. It is, however, not advisable to carry out breeding with these youngsters. The desirable age is five to six months. Meanwhile, it is safer to keep the males and females separated.

Courting is slightly different from the normal pattern pursued by most other Poeciliidae. The male attacks the female suddenly, with lightning speed. She flees to higher levels for safety. She may even jump repeatedly out of the water—a possibility to be considered when setting up the tank so that the females can neither jump clear of the tank nor hurt themselves on the lid. She makes a loud splash on falling back.

For the rest, breeding is the same as with its related species. Feeding this pretty, lively fish is also much the same: a variety of animal food with plant ingredients from time to time is recommended.

Limia nigrofasciata (Regan, 1913)

This fish is native to Haiti. It is well liked, but of late is seldom found in aquariums. A pity, for breeding it is certainly worth the trouble.

Males grow to about 50 mm (2 inches) at most, and females to 60 mm (2⅜ inches). The general coloration is olive green to yellowish brown, and, as the fish grow, the darker tints come gradually to the fore, especially in the fins of the males. The body of mature males also grows deeper and the dorsal fin grows out to an extreme length. It is a beauty that is shown off intensively during courtship. For the rest, see the related species.

903

Genus *Micropoecilia*

A single species of *Micropoecilia* is known, with two sub-species. Three others have been described but are not known to amateurs.

Micropoecilia parae (Eigenmann, 1894)

This species is native to South America—the northern Amazon Basin from the Pará region to the Guianas. Occurrence in Venezuela and Cuba is doubtful. It lives in stagnant water in a very broad, coastal area.

The shape strongly resembles that of the Guppy, a close relative with which it can be easily cross-bred. The offspring form a substantial part of the Guppies with typical designs and fin shapes. The species is far less variable than *Poecilia*; design and fin form, especially, are fairly constant.

The length of females runs to about 30 mm ($1\frac{3}{16}$ inches), of males to about 25 mm (1 inch). The females are relatively much smaller than those of the Guppy. The very large dorsal fin of the male begins half way between the eye and the base of the tail; the small dorsal fin of the female begins much farther back. The caudal fin of both sexes is rounded, that of the males more developed. The base of the anal fin of the female is entirely in front of the dorsal fin; that of the male is shifted forward and deformed into a gonopodium. The mouth is end-positioned, with a small opening directed markedly upward.

The general coloration is light yellow to green. The back is darker, the belly silvery yellow. Above the middle axis of the fish, the scales are edged on the rear side with black, which gives the familiar, reticular pattern. Both sexes show a long, vertical dark spot, edged with a lighter tone between the gill cover and the dorsal fin on the upper half of the body. In front of the vent, where the females show the gravid spot, the males present another black spot, edged with a light tone. Moreover, only the males are decorated with some eight more or less conspicuous, dark, vertical stripes between the gill cover and the base of the tail. A dark spot, often with a light margin, shows up on the caudal stem, and several dark dots and spots appear in the dorsal fin and on the upper half of the caudal fin. The fins are yellowish, the entire body has a purplish shimmer which is seen to best advantage in direct sunlight. The upper lobe of the caudal fin is separated from the lower part by a bright red to red-brown bow-shaped border. The females have no such striking coloration, which is another example of sexual dimorphism.

Keep *Micropoecilia parae* like other small sized, live-bearing toothcarps at temperatures of 20–28 °C (68–82 °F). The brood is rather small, only 10 to 15 young, born at rather long intervals.

There is a very close relationship between this species and *Poecilia reticulata* and *Poecilia vivipara*. Natural hybrids do not occur in the wild—at least, not in large numbers—although they may have given rise to numerous varieties. In the aquarium, cross-breeding is successful (whether you like the idea or not), resulting in a motley hybrid brood lacking the fine characteristics of the original varieties. Perhaps, according to latest notions, it will be found desirable to include this species with the Guppy.

Plate II-246. *Mollienesia sphenops*, male.

Genus *Mollienesia*

Before World War II, numerous varieties of *Mollienesia* were known and kept in home aquariums. Not much has been left, though, for which the fish themselves are mainly responsible. They went on hybridizing with such ease that, in the end, the resulting hodge-podge is hardly worth looking at. Yet, though not all of the hybrids are to be despised, they do, in turn, give us a problem. What are they, actually? The fish generally held to be *Mollienesia velifera* are either *Mollienesia sphenops* or partial crosses between *M. velifera* and either *M. sphenops* or *M. latipinna*.

The group called Sailfin Mollies includes three species—*M. latipinna*, *M. velifera*, and *M. petenensis*. A closely-related variety having normal dorsal fins belongs to a second group, including *M. sphenops*, *M. latipunctata*, and *M. dominicensis*. Another problem with this genus is the inclination its members show to produce what is called melanistic forms—properly called Black Mollies. Black Mollies do not comprise separate species, but were originally produced by selective breeding utilizing black specimens of *M. latipinna* and others which also occur in nature. The name Black Mollie was used in the trade for a medley of hybrids deriving from crosses with the related genera *Poecilia, Gambusia,* and *Poecilistes.* The fish were not always completely black, and in later generations, silvery white patches appeared again.

The male of the real Black Mollie, if a thoroughbred, would always be on the small side, with a small dorsal fin and a full, rounded caudal fin.

In the past 35 years, a great deal has been written about the genus *Mollienesia* and the hybrids deriving from it, so that even a brief summary would take up dozens of pages, out of balance with the rest of the book. Comment, therefore, will be restricted to a few illustrations.

Mollienesia velifera (Regan, 1913)
Giant Sailfin Mollie

Native to Yucatan, Mexico, *Mollienesia velifera* is found in slow-flowing or stagnant waters. In contrast to its relatives, this fish cannot be found in salt or brackish water. Obviously, it is the "king" of the mollies. Little needs to be added to Plate II–247 which shows off all its

Plate II-247. *Mollienesia velifera,* male showing off.

Plate II-248. *Mollienesia velifera,* black variety.

distinguishing marks as compared to *M. latipinna* or *M. sphenops.* The body is markedly compressed in the lateral direction, even more so towards the tail. The females are much rounder in the belly.

The huge dorsal fin to which it owes its name of Sailfin Mollie begins in the male right behind the head and has 16 to 19 rays. The fish can attain a length of 15 cm (6 inches), but the females are usually shorter and fuller around the belly.

A tank of generous size is required for breeding, with dense vegetation, and preferably placed in sunlight. Algae are its essential food, along with all kinds of live or dried animal and vegetable foods. The temperature should be kept at 25–28 °C (77–82 °F). A temperature of 20–22 °C (68–72 °F) is absolutely too low.

908

A fine set of parents can breed as many as 120 young, so that the female can be regarded as one of the most prolific of the family. The young are at once fairly big. They develop fast and make no problems for the aquarist. It takes rather long, however, for the fine dorsal fin of the male to develop to its fullest—usually at least a year. The male's habit of chasing constantly after the females and also after other males is one reason why many aquarists refuse to keep this genus even though the fish never hurt each other.

Through cross-breeding in the aquarium, made easier since the female of the species resembles those of other species, many *M. velifera* hybrids are found that never develop the sailfin. A melanistic form—completely black except for a yellow or red margin to the dorsal fin of the males—is known as the Black Sailfin and should not be confused with the so-called Black Mollie.

Genus *Poecilia*

Poecilia reticulata (Peters, 1860)
(formerly *Lebistes reticulatus*)

Guppy or Millions Fish

Guppies are native to South America—Venezuela, the Guianas, the Amazon country, and the Caribbean islands of Barbados and Trinidad —where they live in stagnant pools or slow-flowing rivers.

The body is elongated, with the tail section compressed laterally. The length of the males reaches a maximum of 35 mm ($1\frac{3}{8}$ inches), of the females, about 60 mm ($2\frac{3}{8}$ inches). It is impossible to describe the males, for they exist in countless variations of coloration and shape. The fins are sometimes rounded, but usually several fin rays are longer than the rest. Plate II–249 is a good example of one of these varieties.

The females have a rather small dorsal fin, but the caudal fin can be fair-sized and rounded. (See Plate II–250.)

The general coloration of both males and females is silver-grey to olive green with a metallic sheen. In addition, the males show an irregular pattern of spots symmetrically on both flanks in various tints

Plate II-249. *Poecilia reticulata*, veil tail, product of breeding; male.

Plate II-250. *Poecilia reticulata,* females.

of green, blue, red, yellow, as well as mixtures of the same tones. Their diversity is so great that even males of the same brood differ from one another to a greater or lesser degree. This fish is happy in any kind of tank, provided there is rich vegetation of fine-leaved plants. It is advisable not to start with a very small tank, as you should keep the future brood in mind. Temperatures of 20–25 °C (68–77 °F) are suitable, but it is advisable to let them winter over at 18–20 °C (64–68 °F). Guppies are not too sensitive to temporarily low temperatures—down to about 10 °C (50 °F)—but the cooling must be gradual. Sudden change in the temperature and temperatures above 28 °C (82 °F) will have an ill effect on the fish.

The Guppy eats anything edible. Along with animal food, plenty of vegetable food must be provided.

As breeding is easy, the process must be carefully controlled to avoid the possibility of degenerative breeding. Like all other viviparous fish, the Guppy is constantly chasing after the females, which does not help growth. It is therefore best to separate the males as soon as their sex can be determined; otherwise the females would bear young too early.

Therefore, at about four weeks of age, put males and females into

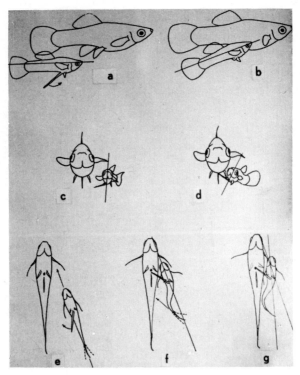

Illus. II-197. Sketches of the different positions assumed by the male Guppy in respect to the female while mating. (Consecutive positions from *a* through *g*.)

separate tanks in order to assure sound growth conditions for both. Male Guppies longer than 25 mm (1 inch) are rarely found. The coloration may be pretty and the design attractive, but they will remain small if they develop coloration ahead of time and reach sexual maturity too soon. The finest specimens should be selected and put aside separately. In about six months, breeding can be undertaken with them.

The Guppy is an ideal aquarium fish. It is small, peaceful and vivid and has a lovely figure. It is easy to breed, is happy in a tank of any size, and is easy to feed and keep comfortable as far as temperature is concerned. From the economic viewpoint, it is useful as a destroyer of malarial mosquitoes (*Anopheles maculipennis*), and has been successfully transplanted into various parts of the world for this purpose. Incidentally, an even greater enemy of the *Anopheles* mosquito larvae is *Gambusia affinis*.

Poecilia vivipara (Bloch, ed. Schneider, 1801)

This toothcarp lives in a very extensive area—all of South America east of Venezuela, and southwards, east of the Andes to the La Plata River.

There is a remarkable difference in size between males and females: 40 and 75 mm respectively ($1\frac{9}{16}$ and 3 inches). The general coloration is greyish yellow; the back is olive brown and the abdomen silver-grey. The stripes on the flanks and the eye-shaped spot are black, and so are the stripes and spots on the dorsal fin. On the whole, there are many varieties, as there are many places of origin. Sometimes there is a red hue on the flanks and on the dorsal and anal fins of the males.

Like the Guppy, it is very prolific.

Illus. II-198. *Poeciliopsis turrubarensis,* male and female.

Sub-family Poeciliopsinae

This sub-family is composed of the old groups Gambusiinae and Poeciliinae. Since 1926, the genera *Poeciliopsis, Poecilistes, Aulophallus, Phallichthys, Phalloptychus* and *Xenophallus,* have been classified under it. Only a few species appear in aquariums, which is regrettable, for they are well above the standards as far as beauty and coloration are concerned. Perhaps this may give a hint to importers.

Poeciliopsinae are native to the area from Arizona to the eastern part of South America (Colombia), including Central America.

Genus *Phallichthys*

Not more than two varieties belong to this genus, *P. amates* and *P. pittieri.* The former is native to Guatemala and Honduras, and the latter to Costa Rica and Panama. It is still doubtful whether they are true species. How would they behave if brought together? It should be kept in mind that differences observed need not necessarily be specific characteristics. Also remember that the problem is not satisfactorily solved by dividing these live-bearing toothcarps into an unlikely number of genera, each having but one or two species. Hubbs gave us a clue for distinguishing the many forms, without, however, tracing their natural relationship.

Illus. II-199. *Phallichthys amates,* **male and female.**

Phallichthys amates (Miller, 1907)
Merry Widow

It appears that Hubbs first thought that the three species names (*P. isthmensis, P. pittieri,* and *P. amates*) actually referred to the same species, and consequently, *amates,* being the oldest, should serve as a type for the species. In 1926, he returned to this subject, describing two species, *P. amates* and *P. pittieri,* with the restriction that the two perhaps do not form separate species.

It is a safer practice to keep the old names, for, without examining a very large series of preserved type specimens, it would be impossible to decide whether the case involved one or two species. The geographic spread suggests that *P. amates* is a series of fish populations with gradual transition between the diverse forms.

P. amates is a most attractive fish, attaining about 50 mm (2 inches) length, the males somewhat less.

Plate II-251. *Gasterosteus,* male.

Order Gasterosteiformes

This order of the so-called sticklebacks is only mentioned here because a number of its species are welcome among aquarists and have been observed in the home aquarium. Parental care makes these fishes particularly interesting.

Order Syngnathiformes

This order includes a number of groups with very strange body structures and adaptations, and with mainly a marine distribution. Evidence of the fresh-water origin of the syngnathid (pipe-shaped) fishes could be found in their present habitat, the mouths of rivers. They live only near the coast and generally do not venture out into the high seas. Some of the species are captured in fresh water, and these are the subjects of this book, which is restricted to fresh-water aquarium fishes.

This order, in which belong the pipefishes and the much better known sea horses, is unique for the peculiar type of parental care.

As a whole (as an older name, Lophobranchii, indicates), the order is characterized by leaf-shaped gills, covered by a single bony opercular plate. The gill opening is simply a small slit. There are no teeth in the mouth, and the snout is tubular with a terminal mouth opening, hence the name *Syngnathus*, referring to the fused jaws' being

Plate II-252. *Microphis boaja* (synonym, *Syngnathus spicifer*).

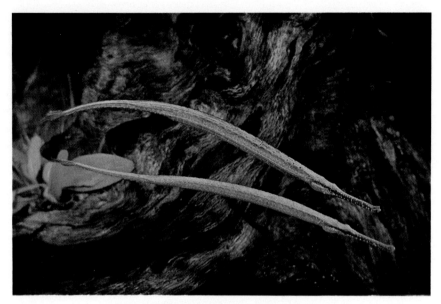

Plate II-253. Pipefish, *Syngnathus acus*.

grown together. The snout is, however, not formed by elongated dentary bones, as was originally thought, but by cranial and orbital bones. The true dental bones are minute and situated at the very end of the tube; they are slightly moveable. What is generally thought to be the mouth is a cylinder or pipe, sometimes trumpet-shaped, which mainly works like a sucking organ. Intake of food is, with real syngnathids, a matter of sucking in the prey, which is only live food, apt for this sucking mouth.

The body is not covered with scales, but with bony plates. There are no ribs or pieces of bone between the muscles; the articular processes of the vertebrae (called PARAPOPHYSES) are considerably elongated and replace ribs in syngnathids. The anterior five or six vertebrae have ankylosed into an immoveable skeletal complex.

The swim bladder, if present, has no open connection with the gut (thus, these fishes are physoclists).

The order Syngnathiformes is divided into two sub-orders, the Aulostomoidei and the Syngnathoidei (or Lophobranchii s.s.), of which the latter is of principal interest to us.

Plate II-254.
Syngnathus pulchellus.

Sub-order Syngnathoidei

The two families belonging in this sub-order are the Solenostomidae, with only a single nostril on either side, and the Syngnathidae, with two nostrils on each side. Again, the latter group is of interest to us.

Family Syngnathidae

This family comprises many genera with numerous species in the tropics and sub-tropics, in brackish and salt-water environments, as well as in fresh and in coastal waters. The bony armour has as many segments as the spinal cord has vertebrae. The fins are weakly developed. The dorsal fin, if one is present, has soft rays only. The pelvic

Illus. II-200. Brood pouch of *Syngnathus acus*, greatly magnified. Note the skin armouring.

fins are entirely lacking and the pectoral fins are located close behind the gill clefts. As recommended by Duncker (1912), this family can best be divided into classes arranged according to the placement of the brood sac in the male. This may be in the ventral region (Gastrophori Duncker=Doryichthyinae Hoedeman, 1956) or in the tail (Urophori Duncker=Syngnathinae).

Sub-family Doryichthyinae

This group includes the genera and species having the brood sac of the male in the ventral region. The genera belonging to the three groups referred to by Berg (1940)—Nerophiini, Gastrotokeini, and Doryichthyini—are all pipefishes with long, slim bodies. The head and body together are longer in proportion than the shorter tail. In other words, the length from snout to dorsal fin is longer than from the dorsal fin to the end of the outstretched tail. Some genera show, in this proportional aspect, a transition towards genera of other sub-families.

Tribe Doryichthyini

In this tribe are classified, among others, those genera with a long snout—*Doryichthys, Microphis,* and *Paramicrophis.*

Imported and more or less successfully kept in the aquarium are: *Doryichthys deokhatoides* (Bleeker, 1853), 18 cm (7 inches), native to Thailand and the Indonesian Archipelago, fresh and brackish coastal waters and river mouths; *Doryichthys lineatus* Kaup, 1856, 20 cm (8 inches), coastal waters from Brazil to Mexico; *Microphis boaja* (Bleeker, 1851), 40 cm (16 inches), coastal waters from South China to the Indonesian Archipelago; *Microphis brachyurus* (Bleeker, 1853) about 20 cm (8 inches), Southern Asia to Japan; *Microphis smithi* Duméril, 1870, to 20 cm (8 inches), in thick vegetation at the mouths of the Niger and Congo Rivers.

The brackish-water varieties can become accustomed to living in water that is almost fresh, though it is recommended that a small quantity of sea salt be added to the water. Among other things, brine shrimp (*Artemia*) and *Asellus* are ideal food for them.

Tribe Nerophiini

To this tribe belongs, among others, the genus *Nerophis*, with the species *Nerophis ophidion* (Linné, 1758), which has a length to about 30 cm (12 inches) and occurs along the European coasts and river mouths of the Mediterranean, and as far north as the Baltic Sea.

Sub-family Syngnathinae

Of this sub-family, only a well known genus with numerous species, *Syngnathus pulchellus* Boulenger, 1915, is suitable for the fresh-water aquarium. Its length is about 15 cm (6 inches) and it is native to fresh and brackish waters of the Congo and Ogowe Rivers.

Plate II-255. *Doryichthys deokhatoides.*

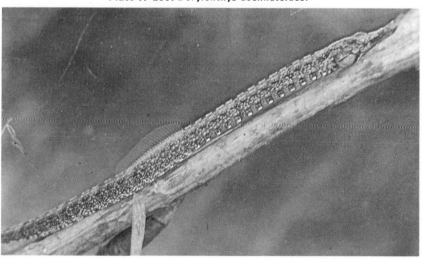

Order Ophicephaliformes

This order of oddly shaped fishes (*Ophicephalus* literally means snake-head) was, up to a short time ago, rather commonly considered to be a member of the order of labyrinth fishes, the Labyrinthici, or else of the sub-order Anabantoidei. Closer investigation made it clear, however, that the auxiliary respiratory organ (the so-called suprabranchial organ) is not in the shape of a labyrinth. It consists of two plates, the first formed by the frontal gill arch (as it is with the labyrinth fishes), and the second an outgrowth of the lower jaw (hyomandibular), which is not found in labyrinth fishes in this form. Although the skeleton corresponds in many ways with that of the perch-like fishes (Perciformes), the skull shows more of a similarity to the Synbranchiformes (a very representative order of eel-like fishes with its gills grown together to form a single gill). Up to now, three genera have been described in this order, which contains but a single family. These are: *Channa* Scopoli, 1777, type species *Channa orientalis;* *Ophicephalus* Bloch, 1793, type species *Ophicephalus punctatus;* and *Parophiocephalus* Senna, 1924, type species *Ophicephalus obscurus*, originally considered a sub-genus of *Ophicephalus*, based on differences of details in the suprabranchial (above the gills) organ.

For the time being, the African *Ophicephalus obscurus* is the only species that is more or less at home as an aquarium fish.

Genus *Ophicephalus*

This genus is distributed throughout tropical Africa and eastern and Southeast Asia. Probably, the African varieties could be classed in the genus *Parophiocephalus*, though it is more suitable for the closely related African varieties to keep the name *Ophicephalus*. In the strictest sense, *Channa* would be the correct name, since it is older than *Ophicephalus* and since it seems scarcely tenable, in fact, to divide the two genera on the single point of presence or absence of ventral fins, the only characteristic difference between *Channa* and *Ophicephalus*.

Ophicephalus obscurus Günther, 1861

These strangely shaped fish, which can attain a length of 350 mm (13¾ inches), inhabit practically all of tropical Africa. The coloration pattern varies somewhat with the locality where it is caught, yet *Ophicephalus obscurus* can be easily distinguished from other species of this genus (60 to 75 scales in length), as they are typified by a certain pattern. Young examples (like many of their relatives) have a practic-

Plate II-256. *Ophicephalus obscurus.*

ally black, lengthwise stripe from head to tail root, with an eye spot (black, edged with whitish yellow) on the lower lobe of the caudal fin. The dark, brownish black and fairly broad band grows more and more marbled as the fish ages, though the lengthwise stripe continues to remain recognizable among the pattern of spots. The band, however, finally does break up into a number of elongated, rounded spots. The edges of the spots are considerably darker (brownish black) than the dirty white to greenish yellow ground coloration. The fins have a somewhat regular pattern of stripes, while the stripes in the dorsal fin (brownish against a yellowish white ground coloration) angle forwards and upwards from the base of the fin. The iris of the eye is reddish brown.

Ophicephalus obscurus is a formidable predator, but a fascinating fish that deserves all the attention that can be given it. The tank should be provided with a cover to keep the fish from jumping out. Although its special auxiliary breathing equipment permits it to live a long time out of water, the middle of a dry, dusty floor is no place for it. Live foods (worms, fish, frogs, and so forth) are a primary dietary requirement, yet it can get used to raw meat.

If more aquarists would undertake to keep this fish, a great deal more information on its living and breeding habits could be made available.

Order Mastacembeliformes

NOTE: Some authorities consider this a sub-order, Mastacembeloidei belonging to the order Perciformes.

This order of so-called spiny eels has as yet been given no definite place in the natural system, nor is it often kept by amateurs, though it certainly deserves to be. Spiny eels are native to southern Asia and Africa, south of the mouths of the Congo River. They appear in fresh inland waters and in some brackish, coastal waters. In the aquarium, they can be kept in fresh water. They prefer muddy water, but quickly accustom themselves to a tank of ample size with a layer of humus (peat moss litter) in the bottom. In many respects, Mastacembeliformes are a great deal like knife fish; they both swim backwards, for example.

Plate II-257. *Mastacembelus armatus.*

924

Plate II-258. *Mastacembelus circumcinctus.*

Plate II-259. *Mastacembelus pancalus.*

Plate II-260. *Mastacembelus erythrotaenia.*

The imported species of Mastacembeliformes are numerous enough to offer a choice for everybody, and no one should be disappointed. These fish are omnivorous, and most of them live on anything and everything edible they happen to find on the bottom. (A number of species, however, will accept only living food.) They are anything but predatory, though the spawn of other fish and the smallest fish larvae are not safe near them. The best known genera are *Macrognathus* and *Mastacembelus.*

Illus. II-201. *Macrognathus aculeatus.*

Order Perciformes

Perciformes is a truly cosmopolitan group of fish found in all waters, rivers, lakes, seas, and oceans. This order of perch-like fishes contains not less than 19 sub-orders with a total of 163 families. Although on the basis of numerous traits these groups must be considered a natural unit, the richness of forms within the order is so huge that a possible variety can hardly be envisaged that is not already represented.

Of the 19 sub-orders, the following four are of interest to us: Percoidei, Anabantoidei, Luciocephaloidei, and Gobioidei. (Although *Luciocephalus pulcher* is an aquarium fish, it will not be discussed here, because it grows quite long and is very voracious.)

Sub-order Percoidei

The 13 super-families of this sub-order include altogether some 58 families. The original family giving rise to the order Mugiliformes is the Centropomidae. Other families from this group, to which some aquarium fishes belong, are the Centrarchidae, Monodactylidae, Toxotidae, Scatophagidae, Nandidae, and Cichlidae.

As a discussion of all of these families would be quite extensive, we shall limit ourselves to a handful of the most important, examining in detail the Cichlidae, a most important and interesting family to aquarists. The families of salt-water fishes will be omitted, with the exception of a few varieties living in both fresh and brackish water.

Family Centropomidae

From this family, only the genus *Chanda* of the sub-family Chandinae will be discussed.

Genus *Chanda*

The species under this genus are very varied in size, and *Chanda lala*, particularly, has conquered the hearts of aquarists. A second species, *Chanda wolffi*, is important from time to time and is about as popular as *Chanda lala*, even though it grows quite a bit larger.

The species *Gymnochanda filamentosa* is closely related to this genus and should be kept like *Chanda lala*. The fin rays of *Gymnochanda filamentosa* are considerably lengthened, hence the species name.

Plate II-261. *Chanda lala.*

Chanda lala Hamilton, 1822
Glassfish
Indian Glassfish
Indian Glass Perch

Asia, the northern part of West Pakistan and Bangladesh are the stamping grounds of this fish. It frequently appears from Calcutta to Burma and is at home in all kinds of water, including rice paddies and creeks, in the coastal plain and even into brackish waters along the coast. The first specimens were introduced into Europe in 1905.

Here again is a fish that has undergone a change of name rather often. The best known synonym to amateurs is *Ambassis lala*. In 1822, in *An Account of the Fishes Found in the River Ganges and its Branches*, Francis Hamilton (Buchanan) described a new genus—*Chanda*—with the type species *Chanda nalua*. Following were descriptions of *Chanda setiver* and of *Chanda ruconius*. Cuvier (1828) assigned *Chanda setiver* to the genus *Gerres*, and *Chanda ruconius* to the genus *Leiognathus* Lacépède, 1902. *Chanda* was classed by Cuvier (1828) under the genus *Ambassis*. However, there seems no reason to reject the genus *Chanda* Hamilton, 1822 (type species *Chanda nalua*), so *Ambassis* is just a synonym for *Chanda*.

In *The Fishes of India, Being a Natural History of the Fishes Known to*

928

Inhabit the Seas and Freshwaters of India, Burma, and Ceylon, Vol. II, 1878, the author Day claimed that *Chanda lala* was only a youthful stage of *Chanda ranga*. This must be contradicted on the grounds that on three separate occasions young have been bred from *Chanda lala* specimens about 45 mm (1$\frac{25}{32}$ inches) long.

It is by no means impossible that extensive comparative investigation should lead to the conclusion that various known species of the *Chanda* genus should more properly be classed as geographic subspecies, strains or varieties of a single species.

The body of *Chanda lala* is strongly compressed sideways and is very high in comparison to its thickness, like a pancake on edge. It is glassily transparent and feels quite fragile. It seldom grows to a length beyond 50 mm (2 inches) in the aquarium. The snout is sharp, with a small, upward-directed mouth. The dorsal fin, like the other fins, is transparent, composed of a spiny part and a soft-rayed part. The spiny part is at the leading edge and is highest; the second spine is the longest, and the following spines quickly fall off in length. The caudal fin is rather deeply incised.

The general coloration is yellowish brown, plainly visible in direct light only. Most of the body is more or less transparent, so that the insides of the fish are clearly visible.

Near the head, the back glistens blue-green, growing lighter towards the tail, resolving into a greenish tint with a reddish purple sheen. The golden yellow iris of the eye has a black margin. Because the body is transparent, it is easy to tell one sex from the other. In the male, the clearly observable swim bladder is pointed on the rear underside, while in the female it is rounded off. The posterior edge of the soft dorsal fin forms a quarter-circle with that of the anal fin. The rear edges of these fins are a bright, light blue. In good, direct light, they show all the hues of the rainbow, and some parts, such as the front part of the skull, the tips of the dorsal fin spines and the first pelvic fin rays, at the base of the fin, are accentuated with black.

This elegant fish is very tolerant and delicate. It should preferably be kept in a community aquarium with smaller fishes, or in a tank by itself. The aquarium should be planted with fine-leaved vegetation, kept in a sunny place, and provided with "stale" water at a temperature of 20–25 °C (68–77 °F). Addition of salt to the water is absolutely unnecessary. *Chanda lala* cannot stand a change in the water composition, so that, when transferring it to another tank, handle it carefully and transfer as much as possible of its accustomed water

Illus. II-202. *Chanda wolffi.*

along with it. It is a quiet fish, preferring to loaf among the vegetation. Recently imported specimens, particularly, are very shy to begin with, though they soon get used to the person caring for them. Although it prefers white worms, it is willing enough to eat other food animals. If necessary, but only then, it can be given dried food, but it does not like it. In any case, it must be animal food. Care must be taken that the diet is richly varied, as monotonous feeding can result in gastric trouble.

A temperature of about 26 °C (79 °F) is required for mating. Following a lively, but not violent, courtship, a few tiny eggs are released in rapid succession. Being sticky, the eggs adhere to the fine leaves of the plants. The females prefer to place the eggs under the roots of floating plants, and on top of *Myriophyllum* or *Najas*. The depth of the water should then be reduced to 10 to 15 cm (4 to 6 inches). The young appear after a day. What to feed the young is a problem, and all breeding attempts usually fail at this stage.

Hoedeman has always been successful at this—that is, he has brought up 10 to 80 young per nest—feeding them cultures (certainly not pure cultures) of *Euglena viridis*, the eye spot protozoan. It is quite possible that it is not the *Euglena* itself that provides the nourishment, but the *Cyclops* nauplii (the larval stage of this microscopic crustacean) which are found among them. However, caution must be shown here, for however plausibly the *Cyclops* nauplii success is explained, it still does not imply that this must be the only proper diet for the young fish. Even after undeniably pioneering work, there is still much to be investigated.

As this fish is easily damaged, a bell jar should be used to catch it. A net should never be used, as the meshes might be contaminated with parasites that would attack this very susceptible fish. Should the fish, after all, become infested, the addition of a little sea salt to the water will sometimes bring good results. In the wild, this fish lives in shallow, fresh and brackish waters.

Illus. II-203. *Elassoma evergladei.*

Family Centrarchidae

This is a very extensive family of unusually small, perch-like fishes, native to North America. The common sun perch (or sunfish) also belongs to this group of cold-water fishes. The little dwarf sun perch of Florida, *Elassoma evergladei*, shares its environment with the tooth-carps *Jordanella floridae, Fundulus chrysotus, Chriopeops goodei, Leptolucania ommata, Heterandria formosa,* and other similar fishes.

A species not often seen in aquariums any more is the Florida pygmy perch, *Elassoma evergladei*, which used to be far more common. It is a very attractive little fish that is easy to keep and has little regard for temperature.

Enneacanthus chaetodon (Baird, 1854)
(formerly known as *Mesogonistius chaetodon*)

Black-Banded Sunfish

A member of the pygmy perch family, this fish is commonly found in North America, particularly in New York, New Jersey, and Maryland, but as far south as South Carolina, in small ponds, slow-flowing streams, lakes, and at the mouths of rivers. Generally not a rare species, *E. chaetodon* is particularly common in some places. Because it is common in the New Jersey area and south, it was, therefore, accessible to nearby exporters so it quickly became known and was among the first imported into Europe. By the end of the 19th century, additional specimens were being repeatedly imported.

The body is strongly compressed laterally and the shape is high, stumpy and perch-like. Ordinarily, neither sex grows longer than

6 cm (2⅜ inches). It is one of the most beautiful, as well as one of the smallest, perch-like fishes suitable for the aquarium.

The dorsal fin consists clearly of two parts, one part spiny and one part soft. The anal fin is shorter than the dorsal fin, but is still rather long in proportion.

The basic coloration of *E. chaetodon* is yellow-brown to glistening silver, turning to grey-brown to black on the back. The belly is lighter in coloration, to whitish. The whole body is covered with dark- and light-tinted irregular spots and dots. Vertically in the flanks run six to eight dark brown to black stripes, the first of which runs across the gold-rimmed eye. The entire body glistens silver-blue in direct light. The dorsal and ventral fins, in the young, are soft red. The pectoral fins are deep black in the young fish, but as the fish ages, the first three rays and the membrane between grow lighter in coloration, and in adult specimens they are a beautiful orange-red.

The sexes can be told apart only at mating time.

As might be supposed from the range of distribution, this lovely fish is proof against low temperatures. In unwarmed home aquariums, as well as in garden aquariums and fish ponds, it is quite at home and is more healthy than in a warmed aquarium. Because North American winters can be generally rather severe while the summers are much warmer, the temperature limits of this fish can be set over a range of about 0–25 °C (32–77 °F). Temperature in the natural habitat differs little from that found in Central Europe, so that, in addition to being a good fish for the home aquarium, *E. chaetodon* is also splendidly suited for European garden aquariums and fish ponds, where it can remain through the winter. In fact, fine, strong brood fish will result if they are brought outdoors in the autumn and allowed to winter over in a fish pond. Kept outside, they can grow to a length of 100 mm (4 inches), but they do not grow to full size in the first year. If a heavy frost is expected, however, it is advisable to bring the fish indoors, but put them into an unheated aquarium. At any rate, it must winter at a temperature below 12° C (54 °F); otherwise, spring will find it run down and worthless. If it is kept in a warmed aquarium, the water must be clear and rich in oxygen. It is very sensitive to strong temperature fluctuations, which may cause it to be covered with fungus within a few hours, and then will soon die. When this fish is transferred from one tank to another, the composition of the aquarium water is quite important, with emphasis on the pH value. The aquarium must always be lushly planted with *Vallisneria* species,

933

Myriophyllum scabratum, M. heterophyllum, M. prismatum, Elodea species, and the like. The bottom should be covered with a layer of sharp river sand at least 5 cm (2 inches) thick. At mating time, the male digs a groove or hole in the sand layer. At a temperature that may vary from 15 to 25 °C (59–77 °F), the female then deposits in the hole a clutch of eggs that looks exactly like sand grains. Brood care is performed as it is by most perch-like fishes—by the male. The young appear in three to seven days and at first are quite helpless. As soon as they begin to move freely about, however, they can be plentifully supplied with dust-fine living and dried food. The parents, too, should be well fed throughout the mating season.

If the tank is large enough, it is not necessary to remove the parents, even though this has often been recommended. Perhaps fewer youngsters will live to grow up than would be the case if the parents were removed, but to leave them in the tank will be better for the survivors. Moreover, it is a splendid sight to see the parents surrounded by a cloud of baby fish swimming about. For the next few weeks, anyway, the parents will not be in any condition to mate again. However, much can be achieved by good feeding. Only fish born in captivity can get used to dried food, yet it can always be noticed that those fed regularly on live food are better looking and more active.

The natural waters *E. chaetodon* inhabits have an acid reaction (a pH value of about 6). As the water in most aquariums comes from natural sources or tap water that is either neutral (pH 7) or slightly alkaline (pH value above 7), this may be the reason why this fish used to be considered a "poor keeper," or highly sensitive to captivity, and was so described in older literature. Indeed, a great deal of the difficulty can be ascribed to the pH of the water. If the transition from acid to neutral or alkaline water is made slowly enough, however, it will be found that the Black-Banded Sunfish is no more susceptible to sickness than any other aquarium fishes.

While it further appears that these little sunfish can breed quite effectively in neutral or alkaline water, they are understandably more at ease in an environment approximating that which was theirs in the wild. They are then noticeably more active and their lovely coloration shines. It must not be thought, of course, that they would waste away in neutral or slightly alkaline water, for they are quite adaptable. Of course, the pH of the water does influence the types of plants and small animals that will live in the water, for they will be different from those which live in water of higher pH value.

Family Nandidae

On the map in Illus. II–204, it appears that this is another family having a peculiar distribution with representatives in the tropics of South America, Africa and Asia (India, Burma, Thailand, the Malay Peninsula and the Indonesian Archipelago). This distribution illustrates the great age of this group. We have already considered fish families having a distribution similar to that of Nandidae. These fishes probably originated in Africa, where this branch diverged from the main stem of the Perciformes some time during the Eocene. From Africa, the first representatives of this family could have found their way in one direction to South America and in the other direction to India. Their distribution in South America must never have differed much from what it is today. The Nandidae were later probably forced out of a large part of Africa by geological or other circumstances, while the fish kept spreading out from India into Asia and later populated the Indonesian Archipelago. The Asiatic representatives can easily be distinguished from other members of this family by the appearance of only three spines in the anal fin.

Therefore, two groups (sub-families) developed, diverging more or less distinctly from the first primitive nandid of the Eocene.

The family Nandidae includes a few species of small, perch-like fish. These are differentiated by a single dorsal fin consisting of two parts, with 12 to 17 spines, and one spine on each of the ventral fins, two pair of nostrils, and a cleft hyoid bone. For further details, see the Classification and Survey of Genera on page 938.

So far, the few members of this family that are known are small

Illus. II-204. Distribution of the family Nandidae.

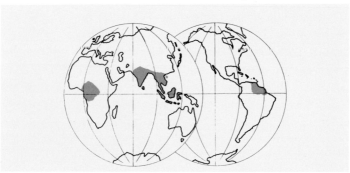

predators which hide among the plants and stones. Generally, they adapt quite well to their environment with a typical form and coloration, for they can change tone suddenly when the need arises. All members can also stand perfectly still in the water, a characteristic which is surely of interest both to the supporters as well as to the opponents of the importance of mimicry. These traits are clearer in these fishes than in many predators which do not hunt their prey but fall upon it as it passes by. This, however, is not observed too much among the aquarium species. *Badis badis*, for example, is considered a very peaceful fish and not predatory, because it seldom chooses the larger fish to prey upon. *Polycentrus schomburgki*, however, as well as its African cousin, *Polycentropsis*, can consume relatively large food, yet are good aquarium companions for fishes that are not too small. The prey must be of such a size that it can be swallowed whole, as Nandidae do not bite or tear off chunks.

As far as breeding is concerned, these are interesting fishes with an unusual form of brood care, which will be taken up with the different genera.

Nandidae are shy, jumpy little fishes that move about more actively as the end of day approaches. According to some authors, they are twilight or nocturnal creatures. However, they do not exhibit this trait in the aquarium, though it depends largely on the environment within the aquarium as well as on the general surroundings of the tank itself. In setting up an aquarium, consideration should be given to the natural environment of the fishes, to make the aquarium environment as much like it as possible. For this, refer to the respective descriptions of the fishes. If the room in which the aquarium is located is quiet and without much movement outside the aquarium panes, then the fishes will not be shy at all but will be moving about the whole day, though less will be seen of them than of barbs or other carp-like fishes. They are not afraid of sunlight, either, as they would be if they were truly nocturnal.

The males like to busy themselves with tidying up the nest, whether it is among plants or stones, and for this they prefer a place that is less brightly lit. Whenever they first appear in the light, they are pitch black, but this soon fades and a suitable coloration appears. The females are usually a little more active, except in the mating season when they leave it up to the males to care for the brood. Any female approaching the nest before it is completely ready is wildly chased away. Later on, when the nest is ready, the females are hospitably

936

Plate II-262. *Nandus nebulosus.*

received. However, when enough eggs have been laid in the nest, the male again chases the female away.

Although Nandidae withstand sudden temperature changes badly, like practically all aquarium fish, they are not considered unusually sensitive provided it is taken into consideration that they are tropical fish.

1. Anal fin with three spines (on exception, four), Asian representatives . . . sub-family Nandinae
   A. Serrated preorbital bone, dorsal fin with 13 to 14 spines and 16 soft rays . . . genus *Pristolepis**
   B. Unserrated preorbital bone, but
      a. Serrated preopercle (front edge of the gill cover), dorsal fin with 12 to 14 spines and 11 to 13 soft fin rays . . . genus *Nandus*
      b. Unserrated preopercle, dorsal fin with 16 to 18 spines and 6 to 10 soft fin rays . . . genus *Badis***
2. Anal fin with more than three spines . . . sub-family Polycentrinae
   A. Dorsal fin with 15 to 17 spines and 9 to 11 soft fin rays, A.IX-XII/8–9*** (Polycentropsini, Africa) . . . genus *Polycentropsis*
   B. Dorsal fin with 16 to 17 spines and 7 to 13 soft fin rays, A.XII-XIV/6-14 (Polycentrini, South America) and
      a. Serrated preopercle, D.XVI-XVII/7-8, A.XIII-XIV/6-8 . . . genus *Polycentrus*
      b. Unserrated preopercle, D.XVI-XVII/12-13, A.XII-XIII/12-14 . . . genus *Monocirrhus*

*NOTE: The genus *Pristolepis* may have preserved most of the primitive characteristics of the family Nandidae.

**NOTE: Recently the genus *Badis* was considered to belong to a distinct family of its own (Badidae), based on behavioral patterns. Its true relationship to the Nandidae is still uncertain.

***NOTE: This is the standard way of formulating fin counts. The Roman numerals refer to bony rays, the Arabic numerals to soft rays. "D" means dorsal, "A" means anal.

Genus *Badis*

Badis badis (Hamilton, 1822)
Blue Perch

Badis badis is rather common in stagnant fresh waters in India. In 1904, the first specimens were brought into Germany and in 1905, the first successful results of breeding were taken into Holland.

In the wild, this lovely little perch grows to a maximum length of 8 cm (3⅛ inches). In the aquarium, however, it seldom grows longer than 5—6 cm (2–2¾ inches), and then is sexually mature. The body is long, low, and squeezed flat sideways. The snout is large and rounded, the mouth opening small, and the underlip projects somewhat forward. As with other perch-like fishes, the dorsal fin is composed of a spiny and a soft-rayed part. The spiny part in front is longer than the soft-rayed part. The much smaller anal fin has only three spiny rays. The soft-rayed parts have longer rays than the spiny parts and are extremely mobile. Pectoral and pelvic fins, as well as the caudal fin, are rounded and well developed. The body is covered with rough-edged scales of moderate size. These overlap each other in regular, oblique rows, and the different tones create an attractive mosaic pattern on the flanks.

Plate II-263. *Badis badis.*

The basic coloration is brownish to greenish blue with beige. The back area is darker to black, the belly is lighter. The coloration varies greatly with environment, temperature and the fish's disposition. From 6 to 12 cross stripes run over the flanks, consisting of an alternating number of black scales, running from bottom to top in the sequence of one scale, then two, then one again, and so on. These vertical stripes run half way through both the dorsal and the anal fin. The soft-rayed part of the dorsal and anal fins, as well as the caudal and ventral fins, may be a lovely blue. Sometimes, however, the tones fade out altogether and, again, the fish will appear almost black, with no other distinguishable coloration or pattern. The pectoral fins are without coloration. A black stripe runs from the snout, through the eye position, and extends as far as the ends of the gill covers, or to the beginning of the dorsal fin.

In the mature fish, the sexes are not difficult to distinguish. It is a difficult judgment to make in the young, however. The males may have a hollow belly—that is, the outline of the belly then curves inwards instead of bulging as in the females.

The Blue Perch is very peaceful and quiet and can, because it is so small, be kept in a community aquarium. Sometimes you can hardly find it in a thickly planted aquarium because it is happily hiding in some hole among the rocks. This pleasure must not be denied it, of course, especially not in the breeding tank, which should be thickly planted and provided with plenty of sheltered nooks. It can stand temperatures from 15 to 30 °C (59–86 °F) without trouble, but it feels most comfortable at 20 °C (68 °F).

Breeding can be undertaken at a temperature of 25–30 °C (77–86 °F) and is a very simple, easy procedure. The tank in which the couple is placed should not be too small—say, 30–40 litres (8–11 gallons) capacity. Almost any type of vegetation will do, as it does not play any particular rôle in the breeding procedure. Broken rocks, stones, and an overturned flower pot provide enough furnishings. A pot about 10 cm (4 inches) across will do, and the bottom hole can be filed or scraped to a larger diameter of 2 to 3 cm (about an inch).

Once the male has discovered a suitable place for breeding, he cleans it up with great care. In the absence of stones or a flower pot, he digs a hole in the sandy bottom, or the eggs may be laid among the plants, but not, however, customarily. When the male has finished his preparatory work, he shows himself off outside the nest in all the grandeur of his darkest hues. This kind of love-making may also be

Plate II-264. *Badis burmanicus.*

observed in other fishes, as well as in other animals. During the love play, the male changes coloration, alternating from very light to pitch black and back again a moment later. The female does not experience such strong, abrupt tone changes. The pair soon disappears into the nest, swimming one behind the other or side by side, and up to 100 or so tiny, sticky eggs are laid on the stones. The performance is repeated three or four times, and each time 20 to 30 eggs are laid, which hatch in 45 to 60 hours. The young fish are quite helpless at first and are in no condition to care for themselves until they are two weeks old.

The main diet for *Badis badis* is Rotifera ("wheel animalcules"), which they consume in great quantities. Both old and young feed exclusively on live food. Aquarists who say that they feed *Badis badis* nothing but dried food delude themselves. It is not the dried food that is eaten, but the infusoria that it produces. The fish grow very slowly or not at all on such a diet. Besides Rotifera and infusoria, *Badis badis* may be fed tubifex, white worms, waterfleas and gnat larvae. In the community aquarium, this fish often goes hungry, as it is rather slow and must be certain of what it is getting before snapping at it. While *Badis badis* is making up its mind, some other fish grabs the food and runs with it.

941

Many breeders remove the parents from the tank in order to get higher results from the breeding. Higher, perhaps, but never better. In a well set-up breeding aquarium with plenty of food, the parents can be left without worry in the tank. If they get really hungry, however, they will eat even the young of live-bearing fishes, which are far less helpless.

A second species regularly imported in recent years is *Badis burmanicus* from Burma, to which the above also applies.

Genus *Polycentrus*

Polycentrus schomburgki Müller and Troschel, 1848

Native to South America, from Venezuela to French Guiana, this fish is also found in Trinidad. It lives in stagnant or slow-flowing waters with humus bottoms, among thick vegetation. It also dwells in ditches between grassy fields, its preferred hangout being under overhanging clumps of grass and in reedy patches along the banks. It was imported into England and bred there in 1907 for the first time.

This nandid has a decidedly perch-like shape to its body—more so than that of the other members of the family. It grows to about 90 mm ($3\frac{9}{16}$ inches) and is then dangerously predatory, attacking not only young fish but adults of smaller species as well, if it gets a chance at them. The big mouth, which can be opened quite wide, enables it to swallow a good-sized prey, the way pike do.

The dorsal fin consists of a spiny part with 15 to 17 spines and an almost invisible (transparent) soft part with 7 to 8 rays. The anal fin is similarly structured and has 13 to 14 spines and 6 to 8 soft rays. The caudal fin is also transparent, which gives the impression that the fish has been chopped off behind the dorsal and anal fins. The very large, outfolding mouth has many rows of teeth in the jaws, pharyngeal bones, and palate.

The ever-varying coloration of this and all other nandids is almost impossible to describe. Except during the mating season, the females are somewhat duller in coloration than the males. At mating time, they can also be recognized, though not easily, by their rounder bellies.

942

The same circumstances that surround this fish in the wild are recommended for the aquarium. It should be provided with a shelter made up of tree roots, dead branches and many dead leaves on the bottom and floating plants on the surface. Though all this is, of course, reproduced in miniature, do not give *Polycentrus schomburgki* too small a tank. It does not have to be deep, but rather long and wide— 90 × 45 × 25 cm (36 × 18 × 10 inches). The temperature should be 20–28 °C (68–82 °F) and the same during the mating period. Low temperatures down to 15 °C (59 °F) can be tolerated temporarily. Mating takes place in a cavity that can be made by piling a few pieces of broken sandstone together. The eggs are deposited against the ceiling of the cavity, and for this the female is obliged to turn over on her back, belly up. The rest of the procedure is as described for *Badis badis*.

The young fish are as greedy as their elders and eat only live food. An ample supply should be provided. A nest of 100 young is a fine result, but up to 500 eggs can be laid.

The following is an entry from the log book of a spawning experiment in a very large, community aquarium (about 600 litres or 160 gallons):

10 December: Eggs deposited on the underside of a large leaf of *Cryptocoryne cordata*.

11 December: The young hang on the underside of the leaf, guarded and fanned by the male parent.

12 December: Clipped off the leaf and transferred it in a bell jar to the nursery tank; the temperature about 25 °C (77 °F), raised in the nursery to 27 °C (81 °F). The young hang from the leaf, their length about 1.7 mm (barely over $\frac{1}{16}$ inch); the mouth and eyes are not yet fully developed. By day's end, a few larvae appear at the surface and on the bottom, occasionally hopping up. A total of 600 eggs was hatched.

13 December: By early afternoon, all the youngsters were swimming and swarming about. Feeding with infusoria begun.

From this nest, about 200 *Polycentrus schomburgki* lived to maturity.

It cannot be confirmed that this is a twilight or night creature, as has often been written. It does, however, prefer a tempered light, which does not encourage plant growth. Only a few floating plants can be suggested, or some marsh varieties of large *Sagittaria* or some species of reed that grows out over the water. A thick bottom cover of thread algae is recommended.

Plate II-265. Mating and egg-laying of *Monocirrhus polyacanthus.*

Polycentrus schomburgki thrives on tadpoles, insect larvae, tubifex and white worms, and tiny crustaceans.

The same applies to the other two more or less well known species of this group, *Monocirrhus polyacanthus* and *Polycentropsis abbreviata*.

Family Monodactylidae

This is an Atlantic-Indo-Pacific family occurring in river mouths. Only one species is of interest to aquarists.

Monodactylus argenteus (Linné, 1758)

Bunga Varu

Mono

Singapore Angelfish

Finger Fish

This fish inhabits waters of the Malaysian-Indonesian-Australian Archipelago, various islands of the Indian Ocean and various points on the Indian Ocean, coasts of Arabia and Africa. It is fairly common in salt, brackish and fresh water.

The body of *Monodactylus argenteus* is flat and practically circular. Its maximum length is about 200 mm (8 inches). Fortunately, it takes a long time for young specimens to grow to 100 mm (4 inches) in the aquarium.

The dorsal and anal fins emerge from long bases, the first fin rays are short and spiny, and the first soft rays are long, diminishing rapidly towards the rear. The caudal fin is rather large, the outer rays somewhat

Plate II-266. *Monodactylus argenteus.*

longer than the middle ones. The jugular ventral fins (pelvic fins placed beneath the throat in front of the pectorals) are very small, consisting of one small spine and two or three greatly reduced soft rays planted close to the anus. The pectoral fins are moderately developed. The tail is about as long as it is broad.

The lateral line runs in a long curve from the upper edge of the gill cover, over the upper half of the body, to the root of the tail. Rather small, rough-edged (ctenoid) scales cover the body all over, including the bases of the dorsal, anal and tail fins. The outward-folding mouth is end-positioned, fairly big, and aimed slightly upwards. The jaws, vomer bone, palate and tongue are all set with tiny, wire-like teeth.

Plate II–266 gives a good idea of what this fish may look like. The silvery body coloration has a mother-of-pearl sheen, while the fins are yellowish. Two vertical, greenish brown to black stripes decorate the head. The first runs across the eye, the second over the base of the pectorals. The leading edge of dorsal and anal fins often are equally dark, considered a continuation of the second cross stripe. The big, goggling eye has a dark, red-rimmed iris.

This dweller of the tropical seas lives not far off the coast, especially frequenting the coral reefs. Young specimens a few centimetres (about an inch) long are found in brackish coastal waters and even in fresh water. In shape and coloration, they are the exact likeness of the adult fish.

Illus. II-205. Habitat of the Toxotidae. The remarkable distribution in southern Australia can be explained by the middle section of the continent having been flooded by the ocean in relatively recent geological time.

Family Toxotidae

As shown on the map in Illus. II–205, the distribution area of the Toxotidae (archer fish) is rather widespread. Occasionally, they can be found at the mouths of large rivers, where they hunt, in their own peculiar way, all kinds of insects that come within range of their "shooting equipment." They are equally comfortable in fresh, brackish and salt water, although they are never found in the open sea. It is strange that Toxotidae are also found on the south coast of Australia, entirely isolated from the habitat of the remainder of the family. It appears obvious, then, that we are dealing with a very old family, for fossil archer fish have been found in the Eocene strata on Sumatra.

In 1910, Max Weber came across a fish, *Toxotes lorentzi*, which is even closer to the fossil fish, hence more primitive in build than the Western species. However, the fossil from Sumatra appears to be even

Illus. II-206. Roof of the mouth with "barrel" and snout with "shooting tongue" of the archer fish.

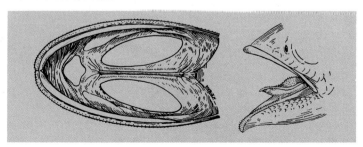

947

more primitive, so that the obvious conclusion is that the *Toxotes* of New Guinea is the link between the fossil form and the current Western species. Toxotidae still survive on Sumatra, completely excluded from salt or brackish waters.

The family includes only a single genus, *Toxotes*, of which six modern species are known to live in the distribution area previously mentioned. These are *Toxotes blythi, T. chatareus, T. jaculator, T. lorentzi, T. microlepis* and *T. oligolepis*. Fossils of *Toxotes beauforti*, among others, were discovered in the highlands of Padang in Sumatra. The body of *Toxotes* is elongated, rather high and perch-like and laterally flattened. The head, too, is flattened out vertically, the mouth is pointed, large, end-positioned and angled upward. The jaws, tongue, alar bone (shoulder bone), palate, and point of the vomer bone are set with tiny teeth. The upper jaw is very thin, the lower jaw can be projected. The spinal column is built up of 10 trunk and 14 caudal vertebrae. The fin ray formulas are: D. IV-V/11-14; A. III/15-18 (see NOTE, page 938). In the fossil *Toxotes beauforti*, these are D. VI/12; A. III/13. The dorsal fin of all species has a long base and is set far to the rear.

Toxotidae require a large, marsh-type aquarium, or at least an aquarium containing several plants growing above water. A special terrarium cover should be placed over the plants so that the live insects that are introduced from time to time cannot escape. The live insects give the fish a chance to "shoot their prey" as they would in the wild. Toxotidae are unusually interesting fishes and are not difficult to keep, as long as they are provided with plenty of food. When night falls, they change their coloration pattern.

Toxotes jaculator (Pallas, 1766)
Archer Fish

Toxotes jaculator occurs along the coasts of the Red Sea, the Indian Ocean, and the Indonesian Archipelago, in the mouths and lower reaches of the rivers, in fresh, salt, and brackish water. It is found on Sumatra in the area of Lake Toba and the Padang uplands. In 1899, P. Nitsche brought, for the first time, two specimens into Europe with him.

Toxotes jaculator attains a length of about 20 cm (8 inches), but seldom gets so big in the aquarium. The dorsal fin consists of a short, spiny section and a longer section of soft rays. The anal fin begins directly under the dorsal fin, and, like the dorsal fin, it consists of a short, spiny section and a longer, soft-rayed length; it is, however,

948

Illus. II-207. *Toxotes jaculator.*

smaller than the dorsal fin. The body, including the base of the soft-rayed sections of the dorsal and anal fins, is covered all over with rough-edged scales.

The general coloration is yellowish grey-green; the back is dark olive green to yellowish brown; the belly is light, silver-white. From the back, four to six dark stripes run halfway down the flanks. The dorsal, caudal, and anal fins are edged with black. The ventral fins are dark brownish; the pectorals are without coloration and transparent. A metallic sheen glimmers all over the body.

This rather large fish should be kept in a roomy aquarium fitted with a high cover to prevent its leaping out. (See also the discussion, just previous, of the family Toxotidae.) The water temperature may not fall below 20 °C (68 °F); the preferable temperature range is from 22 to 26 °C (72–79 °F).

T. jaculator is not a picky eater. Even though it prefers to shoot down its own prey, it gobbles up any animal food—even pieces of meat and fish, as well as crustaceans, wingless ants and insect larvae, etc.—which is either given to it or which happens to fall in the water. The pieces of food must not be large, for, in spite of its big mouth, it appears unable to swallow large chunks. It should subsist mainly on live food, but some frozen and freeze-dried foods, especially floating ones, are also quite acceptable.

This fish has become famous for its peculiar way of hunting. As soon as it notices an insect above the surface of the water, it closes in to within 100 cm (about a yard) or less (it would necessarily be less in an aquarium). With fabulous accuracy, it shoots a drop of water at the coveted insect. Usually the bug is knocked from its perch and tumbles into the water, where it is quickly eaten. This "shooting" has given rise to a special angling technique practiced by tropical fishermen, a technique similar to that used by trout fishermen, who cast flies or other insects for bait on a long light line and let them rest on top of the water.

Although Archer Fish were known to the natives as "sumpit" (Malay *sumpitan* means blow-gun) for a very long time, no author had written up the fish before 1766. About 1763, however, the strange ability of this fish attracted the attention of Hommel, the Dutch physician, who was at that time director of the hospital at Batavia, now Djakarta, Java. John Albert Schlosser introduced the new species to science at a meeting of the Royal Society of London (1764), on the strength of one specimen and the reading aloud of a description of its habits by Hommel. The accompanying specimen, however, was probably a case of mistaken identity, as it appeared not to be a *Toxotes*, but a coral fish, *Chelmo rostratus* (Linné). The natives called both fishes "sumpit sumpit" without attempting to differentiate between them.

In 1766, Pallas introduced the name *Sciaena jaculatrix* for the Archer Fish, but many years later (1817), Cuvier showed that this was not a representative of the genus *Sciaena*. He proposed, instead, the new generic name *Toxotes*.

For a long time after these early reports, the shooting custom of the Archer Fish was considered a misapprehension owing to poor observational methods (Bleeker and others), until the Russian Zolotnisky (1902) and Gill (1909) checked on and confirmed the old observation. The most important points of this study concerned: getting ready for action and aiming the mouth; swimming back to take up a strategic position, in which the fish was actually observed to swim backwards; following the prey with the big, exceptionally moveable eyes; the ability to see well above water; the choice of certain insects for food and the determination of the correct range for shooting down large or small prey. Some authors (Boulenger, 1904, and others) have observed that the fish does not rack up as good a score shooting down insects in flight as when the victim is sitting still.

In 1936, H. M. Smith gave an accurate description of the shooting equipment of this fish, sketched in Illus. II–206. The sketch on the left shows the upper jaw, as seen from inside, with the groove in the palate. This groove serves as the "barrel" of the piece, through which the "bullets" (water drops) are violently expelled. This gun barrel is open on the bottom, but in use is closed off by the tongue, thus forming a kind of blow-gun. It is odd that none of these details was ever discussed in any publication prior to 1936.

When the Archer Fish wants to overcome its prey, it first assumes a suitable position. As it does this, its backward manner of swimming, and the upward, forward and backward movement of the huge eyes, can be observed. Next, the blow-gun is shaped in the fish's mouth, the mouth is closed and the snout is projected only slightly above water. Through a very narrow opening that always remains open, by means of a vigorous squeezing together of the gill covers, a single bullet, or a series of them, machine-gun style, hurtles out. The speed with which the water drops follow upon each other is regulated by the paper-thin point of the tongue.

Toxotes jaculator is shy at first, but soon gets used to the person feeding it and will even take food from his hand. So far, nothing is known about its breeding habits, and even less is known about distinguishing one sex from the other. Here is an interesting field that lies fallow and cries out for further study.

The flesh of the Archer Fish, incidentally, is said to be delicious and high in food value.

Sub-order Anabantoidei

As shown on the map in Illus. II–208, these labyrinth fishes occur at present only in the eastern and southeastern parts of Asia, the Indonesian Archipelago, and part of Africa. They are definitely fresh-water fishes, living in inland waters of the archipelagic islands, but never entering the sea. They inhabit the lower reaches of the rivers, the pools and ponds of the lowland plains, and occur no farther east than Sumatra, Java and Borneo. Many species are also found in flooded rice paddies. The only exception to this general distribution is the genus *Anabas*, the only one inhabiting the Indonesian-Australian region in the Celebes, Amboina, and Halmahera Islands. Whether this distribution is a natural one or is due to human intervention cannot be determined. Since these fishes—especially *Anabas*—have attracted the attention of men for a long time, it is quite possible that men have had something to do with their wide distribution.

It is startling that no representative of these labyrinth fishes is found in East Africa. This is probably due to the complete extinction of fresh-water fish that came about when the sea swept over that part of Africa towards the end of the Cretaceous and the beginning of the Tertiary periods.

The labyrinth fishes owe their name to the peculiar, labyrinth-shaped respiratory organ that permits them to breathe air while out of water (so long as the surroundings are damp) for varying periods of time. For this reason, they are independent of the oxygen content of the water in which they live. This is a splendid and very effective adaptation to the environment.

The body of anabantids is elongated, with an almost oval or laterally

Illus. II-208. Distribution of the labyrinth fish, Anabantoidei.

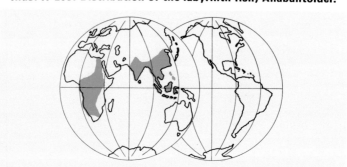

flattened cross-section and is entirely covered with cycloid (smooth) or ctenoid (rough-edged) scales. The mouth is set with fine teeth, usually only on the lower jaw and the intermaxilla, which folds outwards. The pectoral fins are well developed and practically always of a normal fin shape. The ventral fins are usually entirely or partially provided with considerably lengthened fin rays. They are seldom on the belly, but are usually on the breast or under the throat. They are completely absent in the genus *Channa*.

CLASSIFICATION AND SURVEY OF FAMILIES

Three families are often brought together under the name Labyrinthici: Ophicephalidae, Anabantidae, and Luciocephalidae. This arbitrary combining into a single order is highly artificial, since there is no talk of a common origin or ancestry between the first-named and the last two families. The first family, Ophicephalidae, has been discussed earlier as a separate, specialized group and will be included in the separate order, Ophicephaliformes.

The relationship between the other two families does not seem close enough to warrant uniting them, without further research, in one order, for which reason they are distinguished here as two sub-orders of Perciformes. In several ways, both families, Anabantidae and Luciocephalidae, show a remarkable resemblance to representatives of the toothcarp order, Cyprinodontiformes, especially to those of the tribe Rivulini, the African genera and *Aplocheilus*. (This likeness apparently even fooled Valenciennes when he named the species now known as *Betta* under the name *Panchax*, an old name for the toothcarp genus *Aplocheilus*.)

1. The snout is short, with small, outward-folding intermaxilla; has swim bladder; body covered with rough-edged scales . . . sub-order Anabantoidei, family Anabantidae

2. Long snout, pike-like, with large mouth opening and intermaxilla folding far outward; no swim bladder; head covered with cycloid (smooth) scales, body with ctenoid (rough-edged) scales . . . sub-order Luciocephaloidei, family Luciocephalidae

Family Anabantidae

The distribution of this family coincides with that of the entire sub-order, Anabantoidei (see Illus. II–208).

The attraction most anabantids have for the aquarist usually lies in the beautiful, variegated coloration and the graceful shape of these fishes, not to mention their peculiar breeding habits, nest-building, and brood care. As they often like to jump into the air, the tank should be fitted with a cover at all times. Often, while the aquarium is being cleaned, or otherwise being attended to, with the cover temporarily removed and one's hand busy inside, one of the fish makes an exquisite little leap into the air, only to flop ignominiously on the floor.

The body of the anabantids, more or less flattened sideways, is, in many cases, strongly perch-like. Sometimes it is stretched out lengthwise, oval or longish oval in shape, or then again rather stubby and cylindrical or flattened on the sides. The snout is short, with a small, upward-turned, end-positioned mouth. Anabantidae all possess a very large abdominal cavity that extends to just in front of the caudal fin. The entire tail region is taken up by a large swim bladder divided in two. The body—and sometimes the dorsal and anal fin bases —are covered all over with moderately large, rough-edged scales, which run in regular rows. The lateral line organ is either found in all stages of development in the different genera, or else is entirely lacking.

BREEDING AND PARENTAL CARE

The males of the nest-building species of Anabantidae—to which the Kissing Gourami *Helostoma temmincki* does not belong—make a nest of foamy bubbles while showing off their most beautiful coloration. The multitude of bubbles comprising the nest are held together by sticky saliva and are reinforced with bits of plants. The eggs which, after several false attempts, are emitted by the female, are immediately fertilized by the male, usually in a tempestuous embrace. The eggs float upward into the bubble-nest, but some sink slowly down. These are retrieved by either the male or the female and spat out into the nest. The male takes it on himself to care for the spawn, chasing the female angrily away. However, if the space is so small that flight cannot take her far enough away, or if the haven she finds does not afford enough protection, she may suffer a grievous mauling from her erstwhile lover. If anything of this kind is observed coming on, either carefully dip the female out of the tank, or insert an opaque screen between the parents so that they cannot approach each other.

Sub-family Anabantinae

Members of this sub-family have a distribution area coinciding with the entire geographical area covered by the sub-order Anabantoidei.

As said before, the genus *Anabas* has probably been known to man for a long time through the species *A. testudineus* (syn. *A. scandens*), which is doubtless responsible for the sub-family's wide distribution.

The three genera known in aquarist circles are *Ctenopoma*, *Anabas* and *Helostoma*, included here with the genus *Spirobranchus*, still unknown to aquarists. The known genera are distinguished from one another as follows:

1. Dorsal fin with less than 12, and anal fin with less than 15, soft rays; jaws set with tiny, conical teeth . . . tribe Anabantini

    A. Smooth edge to gill cover . . . genus *Ctenopoma*

    B. Serrated edge to gill cover . . . genus *Anabas*

2. Dorsal fin with more than 12, and anal fin with more than 15, soft rays; toothless jaws; small, moveable teeth on the lips . . . tribe Helostomini, genus *Helostoma*

Tribe Anabantini

Of the two genera *Ctenopoma* from Africa and *Anabas* from the Indonesian Archipelago and Asia, only a small number of species have been imported. The species *Anabas testudineus* is sometimes still kept in aquariums, but it is not very popular, so it will not be discussed for the present. However, in the past few years, some promising species of *Ctenopoma* have been imported from Africa.

Plate II-267. *Anabas testudineus.*

Genus *Ctenopoma*

For a long time, up to 1930, this genus was generally included with *Anabas*. This, however, failed to give a correct picture of the relationship, at the same time that there were plenty of reasons why *Ctenopoma* should have been accepted as a separate genus. Besides the difference in the gill covers noted in the table of genera on page 955, there are other important distinguishing marks, such as the more pointed head of *Ctenopoma*. *C. kingsleyae* discussed below is the only species found currently in the aquariums of Holland. It would be useful to both aquarists and to science if these other species were to be imported more often: *C. nanum*, *C. multispinis*, *C. muriei*, *C. damasi*, *C. acutirostre*, *C. argentoventer* and *C. fasciolatum*. They are all rather small species, up to about 100 mm (4 inches).

Ctenopoma acutirostre Pellegrin, 1899

This species comes from the Congo Basin and in the past few years has gained a permanent place among Congo imports destined for the home aquarium, even though not much is known about it. The general coloration is red-brown to deep orange, with dark, irregular spots

Plate II-268. *Ctenopoma acutirostre*.

Plate II-269. *Ctenopoma ansorgei.*

of dark brown to purplish blue or velvet black. It attains a length of about 100 mm (4 inches), and though it is certainly not predatory in the strictest sense, it must be closely watched near fishes small enough to swallow. In conduct, it is somewhat similar to *Colisa lalia* and it is sometimes remindful of the African "Leaf Fish" *Polycentropsis abbreviata*, a cousin of the South American *Polycentrus schomburgki*, except that it is far less voracious.

Illus. II-209. *Ctenopoma kingsleyae.*

Ctenopoma kingsleyae Günther, 1867

This species, very common in the Congo Basin with the exception of Katanga, was reported on by Poll from Stanley Pool, Kinshasa.

It is an attractive fish that attains a length of about 80 mm ($3\frac{3}{16}$ inches). A typical labyrinth fish, it lives in the shallows thickly overgrown with marsh- and water-plants.

The basic coloration is brownish yellow to brown-green with darker black spots and lighter to white spots on the gill covers and in the abdominal region. The caudal fin ends in a milk white border, set off by black. The same black is found along the soft-rayed parts of the dorsal and anal fins. The ventral fins are dark brownish to black with a milk white frontal ray. All in all, *Ctenopoma kingsleyae* is an unusually pretty fish whose conduct is remindful of the various African Nandidae (such as *Polycentropsis abbreviata*) and which can even be as voracious as the better known *Polycentrus schomburgki*. The young thrive and grow quickly on a diet of infusoria.

Ctenopoma nanum Günther, 1896

The first publication in aquarium literature of a description of this import from the Congo appeared in 1956. *Ctenopoma nanum* is certainly one of the most attractive representatives of its genus, especially since it always remains quite small—about 75 mm (3 inches) as compared to 100 to 120 mm (4 to 4¾ inches) for most other species. It is similar in many respects to the Asiatic *Belontia signata*. Hopefully, before too long, more accurate particulars on its life style and breeding will be published. This fish is also a builder of bubble-nests and should be kept as the *Colisa* species.

The dominant coloration of this fish is usually olive brown, and the stripes may also be brownish. However, in no case does this brown coloration predominate, and it appears that, in the proper surroundings, blue takes over. The Congo imports on the market under the name *Anabas fasciolatus* or *Ctenopoma fasciolatum* are probably identical with this variety. In fact, *C. fasciolatum* in Plate II–270 turned out to be only a local variety of *C. nanum*.

A similar situation probably involves the species names *C. kingsleyae*

Plate II-270. *Ctenopoma fasciolatum.*

Plate II-271. *Ctenopoma ocellatum.*

and *C. oxyrhynchus.* As the first is the older name, it will be maintained for the time being, particularly since it may ultimately be revealed that both belong to the same species. Anyhow, it appeared from investigation of preserved specimens from the Congo that the most important characteristic (as specified by Boulenger, 1916)—that is, the serrated or non-serrated edge of the preopercle—is not a constant one. In specimens from the same population, most of the youngsters either had no teeth at all on the preopercle, or the teeth were just barely developed. However, these appeared to develop more and more as the fish grew in size. Moreover, the fish are extremely variable in pattern.

Tribe Helostomini

This tribe classification was set up for the genus *Helostoma*, which has only a single species. This species is so divergent from the other Anabantinae in various characteristics that this classification certainly must be justified.

Genus *Helostoma*

Helostoma temmincki Cuvier, 1831
Kissing Fish
Kissing Gourami

The Kissing Fish (or Kissing Gourami), after some years, is again enjoying a spell of popularity with aquarists, following importation of a few specimens from Singapore. It is native to Sumatra, Java, Borneo, the Malay Peninsula and over into Thailand. It is a typical marsh-dweller, although it also occurs in brooks and streams. Depending on the place of origin, certain strains may grow as long as 300 mm (about 12 inches). By the time they are 150 mm long (6 inches), or sometimes less, they are ready for breeding.

Although it is a labyrinth fish, *Helostoma temmincki* is one of the species that does not make a bubble-nest (there are other species that also deviate in this respect). It often puts its labyrinth organ to good use in its natural waters, for, during the mating season, it often lives in water putrid with all kinds of rotting vegetable refuse. It is precisely there —where the environment is rich in food—that the eggs are laid.

During the western monsoon, under the lash of driving rains, great areas of land are flooded, putting the plant life under water, where most of it dies. The result of this rotting is a lavish development of bacteria, which become food for the micro-organisms infusoria. The richly nourishing waters are well liked as a place for the Kissing Fish getting ready to breed, and they swim up in great numbers, the females leading the males. The former issue their eggs, which, after being fertilized, float lazily to the surface. There they lodge under all kinds of trash and hatch out on the second day. The larvae, like most of their relatives, are each provided with a yolk sac and a tiny bladder containing a drop of oil to keep them afloat. There they live off the rich, natural supply of infusoria and grow quickly. Today's aquarist should have no trouble imitating these natural circumstances, so that tank breeding will be successful.

Helostoma temmincki is named the Kissing Fish because of its strangely-formed lips, with which two individuals often "kiss," sometimes rather violently. The lips are thick and fleshy and set with many tiny teeth. There are no teeth in the jaws. This adaptation is, of course, not really designed for kissing, but is structured, instead, for rasping algae from stones and other objects. The heavy lips with their broad and fine little teeth are convenient for scraping algae off plant stems and other objects.

For the growing fry, a vegetable diet—the same as for their parents—is essential after a few days. Kitchen vegetables, particularly lettuce, can be served to them in the aquarium. Nowadays, a golden yellow variety of Kissing Fish, which has only slightly darker edges to the dorsal and anal fins, is circulating in aquarist circles. This unusual variety is bluish grey with yellow fins, with the darker band which runs from one fin to the other by way of the tail.

Plate II-272. *Macropodus concolor.*

Sub-family Macropodinae

Two genera are of interest to aquarists, *Belontia* Myers, 1923, and *Macropodus* Lacépède, 1802. *Belontia signata* (Günther, 1861), which has been hitherto somewhat rare, has a rather high body, considerably flattened on the sides, which, along with the smooth edge to the gill covers, differentiates it distinctly from the genus *Macropodus*.

Genus *Macropodus*

The genus *Macropodus* can best be considered a rather old genus with diverse forms inhabiting its widespread habitat. It is unnecessary to differentiate sub-genera, as each genus was originally based on a single species (the genus was monotypic). Thus, *Macropodus* includes the species (in chronological order of published description) *M. opercularis*, *M. chinensis* and *M. cupanus*.

Macropodus cupanus (Cuvier, 1831)

Native to Pulu Weh, near Sumatra, to India, Ceylon and the Malay Peninsula, *Macropodus cupanus* is very common in marshy or flooded areas. It also frequents waters under rotting plants floating on the surface, or is found among water plants, where it industriously hunts mosquito larvae. Like the Guppy and *Gambusia*, this fish has made a name for itself as a mosquito exterminator.

Macropodus cupanus is a real bubble-nest builder, comparable in every respect to the larger *M. opercularis*. It reaches a length of 35 to 40 mm (1⅜ to 1⁹⁄₁₆ inches), not counting the tail fin. Several geographic varieties have been differentiated, *M. cupanus cupanus* of Pulu Weh (Lake Anak Laut), which also occurs on the Malay Peninsula, and *M. cupanus dayi* of India.

The basic coloration is chestnut brown with two dark brown to black stripes running lengthwise; the head and ventral region are rust brown; the fins are reddish, edged with blue-green in older specimens. Since *Macropodus cupanus* is an environmental companion of *Betta splendens* and *Trichopsis vittatus*, it is to be kept as they are (see pages 974 and 980).

Macropodus opercularis (Linné, 1758)
Paradise Fish

This fish hails from East Asia and is found in all kinds of waters in China, Korea, and the islands of Taiwan, Hainan and the Ryukyu group. It prefers slow-moving or stagnant, shallow waters with a dark bottom of mud or loam.

The first specimens imported into Europe appeared on the scene in 1869. The body is oblong, high, and flattened in from the sides; the length is about 80 mm (3 inches). The large head has a small, turned-up, end-positioned mouth. The dorsal and anal fins are big and long and consist of soft-rayed and spiny divisions. The caudal fin is also large and runs out into two pointed lobes. The ventral fins are jugular (placed under the neck), with the first fin rays grown together into a kind of wiry support; hence, the name *Macropodus* meaning big foot— *macro* means big and *podus* means foot (with a big foot or fin). Like the dorsal, caudal and anal fins, the pectorals are highly developed.

The coloration depends heavily on all kinds of factors. Under normal conditions, the basic coloration is greenish brown; the back is a dark, brownish purple dotted with black. The flanks bear a number of irregular reddish to bright, carmine red and blue-green stripes, sometimes merging into each other. The head is dark, but under the eye and on the lower half of the gill covers, it is golden yellow to greenish. The trailing part of the gill covers is blazing red with a black spot. From this feature comes the name *opercularis* (opercle means gill cover).

The caudal fin is carmine red to a pretty reddish brown, spotted

with greenish blue. The dorsal fin is bluish with reddish brown cross stripes. The dorsal, caudal and anal fins are all edged in blue; the anal fin is tinted like the caudal fin, except that the blue edge is broader. The soft-rayed part of the ventral fins is greenish to blue; the hard, intergrown rays are brownish. The pectorals are almost without coloration and transparent. The sexes are not hard to tell apart, since the female is not anywhere nearly as distinctly brilliant as the male. Also, the female's fins are not so grotesquely overgrown nor so sharply pointed as the male's.

This fish is probably one of the easiest to keep in an aquarium. One supporting fact is that since it was first imported into Europe in 1869, it has enjoyed an unbroken siege of popularity. Breeding, too, is easily achieved, and this has greatly helped *M. opercularis* to become quickly widespread and well known among aquarists. Although this fish is hardy, a sub-tropical temperature is recommended—15–20 °C (59–68 °F). In the mating season, bring the temperature up to 22–25 °C (72–77 °F) and lower the water depth to 6–10 cm (2$\frac{3}{8}$–4 inches). While mating, which sometimes occurs many times per day, the male embraces the female and fertilizes the eggs as she issues them. The fertilized eggs then float directly upward into the bubble-nest, beneath which the action transpired. If a few eggs sink, the male retrieves them and sees them safely into the nest. After the final mating (a total of 100 to 500 eggs has by now been laid), the male takes it upon himself to care for the spawn. He chases the female from the vicinity of the nest. If he becomes too rough, separate the pair by slipping a partition of frosted glass into the aquarium, if this is possible. If not, remove the female, taking care not to disturb the nest, and put her into another tank. On the second or third day, after 30 to 50 hours, the young fish hatch out. They are very small and must be brought up on infusoria and fine-sieved waterfleas until they grow to a size that can cope with larger food.

These macropods are well suited for the community aquarium, so long as they are in the company of fishes larger than themselves, against whom they cannot give rein to their predatory passions. They will eat anything given them in the way of food.

Some interesting particulars are known about this beautiful and decorative Paradise Fish, bred since ancient times by the Chinese, breeders par excellence, who generally adopted it as an ornamental aquarium dweller. The French consul Simon, residing in Ning-Po, introduced the fish to European aquarists. *Macropodus opercularis* was already known in Europe from earlier times, having been described by Linnaeus (among others), in 1758, in his *Systema Naturae*. In 1869, a French officer named Gérault, under orders from Simon, arrived in Paris aboard the man-o'-war *Impératrice* with 22 survivors of an original shipment of 100 specimens. Twelve males and five females came into the possession of the famous ornamental fish breeder, Pierre Carbonnier, in Paris. Later that same year, Carbonnier announced the successful breeding of these fish. Striking out from Paris, the macropods conquered Europe. At first, ichthyologists mistakenly supposed the fish to be a Chinese breeding product from the root form *Macropodus chinensis*, a species known since 1790. This notion, however, was definitely refuted.

As a final note, a black as well as an albino variety are also known.

Sub-family Sphaerichthyinae

The sub-family Sphaerichthyinae was originally set up for the genus *Sphaerichthys* only, supposing that it was a deviant form, although closely related to the preceding sub-family, Macropodinae. There seemed, however, to be no link with the other members of the family, in the sense that no distinct line of development was plain enough to be followed. But now, a recently discovered genus, *Malpulutta* of Ceylon, clearly links Sphaerichthyinae to Macropodinae. *Malpulutta* possesses the characteristic features of this sub-family, so that two genera can be distinguished, as follows:

. 1. The dorsal fin has 8 to 12 spines and 7 to 10 soft fin rays; anal fin with 8 to 10 spines and 18 to 22 soft fin rays; the body height is contained about 2 times in the standard length (height=$\frac{1}{2}$ length) . . . genus *Sphaerichthys*

2. Dorsal fin with 8 to 10 spines and 6 soft fin rays; anal fin with 16 to 17 spines and 9 to 11 soft fin rays; the body height is contained about

Plate II-274. *Malpulutta kretseri.*

3.5 times in the standard length (height=2/7 length) ... genus *Malpulutta*

Genus *Malpulutta*

Malpulutta is an interesting genus of the labyrinth family of Ceylon. The single known species *Malpulutta kretseri* is a very small fish—only 25 mm (1 inch) or a little bigger, except for tail fin—which has probably already found a place in the aquarium. Superficially, it seems similar to *Macropodus cupanus* or *Trichopsis vitattus*, though the latter species does not occur in Ceylon. The only known species, *Malpulutta kretseri*, inhabits pools and inlets of smaller streams. If frightened, it digs itself into the mud.

Plate II-275. *Sphaerichthys osphromenoides.*

Genus *Sphaerichthys*

One species is known to belong to this genus, *Sphaerichthys osphromenoides* of Sumatra and Malaysia. This fish, known to aquarists as the Chocolate Gourami, is still not too well understood and for that reason has the reputation of being hard to keep. It is not a builder of bubble-nests, but some authors say it lays its eggs on stones, while others consider it to be a mouth-breeder.

Sphaerichthys osphromenoides Canestrini, 1860
Chocolate Gourami

There are few aquarium fishes about which so many are divided as this fish. Is it a bubble-nest builder? Is it a bottom- (on stones) layer? Perhaps it is a mouth-breeder? Or is it all three—or are there several species (or varieties) which are deviant in their brood care? Suppose they all differ in this characteristic brood-biology—can the environment be a factor, at one time a propitious influence for building a bubble-nest, and at another time making that nest a superfluous luxury, so that the fish limit themselves to spawning on stones, or simply to incubating the eggs in their mouths?

Let us examine the three possibilities very critically, taking into account that previous observations should not necessarily be trusted. It then becomes rather clear that, from a biological viewpoint, these three brood methods—bubble-nest, mouth-breeding and bottom-laying—are not, in fact, so very far apart.

A developmental cycle in brood biology must logically have developed from free-laying or bottom-laying. A Chocolate Gourami was observed laying its eggs on a stone, only to have the male take the eggs up in its mouth and spit them out, doing this again and again, until they were finally eaten by the female. The following phase could possibly be either mouth-breeding or bubble-nest building, while a development to bubble-nest building via mouth-breeding must also be considered. It is less probable that development should proceed through bubble-nest building to mouth-breeding.

The question to be more closely investigated—whether or not there are several possible varieties or species—is certainly worth examination before a definite conclusion can be reached. This is all the more so in that a second variety was described by Pellegrin in 1930, *Sphaerichthys vaillanti* from the Kapuas River, Borneo. At first, this variety (at least, the specimens examined) was deemed to be identical to *Ctenops nobilis*.

It can be positively observed right now that the material examined— the original as well as the aquarium imports—had no glands in the mouth for secreting the salivary solution required in the building of a bubble-nest. Neither was there anything to give rise to the supposition that *Sphaerichthys osphromenoides* bear their young alive, since the internal arrangement for this was lacking. These are negative facts, and it can in no way be asserted that no Chocolate Gouramis exist that can meet the necessary requirements. Experience has shown that such things are not impossible.

It must finally be noted that the fish under observation at that time laid their eggs on a stone that was overgrown with fine thread algae. They formed a couple, though it could not be told which was the male and which the female until they could be more closely examined in a preserved state. It had not been possible to determine which of the two had laid the eggs, as neither fish was any thicker through the middle than the other. It appeared that the darker specimen, only 34 mm ($1\frac{11}{32}$ inches) long over-all, was the female; and the larger one, 59 mm ($2\frac{11}{32}$ inches) long over-all, was the male. The male was much lighter in coloration and the stripe pattern hardly showed itself; he took the eggs in his mouth, as noted above.

Sub-family Ctenopinae

The sub-family Ctenopinae was set up for the genera *Ctenops*, *Trichopsis,* and *Betta,* all three native to Southeast Asia, from India to Sumatra, Java, Borneo and Celebes. Its distribution area is shown on the map above. The comparatively small number of species in this sub-family are distinguished from the other anabantids by the rather long anal fin and the short dorsal fin. They are differentiated from the members of the sub-family Osphroneminae, who also have a rather short dorsal fin (for instance, *Trichogaster*), by the only slightly flat body (strongly flattened sideways in the case of *Trichogaster*). *Ctenops nobilis* has a rather severely flattened body, and in this respect is similar to Osphroneminae, but it distinctly differs in the ventral fins, which have indeed a greatly lengthened, second fin ray, yet are in no way rudimentary.

The three genera in this sub-family can be determined by the following criteria:

1. Dorsal fin with only one spine, or, usually, none at all; smooth-edged preorbital (ridge in front of the eye socket) . . . genus *Betta*

2. Dorsal fin with 2 to 6 spines and 6 to 9 soft rays; edge of preorbital serrated

    A. All fins, except the ventral, are rounded, without filamentous, elongated rays; dorsal, 4 to 6 spines; anal, 6 to 7 spines; lateral line rudimentary or missing . . . genus *Ctenops*

    B. All fins with filamentous, elongated rays, or running to a point; dorsal fin, 2 to 4 spines; lateral line absent . . . genus *Trichopsis*

971

Genus *Betta*

This genus includes 12 species, in chronological order: *B. picta, B. anabantoides, B. pugnax, B. bellica, B. rubra, B. macrostoma, B. akarensis, B. fusca, B. bleekeri, B. taeniata, B. splendens,* and *B. fasciata,* to which (De Beaufort, 1933) *B. ocellata* was later added. Almost all these species should be reduced to local varieties or sub-species, and of them all, only *B. splendens* has enjoyed years of popularity with aquarists. This will probably continue to be so for a long time. Occasionally in the past few years, however, other species have been imported in small numbers, to which some attention will be given in the discussion below. These are, in particular, the species (or varieties) *B. picta, B. pugnax,* and *B. taeniata,* the first two probably being synonymous, as one study of *B. pugnax* material has identified it as *B. picta.* Both are mouth-breeders and reach a considerable size.

Betta picta (Valenciennes, 1846)

This species, the first of this genus to be described, gives the impression of being a toothcarp, hence Valenciennes' quite understandable error in describing it as a *Panchax.* However, no one would make this mistake upon seeing it alive in an aquarium, for it shows itself there to be distinctly a *Betta.* Experience with this fish reveals that it is not a bubble-nest builder but a mouth-breeder. It is native to Singapore, Sumatra, Bangka, Belitong, and Java (Indonesia), and grows to a length of about 50 mm (2 inches); unless *B. pugnax* turns out to be only a sub-species, since it can grow as long as 100 mm (4 inches), this can be considered the maximum length for the species. *B. pugnax* is a giant variety localized to the island of Penang, the type-locality for *B. pugnax* s.s. (*sensu strictu,* or in the strictest sense).

The breeding habits of this fish are worth close observation, but this is the only thing recommending this fish to aquarists; it has few other attractions. The general coloration is purplish brown to grey-brown, with dark spots lying in three lengthwise rows. A pattern of five to seven rather broad, vertical bands is sometimes visible if the background coloration is rather light in tone. Furthermore, the males show a dark, purplish blue edge along the anal fin, as seen in Plate II–276. In the female, this edging is weaker or lacking entirely.

To get back to breeding, this fish corresponds a great deal with *Betta splendens* in regard to normal movements, swimming, turning, and standing still. Contrary to *B. splendens,* however, it is a bottom-dweller, even to the point of digging itself in.

The labyrinth organ is only of secondary importance in this species, being used only on rare occasions. Examination has shown that although this organ is present, it is far under-developed, while the gills have undergone hardly any reduction at all. The arrangement of the head-scales is, as are the scales themselves, cyprinoid-like (carp-like), though the scales are only partially toothed and not really ctenoid (rough-edged), but rather ctenocycloid (part rough and part smooth). There may be a link here between the anabantids and the toothcarps (cyprino-donts).

The median eye (a gland in the brain resembling an eye and sometimes called the pineal eye or the third eye) that is strikingly typical in members of the genus *Aplocheilus*, among others, is here a very well developed pineal body (a remnant of an important sense organ in ancestral forms, formerly supposed, by some philosophers, to be the seat of the soul in man).

Mating takes place in the same way as described for *B. splendens* (see page 974), not under a bubble-nest, however, but down near the bottom. The eggs sink down, sometimes into a hole prepared in advance, sometimes simply to the bottom. The female then takes the eggs in her

Plate II-276. *Betta picta.*

mouth, stands some distance off from the male facing her and, one by one, "spits" the eggs at him. The expression "plays ball" is used in the literature, but this is incorrect since it implies a different kind of action—that is, a tossing back and forth—whereas, the male actually simply catches (or misses) them. Often, of course, he manages to catch the eggs in flight. In any case, the final result is that the male holds the spawn in his mouth, not eating the whole time, until the young hatch out, which can take a week to 10 days. If for no other reason than to observe this one-sided game of catch and its final result, these fish are well worth the time and trouble.

Betta splendens Regan, 1910
Siamese Fighting Fish
Betta

Betta splendens is native to Southeast Asia and especially Singapore and Thailand (formerly Siam)—in stagnant waters, ditches and rice paddies,

Plate II-277. The veiled betta, *Betta splendens.*

etc. The first specimens were brought into Europe as early as 1874. The body is elongated and slightly flattened sideways. Its length is about 6 cm (2⅜ inches). The snout is slightly pointed, with a large, up-tilted mouth. The dorsal fin is placed far to the rear. The base is rather short, and the middle fin rays are the longest. The caudal fin is moderately big and rounded. The anal fin is big and pointed and stretches from just in front of the root of the tail to just behind the pectoral fins. The ventral fins are located under the throat and grow out quite long. The pectoral fins are normally developed and rounded.

The basic coloration is dark reddish brown with a blue-green shimmer, with greenish, metallically glittering spots and red dots. The rays of all the fins (except for the pectorals, which are almost transparent or without coloration) are brownish black. The membrane between the fin rays is greenish in the dorsal fin, and in the remaining fins is green, red or blue, while an albino variety is known, having lightly tinted fins. Other combinations are obtained by cross-breeding. *Betta splendens* is absolutely beautiful. The females are less striking in every respect; the fins are smaller and their coloration is dull. In young specimens not yet possessing the striking characteristics of the adults, the females can be recognized by the small, white oviduct.

The tank for this fish has no special requirements; any size is suitable. A roomy aquarium mainly serves to allow you to enjoy the magnificence of this species because roominess is not necessary with most *Betta* species. One important factor that is required is a good deal of warmth. The winter temperature should not be allowed to fall below 24 °C (75 °F). A normal temperature is about 26 °C (79 °F), and in the mating season, 30 °C (86 °F). *B. splendens* is extremely sensitive to temperature variation as well as to a temperature difference between the water and the air it breathes. The aquarium should be in a well lighted location and thickly planted along the glass walls. In addition, there should be a layer of floating plants not quite covering the entire surface. For the sake of the spawn, the breeding tank should be a roomy one.

The bubble-nest of *Betta splendens* is rather small but high, and is preferably constructed among the leaves of floating plants. After a violent courtship during which the female repeatedly attempts to escape the male's impetuous "caresses" by vanishing among the thick vegetation, the male arches his body around her so that she is forced to lie on her back. The anal openings of the two are now so close together that the eggs issued by the female are at once fertilized by the male, as he simultaneously discharges his sperm over them. The eggs, heavier than water, sink to the bottom and the parents (or at least the male) gather up the eggs and spit them out into the floating nest. If the female is caught (by the male) eating any of the eggs, she will find it difficult to keep out of his way, and it would be better to transfer her to another tank.

After 30 to 40 hours, the first of the young begin to hatch out. They are then brought up in the usual way. As soon as they first attempt to swim, it can happen that the parents, confused by the stirring and bustling of the young ones, turn into cannibals. The parents must then be separated from the young and put into another tank, in which the temperature is the same as that in the nursery tank. If the parents are not removed, perhaps no more than a few dozen of the hundred hatched will survive. These, however, will be fine, sturdy fish, the goal of every non-professional breeder. A limited number of fish in an aquarium can more easily withstand the critical period of transition from gill- to labyrinth-breathing.

The Siamese Fighting Fish got its name from the habit of many other fishes to defend a kind of territory. Males of this species are very concerned with watching over their territory, which in nature is usually large enough to keep them apart. When they are, however, forced to share a small area during the mating season, males fight to death. The Siamese people have made this habit a sport like cock fighting, and bet on the winners.

As early as 1874, the famous French ornamental fish breeder, Pierre Carbonnier, began to breed this pretty fish. However, it was not until 1892 that Jeunet raised a few young fish to maturity.

In the wild, this widely known and popular aquarium fish has many varieties, which may differ considerably from the original type, in coloration as well as in shape. These lovely varieties abound especially in the vicinity of Singapore, Penang and Bangkok. Formerly, all these different varieties had names of their own, but are now generally known as *Betta splendens* Regan. The peculiar shape and structure of the fins once so fooled the printing staff of an English journal, that a picture of the fish was published upside-down. The printer unknowingly mistook the big anal fin for the dorsal fin and naturally turned that side of the fish to the top, a mistake that is easy to understand.

A widely known and popular variety of *Betta splendens* is the so-called Veil-Tailed Betta. It is actually nothing but a freak, like the veil-tailed fish that stem from Goldfish (*Carassius auratus*). Older names for this variety are, among others, *Betta cambodia, Betta cyana, Betta splendens* var. *longicaudata*. All that has been said for the type specimen may also be true for the varieties, except that the latter live shorter lives. As far as activity is concerned, however, veiled Bettas are in no sense less active than the parent form, as has sometimes been claimed. All that is known about their origin is that all specimens imported so far have come from dealers of the trade in Singapore. Where they might be found in the wild is unknown and whether they are sometimes found in the wild, or whether they are hybrids bred in captivity and not to be found in the wild, are still unanswered questions. The first veiled Bettas were imported into Europe in 1926.

Betta taeniata Regan, 1909

This little fish, which appears to have a very widespread distribution (Borneo, Sumatra, Malaysia, and Thailand), attains a length of 80 mm ($3\frac{3}{16}$ inches). It is most closely related to *Betta picta* and is probably also a mouth-breeder. In Thailand, it is found in thickly vegetated creeks in company with *Trichopsis, Trichogaster, Nandus, Rasbora*, and *Aplocheilus* species. It has a big head and is called by the natives *pla krim hua mong* ("big-headed krim fish"). As with *B. picta*, the appearance of a broad head, and, hence, the appellation, may come from the mouthful of eggs they carry about on occasion. In truth, the head of this fish, as well as of *B. picta* is hardly broader than that of *B. splendens*.

Illus. II-211. *Betta taeniata.*

Genus *Ctenops*

At the present time, this genus is known to have only a single species representing it.

Ctenops nobilis MacClelland, 1844

Ctenops nobilis is a labyrinth fish that is not very popular among aquarists, supposedly because it is difficult to keep. Evidently, it is a variety from the lowland waters of India and Bangladesh.

It grows to 80 mm ($3\frac{3}{16}$ inches), not counting the caudal fin. The body is fairly high, flattened on the sides, and more or less resembles the *Trichogaster* species, with, however, the differences previously described (under sub-family Ctenopinae on page 971), among others.

The general coloration is brownish, and the fins, especially in the male, have a brownish edge.

Plate II-278. *Trichopsis pumilus.*

Genus *Trichopsis*

To the two species of this genus that were known up to a short time ago, *T. pumilus* and *T. vittatus*, has been added a third species, *T. schalleri*. All three are native to Southeast Asia.

Trichopsis pumilus (Arnold, 1914)
Green Croaking Gourami
Pygmy Purring Gourami

This species was first imported into Germany in 1913 from Saigon in Vietnam. Up to now, there is no certainty that this fish actually does occur in the vicinity of Saigon. Other indications of its occurrence are also unsure, although a wider distribution is probable.

Trichopsis pumilus is one of the smallest anabantids, attaining a length of only 35 mm (1⅜ inches), which is probably the reason it has not yet been reported from other areas. From collections of preserved material, it seems that specimens of *T. pumilus* may be found among *Trichopsis vittatus*, but these are usually considered to be the young of *T. vittatus*. Moreover, it is possible that further study of the material would reveal that *T. pumilus* is a small strain of *T. vittatus*.

The basic coloration of *T. pumilus* is the red of Bordeaux wine, which, if the fish is kept correctly—that is, in a tank with a dark background—

979

turns to reddish brown with a green pattern and a metallic green sheen. If the background of the tank is light, then the green dominates and the lovely, brownish red tints are more retiring, if, indeed, they show up at all. From the point of the snout, a black band runs over the eye to the base of the tail. In adult specimens, this consists of a row of oblong spots. A second, less distinct, band runs from the upper corner of the gill cover (opercle) to the upper edge of the caudal root, while a third, indistinct, band appears above the base of the anal fin. (This pattern of bands is also found in the species *Trichopsis vittatus*.) The fins are reddish with dark points. The sexes are very difficult to tell apart, as the only indication lies in the fins. In the male, these are better developed and somewhat more pointed. Fine specimens can even show elongated fin rays, although in this respect they are different from *T. vittatus*.

Although this fish is tiny, it should be kept in a roomy but not too large aquarium, together with smaller species. It is never advisable to keep several males, not even of related genera, together in a small tank.

Breeding is carried on as it is with other anabantids, but not so violently as is sometimes the case with the larger species. Like *T. vittatus*, this fish builds an unstable nest of bubbles, preferably under a leaf of a floating plant such as *Ceratopteris*. Brood care is taken over by the male, and early on the second day, the young burst out of their eggs. For the first few days, they shoot about inside and around the nest as they actively search for food. Like most of their relatives, the young fish possess a sticky organ on the head, which, in the first few days, is used for clinging to things.

Both male and female Pygmy Purring Gouramis are capable of making a purring or grunting sound, especially heard in the mating season. Hopefully, this lovely little species will get more attention and attain a permanent place in the home aquarium. It is a species that rivals the *Betta* in every respect and is, moreover, less intolerant of other fishes.

Trichopsis vittatus (Cuvier, 1831)
Croaking Gourami

Trichopsis vittatus is a very common species, found especially in the company of *Betta*. Throughout Southeast Asia, it dwells in small creeks thickly grown with vegetation. This species, another Croaking Gourami, is a very attractive and untroublesome aquarium fish which makes few demands of its environment. It is also famed as an exterminator of mosquito larvae.

As may be expected of a species having such a widespread distribution area, local variation is extreme. The fish is generally about 60 mm (2$\frac{3}{8}$

Plate II-279. *Trichopsis vittatus,* variety "schalleri."

inches) long, not counting the long, trailing fin rays. The females are usually somewhat smaller, are also less distinct in coloration, and have smaller fins. On the brownish background, three dark, lengthwise stripes can be seen. The fins show a variety of coloration, generally decorated with red and green specks and spots.

Like all species of this family from Southeast Asia, this fish is kept at a temperature of about 24 °C (75 °F). In the daytime, this can be warmed by the sun to a maximum 30 °C (86 °F), but by night, it should not cool off below 22 °C (72 °F). *T. vittatus* builds an indifferent bubble-nest, compared to *Betta* or *Colisa,* preferably under a large leaf floating on the surface. About 200 eggs are laid during a mating session, which, in the usual manner, are looked after and cared for by the male. A nest of 100 eggs and a hatch of 80 to 100 young is certainly an outstanding breeding accomplishment. For a few days, the young remain under the watchful eye of the male, but shortly thereafter, they become independent and bumble clumsily about, later swimming freely along the surface among the floating plants. After the third week, the young spurt ahead in growth and soon take on the lovely pattern and coloration of mature fish.

The main food of *T. vittatus* consists of mosquito larvae and waterfleas, but the aquarist should not forget that to this fish, like all aquarium dwellers, the micro-organisms in pond and ditch water are an excellent source of nourishment.

Plate II-280. *Colisa chuna* under bubble-nest.

Sub-family Osphroneminae

This sub-family includes three genera, two of which are of interest to the aquarist.

Genus *Colisa*

Two species of this genus are well known in the aquarium, *C. labiosa* and *C. lalia*. A third well known species, *C. fasciata*, is so similar to *C. labiosa* that it has probably caused a great deal of confusion concerning proper nomenclature. Another species long known to science, *Colisa chuna*, the Honey Gourami, was added to this collection of *Colisa* a few years ago.

Colisa labiosa (Day, 1878)
Thick-Lipped Gourami

Colisa labiosa is native to Burma. It was first introduced into Europe in 1904. It can grow up to 95 mm (3¾ inches) but 75 mm (3 inches) is considered usual for the aquarium. The body is oblong, rather high and flattened on the sides. The mouth is turned upward and folds slightly outward. The jaws are set with tiny, conical teeth.

The dorsal and anal fins are very long, though the fin rays are comparatively short. The dorsal fin has its beginning above the bases of the pectoral fins, the anal fin is situated more to the rear. Especially in the male, the dorsal fin is sharply pointed; in both sexes, the anal fin is rounded. The caudal fin is well developed and either curved inward or straight. The lobes are rounded. The ventral fins also have a long, drawn-out, filamentous fin ray.

The basic coloration is a typical, brownish purple, darker or lighter according to circumstances, with eight to ten rearward angling, blue cross stripes which, in fine specimens, are regularly spaced. The tail-side of the bases of the dorsal and anal fins possess several rows of small scales. The difference in the shape of the head, male and female, is remarkable. In the male, the snout is tilted positively upward, and the entire head runs to more of a point than in the female. In addition to the coloration being less distinct on the female, her cross stripes seldom show up across the entire height of the body, since they are localized towards the middle. This gives rise to an irregular, lengthwise stripe which makes it easy to recognize the females in young specimens.

Colisa labiosa should be kept like its related species. The male is an exceptionally tireless "bubble blower." However, since this species does not reinforce the nest with bits of plants or algae, as is done by *Colisa lalia*, the resulting nest is rather flimsy. It covers a large surface, and usually pieces of it float off on their own, long before the nest is finished. Should he start building the nest under a large, floating leaf of

Plate II-281. *Colisa fasciata,* **male.**

some water plant, *C. labiosa* succeeds quite well at blowing a nest that is several centimetres (over an inch) high. During the winter mating season (December to March) the male is very handsome and sometimes so dark that he can hardly be recognized. The points of the dorsal fin spines are always bright red. Together, they form a serrated edge. The coloration of the anal fin is more yellowish to orange-red. When the male is seen head-on, a striking, silver-white band is seen running from eye to eye, down under and along the lower lip. Below this is a dark stripe, then another light one, irregular and broader. The whole pattern takes on the look of a mask.

As a typical dweller of the shallows, of flood areas, rice paddies, etc., this handsome fish should be treated as a labyrinth fish—that is, the water should not be too deep in the tank (maximum 40 cm or about 16 inches), and there should be thick vegetation and, especially, a dark, humus bottom.

Colisa lalia (Hamilton, 1822)
Dwarf Gourami

Colisa lalia is native to India and the drainage basins of the Ganges, Jumna, and Brahmaputra Rivers, and, also in Borneo, of the Baram River. It occurs abundantly in rice paddies. In 1903, it was the first specimen to be imported by a Hamburg breeding establishment, which studied its breeding habits in the same year. *C. lalia* is one of the finest and nicest of labyrinth fishes for the aquarium. The body is flattened on the sides, with a rather stumpy shape. The snout is long with an upward-tilted mouth that sticks out rather far forward. The males run to 60 mm (2⅜ inches) in length, the females to not more than 50 mm (2 inches).

The basic tones are red and blue. Usually, we can speak of a single basic tone, but this fish is blue in the forward parts, and carmine red along the tail. The body is blue, striped with red. The stripes fade out from the back to the belly, and angle slightly rearward. The females are less distinctly patterned and where the male is red, the female is more brownish. The unpaired fins of the male, like his pectorals, are better developed than in the female, and are toned in the same manner as the body. The pectorals are without coloration and transparent, while the ventrals, which are located on the thorax, have the typical filamentous shape and are reddish.

Colisa lalia is a lovable little fish that is easy to keep. A little shy at first, it soon gets used to its surroundings and wanders calmly among the plants and rocks without attracting attention from its fellow aquarium

Plate II-282. *Colisa lalia.*

dwellers. Although it must be kept warm, it can withstand a fairly low temperature—to about 15 °C (59 °F)—provided that the temperature drop comes about slowly. However, it is at its best above 21 °C (70 °F). Outside the mating season, it is best not to let the temperature rise too high. In the daytime, the temperature should be about 24–25 °C (75–77 °F), and at night it can safely drop to 20 °C (68 °F). It prefers fine-leaved plants, and the tank should be well planted with them. It also likes plenty of light and, at the time of mating, this should be provided by the sun. The size of the tank is not important, as long as it is not, naturally, too small. For one couple, a tank 30 cm (12 inches) long is about the minimum for the fish to be comfortable.

Feeding is no problem, for *C. lalia* is not particular and will accept all kinds of live food, as well as dried animal food. Variation in the diet is a good idea.

Mating is a little different from other labyrinth fishes. For breeding, the tank should be set up with several terraces. Also, the vegetation should be fine-leaved plants and algae. Some floating plants, such as *Riccia*, are also needed, as the male uses tiny bits of them in building the bubble-nest. This is the point on which *C. lalia's* way of breeding differs from that of other species. The nest is not large in cross-section, but it may sometimes be several centimetres (over an inch) high. The temperature is brought slowly up to 28 °C (82 °F), preferably not any higher than this, although breeders do it, with the result that the young are "cooked well-done," which is anything but good for their constitution. The water depth must not be allowed to drop too low. In

985

the wild, this is usually a great deal more than 15 cm (6 inches). In the critical change-over from gill- to labyrinth-breathing, some of the young undoubtedly die, though the ones that live through the crisis will be all the stronger, and that is what we set out to achieve in the first place. The goal must be not quantity, but quality.

When the bubble-nest is ready, the male opens his offensive and a series of sham matings follows. Finally, the tiny eggs are issued and fertilized. Some of them fall to the bottom, the remainder float upward into the nest. The whole business of brood care rests on the male, who also takes care of retrieving those eggs that have sunk to the bottom and sees them safely into the nest. To spare the male trouble, carefully remove the female, taking care not to damage the nest. After a day, the eggs hatch and the larvae swarm in the bubble-nest. After three days, they can be contained no longer and swim freely about. Bringing them up on suitable food is accomplished without trouble.

During the period of change-over from gill- to labyrinth-breathing, when the young keep swimming to the surface to gulp down air, it is often recommended that the water in the aquarium be aerated. It is better not to do this, however, because it will drive the oxygen from the water, even though the tank may be thickly planted, as it should be. The plants must be relied upon to oxygenate the water, as blowing air through it will not accomplish the purpose. If the tank has been provided with terraces, then the little fish will have no trouble pulling through this period. If there is a nest of 250 young (out of a total of 750 eggs) that are completely strong and healthy, that is a good result from breeding.

Colisa lalia is so unusual a fish that even in India and Indonesia, its native lands, it is kept as an ornamental fish because of its beauty. In 1889, Francis Day said, "This lovely little fish is the most beautiful amongst the numerous species of freshwater fishes that I have ever seen."

Plate II-283. *Trichogaster cosby.*

Genus *Trichogaster*

This genus is differentiated from *Colisa* by the longer base to its anal fin (A. IX-XIV/25-39) (see page 938) and the three or four soft ventral fin rays.

Plate II-284.
Trichogaster leeri.

Trichogaster leeri **(Bleeker, 1852)**

Diamond Gourami

Lace Gourami

Mosaic Gourami

Pearl Gourami

Native to Sumatra, Borneo, Thailand and Malaysia, *T. leeri* appears in rivers and creeks thickly grown with plants, as well as in stagnant waters among reeds and other such growth.

Undoubtedly, *T. leeri* is one of the finest and most attractive of the labyrinth fishes. During the mating season, the orange-red of the belly can become even more vivid than is shown in Plate II–284.

The body is high, the sides strongly flattened. The maximum length of this fish in the wild is 12 cm ($4\frac{3}{4}$ inches); in the aquarium, however, some specimens, under certain conditions, can grow even bigger. In the males, the fin rays are often excessively elongated. The male dorsal fin is also noticeably longer (reaching farther back over the root of the tail) than it is in the female, and so this is a good criterion for telling the sexes apart. The ventral fins typically grow out in filamentous projections that sometimes reach back beyond the caudal fin. These fins consist of a grown-together, spiny forepart and three to four soft fin rays.

Care and breeding are the same as for *Colisa lalia*. *T. leeri* makes a fine, rather high bubble-nest. The males are more peaceful and less prone to bad temper in respect to the females than most other labyrinth fishes; even less do they yield to eating their eggs or their young—at least so long as conditions are normal. The temperature must not drop below 20 °C (68 °F), and care must also be taken that the room temperature does not markedly differ from that of the tank water on the surface. It is even better if the air the fish breathe is maintained at a warmer temperature.

Trichogaster microlepis Günther, 1861
Moonlight Gourami

This species, belonging to imports from 1953 and after, hails from Thailand, where, although it is known in various localities, it is not known in great numbers. It grows to about 150 mm (6 inches) long and is comparable to the other species of this same genus which already enjoy a widespread acquaintance and popularity.

This species can be promptly recognized by its uniform, silver-white coloration, its very small scales, which count no less than about 60 in the length of the fish, and the very few spines (three or four) in the dorsal fin.

The natives consider this species to be the female of the Two- or Three-Spot Gourami (*Trichogaster trichopterus*). It is an ornamental and especially beautiful fish, in spite of its rather monotonous coloration. Its keeping and breeding are both similar to that of other species of this genus.

Plate II-285. *Trichogaster microlepis.*

Illus. II-212. *Trichogaster pectoralis.*

Trichogaster pectoralis (Regan, 1910)
Snakeskin Gourami

A fine, sturdy species native to Malaysia and Thailand, *T. pectoralis* attains a length of about 200 mm (8 inches). Its most characteristic feature is the large size of the pectoral fins, which gives the fish its name. It has a black stripe running lengthwise. It should be kept the same as *T. trichopterus*.

Plate II-286. *Trichogaster trichopterus.*

Plate II-287. *Trichogaster trichopterus,* "Cosby" or "Opaline" variety.

Trichogaster trichopterus (Pallas, 1770)

Blue Gourami

Golden Gourami

Opaline Gourami

Three-Spot Gourami

This fish is native to Southeast Asia—Malaysia, Thailand, Burma, Vietnam—and the Indonesian Archipelago, including the islands of Sumatra, Bangka, Borneo, Java, Madura and Bali. It has been imported from time to time since 1896.

The body is a stretched-out oval, flattened on the sides. Its length goes to about 150 mm (6 inches). In the wild, however, 110 mm (4⅜ inches) is normal. In a not-too-roomy aquarium, it seldom grows longer than 90–100 mm (3½–4 inches). The head is rather small, while the slightly outward-folded mouth is end-positioned and turned positively upward.

The dorsal fin has a short base and begins halfway back between the eye and the root of the tail. The aftermost fin rays grow, in the male, out past the root of the tail (a sex characteristic). The anal fin has a very long base and stretches from behind the pectorals to the root of the tail. The pectorals are large and, in fine, snappy male specimens are somewhat pointed. The ventral fins are located on the thorax and are filamentous and grow out beyond the root of the tail.

The coloration of the basic species is olive brown, darker on the back and more yellowish brown on the belly. A large number (up to about 20) of angling cross stripes appear more or less distinctly on a lighter background. Sometimes a rather dark stripe is seen running lengthwise, from the eye towards the root of the tail. In young fish and sometimes also in adult specimens, one or several dark spots appear from time to time, especially in the middle of the body, under the dorsal fin. Spattered over the body, as well as on the unpaired fins, are a great many distinct, whitish spots. These fins—the anal fin especially—can be very beautiful in coloration and pattern. The light orange-yellow edging to the anal fin comes on in the mating season, when the males are usually darker in coloration, providing brilliant contrast to its glow.

The Blue Gourami, currently a much-bred species which threatens to crowd out the so-called original brown variety, apparently hails from Sumatra (*T. trichopterus* var. *sumatranus*). Its basic coloration is light blue to dark blue-green. In America, the common variety is a light powder blue, darker in the breeding season, sometimes almost slate blue. An "opaline" or "Cosby" variety has been developed which retains the dark blue coloration at all times. The brown variety is also known in America and is normally a light milk chocolate deepening to dark chocolate at breeding time. A lighter "golden" variety has also been recently introduced.

As mentioned above, the clearest indication of the fish's sex lies in the long, pointed dorsal fin of the males, which is shorter and rounded in the female.

What has been said about the related species (*Trichogaster leeri* and *Colisa lalia* and *C. labiosa*) can be adapted practically entirely to *T. trichopterus*. If anything, it may even be easier to breed. The bubble-nest built by the male, whether or not it is reinforced by bits of plants, is rather large—15 cm (6 inches) or more—and quite high, though not as rugged as the nest built, for instance, by *Colisa lalia*. As soon as the young are hatched, the nest falls apart—if it did not do so to start with. In a not-too-large breeding tank, it is safer to remove the female directly after mating is consummated. *Trichogaster trichopterus* is one of those fish which, in spite of its size, has been readily accepted by the aquarists. It is a pity that it becomes so attached to the tank it grows up in, that large specimens continue to be shy for a long time if they are transferred to another aquarium. It is, therefore, recommended that only young fish be purchased and allowed to grow up in a roomy aquarium. Never keep several males together in a small aquarium.

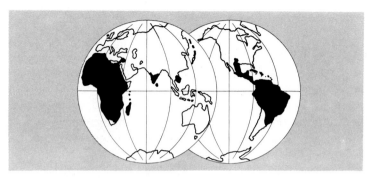

Illus. II-213. Distribution of the family *Cichlidae*.

Family Cichlidae

A striking characteristic of many cichlids is their great variety of gorgeous colorations. This feature induced Günther to describe these fish as chromids (*chroma* means color).

As indicated on the map in Illus. II–213, the distribution area of this family stretches out over Central and South America, Africa, including Madagascar, Israel, India and Ceylon. It is peculiar to find cichlids in Israel, where the fauna is more nearly "palearctic" (see page 52). In Africa, the cichlids predominate over the fish life of the large lakes. In fact, of all the fish species populating Lake Victoria, more than half belong to the family Cichlidae. The original fauna of little Lakes Edward and George was destroyed when their connection to the Nile was broken off, causing the lakes to dry up. However, as soon as the connection was re-established, but this time with a natural obstacle (a waterfall), it was mainly the cichlids that took possession of this new territory. They developed there, undisturbed by large predators, which could not overcome the obstacle of the falls.

It is important to note, however, that there are varieties of cichlids which live in brackish water. This explains how cichlids happen to be living on the island of Madagascar, undoubtedly having migrated there across the sea from the African mainland. That the cichlids did, indeed, have ancestors unafraid of salt water can probably also be deduced since members of the very closely related family Poma-centridae are exclusively true sea dwellers.

The cichlids, without exception, have a more or less perch-like appearance. They are distinguished from the closely related Percidae, Centrarchidae and Nandidae by having only a single pair of nostrils.

The body may be long and slim as well as deep, strongly compressed from the sides or otherwise. The head is large in comparison to the body, with a large mouth and big, lively eyes. Dorsal and anal fins consist of a spiny anterior followed by a soft-rayed posterior portion. The entire body is covered with comparatively large ctenoid (rough) scales. The ventral fins are placed far forward and are usually made up of one spiny ray and five soft ones.

For further characteristics, refer to the descriptions of the sub-families and genera.

These splendidly shaped, gleaming fishes are rather predatory in nature. But quite a few species are plant eaters, and many more are plant destroyers. This is, indeed, one of the reasons why cichlids have been unpopular with hobbyists for a long time. At present, however, aquariums of cichlids are getting to be more and more "the thing." In spite of all their bad qualities, these fishes are also splendid in their life style. When well kept in an aquarium that is properly set up and taken care of, they are very interesting and pleasing objects of study. Their sometimes very remarkable method of brood care causes many a friend of nature to overlook the restraints that have kept him from keeping cichlids.

The breeding of cichlids is extremely interesting. Various species lay their eggs on plants, stones and other objects, other species deposit them in a trench or hole prepared in the sand beforehand. After a few days, the young hatch out of the eggs, and after a week to 10 days, they may be seen swimming freely about. A peculiar brood care may be observed in all species. This is particularly remarkable, however, among the so-called mouth-breeders, where the male or female takes the fertilized eggs into its mouth and holds them there until they hatch. During all that time—usually 10 to 14 days but varying according to species and temperature—they take no food. Later on, the young may hide for a long time, if necessary, in mama's or papa's great "maw." The Angelfish (*Pterophyllum*) is one of the best known and most loved cichlids, often considered by insiders to be the "King of Aquarium Fishes." What friend of nature would not care to possess an aquarium with a school of young Angelfish in it?

CLASSIFICATION OF THE FAMILY

It will occur to most aquarists that nowhere in the literature have attempts been made to break the cichlids down into smaller groups, as has been done so effectively for the toothcarps. It is a case here of finding enough clear, valuable characteristics that are not strongly variable. This has been unusually difficult for this family, but several groups can still be more or less clearly distinguished, on anatomical as well as zoögeographical grounds.

Regan assumes that, for the classification of these perch-like fishes, the piece of bone supporting the uppermost larynx bones is of the utmost importance. In a great number of species, the *Tilapia* group, this piece of bone (pharyngeal apophysis) is formed exlusively by the parasphenoid; in a great number of other species, the *Haplochromis* group, it is formed by the parasphenoid in the middle and the unpaired basioccipital bone on the edges. At least two families are distinguished on these grounds; this difference, then, is characteristic enough to motivate such a division.

For zoögeographical reasons, however, we must go still farther, since the *Tilapia* group, as well as the *Haplochromis* group, are represented both in Africa and in South America. Before the end of the Cretaceous period, Africa and South America formed a single unit of land to which India also belonged at that time. After the Cretaceous, these continents were divided by the ocean, which was certainly a sufficient obstacle to the migration of these cichlids.

If Africa is the cradle of this family, then representatives of both the *Tilapia* and the *Haplochromis* groups must have migrated to South America before the division of the land masses. Against this theory no evidence has been found—quite the reverse.

It is clear that recent cichlids from the *Tilapia* and *Haplochromis* groups, which have been able to develop and specialize independently of each other in both parts of the world for millions of years, are no longer so closely related to each other as they were shortly after the separation of the parts of the world. On these grounds, the *Tilapia* group, as well as the *Haplochromis* group, can thus be divided into African and South American varieties. If this seems somewhat simplified, the *Tilapia* group can be raised up to the sub-family Tilapiinae and the *Haplochromis* group to the sub-family Haplochrominae.

The Indian cichlids still have to be discussed, being most closely related to *Tilapia*. On the basis of several original characteristics and their largely semi-marine way of life, these are best considered relicts of the marine ancestors of the entire family. The only genus known to come from India is *Etroplus*, which the author has classified in the sub-family Etroplinae.

Plate II-288. One of the many cichlids from Lake Malawi not yet classified.

DISTRIBUTION

Distribution has already been briefly discussed, yet it is clear that much more can be written on this subject and that the last word has not been said about it.

For a long time, people have been familiar with representatives of this family. Illustrations have been found on ancient Egyptian buildings, showing the then-most-common species which is also prevalent today, *Tilapia nilotica*, the Nile Mouth-Breeder. Various descriptions, references, and illustrations are known, dating from before Linnaeus, such as the *Historia naturalis Brasiliae*, an 8-volume work about Marcgrave's journey by Piso (1648). This work names three cichlids, which can be immediately recognized from the description as *Cichlasoma bimaculatum, Crenicichla brasiliensis,* and *Cichla* sp. In Linnaeus's *Systema Naturae*, 10th edition (1758), binary nomenclature was employed throughout, making it less complicated to recognize species from their descriptions.

After Linnaeus, many scientists have specialized and chosen for study a certain sub-division of the longer and more expansive material. Well known ichthyologists who have contributed much to the knowledge of the cichlids can be found in the literature list. One may be inclined to ask how to get an idea of the history of the cichlids.

In the Eocene layers of North America (Wyoming), Cope (1877) found remains of a fish, the *Priscacara*, which is quite similar to the cichlids, yet, differs from them, for example, by having teeth on the ploughshare bone (vomer). Woodward, in 1901, mentions remains of an *Acara* sp. (*Aequidens*), found in Tertiary fresh-water deposits of São Paulo, Brazil. Even though *Priscacara* cannot be reckoned among this family, the relationship is so striking that it is obviously a representative of a very closely related family. Indeed, both the *Acara* sp. and the fossil fish described by Cockerell (1924), *Cichlasoma* (*Parapetenia*) *woodringi*, hailing from the Miocene of Haiti, certainly belong to the Cichlidae. This, of course, is not much, but it does give a grip on the situation. Before coming to a conclusion, let us first scan the present-day state of affairs. Cichlids living today are known from Africa, Madagascar and Israel, the eastern and western coasts of India and Ceylon, from South America, and Central America, including Trinidad, Cuba and Jamaica. This region is undoubtedly the largest that this family has ever inhabited; in other words, the present-day distribution is certainly at its greatest extent of expansion, since, in the northern as well as the southern hemispheres, the extreme boundaries, set mainly by the tropical climate, have been reached. The comparatively recent species (*Cichlasoma cyanoguttatum* and others) which have penetrated into North America—Mexico and Texas—are an exception, although the cichlids in Africa today occur as far north as they do in North America. The wealth of varieties, however, clearly decreases to the north (Central America) and to the south (La Plata Basin), which can also be observed in Africa. The Amazon Basin of South America and the Congo Basin of Africa are the focal points. In most areal maps, the northwestern part of Africa is not included in the distribution area. Today, however, *Haplochromis desfontainesii* is known in the vicinity of Algiers and Tunis, so that the entire region of Africa has now become the areal.

The cichlids, as well as the closely related pomacentrids, are undoubtedly of common origin. During the Cretaceous period, a group of fishes diverged from the already strongly differentiated Clupeiformes, and these developed into the spiny-finned fishes. These "primitive spiny fins" populated the "equatorial ocean."

The pomacentrids are considered one of the largest offshoots of the "primitive spiny fins," from which the remaining members of the sub-order Percoidei have sprung.

997

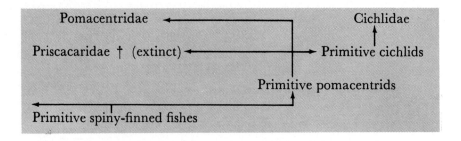

Table II-1. Relationships of the family *Cichlidae*.

The Pomacentridae are marine fishes. The other two families, Priscacaridae † (extinct) and Cichlidae, were fresh-water dwellers, as the recent cichlids still are. The already mentioned fossil *Priscacara* and the equally fossil *Cockerellites* together form the entire family Priscacaridae. Both genera have their origin in the Eocene of North America and cannot be more closely related to the cichlids than represented in Table II–2, for the cichlids arose on the southern primordial continent, and it was only after North and South America became joined that they were able to penetrate into the northern continent by way of the Central American bridge. The same applies to Africa.

DEVELOPMENT OF THE CICHLIDS

The fishes now included in the family Cichlidae are not much more than the extreme tips of the offshoots of the old group, which must have come into existence at the beginning of the Eocene. Among these fishes, relatively little of a close mutual connection has been traced, quite apart from the later genera and species developed from earlier species.

That they are only the tips can be explained relatively simply, for the continents, which were formerly the place of origin of this evolutionary line of fish (the southern primordial continent), had already started to break apart and the Antarctic-Australian region had already come loose.

The most primitive cichlids must not have had such a dislike of sea water as the most recent forms, and possibly the sub-family Etroplinae is a survival of these ancient forms. This sub-family, of which

998

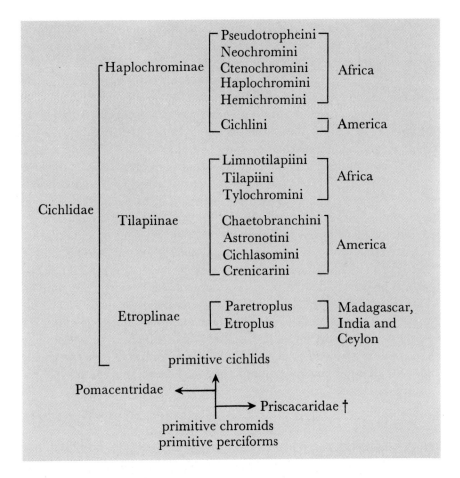

Table II-2. The balance of relationships of the *Cichlidae*.

two genera are considered here—*Paretroplus* from Madagascar and *Etroplus* from India—in former times probably had a substantially larger distribution, but could not maintain themselves against the later-appearing, more specialized varieties, except for those that had become isolated on Madagascar and in India and Ceylon. The other two sub-families distinguished here—the Tilapiinae and the Haplochrominae—can be derived from the Etroplinae.

CLASSIFICATION AND REVIEW OF THE FAMILY

Mutual relationships are more or less present in the various groups of this family. From all three sub-families (Etroplinae, Tilapiinae and Haplochrominae), species have, in the course of time, been imported as aquarium fishes. The most valued species from the tribes Cichla-somini, Astronotini, Tilapiini, Hemichromini, and Haplochromini are now ready for consideration.

It is usually impossible to give information on an entire family with reference to its environment. Many cichlids, however, do live in alkaline water, though, on the contrary, several varieties, especially small ones, live in more or less stagnant, muddy water. In the African lakes, the pH value of the water practically everywhere is in the alkaline region above 7 and can even be as high as 10. The oxygen content of these waters is often rather low, so there is no fear of an oxygen shortage in a sparsely planted cichlid aquarium. (Because cichlids are often large, heavy-bodied fishes which require a substantial amount of oxygen, they are often the first to show signs of distress at oxygen depletion or excessive carbon dioxide by sucking at the top of the water.)

In spite of the predatory nature of several larger species, *all* cichlids that are imported as aquarium fishes are certainly worth the trouble, wherever necessary, of having a separate tank made ready for them. No other group of fishes gives so fine an opportunity to study an unusually interesting method of brood care. Although all species are egg-laying, their methods of reproduction, and of brood care especially, vary to such an extent that only in the smaller groups can there be a detailed discussion.

Illus. II-214. *Etroplus suratensis.*

Illus. II-215. *Etroplus maculatus.*

Sub-family Etroplinae

The only species of this sub-family seen regularly in home aquariums is *Etroplus maculatus* (Bloch, 1795) from India and Ceylon. However, the second species, *Etroplus suratensis* (Bloch, 1790) from the same region, has also been imported off and on since about 1905. They live in fresh as well as brackish water close to the coasts. For cichlid fanciers, it is certainly worth the trouble to try to obtain these fishes. They are tolerant and appreciate a thick growth of water plants. *E. maculatus* grows to about 80 mm ($3\frac{3}{16}$ inches) long. *E. suratensis* may grow as long as 400 mm (16 inches) so only young specimens are suitable.

Sub-family Tilapiinae

Genera from Africa and from South America belong to this sub-family. All members are characterized by the pharyngeal apophysis being formed exclusively by the parasphenoid. This is contrary to the Haplochrominae (see page 1080), among which the basioccipital bone plays a part in this formation, along with the parasphenoid bone.

Besides geographical differences, anatomical differences also exist between the African and American genera, but discussion of these would lead us too far afield.

AFRICAN GENERA

Only the tribe Tilapiini is of significance to aquarists for the time being. Neither of the other two groups in the chart possesses species imported as aquarium fishes.

AMERICAN GENERA

We can be relatively brief on this subject, since the most important member, the tribe Cichlasomini, is treated in the discussion of the genus *Cichlasoma* (see page 1048).

All American cichlids, except the genus *Cichla*, belong to the *Tilapia*-type fishes. Three original genera, which occupy an entirely separate place, must be considered as forerunners of the remaining American tilapiins. These are the genera *Crenicara*, *Batrachops* and *Crenicichla*, tribe Crenicarini. On a somewhat higher level, also directly derived from the ancestral stock, stands the most important tribe, Cichlasomini, to which very highly developed and extremely specialized forms belong, such as *Symphysodon* and *Pterophyllum*. Closely related to the Cichlasomini is the tribe Astronotini, which includes the important genus *Aequidens*. The genus *Aequidens*, in turn, includes the ancestral stock of the tribe Chaetobranchini, a small but very interesting group.

Sometimes there is a very strong but peculiar similarity in build between a number of varieties from Africa and South America, which, however, must be more ascribed to similar living conditions than to a direct relationship. Also, both parts of the world have been separated for so long that most varieties present immediately after the separation have differentiated completely. A similar phenomenon is met with among the characoids and is also established as occurring elsewhere in the animal kingdom.

Tribe Tilapiini

This tribe is spread over all of Africa, including Madagascar, as well as Israel. The fauna is richest in the district south of the Sudan, a region that is streaked with rivers and streams, not to mention the lakes. The Congo Basin and the East African lakes, especially, have unusually large cichlid populations. From the genera belonging to the Tilapiini, only *Ptychochromis* occurs on Madagascar, together with the two species belonging to Etroplinae. In addition to *Tilapia, Parachromis* is the only other genus of this sub-family which has penetrated into Syria and Israel (Sea of Galilee).

No species of the Haplochrominae occur on Madagascar; in Syria or Israel, however, are found several species of the genus *Haplochromis*. If a relationship is determined between the distribution and the number of species in Africa, it soon appears that only a very limited number of genera have a wide distribution, while most of the genera are represented by species more or less confined to particular regions.

Regan and Trewavas have devoted themselves particularly to investigation of the cichlid fauna, and it appears that the Congo, along with Lake Tanganyika, Lake Malawi (formerly Lake Nyasa) and Syria and Israel (on the Sea of Galilee) host a number of genera that are typical for these regions.

As far as the origin of the lakes is concerned, we must go back in time towards the beginning of the Mesozoic, to the Triassic period, when Africa partly sank as a result of geological disturbances, then was again lifted up, torn apart and, along with volcanic eruptions and the like, underwent drastic changes, witnessed today by two more or less clearly distinguished fissures running north and south. In and between these fissures lie the lakes referred to above, as well as the Red Sea and the River Jordan Valley in Israel. The fissures gradually filled with water and the lakes came into being. However, they still had to pass through troublesome times later on before things settled down to their present condition or something close to it.

Although the African lakes lie wholly in the tropics, tropical conditions are far from prevalent all over. Their location at various altitudes plays an important rôle in reducing to sub-tropical several tropical conditions.

Genus *Nannochromis*

At the time that this genus was set up—that is, in 1904—two species were known, *N. nudiceps*, which had been described in 1899 by Boulenger, and *N. dimidiatus* in 1904 by Pellegrin. A third form, *N. squamiceps*, described by Boulenger in 1902, was considered by Pellegrin to be a variety of *N. dimidiatus*, which was undoubtedly correct. It will perhaps be ascertained from a quantity of material that in reality all three species can be reduced to one species.

This African genus, closely related to *Pelmatochromis*, is similar in many respects (also by way of classification) to the South American genus *Apistogramma*. Up to now, only one species, *N. nudiceps*, has become known among aquarists.

Nannochromis nudiceps (Boulenger, 1899)

This species comes from the Upper Congo in Africa—from the vicinity of Kutu on Lake Leopold II and Dolo (Stanley Pool). Its environment is not known for sure, but, considering its conduct, it is probably from about the same vicinity as *Haplochromis multicolor*.

Nannochromis nudiceps is no more predatory than, for example, *Haplochromis multicolor* (Egyptian Mouth-Breeder). This species also attains a reasonable length for an aquarium fish—that is, not more than a total length of 66 mm (2⅝ inches). This species may be compared to its South American relatives, the *Apistogramma* and *Nannacara* species. It is especially similar to the last-named in build as well as in activity, which might lead to the supposition that their relationship is not so far apart as is being expressed in the system of classification. The recently re-imported dweller of the Niger, *Pelmatochromis taeniatus* Boulenger, 1901, is most closely related to *N. nudiceps*. Breeding is the same.

Worthy of note is the pattern in the caudal fin of *N. nudiceps*, which differs from that of the form originally described under this name. It may also be concluded, then, that most imported aquarium specimens represent a local variety (sub-species). This classification is recommended, rather than calling it a new species with nothing but a new import to back it up.

In spite of the rather strongly bulging belly, the fish in Illus. II–217 is a male, characterized by the more sharp-pointed dorsal and anal fins; these are more or less rounded in the female. The body is a bright blue-green, the fins somewhat lighter, translucent with white to ochre yellow stripes and a dark, outer border. In the caudal fin, the stripes next to the yellow-white are sometimes almost black. Near the rearmost

Illus. II-216. *Nannochromis dimidiatus,* male.

point of the gill covers is a dark to black spot, while the upper lip is also blackish.

Although practically nothing has yet been published about this fish, except in scientific works, and only the breeding report of Schuil (1952) gives any particulars about reproduction, it can be assumed (until something more specific shows up) that *N. nudiceps* requires a spacious aquarium, and a sunny location with grouped stones and spots of shade. A bottom soil of sand is recommended, since *N. nudiceps* betrays its relationship to the genus *Tilapia* by digging trenches in it.

The temperature should be about 24 °C (75 °F). Feed predominantly living vegetable and animal food (also infusoria).

N. nudiceps is an exceptional acquisition, so it can be expected to gain greater popularity, even though it is a cichlid. It remains small, and is no more predatory than the South American dwarf cichlids.

Illus. II-217. *Nannochromis nudiceps.*

Plate II-289. *Leptotilapia tinanti.*

Sub-tribe Pelmatochromi

This group was set up, and included as a sub-group of the Tilapiini, for the genera *Pelmatochromis* and *Nannochromis*, along with *Heterochromis*, *Parachromis* and *Cyphotilapia*. The members of the group are the most closely related to the South American members of the tribe Astronotini, particularly the genera *Apistogramma* and *Nannacara*.

Insofar as aquarium fishes are concerned, very little is yet known about the Pelmatochromi, compared to the South American species. Insight into this group has been substantially broadened by the work of the ichthyologists Regan and Trewavas (British Museum of Natural History), Poll and Thys van den Audenaerde (Royal Museum for Central Africa). The genus *Pelmatochromis* with its 50 or so varieties certainly belongs to the most extensive group and, as such, also has the widest distribution, being common in practically every part of Africa. It is an extremely difficult group, from the standpoint of classification, at least. Indeed, a number of fishes are presently included which closer study shows not to belong here. The habitat of various forms described as species of the genus *Pelmatochromis* are sometimes so measurably different that bringing them together on grounds of rigid, classificatory characteristics could be misleading and would not give a correct concept of the true relationship.

1006

Genus *Pelmatochromis*

As a genus, this group is most closely related to *Paratilapia*. The species of interest to aquarists are the smaller ones of the *P. subocellatus* group, which differ so little in nature from the smaller species of the genus *Nannochromis* that it must be asked whether it would not indeed be right to bring all these species together into one genus. A detailed investigation should clear this up, a chore in which the experienced hobbyist-breeder can certainly lend a hand. For the time being, though, the old nomenclature will be maintained.

Hybrids have been yielded by crossing different species, from which it perhaps appears that the biological species within this genus possess numerous species names and the variation is thus much greater than has been assumed for the time being.

COLORATION PATTERN AND RELATIONSHIP

The basic pattern of the different varieties of the *P. subocellatus* complex is based on the patterning of the primitive cichlids, which not only recurs in the South American relatives, but also in many members of the big order of perch-like fishes (Perciformes). If we restrict ourselves to the cichlids, then the rather uniform pattern always becomes noticeable to the breeder in the developing young. There is always a variable number of dark cross bands or vertical stripes combined with one or more lengthwise bands or horizontal stripes.

Pelmatochromis subocellatus, in the different stages of development, shows patterns that can be considered as very original, changing with environment and the personal feelings of the fish. *P. subocellatus* is not regarded here as the most primitive form; however, it is the first form described to avoid a later change of name and it can thus validly be considered the "leader" of the group.

In accordance with the recent distribution of the varieties or species of this group (see Illus. II–218), the heavily populated region of the Niger River delta seems to be where these forms originated. Not less than three of the seven "species" were found there next to each other. Two forms have a westward distribution, *arnoldi* and *annectens*, occurring along the coast and into Liberia. Here, they are taken together as local races of the species *P. ansorgei*.

The third form, *P. ansorgei ansorgei*, can be considered as close to the ancestral stock of the *P. subocellatus* super-species. It has an eastward distribution (and then southward towards the Congo Basin). It changes and is locally substituted for in succession by *P. pulcher*, *P.*

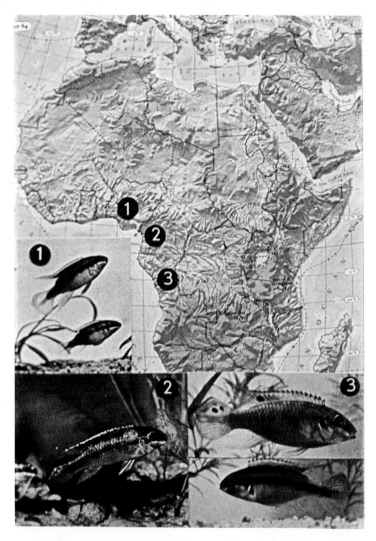

Illus. II-218. Map indicating the type localities of several *Pelmatochromis subocellatus* varieties: 1. *P. subocellatus pulcher*. 2. *P. subocellatus kribensis*. 3. *P. subocellatus* super-species.

taeniatus and *P. subocellatus*. In the Congo Basin, in place of *P. subocellatus*, the genus *Nannochromis* has developed with the species *P. nudiceps*, *P. dimidiatus* and *P. squamiceps*.

The basic pattern, in all varieties, consists of four to nine vertical and one or two horizontal stripes. In the soft-rayed part of the dorsal

Plate II-290. *Pelmatochromis subocellatus kribensis.*

and anal fins and in the caudal fin between the fin rays (on the membrane), a number of dark dots or small spots are present (especially in the males), which sometimes partly make room for a clear lengthwise striping on the caudal fin (*P. subocellatus* from the Lower Congo), or a highly variable number of so-called eye spots on the upper caudal fin lobe. All varieties usually have a plain, dark spot on the projecting points of the gill covers. Just as there is usually a basic pattern in *P. subocellatus*, the vertical and horizontal stripes seldom appear at the same time, but alternate with each other. We can, therefore, observe in these forms a tendency towards reduction in the number of vertical stripes, and an increase in horizontal stripes, even while these, too, are already disappearing. In various forms, either there are only the remains of a single stripe still present or there is no pattern left at all.

Aside from this pattern, there are numerous other characteristics indicating development in this direction. One example is the number of rows of scales on the gill covers (preoperculum) which, in the original forms of *P. ansorgei ansorgei*, consist of three or four, two or three in *P. pulcher*, *P. taeniatus* and *P. subocellatus*. In the species replacing *P. subocellatus*, from which *Nannochromis* species are derived, this reduction

1009

Plate II-291. *Pelmatochromis subocellatus*, male.

goes still farther—two or three rows in *P. squamiceps*, only one or two scales (hence no rows) in *P. dimidiatus*—while the cheek is entirely lacking in scales in *P. nudiceps*.

The so-called ocelli or eye spots seem even more important. These are obviously a recent augmentation to the coloration pattern. In the original forms, the upper caudal fin lobe has a number of more or less regularly arranged, small spots or dots. From the photos of the variations of *P. subocellatus* (see Plate II–291, for example), it may appear that this is certainly not a valid species characteristic.

The notable thing about the specimens imported from the Congo Basin under the name "*Pelmatochromis kribensis*" is that preserved material, upon investigation, could equally well be ascribed to *P. pulcher* and *P. taeniatus* as well as to *P. subocellatus*, and not only on grounds of the spot patterning, but also on an exact interpretation of the key arranged by Boulenger. In order to give the fish a name at this time, we must start from the place of origin (the type localities of the described "species"). The Congo material then belongs, of course, entirely to the species name *Pelmatochromis subocellatus*. In accordance with old material from the regions where the other forms belong—respectively, *P. kribensis* (considered by Thys, 1968, to be a synonym of *P. taeniatus*) (only 3 males and 1 female) and *P. pulcher* (12 males and 8 females)—it cannot be determined whether these species names really represent populations of valid species (or sub-species) or not, because they can, without difficulty, be classed with *P. subocellatus*. The characteristic differences enumerated by Boulenger either lack clarity, or they overlap each other to such an extent that the fish can hardly even be spoken of as a local variety.

Concerning spot patterning, the *P. pulcher* material from Nigeria showed no distinct spots in the fins; in the *P. kribensis* material from Cameroon there was only a small variation in the usual two (in two specimens, only one) eye spots (or dark spots) in the upper caudal fin lobe. In one specimen only the start of a third spot was found. A considerably larger variation was shown by Congo material of *P. subocellatus*, and material from the Chiloango River in Angola and the vicinity of Madimba (Congo) and the Ogowe River in Gabon, which also belongs to *P. subocellatus* s.s. Here, the variation of the eye spots is still greater, from a single, well developed spot to not less than seven weakly developed ones. In the male of this sub-species, moreover, there was a dark border along the bottom lobe of the caudal fin, a prolonging of the dimming lengthwise stripe. In all varieties, the males exhibited a yellow-white, oblique stripe below and contiguous to the black border of the upper lobe, which, in live specimens, is yellow to orange. In the female, this is either not present or is very weakly developed.

This is perhaps one of the clearest differences between the two species, *P. subocellatus* and *P. taeniatus*, the latter having more of an orange-yellow basic coloration as against the purplish red to violet of *P. subocellatus*. The remarkable ventral spot, which stands out so distinctly mainly in the mating season, is purple in the *P. subocellatus* varieties and violet-blue in *P. taeniatus*.

The *P. subocellatus* varieties have hardly any pattern in the lower caudal fin lobe, while in the very same place *P. taeniatus* has a remarkable pattern consisting of five whitish stripes, composed of spots merging together on a dark background, the last stripe being well developed and usually in the form of a "J". In the upper lobe, the dark border and the orange to yellowish, oblique stripe are absent, this being a characteristic of the *P. subocellatus* varieties but, on an orange-yellow background, four to seven dark spots, which may or may not have a light edging around them, do appear.

1011

Plate II-292. *Pelmatochromis subocellatus kribensis.*

In all varieties, the females have a less pronounced pattern, although there are certainly females among them that in this regard are hardly surpassed by the most beautiful males.

Pelmatochromis arnoldi super-species

To this super-species belong the species *Pelmatochromis ansorgei*, *P. arnoldi*, and *P. guentheri*.

The three species reckoned among this group are distinguished from *P. subocellatus*, among other things, by the absence of eye spots on the caudal fin or the dorsal fin, five or six clear cross bands of spots, three or four rows of scales on the cheek (preoperculum), soft-rayed parts of the dorsal and anal fins, and the caudal fin having more or less regularly arranged rows of brownish spots.

None of the three species seems to be kept, at present, in aquariums, although they have been known for a long time as suitable aquarium dwellers.

Pelmatochromis ansorgei Boulenger, 1901

A collection of research material from Abakaliki, Nigeria, includes the three species *P. ansorgei*, *P. pulcher* and *P. taeniatus*, collected, however, as *"Pelmatochromis kribensis."* The sample, consisting for the most part of *P. taeniatus*, indicates that the three do occur side by side in the same water, a situation which does not necessarily imply that they are indeed three true species. We shall assume this provisionally, however, because more extensive material is required, and from several catch locations, in order to come to a conclusion.

Five specimens, one male, three females and a young specimen, could clearly be determined to be *P. ansorgei*. The rather deep body shape is a good indicator here.

The pattern consists of a very dim, lengthwise stripe, a distinct spot on the edge of the gill covers, and three rather wide, easily observed cross stripes, clearest in the male, running from the back to a little below the middle of the flanks. The soft-rayed parts of the dorsal and anal fins, and the entire caudal fin, are spattered with brownish flecks. The basic coloration is yellowish brown.

Pelmatochromis arnoldi Boulenger, 1912
This species is at present known from Nigeria to Liberia, along the coast, partly in brackish coastal waters, yet it is clearly a typical fresh-water dweller. It reproduces exclusively in fresh water. Its length is to about 90 mm ($3\frac{9}{16}$ inches).

The basic pattern consists of a usually very weak lengthwise stripe from the eye to the root of the tail and of five or six cross bands, which are usually not much more than an equal number of dark spots where they cross the horizontal stripe. The fins are the same as among *P. ansorgei*.

Pelmatochromis guentheri (Sauvage, 1882)
Thys, 1968, placed *P. guentheri* in the sub-genus *Chromidotilapia*, which makes the full name *Pelmatochromis (Chromidotilapia) guentheri*.

Pelmatochromis subocellatus super-species
Investigation of some fine, recent material from West Africa and the Congo brings to light that the following, described as true species, form a natural, highly variant population: *P. subocellatus sensu stricto*— *P. pulcher, P. taeniatus, P. kribensis*, and the members of the genus *Nannochromis*. They are listed here in the chronological order of their first description, hence, not in actual order of relationship or development. Viewed from a historic-geographical standpoint, *Pelmatochromis subocellatus* is the valid ancestral form which developed from *P. ansorgei* stock and migrated by way of the fresh coastal waters to the Congo Basin, where the various *Nannochromis* species branched off farther upstream.

On the basis of provisional research, the species *P. subocellatus*, *P. taeniatus* and *P. kribensis* have been lumped together under one species name. Closer study and the experiences of aquarists incline towards the idea that at least *P. taeniatus* can exist next to *P. subocellatus* as a true species. The variety *P. kribensis*, however, should doubtless be classed with *P. subocellatus* s.l. (*sensu lato*, meaning in its widest sense, including all sub-species), as should *P. pulcher*, a species that has indeed been kept by hobbyists, but not yet known by its correct name. The true *P. pulcher* is the fish which has been commonly kept by American aquarists under the name "*P. kribensis*." (Thys, 1968, placed *P. kribensis* as a synonym of *P. taeniatus*, therefore making *P. kribensis* no longer a valid name. Both *P. pulcher* and *P. subocellatus* along with *P. taeniatus* are considered valid species under the sub-genus *Pelvicachromis*.) The author does not agree with this thinking.

This super-species thus includes two species, *P. taeniatus* and *P. subocellatus*, the last with three sub-species, in the order of the migration route of the population, *P. s. pulcher*, *P. s. kribensis* and *P. s. subocellatus*.

Pelmatochromis subocellatus (Günther, 1871)

This species breaks down into three sub-species, which will be successively discussed. A short description applicable to all three varieties is given here, but for details in pattern, refer to the variety under consideration.

As already noted, this species differs clearly in appearance from *P. taeniatus*; the oblique stripe in the upper lobe of the caudal fin, which in live specimens, mainly males, is orange-yellow and towards the outside is set off by a blackish border, is dark towards the inner edge, and may or may not have eye spots. The pattern in the lower caudal fin lobe is, where present, greyish with a series of dark spots on the membrane, rather regularly arranged and hardly forming irregular lines as in *P. taeniatus*.

Pelmatochromis subocellatus kribensis Boulenger, 1911

This form named *P.s. kribensis* seems to be identical to *P. taeniatus* (Boulenger, 1901). It hails from the Kribi River, Cameroon, and not from the Niger, as erroneously indicated by Veldhuizen. The difference between the typical *P. subocellatus* form from Gabon and from the Congo is, if possible, even smaller than that between the Congo form and the *P. s. pulcher* variety.

Although it seems from this that the greater part of the specimens imported as aquarium fishes belong to *P.s. kribensis*, the real *P.*

1014

subocellatus is, however, rather common (certainly in the Netherlands). The mutual differences between the three varieties, as has been indicated, are so small, and the breadth of variation so great, that, in most cases, it is more sensible to talk only about *Pelmatochromis subocellatus*.

Pelmatochromis subocellatus pulcher Boulenger, 1901

The coloration pattern has already been discussed in detail on page 1007. *P. s. pulcher* is a small variety, about 80 mm ($3\frac{3}{16}$ inches) without the caudal fin. The females are a little smaller. The species hails from the delta of the Niger River, Nigeria. It appears that this variety has already been imported into America, but not yet into Europe; at least, no specimens were found among aquarium material.

Pelmatochromis subocellatus subocellatus Günther, 1871

This sub-species inhabits the fresh waters along the West African coast, from Gabon to the Congo, where it is represented by numerous, greatly varying populations. Practically every population shows systematic characteristics of the same rank as those of the varieties *P. s. pulcher* and *P. s. kribensis*, but they are not yet named.

The *P. s. subocellatus* specimens illustrated in Plate II–294 (identical

1015

Plate II-294. *Pelmatochromis subocellatus subocellatus,* male and female.

Plate II-295. Another Malawi cichlid.

Plate II-296. *Pelmatochromis thomasi.*

with those accompanying Meders' article in *l'Aquarium et les Poissons,*
1954) are found in the collections investigated, and there is no doubt
that they belong to this sub-species. The black spot on the dorsal fin,
usually present in both sexes, is found here only in the male. This is
the case not only in these two illustrated specimens, but also in 27 other
specimens from the same place of origin. In another sample, it is just
the opposite—a number of females and young exhibit this spot, and one
male has no spot.

Pelmatochromis taeniatus Boulenger, 1901

This species is probably the same one known to aquarists as
P. kribensis, described here as a species of *P. subocellatus* super-species
(see page 1014).

Genus *Tilapia*

This genus, the largest of the African cichlids, includes dozens of varieties, populating practically every little water-hole over the entire African continent.

Since Boulenger (1915), who gives 100 species names, this has been a rather heterogeneous group, characterized by the presence of teeth in the jaws, the number of dorsal fin rays and spines, and three or four spines in the anal fin. As such, it is certainly not a natural group. A revision is urgently desirable, but it is an enormous job.

Tilapia melanopleura Duméril, 1859

A long series of synonyms has been attached to this fish. It is one of the *Tilapia* species with an especially wide distribution (the distribution area extends from Senegal to Angola, Zambezi and Congo Basins, Bechuanaland and North Natal) and similar variations in form. About 15 forms were conceived with separate names. On the one hand, it is most closely related to *Tilapia zillei* (not *T. zillii*), and on the other to *Tilapia tholloni*.

The basic coloration is bluish, by which it can be directly distinguished from *T. tholloni* (greenish) and *T. zillei* (olive green to yellow-brown). In accordance with the place of origin, *T. melanopleura* is not only an attractive species, but at the same time also one that can be easily bred, although it should be kept in mind that it can grow to a length of not less than 30 cm (almost 12 inches). At about 12 to 15 cm ($4\frac{3}{4}$ to 6 inches), however, it is already sexually mature. *T. melanopleura* is a splendid acquisition for keepers of cichlids, and can always be found among import shipments.

For further particulars, see the discussion of other large cichlids.

Plate II-297. *Tilapia mossambica.*

Tilapia mossambica (Peters, 1852)
Mozambique Mouth-Breeder

T. mossambica, a species that grows to 350 mm (about 14 inches), is from East Africa (Natal). It belongs in large aquariums and may regularly be seen in public aquariums.

Illus. II-219. *Tilapia macrocephala.*

Tilapia nilotica **(Linné, 1766)**
Nile Mouth-Breeder

Very common, even in brackish water, *T. nilotica* comes from Africa—East Africa, Upper Congo, Lake Tanganyika, Lake Chad inlets, the Senegal River, the Niger River—and northeastward, from Syria and Israel.

This perch-like representative of the group Tilapiini will not be much kept in hobbyists' aquariums because of its large size (to 500 mm or almost 20 inches), although young specimens are certainly suitable for keeping over a period of at least two years.

The deep, laterally compressed body merges posteriorly into an extremely narrowed tail section and is entirely covered with rather large, cycloid (smooth) scales. A quite variable species, *Tilapia nilotica* has a large number of varieties spread out over the extensive distribution area.

The basic coloration, as one can expect from so variable a species spread over so wide an area, also differs considerably, yet is always predominantly whitish to yellow-grey with carmine red. The females are easy to recognize by their rounded dorsal and anal fins, which in the males is sharply tapered.

Tilapia tholloni **(Sauvage, 1884)**

This species from West Africa, from the Congo and Ogowe Rivers to Cameroon, grows to a length of about 180 mm (7 inches).

Tribe Astronotini

The habitat of the genera considered to belong to this group—
Astronotus, Aequidens, Geophagus, Apistogramma, Nannacara and *Acaronia*—
entirely covers the area indicated for *Cichlasoma. Aequidens* is the most
important genus for aquarists; moreover, a number of species of the
genera *Apistogramma* and *Nannacara*, the so-called dwarf cichlids, have
introduced aquarists to a more extensive interest in the family of cichlids in general.

Astronotini are distinguished from related tribes by their possession
of only three spines in the anal fin. In this respect, the Astronotini are
connected with the African Tilapiini, especially the genera *Pelmatochromis* and *Nannochromis*. Further valid characteristics are: small teeth,
conical, in bands on the jaws, also conical pharyngeal teeth; scales
are cycloid (smooth) or more or less toothed, but not ctenoid (rough),
about 30 of them lengthwise in the larger genera and 22 or more in
the smaller ones. Spiny and soft-rayed parts of the dorsal fin are not
deeply indented at the division. Weak-rayed parts of the dorsal and
anal fins are unscaled or have a few small basal scales.

Genus *Astronotus*

Astronotus is a monotypical genus, with a wide distribution of its
only species.

Astronotus ocellatus (Cuvier, 1829)
Oscar
Peacock-Eye Cichlid
Velvet Cichlid

In South America, this species comes from the Amazon Basin,
Parana River, Rio Paraguay, Rio Negro, and Guyana. Its natural
environment is unknown.

This fish undoubtedly belongs among the most brilliant cichlids,
but unfortunately, due to its large size and rapacity, is kept by only a
few aquarists. This is indeed a pity, from the standpoint of the
interesting brood care that a pair of these fish always provide. Adult
specimens have a moderately long, laterally compressed body.

The head is blunt and has a large mouth with an oval opening; the
underjaw protrudes somewhat forward. The jaws have well developed
teeth in front and smaller ones on the sides. The median fins all have
rows of scales. The caudal fin and the pectoral fins are rounded; the

Illus. II-220. *Astronotus ocellatus,* head of adult male.

ventral fins have longer frontal rays. The preoperculum (cheek) is notched. The lateral line organ is interrupted, the first part penetrating 19 to 22 scales and the rear part 16 to 20 scales, of which three to four are on the caudal fin.

A description of coloration is extremely difficult here, because it is highly variable, as is also the pattern. Young specimens exhibit a whitish, irregular pattern of bands on a practically black body, with light fins.

Both sexes, which cannot be told apart except in the mating season,

Plate II-299. *Astronotus ocellatus*, young specimen.

can attain a length of 300 mm (about 12 inches). At a length of about 100 mm (4 inches), however, they are already suitable for reproduction.

A very spacious aquarium is a primary requirement for this cichlid. A few sturdy plants can usually be placed in the aquarium without fear of their being destroyed. This is especially so if there are small specimens who will grow up in a tank set up in this manner. It should be given the company of larger fishes, such as other cichlids, loricariids, and other large catfishes.

The food situation is only a question of quantity, for *Astronotus ocellatus* accepts everything! The quantities that even rather small specimens can get away with are enormous. Naturally, it should be fed live food as much as possible, but, if necessary, it will also take pieces of fish and meat.

Reproduction is, as with all other cichlids, always a source of enjoyment for every hobbyist to watch. The eggs are laid, after a mostly stormy courtship, on a previously cleaned stone or somewhere else, are fertilized immediately and are watched over and cared for by both fish in an exemplary manner. About three days after laying, a trench is dug in the sand, into which the young are transferred after hatching. Four or five days later, the young are already swimming freely about in the aquarium.

Genus *Aequidens*

This is a very widespread genus with numerous species, of which only a small number have, up to now, become known in hobbyist circles. A few species have even penetrated into Panama in the north and to the Rio de la Plata in the south. Again the Amazon Basin yields most of the species in this genus, although another important area is the Guiana Highlands.

Aequidens is distinguished from the remaining members of the tribe mainly by the uppermost line of pores of the lateral line organ, which runs along one or more rows of scales below the dorsal fin. The preoperculum has no scales, the body is high and heavily compressed sideways.

Aequidens curviceps (Ahl, 1924)
Flag Cichlid

In South America, *Aequidens curviceps* is found in the drainage basin of the Amazon River, but not including those parts of the river in Peru and Bolivia. Although it was first imported in 1909 by Siggelkow-Hamburg, it is hardly seen any more in hobbyist circles. Re-importation is certainly recommended.

This cichlid can attain a length of 95 mm (3¾ inches), but in the aquarium it seldom grows longer than 80 mm (3 3/16 inches). It is a very attractive fish which does not get too big and, for a cichlid, is rather peaceful and tolerant. The body is a long oval, laterally compressed, with a rather large head.

The large dorsal fin starts just in front of the pectoral fins and continues on back to the typical narrowing of the tail. The soft-rayed part in the males reaches about to the end of the caudal fin, but is somewhat shorter in the females. The anal fin is much smaller than the dorsal fin, extends about as far, yet begins much farther to the rear, about where the extremities of the ventral fins leave off, if these are brought back flat against the body. The ventral fins are located far forward (breast-positioned), but still a little behind the base of the pectoral fins. All fins are well developed. The coloration is very beautiful but highly variable, as it is with most cichlids. The basic coloration is dark brownish green to olive brown. The back is dark due to an intermingling of blue. The fins may have small, light blue spots, arranged in rows, on a greenish yellow background. A lengthwise band runs across the body, but mostly dissolves into three dark (to black) spots—one above the base of the pectoral fins, one above the

Plate II-300. *Aequidens curviceps* **with eggs.**

beginning of the anal fin, and the third on the upper side of the root of the tail. Sometimes, these round spots are entirely or partially merged with the background. Also, vertical bands can appear, depending on the disposition of the fish; these are, however, seldom intense. The area of the head, the gill covers in particular, is decorated with a number of irregularly placed, light blue dots or flecks.

The females' coloration is usually somewhat less distinctive and, besides, can be recognized by the rounder, wider belly, though this may not be so clearly apparent.

Aequidens curviceps, as already mentioned, is very suitable for the home aquarium, something, unfortunately, that cannot be said for all the species. One advantage—which may give opponents of this fish family a reason for changing their minds—is that *Aequidens curviceps* can be kept without trouble in a planted aquarium, even one populated by all kinds of smaller fishes. In a quite roomy aquarium, set up with some large rocks and sturdy plants, it feels so at home that it leaves the plants and even small companions alone, particularly if it is kept well fed. It will also propagate there and take every precaution to protect its progeny from other fishes until the young can take care of themselves. As far as temperature is concerned, this is no more difficult a situation, for it may vary from 15 to 25 °C (59–77 °F). It is absolutely not necessary to raise the temperature in the mating season. It lays as well at 18 °C (64 °F) as at 25 °C (77 °F), as long as there is plenty of room and suitable rocks for laying the eggs on. Sometimes the eggs are laid in a hole between stones and are carefully tended by the male or by both parents standing guard by turns. They also lay their eggs on stiff plants or even against the panes of the aquarium. A total of 200 to 300 eggs can be laid. Depending on the temperature and other factors, the young hatch out after 40 to 100 hours and are not difficult to bring up.

Plate II-301. *Aequidens itanyi.*

Plate II-302. *Aequidens maroni.*

Aequidens maroni (Steindachner, 1881)
Keyhole Cichlid

The distribution of this species remains limited to the eastern Guiana Highlands and, as far as is known, it does not occur in Venezuela, as erroneously indicated by Stoye, Innes and Meinken. The mistake is probably the fault of the first-named author, who confused the Maroni river with the Rio Maroa in Venezuela. The Marowijne running along the border between Surinam and French Guiana is usually called the Maroni by the French. The southern part of the river, no longer serving as the border between the two countries, runs entirely in French Guiana and is called the Marowini.

Aequidens maroni is an exception to the rule that cichlids are always crude and less than enjoyable as aquarium fishes. That is indeed the case with some species, but *A. maroni* is a most pleasant exception. In the first place, it is a smaller species, attaining a maximum length of 80 mm ($3\frac{3}{16}$ inches); it is a calm fish that swims about in a stately fashion; and it is particularly majestic-looking due to the attractive upper outline of the head and back. Moreover, it is not at all predatory, with no tendency to bite or be intolerant of others, so that it scores well in any aquarium that resembles at all a Surinamese environment—

a light current at the edge of open water with some bank growth. *A. maroni* may be kept together with toothcarps (*Rivulus* species and *Poecilia* species) and characins (*Pristella riddlei, Hyphessobrycon callistus, Hyphessobrycon scholzei, Hemigrammus ocellifer, Hemigrammus unilineatus* and the like), hatchet fishes (*Gasteropelecus* and *Carnegiella*), catfishes (*Helogenes marmoratus, Hoplosternum littorale* and *Hoplosternum thoracatum, Corydoras* species). To provide surface dwellers for such a community aquarium, take note of *Copella arnoldi* and Nannostomini.

Aequidens maroni is thus a smaller cichlid with the typical, laterally compressed shape of its genus. The specimen in Plate II–302 came from Surinam and deviates a little in detail from the Guyana variety. This last always shows more or less clearly a dark, round, so-called eye spot with a vertical band dropping from underneath and becoming broader at the bottom. This characteristic has given this fish the popular name in America of Keyhole Cichlid. The Surinamese variety shows this band under the eye spot only sporadically and hardly clearly in older specimens. The eye spot itself is edged with golden yellow. The basic coloration is brownish, more golden brown in young specimens, darker brownish green in older ones.

Reproduction takes place in the same manner as described for *Aequidens pulcher*. It is a very productive species.

Illus. II-221. *Aequidens portalegrensis.*

Aequidens portalegrensis (Hensel, 1870)
Black Acara
Lace Cichlid
Port Acara

This species comes from Porto Alegre (for which it was named), in the state of Rio Grande do Sol, and the State of Santa Catarina, both in Brazil, as well as from Bolivia, Paraguay, and Rio Uruguay. It is very common in the calm waters of the various river drainage basins and in cold highland streams.

Aequidens portalegrensis is very closely related to *Aequidens pulcher*, to which it is most similar in build. Its length is to about 200 mm (8 inches); in the aquarium, however, it seldom grows bigger than 120 mm ($4\frac{3}{4}$ inches) and is already sexually mature at a length of 65 mm ($2\frac{9}{16}$ inches) (all measured without the caudal fin). This species can also be included among the relatively small group of rather calm, peaceful cichlids. Young specimens are in general more predatory than the older ones, although the latter can be rather rough on intruders during the mating season. A great deal of what is said in the discussion of *Aequidens pulcher* applies to this species as well, where a few words are also said about hybrids or cross-breeds, or rather, voluntary mating between the two species.

The green coloration dominates in most cases, especially in young fish and in the parents during the mating season. The head is blue-grey to blue on top. The basic coloration is yellow-green, blue-green, green or green-brown, or greenish brown to brownish, depending on the age and district of origin, changing towards the throat to a reddish

1030

brown tint. The iris of the eye is golden yellow with a dark red upper edge. All scales have a dark edge at the rear, causing a network pattern on the body. From the eye to the root of the tail runs a blackish, rather irregularly formed band, which sometimes resolves into several rather large, dark spots, after which the eight to nine usually less-visible cross bands suddenly appear. On the root of the tail, close to the upper edge, is a usually quite plain, lens-shaped, black or dark blue-green spot, ringed with a light tone. The back is predominantly green, the belly side more blue-grey, light or dark, depending on the circumstances, and quite variable. At times, the fish is entirely black. The dorsal fin is blue-grey to grey-brown, like the anal and caudal fins, spattered with light blue flecks and stripes. The ventral fins are yellow-green, the dorsal fins brownish green to deep, wine red.

The sexes are rather alike in pattern and coloration. Sometimes, however, the slightly more intense blue-green sheen of the male allows the two sexes to be told apart. The lengthened oviduct of the female in the mating season is always a distinguishing characteristic.

Breed the *A. portalegrensis* as described for *A. curviceps* and *A. pulcher*. Although specimens from mountain streams having temperatures about 10 °C (50 °F) are known, it is most sensible not to let the temperature drop below 15 °C (59 °F). As a rule, this fish can be kept in an unheated home aquarium, where it breeds with great willingness at temperatures between 18 and 20 °C (64–68 °F).

Aequidens pulcher (Gill, 1858)
Blue Acara

Aequidens pulcher is found, abundantly, in moderately flowing and stagnant water in Central and South America—in Panama (Magdalena River, Atrato River, San Juan River), Colombia (Cucuta, Rio Pamplonita), Venezuela (Rio Limon, northward from Maracaibo, Isla del Buro, Lago Valencia, Rio Bue, Caripito, Rio Cabriales) and Trinidad.

A typical cichlid, *A. pulcher* has a deep body, which is rather strongly compressed in the tail, and a wide, somewhat flattened head. Although measurements of up to 200 mm (8 inches) have been stated in the aquarium literature, still the biggest specimen among the several hundred fish included in the collection of the Smithsonian Institution in Washington, D.C., measures no longer than 110 mm ($4\frac{3}{8}$ inches), which must be considered its maximum length (without the caudal fin). In the aquarium, it does not usually attain a length greater than 80 mm ($3\frac{3}{16}$ inches). In spite of this somewhat large size, this cichlid is certainly the calmest and most peaceful of all its near relatives. It is fairly variable in proportions and coloration, and there is a substantial difference in pattern between the young and the

Plate II-303. *Aequidens pulcher.*

older fish, but there are still a number of constant characteristics that make it easily distinguishable from its relatives.

The basic coloration of A. pulcher is yellowish to yellow-brown with a somewhat darker, green back. Over the flanks spills a blue glow, which turns to cream on the belly. The five to eight vertical bands are always more distinct than the lengthwise band which is usually vague. The cross bands are widest on the back. The whitish bands located between them show an orange tint.

Every scale is marked with a blue-green to bright blue dot. The gill covers have a number of peculiar, irregularly shaped, bright blue dots and wavy lines, which may also be found under the eye. The lips are also blue-green. The iris of the eye is golden yellow with a bright red ring around the eye. During the mating season and sometimes inbetween the flanks are spattered with a number of golden green, gleaming dots, arranged in rows, which are also usually present on the median fins at the same time.

The dorsal and anal fins are blue-green, the caudal fin is more reddish, but also spilled over with blue. Along the dorsal fin runs a distinct red border. The ventral fins have brownish red fin rays between the blue fin folds; the elongated, second, unbranched ray is a bright green-yellow. All the fins, except the rounded caudal fin, are sharply pointed. The dorsal and anal fins have decidedly tapered middlemost, weak fin rays. Both sexes look so much alike that they cannot easily be told apart. A suitable characteristic, however, is always the lengthened oviduct of the female in the mating season.

The young are without coloration at first, with about five dark (to black) spots in the dorsal region, which practically merge together over the back. The dark spot on the back that is so characteristic of the various related species is absent from the tail root in this case.

Like related cichlids, this species is preferably kept in a very spacious aquarium with a thick layer of sand and a number of big rocks (yellow sandstone or flagstone) on the bottom. Since A. pulcher is one of the few species which can be kept well in a planted aquarium, some sturdy Sagittaria, Ludwigia, Bacopa, and the like can be placed along the sides as long as the middle of the tank remains open (place a few rocks there). A location where a little sunlight can periodically fall into the aquarium will always be appreciated, and the coloration will then show up to its best advantage. The temperature should be between 18 and 30 °C (64–86 °F).

After the usual foreplay, a show that all cichlids put on so beautifully, the egg laying begins. On a stone previously cleaned for the purpose, the female lays her eggs by placing her oviduct on the rock and swimming in a circle. The eggs come down like a veritable necklace of tiny beads and are immediately fertilized by the male. The spawn is fiercely defended against whatever intruders may come along, in which case these fish, which are usually so agreeable, become aggressive in every way possible, at least if the spawn is threatened.

The parents take turns watching and fanning the spawn and after the second day, when the wriggling but still helpless young have hatched out, they are transferred to a hole in the sand. After another day or so in the hole, the young become free-swimming. They are still watched over by the parents and are ready to begin feeding. During this period it is not necessary to provide special food for the young, if the parents are given a good, varied diet, as the parents masticate this into a kind of nourishing porridge which they then spit out among the young. The little fellows grow quickly and after a week or 10 days, the whole school, composed of about 400 little fish or sometimes more, swim about the parents. Often, a young couple, having laid their eggs, will devour the spawn themselves in the course of two days. After that, a second spawning is brought up with the greatest of care. It is especially remarkable in this species, as well as among some relatives, that young just out of the egg have a very tiny head, a great big caudal fin, and a very big yolk sac.

Young hatched out in the spring are sometimes already sexually mature in the fall. However, it is better not to try to breed the fish until they are in their second year. The best results are achieved with fish about two years old.

Mating and egg laying of *Aequidens pulcher* with related varieties such as *Aequidens portalegrensis* and *A. curviceps* have been described many times (page 1026). The mating has rather strange results, however, because it appears that although the eggs can be normally fertilized and their development begun and continued to the height of the "blastula" stage (reached about 10 hours after fertilization), development then ceases and the eggs turn mouldy or simply vanish. That there is any development at all is, at any rate, an indication of the close relationship of the species and possibly even the degree of development is indicative of the degree of relationship.

A successful hybridization—a full development of the eggs and growing up of the young—has not, as far as is known, been reported.

Genus *Apistogramma*

This is a genus of so-called dwarf cichlids with numerous species, of which a number are very well liked among hobbyists.

Apistogramma agassizi (Steindachner, 1875)
Agassiz's Dwarf Cichlid

In South America, *A. agassizi* is found in the middle reaches of the Amazon Basin, the upper reaches of the Parana River and the Rio Paraguay. It is common in moderately flowing waters, and in pools and ponds in periodic contact with the rivers. The first importation of any significance was in 1933 (Hamburg).

Apistogramma agassizi is without doubt one of those cichlids that changed the minds of anti-cichlid aquarists. It is not only an extremely tolerant fish, but it also does not grow too large (about 80 mm or $3\frac{3}{16}$ inches). When young and when older, *A. agassizi* is always a gleaming display jewel of aquarists. The somewhat smaller females are only slightly less attractive than the males. Illus. II–222 shows a male who may be recognized by his pointed fins.

The second ray of the ventral fins, the third and fourth of the soft parts of the dorsal and anal fins, and the middlemost rays of the caudal fin of the male are sometimes lengthened into a thread-like shape.

The coloration and pattern in this species are also very variable and not only dependent on conditions, but at the same time on the place of origin. In general, the basic coloration is yellowish to olive green, the

Illus. II-222. *Apistogramma agassizi,* **male.**

Plate II-304. *Apistogramma borelli*, male.

flanks spilled over with gleaming gold and metallically green, glittering flecks. The two characteristic white bands which run towards each other to the rear appear in the caudal fin of the males, as soon as they are larger than about 40 mm ($1\frac{9}{16}$ inches). The other tones of the body and fins vary from olive green and blue-green to brownish. The dark stripe from the eye that runs backwards and downwards at an angle, typical of many dwarf cichlids, is also present in this species, yet can sometimes be almost entirely lacking, especially in the females. At these times, not much more than a dark spot remains in the middle of the flanks.

A. agassizi is easy to distinguish from the other species of this genus by the lengthened, middlemost caudal fin rays, which gives this fin a pointed look, particularly in the male. It can be distinguished from its close relative *Apistogramma borelli*, which also possesses this characteristic, by the lateral line organ; the topmost part of this extends, in *A. agassizi*, over at least 10 scales, in *A. borelli*, over not more than 9 and usually fewer. Possibly, *A. borelli* will once more be considered a sub-species or a geographical variety of *A. agassizi*.

Like most of its relatives, this dwarf cichlid belongs among those fishes which it is practical to keep in a large community aquarium with small tetras and other attractive little fishes.

A good plant growth is also much appreciated and if it is provided with such, it rewards us with a practically continuous show of its coloration. The temperature limits for this species are 15–30 °C (59–86 °F). At a normal, commonly used temperature of a little over 20 °C (68 °F), *A. agassizi* feels outstandingly well and will spawn spontaneously. It is very sensitive to the addition of chemicals, yet much less sensitive to fungus than is usually asserted. It is just as well for the water to be a little acid as a little alkaline.

All types of food, preferably not dried, are gladly accepted and *A. agassizi* will even eat rather large insect larvae along with certain water insects and snails. In fact, a couple can be very productive, laying up to about 500 whitish to rust-brown eggs, depending on the food served them. The variability of coloration in the eggs is remarkable, even in the same batch, after a certain food in the preceding period has been predominantly given.

Plate II-305. *Apistogramma borelli,* **female with fry.**

Egg laying takes place in the usual manner of cichlids, not only on rocks and panes, but also on large leaves of plants.

Usually, the female takes over the care of the brood by herself and continually chases the male away after fertilization. In a roomy aquarium, the male can either be left in or removed. After two or three days, the female transfers the eggs to a small hole in the sand or between the roots of a robust plant, where they soon hatch out. Sometimes the brood is moved several more times; even the young fish, after hatching, are often transferred several times to some other place.

The young grow quickly without the addition of special infusoria cultures (roomy tank with humus layer) or brine shrimp being served. Of course, to feed them such does no harm (not too much at one time, naturally), but normal feeding with strained waterfleas and wads of ditch algae is sufficient. *A. agassizi* is also quite suitable for an outdoor fish pond, where reproduction, if this is possible, is carried on even more easily.

Plate II-306. *Apistogramma cacatuoides.*

Apistogramma cacatuoides Hoedeman, 1951
Cockatoo Dwarf Cichlid
Crested Dwarf Cichlid

This species hails (insofar as data can be assumed to be trustworthy) from the vicinity of Paramaribo in Surinam. Relatives of this genus are indeed known to come from this region and Guyana.

This species seems not to grow more than about 45 mm ($1\frac{25}{32}$ inches). The female's coloration is somewhat more simple than the male's. It also lacks the substantially lengthened membranes behind the foremost dorsal fin spines and the lengthened rays in the caudal fin, and has rather short ventral fins. Moreover, the dorsal fin is rounded on the end.

The basic coloration of *A. cacatuoides* is olive-yellow with gleaming, metallic blue scales. A dark band, clearly observed in both sexes, runs from the rear edge of the eye towards the base of the caudal fin. Less distinct and sometimes entirely absent is an irregular spot at the base of the last fin rays of the dorsal fin, which sometimes spreads out into a vaguely visible cross stripe, in which case usually two irregular, broad cross stripes run from the tenth to thirteenth and from the sixth to ninth spines of the dorsal fin towards the ventral fin. Back and downwards from the eye towards the edge of the gill cover also runs a usually distinct, dark stripe. The frontal rays of the dorsal fin are deep blue to black; the first ray of the ventral fins and also the first two rays of the anal fin are milk white.

Yellow dominates in the region of the belly and is especially intense above the base of the anal fin. On the head are spattered soft green and orange flecks and stripes.

It may be assumed that practically the same things are true for *A. cacatuoides* as for most other *Apistogramma* spp. It has been observed at egg laying, but the eggs did not hatch because of too thick a population of related varieties. Laying of the eggs takes place, the same as with *Apistogramma agassizi, Nannacara anomala* and *N. taenia.* In a more or less dark place, preferably in a hollow between stones, the female carefully brings everything to a state of readiness. While she is busy cleaning a stone, the male is violently prevented, despite his repeated attempts, from approaching the future nest. Once the female is assured that the time has come, a beautiful courtship begins, which at first seems as if it will develop into a brawl. Each fish nips onto the lower jaw of the other until they are firmly fastened together; then, with powerful wriggles of their bodies, both attempt to swim backwards. It resembles the "beak pulling" that can be observed among birds, a very plain prologue to mating. The fish develop immense speed at this time, which makes us wonder how they can then stand still so quickly, turning their eyes left and right, observing the surroundings.

It is not known to the author how reproduction continues from this point on, after the eggs have been laid, yet it may be supposed that the affair is carried on entirely or almost entirely similarly to the mating and brood care described for *Apistogramma ramirezi* (see page 1042).

This species is no longer being imported into Europe although it first appeared in small numbers among hobbyists in 1949 and 1950 as obvious imports from Surinam. In the United States, however, a variety has been described from time to time under the name (or designation) *Apistogramma* U_2, applied by Innes, which, in all probability, is identical with the variety described here as *Apistogramma cacatuoides*.

The species *Apistogramma ornatipinnis* and *Apistogramma pertense* are much kept, requiring in all respects the same care as the other species of this genus. Reproduction and brood care also follow the same pattern.

Plate II-307. *Apistogramma ortmanni.*

Apistogramma ramirezi Myers & Harry, 1948
Butterfly Fish
Ram
Ramirezi

This species was collected by Manuel Vicente Ramirez and Herman Blass, in April, 1947, in Venezuela, during an 800 km (500 mile) car trip southward across the llanos of the Orinoco River out of Palenque. The locality probably lies on the Rio Meta or Rio Apure. It is, of course, too bad, especially for science, that the fishes caught during the trip were all put together into shipping containers without keeping a memorandum.

The higher and somewhat more thick-set body of *A. ramirezi* deviates from the *Apistogramma* type. In addition, the outgrown spines of the dorsal fin, particularly in the male, are very conspicuous and become longer and longer as the fish continues to grow. This was reason enough for Wickler (1963) to establish the genus *Pseudogeophagus* for this species.

The basic coloration is yellowish pink to lilac or violet, lighter towards the belly side. On the back, at the base of the dorsal fin, are four to five broad, black cross bands, which blur out to nothing in the middle of the flanks. The first band runs through the membrane of the frontal dorsal fin spines. A very intense band runs over the eye in a gentle curve from the back down to the edge of the gill cover. The frontal spines of the ventral fins are usually also black. The fins are otherwise pink to orange-red or light carmine red. On the body are spattered some light blue, metallically gleaming flecks which spread out on the anal and caudal fins.

It can happen that nothing is seen of the band pattern described above, but in place of it, in the middle of the flanks, a little above the middle of the lengthwise axis, a large oval to lens-shaped, vertical black spot may be seen, surrounded by a large number of light blue, gleaming dots.

As seldom happens, this species was successfully bred shortly after it was first imported. That is certainly due in part to the breeders' familiarity with the habitat, an extensive prairie landscape, of the savannah type, with locally thick but mostly sparingly placed growths of trees, from which it appears that the habitat of *A. ramirezi* is only slightly shaded. This is indeed in agreement with the habits of the fish in the aquarium, where it obviously likes to haunt sun-lit places. The air temperature in the catch region in the dry season (November to April) stands at about 22–25 °C (72–77 °F) before sun-up and during the day runs up to not less than 37 °C (100 °F). Of course, the water temperature remains considerably lower than that, but does not fall below 22 °C (72 °F). Considering the geological composition of the region in question, the lime content of the water is bound to be very low, hence the hardness is at a low degree also. Nothing is known of its pH value, so we can only proceed on results and observations in the aquarium. As far as is known at present, *A. ramirezi* is monogamous, thus a male and a female form an ideal pair. Nor must it be just any male and any female, but a couple that is attracted to each other from a group of six or eight fish or more.

The first breeding report (as far as is known) came from the dealer Allen (1948) who, from one pair and 33 egg layings, was able to bring up no less than 13,540 young fish, thus averaging 410 fish per laying. It appeared that the eggs were most frequently laid on a flat stone. Laying on broad leaves of water plants also occurred, while sometimes the fish seemed to dig holes in which to lay their eggs, in the manner of some larger cichlids, such as, among others, the *Tilapia* species.

Allen indicates a pH value of above 7.3. He transferred the stone on which the eggs had been laid, spawn and all, over into another tank and substituted a water-discharge tube for the parents. This is a way, of course, to be sure of getting a certain number of young. The aquarist, however, is hopeful in the first place of being able to study the fish and not to roughly interrupt the mating urge and the further urge to take care of the eggs and the young brood. It is true that in the

1042

method adopted by Allen—and unfortunately not just by him, but by others as well—the parents, through lack of eggs to care for, very soon (within two weeks) are stimulated to a second laying. It will be clear, at any rate, that in the wild, several matings take place per year, considering the great productivity of *A. ramirezi* in the aquarium under usually much less ideal conditions.

The courtship of these fish is easily studied, as it is in the case of many other fishes, of course, and is a delightful experience for every true nature lover. He will get more satisfaction from the courtship alone than can be yielded by the end result, whether that will be 10 or 300 young fish. This courtship, preceding the real laying and fertilization of the eggs, permits us to see the fish with their most beautiful colorations, since, at the same time, they feel at ease, the circumstances being such as to turn them to reproduction. Although it is known that many living organisms are induced to reproduce when environmental circumstances somehow worsen, we must assume that the stimulus that brings on the mating period is a natural one, which, especially in the aquarium, requires optimum conditioning.

Apistogramma ramirezi is a busy fish, so, at any moment that the female is less active, withdrawing from her usual bustle with her belly on the bottom or on a stone, it is indicative that something is about to happen. She may be sick, causing her to act this way, and this will naturally show up in some way, or she is ready to lay, a condition that becomes obvious a day later by the intensifying of the pink coloration near the pectoral fins.

The male has already gone into action in a kind of "play" that Senfft (1950) compares to that of butterflies. The two speed through the tank, fleeing from each other, then return to close association and press themselves against each other and continue the dance. This can last several days before real preparations are made for laying.

Laying is further preceded by cleaning a stone (or sometimes a leaf or some other object). This is not usually done with the care that other cichlids expend on this operation, although both fish do join in the task. Then, the female slides her belly over the stone, turns about once more, finally swims farther, and there appears a row of tiny, light brown eggs, stuck fast to the stone, which are fertilized at once by the male. In doing this, he spreads all his fins out wide, the lengthened spiny rays of the dorsal fin sticking straight up and the tubular anal opening clearly visible as it moves over the eggs. The laying is repeated many times and as the female finally retreats, the male takes up his post by the spawn and fans it, in the manner of cichlids, with his pectoral fins.

Brood care then begins and after some time, the female usually takes over the watch. A good couple will change places as soon as the one on guard swims away to look for food or to chase away an intruder.

Such a nest can contain as many as 500 eggs, and, if they are not alarmed by human hands reaching into the tank, both parent fish will protect the spawn and the hatching young against encroachers. Even some company is advisable, however, as long as the tank, naturally, is big enough and the company is composed of the same size fish or completely peaceable species. It is clear that, as soon as the young hatch out, in about two days, the importance of companions increases as the parents thus lead a busier life. Good feeding ensures that there will be no general attack on the young which, unconscious of any danger, on about the fifth day swim freely about close to the brood location and to the watchful guardian. The young then begin gradually to react to their surroundings and pile in a heap under cover of their parents. Later, they come swarming impudently out, moving even farther from the brood location. Finally, the parents accompany the group of young along the algae-covered rocks, along the bottom or the surface. They grow well and, although some die, after 14 days, there is still a nice crowd of them. Gradually, they begin to go their own way, while the parents make preparations for a new spawning.

Apistogramma reitzigi Ahl, 1939
Reitzig's Dwarf Cichlid
Yellow Dwarf Cichlid

In 1937, the first specimens of *A. reitzigi* were imported into Europe from the middle basin of the Rio Paraguay. Although it was seldom seen after that, it is now being imported again.

A. reitzigi is a small dwarf cichlid, about 45 mm ($1\frac{25}{32}$ inches) (females a little smaller), but with a robust appearance because of the high body build and especially because of the high dorsal fin. The most striking characteristic that immediately distinguishes this species from its relatives is the striping in the last rays of the dorsal fin. In the male, this striping is somewhat clearer than in the female, and sometimes, a similar striping may also be observed in the anal fin of the male. In addition to these differences, the females can always be

Plate II-309. *Apistogramma reitzigi.*

told from the males by the more uniformly flowing line of the back; in the male, this is more or less angular, just in front of the dorsal fin.

A. reitzigi is a very attractive species with a blue-green basic coloration and a bright, light yellow throat, breast and belly. The entire body, with the exception of the ventral region, is spilled over with a splendid, metallic blue sheen.

Depending on the conditions, there is a dark, lengthwise band with about seven, dark cross bands. Owing to a dark edge to their scales, the females are on the whole darker, but at least as attractive as the males. The fins are yellowish green, the frontal part of the dorsal fin blue-green, the first rays being black to brownish black.

This fish, kept the same as its related species and at not too high a temperature (18–24 °C or 64–75 °F), is well suited to a calm aquarium. It reproduces in the aquarium without trouble, and during this period the male is at his most beautiful. The female starts exhibiting a lighter and lighter yellow belly and begins making obvious preparations for mating. Normally, the female takes the care of the brood upon herself, but Andrews (1954) informs us of a deviation in the course of brood care. According to him, after two weeks, part of the young desert the female and seek refuge with the male who takes on his duty in an exemplary manner. The number of young per brood is not large (about 60), but young can be repeatedly brought up in the course of a season.

Apistogramma taeniatum (Günther, 1862)

The distribution area of this species includes the Amazon Basin and the Guianas.

The discussion hereafter applies to all varieties mentioned later which are included in the genus *Apistogramma*, which as aquarium fish are hardly different from each other and, also, can be kept under the same conditions. Where experience has taught that the conditions for certain species may deviate from those customary, this will be mentioned.

The common type of this species shows clearly from the pattern, which, in fact, is also exhibited by the variety *A.t. pertense*. The technical differences between the varieties and the pattern on the body and fins are extremely small. The confusion of nomenclature is here again due to the great variability of forms and the largely overlapping, technical characteristics.

As already mentioned, the fish is hardly distinguishable, if at all, by its activities. Certainly young specimens are not recognizable, which is indeed difficult with all the close relatives until they have attained a length of about 30 mm ($1\frac{3}{16}$ inches).

This species is kept in a roomy aquarium, preferably substantially wider than high, with some fairly large pieces of natural stone (red or yellow sandstone or similar), which become grown over with algae in the course of time. A location where some sunlight can enter the tank is recommended, although the fish does like to hang out among the stones.

At mating time, the female examines the future dwelling place, and finally cleans off a rock with her mouth. Courtship takes place in the usual cichlid fashion and "mouth tugging" begins the real mating. Until then, no mercy is shown the male, who is dragged more or less roughly to the stone, where usually 50 to 200 tiny eggs, obviously without much adhesive power, are laid or possibly deposited in a small hole. After fertilization, which takes place immediately, the male is driven away again and is no longer allowed in the vicinity of the nest, especially not before the young are swimming about absolutely independently and a second nest has been made ready, generally in some other place.

The just-laid and fertilized eggs are carefully watched over by the female, who fans them with her pectoral fins. Dirt and unfertilized eggs are removed. The eggs can hatch after three days at a temperature of about 24 °C (75 °F), but in any case, they are hatched

Plate II-310. *Apistogramma taeniatum.*

within a week. Sometimes, the female then transfers the young over to another place.

Tribe Cichlasomini

In this tribe belong, among others, the genera *Cichlasoma, Petenia, Herichthys, Paraneetroplus, Neetroplus, Herotilapia, Uaru, Symphysodon* and *Pterophyllum*, all with species in South America.

Genus *Cichlasoma*

This genus comes from Central and South America, from Veracruz, Mexico, to Buenos Aires (Rio de la Plata), Argentina, and is found in marshes, lakes, rivers, with rocky or sandy bottom, with slight to heavy plant growth. Some species are found in brackish water and a few even in sea water. Besides, they are also found in some natural springs.

Cichlasoma is the most important genus with the largest number of species (about 60) of the American cichlid stock. Practically without exception, all species may be kept in the aquarium, although several grow quite large (about 350 mm or close to 14 inches).

The body of *Cichlasoma* species is high or stretched out, laterally compressed, covered with large or moderately large, usually ctenoid scales. The lateral line organ consists of two parts. The mouth is small or medium, never really large. The jaws are set with rows of small, conical teeth, which in the outside rows are somewhat larger and sometimes have a typical incisor shape.

There is only one dorsal fin with XIV-XIX/7–15 rays (see page 938), in which the spiny- and soft-rayed parts gradually merge, without a notch in the fin. The anal fin consists of IV-XII/6-14 rays. The pectoral fins are asymmetrical (the anterior rays are longer than the posterior rays) with 12 to 18 rays; the ventral fins are positioned underneath or a little behind the pectoral fins (thoracic or breast-positioned). The caudal fin is truncated or rounded.

For various reasons which are discussed in their own particular place, this genus is particularly interesting, partly due to its development and relationship to related genera.

It might as well be assumed that the genus *Cichlasoma* has been represented since the Eocene—that is to say, it has been in existence for about fifty million years. It is probable and understandable that not only have the primitive *Cichlasoma* been subjected to changes, but also that other forms have sprung from them, having adapted to certain ways of living.

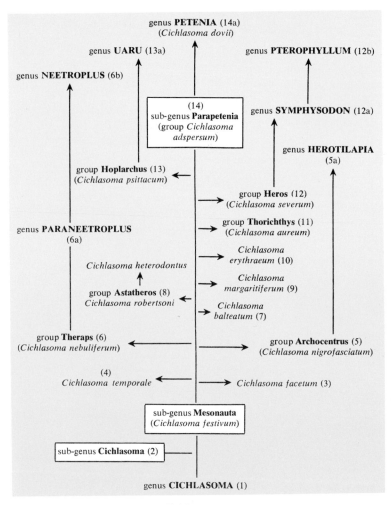

genus **PETENIA** (14a)
(*Cichlasoma dovii*)

genus **UARU** (13a)

genus **PTEROPHYLLUM** (12b)

genus **NEETROPLUS** (6b)

(14)
sub-genus **Parapetenia**
(group *Cichlasoma
adspersum*)

genus **SYMPHYSODON** (12a)

genus **HEROTILAPIA**
(5a)

group **Hoplarchus** (13)
(*Cichlasoma psittacum*)

group **Heros** (12)
(*Cichlasoma severum*)

group **Thorichthys** (11)
(*Cichlasoma aureum*)

genus **PARANEETROPLUS**
(6a)

*Cichlasoma
erythraeum* (10)

Cichlasoma heterodontus

*Cichlasoma
margaritiferum* (9)

group **Astatheros** (8)
Cichlasoma robertsoni

*Cichlasoma
balteatum* (7)

group **Theraps** (6)
(*Cichlasoma nebuliferum*)

group **Archocentrus** (5)
(*Cichlasoma nigrofasciatum*)

(4)
Cichlasoma temporale

Cichlasoma facetum (3)

sub-genus **Mesonauta**
(*Cichlasoma festivum*)

sub-genus **Cichlasoma** (2)

genus **CICHLASOMA** (1)

Table II-3.

It is precisely these ways of living, about which, unfortunately, too little is known, that are of such great interest to aquarists.

On the basis of splitting off from the main stock and adapting to some fixed conditions, a number of groups can be distinguished within this genus, and these can be classified into three sub-genera, which Table II-3 attempts to summarize. Not in any sense does the table represent a family tree or anything of that kind, but it does give an idea of how, on anatomical grounds, species are involved with each other.

1. The chart is to be read from bottom to top, thus beginning with the genus *Cichlasoma*, from which a branch deviates directly to the left.

2. This is the species *Cichlasoma bimaculatum*, which occupies a special place and which is the only representative of the sub-genus *Cichlasoma*. The second sub-genus, *Mesonauta*, is substantially more extensive. It has as characteristic species or type species *Cichlasoma festivum*, and is divided into a number of groups (series), each of which bears one or more fixed characteristics.

3. The first group of the sub-genus *Mesonauta* includes *C. facetum*, *C. autochthon* and *C. oblongum*.

Haseman classifies these three species among *C. facetum*, as there is little difference between them. They all live in the same areas.

4. The second group, with the species *C. temporale*, *C. crassa* and *C. coryphaenoides*, is interesting because it appears that the aquarium hobbyist can, in this regard, be of service to science. Here, too, Haseman includes the species *C. temporale* and *C. coryphaenoides* in a single species on grounds of the complete similarity of the specimens under study. Dr. Ahl, however, has been able to point out a distinction in living specimens which may be sufficient for distinguishing two species: *C. temporale* has an iridescent green pupil to the eye and *C. coryphaenoides* has a completely black pupil. In addition, the coloration patterns of living specimens are remarkably different.

5. Group *Archocentrus* with the species *C. nigrofasciatum*, *C. spilurum*, *C. spinosissimum*, *C. immaculatum* and *C. centrarchus*. Very probably, the genus *Herotilapia* (5a), closely related to *Cichlasoma*, has developed from this group, since its body structure is quite similar to that of *C. nigrofasciatum*.

6. The large group *Theraps* stands once again on a somewhat higher level and includes *C. eigenmanni*, *C. nebuliferum*, *C. maculicauda*, *C. fenestratum*, *C. bifasciatum*, *C. guttulatum*, *C. microphthalmus*, *C. sexfasciatus*, *C. melanurum*, *C. labridens*, *C. gadovii*, *C. intermedium*, *C. guentheri*, *C. pavonaceum*, *C. sieboldii*, *C. godmanni*, *C. irregulare* and *C. lentiginosum*. The genus *Paraneetroplus* (6a), which must have developed from this group, is very closely related to *C. nebuliferum*, differing from it in only a few small sub-parts. The genus *Neetroplus* (6b) follows *Paraneetroplus* in development. Turning back towards the ancestral stock follows the:

1050

7. Nameless group, with *C. balteatum* and *C. nicaraguense*, followed by:

8. Group *Astatheros*, to which belong the species *C. robertsoni, C. longimanus, C. macracanthus, C. heterodontus, C. latifrons* and *C. rostratum*.

9. *Cichlasoma margaritifreum* and *C. citrinellum* together also form a small group, in the same way as:

10. *Cichlasoma erythraeum, C. lobochilus* and *C. labiatum.*

11. Group *Thorichthys* includes *Cichlasoma aureum, C. affine* and *C. callolepis.*

12. Group *Heros* with only a single species, *Cichlasoma severum,* the well known "Heros spurius" of hobbyists is of great importance because of the close relationship between this species and the genera *Symphysodon* and *Pterophyllum,* respectively the Discus Fish and the Angelfish. The genus *Symphysodon* (12a) has undoubtedly developed from this group, in which is included the particularly high body shape of *C. severum. Pterophyllum* (12b) again stands above *Symphysodon,* from which it originates.

13. The group *Hoplarchus,* still represented today by *C. psittacum,* is the forerunner of a distinct genus, *Uaru,* which has only one known species, *Uaru amphiacanthoides* (13a), whose build is most similar to *Cichlasoma psittacum.*

14. The third sub-genus of *Cichlasoma* is *Parapetenia,* to which the most highly developed species belong—*C. adspersum, C. tetracanthus, C. istlanum, C. steindachneri, C. bartoni, C. beani, C. mento, C. festae, C. ornatum, C. octofasciatum, C. cutteri, C. urophthalmus, C. trimaculatum, C. salvini, C. multifasciatum, C. friedrichstahli, C. montaguense, C. manuguense, C. dovii, C. spectabile* and *C. kraussii.* The genus *Petenia* (14) undoubtedly developed from this group by way of *Cichlasoma dovii,* which it most resembles in build.

The above review is given in order to express more clearly the mutual connection that exists between the species, which would have been impossible to bring out in a linear system of classification.

Although only a few of the many species will be discussed, on the basis of this group classification, we can also cover other species in exactly the same way.

Cichlasoma facetum (Jenyns, 1842)
Chanchito or Chameleon Cichlid

In South America—from southern Brazil, Peru, Bolivia, to Uruguay and Argentina—Rio Beni, Rio Pilcomayo, Rio Parana, Rio Uruguay, Rio Negro and their drainage basins—*C. facetum* is very numerous in stagnant and slowly flowing waters. It is also found in brackish coastal waters. It has been a well liked aquarium fish since 1889 when the first specimens were imported into France and acquaintance was first made with this beautiful and interesting cichlid. Moreover, and in spite of its rather robust measurements, it is in no way aggressive.

The body is oblong, elliptical in shape, and laterally compressed. The back, especially in older specimens, is strongly arched. It has a large head with a mouth that is also large and turned upward at an angle. The maximum length in both sexes is about 320 mm ($12\frac{1}{2}$ inches). An aquarium specimen, however, unless the tank is very large, seldom grows to more than 150 mm (6 inches). When it reaches a length of about 100 mm (4 inches), it is ready for reproduction. The difference in appearance between young, half grown and fully grown specimens is large, as far as shape, fin placement and coloration are concerned. The dorsal fin has a long base, the fin rays are, however, rather short, mostly the soft-rayed part is lengthened. The caudal fin is well developed, but not large; the anal fin has a short base.

The dorsal, caudal and anal fins are rounded, and sometimes in larger, finer specimens (male as well as female), the last, soft rays of the dorsal and anal fins are lengthened, so that these fins appear to come to a point. This is not a means of differentiating the sexes. The ventral fins are large and fan-shaped, breast-positioned (thoracic), the frontal rays lengthened. The pectoral fins are well developed and rounded.

The basic coloration is yellow-brown to dark greenish, not practicable to describe more closely, because in different stages of development and under certain conditions, in or out of the mating season, the coloration can vary so much that the name Chameleon Cichlid is correctly chosen. Young specimens exhibit, in addition to a dark (to black) lengthwise stripe, 6 to 10 more or less irregular cross stripes, which show up in varying degrees of clarity. In older specimens, these stripes stand out more from time to time, although the lengthwise stripe has often completely vanished. The iris of the eye, however, is always yellowish, and in the mating season, turns to orange-red. In the mating season, male as well as female can be very dark blue-green with or without stripes, with a bright red border to the fins. It is also difficult to tell the sexes apart in this species, except for the more or less inward curve of the belly line of the males and the more outward curved belly of the females.

This cichlid is eminently suitable for the beginning cichlid fancier. A spacious tank is recommended (for instance, $80 \times 50 \times 50$ cm or $30 \times 12 \times 18$ inches), in which a thick (15 cm or 6-inch) layer of river sand forms the bottom, and the free environment consists of a few fair-sized rocks and a planting along the rear wall of *Sagittaria, Bacopar,* and the like. In many cases, especially if the fish are obtained as young specimens, *Cabomba* is a plant that makes a very attractive background.

Smaller specimens can be kept in company with fishes of the same size. *C. facetum* is peace-loving, although it does look upon smaller fishes as food. It is certainly not a predator in the worst sense of the word.

The temperature range is from 18 to 30 °C (64–86 °F). A special breeding temperature is usually unnecessary, as it is just as happy about laying eggs at 18 °C or even lower as it is at 25 °C (77 °F) and higher. It can withstand fluctuations of temperature very well, provided that these take place gradually over a long period of time. In a heated room, this fish can be kept very well without extra aquarium heat. This has certainly contributed to the firm place *C. facetum* has made for itself among aquarists.

Where food is concerned, it can be given everything that is even slightly considered food, but predominantly live animal food. Regular filtration of the aquarium water is recommended, but siphon it off and replace it with fresh water as little as possible.

A calm surrounding is a first requisite for this gorgeous fish (the same being true for all aquarium fishes), which then treats us to a beautiful brood care procedure. After the usual courtship, which can sometimes be rather boisterous, but seldom results in serious damage (it is best to select a couple that has been formed from a group of young fish), the pair clean off one or more stones. The eggs are then (depending on the size of the female) laid in numbers from 300 to more than 1,000, in straight or spiral rows, and are immediately fertilized by the male. If we watch this process from a short distance (taking care not to frighten them!), we can sometimes see the oviduct of the female, which is several millimetres long, red-ended, and hangs straight down, and the more pointed, backward-turned, anal projection (papilla) of the male. If the aquarium is quite spacious and thickly planted, it is interesting to bring a couple of another species over into the same aquarium. The brood care—mostly attended to by both parents—is then shown off at its best, especially if both couples have a nest to care for, a task which they perform in an exemplary fashion.

About three days after the eggs have been laid, during which the parents take turns keeping watch and busy themselves with digging one or more pits or trenches, the eggs are snapped up by the parents and transferred to a hole. Fanning of the eggs with the pectoral fins, a performance carried on uninterruptedly by one or the other of the parents, is now continued for some time, but from time to time they take the eggs into their mouths and finally free the young from the eggshells. If they have not blocked a view of the hole by digging it behind a stone, the swarming mass can be well observed, the young subsisting at first on the yolk sac, but after a week to 10 days, undertaking their first attempts to explore their surroundings, still carefully guarded by their parents. The period of good feeding with very small, living food may then be interrupted, as they can get along quite well without it, for the parents chew food up fine and spit it out among the young ones, who are not slow about disposing of it. Further progress is normally the same as with related species. The young fish grow quickly, especially if sunlight can fall on the tank and if they are richly fed. For a considerable time, at random and without any visible reason, the parents will periodically snap up one of the young and later spit it out again. A group of young with their parents is a delight for every aquarist to study.

Plate II-311. *Cichlasoma festivum.*

Cichlasoma festivum (Heckel, 1840)
Flag Acara
Festivum

In South America, this species has been found in Brazil (Mato Grosso) and in the drainage basin of the Amazon from Guyana to the Rio de la Plata, in large and small waters, lakes, and pools, ponds and artificial fish ponds created by floods. This cichlid is often found in company with the well liked Brazilian Angelfish (*Pterophyllum scalare*) close to the banks, and in quiet places among thick plant growth. The first specimens were taken in 1908 to Europe, where the first information concerning a successful breeding was published in 1911. There has been some question whether this fish should be called *Cichlasoma festivum* or *Cichlasoma insignis*, and it has, in fact, been included in a great deal of literature under the latter name.

The author of this fish—that is, the biologist who first described it in print—was Heckel. In 1840, an article by him appeared, entitled: *Brasilianische Fluss-Fische* (*Brazilian River Fishes*), in which, among others, two fish were described—a specimen on page 376 to which he gave the name *Heros festivus*, and one on pages 378 and 379, which he describes as *Heros insignis*.

Plate II-312. *Geophagus acuticeps*, an Amazon cichlid.

It was later determined that both these species described were varieties of only a single species. The first name always takes preference, even though this appeared in the same publication only two pages sooner. Thus, the name would have been *Heros festivus* Heckel, were it not that Regan, in 1905, indicated that the genus *Heros* is identical with *Cichlasoma*—at least, that *Heros* differs little from the genus *Cichlasoma* classified by Swainson in 1839, and thus *Heros* deserves to be included in this older genus.

In order to make apparent the slight difference existing between the old *Heros* and the other *Cichlasoma* species, a sub-genus, *Mesonauta*, was inserted, so that at present, the full, complete name of this fish runs: *Cichlasoma* (*Mesonauta*) *festivum* (Heckel, 1840) Regan, 1905. It is obvious that such a long-winded name is used only, and then as an exception, in strictly scientific works.

The body is oblong, high through the dorsal and anal fins, laterally strongly compressed. The maximum length is 15 cm (6 inches). The head is pointed and has a small, only slightly protrusive mouth. The rearmost part of the body narrows abruptly into the short tail section. The dorsal and anal fins are strongly developed; the spiny part merges unostentatiously with the soft-rayed part, the latter part in both fins being quite pointed. In ratio to the dorsal and anal fins, the caudal fin is small and rounded. The ventral fins consist of a normally weak-rayed and a spiny part which is grown out into a long, spiky thread, formed by the second fin ray. The pectoral fins are normal and rounded, the upper rays somewhat longer than the lower ones.

The basic coloration, as in the Angelfish, is a drab yellow-grey with a bright, metallic sheen. This coloration, as well as the shape of the body, works as a natural camouflage, which the fish finds among plants and such in its natural state. The scales are dark-edged and cause the well known, net-like pattern. Very striking is a broad stripe, built up of black scales, which angles upwards from the mouth into the dorsal region, almost unnoticeably merges with the dorsal fin and runs out into the extreme point. In the upper half of the tail root is an eye spot that is also black and ringed with golden yellow. The part of the body lying above the black stripe is brownish to brownish black, the flanks yellowish to yellow-green, and the belly whitish. The strongly varying coloration and pattern are sometimes heightened by brown and green flecks and dots. The lower lip is light blue, the throat of the males dark green. The iris of the eye and the gill covers are gleaming golden yellow. The pectoral fins are without coloration and transparent. The thread-like outgrown ventral fin is reddish gold. In addition to the already-mentioned characteristic, the sexes are not clearly distinguishable until the mating season, when they can readily be told apart by the short, white, pointed sperm duct of the males and the long, blunt oviduct of the females.

In general, refer to the discussion of breeding under *Pterophyllum scalare* (see page 1073). Here, too, a fine, roomy tank is required. The temperature ranges between 22 and 25 °C (72–77 °F), and for breeding, 25–28 °C (77–82 °F). When the breeding fish have made up their minds to go along with each other, a rock or something of the kind is carefully cleaned. In the course of several hours, 150 to 400 eggs are laid. These are glass-clear and small. Brood care is not always ideal. If neither of the parents takes any care of the spawn, or if they are observed eating eggs, they should be transferred to another tank. The water level should be brought down to 10 to 15 cm (4 to 6 inches) deep and a water outflow tube must take over the job of the fanning parents. However, if brood care is observed to be taking place,

1057

so much the better. The young ones hatch out after 40 to 50 hours and the parents "fasten" them to panes, rocks or plants close beneath the surface where they carefully guard them. Upbringing takes place in the usual way with fine food, white worms and daphnia ground to "milk," and so forth. Besides live food and vegetable food, various kinds of dried foods are gratefully accepted. Change of diet is a requirement.

After three to five weeks the youngsters are transferred to a swimming tank. In the breeding tank, the parents can then prepare to start another mating session.

A beautiful and, at the same time, natural environment is a high aquarium with *Vallisneria, Sagittaria, Bacopa* and perhaps some *Heteranthera zosteraefolia*, and, in addition, a number of largish rocks and a rear wall of rocks or concrete, in which the Angelfish swims about among the other fishes in stately fashion. No one will then dare to assert or maintain that cichlids are not suitable for the home aquarium.

A greater ornamentation for the room than *C. festivum* is hardly to be imagined without selling other aquarium fishes short. More than the Angelfish, *Cichlasoma festivum* is sensitive to fright, which in many cases can result in sudden death preceded by spasms or convulsions, which can be likened only to an apoplectic fit or stroke. If all precautions are taken, however, this cichlid, too, will quickly make many friends.

What has been said about the natural environment of *Pterophyllum scalare*, the Brazilian Angelfish (see page 1073), is predominantly applicable to this fish as well. In addition to rocky surroundings, this fish is also often in shallower waters, among numerous dead tree branches, trunks and twigs, real jungle creeks—that is, where it can subsist on algae and all kinds of tiny water creatures that live among these alga pastures.

Along the banks (this fish never occurs in open water) of tributaries, among thick growths of *Cabomba, Myriophyllum* species, *Heteranthera* and *Bacopa*, this fish is found exclusively in the middle and lower reaches of the rivers; farther up, it disappears.

Cichlasoma meeki (Brind, 1918)
Fire-Mouth Cichlid

This species is found in Yucatan, in the vicinity of Merida and Progresso, Mexico, in streams, ponds, springs and underground veins connecting these waters. In 1937, the first specimens were brought into Europe, where they attracted the undivided attention of aquarists.

The body of *C. meeki* is high and laterally compressed, particularly in the tail region. The maximum length is 75 mm (3 inches). The line from the mouth opening to the dorsal fin runs steeply upwards, substantially more so than in, for example, *Cichlasoma aureum*, which can also grow much larger (to 130 mm or $5\frac{1}{8}$ inches). The belly line runs with smooth uniformity. The snout is sharp with a very large, somewhat upward-turned mouth opening. The eyes are placed high in the head, in the middle between the mouth opening and the first dorsal fin ray.

The dorsal and anal fins, as well as the ventral fins, consist of a soft-rayed and a spiny part. The dorsal fin is long and begins above the end of the gill covers. The spiny rays run through to the place where the line of the back bends downwards again; after that comes a short, soft-rayed section of which part of the fin rays are lengthened and the fin runs out to a point. The same can be said for the anal fin, with the understanding that the spiny-rayed part is shorter and begins under the middle of the dorsal fin. The ventral fins are positioned on the breast (thoracic), well developed, with lengthened frontal spiny rays. The pectoral fins are large, somewhat sharpened, and reach as far as the soft-rayed section of the dorsal fin.

The basic coloration is blue-grey with a violet glitter. The rather large scales have a red to red-brown edge. The back is dark (to purplish brown), the belly orange-red to a very distinct carmine which runs partially over the gill covers, the throat and the interior of the mouth. The division of this red coloration from the blue-grey of the upper part of the body is very peculiar. At the division, especially in the region of the head, the pattern is such that it gives the impression that the upper skin is partially rolled up. It is striking that even very young specimens 20 to 30 mm ($\frac{13}{16}$ to $1\frac{3}{16}$ inches) long already exhibit the red throat, although not so bright as in the adult fish. The iris of the eye is a shining blue-green. An irregular black spot on the edge of the gill covers, a second smaller one a little higher, and a third one at the base of the pectoral fins are edged with an iridescent greenish yellow border. In other places, too, similar spots appear, which are somewhat less distinct. The median fins are light red-brown, the fin rays a little darker, the edges having a blue-grey border. The ventral fins are, in general, somewhat darker than the median fins, while the pectorals are black at the base and transparent light brown everywhere else. The frontal rays of the ventral fins are light blue and an edge of a similar hue may sometimes be observed along the dorsal and anal fins. According to conditions, about five more or less clear cross stripes run from the back to halfway down the body. From the edge of the gill cover to the root of the tail runs a lengthwise stripe consisting of irregular black spots, which, like the cross stripes, can disappear entirely.

The sexes can be recognized because the females are less vivid and the dorsal and anal fins run out to less of a point. During the mating season, the female shows a short oviduct and the male a sex papilla. Neither is easy to see. During the mating season, the intensity of the coloration increases in both sexes, especially the red.

This beautiful cichlid is to be kept in a roomy aquarium, planted with sturdy plants. Various soft-leaved plants (*Heteranthera*) quickly turn ugly, since *Cichlasoma meeki*, like its relatives, has a custom of biting a mouthful of the bottom and, after sifting from mud and sand whatever bits of food the chunk contains, spitting it out again. The sand grains, deposited on the plants, can create brown spots on some plants, which finally cause the leaves to die. This, in an ornamental aquarium, is a less than beautiful sight. *Cabomba, Ludwigia, Sagittaria,* and the like are sufficient in good-sized clumps along the walls. A fairly large space must remain open with a thick bottom layer of some sand and a number of rocks, among which can be planted, in order to break up the flatness, a few large clumps of *Acorus* or other low-lying, hardy, well rooting plants.

Because *Cichlasoma meeki* is very calm and peaceful for a cichlid (also in comparison with other, even very small fishes), it can be kept without trouble in a community aquarium, so long as this aquarium fulfils the requirements of size and set-up. It shows off to best advantage, however, in an aquarium with other not-too-predatory fishes. The temperature limits are 20–24 °C (68–75 °F), but raise it to 26 °C (79 °F) during the mating season.

Plate II-313. *Cichlasoma meeki.*

The mating season comes on very rapidly after a couple have chosen each other out of the group. The couple separates from the other fishes and the two are always seen together. They begin their courtship, paying no attention to the other occupants of the tank. However, it is advisable to remove the pair from the tank to enjoy to its fullest the splendid play that follows. In the wedding dress now displayed, the brightest coloration shows up beautifully. The affair begins with bringing a spawning place into readiness, generally by the male alone, though both fish can take part in it. Various grooves or trenches are made in the open sand, the big mouth serving as a shovel, and the job is done rather quickly. Stones are polished smooth, and, punctuating their industriousness, both fish show off their hues, so that it is a delight to watch them. On one of the cleaned stones, finally, the female will lay 100 to 500 eggs, depending on age and other factors. These are at once fertilized by the male.

An exemplary brood care is indulged in by both parents together. It is seldom necessary to provide special food for the young ones. If the parents are fed sufficiently, then they take care of passing on their portion to the young, as has been observed among many other cichlids. As soon as the young are swimming freely about, the parents start spitting a portion of finely chewed food out among the swarm, which grab for it greedily. These fish, too, can be given anything which amounts to food: white worms, tubifex, mosquito larvae, waterfleas, larvae of flies and other water insects (look out for dangerous larvae).

As always, it is a surprisingly attractive sight to see the adult parents swimming about together with their brood of young ones. It is seldom necessary to remove the parents from the tank (to thwart cannibalism), but it is still desirable to keep a sharp eye out. As soon as the parents start making preparations for a new mating, it is better to transfer the youngsters to another tank; by then they are already two to three weeks old and will quickly grow up on good feeding. Personal preference may include letting the young grow up in an open-air fish pond. Of course, this can be done only in the summer months, or when the outdoor temperature at night remains above 18 °C (64 °F). The little outdoor ponds that were used by Hoedeman were only 80 × 40 to 60 cm (32 × 16 to 24 inches) on the surface and 5 to 30 cm (2 to 12 inches) deep.

This splendid fish, first imported (into Germany) in 1937 and into Holland in 1938 (probably earlier into the United States), will always

Plate II-314. *Cichlasoma nigrofasciatum.*

hold the interest of all cichlid fanciers and certainly many hobbyists who feel that they do not want to keep cichlids will change their minds.

At first, *Cichlasoma meeki* was confused with *Cichlasoma aureum* (Günther) which had been known since 1910, to which it is very similar, but which can grow almost twice as big. The similarity of build and appearance of *Cichlasoma meeki* and *Cichlasoma aureum*, on the one hand, and *Cichlasoma ellioti* (Meek), on the other, was reason enough for Meinken to consider the first named as a link between the latter two.

Cichlasoma octofasciatum (Regan, 1903)
Jack Dempsey

Cichlasoma octofasciatum is a species which for many years was known under the wrong name, *C. biocellatum*. Not much was known when the first specimens were described; where it came from and what its place of origin is are still obscure. It is, at present, well established, however, that *C. octofasciatum* is an inhabitant of the Amazon Basin, although that does not tell us much, of course, when we realize the extent of this region. The specimen in Plate II–315 is said to have come from Surinam. The circumstances, however, are such that this report, too, must be considered dubious.

Notwithstanding its obscure origin, *C. octofasciatum* certainly can be reckoned as the most beautiful species of its genus.

For a long time, until about 1934, specimens of *C. octofasciatum* were kept and described under the name *Cichlasoma nigrofasciatum*.

True aquarists and, of course, those who also specialize in keeping cichlids, are always full of praise and admiration for *C. octofasciatum*, not only because of its robust appearance, or its handsome, deep coloration, or because it makes few demands in regard to its environ-

Plate II-315. *Cichlasoma octofasciatum*, male.

Plate II-316. *Cichlasoma octofasciatum,* **female with spawn.**

ment or feeding, but also and particularly because the peculiar brood care of the cichlids is exhibited at its best. It reproduces without difficulty under all conditions, making it an easy-to-keep fish. This has indeed been the most important reason which, for years, has made it the most popular cichlid—until the Angelfish came along and elbowed it largely out of its place.

One characteristic that has caused this fish, along with other cichlids, to be unpopular with aquarists is the tendency to build a nest just any place they feel like it, even in tanks that are not properly set up for their activities, with the consequence that plants and groups of carefully placed stones are all turned upside-down. We should, however, be a little less childish and show some admiration for the instinct that makes itself apparent in the mating season. The tank should be set up in such a manner that the fish can fulfil their passions without creating chaos, which would spoil the whole show.

The appearance of the fish, which can attain a length of 20 cm (8 inches), is less changeable as the fish grows older and becomes less sensitive to influences in its surroundings. At any rate, older specimens react less by changing their coloration than is the case

Plate II-317. *Cichlasoma nigrofasciatum*.

with younger fish. Coloration and pattern are very distinct—as in virtually all other species of this group—in specimens about 5 to 6 cm (2 to 2⅜ inches), when they are about three to four months old. About eight cross bands (hence, *octofasciatum*) can then be clearly seen, especially on the tail. Two black spots are also clear. The first spot lies about under the middle of the dorsal fin, the second in the upper part of the tail root.

The fins, at first virtually glass clear and without coloration, become more striking the longer they get, as can be clearly seen in Plate II–315. The females are always less brilliant. A band present in the embryo runs lengthwise along the body, from the upper edge of the gill covers until it touches the spot on the root of the tail. The band is more distinct in young and female specimens and is considerably less distinct or seldom seen among large males. It is a true characteristic of the *Cichlasoma* and also of the related *Aequidens* species.

Americans call this fish Jack Dempsey, after the ex-world-champion heavy-weight boxer, though it is a misnomer and wholly unjustified. Not that this fish can't give as good as it gets—far from it—

but by naming this species after a champion boxer, the impression is that it is a first class fighting fish. During the mating season, however, most fishes—including not only the cichlids but also stickleback and similar home-protecting species—are thoroughly able to defend their domains against invaders. This species will not fall out of key with the rest of the fishes in the tank without reason or cause. As usual, belligerent activity by a fish, according to many aquarists, is an "attribute of character," and they seem to forget that only when the fish is provided with an environment that in some way approximates its natural one, can its conduct be taken as grounds for concluding whether it is really a pugilist or not. Give it room in accordance with its size (a necessity) and then it will be possible to provide it with the companionship of other fishes that also live in its natural environment. At nest-building time and the period of brood care following thereafter, *C. octofasciatum* reacts violently against related varieties which may constitute a possible threat, while it reacts hardly or not at all towards innocent fishes, such as, for example, the various armoured catfishes like *Corydoras* or *Loricaria* and their relatives, which "accidentally" approach the territory *C. octofasciatum* calls its own. Often, when busy—and well fed, too, of course—*C. octofasciatum* shows no predatory tendencies towards smaller fishes—characins, for example—that can swim back and forth over its territory without being molested.

Plate II-318. *Cichlasoma severum.*

Cichlasoma severum (Heckel, 1840)
Banded Cichlid
Severum

In South America, *C. severum* comes from Brazil, the drainage basin of the Amazon, Rio Japurá; Guyana, Rio Essequibo; and Peru, Rio Marañón and Rio Ucayali and their drainage basins. This splendid cichlid has been known to and kept by European hobbyists since 1904.

The body of *C. severum* is very high, laterally compressed, with a strongly arched head-back line. The maximal length is 180 mm ($7\frac{1}{16}$ inches). By reason of its height, the body is quite rounded, diminishing to a very narrow tail root. All the fins, especially the pectorals, are well developed. The coloration and pattern of this very beautiful cichlid are quite variable and practically indescribable.

The basic coloration is olive green to green-brown, sometimes with blue-green spots. Usually, the young fish possess about eight vertical, dark, brown to blue-green bands, the first one across the eye, the last (sometimes the ninth) on the root of the tail. The next to the last band runs out into the dorsal and anal fins in a more or less round spot. Large specimens gradually lose the cross bands, probably in connection with the different environments occupied by young and old specimens in the wild. Only the next to the last band, which runs out into the dorsal and anal fins, remains present. In addition to the tones named, there is also a peculiar light blue as well as red in the fins and on the body that makes these creatures very attractive. A one hundred per cent method of distinguishing the sexes, as in many cichlids, is impossible to give. As a rule, the females are lighter in coloration, but in the mating season it is often the male that bleaches out entirely from time to time. The shape of the fins is precisely the same in both sexes. *Cichlasoma severum* is very warmth-loving and in no case must the temperature be kept constantly below 20 °C (68 °F), but preferably about 22–24 °C (72–75 °F). Reproduction is carried on as among related species. A total of 200 to 1,000 relatively small, yellowish, transparent eggs are laid.

Cichlasoma severum is found in the wild in various places and environments differing greatly in character. Depending on the habitat, size and age of the specimens caught, these differ so strongly in appearance that it was reason enough for various authors to ascribe many names to this species.

Plate II-319. *Cichlasoma spilurum.*

It is probable that mating takes place in shallow waters, near sand banks and among plant growth. The young remain there for a considerable time. At that time, the typical, vertical banding on the body shows. After a few months, perhaps six, they migrate to deeper water that is not heavily grown with water plants and the cross bands gradually disappear. The specimens living in flowing water without many plants, among rocks rank with algae, are usually the largest. Those specimens from the quiet river bends where many branches of the bank flora overhang the water are half-grown, while the specimens from the shallow creeks, bends and such, close to sand banks heavy with growth, are the very young or parents busy with their brood.

As a rule, *C. severum* lives in company with other cichlids, especially *Cichlasoma festivum* and *Pterophyllum scalare*. After hiding in cracks in the rocks from the fierce sun during the day, in the evening many catfishes show up, such as *Corydoras, Loricaria* and *Hypostomus* species, to enliven the environment.

Another species that is regularly kept at present is *Cichlasoma spilurum*, a rather small variety that must be treated like, for example, *Cichlasoma nigrofasciatum*.

Genus *Nannacara*

Two species of South American dwarf cichlids, of the genus *Nannacara,* have made a special place for themselves among aquarists—*Nannacara anomala* and *Nannacara taenia.*

Nannacara anomala Regan, 1905
Golden-Eyed Dwarf Cichlid

This species comes from Guyana and attains a length of about 75 mm (3 inches), the females a little smaller. It is to be kept the same as *Apistogramma* and smaller *Aequidens* species.

Plate II-321. *Nannacara taenia*, male and female.

Nannacara taenia Regan, 1912
Lattice Dwarf Cichlid

This species hails from the drainage basin of the Amazon and has a wider distribution than *Nannacara anomala*. It reaches a length of about 50 mm (2 inches). At this length, it is one of the most desirable and suitable cichlids for home aquariums and community tank. Also, brood care is carried out completely in the usual cichlid manner without causing any damage to the plants in the tank. For egg laying, *N. taenia* must have available a rocky place or, in any case, a small hollow place or cave. Many aquarists place a flower pot overturned or on its side in the tank in order to meet this desire.

The young hatch out after three to four days and at first are very helpless, requiring complete care from their parents. A week later, however, they are completely self-sufficient.

Genus *Pterophyllum*

Pterophyllum scalare (Cuvier, 1831)
Angelfish
Brazilian Angelfish
Scalare

In Brazil, this species is found in the flood basin of the Amazon and its tributaries, into Peru and eastern Ecuador, and northward towards the Essequibo River. It is also found in Guyana, usually in company with *Cichlasoma festivum*, *Cichlasoma severum* and *Cichla ocellaris* are also found in the same area. The first living specimens of *P. scalare* were brought into Europe in 1911.

As far as the life in the wild of the Angelfish is concerned, very little is known about it, yet such knowledge is very necessary if we wish to provide it with what it needs in the aquarium. The natural domain consists of moderately flowing tributaries and large flood regions in a rocky surrounding where it stays near to and among crannies in the rocks. The entire region is thickly overgrown with algae. This unusually interesting place is inhabited by the above-named species, but as soon as twilight falls, the catfishes, among which are

Plate II-322. Veil form of *Pterophyllum scalare.*

Loricaria and *Hypostomus* species, come popping out of their holes all over, while a number of typical characins are also present, such as *Moenkhausia*, *Chalceus*, *Metynnis*, and others. These last species apparently flee from the burning sun during the day to the protective clefts in the rocks.

This stately fish possesses a deep, strongly compressed body. The shape of the body is more or less like a disc, with large, sickle-shaped dorsal and anal fins. The maximum length is 140 mm ($5\frac{11}{32}$ inches). The first pectoral fin rays are grown out into long, thread-like attachments. The line of the back is sharply bowed above the eye and forms a "saddle" there. The iris of the eye is dark orange-red on the rear edge. The body appears to be symmetrical due to the similarly shaped dorsal and anal fins. The snout is pointed, with a small, upward-turned mouth. The caudal fin is large, rounded and either cut off straight or with lengthened outer fin rays. The entire body and the bases of the fins are covered with tiny ctenoid scales. The basic coloration is olive green to greyish, with a silvery sheen. The area of the back, as usual darker than the belly, is sometimes brownish. Across the body run four vertical stripes, between which are three less distinct stripes, either clearly visible or not so clearly visible, depending on the frame of mind of the fish. The dorsal and anal fins are bluish grey, turning lighter towards the extremities, with a yellowish tint; the anal fin is darker all over than the dorsal fin. The third vertical, black cross stripe runs into the dorsal and anal fins and is the widest and most distinct stripe. The three median fins are decorated with a number of dark grey cross stripes. The ventral fins are grown out into long "feelers," yellowish to blue-green on the base, the long, grown-out fin rays being lemon yellow to orange.

This splendid fish is well worth a fine, well planted tank, which it does require and must have if we want to enjoy its exotic beauty. The tank, which must be at least 50 cm (20 inches) high, preferably even higher, should be planted with thick clumps of *Vallisneria* along the sides, leaving an open swim space in the middle, with some long, erect *Bacopa*, *Myriophyllum* and *Sagittaria*, some fair-sized chunks of rock and, if desired, *Heteranthera zosteraefolia*. In no case must a light be permitted to shine crosswise through the tank. The light must always come from above—indeed, the most beautiful arrangement is a top light only. This can, if necessary, be exclusively artificial light. Such a cichlid tank will be a pleasure to the eye of even an opponent of cichlids; there will be no plant destruction or spoiling of the water with the bottom soil. The water temperature is normally kept at 24–26 °C (75–79 °F), and this must not fall below 22 °C (72 °F) in the winter. Breeding temperature is 26–30 °C (79–86 °F). So far as the formation of couples is concerned, refer to what is said about this under *Haplochromis multicolor* (see page 1085). Fresh stock added among the breed fish at the correct time can prevent many disappointments and will be a profit to the hobby. The eggs are laid on the broad, ribbon-like leaves of *Vallisneria* and *Sagittaria*, where they are immediately fertilized by the male. A good breeding pair at once takes over care of the brood and the parents start fanning the eggs with their pectoral fins.

Distinguishing the sexes is still a constant question, sometimes even for the fish themselves. Some authors indicate that the females can be distinguished by the black stripe behind the gill covers not running entirely through to the belly line, others see in the males a broadening of the back between the saddle and the first dorsal fin ray. An adequate indication occurs when young have been born from a certain couple, for though eggs can be obtained from two females, these turn mouldy because no male is present to fertilize them.

It is superfluous to say that a more beautiful or more suitable fish for the home aquarium can seldom be found. This fish has been kept so much, and is so discussed and illustrated, that it has attracted attention in circles having nothing to do with aquarists. Its great suitability may be further illustrated since there are hobbyists who have cared for the same couple for more than 12 years. If well taken care of, Angelfish can enjoy a very long life.

A group of Angelfish found by Ladiges near Rockstone, Guyana, was particularly striking, living in water that was opaque, filthy and polluted with the excrement of mammals. Directly after being caught, the fish showed none of their characteristic stripes; after a few days of swimming about in clear water, however, the dark, vertical stripes again appeared. The region investigated by Ladiges, on the Essequibo River, had no reed growth where the Angelfish were found. Farther south, in the actual Amazon flood basin, there was always reed growth along the banks where the Angelfish were found. Moreover, though *Cabomba aquatica* is a submerged type of aquatic plant, it was often found decorating their habitat. The floating plants found here are, among others, *Eichhornia* and *Pistia*, in addition to *Victoria regia* and *Nymphaea* species. Probably also various *Sagittaria* species have a part in *P. scalare's* routine, perhaps a principal one during the mating

1075

season, since it is the main plant on which the Angelfish lay their eggs in the aquarium (they also show a great preference for the Amazon sword plant, *Echinodorus* spp.). They have also been known to lay eggs on stones and reed stems, wholly apart from artificial "laying places" such as glass rods and similar places.

It will certainly be quite necessary to collect more data from the country of origin of these as well as other fishes, before we will be able to unveil many of the mysteries surrounding them.

Two other species, *P. altum* and *P. dumerilli* have also been available upon occasion.

Plate II-323. One of the varieties of *Symphysodon discus*.

Genus *Symphysodon*

It is most likely that the species *S. aequifasciata* Pellegrin, as described by Schultz, along with the supposed sub-species *S.a. aequifasciata*, *S.a. haraldi* and *S.a. axelrodi*, are merely varieties of *S. discus*. They are not found together anywhere in the same natural biotope, which supports the opinion that these forms should be considered local populations of the single species.

Symphysodon discus Heckel, 1846
Discus
Heckel Discus
Pompadour Fish

The Discus, like the Angelfish (*Pterophyllum*) and *Cichlasoma festivum*, inhabits the gigantic region included under the name Amazonas, extending from the middle reaches of the Amazon River to far into the jungles of the Venezuelan and Peruvian flood basins. The Discus is quite commonly found there among profuse plant growth in the quiet bends of the rivers, under overhanging banks, and among rock crannies. In the shallow areas, it cares for its young beneath the numerous leaves of various *Nymphaea* species.

Considered from the standpoint of classification, the Discus occupies a place between the genus *Cichlasoma*, on the one hand, and the genus *Pterophyllum* on the other, and therefore connects these two genera together within the tribe Cichlasomini. For aquarists who have bred representatives of all three genera, there is no longer any doubt about this. The young of *Symphysodon* and *Pterophyllum* are, in their early stages, almost identical to the young and mature specimens of the species belonging to the genus *Cichlasoma*. The reason why two species (genera) out of one tribe have specialized and developed to such an extent that their external appearance deviates severely from the basic type must first be searched for in environmental factors and adaptation to special conditions. That a few species also living in the same region and belonging to the genus *Cichlasoma*, such as *C. festivum*, for instance, have not experienced such a metamorphosis, is not just yet so easy to explain.

The Discus was, for several years, considered the "problem fish" number one, and aquarists perhaps asked themselves, "Why?"

Until the late 1950's, breeding the Discus Fish was still a special occasion, and the term "problem fish" was entirely applicable. Today, any experienced aquarist can put these fish through their reproductive phase without too much difficulty. The first problem with these fish directly concerns how they are kept—to keep them alive and in good condition after they have been imported. If that is successful, then the possibility hardly exists that the fish, if we have at least a suitable couple, cannot prepare themselves for reproduction. The difficulty with the imported fish is probably no greater than the difficulties encountered with many other aquarium fishes.

However, when an American, Armbruster of Philadelphia, succeeded, in 1934, in raising about 35 young Discus, the gates were opened. A series of attempts, with or without success, followed in the years thereafter, including the first time in Europe by Beierlein in 1935. The parents were always taken away from the eggs and the young, until, in 1939, Hoffman succeeded in allowing the parents to bring up a brood of 30 young by themselves.

Now concerning the Discus itself. It grows to a total length of about 200 mm (8 inches). A description of the shape and coloration in addition to Plate II–323 is utterly superfluous. A review of the observations of various aquarists who have kept this fish is perhaps the most interesting for future owners of this "imperial fish."

The variegated coloration is not continuously present, for it can quickly change over from practically white to a deep blackish, according to the fish's surroundings or frame of mind. The sky blue lines, stripes and flecks in the fins and on the head of adult males are softer blue to blue-grey in the female. The coloration of the iris of the eye cannot be taken as a sex characteristic; however, as is the case with most cichlids, the shape of the anal papilla can indeed so serve, being round and blunt in the female and pointed in the male. This papilla or oviduct shows up quite clearly during the mating season.

As far as breeding is concerned, the whole line of activities described for the Angelfish can, in fact, be observed in this fish. A temperature of about 25 °C (77 °F) is sufficient. A refreshing of the water (preferably with rain water or an artificial rain shower) can get the mating season off to a good start. It is neither necessary nor desirable to allow the temperature to rise to 28 °C (82 °F) or higher, for even in the natural environment, such temperatures hardly ever occur, at least, they do not last over any lengthy period of time. For the Angelfish, too, very high temperatures or temperature rises were advised, but this has been settled once and for all. The main criterion will be a change in the composition of the water, such as that found in the wild at the time of the rainy season.

As soon as the fry have reached the free-swimming stage, a remarkable adaptation to the struggle for life and parental care in these highly advanced cichlids can be observed.

The parents produce natural food for the fry by excreting highly protein-rich food particles from their skin. These excretions are not the production of the ordinary slime-skin, as is typical for all fish, but special products upon which the young fish feed for almost a month. It is noteworthy that the parents take turns in offering this special food to their offspring; as soon as one of them is "cleaned," the parent takes off quickly from the young, and its place is taken over by the other parent. It is of no use, during the first 10-day period from the start of this procedure, to feed the fry anything else, but then you may try brine shrimp to see whether or not the fry are ready for them. If so, continue to feed them regularly. From the time they accept this kind of food, a rather large quantity is needed in order to make the young grow properly. Later on, feed the fish larger crustaceans and worms.

Changing from one living food to another—*Artemia*, various kinds and sizes of waterfleas, grindal worms, mosquito larvae, tubifex and white worms—and feeding in quantity with a variety of ditch infusoria is essential.

Experiments have shown that raw egg white has, in some instances, possibly replaced the skin proteins of the parents, but merely in time of emergency.

Plate II-324. *Julidochromis ornatus.*

Sub-family Haplochrominae

Like the sub-family Tilapiinae, the Haplochrominae are divided into two tribes, the African and the South American genera. The entire sub-family is distinguished from the Tilapiinae by the frequently mentioned pharyngeal apophysis being formed here by the parasphenoid bone in the middle and the basioccipital bones to either side of it. Compare also its structure with that of the Tilapiinae (see page 1002). Again, we shall discuss the African and the South American genera separately and make the following classification: the African Haplochrominae and the South American Haplochrominae, tribe Cichlini.

AFRICAN GENERA

Their native habitat is the same as for the Tilapiini, thus including all of Africa, along with Jordan, Israel and Syria. However, Haplochrominae are entirely absent on Madagascar. The focal points of this group lie in other places than those of the Tilapiinae. The most important point at present is undoubtedly Lake Malawi (formerly Nyasa), while that for the *Tilapia* types was Lake Tanganyika. We shall return to this in more detail, but first let us trace the development of this group of cichlids.

The rich-in-species genus *Haplochromis*, the most extensive of the entire group, must likewise be considered the original group, from which the other genera have sprung.

Also, only the genus *Haplochromis* is found in the entire region. As the only exception, the genus *Hemichromis*, like *Tylochromis* among the Tilapiinae, occupies a special place and also inhabits a very large region. *Hemichromis* and *Haplochromis* have both sprung from a primitive cichlid form and today stand next to each other, with the difference that all other genera can be derived from *Haplochromis*.

Here, too, we shall treat separately the most important regions, where an important part of the fresh-water fauna is composed of Haplochromini, but we will begin with Africa as a whole.

A number of species that have not penetrated into the lakes, or are confined to them, belong to the genus *Haplochromis* and are mutually very closely related. According to Regan, we must bring together these species—that is, those outside the lakes—in the sub-genus *Ctenochromis*. It may also be further concluded that the species from the sub-genus *Ctenochromis* are more original and directly or indirectly can be derived from the primitive cichlid stock.

Regan makes a classification within the sub-genus in accordance with geographical distribution and distinguishes three regions, which, of course, are not too sharply demarcated.

SOUTH AFRICAN REGION—This is the region south of the Zambezi River, including the river itself, where about 11 *Haplochromis* species live. The genera *Sarichochromis* and *Serranochromis* are each represented here by three species.

Illus. II-223. *Julidochromis marlieri.*

Illus. II-224. *Lamprologus congolensis*, male.

CONGO REGION—This region is more plentiful in species than the other regions, since, in addition to the big lakes, there is the extensive drainage basin of the Congo. Nevertheless, *Haplochromis* is represented here by only about five species, *Hemichromis* by two, *Serranochromis* by two, and *Steatocranus* by one, while *Lamprologus* is represented by three species. In regard to the last named genus, it should be noted that the three Congo species obviously belong to a recent invasion from Lake Tanganyika.

NORTHERN REGION—The northern region includes North Africa, East Africa except for the lakes, and Syria. Eight *Haplochromis* species are found here and as far as Jordan, Israel and Syria are concerned, this probably indicates a relatively recent invasion. Other Haplochromini have not yet penetrated into this region.

Illus. II-225. *Steatocranus gibbiceps.*

Genus *Haplochromis*

***Haplochromis multicolor* (Hilgendorf, 1903)**

Egyptian Mouth-Breeder

In North and East Africa, *H. multicolor* is found east of the Nile, as far as the lakes—in Alexandria, the entire Nile, Bahr-el-Jebel, Lake Albert, Semliki River, and Lake Victoria, usually abundantly and in shallow waters.

The body of this simple but very handsome fish is moderately high, long, and laterally compressed. The maximum length is 80 mm ($3\frac{3}{16}$ inches). The large mouth is directed obliquely upwards. All the fins are well developed; the dorsal fin is long and consists of a relatively low, spiny-rayed section and a smaller, soft-rayed section which has fin rays that are somewhat longer. The anal fin is much shorter, but also consists of a very small spiny section and a larger, soft-rayed section. In the male, both fins are pointed at the rear.

The caudal fin is large, fan-shaped and rounded. The ventral and

Plate II-325. *Haplochromis multicolor.*

Plate II-326. *Haplochromis burtoni* with fry.

Plate II-327. *Haplochromis burtoni,* male.

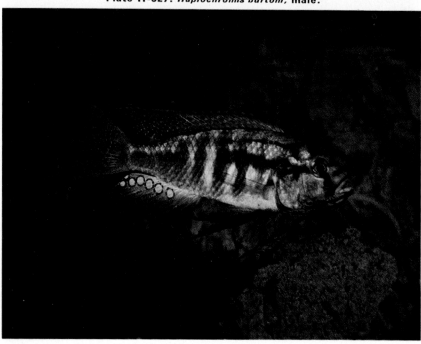

pectoral fins are large, the ventral fins being implanted just behind the pectoral fins. Both these fins are also pointed, in the male as well as in the female.

The body of *H. multicolor* is covered with rather large ctenoid scales, which are uniform in size and are laid out in regular rows.

The basic coloration is yellowish grey to yellow-brown, sometimes with a purple-blue glow. The area of the back is darker, growing lighter across the flanks and turning silver-yellow to faded whitish lilac towards the belly. In the soft-rayed parts of the dorsal and anal fins, the brownish background is set off by three yellow to whitish curved lines. In the caudal fin, there are five of these curved lines, though they are more bluish. The extreme tip of the anal fin is red in the male, and this is especially noticeable during the mating season. The males are then well worth whatever trouble they may be, as light blue breaks through over all the body and the region of the head and the gill covers become bright yellow. The throat is then nearly black, the whole body covered with scales of gleaming gold. Plate II–325 plainly shows all these details.

It is certainly not too much to say that this fish is among the most enjoyable and attractive of the cichlids. This is not only because of its interesting way of breeding, but also because it does not keep the hobbyist with his hands full of work, like many other of its larger fellow species do.

Any tank of more than 20 litres (21 quarts) is suitable, with the understanding that it is heavily planted, with *Myriophyllum* and *Aponogeton* species, for instance, supplied with a few rocks and a layer of not-too-fine river sand. The tank should be so placed that now and then a little sunlight can penetrate it, and the background should be made dark (hence, a direct downfall of light, but not cross- or through-light, is preferable), and then you can enjoy yourself to your heart's content watching a pair of these fish. The temperature should not be allowed to drop below 18 °C (64 °F) and in the summer it can rise as high as 25 °C (77 °F). It is preferable to breed in the same tank and it is not necessary to raise the summer temperature any higher for breeding.

Once the mating season has begun, a tank set up in the above manner will present an interesting show. Both fish in their bridal garments introduce the actual mating with a courtship that can sometimes last for quite a while, during which the male tries to drive the female into the hole or trench previously made ready. Because a male from the same nest is usually sexually mature earlier than a female, it can happen that the female wants nothing to do with him, and then special care must be taken. Should the male's attack become too violent, and if it can be clearly seen that the female is taking no interest in the affair, then it is better to separate them for a few weeks by means of an opaque, sliding panel in the tank, and then to feed the female well with a wide variety of foods to bring her into readiness. It is not very easy to tell when a female is ready to lay, for the belly is seldom swollen from its content of eggs.

As for what constitutes a good pair, it is often advised (as for other cichlids) to let the fish choose each other from a large nest. The sexes may be told apart quite early by the more faded coloration of the female and the sharper fins of the males.

The actual mating takes place rather quickly. After both fish have swum violently around and around each other for a while, each with its head against the flank of its partner, 20 to 100 eggs are laid in less than an hour's time. From 5 to 12 eggs at a time are emitted by the female and immediately fertilized by the male, after which the female takes them into her mouth, where they remain until the young hatch out. Hatching can be observed quite well, as the eggs can be dimly seen through the thin throat sac of the female. After about 10 days, the first young are hatched. After 14 days, all the young have hatched out and the most precocious of them leave "mama's" mouth for a brief outing.

It is quite possible to leave the father in the tank, but he may become too active and give the female a hard time while the eggs are developing, during which period she takes no nourishment at all. In that case, reach in carefully and take him out, because, if the female is frightened too much, she will swallow every last egg in one fatal gulp, and then there will be no young.

The eggs in the throat sac are about the same size as a medium-sized grain of sand, and are yellowish. They continually darken until after a week when the larvae can be seen inside them. When the young are "let out" for the first time, they are about 6 to 8 mm ($\frac{1}{4}$ to $\frac{5}{16}$ inch) long and in every respect look like other young cichlids.

Bringing them up is quite simple, for actually, it is enough just to feed the adult fish plentifully. The adults chew their food up fine and spit it out again for the young ones, so that the young never go hungry. It is superfluous to feed them infusoria, though strained waterfleas are very welcome. However, live food must still be the main dish, also for the

Illus. II-226. *Haplochromis desfontainesi.*

parents. A menu of tubifex, white worms, waterfleas, other crustaceans, insects and their larvae, small earthworms, minced lean beef, and such, is certainly sufficient.

Haplochromis multicolor is an especially suitable fish for a quiet community tank containing larger species—that is, from 5 to 10 cm (2 to 4 inches). It is positively not a plant destroyer, though specimens may be found that are totally unsuited to keeping as aquarium fish, because of their "disagreeableness," and their predatory and destructive tendencies. Luckily, such tendencies are the exception. If you should obtain such a specimen, though, it is better to do away with it and go buy another, because you will never get any pleasure from it.

Although it is only when the period of mating begins that *H. multicolor* shows off the full glory of its coloration, that does not mean that it is not an attractive fish outside the mating season. Its appearance then depends on the combinations of other fishes in the tank and on a suitable growth of plants. Soft-leaved plants (*Heteranthera*) must not be

Illus. II-227. *Haplochromis wingati,* close relative of a local variety of *Haplochromis desfontainesi.*

put in its tank, since it has a habit of occasionally snapping up a mouthful of sand from the bottom, while looking for something edible, and then it swims upwards with it and spits it out again, letting some of the sand escape through its gills. The sand grains then sink down and rest on the fine leaves of the plants and there they lie, spoiling the plants' beauty and health.

As a peculiarity concerning breeding, it can be mentioned that bigamy and even polygamy are rife among these mouth-breeders (these are also not rare elsewhere in the animal kingdom). If a number of these fish are kept together in a large aquarium, it may happen that a single male courts several females and fertilizes their eggs. If the plant growth is thick enough, every nesting can grow up well. Youngsters that have swum from their mother's mouth and have penetrated deeply into the area of another's progeny, may, in case of danger, be taken up into the mouth of the latter mother. Although under normal conditions, cannibalism is rarely observed, *H. multicolor* show no mercy to the young of other kinds of fish.

Due to peculiar activities, *H. multicolor* has recently been given distinct generic recognition in the genus *Hemihaplochromis* Wickler.

Plate II-328. *Hemichromis bimaculatus.*

Genus *Hemichromis*

Hemichromis bimaculatus Gill, 1862
Jewel Fish
Red Cichlid
Jewel Cichlid

This fish is found in all of Africa south of the Atlas Mountains of Morocco to the Cape of Good Hope, in all waters, even brackish coastal lagoons. It is one of the few cichlids having so wide a distribution area, which is an indication of the great age of the species of this genus. It

1089

Plate II-329. *Hemichromis fasciatus.*

can thus be assumed that *Hemichromis* is either older than *Haplochromis,* or that they spring from a common stock.

The species described under the synonyms are considered varieties or geographical races of the root form.

The body of this splendid fish is oblong, the line of the back more arched and the line of the belly less so, laterally compressed, and clearly perch-like. Its length in the wild runs to about 200 mm (8 inches), in large aquariums to 175 mm (7 inches), and in ordinary home aquariums seldom more than 150 mm (6 inches). At a length of 80 to 100 mm ($3\frac{3}{16}$ to 4 inches), it is usually already mature enough for reproduction. The shape of the body changes with age, and as a rule the larger growth of the fish depends on the amount of space available in the tank.

The basic coloration is red-brown to yellowish olive green, becoming darker towards the back. During the mating season, the coloration is usually its most intense. Although the sexes are generally hard to tell apart, it is remarkable that the most beautiful fish of a *H. bimaculatus* couple is not the male but the female—the male is much darker, and the female very red. The two dark (to brownish) spots can disappear entirely and from time to time a faint pattern of dark,

1090

vertical bands can be observed. Also, in good-sized specimens, the rounder belly of the female is quite noticeable, but others can be distinguished only in the mating season, at which time the female exhibits a short, blunt oviduct.

Reproduction takes place the same way as with other cichlids. It is only a matter of the couples finding each other. If two fish cannot stand each other, they must not be allowed to come together, since one or the other will always get the worst of it. Also, fish that are not about the same size and age cannot be brought together for breeding. Depending on the size and age of the fish, 100 to 500 eggs can be laid, preferably on a flat rock, sometimes against a pane, though the fish apparently do not like that so well. The natural depth of water is not more than 20 to 45 cm (8 to 18 inches), and the temperature, too, must be maintained as near as possible to what it would be in the wild. In the shallow waters where it reproduces, this is 25–28 °C (77–82 °F). During the rainy season, this drops to about 18 °C (64 °F).

Much pleasure is to be had from *H. bimaculatus*. It has shown itself to be not nearly so wild and stand-offish as has been reported. The plants recommended are fair-size "bushes" of *Acorus* species, *Aponogeton, Sagittaria* and *Ludwigia* to which neither young fish nor old have ever done any damage worth mentioning. In one case, the parents were 123 and 127 mm (4⅞ and 5 inches) long, but were not imported fish. Fish imported from certain districts where they are not familiar with plant growth are usually terrible plant destroyers, but their progeny, when kept in well planted tanks, seldom do violence to the plant growth. The same can be said for fish imported from natural waters having plant growth.

Depending on the district, *H. bimaculatus* occurs throughout practically all of Africa. The Red Cichlid lives in company with *Tilapia zillei* and *T. heudeloti, Pelmatochromis ansorgei*, its cousin *Hemichromis fasciatus* and several other species of cichlids. Hybrid varieties have, of course, been described; there is not, however, enough data on hand concerning these.

In the past few years, several genera have appeared on the market—among others, *Lamprologus*, including the species *L. congolensis*, *L. leloupi* and *L. werneri*; *Steatocranus*, especially the species *S. gibbiceps*; and *Pseudotropheus* with the species *P. auratus*, and many more.

Recently, the Malawi district (Lake Malawi) has been the source of many new cichlids, most of whom are mouth-breeders of the *Haplochromis* type, beautifully hued and reasonably sized (up to about 10 cm or 4 inches). They should all be kept in water of a recommended hardness of about 8 to 15 °DH, and a temperature range from 22 to 28 °C (72–82 °F). These fish are absolutely not suitable for the community tank since they are mostly voracious and will eat specimens of even almost their own size.

So far, the following specimens have been imported, though the dissimilarity of the sexes is extraordinary and may mislead the beginner. In some instances, in fact, it is difficult to determine that males and females belong to the same species. The species are: *Labeotropheus fuelleborni* and *L. trewavasae*; *Petrotilapia tridentiger*; and *Pseudotropheus auratus* and *P. zebra*.

Illus. II-229. *Labeotropheus trewavasae,* a cichlid entirely adapted to a diet of tiny vegetable and animal organisms. Its snout is similar to that of a *Labeo*.

Plate II-330. *Pseudotropheus zebra.*

Another species rather new to aquarists is *Tropheus duboisi*, about 6 cm (2⅜ inches) long, originating from Lake Tanganyika. This fish is also a mouth-breeder, showing the same type of parental care as the other species.

Illus. II-230. *Pseudotropheus novemfasciatus.*

Plate II-331. *Pseudotropheus auratus*, female.

Plate II-332. *Pseudotropheus auratus*, male.

Sub-order Gobioidei

Of the gobies or gudgeons, extremely few species are known to aquarists. Actually, any hobbyist knows only the Bumblebee Goby well, and all the other varieties are new to him. Although a few times some imported species have been added to the series as aquarium fish, it is difficult to understand why more varieties of this extensive group have not found their way into the aquariums of amateurs. Dozens of splendid species that remain small in size live in fresh, brackish and salt coastal waters all over the world. Therefore, it should not be much trouble for the collectors to involve themselves with a few more of these species, while the importers should certainly be able to do good business with them. These fishes are just the thing for setting up an environmental or regional aquarium, since they represent an interesting group of fishes, particularly where reproductive biology is concerned.

Because so little is, in fact, known about the living fishes, their nomenclature is still a hopeless muddle. Numerous species have had several names bestowed upon them, partly because their developmental cycle remains unknown, and partly because the enormous variety of this rather young group cannot be estimated. Also, the areas of distribution of many varieties still pose a question. The characteristics for distinguishing the varieties and species that have been and are being used are, in part, connected only with a certain stage of development and are partly of a local nature. However, we shall not delve more deeply into this. In the course of time, nomenclature will still undergo some change, but it is safer for the researcher not to be a constant maker of changes but to seek a more solid foundation from the specialists who are well acquainted with the varieties in question.

Gobies are distributed over the entire world and occur in fresh and brackish water as well as in sea water. A large number of species spawn in estuaries, but otherwise carry on their lives in fresh water. It is clear that it would be difficult to create a suitable environment in the home aquarium for these species.

Two large groups that include several families each, of which the two most important include a few aquarium fishes, can be distinguished.

Plate II-333. *Eleotris lebretonis.*

Super-family Eleotrioidea
Family Eleotridae

This family, usually indicated as the family of "sleepers," includes many species which grow really large (a metre, about 40 inches, or more) and is represented in all parts of the world. As a family, they are distinguished from other families of gobies by the ventral fins, which are implanted very close to each other, but which are not grown together, and are throat-positioned (located in front of the pectoral fins).

A few species are suitable for the home aquarium. One is *Butis butis* (Hamilton-Buchanan) from India, Thailand, Indonesia, the Philippines and Australia. Its length is to about 150 mm (6 inches). It dwells in brackish coastal waters, river estuaries and mangrove swamps. It has difficulty getting accustomed to fully salt water.

Eleotris pisonis (Gmelin) lives in the estuaries of southern Florida and the Caribbean islands, but is found as far as Rio de Janeiro, Brazil. Its length runs up to about 175 mm (7 inches).

Illus. II-231. *Eleotris marmoratus.*

Eleotris vittata Duméril comes from West Africa—from Senegal to Angola—from fresh and brackish water. Its length is to about 200 mm (8 inches).

Mogurnda mogurnda (Richardson) is an Australian species which is being offered regularly at present. Its length is to 150 mm (6 inches). Found in fresh and brackish water, it is a very lively species and, where shape and coloration are concerned, particularly attractive.

In general, very little is known about the gobies, and although some species also reproduce in the aquarium, a closer study of activities and reproductive biology is desirable.

Plate II-334. *Hypseleotris cyprinoides.*

Illus. II-232. *Dormitator latifrons.*

Genus *Dormitator*

Dormitator lophocephalus Hoedeman, 1951

This small species of goby has ventral fins grown together in the male. It is possible that the species was formerly kept in the aquarium, where it reproduced, in which case, so far as is known, it was described under the name *Dormitator maculatus*. *Dormitator maculatus* (Bloch, 1785), however, is a species which can grow to 700 mm (27½ inches) and is not sexually mature until it reaches a length of about 200 mm (8 inches). The form described here is sexually mature at about 70 mm (2$\frac{25}{32}$ inches).

Very probably, *Dormitator lophocephalus* is a rather common species in the lowland waters of the Guianas of South America, where it probably also occurs in brackish water. It is known with certainty to come from Surinam in the vicinity of Paramaribo, from where the type specimens originated.

The body is shaped like a club (the tail is the narrowest part), strongly compressed sideways. The body in front of the dorsal fin is high and broad. A typical peculiarity, which appears more among the eleotrids (although a typical characteristic for the family Gobiidae), is the way the ventral fins of the male are grown together. In the female, they are completely free of each other.

The coloration of live specimens is brownish to black on the back, the head lighter; about eight narrow to rather broad, light (to white) bands cross the flanks, vanishing towards the belly side. Depending on conditions (the mood of the fish), these bands can be entirely absent. A median lengthwise stripe of black dots or flecks runs from the upper back corner of the gill cover to the root of the tail. Above this rather clearly stippled line run two other less distinct stippled lines in the male (not in the female), and three or four under it, which are also found in the female.

In both sexes, the belly is golden yellow to olive green, with a metallic sheen. The male has a few extra blue flecks and dots. The cheeks are bluish brown with dark brown, unclear stippled lines from the eye ring backwards. The iris of the eye is blue with a corner of gleaming gold on the upper fore edge. The ventral and pectoral fins are transparent, with a blue-gold shine in sunlight and under artificial light. The median fins are yellowish in both sexes, somewhat more brilliant in the male, with stippled lines, the stipples, or dots, being black at the base and brown towards the edge. The dorsal fins are bordered with orange-yellow; the caudal fin has a border of greenish blue. The over-all coloration is quite variable.

Family Gobiidae

Genus *Acentrogobius*

This is a genus possessing many varieties with a distribution in Southeast Asia and the Indonesian-Australian Archipelago. Typical dwellers of brackish coastal areas, they have a tendency to migrate farther upstream into fresh water for the mating season.

Acentrogobius is distinguished from the closely related *Ctenogobius* and *Vaimosa* by its frontal scalation as far as the eye; the gill covers are either scaled or not.

Acentrogobius balteatus (Herre, 1935)

This fish, which can reach a length of about 200 mm (8 inches), inhabits the coastal waters of Borneo and the Philippines. Statements to the effect that its place of origin is Ceylon still appear improbable. Its environment includes the fresh and brackish coastal waters and the very brackish to salt mangrove swamps along the coasts. Reproduction appears to take place farther inland in fresh water.

Although the coloration of this fish is limited to a few soft, pastel tints on the flanks and in the fins, from soft yellowish to silvery ice blue, the deep black bands give a lift to the over-all appearance and make the fish extremely attractive. The typical pattern shows up well in Illus. II–233.

Illus. II-233. *Acentrogobius balteatus*.

Plate II-335. *Brachygobius nunus.*

Genus *Brachygobius*

This is a genus with a comparatively small number of species, but with a rather wide distribution. A number of the species are similar to each other, in pattern, in the scaling of the head, which is considered typifying, and in the gill covers. Such a young group, obviously still in the middle of its development, cannot yet be classified on the basis of a small number of constant characteristics.

Brachygobius nunus (Hamilton, 1822)
Bumblebee Goby
Yellow-Banded Goby
This species comes from India, Burma, Thailand, Malaysia, and Indonesia, including Borneo and Java, in the lowland waters close to the coast, into the brackish water zone.

This little goby has a conical, rounded body, the tail somewhat laterally compressed, and the head a little flattened in front of the eyes. The body is covered with 25 to 27 ctenoid scales, lengthwise. The head is unscaled, the only scales being on the gill covers. The

1101

mouth is end-positioned, the lower lip a little protrusive. Both jaws have several rows of teeth. The dorsal fins are located far apart. Plate II–335 gives a clear view of other particulars. The total length is about 40 mm (1 9/16 inches).

Brachygobius nunus is one of the most sociable aquarium fishes in the gobioid order. All in all, it gives no trouble at all, neither with keeping nor with breeding. Any aquarium, actually, is suitable and it may be kept in company with even rather large fishes. Although in the wild it appears to live in waters so close to the coast that a quantity of sea water regularly mingles with the river water, it can be kept for several years in nothing but fresh water without its being discomforted in the least. The salt content of the water also seems to be of little importance in regard to reproduction. Apparently, though, it is important to keep the water slightly alkaline (pH 7 to 7.4).

The required temperature is rather high, 25–30 °C (77–86 °F). *B. nunus* can withstand very nicely a nightly cooling off to 20 °C (68 °F), which indeed is a natural condition.

The tank should be planted with some Indian plants with a few pieces of sandstone added. The latter is needed because of the preference of this fish for laying its eggs against the underside of stones, which makes the stones indispensable for breeding. (Half a flower pot split vertically makes a perfect cave for its breeding.) The female lays her eggs (50 to 100 of them) with her belly turned upwards against the underside of a stone that has been previously cleaned by the male. After that, the male takes over care of the spawn and fans fresh water over them regularly with his pectoral fins.

The young hatch out after six to ten days. They are then as clear as glass, about 8 mm (5/16 inch) long, with two jet black, beady little eyes and a dark swim bladder. They eat heartily and grow quickly. Both parents and young eat mainly live animal food. The parents must be well fed just before the mating season. The female fasts one or two days during the laying of eggs. The mating play is very interesting due to the great activity of the male, who is then golden yellow almost all over.

Illus. II-234. *Stigmatogobius sadanundio*.

Genus *Stigmatogobius*

This is a genus having considerably fewer varieties than *Brachygobius*; however, several of the species do have a very wide distribution. The total region of distribution stretches from India (Ganges, Calcutta) to Burma, Malaysia, Singapore, China (Hong Kong), the Indonesian-Australian Archipelago and Samoa.

Stigmatogobius is most closely related to *Vaimosa*, with a head scaling that runs farther forward. The foremost scale on the head is unpaired and enlarged. The gill cover is scaled.

Stigmatogobius sadanundio (Hamilton, 1822)

This species is found in rivers and brackish waters close to the coast; however, it is probably less salt tolerant than *Acentrogobius balteatus*— at least, it is not found in the heavily salted mangrove swamps. It mates in water that is more fresh. Its length runs to about 85 mm ($3\frac{3}{8}$ inches). Smith gives (for material from Thailand) a maximum length of 70 mm ($2\frac{25}{32}$ inches). The distribution area includes India (not reported from Ceylon), Malaysia, the Indonesian-Australian Archipelago, Thailand and Burma.

Its food consists mainly of mosquito larvae. The basic coloration is silver-white to milk white with dark (to nearly black) spots on the body and in the fins. This pattern is outstandingly illustrated in Illus. II–234.

1103

Family Periophthalmidae

This family of so-called mudskippers can be found on tropical strands and especially on mud banks along Africa, southern Asia, Indonesia, the Philippines, Australia and the Pacific islands.

The best known genera are *Periophthalmus* and *Boleophthalmus*. Neither are ordinary aquarium fishes and require a kind of coastal or bank aquarium to show them off at their best. They spend a great deal of time on land, skipping about in great crowds on the mud banks among the mangroves. The air and water temperatures must not differ too greatly and should be above 22 °C (72 °F). They live on insects, young fish, worms, and everything else in their biotope they can find in the way of fly maggots, insect larvae, and crustaceans, slugs, etc.

The species most kept in the aquarium is *Periophthalmus papilio* Bloch, which hails from the west coast of Africa and Madagascar. From the Indian Ocean to Japan and Australia are found a number

Plate II-336. *Periophthalmus barbarus.*

Illus. II-235. Close-up of *Periophthalmus barbarus.*

of representatives of the genus *Boleophthalmus*, as well as *Periophthalmus*. *Boleophthalmus* spp. usually have more coloration.

It would be more desirable for hobbyists, and, naturally, the importers as well, to pay somewhat more attention to this group of fishes. Seen a few times in public aquariums, these fishes would stir hobbyists into considering them something special which they would want to keep themselves.

Order Tetraodontiformes

Finally, something about this order of "quadri-toothed" (four-toothed) fishes, which is the literal translation of Tetraodontiformes. This name refers to the beak-like, fusiform or grown-together teeth in the upper and lower jaws, each of which is split into a left and a right half, which gives the impression of being "quadri-toothed." The more familiar name for many of these fishes is "blow fish" or "puffers," which originated because of the ability of representatives of this order to greatly enlarge (blow up) the belly part of the body by taking in air or water. We must consider this "blowing up" as a defence mechanism against attackers, which are frightened away when their prey suddenly swells up to twice its size. These fishes are of no economic significance other than as aquarium fish, because the flesh is usually poisonous.

Plate II-337. *Carinotetraodon somphongsi.*

Plate II-338. *Tetraodon palembangensis.*

Boys in the regions that Tetraodontiformes inhabit blow up some species and use them for footballs, a practice that we, as nature lovers, of course, should disapprove of, but which clearly demonstrates how effective this blowing-up can be.

Although most members of this order are sea dwellers, a number of varieties occur in brackish and fresh coastal waters; a few even live rather far inland in the rivers.

The genus *Tetraodon* has numerous species, of which the smaller five species so far imported are fine for the aquarium; some have even gained a certain amount of popularity: *Tetraodon cutcutia* (Hamilton-Buchanan), which grows to about 80 mm ($3\frac{3}{16}$ inches); *T. leiurus* Bleeker, which grows to 130 mm ($5\frac{1}{8}$ inches), and is a purely fresh-water species; *T. miurus* Boulenger, which grows to about 140 mm ($5\frac{11}{32}$ inches), and is also a purely fresh-water species, like *T. palembangensis* Bleeker, which grows to 200 mm (8 inches), and *T. schoutedeni* (Pellegrin), which grows to 100 mm (4 inches).

Bibliography

This is a bibliography of ichthyologists and works which are either referred to throughout this book or which contain further information for your own reference.

Because one author frequently published many different articles in the same journal or work, only the author, title of the publication and the year are listed here, not specific articles, issues or pages. Because references in the text refer to the author and the date, you should be able to use this list to identify the specific work referred to.

The full names of the publications are written in a list preceding this bibliography. Future references to that work, under the author's names, are abbreviated.

ABBREVIATIONS USED IN BIBLIOGRAPHY

Acta Soc. Sci. Indo-Neerl.: Acta Société Scientifique Indo-Neerlandaises
Amer. Mus. Novit.: American Museum Novitates
Ann. Carnegie Mus.: Annals of the Carnegie Museum
Ann. Congo Mus.: Annals of the Congo Museum
Ann. Lyc. Nat. Hist. N.Y.: Annals of the Lyceum of Natural History, New York
Ann. Mag. Nat. Hist.: Annals and Magazine of Natural History
Ann. Mus. Congo (Zool.): Annales du Musée du Congo, Zoölogie
Ann. N.Y. Acad. Sci.: Annals of the New York Academy of Science
Ann. Wien Mus. Naturgesch.: Annalen des Wiener Museum für Naturgeschichte
Anz. Akad. Wiss. Wien: Anzeiger der Akademic von Wissenschaften
Aq. f. W. u. B.: Aquarienfische in Wort und Bild
Aq. Journ.: The Aquarium Journal
Aquar. Terrar.: Aquarien und Terrarien (Leipzig)
Aquarist: The Aquarist and Pondkeeper
Ark. Zool.: Arkiv for Zoologie
Arq. Mus. Nac.: Arquivos dei Museo Nacional
Arr. fam. Fish: Arrangement of the families of Fish
Asiat. Res.: Asiatic Research (book series)
As. Soc. Bengal: Journal of the Asiatic Society of Bengal
Atl. Ichthyol.: Atlas Ichthyologique des Indes Orientales
Atl. Vert. Ceylon: Atlas of the Vertebrates of Ceylon
Beaufortia: Beaufortia, series of Miscellaneous Publications of the Zoological Museum, Amsterdam
Bibl. Aq. u. Terr. k.: Bibliothek für Aquarien und Terrarienkunde
Blätt.: Blätter für Aquarien und Terrarien
Blätt. Aq. Terr. k.: Blätter für Aquarien und Terrarienkunde
Bol. Mus. Nac. (Zool.): Boletino dei Museo Nacional (Zool.)
Bull. Aquatic Biol.: Bulletin of Aquatic Biology
Bull. Raffles Mus.: Bulletin of the Raffles Museum (Singapore)
Bull. Soc. Etud. Indochin.: Bulletin de la Société de l'étude à l'Indochine
Bull. Soc. Zool.: Bulletin du Société Zoologique
Bull. Zool. Nomencl.: Bulletin of Zoological Nomenclature (London)

Cat. Fish. Afr.: Catalogue of the Fishes of Africa
Cat. Fish. Brit. Mus.: Catalogue of the Fishes in the British Museum (Natural History)
Cat. Fresh-Water Fishes Afr.: Catalogue of the Fresh-Water Fishes of Africa
Das Aq.: Das Aquarium
D.A.T.Z.: Die Aquarien und Terrarien Zeitschrift
Dict. Sci. Nat.: Dictionaire des Sciences Naturèlles
Ency. Aquariumhouder: Encyclopedie voor de Aquariumhouder
Exotic Aq. Fish.: Exotic Aquarium Fishes
Exp. part centr. Amer. Sud.: Expédition au part centrale de l'Amérique du Sud
Fauna Brit. India: Fauna of British India
Fischfauna Magdalenenstroms, Denkschr. Akad. Wiss. Wien: Deukschriften der Akademie von Wissenschaften, Wien
Fish. India: Fishes of India
Fish. Indo-Austr. Arch.: Fishes of the Indo-Australian Archipelago
Fish. Nile: Fishes of the Nile
Fish. Western S. America: Fishes of Western South America
Handb. Aq. Liefh.: Handbook voor de Aquariumliefhebber
Het Aq.: Het Aquarium
Hist. Nat. Poiss.: Histoire Naturelle des Poissons
Hist. Nat. Zool.: Historiae Naturalae Zoologicae
Ichth. Arch. Ind. Prodr.: Ichthyologiae Archipelago Indiae Prodome
Ichth. Hist. Nat.: Ichthyologiae Historae Naturale
Indian Zool. Zool. Misc.: Indian Zoology in Zoologiae Miscellanea
Ind. Cypr. As. Res.: Indian Cyprinids (in Asiatic Research)
Inst. Sci. & Technol.: Institute of Science and Technology
Intr. Hist. Nat.: Introdusione de Historia Naturale
J. Bombay Nat. Hist. Soc.: Journal of the Bombay Natural History Society
Journ. Siam. Soc. Nat. Hist. Suppl.: Journal of the Siamese Society of Natural History Supplement
l'Aq. Poiss.: l'Aquarium et les Poissons (Paris)
Mem. Acad. Sci.: Mémoires de l'Académie des Sciences
Madras Journ. Lit. & Sci.: Madras Journal of Literature & Science
Mem. Indian Mus.: Memoirs of the Indian Museum (Calcutta)
Mem. Carnegie Mus.: Memoirs of the Carnegie Museum
Mem. Ind. Mus.: Memoirs of the Indian Museum
Mitt. bl. V.D.A.: Mitteilungsblatt Verein Deutscher Aquarianer
Mitt. Zool. Mus.: Mitteilungen des Zoologischen Museums, Hamburg
Nat. Hist. class. fish etc.: Natural History; classification of fishes
Nat. Tijdschr. Ned. Ind.: Natuurkundig Tijdschrift voor Nederlandsch Indië
Naturgesch. Ausl. Fische: Naturgeschichte Ausländischer Fische
Notos prel. Rev. Mus. Pauliston: Notos preliminare, Revista Museo Pauliston
Nouv. Arch. Mus. Hist. Nat. Poiss.: Nouveaux Archives du Musée d'histoire Naturel (section Poissons)
Phil. Biol. Soc.: Philosophical and Biological Society (N.Y.)
Philos. Trans.: Philosophical Transactions, London
Poiss. Afr. Occ.: Les Poissons de l'Afrique Occidentale
Poiss. Bass. Congo: Poissons du Bassin du Congo
Proc. Acad. Nat. Sci. Phila.: Proceedings of the Academy of Natural Sciences, Philadelphia
Proc. Amer. Philos. Soc.: Proceedings of the American Philosophical Society
Proc. Biol. Soc. Washington: Proceedings of the Biological Society of Washington
Proc. Calif. Acad. Nat. Sci.: Proceedings of the California Academy of Natural Sciences
Proc. Zool. Soc. London: Proceedings of the Zoological Society of London
Rec. Indian Mus.: Records of the Indian Museum (Calcutta)
Rec. Malaria Surv. India: Records of the Malaria Survey of India
Rev. Bras. Biol. Rio: Revista Brasiliense Biologiae, Rio de Janeiro

Rev. Mus. Paul.: Revista Museo Pauliston
Rev. Zool. Afr.: Revue Zoologique Africaine
Rev. Zool. Bot. Afr.: Revue Zoologique et Botanique Africaine
Sel. gen. spec. pisc.: Selecta genere et species piscium
Senck. Biol.: Senckenbergia Biologica
Sitzber. Akad. Wiss. Wien: Sitzungsberichte der Akademie von Wissenschaften Wien
Smithsonian Misc. Coll.: Smithsonian Miscellaneous Collections
Smithsonian Inst. U.S. Nat. Mus.: Smithsonian Institution, U.S. National Museum
Stanford Ichth. Bull.: Stanford Ichthyological Bulletin
Stanford Univ. Publ. (Biol. Ser.): Stanford University Publications (Biological Series)
T.F.H.: Tropical Fish Hobbyist
Ver. Bat. Gen.: Verhandelingen van het Bataafs Genootschap
Woch. A.T.: Wochenschrift für Aquarien und Terrarien
Zool. Anz.: Zoologische Anzeiger
Zool. Eigebn. Reise Niederl. Ost-Ind.: Zoologische Eigebnisse einer Reise in Niederländisch Ost-Indien
Zool. Meded.: Zoölogische Mededelingen, Leiden
Zool. Voy. Beagle: Zoologica, Voyage of the Beagle (volume of Darwin's book)

AGASSIZ
1829 Sel. gen. spec. pisc.
AHL
1924 Mitt. Zool. Mus.
1925 Mitt. Zool. Mus.
1929 Das Aq.
1938 Zool. Anz.
APELT
1955 D.A.T.Z.
ATZ
1972 *Aquarium Fishes*
AXELROD
1954 T.F.H.
AXELROD, et. al.
1962 *Exotic Tropical Fishes*
AXELROD & SCHULTZ
1955 *Handbook of Tropical Aquarium Fishes*
AXELROD & VORDERWINKLER
1959 *Encyclopedia of Tropical Fishes*
BERG
1940 Classification of fishes, both recent and fossil, Ann Arbor Univ. Press (American Edition, 1947)
BERTOLINI
1952 Aq. Journ.
BLEEKER
1853 Ver. Bat. Gen.
1855 and later Atl. Ichthyol.
1858 Acta. Soc. Sci. Indo-Neerl.
1858 Ichth. Arch. Ind. Prodr.
1860 Acta. Soc. Sci. Indo-Neerl. (Cyprinorum)
1860 Nat. Tijdschr. Ned. Ind.

1862 Atl. Ichthyol.
1863–65 Nederl. Tijdsch. Dierk.
BLOCH
1785, 94 Naturgesch. Ausl. Fische
1797 Ichthyologie
1797 Ichth. Hist. Nat.
BLYTH
1860 As. Soc. Bengal
BOESEMAN
1952, 53 Zool. Meded.
BÖHLKE
1955 Notulae Naturae
BOULENGER
1887 Proc. Zool. Soc. London
1894 Ann. Mag. Nat. Hist.
1899 Ann. Mus. Congo Zool.
1901 Ann. Mag. Nat. Hist. ser. 7, 8
1901 Poiss. Bass. Congo
1901 Proc. Zool. Soc. London
1904 Ann. Congo Mus.
1905 Ann. Mag. Nat. Hist.
1907 Fish. Nile
1909 Cat. Fish. Afr.
1911 Ann. Mag. Nat. Hist.
1911 Blätt Aq. Terr. k.
1911 Cat. Fresh-Water Fishes Afr.
1913 Rev. Zool. Afr.
1916 Cat. Fish. Afr.
1919 Rev. Zool. Afr.
1920 Ann. Mus. Congo, (Zool.)
1921 Ann. Mus. Congo
BRITTAN
1954 A Revision of the Indo-Malayan Fresh-water Fish Genus *Rasbora*

1111

(thesis), Inst. Sci. & Technol., Manila
BURNEL
1953 Water Life
CASTELNAU
1855 Exp. part. centr. Amer. Sud.
CHAUDHURI
1916 Mem. Ind. Mus.
COPE
1871 Proc. Acad. Nat. Sci. Phila.
1872 Proc. Acad. Nat. Sci. Phila.
1878 Proc. Amer. Philos. Soc.
1894 Proc. Amer. Philos. Soc.
CUVIER
1817 Regne Animal
1831 Hist. Nat. Poiss.
CUVIER & CLOQUET
1816 Dict. Sci. Nat.
DADIBURJOR
1955 Water Life
DAVID
1936 Rev. Zool. Bot. Afr.
DAY
1865 Proc. Zool. Soc.
1865, 69 Proc. Zool. Soc. London
1877, 78, 88 Fish. India
1889 Fauna Brit. India
DERANIYAGALA
1929 Spolia Zeylanica
1952 Atl. Vert. Ceylon
DUMERIL
1856 Mem. Acad. Sci.
DUNCKER
1904, 12 Mitt. Naturh. Mus. Hamburg
EDDY
1957 How to Know the Freshwater Fishes
EIGENMANN
1912 Mem. Carnegie Mus.
1913 Ann. Carnegie Mus.
EIGENMANN & ALLEN
1942 Fish. Western S. America
EIGENMANN & EIGENMANN
1888 Proc. Calif. Acad. Nat. Sci.
1889 Ann. N.Y. Acad. Sci.
1890 Occ. Pap. Cal. Acad. Sci.
EIGENMANN & KENNEDY
1903 Proc. Acad. Nat. Sci. Phila.
EIGENMANN & WARD
1907 Ann. Carnegie Mus.
ELLIS
1913 Ann. Carnegie Mus.
ELWIN
1939 Ann. Mag. Nat. Hist.
EMMENS
1960 How To Keep and Breed Tropical
Fish
FAHRIG
1962 D.A.T.Z.
FEIGS

1954 D.A.T.Z.
1954 Mitt. bl. V.D.A.
1954 Mitt. bl. V.D.A.
1955 Mitt. bl. V.D.A.
FOWLER
1905 Proc. Acad. Nat. Sci. Phila.
1932 Proc. Acad. Nat. Sci.
1934 Proc. Acad. Nat. Sci.
1935 Proc. Acad. Nat. Sci.
1937 Proc. Acad. Nat. Sci.
1940 Proc. Acad. Nat. Sci.
FRANKE
1954 Aquar. Terrar.
1961 Aquar. Terrar.
1966 Aquar. Terrar.
FRANZ
1962 Aquar. Terrar.
FRASER-BRUNNER
1940 Ann. Mag. Nat. Hist.
1947 The Aquarium
1947 Proc. Zool. Soc. London
1954 Aquarist
1955 Aquarist
FREY
1960 Illustrated Dictionary of Tropical
Fishes
FRISWOLD
1937 The Aquarium
FRYER & ILES
1972 The Cichlid Fishes of The Great
Lakes of Africa
FUTTERER
1951 D.A.T.Z.
GHADIALLY
1954 Water Life
1969 Advanced Aquarist Guide
GILL
1855 Ann. Lyc. Nat. Hist. N.Y.
1958 Ann. Lyc. Nat. Hist. N.Y.
1861 Proc. Acad. Nat. Sci., appendix
11, 56
1872 Arr. fam. Fish
1872 Smithsonian Misc. Coll.
GOLDSTEIN
1970 Cichlids
GOSLINE
1940 Stanford Ichth. Bull.
1945 Bol. Mus. Nac. (Zool.)
1947 Arq. Mus. Nac.
GRAMBOW
1965 Aquar. Terrar.
GRAY
1830–32 Indian Zool. Zool. Misc.
GREENWOOD, ROSEN, WEITZMAN, &
MYERS
1966 Phyletic Studies of Teleostean Fishes,
With a Provisional Classification of Living
Forms

GRINDAL
  1952 Aquarist
GÜNTHER
  1863 Ann. Mag. Nat. Hist.
  1864, p.p., Cat. Fish. Brit. Mus.
  1868 Cat. Fish. Brit. Mus.
  1871 Proc. Zool. Soc. London
  1874 Ann. Mag. Nat. Hist.
HAGENBUCHLI
  1951 D.A.T.Z.
  1952 D.A.T.Z.
HAMILTON
  1822 Fish. Ganges (An Account of
  the fishes found in the River Ganges
  and its branches)
HARDT
  1953 D.A.T.Z.
HARRY
  1947 Aq. Journ.
  1949 Phil. Biol. Soc.
HECKEL
  1840 Ann. Wien Mus. Naturgesch.
  1843 *Russeger's Reisen* (book)
HEGENER
  1932 Blatt. Aq. Terr.
HELFFER & MILON
  1956 l'Aq. Poiss.
HEINECK
  1967 Aquar. Terrar.
HEMMING
  1955 Water Life
HEMS
  1955 Aquarist
HENTSCHEL
  1964 D.A.T.Z.
HERALD
  1961 *Living Fishes of the World*
HERMS
  1949 D.A.T.Z.
HERRE & MYERS
  1937 Bull. Raffles Mus.
HILDEBRANDT
  1962 Aquar. Terrar.
HOEDEMAN
  1947–1951 Ency. Aquariumhouder
  1952–57 Beaufortia
  1954–58 Aquariumvissen
  Encyclopedie
  1956 l'Aq. et Poiss.
  1957–71 Bull. Aquatic Biol.
  1961 Bull. Zool. Nomencl.
HOLLY
  1939 Zool. Anz.
  1940 Anz. Akad. Wiss. Wien
  1949 Woch. A. T.
HORA
  1929 Mem. Indian Mus.
  1931, 35, 37, 40, 41 Rec. Indian Mus.

HORA & GUPTA
  1941 Bull. Raffles Mus.
HORA & MUKERJI
  1928 Rec. Indian Mus.
HORA & NAIR
  1941 Rec. Indian Mus.
INNES
  1949, 52, 66 Exotic Aq. Fish.
  1950, 56 The Aquarium
JACOBS
  1971 *Livebearing Aquarium Fishes*
JAYARAM
  1954 Rec. Indian Mus.
  1955 Proc. Nat. Inst. Sci.
JENYNS
  1842 Zool. Voy. Beagle
JERDON
  1849 Madras Journ. Lit. & Sci.
JOANNIS
  1835 Mag. Zool.
JOHN
  1936 J. Bombay Nat. Hist. Soc.
JORDAN
  1923 Stanford Univ. Publ. (Biol. Ser.)
KARAMAN
  1929 Zool. Anz.
KELLNER
  1951 D.A.T.Z.
KELLY
  1969 *Aquarist Guide*
KLAUSEWITZ
  1955 Senck. Biol.
  1959 D.A.T.Z.
KNAACK
  1955, 56, 62, 63, 64, 66 Aquar. Terrar.
  1962, 67 D.A.T.Z.
KOKERT
  1966 Aquar. Terrar.
KRIESE
  1955 Aquar. Terrar.
KRIETSCH
  1967 Aquar. Terrar.
LACÉPÈDE
  1302, 03 Hist. Nat. Poiss.
LADIGES
  1949 Woch. A.T.
  1952 D.A.T.Z.
LAGLER, BARDACH & MILLER
  1962 *Ichthyology*
LA MONTE
  1941 Zoologica
LEHMANN
  1959 D.A.T.Z.
LINNÉ (LINNAEUS)
  1758, 62 *Systema Naturae* (10th, 12th
  editions)
LÖNNBERG & RENDAHL
  1930 Ark. Zool.

MacClelland
1838 Asiat. Res.
1839 Asiat. Res.
1839 Ind. Cypr. As. Res.
Machlin
1965 Aquar. Terrar.
Marsack
1948 The Aq.
Masya & Indrambarya
1932 Journ. Siam. Soc. Nat. Hist.
Suppl. 8
Mayr
1969 *Principles of Systematic Zoology*
Meinken
1926 Bibl. Aq. u. Terr. k.
1933 Blatt
1934, 49 Aq. f. W. u. B.
1936, 38, 48, 49 Woch. Aq. Terr. k.
1950, 54, 56 D.A.T.Z.
1955 Handb. Aq. Liefh.
1963 Aquar. Terrar.
Mihatsch
1966 Aquar. Terrar.
Milon
1955 l'Aquar. & Poiss.
Miranda-Ribeiro
1907 Lavoura (journal)
1912 Hist. Nat. Zool.
1942 Rev. Bras. Biol. Rio
Myers
1924, 27, 34 Amer. Mus. Novit.
1931 Stanford Univ. Publ. (Biol. Sci.)
1932 The Aq.
1933, 38, 40 Copeia
1942 Stanford Ichth. Bull.
1952, 54 Aq. Journ.
1954 Proc. Biol. Soc. Washington
Myers & Weitzman
1954 Aq. Journ.
1956 Stanford Ichth. Bull.
Nicholas
1952 Het Aq.
Nichols & La Monte
1933 Amer. Mus. Novit. 656
Nijssen & Isbrücker
1967 Zool. Meded.
Norman
1958 *A History of Fishes*
Ostermöller
1967 D.A.T.Z.
Ommanney
1964 *The Fishes*
Pallas
1766 Philos. Trans.
Pellegrin
1923 Poiss. Afr. Occ.
1928 Ann. Mus. Congo (Zool.)
1930 Bull. Soc. Zool.

Pinter
1955 D.A.T.Z.
1955 Aquar. Terrar.
Pisces
1954 Aquar.
1955 Aquarist.
Poll
1939 Ann. Mus. Congo Belge
Polutzke
1955 Aquar. Terrar.
Popta
1905 Notes Leyden Museum
Prashad & Hora
1936 Rec. Malaria Surv. India
Quoy & Gaimard
1842 Voyage autour du monde etc.
Rao
1920 Ann. Mag. Nat. Hist.
Regan
1904 Trans. Zool. Soc.
1909, 11, 12, 13 Ann. Mag. Nat. Hist.
Rössel
1961, 63 Senck. Biol.
1967 D.A.T.Z.
Sauvage
1881 Nouv. Arch. Mus. Hist. Nat.
Poiss.
Scheel
1968 *Rivulins of the Old World*
Schultz
1944 Proc. U.S. Nat. Mus.
1956 T.F.H.
1963 Het. Aq.
1971 *The Ways of Fishes*
Scopoli
1777 Intr. Hist. Nat.
Seleuthner
1950 D.A.T.Z.
Senfft
1950 Woch. Ap. Terr. k.
Silas
1956 Copeia
Smith
1931 Proc. U.S. Natl. Mus.
1934 The Aq.
1934 Journ. Siam. Soc. Nat. Hist.
Suppl. 9
1945 Bull. 188 U.S. Nat. Mus.
1945 (Fish. Siam) Bull. 188 Smithsonian Inst. U.S. Natl. Mus.
1945 *The Freshwater Fishes of Siam, or
Thailand*
1949 Water Life (England)
Steindachner
1877 Sitzber. Akad. Wiss. Wien
1878 Fischfauna Magdalenenstroms,
Denkschr. Akad. Wiss. Wien
1879 Denkschr. Akad. Wiss. Wien

1906, 10 Anz. Akad. Wiss. Wien
STERBA
1963 *Freshwater Fishes of the World*
STOYE
1951 Het. Aq.
SWAINSON
1839 Nat. Hist. class. fish etc. 1
TIRANT
1883 Bull. Soc. Etud. Indochin.
TREWAVAS
1943 Proc. Zool. Soc. London
VAILLANT
1902 Notes Leyden Mus.
VALENCIENNES
1839 Hist. Nat. Poiss.
1840 Hist. Nat. Poiss.
1842 Hist. Nat. Poiss.
1844 Hist. Nat. Poiss.
1846 Cuvier & Valenciennes

VON IHERING
1907 Notos prel. Rev. Mus. Pauliston
1911 Rev. Mus. Paul.
WALKER
1971 *Tropical Fish Identifier*
WARD-SMITH
1949 Aquarist
WEBER
1849 *Zool. Eigebn. Reise Niederl. Ost-Ind.* (book)
WEBER & DE BEAUFORT
1912 in Maass: Durch Zentral-Sumatra
1913–47 Fish. Indo-Austr. Arch.
WEITZMAN
1955 Aq. Journ.
WHITLEY
1935 Rec. Austr. Mus.
WOLFSHEIMER
1954, 55, 62 Aq. Journ.

Glossary-Index

(italic page numbers indicate photographs)

abdominal system:
  the part of the venous system that includes the head and body, 125
Abramites (genus), 606
  hypselonotus, 606, 607
Acanthocleithron (genus), 396
Acanthodiformes (order), 33
Acanthodii (class), 33, 210
Acanthodoras spinosissimus, 391–392
Acanthophthalmus (genus), 441, 442
  kuhlii, 431, *442–444*
Acanthopsini (tribe), 441
Acanthopsis (genus), 441, 445
  choirorhynchus, 445, 524
Acanthopteri (sub-class), 314
Acanthopterygii, 61, 304, 313
Acara (genus), 997
Acaronia (genus), 1022
Account of the Fishes Found in the River Ganges and Its Branches, 169, 928
Acentrogobius (genus), 1100
  balteatus, 1100, 1103
Acipenseriformes (order), 313, 698
Acrania:
  animals which have no skull; generally considered the most primitive group of chordates, 27, 211
Actinistia (super-order), 44, 311–312
Actinopteri (infra-class), 304, 313, 314
Actinopterygii (sub-class):
  non-spiny-finned (ray-finned) bony fishes, 211, 304, 313–314
adaptation, 63, 65, 138, 156
  annual fish, 157–158
Adiposia (genus), 429
Aeneus Catfish, 338
Aequidens (genus), 187, 997, 1002, 1022, 1025
  curviceps, 1025–1027, *1026*
  itanyi, 1027
  *maroni, 1028–*1029
  portalegrensis, 582, *1030–*1031
  pulcher, 1029, 1030, *1032–*1034
aeration of aquarium, 272–273, 274
African Bagrinae, 406
African Featherfin, 708
African Glass Catfish, 417
African Knife Fish, 711
African Long-Finned Tetra, 628
African Mud Fish, 714

African Striped Glass Catfish, 416
African Upside-Down Catfish, 400
Agassiz, (John) Louis (Rodolphe), 164, 167, 168, 211
Agassiz's Dwarf Cichlid, 1035
Ageneiosus ucayalensis, 656
Agnatha:
  primitive fish characterized by the lack of true jaws, 26, 32, 211, 300
Agonostomus (genus), 717
  monticola, 717
air bladder, *see* bladder, air
Akysis variegatus, 384, *385*
Alaspis (genus), 66
albumin:
  one of the constituent proteins in the blood, 124
Alessandri, Alessandro, 22
Alestes (genus)
  emberii, 624
  nurse, 624
Alestinae (sub-family), 614, 624
Alestopetersius (genus), 624, 625
  hilgendorfi, 625
    grandi, 625
    hilgendorfi, 625
    kribensis, 625
Alexander the Great, 160
Alfarinae (sub-family), 872
algae, 289
  removal from tank, 276
alkaloids, 107
Allodontichthys (genus), 867
  zonistius, 868
Alloophorus (genus), 867
  robustus, 868
allopatric species:
  species of the same genus from different distribution areas, 209
Allopoecilia (genus), 901
Allotoca (genus), 867
  dugesii, 868
Amarginops (genus), 407
Ambassis (genus), 928
  lala, 928
Amblycepitidae (family), 384, 426
Amblydoras hancocki, 392, 393
Amblyopsidae (family), 742
Amblyopsis (genus), 742
Amblyopsoidei (sub-order), 742

American Characidae, 170
American Flag Fish, 847
Amia (genus), 162, 566
  calva, 715
Amiidae (family), 715
Amiiformes (order), 545, 565, 715
Amphibia (class), 44, 310, 699
Amphiliidae (family), 109, 384
Amphilius (genus), 384
Amphioxi, 27
Amphioxiformes (order), 27, 30, 300, 302
Amphioxus lanceolatus, 27
Anabantidae (family), 143, 953–954
Anabantinae (sub-family), 954–955
Anabantini (tribe), 955
Anabantoidei (sub-order), 922, 927, 952–953, 954
Anabas (genus), 952, 955, 956
  fasciolatus, 959
  scandens, 955
  testudineus, 524, *955*
Anablepidae (family), 866
Anableps (genus), 235
anal opening (anus), 118, 120
Anaspida (sub-class), 30, 31, 300
Anatolichthys (genus), 832, 833
  burdurensis, 833
  splendens, *832*, 833–834
  transgrediens, 833
anatomy, 83–135
  blood circulation, 124–125
  body shape, 84–89
  excretory organs, 120
  fins, 97–104
  musculature, 111–112
  nervous system and sense organs, 126–135
  reproductive organs, 121–122
  respiratory and digestive organs, 113–119
  scales, 109–110
  skeletons, 90–106
  skin, 107–108
Ancistrus (genus), 66, 361, 362, 371
  oligospilus, 362
Andersonia (genus), 384
Angara:
  the northern primordial continent, 52, 57
Angelfish, *88*, 244, 246, 994, 1051, 1073, 1077, 1078
Anglaspis (genus), *30*
angle-iron aquarium, 241
Angler Fish, 89, 218
Anguilla anguilla, *87*
Anguilliformes (order), 69, 697, 698
Anisitsia (genus), *601*
"anjoemara," 253

annual fish, 157–158, 796, 821
  life cycle, *64*, 158
Anodonta cygnea (swan mussel), 541
Anopheles maculipinnis, 293–294, 912
Anoptichthys (genus), 632, 633
  jordani, 633–636, *634*, 639
Anostominae (sub-family), 603
Anostomus (genus), 603
  anostomus, 603–605, *604*
  taeniatus, 605
  trimaculatus, *605*
Ansorgia (genus), 415
Ansorgiichthys (genus), 415
Antiarchi (sub-class), 32
Anura:
  amphibians which have tails only in the larval stage, 44
anus, 118, 120
Aphaniini (tribe), 740, *741*, 832, 840, 841
Aphaniops (genus), 832, 835
  dispar, 835
Aphanius (genus), 832, 833, 835, 836
  apodus, 837
  chantrei, *837–838*
    chantrei, 838
    litoralis, 838
    maeandricus, 838
    parvus, 838
    venustus, 838
  cypris, 837
  fasciatus, 838
  iberus, 838
  sophiae, 837, 839
    mentoides, 839
    similis, 839
Aphiosemion, 777
Aphyocharacini (tribe), 614
Aphyocharax (genus), 614, 615
  alburnus, 615
  rubropinnis, 245, *615*–616, 623, 640
Aphyoplatys duboisi, 761
Aphyosemion (genus), 65, 158, 750, 768–774, *792*, 796, 803
  arnoldi, 770, *773*
  australe, 171, 246, 768, 769, 771, 775–777, *776*
    hjerreseni, *787*
  batesi, 770
  beauforti, 770
  bitaeniatum, 770
  bivittatum, 768, 770, 772, 774, 777–*778*, 824
  bualanum, *778*
  calabaricus, *781*
  calliurum, 768, 769, 771, 774, 779
  cameronensis, 775
  castaneum, 780
  christyi, 768, 769, 771, 779–781, *780*

1117

brevis, 730
sclerolepis, 730
arrow-shaped body, 86
Artedi, Peter, 161–162, 166, 174
Artemia salina, 292
arterial system:
    entire system of vessels which carry
    the blood away from the heart,
    through an oxygen-enriching process
    in the gills, and then into the rest of
    the body, 125
Arthrodira (sub-class), 32, 33, 38
Arthropoda:
    the largest division of the animal
    kingdom, which includes centipedes,
    spiders, shrimps, crabs and insects
Asian Mystinae, 406
Aspidoradini (tribe), 332, 357
Aspidoras (genus), 332, 352, 357
    rochai, 357
Aspredinidae (family), 386
Aspredininae (sub-family), 386
Astatheros, 1051
Asterolepiformes (order), 32
Astroblepinae (sub-family), 383
Astronotini (tribe), 1000, 1002, 1006,
    1022
Astronotus (genus), 1022
    ocellatus, 1022–1024, 1023
Astyanax (genus), 262, 632, 633, 636, 637,
    643
    abramoides, 639
    bimaculatus, 638
    fasciatus, 639
    mexicanus, 636, 639, 894
    potaroensis, 639
Asymmetron lanceolatum, 27
Ataeniobiinae (sub-family), 867, 868
Ataeniobius (genus), 867
    toweri, 867
Atherina (genus), 162
Atherinidae (family), 61, 717
Atherininae (sub-family), 717, 718
Atherinini (tribe), 718
atlas-axis complex, 92
Atlas ichthyologique des Indes Orientales
    Néerlandaises, 166–167
Atopochilus (genus), 396
atrium:
    the second of the chambers of the
    heart, located between the sinus
    venosus and the ventricle, 125
Auchenipteridae (family), 394
Auchenoglanis (genus), 407
auditory capsule:
    the location of the inner ear, situated
    on either side of the skull, 130, 135
auditory organ, 114–115, 131–132, 133

Aulophallus (genus), 914
Aulostomoidei (sub-order), 918
"auratus," 830
Australian area:
    a general biogeographical region in-
    cluding Australia and New Zealand,
    52
Australian Rainbow Fish, 722
autumn plague, 248
auxiliary respiratory organ, 40, 187
axial skeleton, 90, 98
Azoic, see Archaic
Aztecs, 237
Bacopa amplexicaulis, 840
Badidae (family), 938
Badis (genus), 938, 939
    badis, 936, 939–942
    burmanicus, 941, 942
Bagrichthys (genus), 408
Bagridae (family), 406
Bagrinae (sub-family), 406–407
Bagroides (genus), 408
Bagrus (genus), 407, 409
Baird, Spencer Fullerton, 168
"bait flaps," 216
balance, 112, 115, 131, 132
Balantiocheilus (genus), 450
    melanopterus, 450
Baldner, Leonhard, 238
Balitora (genus), 425
Balitoropsis (genus), 425
Balsadichthys (genus), 867
    whitei, 868
Banded Anostomus, 605
Banded Astyanax, 639
Banded Cichlid, 1068
Banded Corydoras, 340
Banded Epiplatys, 762
Banded Killie (Killifish), 853
Banded Knife Fish, 547
Bandit Corydoras, 346
Banjo Catfish, 387
barbel, 449
barbels, 318–319
Barbodes (genus), 466
Barbus (genus), 451–452, 495, 754, 782
    anchisporus, 473
    arulius, 452
    barbus, 452
    bariliodes, 477
    belinka, 524
    binotatus, 458, 524
    chola, 453
    conchonius, 171, 453–454, 469
    congicus, 455–456
    cumingi, 456–457, 474
    deserti, 466
    dorsalis, 462

Black Shark, 496
Black Spotted Corydoras, 345
Black Spotted Upside-Down Catfish, 402
Black-Striped Rasbora, 531
Black Swallower, *220, 221*
"Black" Swordtail, 890
Black Tetra, 644
Black Widow (U.K.), 644
bladder, air (swim), 39, 40, 65, 72, 85, 114–116, 133, 134–135, 164, 248–249
bladder, gas, 134
bladderwort, 191
Blaka Creek, 189
blastula:
the compact spherical mass of cells formed by cleavage of the fertilized egg; also called morula stage, 44
bleak, *449*
Bleeding Heart Tetra, 673
Bleeker, Pieter, 166–167, 169, 227
Blind Barb, 489
Blind Cave Characin, 633
Blind Cave Tetra, 633
"Bloch, ed. Schneider, 1801," 163
Block, Marc Elezier, 162–163, 166
blood, 124
circulation of, *123*, 125
Bloodfin, 615
Blood Spot Tetra, 673
blowfish, 89, 1106
Blue Acara, 1032
Blue Aphyosemion, 788
Blue Corydoras, 348
Bluefin Killie, 849
Blue Gourami, 242, 244, 991
Blue Gularis, 768, 782
Blue Perch, 939
Blyth, 173
Bocage, 169
body segments, 90
body shapes, 84–90
arrow-shaped, 86
compressed, 88–89
eel-shaped, 86
flattened, 86, 88
special, 89
spindle, 85–86
Boehlkea fredcochui, 640
Boehlke's Penguin Fish, 685
Boeseman, 227
Boleophthalmus (genus), 1104–1105
bony fishes, 32, 39–41, 43, 90, 114, 161, 211, 298, 304–305
Borapet Rasbora, 516
Borelli, Giovanni, Alfonso, 161
Bosbivak Zanderij, 195–196
Bosmina, 292
Bothriolepis, 31

Botia (genus), 62, 428, 432–433
horae, 433
hymenophysa, 431, 432, *434*, 436, 440, 524
lohachata, 435
lucasbahi, 435
macracantha, 432, 434, *436*–437
modesta, 433, *438*
sidthimunki, 439
striata, 439–*440*
Botiinae (sub-family), 428, 432–433
Boulenger, George Albert, 167
Brachychalcinus, 261
Brachydanio (genus), 499, 500
albolineatus, 173, *500*–*501*, 502, 503, 524
kerri, 502
nigrofasciatus, 502–*503*
rerio, 82, 245, 478, 479, 501, 502, 503, *504*–507
frankei, 507
Brachygobius (genus), 1101
nunus, 1101–1102
brain, 97, 126, 128
Branchiostegi:
one of Artedi's five orders, 161
Branchiostoma lanceolata, 27
Brasilianische Naturgegenstände, 160
Brazil, 68, 160
Brazilian Angel Fish, 1073
breeding in an aquarium, 140
cross-breeding, 146
breeding plants, 289–291
Bregmaceros macclelandi, 220, 221
brine shrimp, 292
British Museum of Natural History (London), 150, 199, 204
Brochis (genus), 333
coerulens, 333
splendens, 333
Brokopondo Plan, 227
Bronze Catfish, 338
Brown Hoplo Catfish, 325
Brown Rivulus, 810
Bryconalestes (genus), 624, 628
longipinnis, 628
chaperi, 628
longipinnis, 628
Bryconini (tribe), 614
bubble-nest, 143, 242
buccal glands (mouth glands), 113
Budgett, J. S., 151
Buenos Aires Tetra, 650
Buffon, George Louis, 22
Bullhead, 89
Bullhead Minnow, 535
Bumblebee Catfish, 408
Bumblebee Goby, 1095, 1101

Bunga Varu, 945
Bunocephalinae (sub-family), 386
Bunocephalus (genus)
  amaurus, 386, 387
  chamaizelus, 594
"burnt-tailed fish," 450
Butis butis, 1096
Butterfly Fish, 705, 1041
Butterfly Tetra, 644
Cabomba (genus of water plants)
  aquatica, 281
  caroliniana, 281
Caecobarbus geertsi, 489, 633
Calamoichthys (genus), 699, 702
  calabaricus, 702
caliper, vernier, 179
Callichrous (genus), 413
Callichthyidae (family), 98, 109, 235, 318
Callichthyinae (sub-family), 319, 334
Callichthyini (tribe), 319, 320–323, 329, 334
Callichthys (genus), 143, 187, 319, 322, 324, 325, 392
  callichthys, 324, 656
  cartilaginous skull of, 94, 95
  larval development of, 93
Callionymus (genus), 162
Callistus Tetra, 659
Calliurum, 779
Callopanchax (sub-genus), 770, 773
"cambona" (Protopterus annectens), 151
Cambrian:
  the first geological epoch in the Palaeozoic era, which lasted from about 550 to 480 million years ago, 28
camera work, 183–184
cannibalism, 148
  cure for, 148–149
Canton Danio, 536
Cape Lopez Lyretail, 246, 775
"Carapo," 546
Carassius auratus, 490–491, 977
Carboniferous:
  the fifth geological epoch in the Palaeozoic, from about 300 to 230 million years ago, characterized by the formation of extensive coal beds, 36, 38, 41, 57, 247
Cardinal Tetra, 617–619
Carinotetraodon somphongsi, 1106
Carmine Nothobranchius, 793
Carnegiella (genus), 691, 1029
  marthae, 691
  myersi, 691
  strigata, 690, 691, 692–693, 694
carp, 61, 138, 449
cartilage, 90

cartilaginous fishes, 32–33, 36–38, 39, 161, 211, 298
Cascadura (genus), 319
Castelnau, Comte François L. de Laporte de, 150, 168
Catalogue of Fishes of the British Museum, 162, 164
Catalogue of the Fresh-Water Fishes of Africa, 167
cataloguing specimens, 199–200
Cataphractops (genus), 328
catfish, 31, 57, 61, 65, 68, 74, 82, 88, 89, 104, 110, 117, 129, 134, 250, 316–317
  respiration in, 249
Catostomidae (family), 422, 446–447, 448
caudal fin, 92, 97–98
Celebes Rainbow Fish, 718
center of gravity, 112
central nervous system, 126, 128, 129
Centrarchidae (family), 927, 932, 993
Centriscus (genus), 162
Centromochlus (genus)
  aulopygius, 394
  creutzbergi, 395
Centropomidae (family), 927
Cephalaspida (sub-class), 30, 31, 210, 300
Cephalaspis salweyi, 21, 39
Cephalochordata:
  a sub-phylum of Chordata whose members have the notochord continued into the head; lancelets are classified here, 15, 26, 27, 302
Cepola (genus), 162
Ceratodi, 41
Ceratodiformes (order), 307–308
Ceratodus (genus), 150
  forsteri, 150
Ceratopteris (genus), 285
  thalictroides, 284–285
    forma cornuta, 285
cerebellum, 128
Ceylonese Dwarf Rasbora, 534
Chaetobranchini (tribe), 1002
Chalceus (genus), 1074
Challenger Deep, 222
"Challenger" expedition, 47, 219–222
Chameleon Cichlid, 1052
Chanchito, 1052
Chanda (genus), 524, 927
  lala, 927, 928–931
  nalua, 928
  ranga, 929
  ruconius, 928
  setiver, 928
  wolffi, 927, 930
Chandinae (sub-family), 927

1127

1128

Gastromyzontinae (sub-family), 425
Gastrophori (genus), 920
Gastrostomus (genus), *220, 221*
Gastrotokeini (tribe), 920
gastrula:
a two-layered sac enclosing a central cavity developed from the blastula, 144
gastrulation, 144
genera:
plural of genus, 209
generic concept, 162
genes, 144
genitourinary system:
the urogenital system, 121
genus:
a category of plants or animals ranking above the species and below the tribe, 172, 209
geological eras, 18–20
table of, 18
Geophagus (genus), 235, 1022
acuticeps, 1056
brasiliensis, 240, 800
jurupari, 240
Georgette's Tetra, 664
Gephyroglanis (genus), 407
Gephyromochlus (genus), 394
Gerres (genus), 928
setiver, 928
Géry, Jacques, 259–262
Giant Danio, 508
Giant Rivulus, 813
Giant Sailfin Mollie, 907
Gilbert, Charles Henry, 168
gill arches:
cartilaginous elements in the rear half of the pharyngeal cavity, 114, 125
gill basket:
primitive respiratory and digestive organ, 26–27, 32, 113
gill lamellae:
folds of tissue in the gills which serve as the place of gas exchange, 114, 746
gill pouches, 132, 134
gill rakers:
small processes on the oral-cavity side of the gill arches which serve as food strainers, 114
gills, 40, 125
Gill, Theodore Nicholas, 169
Girard, Charles Frederic, 168
Girardinichthyinae (sub-family), 867, 868–869
Girardinichthys (genus), 867
innominatus, 868
Girardiniini (tribe), 873, 885, 886
Girardinus (genus), 872, 886

metallicus, 886
glands, skin, 107
Glandulocaudini, 614
Glaridichthys (genus), 885, 886
Glass Catfish, 416, 419
Glassfish, 928
Glass Knife Fish, 548
Glass Tetra, 680
globulin:
one of the constituent proteins in the blood, 124
Glowlight Tetra, 652
Gmelin, Johann Frederick, 162
Gnathobagrus (genus), 406
Gnathonemus (genus), 712, 713
schilthuisiae, 713
Gnathostomata:
fish that have jaws, 26, 32, 211
Gobiidae (family), 1098, 1100
Gobioidei (sub-order), 61, 927, 1095
Gobioinae (sub-family), 448
Gold Banded Characin, 641
Gold Barb, 476
Gold-Crowned Aphyocharax, 615
Golden Danio, 500
Golden Dwarf Barb, 463
Golden-Eared Killie, 851
Golden-Eyed Dwarf Cichlid, 1071
Golden Gambusia, 888
Golden Gourami, 991
Golden Pheasant, 790
Golden Rivulus, 816
Golden Shiner, 535
Golden Tetra, 648
Gold-Eyed Fundulus, 851
Gold-Eyed Killie, 851
Goldfish, 237–238, 241, 490
variations of, *491*
Gold Spotted Rio, 666
gonads:
either of the sex glands, 144
Gondwana:
the southern primordial continent, 52, 57, 66, 447
Gondwanaland:
the single primordial continent, 52, 57, 66, 68, 447
gonopodium:
the male copulatory organ, 860, 861–*862, 864*
Goodea (genus), 867
atripinnis, 868, 869
gracilis, 868
Goodeidae (family), 861, 865, 867, 870
Goodeinae (sub-family), 867, 868
Goodrich, E. S., 210
Graceful Catfish, 404
Green Catfish, 333

1133

One-Spot Platy, 892
Oodinium pillularis, 295
Opaline Gourami, 991
operculum:
  gill cover, 114
Ophicephalidae (family), 953
Ophicephaliformes (order), 922, 953
Ophicephalus (genus), 478, 922
  obscurus, 922–*923*
  punctatus, 82, 479, 922
Ophiolepis (genus), 66
orbital region:
  the area in the skull which houses the sight organs, 97
order:
  a category of plants or animals formed of sub-orders; orders are ultimately classed into a few main groups, 209, 210
Ordovician:
  the second geological epoch in the Palaeozoic era, which took place from 480 to 390 million years ago, 28, 30, 32, 39, 299, 304
Orestias (genus), 750
Orestiatidae (family), 745, 750
Orestiatinae (sub-family), 750
Oriental area:
  a general biogeographical region consisting of Asia south of the Himalayas, 52
Origin of Species, 147
Oryzias (genus), 753, 754, 824, 827–828
  celebensis, 827, 831
  javanicus, 827, *829*
  latipes, 827, 829, *830*
  melastigma, 827, 831
Oryziatini (tribe), 823, 824, 827
Oscar, 1022
Osphroneminae (sub-family), 971, 982
Ostariophysi (super-order), 61, 65, 66, 97, 112, 115, 132, 133, 134, 135, 304, 313, 315, 421, 543, 545, 552, 554, 697–698, 715
Osteichthyes (class), 39, 304–305
Osteochilus (genus), 498
  hasselti, 524
  vittatus, 466, 493, *498*
osteocranium:
  the bony part of the skull, 92–93
Osteoglossidae (family), 545, 703, 714
Osteoglossiformes (order), 68, 697, 703–704
  distribution, *54*
Osteoglossoidei (sub-order), 703
Osteoglossum (genus)
  albifrons, *704*
  bicirrhosum, *703*

Osteolepidae (family), 309
Osteolepiformes (order), 44, 309
Osteolepis (genus), *42*
Ostracodermi (class), 28, 30, 31, 32, 39, 66, 92, 112, 299–301, 313, 315
otic region:
  the area in the skull where the hearing organs are located, 97
Otocinclus (genus), 342, 374, 800
  flexilis, *374*
  vestitus, *375–376*
  vittatus, 377
otoliths:
  solidified calcareous jelly; also called ear-stones, 131–132
ova:
  plural of ovum, 122
oval organ:
  special organ in certain fish (called physoclysti) which regulates the amount of gas in the swim bladder, 116
ovaries:
  female reproductive organs, 121, 122
oviduct, 121
oviparous:
  an egg-layer, 746
ovipositor:
  the tubular organ at the extremity of the abdomen by which eggs are deposited, used especially by bitterlings in their co-operative reproduction with mussels, 542
ovoviviparous:
  producing eggs that are incubated and hatched within the parent's body; an egg live-bearer, 861
ovum:
  fish eggs, 122
Owen, Richard, 150
oxygen content of water, 153, 155
Pachypanchax (genus), 750, 766, 832
  homalonotus, *766*
  nuchimaculatus, 766
  playfairi, 766, *767*
  sakaramyi, 766
Pacific area:
  a general biogeographical region including Polynesia, Oceania and the Pacific Islands to Hawaii, 52
Paddlefish, *43*
paedogenesis:
  the occurrence in nature in which an organism only develops up to a certain point at which it remains even after it reaches sexual maturity and reproduces, 31
paedomorphosis:

1140

another term, like neotony and paedo-genesis, having to do with the indefinite prolongment of the period of immaturity (retaining larval char-acteristics), 31, 302
painter's mussel, 540
paired fins (limbs), 98, 101, 112
Palaeonisciformes (order), 314, 698
Palaeoniscus (genus), *43*, 314
palaeontology, science of, 22–23, 212
Palaeopterygi:
  primitive-finned fishes, 314
Palaeopterygii (sub-class), 210
Palaeospondyli (class), 211
Palaeozoic:
  a geological era divided into six epochs which saw the ice ages, the first fish, amphibians and reptiles; it ran from about 550 to 200 million years ago, 20, 38, 41, 52
Palearctic area:
  a general biogeographical region that consists of Europe, North Africa and Asia north of the Himalayas, 52
Pamphoriini (tribe), 889
Panaque (genus), *361*
  dentex, 656
Panchax, 753, 766
Panchax (genus), 953, 972
pancreas, 119
Pangasianodon gigas, 316
Pangasiinae (sub-family), 419
Pantodon buchholzi, *705–706*
Pantodontidae (family), 705
Pantodontoidei (sub-order), 704
Paracheirodon (genus), 617, 618, 620
  innesi, 617, 618, 620–622, 653, 656, 668
Parachromis (genus), 1003, 1006
Paradise Fish, 241–242, 244, 964
Paradon (genus), 584
Parailia (genus), 415
Paramicrophis (genus), 920
Paramphilius (genus), 384
Paraneetroplus (genus), 1048, 1050
Parapetenia (sub-genus), 997, 1051
Parapoecilia (genus), 901
parapophyses:
  elongated protrusions on the verte-brae which replace the ribs in pipefish, 918
Para River, 189, 194
Parasilurus (genus), 412
parasite, 295
Paratilapia (genus), 1007
paratype:
  any other specimen, in a typical series of a new species upon which the de-scription is based, other than the

unique holotype, 205
Paranchenoglanis (genus), 407
  macrostoma, *407*
parental care of eggs, 143, 147–158
Paretroplus (genus), 999
Pareutropius (genus), 415
Parodon guganensis, 261
Parophiocephalus (genus), 922
Parupygus (genus), 548, 550
  litaniensis, 550
  savannensis, *550*
Paulicea lutkeni, 316
Peacock-Eye Cichlid, 1022
Pearl Danio, 500
Pearl Gourami, 242, 244, 988
Pearly Rasbora, 534
pectoral fins, 98, 101–102
pectoral girdle:
  a support complex for the fins formed of the fin ray elements and elements of the internal skeleton combined with the dermal ossifications; also called shoulder girdle, 101–103
pediments:
  bony rings in the corium layer from which the bony plates arise, 109
peduncle, 872
Pegasus (genus), 162
pelicans, *842*
Pellegrin, Jacques, 167
Pelmatochromi (tribe), 1006
Pelmatochromis (genus), 1004, 1006–1012, 1022
  annectens, 1007
  ansorgei, 1007, 1012–1013, 1091
    ansorgei, 1007, 1013
  arnoldi, 1007, 1013
  arnoldi super-species, 1012
  (Chromidotilapia) guentheri, 1013
  dimidiatus, 1007, 1010
  guentheri, 1013
  kribensis, 1011, 1014
  nudiceps, 1008, 1010
  pulcher, 1007, 1009, 1010, 1011, 1012, 1013, 1014
  squamiceps, 1008, 1010
  subocellatus, 1007, 1008, 1009, *1010*, 1011, 1014
    kribensis, *1009*, *1012*, 1014–1015
    pulcher, *1015*
    subocellatus, 1015, *1016*
  subocellatus super-species, 1013–1014
  taeniatus, 1004, 1008, 1009, 1010, 1011, 1012, 1013–1014, 1017
  thomasi, *1017*
"*Pelmatochromis kribensis*," 1010, 1012, 1013–1014
Peltobagrus (genus), 408

processes:
  protrusions on each side of each of the vertebra; the upper pair of processes on each vertebra form the neural arch and the lower pair form the hemal arch, 90, 91
Prochilodus insignis, 608
Profundulus (genus), 746, 750, 858, 859
  candalarius, 858
  hildebrandi, 858
  labialis, 858
  oaxacae, 858
  punctatus, 858
prosencephalon:
  the primitive forebrain, 128
Proterozoic:
  a geological epoch in the Archaeozoic era; the age of primitive and mostly single-celled organisms, which ran from 2,000 to 550 million years ago, 17, 20
Protista:
  a kingdom of one-celled beings, either plant or animal, 15
protocol, 200–201, 202
Protophyta:
  any single-celled plants, 15
protoplasm, 144
Protopteridae (family), 307
Protopterus (genus)
  aethiopicus, 306, 307, *308*
  amphibius, 307
  annectens, 151, *306,* 307
  dolloi, 307
Protoselachii, 36
Protozoa:
  a phylum of single-celled animals, 15
protrusile mouth:
  a mouth adapted to be stuck out quickly and rapidly, 427
Psectrogaster amazonicus, 656
Pseudacanthicus (genus), 66
Pseuderrythinus rosapinnis, 581–583
Pseudobagrus (genus), 408
Pseudogeophagus (genus), 1041
Pseudomugil (genus), 720
Pseudo-Swordtail, 876
Pseudotropheus (genus), 1092
  auratus, 1092, *1094*
  novemfasciatus, 1093
  zebra, 1092, *1093*
Pseudoxiphophorus (genus), 873, 876, 884, 894
  bimaculatus, 876–877
  taeniatus, 876
Pteraspida (sub-class), 30, 31, 210, 300
Pterichthyes (class), 211
Pterichthyodes (genus), 32, *33*

Pterodiscus levis, 694
Pterohemiodus (genus), *601*
Pterolebias (genus), 750, 807, 820
  bockermanni, 820
  longipinnis, 820, *821*
  peruensis, 820, *822*
  zonatus, 820, 822
Pterolepis (genus), *31*
Pterophyllum (genus), 994, 1002, 1048, 1051
  altum, 1076
  dumerilli, 1076
  scalare, 243, 244, 1055, 1070, *1073*–1076
Pterygoplichthys (genus), 360, 361
  gibbiceps, 373
  multiradiatus, 373
Ptychocheilus (genus), 535
  lucius, 535
Ptychochromis (genus), 1003
publication, steps in
  comparative material, 204
  description, 205–206
  determination, 205
  documentation, 201
  literature, 201–202
  name and nomenclature, 205
  protocol, 200–201
  "Zoological Record," 204
puffers, 1106
Pulcher Tetra, 655
pump, aquarium, 272–273
Puntius (genus), 451–452
Purple-Headed Barb, 467
Pygidium (genus), 383
Pygmy Corydoras, 342
pygmy perch, 932
Pygmy Purring Gourami, 979
Pygmy Swordtail, 894
pylorus:
  the ring-muscle between the stomach and the mid-gut, 117
Pyrrhulina (genus), 81, 143, 187, 201–202, 566, 567, 572, 654
  argyrops, 566, 567
  australe, 567
  beni, 567
  brevis, 566, 576, 578
  callolepis, 567
  carsevennensis, 567
  compta, 567
  eigenmanni, 567
  eleanorae, 567
  filamentosa, 566, 567, *576,* 578
  laeta, 566, *577*
  lugubris, 567
  maxima, 567
  melanostoma, 566, 587

reproductive organs, 121–122
Rerum Naturalium Brasiliae, libri VIII, 161
research, scientific
  cataloguing, 199–200
  collecting the material, 185–196
  deep-sea, 217–218, 219–220, 222
  elaboration of material, 197–200
  equipment for, 179
  fisheries, 225–226
  labelling specimens, 198
  preservation of material, 198–199
  publication, 200–206
  recording, 177–179
  steps in (table), 178
  storage, 199–200
respiration
  dermal, 65, 107
  intestinal, 40, 41, 65, 113, 248–249
  problems and solutions, 248–255
respiratory organs, 113–117
respiratory system, 40–41, 65, 107, 114–117
Reticulated Corydoras, 354
retractores arcuum branchialium:
  muscles used to retract the gill arches, 304–305, 313
Rhamphichthyidae (family), 548
Rhamphichthys (genus), 548
Rhinichthys (genus), 535
Rhipidistia (super-order), 44, 305, 309–310
Rhizodontidae (family), 309
Rhodeinae (sub-family), 510
Rhodeus (genus)
  amarus, 540–542
rhombencephalon:
  the embryonic hindbrain, 128
ribs, 92
rice fish, 827–828
Richardson, Sir John, 168
Rita (genus), 408
Rivulid Fishes of the Antilles, 172
Rivulinae (sub-family), 740, 750
  scale patterns, *748–749*
Rivulini (tribe), 750, 796, 804, 843, 953
Rivulus (genus), 201–202, 232–234, 643, 743–744, 750, 771, 796, 802, 804–809, 857, 1029
  agilae, 808, 809, *810*
  as insect destroyer, 232–234
  beniensis, 808
  bondi, 808
  brasiliensis, 808
  breviceps, 804, 806, 808–809, 810
  compactus, 808
  cylindraceus, 233, 804, 805–806, 807–808, 810–812

dibaphus, 809, 810
dorni, 809
elegans, 808
frenatus, 809
geayi, 809, 810
harti, 173, 808, *813*
heyei, 807
hildebrandi, 806
holmiae, 172–173, 806, 808, 813, *814–815*
isthmensis, 804, 806
lanceolatus, 806
marmoratus, 233, 804–806
mazaruni, 808
micropus, 806, 808, 813
milesi, 815
obscurus, 809
ocellatus, 804
ornatus, 809, 810
peruanus, 806
roloffi, 809
santensis, 806
scale pattern of, *743, 748*
stagnatus, 806
strigatus, 809
taeniatus, 809
urophthalmus, 172, 804, 806–807, *816–818*
volcanus, 806
waimacui, 804
xanthonotus, 806, 818–819
zygonectes, 807
roach, *449*
Roberti, *678*
Roloffia (genus), 774
  geryi, 774
  liberiensis, 775
  occidentalis, 768, *769*, 774
Rondelet, 160
Rosaceus, 670
Rossmässler, 239
Rosy Barb, 453
Rosy Tetra, 670
Rotifera, 239
Round mouth, *220, 221*
rudd, *449*
Rummy-Nosed Tetra, 657
Sabakoe Creek (Coca-Cola Creek), 189, *192, 193*
Sabakoe River, 190–191
sacculus:
  one of the sacs in the ear labyrinth, 131
Sailfin Mollies, 906, 908
Sailfish Characin, 554
salamander, 241, 310
salinity, affect on population, 60–61
Salmonidae (family), 69, 72, 152
Salmoniformes (order), 697, 698

1147

Sipaliwini River, 253, 255
Siren (genus), 150
Sisoridae (family), 384, 426
Six-Banded Barb, 473
Skate, *37*, 88
Skeleton, 90–106
  internal, 26
Skiffia (genus), 867
  bilineata, 869
  lermae, 869
  variegata, 869
skin, 107–108, 112
  denticles, 108, 109, 113
  glands, 107
skipjacks, 320
skull, 27, 92–93, *96, 97*
Skunk Corydoras, 339
Skunk Loach, 433
slide rule, 182–183
Small-Headed Abramites, 606
smell, 129–130
Smith, Professor J. L. B., 311–312
Smithsonian Institution (Washington), 199
Smoky Glass Catfish, 418
Snake Fish, 302
Snakehead Fish, 82
Snakeskin Gourami, 990
Snellius expedition, 47
Snyder, John Otterbein, 169
soil, 77
Solenostomidae (family), 919
Sorubim lima, 410
Spallanzani, Lazzaro, 238
Spanish Toothcarp, 859
Spanner Barb, 464
spawn:
  fish eggs, 122
spawning grounds, 152
species:
  a category of plants or animals ranking below the genus but above a breed, strain or variety, 172, 208–209
species
  classification of, 172–174
  differentiation of, 78, 81
  ideal, *see* ideal species
  isolation of, 49
  number of, 164
"species inquirendum":
  a species with a dubious name about which further research is required, 451
spermatozoa:
  scientific term for motile sperm cells, 122, 144
spermatophores:
  sperm capsules, 141
sperm duct, 121

Sphaerichthyinae (sub-family), 967–968
Sphaerichthys (genus), 967, 969
  osphromenoides, 524, *969*–970
  vaillanti, 970
spinal column, 24–26, 84, 90–92, 98, 128
  extremities of, 92
spinal cord, 91, 92, 126, *127*
spindle-shaped body, 85–86
Spined Loach, 441
spines, 98, 101
spiny eels, 924
Spirobranchus (genus), 955
Splashing Samlet, 572
spleen, 119, 124
Spoon-Billed Catfish, *43*
Spot-Tail Shiner, 535
Spotted "Callichthys," 327
Spotted Catfish, 351
Spotted Characin, 572
Spotted Danio, 502
Spotted Head Stander, 607
Spotted Panzerwels, 327
Spotted Profundulus, 858
Spotted Rasbora, 526
Spotted Suckermouth Catfish, 368
Spotted Weatherfish, 441
Spraying Characin, 572
Squawfish, 535
standard length, 183
Stargazer, 238
Steatocranus (genus), 1082, 1092
  gibbiceps, *1082*, 1092
Steatogenys (genus), 548, 550
  elegans, *550*
Stegotrachelus (genus), 314
Steindachner, Franz, 168
Stensiö, 210
stereo-microscope, binocular, 179–182
Sternopygus (genus), 548, 551
  macrurus, *551*
Stethaprionini (tribe), 614, 632, 680, 688
sticklebacks, 61, 916
Stigmatogobius (genus), 1103
  sadanundio, *1103*
Stingray, *37*
Stoll, Caspar, 227
stomach, 117, 119
Stone-Lapping Fish, 494
Stone Loach, 429
Striped Anostomus, 603
Striped Barb, 460
Striped Dwarf Sucker Catfish, 777
Striped Head Stander, 606
Striped Hoplo, 326
Striped Killie (Killifish), 855
Striped Mystus, 410

Striped "Porthole," 326
Striped Pyrrhulina, 579
Striped Synodontis, 403
sturgeon, 39, 210
sub-family:
  a category of plants or animals formed of tribes, ranking below a family, 209, 210
sub-order:
  a category of plants or animals formed of families which form into orders, 209, 210
sub-species, 146
"Suckermouth" Catfish, 367
"suckers," 448
Sucking Loach, 424
Suess, Sir Edward, 52
suffixes, 210
Sumatra, 49
Sumatra Barb, 470
"sumpit," 950
Sunda Shelf, 49
Sunder Lal Hora, 169
sunfish, 932
sun perch, 932
super-family, 210
super-species:
  a monophyletic group of closely related and largely or entirely allopatric species, 209, 210
supra-branchial organ, *see* auxiliary respiratory organ, 922
Surinam, 185–193, 226–227, 247
  geography, 185–186, 189
  maps, *186, 187, 229, 252, 258*
Surinam River, 227
Svenson, 151
Swallower Eel, *220, 221*
Swammerdam, Jan, 161
Swamp Barb, 453
Swamp Killie, 857
swamps, 152–153, *154*
swan mussel, 541
swim bladder, *see* bladder, air
Swordtail, 244
Symphysodon (genus), 1002, 1048, 1057, 1077
  aequifasciata, 1077
    aequifasciata, 1077
    axelrodi, 1077
    haraldi, 1077
  discus, 1076, 1077–1079
synapse:
  the junction point between two neurons across which the nerve impulse passes, 126, 127, 129
Synbranchiformes (order), 922
Synentognathi, 723

Syngnathidae (family), 919–920
Syngnathiformes (order), 917–918
Syngnathinae (sub-family), 920, 921
Syngnathoidei (sub-order), 918, 919
Syngnathus (genus), 917
  acus, 918, 920
  pulchellus, 919, 921
  spicifer, 917
Synodontis (genus), 396, 406, 437
  alberti, 396–*397*
  angelicus, 398–399
  decorus, 399
  flavitaeniatus, 400
  nigriventris, 396, 400–*401*
  nigromaculatus, 402, 403
  vittatus, 403
Synopsis of the Fishes of North America, 168
Systema Naturae, 162, 172, 996
systematics, 171, 175–176, 207–212
Tabatinga Catfish, 339
tail, 86
  movement of, 91
Talking Catfish, 391
Tanichthys (genus), 536
  albonubes, 536–539
tank, aquarium, 264–266
  filling of, 268–269
Tarassiformes (order), 313
taste buds, 129, *131*
tautonym:
  a binomial name in which the generic and specific names are alike, such as *Puntius puntius,* 451
taxonomic studies, 169–170
T Barb, 464
teeth, 109, 114
telencephalon:
  the endbrain, which, with the thalamus, forms the forebrain, 128
Teleostei (super-order), 164, 210, 307, 697, 715, 717
Teleostomi (class), 211, 305
Telescope Fish, 238, *491*
Tellia (genus), 837
Telmatherina (genus), 718
  ladigesi, 717, 718–719
tench, *449*
terraces, aquarium, 277, 288
Tertiary:
  a geological period covering the first part of the Neozoic era from the Eocene to the Pliocene; it lasted from 60 to 21 million years ago, *59,* 60, 66, 68
testes:
  male reproductive organs, 121, 122
Tethys:
  the equatorial sea posited by Suess to

1150

Two-Spot Gourami, 989
Two-Spot Platy, 892
Two-Spotted Astyanax, 638
Tylochromis (genus), 1081
type species:
the species of a genus upon which the generic name depends, 205, 451
type specimen:
the holotype and paratypes, 205
Typhlichthys, 742
Typhlonus (genus), 216
Uaru (genus), 1048, 1051
  amphiacanthoides, 1051
Über den Bau und die Grenzen der Ganoiden, 164, 210
Umbra (genus), 858
Unionidae (mussel), 540
Unio pictorum (painter's mussel), 540
unpaired fin, *see* median fin
Uranoscopus (genus), 162
ureter, 121
urinophile:
members of the catfish family Trichomyeteridae which, if allowed, will penetrate the urinary tract of men and animals, 236, 383
Urochordata:
a sub-phylum of small marine chordata which have, in the adult stage, a cylindrical sac-like body covered with a transparent membrane; also called Tunicata, 15, 25, 28
Urodela:
the second branch of amphibians which retain tails as adults, 44
urogential system:
the combination of the reproductive and excretory systems; also called genitoninary system, 121
Urophori (genus), 920
urostyle:
the extension of the spinal column which runs out into the tail, 128
Utiarichthys (genus), 261
Utricularia (bladderwort), 191, 192
utriculus:
one of the sacs in the ear labyrinth, 131
Vaimosa (genus), 1100, 1103
Valencia (genus), 739, 832, 859
  hispanica, 859
Valenciennes, A., 163, 166
Vallisneria, 239, 284, 288
Van der Kamp, J., 193, 195
Van der Stigchel, 227
Varicorhinus (genus), 495
Veil-Finned Angelfish, 242
Veiltail, 238
Veil-Tailed Betta, 977

Velvet, 295
Velvet Cichlid, 1022
venous system:
the system of tubes (veins) that serves to return the blood back to the liver and heart, 125
ventral aorta:
the artery located on the belly, which conducts oxygen-poor blood from the heart to the gills, 125
ventral fins, 98, 101, 103, 104
ventricule:
the main pumping chamber in the heart, 125
Vermes:
segmented and unsegmented worms, 15
vertebrae, 90–92
  ultimate, *100*
Vertebrata:
a sub-phylum of chordata characterized by a segmented spinal column and a symmetrically constructed body, 15, 84
vertical distribution, 73–74
Viperfish, *220, 221*
vivaria:
a place for keeping and maintaining live creatures, 237, 239
Viviparous Dwarf Pike, 884
viviparous fish:
true live-bearing fish, 861
Von Chamisso, Adalbert, 47
Von Humboldt, Alexander, 47, 51, 167, 207, 238
Von Siebold, 169
Wagtail, 892
Walking Catfish, 390
Wallago (genus), 412
Wallagonia (genus), 412
Ward, 239
water composition, 267–269
waterfleas, 292–293, 294
water temperature, 61, 269–271
Weather Fish, 238
Weberian apparatus, 65, 97, 132, 133–135, 421
  ossicles, 115, 135
Weber, Max, 47, 51, 167, 169, 500
whale, 161
Whiptailed Catfish, 379
White Cloud, 536
White Cloud Mountain Fish, 536
white worms, 292
Willoughby, Francis, 161, 211
wrasses, 117
Wrestling Half-Beak, 735
Xenacanthiformes (order), 36
Xenocara (genus), 361, 369, 371, 800

Glossary-Index prepared by Sean Sullivan